The Best of

LONDON

4th Revised

Editor-in-Chief: André Gayot

Editor: Mary Anne Evans

Restaurant contributors: Lindsey Bareham, Matthew Fort, Henri Gault, Christian Millau, Michael North, Stuart Walton, David Wolfe

Contributors: David Evans, James Fairhead, Carole Hirschhorn, Lucy Koserski, Ossi Laurila, Susan Low, Maureen Mills, Kay Roberts

Coordination: Sophie Gayot

Publisher: Alain Gayot

Gault Millau

ANDRÉ GAYOT PUBLICATIONS

Paris ■ Los Angeles ■ New York ■ London ■ Munich ■ San Francisco ■ Vienna

ANDRÉ GAYOT PUBLICATIONS
Bring You

The Best of Chicago	The Best of New England
The Best of Florida	The Best of New Orleans
The Best of France	The Best of New York
The Best of Germany	The Best of Paris
The Best of Hawaii	The Best of San Francisco
The Best of Hong Kong	The Best of Thailand
The Best of Italy	The Best of Toronto
The Best of London	The Best of Washington, D.C.
The Best of Los Angeles	The Best Wineries of America

The Food Paper
Tastes Newsletter

Copyright © 1982, 1986, 1990, 1994 by Gault Millau, Inc.

Published by Gault Millau, Inc.
5900 Wilshire Blvd.
Los Angeles, CA 90036

Please address all comments regarding
The Best of London to:
Gault Millau, Inc.
P.O. Box 361144
Los Angeles, CA 90036
fax (213) 936-2883

Library of Congress Cataloging-in-Publication Data

The Best of London / editor-in-chief, André Gayot;
editor, Mary Anne Evans.—4th rev. ed.
p. cm.
"An André Gayot publication."
Includes index.
ISBN 1-881066-11-8: $20.00
1. London (England)—Guidebooks.
I. Gayot, André. II. Evans, Mary Anne.
DA679.B47 1994
914.2104'859—dc20
94-6494
CIP

Printed in the United States of America

CONTENTS

■ INTRODUCTION 5

■ RESTAURANTS 7

André Gayot/Gault Millau's penchant for observing everything that's good (and bad) about food and the experience of dining has made these guides popular and yes, indispensible. Here we give you candid, penetrating, witty reviews of the very top, the new, and the newly-discovered. Listed by area. Includes the famous Toque Tally.

■ HOTELS 93

A hotel guide for every taste and every pocket.

■ REFRESHMENTS & QUICK BITES 125

London's quick bites range from traditional fish and chips (though we can no longer rely on them coming wrapped in newspaper as of old!) to sophisticated food in former pubs. And not forgetting the innumerable excellent pubs that remain, the sophisticated wine bars and bars and of course where to find the best cup of tea in town.

■ NIGHTLIFE 165

A round-up of the best that London has to offer, where to dance the night away, enjoy British comedy at its best (and its worst!) and join the clubbers.

■ SHOPS 175

From antique books to porcelain miniatures... young British fashion to traditional British tailoring. André Gayot/Gault Millau direct you to the best.

■ ARTS & LEISURE 269

Where to discover the best, most interesting galleries and museums London has to offer from the off-beat to the mainstream.

■ OUT OF LONDON 309

All you need to know about where to spend a day or two, or three or four outside London in England's green and pleasant countryside.

■ BASICS 337

Everything you need to know about getting around London.

■ MENU SAVVY 346

Glossaries of international cuisine terms.

■ INDEX 352

A disclaimer

Readers are advised that prices and conditions change over the course of time. The restaurants, hotels, shops, and other establishments reviewed in this book have been reviewed over a period of time, and the reviews reflect the personal experiences and opinions of the reviewers. The reviewers and publishers cannot be held responsible for the experiences of the reader related to establishments reviewed. Readers are invited to write to the publisher with ideas, comments, and suggestions for future editions.

LONDON

LIKE NOWHERE IN THE WORLD...

No two people will see London with the same eyes nor recall it in the same manner. In the whirlwind of images it projects on us, it is hard to capture them all for they flash by too rapidly and too intensely to be entirely perceived and recorded. Never mind: we are here to help you take a fuller bite of this great city.

Whether you want to stroll in the tree-filled squares of Kensington, down the small alleyways in the City, worship in sixteenth-century churches, contemplate the massive monuments or the impressive houses and palaces of past residents, eat the most exotic foods or the most local ones, buy rare teas or invaluable spirits, dance the night away, acquire precious silver and antiques, spend an unforgett-able evening in a theatre and retire to a cosy hotel that makes you feel instantly at home, we will lead you to the places and the people on which you can rely to help you fully enjoy London.

You don't need us to look around at the street life, to see well-dressed people up from the country hurrying along to the latest exhibition at the Royal Academy, punk rockers with Mohican hair-cuts being photographed in Camden Lock market, bowler-hatted gentlemen (still) in the City, lawyers in wigs and gowns in the Inns of Court, and red-coated mounted soldiers trotting along Bird Cage Walk on their way to the Changing of the Guard.

You cannot see the centuries of endeavour with threads stretching back to the very beginnings and precisely to those days in AD 43 when the Romans decided to build a tiny wooden bridge over the river now called the Thames. Rather than trying to guide you through the meanderings of history from the Romans, the Anglo-Saxons, the Vikings and the Frenchmen of William the Conqueror or to horrify you with the gigantic fire that destroyed the city in 1666, we recommend you visit the Museum of London (see *Arts & Leisure* chapter). Browse through the past in room settings that resurrect the daily life of Londoners since the days of the Romans to the terrifying nights of the Blitz in 1940.

In the course of the centuries, London has welcomed a constant stream of visitors from overseas, but nowadays the flow has reached the size of the Amazon. Ten million of them according to the British Tourist Authority rush annually to discover London—and sometime stay there. Not all of them are as well known as those whose names are immortalised on the famous 'blue plaques' on many of London's houses. Mozart wrote his first symphony in Ebury Street, Voltaire stayed in Maiden Lane and Benjamin Franklin so delighted his landlady with his wit and wisdom in Duke Street that she halved the rent in order to keep him.

A penetrating visitor by the name of Nathaniel Hawthorne wrote in 1863 'Day after day, I had trodden the thronged labyrinthine courts, the parks, the gardens and enclosures of ancient studious societies, so retired and silent amid the city uproar, the markets, the streets along the river-side, the bridges. I had sought all parts of the metropolis with an unweariable and indiscriminating curiosity. The result was, that I acquired a home-feeling there, as nowhere in the world.'

Our British team of writers and journalists, and Mssrs. Gault et Millau as well, have followed in the footsteps of Nathaniel Hawthorne. Not only have they trodden the thronged thoroughfares but also eaten in countless eateries, slept in innumerable hotel beds and drank an unspecified number of bottles of wine as well as pints of beer.

Experiencing for themselves the Best and sometimes the not so Best of London, they have paved a sure way to pleasure, enjoyment and understanding of this awesome city for our faithful readers.

André Gayot

RESTAURANTS

INTRODUCTION

BRITISH GASTRONOMY HAS COME A LONG WAY...

The gastronome who has not visited London for some time may find it hard to swallow but yes, London has become a great restaurant city. It already had a reputation as a centre for ethnic restaurants, particularly Indian and Chinese, which draw visitors from all over the world. But in the past few years London as a gourmet experience has come into its own, encouraged by an increasingly wide and sophisticated choice of eating places, a generation of clients with the means and the knowledge to enjoy good food, and most important of all a group of young, innovative chefs. These new names have broken free of the traditions of their masters to go their own way and establish a new, exciting cuisine which has come to be known as 'Modern British'.

While finding it difficult to recommend a handful out of such a range, we would urge those who have up to now thought of British cuisine as meat and two veg to venture to Alastair Little's restaurant in Soho for a meal our reviewer described as 'unfettered and free', or to Bibendum for Simon Hopkinson's robust cuisine, or to The Square for the cooking of Philip Howard.

The masters remain, of course, chefs like Pierre Koffmann at Tante Claire (who has the highly deserved distinction of being awarded the highest toque rating in this guide), Raymond Blanc at Le Manoir aux Quat' Saisons, Nico Ladenis at Nico at Ninety and the Roux family and they still set the standards many chefs aspire to in their elegant, beautifully run restaurants. A meal at one of the top establishments is an experience not to be missed.

All this, of course, does not happen without the usual proportion of failures, exaggerations, ephemeral stunts and rip-offs. But at the same time, the proliferation of first-rate new restaurants serving a cuisine which searches the world for its inspiration offers the restaurant-goer an enormously wide choice. London has always been a cultural melting-pot and it shows in its restaurants and in the attitude towards food which is now more open than that of previous generations. Londoners are prepared to accept innovations in tastes and applaud the results. Young chefs are making their mark as never before. What about Gordon Ramsey at Aubergine, Henry Harris at The Fifth Floor Restaurant, Bruno Loubet, and Marco Pierre White at The Restaurant? We encourage you to try them all.

There have been other trends in the recent past. Many chefs are favouring the food rather than the décor, taking over a room in a pub or even the whole place, doing a quick painting job and relying on the quality of the food to bring in the customers. And it is working superbly. Part of the success of such places is that they give value for money, another serious consideration in today's tougher, more realistic world. Top chefs at top restaurants are also looking to ways to serve the best food at prices most of us can afford, and it is worth looking out for special prix-fixe menus (often

9

at lunch) which can give you the chance to eat first-rate food at reasonable prices. One further and interesting trend, in part spearheaded by the young British chefs, is that chefs are looking more and more to hitherto humble ingredients, and familiar dishes with a new, light modern touch are making regular appearances on many menus.

One of the many strengths of the Gault Millau guides is their lack of preconceptions and prejudices. We have therefore made a conscious effort in this guide to seek out the very best of the very many ethnic restaurants in London. Many people may be surprised that we have awarded such high marks to the Japanese restaurant Tatsuso, or the tiny Indian vegetarian Sabras in Willesden. Again we would urge you to try these restaurants. You will be delightfully surprised, but not too surprised; we have included a lot of interesting general information on Chinese, Japanese, Indian, Goan and other cuisines within the reviews.

So we suggest you come to London with an open mind, try as many restaurants as your purse and your tastes can take and enjoy the whole experience. You will find some unexpected culinary bombshells.

RESTAURANT SAVVY

• **You will have to book the top restaurants** in advance, and some might require a few weeks' notice. Be prepared to give your telephone number and expect at popular times like Christmas for the restaurant to re-confirm the booking. There have been so many cases of no-shows in the past that restaurants have found themselves with empty tables on busy nights that they can ill afford.

• **Dress is fairly casual**, though at the better restaurants women may feel out of place in pantsuits. **Men should wear** a jacket and tie. Although there is no formal dress code, many people these days dress up for an evening out, so you may feel out of place if you are too casually dressed.

• At any of the top restaurants, it is always a good idea to **ask the head waiter for suggestions**. Remember, too, that the wine waiter is there to offer expert advice, and never be afraid to ask.

• **Lunch is served** from 12.30pm to around 2.30pm, **dinner** from 7.30pm onwards. However many restaurants now offer pre- or post-theatre menus. These can be very good value and are worth trying. Another recent innovation (although centuries-old in Chinese restaurants) is the **prix-fixe menu**, which can offer good value and often the best efforts of the chef.

• Some restaurants add on a **service charge** (this should be printed on the menu), others will leave the service charge up to you. Fifteen percent has become the norm. But always double check your bill as cases have been recorded of the bad practice of adding on the service charge then leaving the final total free, and customers have added on yet again without realising.

• In today's changing world, **chefs change** too, which means a restaurant might not be as described. Chef-owned restaurants are more stable, though they can also change. If you experience any of this, please don't hold us responsible!

ABOUT THE REVIEWS

RATINGS & TOQUES

Gault Millau ranks restaurants in the same manner that French students are graded: on a scale of zero to twenty, twenty being unattainable perfection. The rankings reflect only the quality of the cooking; décor, service, reception and atmosphere do not influence the rating, though they are explicitly commented on within the reviews. Restaurants ranked thirteen and above are distinguished with toques (chef's hats), according to the following table:

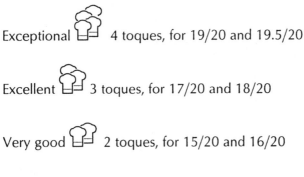

Exceptional 4 toques, for 19/20 and 19.5/20

Excellent 3 toques, for 17/20 and 18/20

Very good 2 toques, for 15/20 and 16/20

Good 1 toque, for 13/20 and 14/20

Keep in mind that these ranks are relative. One toque or 13/20 is not a very good rating for a highly reputed (and very expensive) restaurant, but it is complimentary for a small place without much pretension.

PRICES

At the end of each restaurant review, prices are given—either **C** (A la carte) or **Set L**, **Set D** or **Set menus** (set lunch, set dinner, set menus at any time, all for fixed price meals). A la carte prices are those of an average meal (appetiser, main course, dessert and coffee) for one person, including service but no wine or beer. The fixed price meals quoted are for a complete multi-course meal for one person, excluding service and drink. These fixed-price menus often give diners a chance to sample the cuisine of an otherwise expensive restaurant.

TOQUE TALLY

Four Toques (19/20)

La Tante Claire, *(Chelsea)*

Three Toques (18/20)

Le Manoir aux Quat'Saisons, *(Great Milton, see Oxford)*
Tatsuso, *(The City)*

Three Toques (17/20)

Fung Shing, *(Chinatown)*
Le Gavroche, *(Mayfair)*
Nico at Ninety, *(Mayfair)*
The Oak Room, *(Piccadilly)*
Les Saveurs, *(Mayfair)*
Waterside Inn, *(Bray-on-Thames, see Windsor)*

Two toques (16/20)

Alastair Little, *(Soho)*
Aubergine, *(Chelsea)*
Bibendum, *(South Kensington)*
Bistrot Bruno, *(Soho)*
The Connaught Restaurant and Grill, *(Mayfair)*
Inaho, *(Bayswater)*

Mijanou, *(Belgravia)*
L'Ortolan, *(Shinfield, see Windsor)*
The Regent Dining Room, *(Marylebone)*
The Restaurant, *(Knightsbridge)*
Sabras, *(Willesden)*

Two toques (15/20)

The Argyll, *(Chelsea)*
Café Royal Grill Room, *(Piccadilly)*
Clarke's, *(Kensington)*
The Fifth Floor Restaurant, *(Knightsbridge)*
The Greenhouse, *(Mayfair)*
Masako, *(Oxford Street)*
Matsuri, *(Piccadilly)*
Nico Central, *(Tottenham Court Road)*
Pied-à-Terre, *(Tottenham Court Road)*
Le Pont de la Tour, *(Tower Bridge)*
Riva, *(Barnes)*
The Square, *(Piccadilly)*
Tatsuso Teppan Room, *(The City)*

One toque (14/20)

Albero & Grana, *(Chelsea)*
Al San Vincenzo, *(Marble Arch)*
Bistrot 190, *(South Kensington)*
Blue Print Café, *(Tower Bridge)*
The Brackenbury, *(Shepherd's Bush)*
Boyd's, *(Kensington)*
The Capital, *(Knightsbridge)*
Le Caprice, *(Piccadilly)*
Chinon, *(Shepherd's Bush)*
Clos du Roy, *(Bath)*
dell 'Ugo, *(Soho)*
Dorchester Terrace, *(Mayfair)*
Downstairs at One Ninety, *(South Kensington)*

L'Escargot, *(Soho)*
Harbour City, *(Chinatown)*
Imperial City, *(The City)*
The Ivy, *(Covent Garden)*
Kensington Place, *(Kensington)*
Leith's, *(Notting Hill Gate)*
Mandarin Kitchen, *(Bayswater)*
Ming, *(Soho)*
Miyama, *(Mayfair)*
Odette's, *(Primrose Hill)*
Pearl of Knightsbridge, *(Knightsbridge)*
Quality Chop House, *(Clerkenwell)*
River Café, *(Hammersmith)*
The River Restaurant, *(Strand)*
Saga, *(Mayfair)*
Snows on the Green, *(Shepherd's Bush)*
Le Soufflé, *(Mayfair)*
Suntory, *(Piccadilly)*
Turner's, *(South Kensington)*

One toque (13/20)

L'Altro, *(Notting Hill Gate)*
Bahn Thai, *(Soho)*
Bath Place Restaurant, *(Oxford)*
Butlers Wharf Chop
  House, *(Tower Bridge)*
Byblos, *(Kensington)*
The Canteen, *(Chelsea)*
Chez Moi, *(Holland Park)*
City Singapura, *(The City)*
Claridge's, *(Mayfair)*

Dower House Restaurant, *(Bath)*
15 North Parade, *(Oxford)*
Four Seasons Restaurant, *(Mayfair)*
La Gaulette, *(Tottenham Court Road)*
Gopal's of Soho, *(Soho)*
Granita, *(Islington)*
Green's Restaurant and
  Oyster Bar, *(Piccadilly)*
Hilaire, *(South Kensington)*
Homewood Park Restaurant, *(Hinton
  Charterhouse, see Bath)*
Hunan, *(Pimlico)*
Joes's Café, *(South Kensington)*
Lou Pescadou, *(South Kensington)*
Lucknam Park Restaurant, *(Colerne,
  see Bath)*
Midsummer House, *(Cambridge)*
Mr Ke, *(Finchley Road)*
Mr Kong, *(Chinatown)*
Mulligans of Mayfair, *(Mayfair)*
Museum Street Café, *(Bloomsbury)*
New Moon, *(Bath)*
Olive Tree Restaurant, *(Bath)*
Orso, *(Covent Garden)*
Le Petit Max, *(Hampton Court)*
Phœnicia, *(Kensington)*
Priory Hotel Restaurant, *(Bath)*
Red Fort, *(Soho)*
The Ritz Restaurant, *(Piccadilly)*
The Room at the
  Halcyon, *(Holland Park)*
St Quentin, *(Knightsbridge)*
San Martino, *(South Kensington)*
Stephen Bull, *(Marylebone)*
Stephen Bull's Bistro and Bar, *(The City)*
Walton's, *(South Kensington)*

BY CUISINE

There are so many cross-overs in modern cooking that it is difficult to pinpoint the inspiration behind many restaurants. However we have taken the predominant tastes to classify restaurants by their cuisine.

AFGHAN

Caravan Serai, *(Marylebone)*

AMERICAN

Christopher's American
  Grill, *(Covent Garden)*
Clarke's, *(Kensington)*
Joe Allen, *(Covent Garden)*
PJ's Bar & Grill, *(Covent Garden)*

BELGIAN

Belgo, *(Camden Town/Chalk Farm)*

BRITISH

Bottoms Restaurant, *(Brighton)*
Buchan's, *(Battersea)*
Cherwell Boathouse, *(Oxford)*
The English Garden, *(Chelsea)*
Foxtrot Oscar, *(Chelsea)*
French House Dining Room, *(Soho)*
Green's Restaurant and
  Oyster Bar, *(Piccadilly)*
The Grill Room, *(Strand)*
Leith's, *(Notting Hill Gate)*
Quincy's, *(Golders Green)*
The Regent Dining Room, *(Marylebone)*
Rules, *(Covent Garden)*
Simpson's-in-the-Strand, *(Strand)*
Sweetings, *(The City)*
Tate Gallery Restaurant, *(Pimlico)*
Walsh's, *(Tottenham Court Road)*
Walton's, *(South Kensington)*
Wiltons, *(Piccadilly)*

CHINESE

Fung Shing, *(Chinatown)*
Harbour City, *(Chinatown)*
Hunan, *(Pimlico)*
Imperial City, *(The City)*
Jade Garden, *(Chinatown)*
Mandarin Kitchen, *(Bayswater)*

Ming, *(Soho)*
Mr Ke, *(Golders Green)*
Mr Kong, *(Chinatown)*
Oriental, *(Mayfair)*
Pearl of Knightsbridge, *(Knightsbridge)*
Vegetarian Cottage,
  (Camden Town/Chalk Farm)
Zen, *(Chelsea)*

EAST EUROPEAN

The Gay Hussar, *(Soho)*
Ognisko Polskie, *(South Kensington)*
Wódka, *(Kensington)*

FRENCH

Les Associés, *(Crouch End)*
Bath Place Restaurant, *(Oxford)*
Bistrot Bruno, *(Soho)*
Bottoms Restaurant, *(Brighton)*
La Brasserie, *(South Kensington)*
Café des Arts, *(Hampstead)*
Café du Marché, *(The City)*
Café Pelican, *(Covent Garden)*
Café Royal Grill Room, *(Piccadilly)*
Camden Brasserie,
  (Camden Town/Chalk Farm)
Chez Gérard, *(Tottenham Court Road)*
Chez Moi, *(Holland Park)*
Chinon, *(Shepherd's Bush)*
Claridge's, *(Mayfair)*
Clos du Roy, *(Bath)*
Dan's, *(South Kensington)*
Dorchester Terrace, *(Mayfair)*
La Dordogne, *(Chiswick)*
Dower House Restaurant, *(Bath)*
L'Epicure, *(Soho)*
L'Escargot, *(Soho)*
L'Estaminet, *(Covent Garden)*
L'Express, *(Chelsea)*
15 North Parade, *(Oxford)*
Four Seasons Restaurant, *(Mayfair)*
Le Gavroche, *(Mayfair)*
Grill St Quentin, *(South Kensington)*
Homewood Park Restaurant, *(Bath)*

Lou Pescadou, *(South Kensington)*
Le Manoir aux Quat'Saisons, *(Great Milton, see Oxford)*
Mijanou, *(Belgravia)*
Mon Petit Plaisir, *(Kensington)*
Mon Plaisir, *(Covent Garden)*
New Moon, *(Bath)*
Nico Central, *(Tottenham Court Road)*
Nico at Ninety, *(Mayfair)*
The Oak Room, *(Piccadilly)*
L'Ortolan, *(Shinfield, see Windsor)*
Le Palais du Jardin, *(Covent Garden)*
Le Petit Max, *(Hampton Court)*
Pied-à-Terre, *(Tottenham Court Road)*
La Poule au Pot, *(Victoria)*
Restaurant Elizabeth, *(Oxford)*
The River Restaurant, *(Strand)*
The Rotisserie, *(Shepherd's Bush)*
Les Saveurs, *(Mayfair)*
Simply Nico, *(Pimlico)*
St Quentin, *(Knightsbridge)*
Sir Toby's, *(Stratford-upon-Avon)*
Le Soufflé, *(Mayfair)*
Le Suquet, *(South Kensington)*
La Tante Claire, *(Chelsea)*
Turner's, *(South Kensington)*
Villandry Dining Room, *(Marylebone)*
Waterside Inn, *(Bray-on-Thames, see Windsor)*
Whites, *(Oxford)*

FRENCH/ BRITISH

The Connaught Grill and Restaurant, *(Mayfair)*

GREEK

Kalamaras, *(Bayswater)*

INDIAN

Bombay Brasserie, *(South Kensington)*
Chutney Mary, *(Fulham)*
Gopal's of Soho, *(Soho)*
Ma Goa, *(Richmond)*
Ragam, *(Tottenham Court Road)*
Red Fort, *(Soho)*
Sabras, *(Willesden)*
Salloos, *(Belgravia)*
Star of India, *(South Kensington)*

INTERNATIONAL

Alfresco Restaurant, *(Bath)*
Bell Bistro, *(Alderminster, see Stratford-upon-Avon)*

Brasserie du Marché aux Puces, *(Notting Hill Gate)*
Browns, *(Brighton)*
Browns, *(Cambridge)*
Browns, *(Oxford)*
Caffé Graffiti, *(Hampstead)*
Deals, *(Chelsea)*
Langan's Bistro, *(Brighton)*
Melton's, *(York)*
Midsummer House, *(Cambridge)*
Olive Tree Restaurant, *(Bath)*
Palio, *(Notting Hill Gate)*
Priory Hotel Restaurant, *(Bath)*
Stephen Bull's Bistro and Bar, *(The City)*
Twenty Two, *(Cambridge)*
Vellore Restaurant, *(Bath)*
Zoe, *(Oxford Street)*

IRISH

Mulligans of Mayfair, *(Mayfair)*

ITALIAN

L'Accento Italiano, *(Notting Hill Gate)*
L'Altro, *(Notting Hill Gate)*
Al San Vincenzo, *(Marble Arch)*
Arts Theatre Café, *(Covent Garden)*
Casale Franco, *(Islington)*
Cibo, *(Kensington)*
Daphne's, *(Chelsea)*
Del Buongustaio, *(Putney)*
La Famiglia, *(Chelsea)*
L'Incontro, *(Pimlico)*
Manzi's, *(Soho)*
Neal Street Restaurant, *(Covent Garden)*
Olivo, *(Belgravia)*
Orsino, *(Notting Hill Gate)*
Orso, *(Covent Garden)*
Osteria Antica Bologna, *(Battersea)*
The Regent Dining Room, *(Marylebone)*
Riva, *(Barnes)*
River Café, *(Hammersmith)*
San Lorenzo, *(South Kensington)*
San Martino, *(South Kensington)*

JAPANESE/SUSHI

Ginnan, *(Clerkenwell)*
Inaho, *(Bayswater)*
Masako, *(Oxford Street)*
Matsuri, *(Piccadilly)*
Matsuri Teppan Bar, *(Piccadilly)*
Miyama, *(Mayfair)*
Saga, *(Mayfair)*
Shogun, *(Mayfair)*
Suntory, *(Piccadilly)*

Tatsuso, *(The City)*
Tatsuso Teppan Room, *(The City)*
Wakaba, *(Finchley Road)*

LEBANESE

Al Hamra, *(Mayfair)*
Al-Shami, *(Oxford)*
Byblos, *(Kensington)*
Phœnicia, *(Kensington)*

MAURITIAN

La Gaulette, *(Tottenham Court Road)*

MEDITERRANEAN

Cantina del Ponte, *(Tower Bridge)*
Criterion Brasserie, *(Piccadilly)*
dell 'Ugo, *(Soho)*
est, *(Soho)*
Granita, *(Islington)*
Odette's, *(Primrose Hill)*
Soho Soho, *(Soho)*

MODERN BRITISH

Alastair Little, *(Soho)*
The Argyll, *(Chelsea)*
The Ark, *(Kensington)*
Aubergine, *(Chelsea)*
The Belvedere, *(Holland Park)*
Bibendum, *(South Kensington)*
Bibendum Oyster
  Bar, *(South Kensington)*
Big Night Out, *(Primrose Hill)*
Billesley Manor
  Restaurant, *(Stratford-upon-Avon)*
Bistrot 190, *(South Kensington)*
Blue Print Café, *(Tower Bridge)*
Boyd's, *(Kensington)*
The Brackenbury, *(Shepherd's Bush)*
Butlers Wharf
  Chop House, *(Tower Bridge)*
The Canteen, *(Chelsea)*
The Capital, *(Knightsbridge)*
Le Caprice, *(Piccadilly)*
Clarke's, *(Kensington)*
Downstairs at One
  Ninety, *(South Kensington)*
The Fifth Floor
  Restaurant, *(Knightsbridge)*
First Floor, *(Notting Hill Gate)*
Garlands Restaurant, *(Bath)*
Gilbert's, *(South Kensington)*
The Greenhouse, *(Mayfair)*
Hilaire, *(South Kensington)*

The Ivy, *(Covent Garden)*
Ivy Restaurant, *(York)*
Joe's Café, *(South Kensington)*
Kensington Place, *(Kensington)*
Langan's Brasserie, *(Mayfair)*
Launceston Place, *(Kensington)*
The Lexington, *(Soho)*
Lucknam Park Restaurant, *(Bath)*
Middlethorpe Hall Restaurant, *(York)*
Mosimann's, *(Belgravia)*
Museum Street Café, *(Bloomsbury)*
19 Grape Lane, *(York)*
192, *(Notting Hill Gate)*
Le Pont de la Tour, *(Tower Bridge)*
Quaglino's, *(Piccadilly)*
Quality Chop House, *(Clerkenwell)*
Ransome's Dock, *(Battersea)*
The Restaurant, *(Knightsbridge)*
The Ritz Restaurant, *(Piccadilly)*
The Room at the
  Halcyon, *(Holland Park)*
RSJ, *(South Bank)*
Smith's, *(Covent Garden)*
Snows on the Green, *(Shepherd's Bush)*
Sonny's, *(Barnes)*
The Square, *(Piccadilly)*
Stephen Bull, *(Marylebone)*

RUSSIAN/FRENCH

Caviar House, La Brasserie, *(Piccadilly)*
Caviar Kaspia, *(Mayfair)*

SOUTH-EAST ASIAN

City Singapura, *(The City)*
Melati, *(Soho)*
Minang, *(Soho)*

SPANISH

Albero & Grana, *(Chelsea)*

SWEDISH

Anna's Place, *(Islington)*

THAI

Bahn Thai, *(Soho)*
Blue Elephant, *(Fulham)*
Chiang Mai, *(Soho)*
Khun Akorn, *(Knightsbridge)*
Sri Siam, *(Soho)*

TURKISH

BY NOTABLE FEATURES

FISH

**Restaurants serving exclusively
or predominantly fish.**

L'Altro, (Notting Hill Gate)
Bibendum Oyster Bar, (South Kensington)
Downstairs at One
  Ninety, (South Kensington)
La Gaulette, (Tottenham Court Road)
Green's Oyster Bar, (Piccadilly)
Lou Pescadou, (South Kensington)
Manzi's, (Soho)
Le Suquet, (South Kensington)
Sweetings, (The City)
Walsh's, (Tottenham Court Road)

LATE-NIGHT

Last orders at 11pm.

L'Accento Italiano, (Notting Hill Gate)
Al Hamra, (Mayfair)
Alastair Little, (Soho)
L'Altro, (Notting Hill Gate)
The Argyll, (Chelsea)
The Ark, (Kensington)
Aubergine, (Chelsea)
Bahn Thai, (Soho)
Belgo, (Camden Town/Chalk Farm)
Bibendum, (South Kensington)
Big Night Out, (Primerose Hill)
Bistrot Bruno, (Soho)
Blue Print Café, (Tower Bridge)
Boyd's, (Kensington)
La Brasserie, (South Kensington)
Brasserie du Marché
  aux Puces, (Notting Hill Gate)
Byblos, (Kensington)
Café des Arts, (Hampstead)
Café Pelican, (Covent Garden)
Caffé Graffiti, (Hampstead)
Camden Brasserie, (Camden Town/
  Chalk Farm)
Cantina del Ponte, (Tower Bridge)
The Capital, (Knightsbridge)
Caravan Serai, (Marylebone)
Casale Franco, (Islington)
Caviar House, La Brasserie (Piccadilly)
Caviar Kaspia, (Mayfair)
Chez Gérard, (Tottenham Court Road)

Chez Moi, (Holland Park)
Chiang Mai, (Soho)
Chinon, (Shepherd's Bush)
Christopher's American
  Grill, (Covent Garden)
Chutney Mary, (Fulham)
Cibo, (Kensington)
Claridge's, (Mayfair)
Criterion Brasserie, (Piccadilly)
Deals, (Chelsea)
Del Buongustaio, (Putney)
Dorchester Terrace, (Mayfair)
La Dordogne, (Chiswick)
The English Garden, (Chelsea)
est, (Soho)
L'Estaminet, (Covent Garden)
La Famiglia, (Chelsea)
The Fifth Floor Restaurant, (Knightsbridge)
Four Seasons Restaurant, (Mayfair)
French House Dining Room, (Soho)
Fung Shing, (Chinatown)
La Gaulette, (Tottenham Court Road)
Le Gavroche, (Mayfair)
Gay Hussar, (Soho)
Gopal's of Soho, (Soho)
The Greenhouse, (Mayfair)
Green's Restaurant and
  Oyster Bar, (Piccadilly)
The Grill Room, (Strand)
Grill St Quentin, (South Kensington)
Hilaire, (South Kensington)
Hunan, (Pimlico)
Inaho, (Bayswater)
L'Incontro, (Pimlico)
Jade Garden, (Chinatown)
Joe's Café, (South Kensington)
Kensington Place, (Kensington)
Khun Akorn, (Knightsbridge)
Mr Ke, (Finchley Road)
Ma Goa, (Richmond)
Mandarin Kitchen, (Bayswater)
Manzi's, (Soho)
Melati, (Soho)
Mijanou, (Belgravia)
Ming, (Soho)
Mon Plaisir, (Covent Garden)
Mulligans of Mayfair, (Mayfair)
Neal Street Restaurant, (Covent Garden)
Nico Central, (Tottenham Court Road)
Nico at Ninety, (Mayfair)

17

Odette's, (Primrose Hill)
Ognisko Polskie, (South Kensington)
Olivo, (Belgravia)
192, (Notting Hill Gate)
Oriental, (Mayfair)
Orsino, (Notting Hill Gate)
Osteria Antica Bologna, (Battersea)
Palio, (Notting Hill Gate)
Pearl of Knightsbridge, (Knightsbridge)
La Poule au Pot, (Victoria)
Quincy's, (Golders Green)
Ragam, (Tottenham Court Road)
Red Fort, (Soho)
The Regent Dining Room, (Marylebone)
The Restaurant, (Knightsbridge)
The Ritz Restaurant, (Piccadilly)
Riva, (Barnes)
The River Restaurant, (Strand)
The Room at the Halcyon, (Holland Park)
The Rotisserie, (Shepherd's Bush)
RSJ, (South Bank)
St Quentin, (Knightsbridge)
Salloos, (Belgravia)
San Lorenzo, (South Kensington)
San Martino, (South Kensington)
Shogun, (Mayfair)
Simply Nico, (Pimlico)
Smith's, (Covent Garden)
Snows on the Green, (Shepherd's Bush)
Sonny's, (Barnes)
Le Soufflé, (Mayfair)
Sri Siam, (Soho)
Le Suquet, (South Kensington)
La Tante Claire, (Chelsea)
Topkapi, (Marylebone)
Turner's, (South Kensington)
Wakaba, (Hampstead)
Walsh's, (Tottenham Court Road)
Walton's, (South Kensington)
Wódka, (Kensington)
Zen, (Chelsea)
Zoe, (Oxford Street)

LATE-LATE NIGHT

Restaurants with last orders between 11.30pm and midnight, though it's best to double-check. If it's a quiet night, then the restaurant may close earlier than its stated time.

Albero & Grana, (Chelsea)
Bistrot 190, (South Kensington)
Blue Elephant, (Fulham)
Bombay Brasserie, (South Kensington)
The Canteen, (Chelsea)
Le Caprice, (Piccadilly)

Daphne's, (Chelsea)
dell 'Ugo, (Soho)
Downstairs at One
  Ninety, (South Kensington)
Harbour City, (Chinatown)
The Ivy, (Covent Garden)
Joe Allen, (Covent Garden)
Kalamaras, (Bayswater)
Lou Pescadou, (South Kensington)
Mr Kong, (Chinatown)
Orso, (Covent Garden)
PJ's Bar & Grill, (Covent Garden)
Le Palais du Jardin, (Covent Garden)
Phœnicia, (Kensington)
Le Pont de la Tour, (Tower Bridge)
Quaglino's, (Piccadilly)
Quality Chop House, (Clerkenwell)
Ransome's Dock, (Battersea)
Rules, (Covent Garden)
Sofra, (Mayfair)
Soho Soho, (Soho)
The Square, (Piccadilly)
Star of India, (South Kensington)

VEGETARIAN

Most restaurants have one or two dishes for appetisers and main courses. We have listed here only restaurants serving a substantial number of vegetarian dishes or with a separate vegetarian menu.

Al Hamra, (Mayfair)
Bistrot 190, (South Kensington)
Bombay Brasserie, (South Kensington)
Byblos, (Kensington)
Ma Goa, (Richmond)
Ragam, (Tottenham Court Road)
The Room at the Halcyon, (Holland Park)
Sabras, (Willesden)
Sofra, (Mayfair)
Star of India, (South Kensington)
Vegetarian Cottage,
  (Camden Town/Chalk Farm)

OPEN ON A SUNDAY

(L) means lunch only,
(D) means dinner only.

L'Accento Italiano, (Notting Hill Gate)
Al Hamra, (Mayfair)
L'Altro (L), (Notting Hill Gate)
The Ark (D), (Kensington)
Bahn Thai, (Soho)
Belgo, (Camden Town/Chalk Farm)
The Belvedere (L), (Holland Park)
Bibendum, (South Kensington)

Bibendum Oyster Bar, *(South Kensington)*
Big Night Out (L), *(Primerose Hill)*
Bistrot 190, *(South Kensington)*
Blue Elephant, *(Fulham)*
Blue Print Café (L), *(Tower Bridge)*
Bombay Brasserie, *(South Kensington)*
The Brackenbury (L), *(Shepherd's Bush)*
La Brasserie, *(South Kensington)*
Brasserie du Marché
   aux Puces (L), *(Notting Hill Gate)*
Buchan's, *(Battersea)*
Butlers Wharf Chop
   House (L), *(Tower Bridge)*
Byblos, *(Kensington)*
Café des Arts, *(Hampstead)*
Café Pelican, *(Covent Garden)*
Caffé Graffiti, *(Hampstead)*
Camden Brasserie, *(Camden Town/*
   Chalk Farm)
Cantina del Ponte (L), *(Tower Bridge)*
The Canteen, *(Chelsea)*
The Capital, *(Knightsbridge)*
Le Caprice, *(Piccadilly)*
Caravan Serai, *(Marylebone)*
Casale Franco, *(Islington)*
Chez Gérard (D), *(Tottenham Court Road)*
Chiang Mai (D), *(Soho)*
Christopher's American
   Grill (L), *(Covent Garden)*
Chutney Mary, *(Fulham)*
Cibo, *(Kensington)*
Claridge's, *(Mayfair)*
The Connaught Restaurant, *(Mayfair)*
Criterion Brasserie, *(Piccadilly)*
Daphne's, *(Chelsea)*
Del Buongustaio (L), *(Putney)*
Deals, *(Chelsea)*
Downstairs at One
   Ninety, *(South Kensington)*
La Dordogne (D), *(Chiswick)*
The English Garden, *(Chelsea)*
La Famiglia, *(Chelsea)*
First Floor, *(Notting Hill Gate)*
Four Seasons Restaurant, *(Mayfair)*
Foxtrot Oscar, *(Chelsea)*
Fung Shing, *(Chinatown)*
Gopal's of Soho, *(Soho)*
Granita, *(Islington)*
The Greenhouse, *(Mayfair)*
Green's Restaurant and
   Oyster Bar (L), *(Piccadilly)*
Grill St Quentin, *(South Kensington)*
Harbour City, *(Chinatown)*
Hunan (D), *(Pimlico)*
L'Incontro (D), *(Pimlico)*
The Ivy, *(Covent Garden)*
Jade Garden, *(Chinatown)*

Joe's Café (L), *(South Kensington)*
Joe Allen, *(Covent Garden)*
Kensington Place, *(Kensington)*
Khun Akorn, *(Knightsbridge)*
Launceston Place (L), *(Kensington)*
Leith's (D), *(Notting Hill Gate)*
Lou Pescadou, *(South Kensington)*
Mandarin Kitchen, *(Bayswater)*
Ma Goa, *(Richmond)*
Melati, *(Soho)*
Minang, *(Soho)*
Mr Ke, *(Finchley Road)*
Mr Kong, *(Chinatown)*
Miyama (D), *(Mayfair)*
Odette's (L), *(Primrose Hill)*
Ognisko Polskie, *(South Kensington)*
192, *(Notting Hill Gate)*
Orso, *(Covent Garden)*
Orsino, *(Notting Hill Gate)*
Osteria Antica Bologna, *(Battersea)*
Le Palais du Jardin, *(Covent Garden)*
Palio, *(Notting Hill Gate)*
Pearl of Knightsbridge, *(Knightsbridge)*
PJ's Bar & Grill, *(Covent Garden)*
Phœnicia, *(Kensington)*
Le Pont de la Tour, *(Tower Bridge)*
La Poule au Pot, *(Victoria)*
Quaglino's, *(Piccadilly)*
Quality Chop House, *(Clerkenwell)*
Ragam, *(Tottenham Court Road)*
Ransome's Dock (L), *(Battersea)*
Red Fort, *(Soho)*
The Regent Dining Room, *(Marylebone)*
The Ritz Restaurant, *(Piccadilly)*
Riva (D), *(Barnes)*
River Café (L), *(Hammersmith)*
The River Restaurant, *(Strand)*
The Room at the Halcyon, *(Holland Park)*
Rules, *(Covent Garden)*
St Quentin, *(Knightsbridge)*
Sabras (D), *(Willesden)*
Saga, *(Mayfair)*
San Martino, *(South Kensington)*
Shogun (D), *(Mayfair)*
Simpson's-in-the-Strand, *(Strand)*
Snows on the
   Green (L), *(Shepherd's Bush)*
Sofra, *(Mayfair)*
Sonny's (L), *(Barnes)*
The Square (D), *(Piccadilly)*
Sri Siam (D), *(Soho)*
Star of India, *(South Kensington)*
Le Suquet, *(South Kensington)*
Topkapi, *(Marylebone)*
Turner's, *(South Kensington)*
Vegetarian Cottage, *(Camden*
   Town/Chalk Farm)

Walton's, (South Kensington)
Wódka (L), (Kensington)
Zen, (Chelsea)
Zoe (L), (Oxford Street)

UNDER £25

L'Accento Italiano, (Notting Hill Gate)
Anna's Place, (Islington)
The Argyll, (Chelsea)
The Ark, (Kensington)
Arts Theatre Café, (Covent Garden)
Les Associés, (Crouch End)
Bahn Thai, (Soho)
Belgo, (Camden Town/Chalk Farm)
The Belvedere, (Holland Park)
Big Night Out, (Primrose Hill)
Bistrot 190, (South Kensington)
The Brackenbury, (Shepherd's Bush)
La Brasserie, (South Kensington)
Brasserie du Marché
  aux Puces, (Notting Hill Gate)
Buchan's, (Battersea)
Byblos, (Kensington)
Café des Arts, (Hampstead)
Café du Marché, (The City)
Café Royal Brasserie, (Piccadilly)
Caffè Graffiti, (Hampstead)
Camden Brasserie, (Camden Town/
  Chalk Farm)
Cantina del Ponte, (Tower Bridge)
Caravan Serai, (Marylebone)
Casale Franco, (Islington)
City Singapura, (The City)
Criterion Brasserie, (Piccadilly)
Dan's, (South Kensington)
Deals, (Chelsea)
Del Buongustaio, (Putney)
dell 'Ugo, (Soho)
La Dordogne, (Chiswick)
L'Estaminet, (Covent Garden)
L'Express, (Chelsea)
La Famiglia, (Chelsea)
First Floor, (Notting Hill Gate)
Foxtrot Oscar, (Chelsea)
The French House Dining Room, (Soho)
Fung Shing, (Chinatown)
Gilbert's, (South Kensington)
Gopal's of Soho, (Soho)
Granita, (Islington)
Grill St Quentin, (South Kensington)
Harbour City, (Chinatown)
Hunan, (Pimlico)
Imperial City, (The City)
Inaho, (Bayswater)
Jade Garden, (Chinatown)

Joe Allen, (Covent Garden)
Joe's Café, (South Kensington)
Kalamaras, (Bayswater)
The Lexington, (Soho)
Ma Goa, (Richmond)
Manzi's, (Soho)
Melati, (Soho)
Minang, (Soho)
Ming, (Soho)
Mr Ke, (Finchley Road)
Mr Kong, (Chinatown)
Mon Plaisir, (Covent Garden)
Mon Petit Plaisir, (Kensington)
Museum Street Café, (Bloomsbury)
Ognisko Polskie, (South Kensington)
192, (Notting Hill Gate)
Osteria Antica Bologna, (Battersea)
Le Palais du Jardin, (Covent Garden)
Palio, (Notting Hill Gate)
PJ's Bar & Grill, (Covent Garden)
Phœnicia, (Kensington)
La Poule au Pot, (Victoria)
Quality Chop House, (Clerkenwell)
Quincy's, (Golders Green)
Ragam, (Tottenham Court Road)
The Rotisserie, (Shepherd's Bush)
St Quentin, (Knightsbridge)
Sabras, (Willesden)
San Martino, (South Kensington)
Smith's, (Covent Garden)
Snows on the Green, (Shepherd's Bush)
Sofra, (Mayfair)
Soho Soho, (Soho)
Sonny's, (Barnes)
Sri Siam, (Soho)
Stephen Bull's Bistro and Bar, (The City)
Sweetings, (The City)
Tate Gallery Restaurant, (Pimlico)
Topkapi, (Marylebone)
Vegetarian Cottage,
  (Camden Town/Chalk Farm)
Villandry Dining Room, (Marylebone)
Wódka, (Kensington)
Zoe, (Oxford Street)

BETWEEN £25 AND £40

Alastair Little, (Soho)
Albero & Grana, (Chelsea)
Al Hamra, (Mayfair)
L'Altro, (Notting Hill Gate)
Al San Vincenzo, (Marble Arch)
Aubergine, (Chelsea)
Bibendum Oyster Bar, (South Kensington)
Bistrot Bruno, (Soho)
Blue Elephant, (Fulham)

Blue Print Café, *(Tower Bridge)*
Bombay Brasserie, *(South Kensington)*
Boyd's, *(Kensington)*
Butlers Wharf Chop
   House, *(Tower Bridge)*
Café Pelican, *(Covent Garden)*
The Canteen, *(Chelsea)*
The Capital, *(Knightsbridge)*
Le Caprice, *(Piccadilly)*
Caviar House, La Brasserie, *(Piccadilly)*
Caviar Kaspia, *(Mayfair)*
Chez Gérard, *(Tottenham Court Road)*
Chez Moi, *(Holland Park)*
Chiang Mai, *(Soho)*
Chinon, *(Shepherd's Bush)*
Christopher's American
   Grill, *(Covent Garden)*
Chutney Mary, *(Fulham)*
Cibo, *(Kensington)*
Clarke's, *(Kensington)*
The Connaught Restaurant and
   Grill, *(Mayfair)*
Daphne's, *(Chelsea)*
Downstairs at One
   Ninety, *(South Kensington)*
The English Garden, *(Chelsea)*
L'Epicure, *(Soho)*
L'Escargot, *(Soho)*
est, *(Soho)*
The Fifth Floor Restaurant, *(Knightsbridge)*
La Gaulette, *(Tottenham Court Road)*
The Gay Hussar, *(Soho)*
Ginnan, *(Clerkenwell)*
Green's Restaurant and
   Oyster Bar, *(Piccadilly)*
The Greenhouse, *(Mayfair)*
Hilaire, *(South Kensington)*
L'Incontro, *(Pimlico)*
The Ivy, *(Covent Garden)*
Kensington Place, *(Kensington)*
Khun Akorn, *(Knightsbridge)*
Langan's Brasserie, *(Mayfair)*
Launceston Place, *(Kensington)*
Lou Pescadou, *(South Kensington)*
Mandarin Kitchen, *(Bayswater)*
Masako, *(Oxford Street)*
Mijanou, *(Belgravia)*
Miyama, *(Mayfair)*
Mulligans of Mayfair, *(Mayfair)*
Neal Street Restaurant, *(Covent Garden)*
Nico Central, *(Tottenham Court Road)*
Odette's, *(Primrose Hill)*
Olivo, *(Belgravia)*

Oriental, *(Mayfair)*
Orso, *(Covent Garden)*
Orsino, *(Notting Hill Gate)*
Pearl of Knightsbridge, *(Knightsbridge)*
Pied-à-Terre, *(Tottenham Court Road)*
Le Pont de la Tour, *(Tower Bridge)*
Quaglino's, *(Piccadilly)*
Red Fort, *(Soho)*
The Regent Dining Room, *(Marylebone)*
Riva, *(Barnes)*
River Café, *(Hammersmith)*
The Room at the Halcyon, *(Holland Park)*
RSJ, *(South Bank)*
Rules, *(Covent Garden)*
Salloos, *(Belgravia)*
San Lorenzo, *(South Kensington)*
Shogun, *(Mayfair)*
Simply Nico, *(Pimlico)*
Simpson's-in-the-Strand, *(Strand)*
Soho Soho, *(Soho)*
The Square, *(Piccadilly)*
Star of India, *(South Kensington)*
Stephen Bull, *(Marylebone)*
Le Suquet, *(South Kensington)*
Tatsuso, *(The City)*
Turner's, *(South Kensington)*
Wakaba, *(Hampstead)*
Walton's, *(South Kensington)*
Walsh's, *(Tottenham Court Road)*
Zen, *(Chelsea)*

OVER £40

Bibendum, *(South Kensington)*
Café Royal Grill Room, *(Piccadilly)*
Claridge's, *(Mayfair)*
Dorchester Terrace, *(Mayfair)*
Four Seasons Restaurant, *(Mayfair)*
Le Gavroche, *(Mayfair)*
The Grill Room, *(Strand)*
Leith's, *(Notting Hill Gate)*
Matsuri, *(Piccadilly)*
Nico at Ninety, *(Mayfair)*
The Oak Room, *(Piccadilly)*
The Restaurant, *(Knightsbridge)*
The Ritz Restaurant, *(Piccadilly)*
The River Restaurant, *(Strand)*
Saga, *(Mayfair)*
Les Saveurs, *(Mayfair)*
Le Soufflé, *(Mayfair)*
Suntory, *(Piccadilly)*
La Tante Claire, *(Chelsea)*
Wiltons, *(Piccadilly)*

BARNES

 Riva

169 Church Rd, SW13 - 081-748 0434
ITALIAN
Open Lunch Mon-Sat, Dinner daily.

Proprietor Andrea Riva's love child continues to wow London with its menu of northern Italian food, invariably well cooked by Francesco Zanchetta, late of The Cipriani in Venice. The menu changes with the seasons and is strong on braised and casseroled dishes, seafood and pasta. Certain dishes, notably creamed salt cod with grilled polenta (baccala Mantecato) and grilled and sliced rib eye steak (tagliata di manzo) are too popular to rotate. Tiramisù is like biting into alcoholic cream clouds and panna cotta is manna from heaven. The Italian wine list is short and to the point but befriending the boss may well lead to unpublished discoveries. The grappa selection is unparalleled. Riva, a converted shop, is a long narrow room 'widened' by a mirror wall that reflects the Palladian prints and nicotine colour scheme, though many tables are quite cramped. **C** £25.

12/20 Sonny's

94 Church Rd, SW13 - 081-748 0393
MODERN BRITISH
Open Lunch daily, Dinner Mon-Sat.

Restaurant, bar then deli and now café too, Sonny's has something for everyone whatever the occasion. Neighbourhood restaurant it might be, but Sonny's understated style and interesting menu lures others to leafy Barnes too, so it's essential to book. Although it's not a chef-led restaurant, Sonny's kitchen has nurtured a succession of trend setters and stands forever at the sharp end of food fashions. Hence flavours are Mediterranean-cum-Californian-cum-Asian with a sprinkling of classic British and French dishes. This is a good place for a family Sunday lunch and is the ideal choice for vegetarians and meat lovers eating together. The wine list is similarly mixed but well chosen and good value. **C** £20. **Set L** £12.50.

BATTERSEA

11/20 Buchan's

62 Battersea Bridge Rd, SW11 - 071-228 0888
BRITISH
Open Lunch & Dinner daily.

With its lively ambience, this pleasant brasserie attracts a youngish crowd. Its décor, and the contents of the bookcase in the main restaurant room are Scottish without tartanry, and the same could be said of much of the menu. Haggis with neeps and tatties is one starter, Loch Fyne oysters another. But the 'auld alliance' between Scotland and France is recalled by such dishes as a creamy Roquefort and whisky mousse, lamb shank Bourguignon, wild boar sausages with Calvados and the selection of Scottish and French cheeses. Special menus are offered for Saturday and Sunday brunch, the latter including roast beef; there are four options in each course at a modest £8.50 for two courses, £10.50 for three. On Mondays the £5 dinner helps fill the restaurant. A dozen wines by the glass are offered, but whilst applauding patriotism we cannot recommend the one from Scotland. At £8.50 to £26.50 (Champagne excepted) some very decent bottles are listed. The cooking is generally sound although some desserts taste less exciting than they look. Service is informal and friendly but efficient. **C** £21. **Set L** (Sat, Sun) £8.50, £10.50, **Set D** (Mon) £5.

12/20 Osteria Antica Bologna

23 Northcote Rd, SW11
071-978 4771
ITALIAN
Open Lunch & Dinner daily.

Noisy, busy and bustling. Do not go to the Osteria for intimate elegance, or refined cucina nuova. The place is like a family kitchen, and the cooking as honest and direct and filling as Italian domestic cooking should be. Aurelio Spagnuolo comes from Sicily, but he does not allow that to restrict the dishes that he serves which seem to be selected at random from all over the country—spicy Sicilian suppli, grilled sausages, fried spleen on focaccia, polenta with various accompaniments, mushrooms and Pecorino cheesecake, fried fennel in bread crumbs, swordfish marinated in lemon, kid cooked in almond and tomato sauce, and generally reliable pasta. The kitchen occasionally cracks under the strain of it all, but the customers don't. The same team have opened Del Buongustaio at 283 Putney Bridge Rd, SW15, 081-780 9361. C £15. Set L £6.50.

12/20 Ransome's Dock

35 Parkgate Rd, SW11 - 071-223 1611
MODERN BRITISH
Open Lunch daily, Dinner Mon-Sat.
 Set in the courtyard of a modern office development, once a Victorian ice warehouse, the restaurant overlooks a sleepy dock containing urban debris, a heron, a few mallards and a pair of coots. Sliding windows give a feel of the outdoors to the pleasing and comfortable blue-green rooms, but the front and dockside terrace is a fume-free haven for al fresco meals. Martin Lam used to cook at Le Caprice, and decamped here from L'Escargot, creating a menu that ranges round the world but is under-pinned by France. Morecombe Bay potted shrimps with granary toast is rarely off a frequently changing menu that might include cassoulet, rabbit stew with herb dumplings and baked sea bream in a beurre blanc accompanied by samphire. Lam's wife Vanessa, a patissière, produces a fine and varied selection of desserts. A short and interesting wine list is notable for its inclusion of several house wines and decent wines by the glass. An interesting location for a family weekend brunch. **C** £20. **Set L** £10.50.

BAYSWATER

16 Inaho

4 Hereford Rd, W2 - 071-221 8495
JAPANESE/SUSHI
Open Lunch Mon-Fri, Dinner Mon-Sat.
 This tiny 'hut' seats just twenty on wooden chairs at wooden tables. On each sits a wicker basket shaped like a half-open clam shell, filled with dried flowers. You will see prints on the walls and a few oddments, plus one item rarely found in London's Japanese restaurants—a cuckoo clock proclaiming its full working order every half-hour. More startling: this totally unpretentious eating house serves some of the best Japanese food in London. A short conventional menu is supplemented by seasonal specialities listed on wooden tablets hanging on the wall, or placed on the table. They give the Japanese names in Roman script, short English descriptions, and prices. A separate menu offers a limited selection of sushi on Wednesday to Saturday evenings only. It would be a pity to restrict yourself to the set menus unless you are new to Japanese cuisine. Among seasonal specialities you may find edamame—boiled green soya beans in their salted pods, grilled salmon skins in a dipping sauce, and kabocha—earthy chunks of pumpkin in broth. To appreciate the finesse of the cooking, taste such classic dishes as sunomono of mackerel, crab-stick, vegetable and two sorts of seaweed in seasoned vinegar. Modern-style sushi—half the rice in each piece, 90 per cent of the fish—include tender squid and ark (clam) shell, both often dentally challenging elsewhere. Miso soup, a perfect side dish with sushi, is fully yet delicately flavoured. Even simple yaki udon—fried noodles 'Japanese style', here meaning with pieces of prawn—deserve high praise. The chef helps the single waiter take the orders when necessary. He has minimal help in the minute kitchen so service is not always speedy. But when this means that dishes, hot or cold, come to the table one by one instead of all together, you may actually find that a virtue. **C** £23. **Set L** £8, £10, **Set D** £20, £22.

12/20 Kalamaras

76-78 Inverness St, W2 - 071-727 9122/2564
GREEK
Open Dinner Mon-Sat.
 Coming up for its twentieth anniversary, Kalamaras still serves some of the most interesting and authentic Greek food in London. Owner Stelias Platonos—one of those precious breed of restaurateurs who sustain a love of their restaurant—runs the place with total dedication, patrolling it continually with a beady eye on all aspects. The place looks and feels exactly like the real thing with low ceilings and colourful rugs on the white-washed walls, those ladderback chairs and the inevitable bazouki music. If

you show more than a passing interest in the food (the menu is translated for every customer), you'll be whisked off to the kitchen to pick and choose the ingredients for your meal. The 28-strong meze is not the standard selection; here you are offered fried salt cod with garlic dip, grilled mussels, and flaky, plump filo pastries stuffed with feta and oregano. Moussaka is dependably rich but fish is a speciality here, as well as casseroled lamb with spinach and lemon juice. The all-Greek wine list, chosen with value-for-money in mind, is none the worse for that. C £25. Set D £15.50.

 Mandarin Kitchen

14-16 Queensway, W2
071-727 9012
CHINESE
Open Lunch & Dinner daily.
Bayswater's top Chinese restaurants are popular with Hong Kong businessmen looking for more comfort and smoother service than Chinatown provides. In this one, which is not that far above Chinatown's standards, tables are placed close together in the rather characterless room, and service may be brusque even at a quiet time of day. At busier periods even reserved tables may not always be ready. The long menu solicits requests for dishes not listed. It is Cantonese with few forays into other areas—duck for example, either Peking or aeromatic (sic) crispy style. Set dinner menus at £8.90 per head are good value although boringly conventional.

Standards of cooking match fine ingredients with delicate flavours and no sign of MSG. Although seafood is the speciality, and lobsters, crabs, scallops, whelks, mussels, eel and carp are all kept live, meat is not neglected. An outstanding starter consists of deep-fried shredded smoked chicken, cut thicker than usual with succulent results. Its success is confirmed by its reappearance in smoked chicken fried rice and in a special dish of Mandarin smoked chicken pancake roll. The menu is not always decoded. In deep-fried sesame soft-shell crab for example, the sesame is on a layer of minced prawn (as in prawn toasts) which is pressed on the crab. Eel with pork and straw mushroom is 'sizzled' on an iron platter but to compensate, the advertised mushrooms may be replaced by the more expensive black variety. 'Crystal King Prawn with an Unexpected Taste' lived up to its titillating name; its curious undertaste remains so far unidentified. Finish the meal with another north Chinese dish—red bean pancake. Although it looks oily, it is light and crisp with a pleasantly unsweet filling. Also at 249 Upper St, N1, 071-226 0208. C £26. **Set L & D** £8.90.

BELGRAVIA

 Mijanou

143 Ebury St, SW1 - 071-730 4099
FRENCH
Open Lunch & Dinner Mon-Fri.
Sonia Blech's cooking was always unusual. It has now evolved into something quite unique. Whilst her menus are truly seasonal, the word that best describes the style is 'spring-like'. Even in the darkest days of winter, young vegetables, herbs and nuts provide brightness and colour—not just visually, but also in terms of taste and texture.
In the starter ravioles de coquilles St Jacques au fumet à la citronelle et julienne de légumes there are no strong flavours, but the balanced delicacy of the green pasta, the subtle scallops and the vegetables in their broth make it memorable. And note the warm flavour of a risotto of wild rice, lentils and foie gras which may accompany game or poultry. Another flavour remarkable in itself and for its freshness is that of Christmas pudding—as in Christmas pudding ice cream—a much-copied notion which she invented. Composer Saint-Saëns said that it is not the absence of defects, but the presence of merit which makes art great. Mrs Blech qualifies as a great artist on both sides of the equation. Mijanou is now fourteen years old and a few details show its age. The seats make us wonder at the temerity of those who would wish to sit on a throne, even an upholstered wooden one. More recent are 'medieval' murals, dating from the restaurant's refurbishment three years ago and executed by a daughter of the

talented family. Neville Blech has progressed from being a restaurateur with one of London's best wine lists to being a wine merchant also, sharing with the public and other restaurateurs both fine classic wines and discoveries from his travels. This intimate restaurant has many distinguished regular customers. But if you recognise a fellow diner's face, the discretion of the establishment might prevent your confirming the identification. There is no smoking in the ground-floor room, but it is permitted in the (well-ventilated) basement. **C** £35. **Set L** £12.50, £15, **Set D** £21, £25.

Mosimann's

110 West Halkin St, Belgrave Sq, SW1 - 071-235 9625
MODERN BRITISH
Open Lunch & Dinner daily.
Is it wise, we wonder, to write glowing reviews of restaurants where non-members (most of our readers, in other words) are not admitted? We decided to take the risk...After all, who knows? Nothing prevents you from obtaining a club card, or perhaps you'll be invited as the guest of one of the 2,000 privileged members.
Some fifteen years ago, Gault Millau were the first to celebrate the talent of Swiss native Anton Mosimann, the chef who brought the Dorchester's kitchens back to life. When at length, he decided to strike out on his own, Mosimann turned up in elegant Belgravia, in rather unlikely premises: a neo-Gothic chapel which had been a club. There he fitted

out a handsome ground-floor dining room and bar with his superb collection of antique menus and transformed the gallery into a wine bar and the upper floors into a half-dozen smaller rooms which members may reserve for private parties. From the start, the club was a roaring success. The smart set crowd in at noon and in the evening, en-raptured by the highly orig-inal, utterly charming atmosphere. Mosimann himself heads the kitchen's large brigade. He has com-posed a savoury, eclectic menu that brings the flavours of France, Eng-land, Italy and southeast Asia together in a delect-able harmony with such offerings as braised oxtail, Scottish salmon accented with lemon thyme, mush-room risotto, jasmine tea-smoked trout, Thai-style warm chicken salad, the best bread and butter pudding in London, and a Christmas pudding that owes its ineffable lightness to vegetable oil, which Mosimann uses in place of the traditional beef suet. (Mosimann's Christmas pudding, incidentally, may be purchased in fine food shops).
It would not be cricket for us to rate a private es-tablishment; but we may surely say, without bending the rules, that Mosimann's food is excellent. **C** £45.

12/20 Olivo

21 Eccleston St, SW1 - 071-730 2505
ITALIAN
Open Lunch Mon-Fri, Dinner Mon-Sat.
Market forces and the trend away from French to

Italian cooking led Ciboure's owners to re-invent their little restaurant as Olivo. In keeping with the new mood of restaurant in-formality, the L-shaped din-ing room has been given a rustic look with lots of grainy wood and a dark blue-and-ochre colour scheme. French and Italian waiters are hard-pressed to keep up with Olivo's sus-tained success and adv-ance booking is essential. The Italian food on offer here originates from Sardinia, which translates as fresh-tasting, simple food, generously served and nicely presented. Pasta, home-made and variously stuffed, and polenta are specialities, and char-grilling the favoured way of cooking meat and fish. The simpler desserts, including vanilla ice cream with espresso or Italian cheeses, are the best choices from a short list. The menu is frequently modified and the outstand-ing set lunch changes weekly. The Italian wine list is reasonably priced. **C** £25. **Set L** £13, £15.

11/20 Salloos

62-64 Kinnerton St, SW1
071-235 6845
INDIAN
Open Lunch & Dinner Mon-Sat.
Tucked away in a mews house on the fringes of Belgravia and Knights-bridge makes an unlikely location for a restaurant serving fine Pakistani food. You enter a small, often un-attended lobby at street level; the restaurant is up a short flight of stairs. This is pleasant enough, in a sub-dued opulent kind of way, but the thing here is the

food. And you pay dearly for the privilege of knowing that the ingredients have been virtually hand-picked and that many dishes on the rarely changing menu are cooked to order. Dedication to quality is declared on the menu—lamb is well hung, tandoori meats are fat-free and untainted by artificial colours—and there are certain dishes that are marvellous. Tandoori lamb chops arrive exquisitely crisp on the outside yet moist and pink inside, and marinated chicken taimuri is deep fried in a batter made with added onions and tomatoes. Corney & Barrow's wine list is almost exclusively French and pricey. **C** £25.

BLOOMSBURY

Museum Street Café

47 Museum St, WC1 - 071-405 3211
MODERN BRITISH
Open Lunch & Dinner Mon-Fri. No cards.
Gail Koerber, a baker who perfected her skills at Clarke's, and Mark Nathan, a grill chef who 'graduated' through the River Café took on this tiny, unlicensed Bloomsbury café four years ago and tuned their talents to meet the confines of the premises and market needs. Short lunch and dinner menus change daily and are prix-fixe. From their tiny kitchen comes food that you'd pay double for elsewhere and if you don't mind elbows in your back—it is ex-

ceedingly cramped and very busy—it is a gem of a place. Careful, seasonal buying and imaginative use of modest ingredients keep the prices down and the onus is on simplicity and honest, gutsy flavours. Hence these first-rate dishes from recent blackboards: chick pea soup with rosemary and red pepper purée and basil oil, char-grilled corn-fed chicken with sweet potato ravioli, lemon tart, and Gail's excellent bread with cheeses supplied by reputed Neal's Yard Dairy. They are unlicensed and don't charge corkage, yet another advantage of this honest 'people's restaurant'. **Set L** £12, £14, **Set D** £21.

CAMDEN TOWN/ CHALK FARM

10/20 Belgo

72 Chalk Farm Rd, NW1
071-267 0718
BELGIAN
Open Lunch & Dinner daily.
This restaurant should have been a recipe for disaster—a concrete-walled joint with words by Rabelais cut into the décor, an unobtrusive entrance at the wrong end of Chalk Farm Road, Belgian food (and mussels and beer at that) and waiters dressed as monks. Oh yes, and you walk into a narrow entrance way that looks like a high-tech version of Dante's Inferno. But it has turned out to be one of the great restaurant successes. The food is genuinely good and unpretentious; moules

are done all sorts of ways, though on the set menu the choice is restricted to moules marinières or moules provençales; pommes frites are crisp, and the desserts as you would imagine Belgian desserts to be, rich and filling. Although you can drink wine and eat meat (stoemp and wild boar sausages at £7.50, roast pheasant with green peppercorn sauce and roasted parsnips at £10.25), the point here is mussels and beer. The beer list is, by any standards, formidable. In the 'mad brewers' selection comes a dark, sweet, spicy, cinnamon Oerbier at a huge 7.5 percent and costing £3.25 a glass, or a triple Witkap (£2.75) or the aptly named delirium tremens at 9% percent. For the connoisseur, the trappist monasteries of Belgium have come up with Chimay rouge or the more expensive Chimay grande réserve at £7.75. This is not a restaurant for a delicate eater or a teetotaller. **C** £20. **Set menu** £10.

11/20 Camden Brasserie

216 Camden High St, NW1
071-482 2114
FRENCH
Open Lunch & Dinner daily.
If it works, why change it? The Camden Brasserie has been serving the same dishes for years now and has kept its loyal, predominantly local clientele quite happy. One reason is that they buy their meat well, the other is that they cook it well. Simple grilled fillet of Scottish salmon with hollandaise sauce at £8.75 or beef brochette

teriyaki marinated in sherry, soya and ginger at £8.95 are invariably cooked exactly how you ask them to. Starters include soup, gravlax with dill mustard sauce and baby spinach with goat's cheese dressing and toasted almonds. The wine list, too, rarely strays beyond its formula of solid French and Spanish with the odd New World offering.

This is a real neighbourhood restaurant with a simple wooden décor and photographs of the area on the walls. The two brothers who own it are here almost every night. They care for their customers and greet everyone they know without making those who are new here feel out of place, which is quite a gift. **C** £20.

12/20 Vegetarian Cottage

91 Haverstock Hill, NW3
071-5866 1257
CHINESE/VEGETARIAN
Open Lunch Sat, Sun, Dinner daily.

Despite its name, Vegetarian Cottage is not strictly vegetarian. Its menu includes fish and shellfish, in addition to dishes in what is often called the Chinese Buddhist style, although the history of these vegetarian dishes pre-dates the arrival of Buddhism in China. Major ingredients of this strange cuisine are wheat gluten and tofu—soya bean curd. They are used in a whole range of imitation meat, fowl and fish dishes. First impressions are usually favourable but carnivores may complain of a lack of variety in this food. Sweet-

and-sour 'fish' makes a welcome alternative as it is made of yam. The cooking achieves high standards. Unusually for an oriental vegetarian restaurant, some fresh green vegetables are offered, but more would be welcome. Prices of vegetarian dishes are very modest; choosing fish, especially shellfish, can greatly increase the bill.

The attractive décor is in modern Chinese style, with black woodwork setting off white, textured walls. Service is a strong point—slightly formal, yet relaxed and friendly. **C** £15.

CHELSEA

Albero & Grana

Chelsea Cloisters, 89 Sloane Ave, SW3 - 071-225 1048, Fax 071-581 3259
SPANISH
Open Dinner Mon-Sat.

Blood and sand, red and black and white, substantial and serious Spanish cooking. The bar in front heaves with be-braced and jacketed youth bellowing like bullocks as they down some of the best tapas in town. Those of a more inquiring, not to say retiring, disposition make their way to the elegant and striking restaurant at the back for such goodies as lasagne of black pudding with pimento sauce, veal kidney with a sherry sauce, sword fish on an orange sauce or lamb stew on a sherry and saffron and cumin sauce, dishes which deliver flavours forcefully but with surprising subtlety. With

the fixed-price menus you can explore the regional nature of Spanish cooking. The all-Spanish wine list reflects the weaknesses apparent in Spanish wine production generally. **C** £25.

 ## The Argyll

316 King's Rd, SW3 - 071-352 0025
MODERN BRITISH
Open Lunch Tues-Sat, Dinner Mon-Sat.

Premises that have seen many restaurants come and go are settled under this ownership thanks to the elegant finesse of Anand Sastry's cooking. Sastry, who made a name for himself cooking at the country house hotel Woolley Grange in Bradford-on-Avon presents simple, eclectic though fancily presented food. For example, recent samplings have been as diverse as oxtail braised with salsify and wild mushrooms, and ravioli stuffed with foie gras served on a Sauternes-laced, creamy compôte of lentils. There are occasional lapses of form when too many ingredients result in confused flavours. Vegetables, however, can be outstanding and are always served as a selection. The multi-faceted desserts are a pudding freak's delight. Banana parfait comes with caramelised bananas, and lemon tart is served with meringue lemon curd sandwich *and* vodka and celery sorbet. The set lunch is one of London's finest gastronomic bargains. Bargains, however, are few and far between on the short, up-to-date wine list. The restaurant's bleached floor, stark white décor and random collection of old dining chairs provide a pleasing mix of chic formality, especially attractive in the summer when the doors fold back to the street. **C** £25. **Set L** £8.50, £10.

Aubergine

11 Park Walk, SW10 - 071-352 3449
MODERN BRITISH
Open Lunch Mon-Fri, Dinner Mon-Sat.
Owner/chef Gordon Ramsay heads a team at Aubergine that replicates and echoes his years in Paris working with Guy Savoy and Joël Robuchon at Jamin. Thus the food is light, fresh-tasting, intelligent and exquisite—contemporary French cooking, though here with some Italian influences. A single oyster swims in perfectly balanced vichyssoise seasoned with a dollop of chive chantilly, a quick-roasted and jointed guinea fowl sits on tagliatelle of leeks and a jus of thyme, and a tarte citron trembles on this side of collapse. Menus change about every two weeks, although some favourites, such as tortellini of lobster with a vinaigrette crustacés, and many of the quite exquisite desserts remain. The set-price lunch has a choice of two starters, two main courses and desserts; the set dinner offers a choice of eight starters and eight main courses. Many dishes on the menu here also grace the list at The Canteen and The Restaurant at the Hyde Park Hotel. The link is the young chef Marco Pierre White, with

whom Gordon Ramsay trained. The wine list, intelligently chosen, includes Madiran André Daguin from Gascony and Penfolds Kirkton Vale Semillon Chardonnay, both under £15.

Until recently Aubergine was Eleven Park Walk, an Italian restaurant where most of the action took place downstairs. Great changes make it unrecognisable. The ground floor appears to have tripled in size to provide plenty of room for a reception bar and a decent-sized, spacious dining room, and the kitchen now monopolises the basement. The overall effect, aided by clever use of mirrors, a bleached wooden floor and a pale primrose colour scheme, is country kitchen meets town chic. Finally the service is first-rate: attentive, knowledgeable and enthusiastic. **Set L** £18, **Set D** £26.

The Canteen

Unit G4, Harbour Yard, Chelsea Harbour, SW10
071-351 7330
MODERN BRITISH
Open Lunch & Dinner daily.
The Canteen has the prime site in the American-style apartment and leisure complex on the river beyond Lots Road, lately known as South Chelsea. Canteen it is not. Owned by film star Michael Caine and chef Marco Pierre White, the large split-level room is cool and elegant, decked out on a theme of harlequinade and playing cards. A conservatory annexe—the prime tables—overlooks a marina full of

boats that go nowhere. Conceived as the brasserie equivalent of Harvey's, before MPW decamped to The Restaurant in the Hyde Park Hotel, the food here is less haute and more simple. Hence the menu has a dual personality and people report startlingly different experiences of meals eaten here. The simpler brasserie dishes are sometimes too prissily treated and the grander compositions, made with ingredients that require precise handling, can suffer in this large operation. Be warned, too, that although the menu doesn't change much, dishes are often changed slightly, and sometimes differ radically from what's written on the menu. Desserts are more consistent, and the lemon tart and tarte tatin of pears are outstanding. The state-of-the-art wine list is sensibly listed by price and is unique in including alcohol volumes. But why no half bottles? **C** £25.

12/20 Daphne's

112 Draycott Ave, SW3
071-589 4257, Fax 071-581 2232
ITALIAN
Open Lunch & Dinner daily.
Recent newcomer to the restaurant scene and former designer, Mogens Tholstrup, has a certain knack of appealing to the 'in' crowd. With Daphne, which opened late summer 1993, Tholstrup has ventured into fashion-conscious South Kensington with a dazzling refurbishment. (His first restaurant venture, est, is packed tight every evening with a smart crowd in Soho). Three light-filled

connecting rooms, seating one hundred and twenty people, are designed with distinct Italian influences—a Florentine-inspired set of metal gates, rich burnt-umber walls, rustic flagstone floor, several working fireplaces and an impressive sliding glass roof in the garden room at the back. The menu is modern European with the emphasis on northern Italy. Pasta and risotto take pride of place, with dishes like cheese and mushroom soufflé and grilled goat's cheese with aubergine, peppers and radicchio just as well prepared. There is also a good mix of fish like a highly recommended roast sea bass with artichokes, and grills. Desserts are traditional, like tiramisù, a sinful pot au chocolat and a slightly insipid lemon tart. Service tends to indifference but the ambience is conducive to people-watching. **C £25.**

10/20 Deals

Harbour Yard, Chelsea Harbour, SW10 - 071-352 5887
INTERNATIONAL
Open Lunch & Dinner daily.
When Viscount Linley, Lord Lichfield and restaurateur Edward Lim opened up shop in the new Chelsea Harbour some people showed scepticism. Stylistically they created a slice of New England with a rustically-hewn diner styled with farmyard antiquities and dominated by a huge central bar. The barn-like premises is hidden behind wooden blinds and is broken up by a series of semi-private booths created by high-backed wooden banquettes. Staff

belong to the resting actor category and the place buzzes with sixties music. It is a 'fun' concept much appreciated by the fashionable Chelsea crowd—of all ages. At weekends it is particularly popular with families, perhaps hoping to spot Princess Diana on one of her visits with the young princes, William and Harry. Their menu was ahead of its time—a clever mix of popular international dishes including Thai curries, Indonesian satay, tacos and nachos and D-I-Y griddle dishes, as well as ribs, burgers, steak sandwiches and salads. The opening in 1994 of a new branch in Hammersmith Mall (Bradmore House, Queen Caroline St, W6, 081-563 1001) has prompted more southeast Asian dishes. Deals is a cut above one's expectations, largely because it has a proper kitchen presided over by a talented Thai chef. The drinks list encompasses all and the wines are as varied as the food. **C £20.**

11/20 The English Garden

10 Lincoln St, Draycott Ave, SW3 - 071-584 7272, Fax 071-581 2848
BRITISH
Open Lunch & Dinner daily.
Down a quiet residential street not far from Sloane Square, the English Garden offers the sort of traditional British fare that sometimes throws up odd surprises gleaned from nineteenth-century culinary research. A sombre, many-mirrored room at the front should if possible be forsaken in favour of the cheerier conservatory to the rear. The vapid fish terrine with

prawns should likewise be passed over for excellent shredded crabmeat on croûtons with a high-octane saffron sauce. On occasions we've found the lamb encrusted with chopped hazelnuts insufficiently cooked to render enough of the plentiful fat, while individual pies in round dishes encircled by paper collars contain—under their browned puff-pastry lids—copious chicken breast meat and strongly tarragoned white sauce. Flavours of old England inspire puddings such as gooseberry fool with unctuous elderflower syrup. Expect to sit cheek-by-jowl with your neighbours. A good choice of pedigree French wines. You'll appreciate the courteous, informed service. **C £28. Set L £14.75.**

10/20 L'Express

126 Sloane St, SW3 - 071-235 9869
FRENCH
Open Breakfast & Lunch Mon-Sat.
L'Express, a minimalist, stark, black-and-white narrow restaurant below a frock shop in the same ownership (Joseph Ettedgui), provides the backdrop for ladies who shop. It also serves as a reminder that Joseph was the original boss of the hugely popular Le Caprice. Here the bar stretches the entire length of the room, with little black tables crammed into the rest of the space. It's not a place to linger at lunchtime, indeed people often queue up the stairs, but it's perfect if you're eating alone or want breakfast at 11am or lunch at 4.30pm. The menu is sim-

ple, wholesome, healthy and seductively indulgent. Its linchpin is a selection of superior salads, and there is a daily different choice of three pure vegetable soups, a couple of fashionable hot dishes such as salmon fish cakes with pommes frites, and ravioli of wild mushrooms. They are licensed but specialise in fresh fruit juices. C £18.

12/20 La Famiglia
5-7 Langton St, SW10 - 071-351 0761
ITALIAN
Open Lunch & Dinner daily.
A Chelsea landmark celebrating its 30th anniversary, it's like summer all year round with its startling white walls, Mediterranean tiles and pretty, large, awning-covered garden which is an oasis most of the year. Family run, as its name suggests, the restaurant has a jolly atmosphere and Sunday lunches become real Italian family celebrations. It doesn't, wisely, try to compete with the new wave of modern Mediterranean food. Tuscan specialities can tend to the mundane, but noteworthy dishes include fantasia di pasta, panzanella salad and sea bream with fennel and Sambuca. There is a well-priced wine list. C £20.

12/20 Foxtrot Oscar
79 Royal Hospital Rd, SW3
071-352 7179
BRITISH
Open Lunch & Dinner daily.
Does the name refer, as some think, to a rather rude suggestion based on the Royal Air Force's identification of letters of the alphabet? A vestige of the 1960s, it has changed little in its neighbourly appeal to the Chelsea smart set. Informality is the key to its success—the no-fuss bistro décor of crowded tables and basic British menu on the blackboard, the laid-back service with wine and food plonked down on the table, but with a smile. Steak, kidney and oyster pie is good, as is the cottage pie. Burgers, big salads and sausages with mash and onions in huge portions are ably prepared. Nothing is fussy or fancy but the quality and quantity are both reliable. There tends to be a camaraderie among diners by the end of the evening, although Saturday lunch, too, is a jolly affair to kick off the weekend. C £20. **Set menus** £14.50, £16.75.

La Tante Claire
68 Royal Hospital Rd, SW3 - 071-352 6045/071-351 0227, Fax 071-352 3257
FRENCH
Open Lunch & Dinner Mon-Fri.
You may remember that Gault Millau awarded La Tante Claire its third toque in 1982, a time when no other restaurant in London had even one. It amuses us to remember that back in the early 80s, the same fashionable set who today swoon at the very mention of La Tante Claire, regarded it as nothing more than a 'good little bistro'. But we knew that Pierre Koffmann, a man of excellent taste, was running a charming, very special restaurant. Since its redecoration in luminous tones, it is a stunning, original space with attractive modern prints and water-colours on the walls, chairs skirted in yellow fabric, and lighting that is both precise and flattering. The overall effect is one of elegant simplicity, far removed from the staid, ponderous sort of décor that encumbers so many first-class restaurants.

The dining-room staff, urbanely directed by Jean-Pierre Durantet, go about their work unobtrusively, with no fawning or flourishes. Each plate that Koffmann sends forth from the kitchen is a small masterpiece: nothing precious or contrived here, just beautiful food presented on exquisite dishes in an artful harmony of colours.

It is hard to believe that Koffmann was trained by the Roux brothers, back in the days when elaborate 'decorator' food was the rule at Le Gavroche. The Gascon-born Koffmann is a resolutely modern chef, one who would rather invent felicitous combinations of flavours and colours than erect ornamental pièces montées. His is a muscular culinary style, characterised by potent, occasionally rustic savours—witness his morel-stuffed pig's trotter served with a split-pea purée; or the winy ox-cheek daube; or the saddle of rabbit with lentils. Yet even these vigorous dishes reflect Koffmann's pursuit of purity and his personal, subtle touch. There is something of Joël Robuchon in these dishes; even more evident is the influence of four-toque chef Bernard Pacaud of L'Ambroisie in Paris. Like him, or like Claude Peyrot of Le Vivarois, Koffmann has a gift for constructing distinct layers of flavours, which a lesser talent would inevitably muddle together. He orchestrates an ideal harmony, for example, with sea-sweet coquilles Saint-Jacques, garlic cream, bell pepper and squid ink; likewise a hint of cumin lends haunting depth to red mullet in a gently spiced broth. Koffmann's sure hand adds just enough thyme to perfume a pigeon en cocotte without overwhelming its delicate flesh. Each dish on the concise menu deserves mention, from the thin tart topped with chicory and scallops, the Sauternes-laced galette de foie gras with roasted shallots, or the lotte with celeriac, capers and saffron, to the admirable fillet of hare with mustard. You will not be surprised to learn that La Tante Claire's prices are stiff (around £60 to £70 with a reasonably inexpensive wine), especially if you indulge in the wonders proposed by the splendidly intelligent, exclusively French wine list. At lunch, however, the two manageably tariffed prix-fixe meals (£25) keep La Tante Claire in the accessible category. We therefore see no reason why we should forego the pleasure of making La Tante Claire London's first—and for the moment, only—four-toque restaurant. The award may encourage Pierre Koffmann to leave his kitchens long enough, on our next visit, to accept our congratulations, along with our compliments! **C** £55-£60. **Set L** £24.50.

12/20 **Zen**
Chelsea Cloisters, Sloane Ave, SW3 - 071-589 1781, Fax 071-437 0641
CHINESE
Open Lunch & Dinner daily.

Zen, a highly successful chain of fashionable Chinese restaurants, began in Chelsea Cloisters and has since expanded to several other branches, the most recent being at The Hilton, Terminal 4, Heathrow. The later restaurants are designed by architect Rick Mather to include lavish and inventive use of glass, steel and water; the Chelsea Cloisters Zen remains an old-fashioned, slightly garish place with low ceilings and a small waterfall near the entrance. The menu here, as at all the restaurants, is huge: 32 starters alone plus soups before you get into the main courses. Included are all the favourites: spring rolls wrapped with lettuce, mixed seafood with prawn crackers and a good selection of dim sum. 'A Feast on it's own' includes dishes like roasted Peking duck with spring onions, cucumber and pancakes, or for the rich, specialities like braised fluffy supreme shark's fin in spicy sauce for two people. Recommended are baked sea bass with garlic wrapped in banana leaves, a sizzling dish of chicken fillet sautéed with whole black beans, and Tao Peng prawn balls which are hot and fierce as advertised, and for vegetarians (who are well catered for here), French bean foo yung in a spicy sauce. The Zen restaurants have a policy of rotating their chefs and standards can fluctuate as

a result. Now and Zen has introduced an eat-as-much-as-you-like set price menu of pick-and-mix from 149 dishes for £16. **C** £30. **Set menus** £18-£38. Also **Now and Zen**, 48 Upper St Martin's Lane, WC2, 071-497 0376. **Zen Central**, 20 Queen St, W1, 071-629 8089. **Zen W3**, 81 Hampstead High St, NW3, 071-794 7863.

CHINATOWN

 Fung Shing
15 Lisle St, WC2
071-437 1539
CHINESE
Open Lunch & Dinner daily.

What should be expected of a top Chinese chef? The same as one expects of a top chef of any school of cooking. (The detailed specifications are outlined in the notes on our rating system in the introduction), and the only difference in the case of a Chinese chef is that creativity is less important. We expect occidental chefs to produce a succession of original dishes, at least early in their careers—although after a number of years at the top they can continue to offer the same 'signature dishes' for an undetermined length of time. In major oriental cuisines strict adherence to classic recipes is the road to success and recognition. Only in recent years has it become possible for a great Chinese or Japanese chef to introduce something new every few years, without being accused of being a dangerous gastronomic revolutionary. A requirement not mentioned, perhaps because it is understood, is the major one of staff training. The kitchen must produce dishes of the same standard in the chef's absence as in his presence. In the case of a restaurant like Fung Shing which is open all day, every day, and whose chef is not young, it is absolutely vital. So it is a positive, not negative, indication when the chef may be seen relaxing with a family party in the restaurant, while we enjoy the brilliant cooking from his kitchen.

A feature of Chinese restauration which has reached western establishments only in recent years is the Menu Dégustation. In Chinese restaurants it is everyday practice to agree a price for a special meal, leaving the actual choice of dishes to the chef. The customer can specify particular dishes or ingredients to be included, or excluded. Such a meal at Fung Shing might include such delicacies as braised whole abalone (£45), doubled-boiled fluffy supreme shark's fin (£50), or various styles of lobster. It might also include dishes as homely as crispy spicy eel, pak choy with garlic, or a soup with sliced pork, green vegetables and separately beaten egg-white and beaten salted duck egg yolk. Even more surprising was the inclusion in one such meal of Singapore noodles where the normal coarse curry flavour was transmuted to a fine, delicate hint of warm spices. Refinement and elegance are the key-

notes of this kitchen. These are not words that come readily to mind in describing the Cantonese repertoire from which the vast majority of the 150 items on the carte come. Further examples include the perfection of steamed scallops with soya sauce; and the subtle flavours and textures of one of the few Cantonese cold dishes—spicy jellyfish with chicken and mustard. Only a few northern and Szechuen dishes have crept into the menu.

There seems little point in visiting this restaurant and choosing set menus for they are unadventurous although well balanced. Smooth, efficient and pleasant service contribute to the ambience of Fung Shing which is much more agreeable than in most Chinatown restaurants. Cream walls with classic and modern water-colours combine harmoniously with the unifying greenness of carpet, table linen and upholstery of the cane-back chairs. Tables are fairly close together but not intolerably so, and the noise level does not reach too high a level for a restaurant which is always busy. **C** £24. **Set menus** £20, £25, £30.

🏠 Harbour City

46 Gerrard St, W1 - 071-439 7859
CHINESE
Open Lunch & Dinner daily.
The décor of this busy restaurant on three floors is just above basic Chinatown level, service is usually well above it, and dim sum are very superior indeed—our rating is for dim

sum only. They are probably the best in London, helped by their being ordered from the kitchen and served freshly cooked, as opposed to being kept in hot cabinets on trolleys. Page one of the dim sum menu offers the normal range of these snacks, steamed and fried, of which three to six make a satisfying lunch. 'Exotic dim sum' which follow are a mixed lot, with more dumplings and small plates of such far-out delicacies as beef intestines, ducks' tongues, and steamed cockles, in various sauces; there is congee—Chinese rice porridge—and a few Vietnamese items such as spring rolls (Nem) and fried cuttle fish ball. Choose from several sections of the menu to balance fried and steamed dishes. Fried are usually eaten first. If the temperature of food matters greatly to you, order in two 'courses', requesting a second assortment later, but bear in mind that steaming takes longer than frying.

Plate dishes of rice and noodles in different ways include Fook Jing fried rice, with egg, roast duck, peas and mushrooms in a rich sauce, always good although never identical twice running. Chinese eat the sweet dim sum along with the rest but if you want a dessert, egg tart—baked egg yolk in ethereally light flaky pastry—may be the best choice. To drink there is jasmine tea, or much better Po Li, a softer tasting brown tea, which many find more digestible. Tsing Tao beer is good, and so is red wine, but the flavour of most whites is too weak to complement the spicy food. Dim sum are served until 5pm in theory but many will be sold out at least an hour earlier. The conventional menu is usually well cooked but cheap pre-theatre menus seem intended only for westerners unused to real Chinese food. **C** dim sum £9.50. **Set menus** from £10.50

12/20 Jade Garden

15 Wardour St, W1 - 071-439 7851
CHINESE
Open Lunch & Dinner daily.
This medium-sized restaurant is typical of renovated Chinatown style, although a sweeping staircase to the balcony adds distinction, and the tables beside the balcony railing have a splendid view of the sometimes frenetic action in the main room. Service, even at the height of the rush hour, only rarely descends to the brutalist Chinatown level, and is usually efficient. Dim sum have long been highly reputed here, but the main kitchen produces serious cooking too. This is a good place for the most egalitarian of finger foods, crab with chilli and black bean sauce, while other lively Cantonese seafood dishes include fried squid with seasonal vegetables, and stewed eel with roast pork. Less successful is steamed sliced chicken with ham and vegetables—in this would-be haute cuisine delicacy the 'ham' seems to be from a can, and not unrelated to spam or pork luncheon meat. Portions are large and among the set menus from £9.50 per

head are good selections of seafood at £15 to £17. Fresh orange segments are free. **C** £17.50. **Set menus** from £9.50 per head.

Mr Kong

21 Lisle St, WC2 - 071-437 7341
CHINESE
Open Lunch & Dinner daily.
For many years this restaurant's 'signature dish' has been spare ribs baked in a paper bag, but it never appeared on the menu. If you asked why, the invariable reply was 'but everyone knows about it'. It is now on the menu, lightly disguised as baked spare ribs with chilli, and if you ask why there is no mention of the paper bag the answer is 'but everyone knows about it.' It is one of many interesting dishes on the very long à la carte menu which offers more variety of standard dishes than most, as well as a long list of 'miscellaneous dishes'. But many of the best things are on the supplementary 'Chef Special' menu of another 40 items. Ten years after opening the restaurant, Mr Kong himself still supervises the kitchen to good effect.
The décor has recently been refreshed with cream walls setting off a splash of crimson on the 'roof' of the service bar at the back, and faded pink-purple table cloths. Tables are rather too close for comfort. Service is generally pleasant and the normal Chinese rule of anonymity is broken by a board at the door showing the name of the duty manager. Set menus at £8.60 to £11 are

dull, and even 'Mr Kong's Special Set Dinners' at £15 to £21 per person are quite conventional. **C** £18. **Set menus** £8.60-£21.

CHISWICK

11/20 La Dordogne

5 Devonshire Rd, W1 - 081-747 1836
FRENCH
Open Lunch Mon-Fri, Dinner daily.
The Dordogne region in France is much loved by the British ex-pat brigade and holiday makers, and this slightly gloomy—or atmospheric, depending on your point of view—establishment, with its dark green walls, red curtains and Victorian light fittings just off Chiswick High Street has its own band of enthusiastic and highly respectable followers. It has a nice line in oyster and lobsters. Other dishes are of the robust variety: salade gourmande, boudin blanc with foie gras, monkfish with bacon and port, fillet of beef with Cahors sauce, potato pancake and wild mushrooms. The wine list is a shrine to France, with some interesting specialities from Cahors and Jurançon. **C** £20.

*We're always happy to hear about your discoveries and receive your comments on ours. We want to give your letters the attention they deserve, so when you **write to Gault Millau**, please state clearly what you liked or disliked. Be concise but convincing, and take the time to argue your point.*

THE CITY

10/20 Café du Marché

22 Charterhouse Sq, Charterhouse Mews, EC1
071-608 1609
FRENCH
Open Lunch Mon-Fri, Dinner Mon-Sat.

Once a corset factory and now a busy two-floor restaurant, the Café du Marché has been lovingly converted to reveal sandy brick walls and pale wooden rafters. It's a bohemian sort of place that gets packed out with the business fraternity at lunchtime but comes into its own at night when it's lit with candles. Their style of French food is rooted in familiar French provincial cooking but strays into less tried-and-tested combinations. Hence it's advisable to stick to bistro classics such as soupe de poisson, confit de canard and côte de boeuf sauce béarnaise. Grills, incidentally, are the speciality of the first floor Le Grenier. Both rooms operate prix-fixe menus. C £20. **Set menu** £19.50.

City Singapura

78-79 Leadenhall St, EC3
071-929 0089
SOUTHEAST ASIAN
Open Lunch & Dinner Mon-Fri.

Go out of your way to eat at this restaurant for it offers good and unusual food at reasonable prices. Only recently moved from Fulham, it is already difficult to get into at peak lunchtime hours. Our advice is to skip breakfast, telephone and go early. This not only gets you a seat, it allows you to do full justice to the generous servings. Connoisseurs will appreciate the way chef and co-owner Maureen Aruymainayagam uses only the freshest ingredients and selects deftly from the culinary possibilities offered by southeast Asia. Both connoisseurs and novices will appreciate the variety of the set menus. These begin with a selection of delicate starters—Indonesian satay, Vietnamese prawn spring rolls, marinated prawns in wanton pastry, and 'lettuce-boats' of minced chicken with fresh coriander from Laos—and are followed by a variety of other dishes from which to pick and choose in traditional fashion. Savour particularly the gloriously mellow siput (mussels stir-fried with lemon grass, lime leaves, chillies and ginger in sherry sauce), and enjoy the contrast with the exuberant sunshine flavour of ayam lemak (breast of chicken and bamboo shoots cooked in lemon grass, turmeric and spices, and enriched with coconut cream). To finish, jettison all preconceptions about ice cream and try either the home-made brown bread and marmalade flavours, or the Earl Grey and ginger. Finally, stumble out into the City and look at the Lloyds building opposite through new eyes. C £24. **Set menus** £12.95, £15.95.

Imperial City

Royal Exchange, Cornhill, EC3 - 071-626 3437, Fax 071-338 0125
CHINESE
Open Lunch & Dinner Mon-Fri.

In the basement of the grand old Royal Exchange building, this recently opened Chinese restaurant has, under the influence of writer and broadcaster Ken Hom, brought good-value ethnic eating to the heart of the City. The dining room has a light and airy California feel to it, with split levels and nicely intimate alcoves. It suffers the fate of many City restaurants in that it tends to be thinly attended in the evening, but the food should convince lunchers to return. Classics such as Peking duck with exquisite plum sauce are supported by less familiar offerings like Shanghai lion's-head dumplings of minced pork or Cantonese curried chicken with peppers. Accompaniments such as stir-fried Chinese cabbage with garlic and crisp, deep-fried rice balls add plenty of texture. There is no stinting the chilli in a bright red sauce with king prawns, nor in the Szechuan noodles with pork and spring onion. Linger over the wine list which contains many of today's pace-setting names at sensible prices. C £22. **Set L** from £13.50.

Stephen Bull's Bistro and Bar

71 St John St, EC1 - 071-490 1750
INTERNATIONAL
Open Lunch Mon-Fri, Dinner Mon-Sat.

The striking décor of this noisy, buzzing bistro seems to be designed for somewhere other than its actual location near

Smithfield Market. White walls, fine parquet flooring and a floating staircase suggest a smart Japanese place in Mayfair. The brilliantly coloured recesses, papier-mâché panels and sculptures could decorate a modern art gallery. The visual style is an appropriate metaphor for the nature of Stephen Bull's cooking. The sheer brilliance of one dish may be as surprising as the mismatching of flavours and textures in another. Fortunately, triumphs far outnumber turkeys in menus which change twice daily. Typical recent dishes have included a dire multi-ethnic smoked tandoori duck with tzatziki. The flesh of the duck was good but separated from its spicy dark skin by a thick layer of fat, while the tzatziki was a travesty of the eastern Mediterranean minted yoghurt with cucumber. But by contrast, a fava bean, marjoram and sun-dried tomato tart of crisp pastry creamily filled with tiny broad beans was highly successful. So was spiced salt beef with a confit of root vegetables, mustard and parsley sauce, all as promised, with a bonus of pungent home-made piccalilli. Casual eating is encouraged by dual pricing of many starters also as main dishes. Over 40 wines are listed, few over £20, none over £30. By the glass are fifteen choices, with dessert wines and Champagne at £5. Among fine bottles, classic and unknown, Australian Madfish Bay Chardonnay and Californian Duxoup (pronounced duck soup) Charbono may be listed partly for their names. Beer drinkers can choose from nine beauties including Scottish Orkney Skullsplitter. C £24.

10/20 Sweetings
39 Queen Victoria St, EC4
071-248 3062
BRITISH
Open Lunch Mon-Fri. No cards.

The Sweeting family opened their Victorian fish 'ordinary' at these premises in 1906 and not much has changed since. It has the atmosphere and look of a pub, and customers take their chances at one of the three bars or queue for a seat at the refectory tables in the tiny adjoining canteen. By noon it is packed to the gunnels with pinstriped City gents, and fever pitch is reached by 1pm. Miraculously, it is almost always over by 2pm. Turnaround is fast and if you want to reflect into your oysters (Colchester's finest), or linger over your poached turbot and steamed syrup pudding go late. Their cod's roe, fish pie, haddock topped with a poached egg, chips and suet pudding are the finest in town. Drink draught Guinness, chilled Chablis or Champagne by the glass. C £22.

 Tatsuso
32 Broadgate Circle, EC2 - 071-638 5863, Fax 071-638 5864
JAPANESE
Open Lunch & Dinner Mon-Fri.

Japanese reverence for established names means that the absolute excellence of this restaurant is only now beginning to receive due recognition. It is located in one of the City of London's few modern architectural successes and its interior is equally attractive. After passing through the small entrance lobby with its suit of samurai armour you go straight to your table, for the one thing this restaurant lacks is a bar. The teppan-yaki room is on the upper floor with the main restaurant below. It is quietly and pleasantly decorated with fine veneer panelling and comfortable seats. Wood, and hand-printed papers, add up to a warm and relaxing background, and the ambience is less formal than in some top Japanese restaurants. Nonetheless service is everything it should be, and an international management team ensures that there is no language problem, even if the elegant waitresses do not all speak English. Lunch set menus are from £19 to £35 and oddly only the cheapest includes beer.

In meals which justify the high rating, we have eaten from most sections of the menu, except for dishes cooked at the table. As always with Japanese food, presentation ranges from homely—there is no way of making vegetables in broth look exciting—to elegance without fussiness in sushi, sashimi and some of the appetisers. Typical of the simplicity of style was kur-age-su, a sunomono, or vinegared dish of jellyfish with cucumber and two sorts of seaweed in the mildest of vinegars. A sensational, but un-named appetiser of the day could be sorrel mixed with seaweed in a subtle dressing with three layers of flavour: first a bland sea-taste, then a faint bitterness and finally a hint of red pepper hotness. An example of the kitchen's skill is chawanmushi, listed under 'Tofu and Egg Dishes'. This is a steamed savoury egg-custard served in a small pot, and uniquely amongst Japanese dishes, eaten with a spoon. When brillliantly cooked as this is, the custard trembles on the edge of liquidity in the same way as an ideal jellied consommé. The usual garnish is one piece each of a whole range of fish, meat and vegetables, but here there are only thickly sliced black mushrooms, green soya beans, small fresh prawns, and chunks of chicken. The delicious shiso leaf, perilla or beefsteak plant is used both in sushi and in the special sashimi which may include yellowtail and turbot as well as the usual tuna, sea bass, salmon and scallops. More conventional items—from tempura to boiled rice with pickles and miso soup—are perfectly balanced and delicate. There is no under- nor over-seasoning nor any MSG. Desserts are usually the least interesting part of Japanese meals but in the dish of three ice creams is a richly flavoured green tea, and a splendid purple-blue-grey toasted sesame, with a curious, slightly bitter undertaste. If you have not realised that Japanese cuisine is one of the glories of world gastronomy, then

this is the restaurant to convince you.

One does not expect the same standards in a teppan room as in a classic Japanese restaurant. However, the one at Tatsuso, much used by businessmen at both lunch and dinner, is one of the best. There is a short à la carte and set lunches. All menus include either Japanese clear soup or dobin-mushi, a superb consommé served in a tea pot. At £66 you also have sashimi, and a champagne sorbet—served in a large cocktail glass and topped up from a bottle of Perrier-Jouet. Main courses are giant prawns, salmon and turbot, followed, after a salad, by thinly sliced entrecôte and a large fillet steak—a Japanese customer told us that the equivalent in Tokyo would cost about £200 just for the steak, which would be only marginally superior. Ingredients are of the highest quality, portions generous to a fault, and the cooking is skilled yet discreet—neither food nor knives are tossed in the air for show. C £34. Set L from £19, Set D £35-£70.

🍴 Tatsuso Teppan Room

32 Broadgate Circle, EC2
071-638 5863, Fax 071-638 5864
JAPANESE
Open Lunch & Dinner Mon-Fri.
    See *text* above. **Set L** £20-£35, **Set D** £38-£66.

> The **prices** *in this guide reflect what establishments were charging at the time of going to press.*

CLERKENWELL

12/20 Ginnan

1-2 Roseberry Ct, Roseberry Ave, EC1 - 071-278 0008
JAPANESE
Open Lunch Mon-Fri, Dinner Mon-Sat.

In this Japanese version of a pub, much of the food is meant to casually accompany drinks. The large, bare room is filled with wooden screens, tables and chairs in grey-brown wood, and upholstery in equally dull purple-red. Sit at the short bar to watch your food being prepared and chat with the cook despite the language barrier—a Durham accent is not readily accessible to all English speakers. This bar offers neither sushi nor tempura (both prepared in the kitchen) but kushiyaki—small barbecued bamboo skewers. The twelve listed are mainly chicken and chicken giblets, but one of the best is beef tongue. Also behind the bar are bains-maries of oden (boiled fish cake and vegetables) and deep frying pans for skewered meat or vegetable kushiage. A remarkably international kitchen brigade—two Sri Lankans, a Russian and the Englishman from Durham—produces cooking to satisfy Japanese customers as well as natives. Of more than 80 dishes on the menu a handful are untranslated to prevent non-Japanese ordering something they might find unpleasant. But some of us actually enjoy octopus and would prefer to decide for ourselves. As usual set lunches are the best value. There are thirteen from £6.80 to £11, plus a bento (boxed picnic) at £15, and a generous multi-course lunch at £20. C £32. **Set menus** £6.80-£20.

 Quality Chop House
94 Farringdon Rd, EC1 - 071-837 5093
MODERN BRITISH
Open Lunch Sun-Fri, Dinner daily. No cards.

The Quality Chop House was famous in its day before Charles Fontaine, formerly at the celebrated Le Caprice, breathed new life through its Victorian frame. Launched as a 'Progressive working class caterers', these days the workers are fed on an accomplished French chef's interpretation of everyday grub. You can eat within the vernacular with dishes like egg, bacon and chips, or sausages and mash with onion gravy (although the sausages will have come from Toulouse), and treacle pudding. But it wasn't for nothing that Charles Fontaine presided over the kitchens at Le Caprice for nine years, and the menu is peppered with his signature dishes like bang-bang chicken, Caesar salad and salmon fish cakes with sorrel sauce. The short menu changes slightly every day. Its hallmarks are simplicity, accuracy of cooking and generosity. Apart from the food, many people may remember the uncomfortable bench seating and the fact that they might be asked to share a table. Its spartan design is not a gimmick but an al-

most exact replica of the 120-year-old original. There's an appropriate drinks list with Champagne by the glass, a decent range of beers and modestly priced wines. C £18.

COVENT GARDEN

12/20 Arts Theatre Café
6-7 Gt Newport St, WC2
071-497 8014
ITALIAN
Open Lunch & Dinner Mon-Fri. No cards.

The Italian cooking here is exciting in the modern Italian style made so fashionably popular by the River Café and Cibo, and of a similar standard, quite a suprise in this small, candle-lit, old-fashioned basement. Chef Philip Owens produces a simple daily-changing menu with starters like Swiss chard, potato and garlic soup flavoured with nutmeg, bruschetta and parmesan. Main dishes might include succulent braised duck with onions, mint and vinegar served with a crisp polenta, and grilled meat with spicy Puy lentils. For this elegant and light cooking, prices are very reasonable indeed, with starters around £4 and main dishes £8 to £9 while set meals at £11.50 are excellent value. A well-chosen Italian wine list is an extra pleasure. C £15. **Set L & D** £11.50.

10/20 Café Pelican
45 St Martin's Lane, WC2
071-379 0309
FRENCH

Open Lunch & Dinner daily.

This long, elegant bar-cum-restaurant seems to stretch for miles as you leave the street behind you. Taped jazz is played a shade too loudly, and the place has the decorative feel of a slightly faded ocean-liner. The menu deals in French bistro dishes, tolerable renditions of 'cuisine bourgeoise' that may be vapid in the case of a plate of Bayonne ham with cinnamon pears or earthily heartwarming as in thick slices of smoked saucisse de Toulouse and new potato on spinach leaves. Coq au vin will wow the Burgundophiles, while the duck confit is the real thing, thrown onto a bed of green lentils and onions, and served, if you like, with wonderful frites. Pastry leaves room for improvement; we found the lemon tart with lemon caramel tough and the filo encasing a truffe au chocolat savoury and papery. The wine list is short but well-chosen. Be warned that service, even when the place is only half-full, can be pathetically slow. C £26.

11/20 Christopher's American Grill
18 Wellington St, WC2
071-240 4222
AMERICAN
Open Lunch Mon-Fri, Dinner Mon-Sat, Sun Brunch.

Christopher Gilmour is the Christopher in question—son of the former Thatcher Cabinet minister, Sir Ian Gilmour—who returned to London after eleven years as a commodity broker in the Windy City. His restaurant has ideal premises, an impressive corner site with room for a bar/café on the ground floor and a large dining room at the top of a sweeping stone staircase. Opinion divides about the over-designed dining room that is aiming to be antique and modern all at once. The menu is unashamedly modelled on the grand steak and lobster houses and grills of the east coast of America, so un-adulterated protein is the name of the game. That aside, there are some odd-sounding but delicious-tasting appetisers and side dishes. Lobster coleslaw, made with finely shredded Chinese leaf, rolled with lobster and carrot in blanched savoy cabbage, is sliced and served sushi-style. Sweet potato hash, decent fries, and celeriac mash take some beating. Overall the cooking succeeds but occasional lapses in seasoning and technique (smoking tomatoes for a soup does not work) have earned Christopher's a reputation for inconsistency. **C** £30.

11/20 **L'Estaminet**
14 Garrick St, WC2 - 071-379 1432
FRENCH
Open Lunch & Dinner Mon-Sat.
An establishment on the site of the late, un-lamented, over-rated Inigo Jones restaurant must be an improvement, but l'Estaminet would be welcome anywhere. It combines the vitality of a brasserie with some of the more agreeable aspects of a small restaurant. Somewhere we can converse without shouting is quite unusual in this part of

London. The décor—basically interesting modern paintings on brick walls—is another attraction, and the wine bar downstairs brings in a young crowd to leaven the preponderance of business people. The menu, a brief à la carte, supplemented by plats du jour, is mainly traditional bistro-brasserie. Moules mari-nières, herring salad and omelette aux choix are balanced by tarte au chèvre tiède as a gesture to the nineties. The best main dishes are as simple as bangers and mash, liver and bacon, and well-hung, grilled steaks. Excellent fruit tarts are the dessert speciality. Cheese is charged at £1.40 for each piece chosen. The short wine list includes some promising modest bottles, although fuller descriptions are needed. Service is friendly. **C** £22.50.

 ### The Ivy
1 West St, WC2 - 071-836 4751, Fax 071-497 3644
MODERN BRITISH
Open Lunch & Dinner daily.
The blue-green leaded lights, which cast an eerie glow across the Ivy's large dining room, are the only original feature of London's oldest theatre restaurant, where Noel Coward rubbed shoulders with Sybil Thorndike. The oak panelling that looks so well seasoned is new, and the green leather banquettes were especially made. Its owners are also the power behind Le Caprice, arguably London's most consistently busy restaurant, and the Ivy's design appears sedate by comparison. Dotted

around on its walls, however, you'll see work by many leading contemporary British artists. Dining under a Howard Hodgkin or an Alan Jones is the icing on a very smooth cake. The menu is not easy to categorise. On the one hand it reads like a grill menu, yet both classical (French and English), it also reflects the fashionable Mediterranean flavours. All in all a clever menu with unlimited appeal for its regulars, of which there are many. As befits a show-biz restaurant, the Ivy opens at 5.30pm and takes last orders at midnight—an additional attraction for its many customers of stage and screen. **C** £35. **Set menu Sat, Sun** £12.50.

11/20 **Joe Allen**
13 Exeter St, WC2 - 071-836 0651, Fax 071-497 2148
AMERICAN
Open Lunch & Dinner daily.
No cards.
Regulars describe the clientele as 'Prima donnas by the barrow load' at this discreetly located basement replica of New York's famous theatre restaurant. Now sixteen years old, its clubby atmosphere and brusque style, not to mention a 12.45am last order call, keep it popular with London's luvvies, and it's an established favourite of lunchers in the opinion and service industries. The formula rests on a long cocktail bar, dim lighting, red gingham table cloths, bare brick walls covered with theatrical posters, and a huge blackboard menu. The menu has developed over the years but it rules supreme at brunch dishes–

eggs Benedict, smoked salmon and scrambled egg and omelettes. They are justly famous for their chips and though no burger appears on the menu, if you ask for one and specify how you would like it cooked, it will be done. This is an old tip from Rowley Leigh, once a Joe Allen grill chef and now chef/patron of Kensington Place. It is useful to know that Joe's is open all day, every day, and off-peak meals are often the nicest. **C £25.**

10/20 Mon Plaisir

21 Monmouth St, WC2
071-836 7243
FRENCH
Open Lunch Mon-Fri, Dinner Mon-Sat.

Now on two floors and with a generous back extension, Mon Plaisir is coming up for its fiftieth anniversary and is London's premier quintessentially French bistro. Little changed on the outside, its pleasingly tatty original 30-cover dining room has been extended with its character retained, an upstairs room opened, and a twenties-inspired bar sandwiched between the two. The menu has expanded, but remains firmly rooted in straightforward bourgeois cooking. Hence you can start the meal with a traditional gratinée à l'oignon or escargots à l'ail and follow with entrecôte béarnaise and excellent pommes allumettes. In fact, this is arguably the best meal at Mon Plaisir, particularly if you conclude with a selection from their outstanding cheeseboard. This is not a place to take a vegetarian but it is useful for pre- and post-theatre meals. **C £18. Set L & D £13.95.**

11/20 Neal Street Restaurant

26 Neal St, WC2 - 071-836 8368
ITALIAN
Open Lunch & Dinner Mon-Sat.

Chef/owner Antonio Carluccio, who's become synonymous with wild mushrooms (which you can buy in his food shop next door), is married to the restaurateur Sir Terence Conran's sister. Hence Sir 'Tel' as he is often called, had a hand in its elegant and glamorous design and it has stood the test of time. Twenty years is a long time for a restaurant to remain fashionable but despite outrageously high prices, the Neal Street Restaurant has never faltered as a style leader. The walls are hung with a fine collection of contemporary British art, originally chosen by the art dealer Kasmin, and the menu is designed around a David Hockney print. Funghi has a noticeable presence—porcini and tartufi in season—and so too do other obscure Italian specialities such as bottarga (dried mullet roe), mostarda di Cremona and miniature rocket. Very particular ingredients have always been an obsession here (many can now be bought in the shop), and the simplicity of some dishes, such as a plate of hand-cut raw ham or veal cooked with butter and sage, is a hallmark of the Neal Street Restaurant. About half the wine list is Italian, rising from four commendable house wines to class acts such as Mastroberaddino and Jermann. Watch out for the grappa trolley. **C £35.**

 Orso

27 Wellington St, WC2
071-240 5269, Fax 071-497 2148
ITALIAN
Open Lunch & Dinner daily. No cards.

This, the Italian arm of Joe Allen, has a similarly low-key entrance and high-profile clientele. In the vast basement with low ceilings and photos of stars of stage and screen on its wood-panelled walls, the gorgeous parquet floor is much envied. Like its parent, you'll hear no music and the curious acoustics muffle the non-stop babble. Orso pioneered the style of sophisticated rustic cooking that's now a feature of many Italian London menus. Theirs changes daily and is a list of tempting and fashionable goodies such as pork chops with mozzarella, sun-dried tomatoes, basil and pine kernels, and roast suckling pig with garlic potatoes. Spinach and broccoli are served lukewarm with a dressing of olive oil and lemon. One speciality is super-thin, mini pizzas with simple toppings such as anchovies and olives. The dessert consists of a slice of Pecorino cheese with a pear. The wine list is Italian, short and to the point. Note that Orso, like Joe Allen, is open all day and every day, including many Bank holidays. **C £30.**

12/20 Le Palais du Jardin

136 Long Acre, WC2 - 071-379 5353
FRENCH
Open Lunch & Dinner daily.

Lovers of Parisian brasseries will enjoy this large—200-seat—place buzzing with life at virtually any time. Drinks, coffee and casual meals are served in the seafood bar area which opens onto the street in fine weather. Beyond the enormous bar stretches the restaurant with its white walls, bare of decoration other than wheat sheaves in black velvet bows. Colour is provided by the customers, who can be specially viewed from the small gallery at the end of the room. The seafood bar displays crustaceans and molluscs at modest prices, with frequent, and irresistible, special offers on lobsters, crab or oysters. A gargantuan plateau de fruits de mer is £16.50 per head. The main menu offers a wide choice of typical brasserie dishes. Among the favourites are hors d'oeuvres of baby scallops with bacon and spinach, and salads such as rabbit, quail and duck liver, well put together and decently dressed. Another section of the menu offers 'cuisine grand-mère'—from fish cakes and sausage and mash at £5.75 to braised gigot of lamb at £8.25. Grills include good steaks, with some of London's best pommes frites and fresh vegetables. Wines are from £8.50 to £17.50 (except Champagne) and the 40-strong list includes some decent bottles. Service is polite and cheerful and telephone bookings are courteously welcomed. **C £21.**

10/20 PJ's Bar & Grill

30 Wellington St, WC2
071-240 7529
AMERICAN
Open Lunch & Dinner daily.

Various restaurants have come and gone on this site—a long, rather awkward room that snakes its way from Wellington Street to Catherine Street. But PJ's seems here to stay. An off-shoot of the very successful and fun PJ's Bar in Fulham Road, it is decorated with such oddities as polo sticks and sporting pictures on the walls and a lot of mahogany and brass. It serves honest American food in the honest American food category: spicy creole fish cakes with tomato relish and clam chowder for starters, New Orleans seafood gumbo or from the grill, fillet steak béarnaise with mushrooms, good juicy hamburgers and Janes best barbecued ribs and puddings like crème brûlée, pecan pie and the de rigeur New York cheesecake. Atmosphere is fun, particularly later in the evening when the young gather around the bar, and service is good. Children (and their parents) love the Sunday lunchtime feast. Long may PJ's remain in an area which has plenty of indifferent joints. **C £18.**

11/20 Rules

35 Maiden Lane, WC2 - 071-836 5314, Fax 071-497 1080
BRITISH
Open Lunch & Dinner daily.

Everybody should try Rules once. One hears too much talk of restaurants as institutions, but Rules is fast approaching its bicentennial—making it the oldest eatery in London. An ambience of the senior common room, with oak panelling and framed prints of old cartoons, gives adequate indication of the style of food to expect. Plates of smoked salmon satisfy traditionalists, though we have been known to go into raptures over a salad of bacon and black pudding with poached egg, for all that 8pm might seem a little late for breakfast. Much seasonal game is offered, usually with old-school farinaceous sauces, but the meat is powerfully gamey. Moules marinières served in a huge bowl please seafood lovers, and fish is always admirably fresh. Fans of English puddings will get their money's worth with the apple sponge, the bread and butter pudding or the sticky toffee confection ladled with lumpy custard; fainthearts take comfort in home-made ices and sorbets. For its brevity, the wine list needs much better selection, and we were dismayed to find a Cabernet Sauvignon ruined by being served too warm. **C £28.**

11/20 Smith's

25 Neal St, WC2 - 071-379 0310
MODERN BRITISH
Open Lunch & Dinner Mon-Sat.

Located in a basement on a corner of Neal Street, the long vaulted, whitewashed room is made colourful with modern paintings supplied by the upstairs gallery. It's a fun restaurant serving basically British food with some strongly Mediterranean-influenced dishes like grilled goat's cheese salad and baked tuna with grilled peppers and feta cheese. Portions are generous, the wine list is wide ranging and the wine bar at the front of the restaurant adds to the noise level and the varied clientele. Service can be a little chaotic at times, but is usually willing. A reliable, permanent fixture in Covent Garden where restaurants change hands too often to become favourite places. **C** £20. **Set D** £10.75.

CROUCH END

12/20 Les Associés
172 Park Rd, N8 - 081-348 8944
FRENCH
Open Lunch Wed-Fri, Dinner Tues-Sat.
Three Burgundians became 'les associés' to run this cosy little restaurant with a friendly intimacy. It's the sort of place that the English dream of discovering in France and here it is in Crouch End. Gilles Charvet's half-a-dozen starters and main dishes rotate regularly but he has a predilection for first courses in pastry—miniature feuilletés of snails are particularly special. He is adept, too, at daubes and dishes that require gentle braising to produce rich and well-seasoned flavours. One such technique, rarely seen on menus and called a

chartreuse, seems to be a speciality. Vegetables are braised in a mould with a main ingredient, and then turned out onto the plate. The side vegetable dishes, included in the main course price, are exceptional. Cheeses are kept in fine condition and few people can resist the platter of desserts. A far simpler menu, featuring soup, charcuterie and cheese, is the order of the day at lunch. **C** £25. **Set L** £15.95.

FINCHLEY ROAD

  Mr Ke
7 New College Parade, Finchley Rd, NW3 - 071-722 8474
CHINESE
Open Lunch & Dinner daily.
This restaurant's bright modern décor could be Italian, Japanese or Indian— yet more than the pictures immediately identify it as Chinese. About the menu there is no confusion, for chef/patron Mr Ke sticks firmly to the northern Peking, Szechuan styles and that of Jiangnan in the southeast. That so many of the dishes are now found in Cantonese places may sadden purists, but clearly points to their wide appeal. Here they are cooked with rare skill, and their authenticity adds to the pleasure. Stir-fried 'lover's prawns' are a single dish of white and contrasting pink crustaceans, cleverly sauced. Sliced fish in hot bean sauce 'Jiangnan' style, although not very hot, is highly spiced, and

sea-spiced aubergine with pork is another piquant success. For lovers of the really hot, quick-fried spiced squid is an ideal starter. Set menus are more expensive than most, and correspondingly more interesting. Some menus include superb poached Peking dumplings, then wok-fried; Szechuan dumplings served with hot sauce have a subtly different texture but these are offered only à la carte. **C** £20. **Set menus** £14-£25.

12/20 **Wakaba**
122a Finchley Rd, NW3
071-586 7960
JAPANESE
Open Dinner Mon-Sat.
Huge panes of frosted plate glass conceal the stark, white minimalism of architect John Pawson's dramatic interior that never fails to provoke strong reactions from new customers. Many people never make it past the sushi bar which others find intimidating, but it has to be passed to get to the main dining area. Here the chef wields his knife to produce some of the best, and freshest, sushi and sashimi in town. A greater choice of food is served in the austere restaurant, and set meals are the most economical way to explore the food. These centre round popular styles of cooking such as tempura, teriyaki and shabu shabu. But there's something for all tastes here, from the popular fondue-style dishes that are cooked at the table to dishes like suzukuri— thinly sliced raw turbot with a tangy ponzu sauce. Drink saké, green tea or Japanese beer. **C** £35.

FULHAM

11/20 **Blue Elephant**
4-6 Fulham Broadway, SW6
071-0385 6595, Fax 071-386 7665
THAI
Open Lunch Mon-Fri, Sun, Dinner daily, Sun Brunch.

The staff flit around like butterflies in an enchanted tropical garden at this extraordinarily adept, glamourised interpretation of a Thai village. The profusion of tropical plants and flowers aside, an ornate bridge spans a wishing lake, stilt huts enclose tables, and the abundance of Thai antiquities and statues would furnish a shop. Since it opened eight years ago, with the intention of serving authentic royal cuisine, the Blue Elephant's food has had its ups and downs. The menu has broadened, now also encompassing street snacks from Bangkok, stews and grills from the provinces, and lately a new range of interesting vegetarian dishes. Prices have also shot skyward, enhancing its reputation as London's most expensive Thai restaurant. It is certainly reserved, by many people, for high days and holidays. The staff are charming and attentive, it looks very pretty with candlelight reflecting off the water, and orchids are given to departing women guests. To eat here is an event, which explains why so many people are prepared to put up with small portions of food that is often better elsewhere. Thai beer is the only reasonable alternative to a good but expensive wine list. C £35. Set D £28.

11/20 **Chutney Mary**
535 King's Rd, SW10 - 071-351 3113, Fax 071-351 7694
INDIAN
Open Lunch & Dinner daily.

Chutney Mary was a term coined by conservative Indians during the British rule of India to describe a westernised Indian woman. It seems an appropriate enough name to give a restaurant that celebrates Anglo-Indian food served in an appropriately colonial setting. The menu provides a little history lesson to explain itself and is awesome in its variety. It is divided between the cuisine of the Christian communities of India, dishes they unabashedly call Indian, and Anglo-Indian specialities such as Bangalore bangers and mash and salmon khitchri (the forerunner of kedgeree). The starters are particularly enticing: yoghurt medley, where small dumplings, chickpeas and potatoes are beaten in yoghurt and drizzled with three chutneys, and spicy crab cakes served with fresh coriander and mint chutney. Unlike most other Indian restaurants, here the food is served French-style and sharing dishes is not the order of the day. The upstairs bar serves an interesting selection of snacks. The concept is taken to its limits with a wine list that encompasses the British habit of drinking Madeira through an Indian meal and claret at its end. C £25. Set menus £10, £12.95.

GOLDERS GREEN

12/20 **Quincy's**
675 Finchley Rd, NW2 - 071-794 8499
BRITISH
Open Dinner Tues-Sat.

In the environs of Golders Green, this friendly neighbourhood restaurant enjoys a solid local following who enjoy the informal approach, pleasant hubbub and quietly accomplished cooking on offer. Depending on the mood, this can be over-artful, as in a starter of ravioli filled with salmon mousse with a saffron sauce. Other dishes, however, are effective such as the dead simple, quick roasting of lamb with a rosemary-scented stock. We have often had good soups here such as thick carrot and coriander, while game is always offered in season and has usually been properly hung. Desserts run a British gamut, with the bread and butter pudding especially praiseworthy for the lightest custard and plentiful dried fruit. Cheeses are always up to the mark, while the short and only adequate wine list is fairly priced and knowledgeably served. C £25. Set D £22.

HAMMERSMITH

River Café
Thames Wharf Studios, Rainville Rd, W6 - 071-381 8824, Fax 071-381 6217
ITALIAN

Open Lunch daily, Dinner Mon-Sat.

The reasons for the brilliant success of this improbable restaurant are varied and contradictory. First, its location in far-flung Hammersmith, in a warren of one-way streets that drives cabbies wild, ought to discourage the fashionable foodies who flock here. But reflect for a moment: if the city is at your back, the River Thames is before you, flowing just beyond the restaurant's terrace where lunch is served in summer. On the far bank, the sight of green fields at the edge of a bustling metropolis is a city-dweller's dream. The décor of this former architects' canteen may also startle you, unless you know Sir Richard Roger's other works, notably the Pompidou Centre in Paris. Although the River Café doesn't resemble the multi-coloured factory in Beaubourg, the stark, spacious, white room, with bay windows bordered in blue, is a trifle disconcerting. And for a restaurant that posts such heavy tariffs (you will easily spend £40), the setting and paper-clothed minimalist tables seem awfully bare. Yet this is the kind of dining room the minimalist snobs of the chattering classes—socialites, journalists, businessmen—prefer, whether it be in New York, Rome or Paris. Likewise the service, studiedly casual but sly and efficient, is the height of chic.

Designed, directed and executed by Ruthie Rogers (Richard Rogers' wife) and Rosie Gray and a team of Englishwomen with vague Italian roots or credentials in their background, the food served at the River Café is as ambiguous and perplexing as the rest. The concise menu lists five starters, five main dishes and five desserts, all Italian-inspired. But this food springs from an imagination fertilised by influences both rustic and urban, Mediterranean and British; it mirrors the enthusiasm of the keen amateur cook as well as the professional's concern for detail and quality. Superior ingredients, a penchant for lightness and uncommon flavour combinations, a pronounced preference for grills and marinades (no ragouts) are all features of the River Café's kitchen; above all, it swears exclusive allegiance to the foundations of Italian gastronomy: olive oil, basil, tomatoes, sage and marjoram.

The food pleasingly demonstrates this new Anglo-Italian hybrid, cooking of a sort one would never encounter in Rome or Apulia. Among the offerings are a chicken and cabbage bouillon with cheese and anchovies; ham with grilled polenta; delicious marinated sweet peppers with a jolt of hot chilli; broad tagliatelle (only one pasta dish listed) with ultrafresh mussels, garlic and herbs; butterflied (sic) lamb marinated with fennel accompanied by a fine chicory gratin; plump scallops briefly seared al ferro (grilled); calf's liver (undercooked, as it always is in Britain) with dandelion greens, bacon and cranberry beans; a powerfully flavourful chocolate cake ('the Nemesis') and a delicate iced zabaglione al marsala. Add to that a rich and diverse list of exclusively Italian wines, selected with discernment and annotated with as much care as enthusiasm in an unfortunately muddled index. **C £30.**

HAMPSTEAD

12/20 Café des Arts
82 Hampstead High St, NW3 - 071-435 3608
FRENCH
Open Lunch & Dinner daily.

Hampstead is long overdue a few decent, reasonably priced places to eat, and Café des Arts is a welcome arrival. Born out of Fagin's Kitchen, which had its day twenty years ago, the décor is still pine panelling, open fireplaces and terracotta tiles. An exhibition of paintings, all of which are for sale, changes continually. In the summer tables are placed outside. The menu is short, to the point and a cross-cultural balance of Mediterranean and southeast Asian flavours. Many dishes can be chosen as a small or large portion thus waiving the traditional menu boundaries. Some interesting ideas appear here: wafer-thin sheets of celeriac with Caesar dressing, roast pork fillet seasoned with soya and lime and served with a spicy noodle salad, and bread and butter pudding made with panettone. The similarly eclectic wine list concentrates on wines under £15. **C** £20.

12/20 Caffé Graffiti
71 Hampstead High St, NW3 - 071-431 7579
INTERNATIONAL
Open Lunch & Dinner daily.
At last, we have another restaurant to brighten the otherwise uninspiring culinary environs of Hampstead. The style is full of buzz, even if the long room may somewhat resemble a railway carriage. A menu offering an eclectic selection of dishes is supplemented by daily specials chalked on a blackboard. We were astonished at the quality of a dish of fresh squid-ink linguine with char-grilled salmon, while confidence with flavour also comes out in simple gnocchi with tomatoes, goat's cheese and slivered black olives, spiked with plenty of cracked black pepper. Meat is well-bought, and the beef fillet gratinated with Gorgonzola and served with an onion and mushroom compôte impresses for its resonant tastes. Chicken breast stuffed with artichoke and pine nuts is less convincing, and the sage fettucine that comes with it was underseasoned. Comfort is found in the French-inspired desserts. The crème brûlée is richly rewarding, and pastrywork also shows a sure touch. An international wine list demonstrates the same savoir-faire as the food. This is a welcome

arrival—long may it reign. **C** £22.

HOLLAND PARK

11/20 The Belvedere
In Holland Park, Abbotsbury Rd, W8 - 071-602 1238
MODERN BRITISH
Open Lunch daily, Dinner Mon-Sat.
For over 30 years, this restaurant, housed in what was the summer ballroom of Holland House on the edge of Holland Park, has been one of London's restaurant travesties. In the past it offered pretentious food at inflated prices but all that has changed. Under new ownership, with a new contemporary look and outlook, the Belvedere has joined the ranks of London's most fashionable places to eat. The company who conceived the new concept are victims of the recession and their chef, Jeremy Strode, whose menu was both modern and inexpensive, has moved on, but their legacy has been embraced by new owner Johnny Gold (of the night club Tramps). The menu, designed to be flexible, is both fashionable and health-conscious. Thus confit de canard, risotto, fish cakes, onion and sundried tomato tart, and home-made ices. It is a beautiful restaurant with its high ceilings and vast windows in the downstairs ballroom and the more for-

mal galleried dining room upstairs looking out across the park which is floodlit at night. On sunny days tables are placed on a small terrace outside. **C** £20.

 Chez Moi
1 Addison Ave, W11 - 071-603 8267
FRENCH
Open Lunch Mon-Fri, Dinner Mon-Sat.
Here we have a *restaurant de quartier* of the old school. Established in the late sixties by partners Richard Walton and Colin Smith, Chez Moi remains faithful, as the decades turn and others go in search of the undiscovered, to a stolid but successful formula. In a pleasing if slightly faded ambience of warm red walls and formally attired waiters, a menu of two halves is offered. One side designates dishes that are 'traditionnel': from this we have repeatedly enjoyed the rack of lamb with its mustard-spiked herb crust, though doubting whether the turbot quenelles in a creamily rich lobster sauce are quite substantial enough to qualify as an entrée. A simple salad of chicken livers, however, makes for an appetising hors d'oeuvre. The other half of the menu is headed *Quelque chose de différent* and represent a regularly changing slate of more experimental dishes to demonstrate that today's culinary fashions hold no fear. We were a trifle bemused recently to encounter chicken with southeast Asian seasonings but desserts bring us firmly back to bistro stalwarts, such as densely filling

---

Gault Millau's ratings are based solely on the restaurant's cuisine. We do not take into account the atmosphere, décor, service and so on; these are commented upon within the review.

crème brûlée and the house speciality—a pot au chocolat with Cointreau or some other liqueur poured carefully over the surface. The wine list will not impress for geographical breadth, but makes a good fist of the classic French regions. An impressively loyal clientele keeps coming back for more. **C £32. Set L £14.**

The Room at the Halcyon

The Halcyon, 129 Holland Park Ave, W11 - 071-221 5411, Fax 071-229 8516
MODERN BRITISH
Open Lunch Sun-Fri, Dinner daily.

The Room at the Halcyon escapes the hotel restaurant feeling by having its own separate entrance to the street, a small, pretty terrace for summer eating which is especially good for lunch and tea, and a décor that manages to combine a Mediterranean feel with a slight air of decadence. Perhaps this goes some way to explain its success; this is a place for celebrity-spotting, a favourite royal haunt and a regular dining spot for the powers-that-be at BBC Television Centre (particularly those in the drama department), and people from the movie and fashion business. The other reason for its popularity is some good, inventive but not startling modern cooking from Martin Hadden who has worked in the kitchens of Nico Ladenis in London and Shaun Hill at Gidleigh Park, Devon.

A successful starter at a recent lunch was grilled red mullet fillet—not an easy choice for a starter—on a bed of basil-mashed potatoes with a piquant tomato, bacon and red pepper sauce. Pan-fried scallops on a marinated cucumber salad flavoured with the mustard-like wasabi (usually found added to the rice balls in sushi), was slightly salty. Portions are almost too generous: three pieces of salmon fillet grilled with tapenade which just managed to let the taste of the salmon through, with mussels and provençal vegetables, was just one piece too many. Excellent, pink roast rack of lamb with creamy garlic potatoes, mangetout and carrots added up to another honest portion. There was just room for a good lemon tart with blackcurrant sorbet and refreshing mint and lemon sorbet. The Room caters handsomely for vegetarians with a complete vegetarian menu, and the three-course set meals which include tax but not service are particularly good value. With rich cooking and large portions, dinner is the better bet. The wine list is short and reasonably-priced, which comes as a surprise in this ultra-fashionable joint. Perhaps everyone stocks up at the vodka bar at the restaurant entrance. **C £30. Set L £12.95, Set D £17.**

> *The **C** (A la carte) restaurant prices given are for a complete three-course meal for one, and service. **Set L or D or menus** prices are for a complete fixed-price meal for one, excluding wine (unless otherwise noted).*

11/20 Anna's Place
90 Mildmay Park, Newington Green, N1 - 071-249 9379
SWEDISH
Open Lunch & Dinner Tues-Sat. No cards.

Anna Hegarty is known for the warmth of her personality and her interesting Swedish menu. An institution in Newington Green, the tiny dining room with its polished wooden floor, subdued colours and displays of greenery is a pleasant home-from-home. A second more spacious bar room gives way to a garden which is worth remembering during the summer. The menu doesn't change much and Anna, her daughter and staff, take pride in giving a detailed description of each dish to every table. The soundly traditional dishes such as gravlax, silky-mild Swedish marinated herrings, Jansson's frestielse (an oven-baked hot-pot of potatoes, onions, Swedish anchovies and cream), and biff Strindberg (a piquant stew served with spiced potatoes and cucumber salad), followed by Swedish waffles with blueberries and cream, are worth going out of your way for. A reasonably priced and well-chosen wine list, with several half bottles, helps make this a popular neighbourhood restaurant. **C £20.**

11/20 Casale Franco
134 Upper St, N1 - 071-226 8994
ITALIAN

Open Lunch Fri-Sun, Dinner Tues-Sun.

Islington's Citroen dealers were first off the block to try Casale Franco when it opened four years ago, hidden as it is in an alley opposite their garages. Since then, its no-booking policy and the consequent queues might well have sold a few cars. What was a warehouse has been cleverly and cheaply converted to make a feature of bare brick walls, with part of the brass wiring culminating in eccentric spaghetti-like central lighting. Although it is a big place and also has a second more cramped upstairs room, it buzzes with a frantic atmosphere. The speciality, pizzas (not served at lunchtime), arrive thin, crusty and misshapen, and are excellent. Otherwise the simpler dishes, particularly the seafood, are the most successful. The house wine is good and good value, thereafter prices rise steeply. **C** £20.

 Granita

127 Upper St, N1 - 071-226 3222
MEDITERRANEAN
Open Lunch Wed-Sun, Dinner Tues-Sun.

Minimalism veers on the side of austerity at this long, narrow and fundamentally Italian restaurant. But don't let its dour concrete frontage put you off, because once you start eating all thoughts of décor will be forgotten. Details such as a dish of olives and a tub of unsalted French butter, and offers of good home-made breads bode well for the meal to follow. The chef, Ahmed Kharshoum, writes his short weekly

changing menus with explicit truthfulness. Hence when you order spinach cake with shitake mushrooms and goat's cheese, smoked salmon and crème fraîche, or fillet of yellowfin tuna (pink) char-grilled, slow-roasted red pepper and garlic, crispy roast potatoes and mangetout, you know exactly what to expect. Desserts are similarly interesting and show a good understanding of textures and flavours. The drinks list, carefully chosen, comprises moderately priced wines and a thoughtful selection of non-alcoholic alternatives. The intention has been to create a neighbourhood restaurant serving fresh, interesting food at affordable prices. They have succeeded; do book. **C** £20.

KENSINGTON

12/20 The Ark

Kensington High St, W8
071-937 4294
MODERN BRITISH
Open Lunch Mon-Fri, Dinner daily.

Set back from the main road in Kensington Court, the large, heavy wooden entrance suggests a classy venue. Indeed the Ark has the atmosphere and the look of a restaurant that means business. Starched white tablecloths, heavy white china, lots of dark wood panelling, period prints and mirrors and banquette seating give the ground-floor room a cosy but professional feel. Until recently the Ark's food was

a let-down, but since the arrival of Nicky Barraclough, who has worked in the kitchens of Bibendum and before that at the Carved Angel in Devon, things have begun to improve radically. Now the bistro food has soul and flavour and the frequently changing menus are something to look forward too. Pâtés and terrines are richly flavoured and accompanied by onion chutney and cornichons, rabbit is stewed to a melting tenderness and lamb shanks are braised with aubergine. The kitchen cooks with the seasons and much use is made of ordinary, inexpensive ingredients, thus keeping prices down. Sensible and realistically priced wine list. **C** £25.

 Boyd's

135 Kensington Church St, W8 - 071 727 5452
MODERN BRITISH
Open Lunch & Dinner Mon-Sat.

Boyd's, located between two centres of foodie fashionability (Kensington Place and Clarke's), can safely hold its own. Chef/patron Boyd Gilmour is mostly self-taught but the surety of his cooking bespeaks no amateurism; he combines professional simplicity with inspiration. Starters highlight a liking for grilled fish/seafood with subtle dressings and luscious salad leaves, as in perfect scallops with rocket and Chinese vinaigrette, and tender grilled squid, red onion and linguine salad on char-grilled aubergines. Main courses marry meats with herbs and citrus flavours, deft, not overpowering though, as in grilled rib eye of Scotch beef marinated in orange and ginger, and roast breast of pheasant with a wild mushroom farcie and blackcurrant sauce. Puddings are straightforward but appealing: the passion fruit brulée had a creamy zing, the lemon parfait was nicely lemony. There's a good cheese board. The wine list (chosen by Neville Blech of Mijanou) has some real beauties, and a strong leaning to the New World, with many half bottles, regular bin ends and decent house wines, also by the glass. The restaurant has a pretty, green conservatory look with a relaxed garden air and the service by pleasant young staff is adroit. This is a popular *restaurant de quartier* with many well-heeled Kensington residents. Our one cavil is that prices for dinner should come down a notch. C £28. Set L £14.

Byblos

262 Kensington High St, W8
071-603 4422
LEBANESE
Open Lunch & Dinner daily.
London abounds with Lebanese restaurants of excellent quality but you'd sometimes be hard pressed to tell one from another, as so many sport much business-like marble and glass in the Arab international style. All these restaurants cater magnificently for vegetarians and meat-eaters alike—but usually at a price. Byblos is unusual because it manages to combine high standards with excellent value, in a setting that is cosy and idiosyncratic. It is very much the personal fiefdom of chef-proprietor Rafic Kreidi, resident in London for more that 30 years, whose dead-pan observations and anecdotes, on any subject you care to mention, are in themselves worth a detour. So if you need some culinary pointers, don't be afraid to ask. Otherwise he will leave you to your own devices. The basic culinary currency is the meze—a profusion of little dishes, plucked and jabbed at with fork or unleavened bread, whose taste combinations you will soon be playing like an orchestral maestro. You won't necessarily like all of them, but whatever you do, don't miss the smoky taste sensation of moutabal (purée of aubergines) or the summery freshness of tabbouleh. In between, if you're feeling experimental, try making up a finger-version of a staple Beiruti street snack: tear up your bread into a tiny envelope, line it with chawarma (spit-grilled sliced lamb) and then use it as a scoop to dip into the hummus. In summer, try lining your bread instead with fresh sprigs of mint or a radish. If you're really hungry or just curious to explore the furthest reaches of the cuisine, go for the 'Lebanese Feast' menu which takes you past the basic meze into a range of kebabs before delivering you into the cosy self-indulgence of Lebanese semolina pudding drizzled with honey and pistachio nuts, and Turkish coffee or mint tea. The house wine is £7.85 a bottle, but try the excellent Château Musar from Lebanon at £13.85. C £14. **Set menus £7.35, £9.35, £13.65.**

11/20 Cibo

3 Russell Gdns, W14 - 071-371 6271
ITALIAN
Open Lunch & Dinner daily.
A generous spirit reigns at Cibo. Everyone gets free nibbles—antipasti—and home-made chocolates with coffee, there's no cover charge and most main dishes come with vegetables. On balance, however, prices are high. They were one of the first London restaurants to serve bruschetta and the freshly seasoned stews and char-grills that have become known as new-wave Italian cooking. The menu changes frequently but is dominated by seafood, which is often marinated then char-grilled, and specialises in risotto and simply cooked meat dishes. Cibo is a jolly place, chic in a casual sort of way. A main dining room gives way to two smaller rooms and the kitchen (and lavatories) are at the foot of a perilously narrow staircase. The wine list is usefully annotated and includes several bottles under £15. C £30. **Set L £10.**

Clarke's

124 Kensington Church St, W8 - 071-221 9225, Fax 071-229 4564
CALIFORNIAN/ MODERN BRITISH
Open Lunch & Dinner Mon-Fri.
When Sally Clarke opened her Hobson's choice restaurant that modelled its style on the trend-setting restaurants of

California, most people thought it was doomed to fail. Ten years and many laudatory reviews later, Clarke's is firmly established amongst London's top restaurants and clearly hasn't suffered by its no-choice menu. The week's menus are posted outside the restaurant but such is the fine balance of foods and inspiring ways of cooking them that most people are happy to take pot luck. At lunch there are three choices per course. Some people prefer the original upstairs restaurant, its walls hung with contemporary art, but others like the larger basement with its views into the kitchen. Fresh pasta, often stuffed and simply sauced with top-notch olive oil, elegant and interesting salads, marinated and then char-grilled fish, game and meat, are much in evidence. Soups are a speciality, as in leek and wild mushroom broth with fresh pasta, scallops, thyme and truffle shavings, so are breads and biscuits (from their next door bakery/food and wine store) and cheeses are farmhouse British. The keenly priced wine list also takes its lead from California and includes a good selection of wines by the glass. **Set L** £22, £26, **Set D** £37.

 ### Kensington Place

205 Kensington Church St, W8 - 071-727 3184
MODERN BRITISH
Open Lunch & Dinner daily.
  Few restaurants divide opinion quite so much as Kensington Place, or KP as it is known to its regulars.

For admirers it encapsulates what a buzzing metropolitan place should be: crowded, noisy and with an inventive, good-value menu remarkable for its consistency. Its non-admirers dislike the effect of eating in a goldfish bowl created by its glass frontage, and find Julian Wickham's space-age design—particularly the chairs—uncomfortable. Occasionally people complain about the food, but considering that there are now 130 covers and several sittings for each service, the kitchen does an admirable job. On the flexible menu it's possible to eat anything from an omelette to a sophisticated four-course meal, with the option of a different daily set menu. Rowley Leigh's cooking owes much to his years with the celebrated Roux brothers (he was head chef at Le Poulbot in the City) and at KP it is a commendable marriage of the Roux style of haute cuisine and classic British and brasserie dishes. Scallops with minted split-pea purée, vinaigrette of red peppers with anchovies, chicken and goat's cheese mousse with olives, and griddled foie gras with sweet corn pancake, are in such demand that they rarely leave the menu. **C** £25. **Set L** £13.50.

12/20 Launceston Place

1a Launceston Pl, W8 - 071-937 6912, Fax 071-938 2412

MODERN BRITISH
Open Lunch Sun-Fri, Dinner Mon-Sat.
  The parent and very much the grown-up rela-

tive of Kensington Place, at Launceston Place the look and mood is tasteful tranquillity, somewhere to go for a civilised meal out. The elegant table settings, comfortable chairs, period oil paintings and lights dimmed to a romantic level, are in exact contrast to Simon Slater and Nick Smallwood's other restaurant, the noisy and buzzing Kensington Place. The food is masterminded by KP's chef Rowley Leigh. Straightforward treatment of classic British dishes rub shoulders with eclectic compositions using all the latest fashionable ingredients and seasoning. Hence Sunday lunch is likely to begin with char-grilled Mediterranean vegetables or a vivid green parsley soup and continue with traditional roast beef served with Yorkshire pudding and simply cooked vegetables. Puddings are always interesting; there is a well-kept cheese board and a serious wine list. **C** £30. **Set menu** £15.50 (to 8pm).

10/20 Mon Petit Plaisir

33c Holland St, W8 - 071-937 3224
FRENCH
Open Lunch & Dinner Mon-Fri.
  The second sibling to the thirty-year old Covent Garden bistro Mon Plaisir (a third, Mon Plaisir du Nord, is handy for Camden Passage antiques market), tucked away in a back street behind Kensington High Street is tiny with a quintessential bistro design. Bare brick walls are hung with copper pans, bread baskets and

atmospheric pictures. It's a good place to remember for sunny days when almost as many tables can be accommodated on the pavement outside. Part of its charm is the straightforward bistro cooking that is generally very successful. Traditional dishes such as onion soup with Gruyère cheese, potato salad with anchovies and tapenade and entrecôte béarnaise with frites are reliably good. They keep an excellent cheese board and the small selection of classic desserts includes a good crème brûlée and decent tarte du jour. **C** £18. **Set L** £13.50, **Set D** £13.70 (6.30-7.30pm).

Phœnicia
11-13 Abingdon Rd, W8
071-937 0120, Fax 071-937 7668
LEBANESE
Open Lunch & Dinner daily.
The key to the success of this fifteen year-old restaurant is the energy that Hani Khaliffe and his family, who own and run it, put into maintaining the consistency of the food and the welcome. This relaxed and comfortable place is sometimes enlivened with a celebration that calls for a belly dancer. At lunchtime an impressive buffet of hot and cold dishes provides the perfect introduction to this interesting cuisine. As is the tradition of Lebanese restaurants, tables are laid with a bowl of uncut salad, olives and sweet pickled peppers. These, and wafer-thin pitta-style bread which arrives puffed like a ball, are used as scoops for the dips and salads of the meze. These vividly

flavoured snacks can be ordered either as appetisers or to make up a complete meal. Main dishes tend to be grilled variations on the kebab, but there is always a homely stew-style dish of the day. Home-made baklava-style pastries and pancakes stuffed with cream cheese and studded with pistachios, make a fitting end to the meal. Try arak, an aniseedy spirit diluted with water, as an aperitif, followed by Château Musar, a wine from the homeland, an appropriate choice. **C** £20. **Set L** £9.95, **Set D** £15.30, £22.70.

10/20 Wódka
12 St Alban's Grove, W8
071-937 6513
EAST EUROPEAN
Open Lunch Mon-Fri, Dinner daily.
Until the arrival of Wódka six years ago, London's Polish restaurants were, well, very Polish. Here the look is minimalist. A feature has been made of the white-and-green period tiles that date back to 1880 and its days as a dairy. A short menu centres around blinis—with herring, smoked salmon and various caviars—and an enticing selection of robust dishes such as venison and wild boar sausages with olive oil and garlic mash and cabbage stuffed with pork and wild rice. However, a great attraction is the fifteen-strong list of flavoured vodkas served ice-cold, or indeed sometimes warmed. Comforting puddings include white chocolate cheesecake, chocolate cup with sour cherry and chocolate ice

cream, and crème brûlée with Krupnic. **C** £20.

 ### The Capital
22-24 Basil St, SW3 - 071-589 5171
MODERN BRITISH
Open Lunch & Dinner daily.
Londoners harbour no inborn prejudices against hotel restaurants. Consequently, hoteliers and those that govern these establishments invest bountifully in top chefs, kitchens and dining-room décor. The efforts yield convincing results, for a large proportion of London's hotel restaurants win high ratings in the various guidebooks.
The rousing success of The Capital, the dining room of a charming small-scale luxury hotel must be attributed to this trend, rather than to the superiority of its cuisine. No complaints about the décor of the small, narrow dining room, done up in 'boudoir' shades of salmon-pink and given an air of stateliness with ornate chandeliers, heavy flounced curtains, painted panels and Adam-style furniture. Our compliments to the serving staff, more or less French, well-bred and obliging, overseen by the hotel's gracious manager, Jonathan Orr-Ewing. And the excellent sommelier speaks knowledgeably of his great and modest French wines, as well as his bottlings from Italy and Australia (we noted with interest Tyrrell's powerful '91 Pinot Noir).

We wonder, however, about the usefulness of offering a £25 single-price menu at dinner when every option offered has a supplement tacked on (there is also a seafood menu priced at £37.50). The perusal of this explicitly annotated menu is beguiling indeed, for it abounds in such modern, elegant possibilities as soufflé de coquilles Saint-Jacques aux langoustines; asparagus and foie gras au gratin; baked sea bass with a truffle salad; slices of grilled lamb and lamb's kidneys marinated in Port; ginger-scented beef fillet with cèpes; casserole-roasted pigeon with root vegetables; an Armagnac-spiked parfait; and apricot soufflé.

Yet a sampling of these dishes left us perplexed. Our potage Germiny, in principle a sorrel soup surely, featured raw Jerusalem artichokes and bits of foie gras, but an underdone of tartness was the only relation it bore to its namesake. Similarly, a 'croustillon' of sweetbreads had been cooked nearly to death, but was revived by a vivid and delicious green-pea coulis. Happily, the young English chef, Philip Britten, shows his mastery of cooking times and delicacy of touch with an attractive terrine of sole, red mullet and leeks accented with dill and olive oil. Most exquisite was a generous portion of lobster beignets, coated with a diaphanous tempura-style batter, accompanied by a beautifully rendered but utterly inappropriate beurre blanc sauce. To finish, there was a very clever pudding flavoured with lemon, orange, and lavender honey. Britten is yet another representative of the many young English chefs who are still 'feeling their way', working towards a future which seems assured, if only they manage to channel their energies and rein in their imagination. **C** £40. **Set L** £21.50, £25, **Set D** £25, £37.50.

 ## The Fifth Floor Restaurant

Harvey Nichols, SW1 - 071-235 5250, Fax 071-235 5020
MODERN BRITISH
Open Lunch & Dinner Mon-Sat.

The fifth floor of the revitalised Harvey Nichols, the other Knightsbridge store, is devoted to food and wine. An express lift whisks you to the top where there's a specialist food store, 'open-air' market, café and wine shop. Overlooking and running the entire length of the market is this large and stylish restaurant, with its own separate café/bar, designed by the Kensington Place architect, Julian Wickham. Windows on one side overlook the Hyde Park Hotel, giving the room incredible light. The chef, Henry Harris, worked for many years as Simon Hopkinson's right-hand man at the famous restaurant Bibendum. His menu is deceptive in its simplicity. Pork rillettes, rich and unctuous, are served with an intensely flavoured onion confit, a stew of mussels is enriched with chick peas and chorizo, and roast fillet of cod is dressed with a black bean and spring onion dressing. English nursery puddings and refinements of clichéd dishes such as rum baba, achieve new heights of pleasure in Harris's capable hands. The menu changes with seasonal specialities—roast grouse with exceptional bread sauce for instance—and a daily different set meal is terrific value. The vast wine list is fuelled by the wine shop. **C** £25. **Set menus** £16.50, £19.50.

10/20 Khun Akorn

136 Brompton Rd, SW3
071-225 2688, Fax 071-225 2680
THAI
Open Lunch & Dinner daily.

The proliferation of Thai cooking in London has spawned a fair amount of regional diversity, but for those looking for standard dishes served in glitzy surroundings by waitresses who actually kneel to take your order, Khun Akorn is the place. We enjoy the fiery soups of prawn, lemon-grass and coriander in a chilli-and-ginger broth, and the succulent Thai fish cakes with dipping sauces. Presentation of centre-piece dishes is reliably painstaking, with strips of rare beef in spicy peanut sauce becomingly garnished with orchids. Nor do desserts let the side down; the lavishly sculpted tropical fruits and even the coconut ice cream are usually enjoyable. Prices tend to be steep when incidentals are added, but remember—you are only a stone's throw from Harrod's. There are no great surprises on the wine list. We suggest Alsace wines as the best choice for Thai food. **C** £32. **Set L** £12.50, **Set D** £17.50, £24.

Pearl of Knightsbridge

22 Brompton Rd, Knightsbridge Green, SW1
071-225 3888
CHINESE
Open Lunch & Dinner daily.
Conveniently sited for shoppers, this bright restaurant exemplifies the modern oriental style. White walls carry unusual pictures and murals. White tablecloths set off dramatic, high-backed, black wooden chairs each crowned with a flash of red. Service by Chinese and European waiters is smooth and efficient, and they can clarify (most of) the few enigmas on the menus. They are few because this short menu is as far removed as possible from Chinatown's almost infinite list of permutations. It features rare and unashamedly expensive delicacies with more mundane dishes in support. All the main Chinese regional schools are well represented particularly in the wide range of appetisers, both hot and cold, with a few for vegetarians. Lobster on a bed of noodles is offered in five ways, and as well as the usual ducks, crispy aromatic chicken and lamb are available. The specialities are shark's fin (from £50), whole abalone (from £38) and whole suckling pig. As the helpful staff could not adequately explain 'Baby Ribs in Hot Vinegar Sauce' we tried it, and enjoyed an exotic but engaging flavour combining a hint of caramel with vinegar. We also enjoyed the tender texture in Peking 'double-cooked' pork. A longer than normal dessert menu also included a novelty in the form of deep-fried crispy buns with custard filling, more pleasing than the name suggests. The fine cooking here will not offend delicate occidental sensibilities; more robust palates can turn to the chilli sauce and chilli oil which appear on the table automatically. **C** £35. **Set L** from £12.50, **Set D** from £25.

The Restaurant

Hyde Park Hotel, 66 Knightsbridge, SW1 - 071-235 2000, Fax 071-235 4552
MODERN BRITISH
Open Lunch Mon-Fri, Dinner Mon-Sat.
What you've heard is true: Marco Pierre White is unbearable. He looks like a hoodlum with his long, greasy hair; while his angry outbursts, his insults directed at diners, food critics (though he claims to adore both Gault Millau) and establishment types, his gutter vocabulary, his false modesty and megalomania, his contradictions and blatant scorn for colleagues all contribute to White's badboy image. Not to mention the tabloid accounts of MPW's taste for fashion models and money! Some people find his cooking equally offensive. They call it incoherent and sloppy, overladen with costly foie gras, truffles and caviar, which with expensive wines can bring bills to a burdensome £120 a head. The cooking of this Anglo-Italian colossus is as hugely engaging as White himself. Provocative, even excessive in certain juxtapositions of flavour, always daring, his dishes leave a strong impression. Take, for example, his saffron-tinged scallops with caviar; or a remarkable foie gras that is nearly overpowered by its rough-and-ready gelée; or the savoury, delicately cooked salmon aptly finished with a lie-de-vin sauce; or his luminous, lovely terrine of languoustines and leeks: a marvel of freshness in its lacy mantle of green bell pepper, yet with a curious metallic aftertaste. We'll skip over the unsuccessful combination of oysters, leeks and caviar (again!), blunted by a quasi beurre blanc, as well as the misbegotten marriage of cod and whipped potatoes, and the fiddly 'andouillette' of brill and smoked salmon with mustard. Yet what a glorious talent shines through in White's more raffish options: we're thinking of the pig's head with baby vegetables in a sauce with a keen touch of orange; smoked oxtail braised with carrots and celery; a white-bean velouté with truffled morsels of duck confit; and then there is the miraculously sapid pig's trotter stuffed with veal and poached sweetbreads, then braised in a reduced tripe stock. This culinary masterpiece is the only offering on the menu not listed with a date (the oldest dish is from 1987: leeks, lobster and caviar vinai-

grette), for it is the brain-child of Pierre Koffmann of La Tante Claire. White reproduces it here with dazzling grace.

White's cooking is certainly open to criticism, but in our opinion, this culinary genius-in-the-rough should be encouraged for what he has already accomplished, and bids fair to achieve in the future. Indeed, we predict that before long this restaurant will indeed be, as the unbearable Marco Pierre calls it with his accustomed modesty: The Restaurant. **Set L** £22.50. **Set D** £60.

 St Quentin

243 Brompton Rd, SW3
071-581 5131, Fax 071-584 6064
FRENCH
Open Lunch & Dinner daily.

The St Quentin, now part of the Savoy Group, seems to have been here for ever. Remember the Brompton Grill? And the décor remains very much the same—an elegant belle-époque interior with pillars and plenty of mirrors to brighten the dark wood, brass, banquettes and flowers. The staff is mainly young and French and has had a change of heart: they are extremely polite, helpful and friendly. The kitchen is now under the sway of Nigel Davies who heads a British staff and produces a robust menu of mainly southwest French dishes in generous portions. The dishes remain traditional but are cooked with a due regard for the integrity of the fresh ingredients. Lamb, suitably pink, is invariably delicious

and starters of jambon de Bayonne, creamed wild mushroom soup and smoked salmon are excellent. The mainly French wine list is sensible, with a good choice of well priced half bottles. **C** £22. **Set L** £10.50, **Set D** £15.25.

MARBLE ARCH

 Al San Vincenzo

30 Connaught St, W1 - 071-262 9623
ITALIAN
Open Lunch Mon-Fri, Dinner Mon-Sat.

Vincenzo and Elaine Borgonzolo moved to this small, smart site in a quiet, smart Paddington Street after building up a loyal following in Cheam over a decade or so. They struggled a bit at first, but now the restaurant has settled down and is supplying the best southern Italian cooking, indeed some of the best Italian cooking, north or south, to be found in London. Although Neopolitan by birth, Vincenzo is not a slave to the classics of his native city. He judiciously uses the hallmarks of the region—garlic, olive oil, and above all, parsley and chilli—to bring dash and depth to such dishes as carpaccio of tuna in olive oil with caramelised onions, fried chilli, lemon juice, parsley and olive oil; a soup of cannellini made thick with stale bread; salt cod with potatoes; sea bass roasted with tarragon, mint, basil and parsley. The

wine list is short but serious and entirely Italian. **C** £25.

MARYLEBONE

12/20 **Caravan Serai**
50 Paddington St, W1 - 071-935 1208
AFGHAN
Open Lunch & Dinner daily.

Offspring of the Buzkash in Putney, Caravan Serai offers a slice of Afghani culture as well as its food. Almost every surface is covered or hung with mementoes, making an Aladdin's cave of rugs and other Afghani treasures. Afghan food is a mixture of the spices, curries and tandoori-oven cooking of northern India, mixed with the finesse of Arab food. It is rarely hot, and often incorporates fruit, nuts and seeds. The menu is helpfully explicit and there is much to choose from. Meals begin with a dish of pickled carrot and a potato fritter with a minty yoghurt sauce. These, like the tiny apricot sorbet that punctuates the meal and rye-flavoured pastry twists that conclude it, are complimentary. The wine list and dessert choice is cursory; Muscadet would be an appropriate choice. **C** £25. **Set L** £9.95.

 The Regent Dining Room

The Regent London, 222 Marylebone Rd, NW1 - 071-631 8000
ITALIAN/BRITISH
Open Lunch & Dinner daily.

The superlative north Italian cooking here is one of London's best kept secrets.

Critics have not always appreciated the peasant earthiness of some dishes, nor the subtlety of others; and the hotel's position near Baker Street station makes it all the more surprising. The quality is signalled by the bread basket where white rolls, olive bread, walnut bread, dark rye bread with caraway are excelled only by home-made grissini and a circle of pizza dough rolled out to the thickness of a poppadum, then brushed with oil and herbs and baked for exactly 30 seconds so it is also as crisp as a poppadum.

On a recent visit the à la carte at dinner offered six appetising pasta dishes, but not one with a tomato-based sauce. Also listed were ten starters of which beef broth, tortellini and old sherry was a perfect soup, though superb 'Bresaola with pickled mushrooms and pomegranates' lacked the promised pomegranates. Main courses also include such simple traditional English offerings as Dover sole, grilled or meunière, and a roast from the trolley is always on the lunch menu. The chef's well justified confidence in the cooks' skill is shown in such clever combinations as the near al dente chopped aubergine with roast fillet of rabbit and basil sauce, and smooth celeriac purée with breast of duck. Most desserts are served from a trolley. Only about eight are offered, with the emphasis on fresh fruit, alone or in pastry, all unsweetened. Variations on crème brûlée rarely work,

but the rum-flavoured version here is an exception. And pink grapefruit sorbet has more flavour than the fruit itself, again with minimum sugar and no alcohol. While the £27 menu includes a half bottle of wine per person, the extraordinary bargain here is the set dinner of five courses for £25 which includes coffee with biscotti—a plate of tempting truffles, fruit pastries and amaretti. The formally dressed staff serve with charm, skill and enthusiasm.

Our one reservation about this dining room is the décor and lighting. The colours are more English drab than Italian lustrous, and the three magnificent candelabra fail to shed enough light from the stratospheric ceiling. But the management are planning improvements. The wine list is worthy of the cooking, but expensive. The range of Italian wines is probably unequalled in this country, and seldom in Italy. Wines by the glass include a fine Soave at £4.50 and the vivacious little-known red Franciacorta from Lombardy at £4.80. Most of the great Italian winemakers are represented, but some of their big red wines are too young. Not so the exciting Californian Cabernet Sauvignons, which go back to 1984. French wines include some serious clarets, and a welcome feature is the list of largely Italian sweet wines to match the desserts, such as glorious Reciotos and Moscatos. **C** £33. **Set L** £19.50, £27, **Set D** £25.

Stephen Bull

5-7 Blandford St, W1 - 071-486 9696
MODERN BRITISH
Open Lunch Mon-Fri, Dinner Mon-Sat.

Stephen Bull is one of a handful of top British chefs (Alastair Little is another) who are self taught. When he opened here, after several years of running a quite formal restaurant in Richmond, he put into practise his belief that eating out should not be surrounded by a lot of unnecessary trappings. So his décor is simple and plain and his menus are written without fuss or whimsy. Unconstrained by classical training, his cooking has never courted fashion and has evolved its own eclectic, magpie style. He seems preoccupied with providing value-for-money and this has led to some interesting ways with root vegetables, pulses and grains. Dishes such as salad of lentils with anchoiade croûtons, and the unexpected coupling of black bream with polenta and a provençale red wine sauce. Favouring fish, he serves a warm terrine of hake and salmon, a carpaccio of salmon with a lime jelly, and was one of the first to serve baked cod with a crab crust. The consistency of the set lunch has made it extremely popular. An intelligent wine list includes several decent half bottles. **C** £25. **Set L** £14.50, £17.50.

> Remember to call ahead to **reserve your table**, and please, if you cannot honour your reservation, be courteous and let the restaurant know.

10/20 Topkapi

25 Marylebone High St, W1
071-486 1872
TURKISH
Open Lunch & Dinner daily.
Topkapi, a reliable Turkish restaurant, won a London Capital Radio award way back in 1984 and, rather endearingly, still announces it proudly on their menus. We've been going for years and the menu and the standards have barely changed. Mixed meze offers a good selection of starters like cacik (yoghurt salad with chopped cucumber and garlic), hummus (chickpea purée with lemon, sesame cream and garlic), taramasalata, and bean salad. Char-grilled chicken with a mixture of peppers, onions and rice is always a good bet, as is saslik kebab (thinly sliced lamb fillet marinated and cooked with onions and green peppers). The long thin entranceway broadens out into a larger room at the back, hung with colourful views of Turkey in suitably bright colours and a lot of brass. A mock gas fire burns in winter. Try not to sit at the front near the glass display cabinet. Service can be charming or surly depending on the waiter. It doesn't seem to bother the regulars; this is an enjoyable restaurant with a loyal following. **C £18. Set menus** from £12.50.

11/20 Villandry Dining Room

89 Marylebone High St, W1
071-224 3799
FRENCH
Open Lunch Mon-Sat.
This seethingly popular Marylebone lunch-venue is an extension of an excellent delicatessen of the same name. Tables are packed in anywhere and everywhere, and even spill out into the back of the shop. One's digestion is not improved by browsers crowding against the table in order to peer at the wine shelves. Pressure of numbers can befuddle the staff so that orders are in danger of getting mixed up. Soups come in large tureens (the waitress on one occasion setting it directly in front of the diner as if she thought it a particularly generous bowl) and we appreciate the likes of the hearty cauliflower and stilton version served on a bitterly cold day. Casserole dishes proliferate, whether of mixed fish, squid and saffron, or of cubed veal with tomatoes, both served with accurately cooked rice. Tarts are well-made, with proper tatin, or frangipane-based pear tart with cream. Wines are bought directly from Paris and offer a chance to taste vintages unavailable elsewhere in London. We recommend the Villandry, while wishing it were just a touch cheaper. **C £22.**

> **Plan to travel?** Look for *Gault Millau's* other Best of guides to Chicago, Florida, France, Germany, Hawaii, Hong Kong, Italy, Los Angeles, New England, New Orleans, New York, Paris, San Francisco, Thailand, Toronto, and Washington, D.C.

MAYFAIR

11/20 Al Hamra

31 Shepherd Market, W1
071-493 1954
LEBANESE
Open Lunch & Dinner daily.
Located in the heart of Mayfair's notorious Shepherd's Market, in summer it is fun to secure an outside table and watch this expensive playground at work. Inside the restaurant is pleasant and comfortable but the point here is the food. Over 40 items of meze dominate the menu and dishes like creamy aubergine moutabal, hummus topped with diced lamb and toasted pine-nuts and falafel, are just a hint of its delights. There is a hefty cover charge of £2.50 which includes unlimited salad and bread. Many people never graduate onto the main courses which centre around the char-grill, mainly poultry and lamb. Specialities, such as raw lamb kibbeh, eaten with raw onion and mint, and raw liver are an acquired taste. Freshly sliced and elegantly presented fruit might be a more fitting end to the meal than the sugar-water drenched pastries. Drink aniseedy Arak, Iyran yoghurt or Lebanese wines, and choose between authentic mint tea and Turkish coffee. **C £35.**

12/20 Caviar Kaspia

18/18a Bruton Pl, W1 - 071-493 2612
RUSSIAN/FRENCH

Open Lunch & Dinner Mon-Sat.

You can eat caviar in select London venues, but no better than here, where it reaches its apogee. This is the sister restaurant to the famous Paris Salle de Dégustation, opened in 1927. Five types of caviar include notable Sevruga, Oscietre and Beluga in 30g, 50g and 125g servings, with prices ranging from £16.70 to £237. Expense is obviously no deterrent. The panelled restaurant, decorated with gleaming samovars and Tsarist porcelain, is reached through its own shop offering various delicacies and Russian objets d'art. Whilst the chef Annabel Job does not ignore the central culinary premise, served in small jars rested on buckets of ice (with a choice of sixteen shots of vodka, many peppery), she has also introduced modern interpretations of White Russian cuisine. Such specialities include creamy beef Stroganoff (properly made with fillet), robust fish cakes with a sorrel sauce, or extravagantly layered lobster lasagne. Puddings comprise unusual out-of-season fruits and well-made tarts, and there is a well selected cheese board. Wines include eleven Champagnes (notable a Krug '82), but a glass of house Sancerre does not short change. However, we found the service erratic. Kaspia exudes a club-like atmosphere of quiet understated wealth, where 'society ladies who lunch', the establishment and the aristocracy hole up, confident their pres-

ence is undisturbed. The Princess of Wales is a regular and Her Majesty the Queen is reported to have dined here. It's the sort of place where, caviar notwithstanding, food is not wholly the point. That said, you can dine modestly. C £30. **Set menu £27.**

Claridge's
Claridge's, Brook St, W1
071-629 8860
FRENCH
Open Lunch & Dinner daily.

Distinguished, gracious and sumptuous are all words to describe Basil Ionides' art deco restaurant at the rear of this great hotel. A golden pink colour scheme is picked out by extraordinary fluted wall lights that play off a stunning mirror mural. Customers pick their way past palms and a piano (dinner dances are a regular event) to one of the well-spaced and impeccably dressed tables. The whole experience of a meal here, the wonderfully attentive staff and rather good food make it an occasion to savour and an experience to remember. The luncheon menu is affordable—from £24 if you stick to a main course and a dessert from the trolley—and is interesting, up-to-the-minute and staunchly traditional, Recent choices of warm black pudding with potato and apple salad, and baked crottin with pimento and coriander chutney were commendable. The trolley offers a different meat each day and the well-stocked dessert trolley has a number of freshly made pastries. Luxury is the name of

the game in the à la carte menu. Light, elegant dishes such as lobster and crab fritters with soft quail eggs, and fillet of new season lamb with minted vegetable and celery sauce, show that chef Marjan Lesnik keeps his finger on the pulse. Serious wine list. C £40. **Set L from £24.**

The Connaught Restaurant and Grill
Carlos Pl, W1 - 071-499 7070, Fax 071-495 3262
FRENCH/BRITISH
Open Restaurant: Lunch & Dinner daily. Grill Lunch & Dinner Mon-Fri.

We could take up every page in this guide and still lack space to detail the professional career, the passions, the ideas, the deeds and the wise proclamations of Michel Bourdin, former sous-chef at Maxim's (until 1972), now master of the Connaught's kitchens and patron saint of classic cuisine in Britain. Classic, but not hidebound. His cooking encompasses elaborate creations in the grand tradition but also embraces more homespun dishes, particularly those English recipes that are so unjustly disdained but can be so satisfying when prepared with a light hand and panache.

In nearly a hundred years of well-deserved fame, the Connaught has employed only five chefs (and five managers; the devoted and urbane Paolo Zago is the current curator of this living museum). Proof enough that no flightiness or erraticism is tolerated here. A culinary Academician like Bourdin is just the man to maintain a steady course in the kitchen, advancing to meet modernity by only the smallest increments, thus suiting an élite clientele that regard the Connaught as their private club.

The difference between the Restaurant and the Grill is significant. The former, lined in dark mahogany, is the haunt of wealthy Continentals who come to dine and do business. The smaller, green Grill is a favourite lunch-hour venue for American gentlemen, who come to share the graceful manners of the English clubmen. Otherwise, the cooking served in both rooms is identical, delivered by distinguished, efficient Italian waiters who skilfully manoeuvre the trolleys and broad serving trays (the kitchen spurns the current fashion for ready-arranged plates).

For seventeen years Michel Bourdin has each day renewed fifteen of the menu's innumerable dishes. His prudent suggestions to three generations of habitués have included such familiar delights as oxtail, steak and kidney pie, sirloin of Scottish beef served with its juices moistening a Yorkshire pudding, and a gâteau of Sherry-soaked biscuits. The Connaught's food is remarkable for its consistency, impeccable quality, and staggering diversity. Bold creations, however, are not to be expected. Alongside gastronomic showpieces with lyrical, slightly ridiculous names— 'turbot au homard sauce Pudeur, crustacés

Amoureux, galette aux Diamants Noirs, salade Aphrodite and Feuilles d'Automne en Surprise'— you will find any number of simpler, more forthright, rustic and (dare we say?) modern offerings. There is the light and savoury terrine Connaught, for instance, created by Maxim's chef Alex Humbert, featuring pheasant (or duck) and pork, or the mosaique de gibier with fruit jelly, a powerfully flavourful assemblage of ten kinds of furred and feathered game, an updated version of the late Alexandre Dumaine's famed Oreiller de la Belle Aurore. Also on hand are a simple kipper pâté that incorporates herring, bacon, onions and whisky, tiny minced-sirloin steaks with sauce Saint-Hubert (delicious forerunners of today's hamburgers with ketchup), and a rousing Irish stew made with real mutton rather than weak-flavoured lamb. To finish, sample some tip-top Stilton or Cheddar, silken crème brûlée, a delectable, rib-sticking, bread and butter pudding, or the latest addition to the sweets list: the Misses Powers quince tart, a creation of the twin sisters who are the Connaught's pastry chefs. With a superb wine from the Italian, German or (mostly) French cellar, the bill for a delightfully English meal of Palaeo-French cuisine will not necessarily rise much above £50. Foreign visitors hungry for a taste of Old England should make a point of eating at the Connaught; nostalgic Brits too, will enjoy the chance to revisit their culinary

roots. **C** £36. **Set L** £25 (£30 Sun), **Set D** £30 (Grill only).

 ## Dorchester Terrace

The Dorchester, Park Lane, W1 - 071-629 8888, Fax 071-409 0114
FRENCH
Open Lunch & Dinner Tues-Sat.

Once again one of London's smartest grand-hotel dining rooms, the Terrace restaurant constitutes a luxurious package (with prices to match) for those who want to see how things used to be done in more recklessly opulent times. A small ensemble plays popular tunes, and if your digestive powers are sound enough, you may feel inclined to teeter on to the dance floor. Chef Willi Elsner carries the torch for a style of haute cuisine that still bears the stamp of his predecessor Anton Mosimann. What may surprise is that flavours can be delicate to the point of evanescence in certain dishes. We applaud the sautéed goose foie gras on a salad of new potatoes infused with chervil and honey vinegar. These are flavours and textures that cosset rather than startle, but who eats in a five-star hotel to be startled? A more modern accent, and greater assertiveness, is evidenced in a wing of skate on tomatoes and capers with sesame oil and coriander. (Ignore the boring tofu that comes with it.) Entrées range from a glorious panaché of sea bass, turbot, red mullet and prawns with aubergine and tomato and a daring hint of chilli, through sautéed veal fillet with kidneys and noodles to a mightily filling roast venison with walnuts, chestnuts and cabbage given a little bite by an infusion of dried mandarin peel. A good value prix-fixe menu is offered, as is a health-conscious table d'hôte that rewards the abstemious with an exquisite pink champagne sorbet at the end. Otherwise, the beautiful arrangements of exotic fruit that may be crowned with an almond tuile containing coconut ice cream demonstrate that infinite care is taken all the way through. The wine list is very fine, but be prepared to pay dearly for its wares. C £45. Set D £25 & £30.

Four Seasons Restaurant

The Four Seasons Hotel, Hamilton Pl, Park Lane, W1 071-499 0888, Fax 071-493 1895
FRENCH
Open Lunch & Dinner daily.
Jean-Christophe Novelli who has succeeded the excellent Bruno Loubet in the kitchens of the Four Seasons is certainly a good chef, but he tends to overdo. His dishes come carefully garnished in a style that might remind you of entries in a cooking competition. A note of excess is struck on the menu, with the oddly named 'charlotte léger des sous-bois sauvages en fine crêpe', 'joue de lotte en vapeur au jus de bettrave façon Wheeler', or 'danse du cygne, glace au fromage blanc'. One wonders what is in store.
The kitchen is supplied

with magnificent raw materials, and when the chef keeps things simple, his cooking is very good indeed. But simplicity is often not his style; witness the ill-assorted escargots, sweetbreads and chanterelles that compose his 'bafouille bourgui-gnonne' in a wine fumet; or the overdose of vanilla that annihilated the sauce napping flawless, superbly cooked langoustines and scallops. While the saddle of rabbit with coarse-grain mustard is above reproach, the Stilton cheese mousse-soufflé accompanying lamb cutlets is superfluous. Yet some dishes work superbly, like a tartine of marinated salmon with crab meat, with cucumber, quail's egg and a touch of caviar. A simple ox cheek with escargots cooked slowly in a red wine sauce reminded us of the days of classic French cooking, though done here with a modern touch that took the heaviness out of this robust dish. Jean-Christophe Novelli treads a narrow path with his mixings and occasional mis-matchings. Were the kitchens to exercise just a llittle restraint, the Four Seasons could well become one of London's best hotel restaurants, and we look forward to it in the next edition. The service is already perfect and the wide-ranging cellar merits nothing but praise. C £50. **Set L** Mon-Sat £25, Sun £28.

*Find the address you are looking for, quickly and easily, in the **index**.*

 ## Le Gavroche
43 Upper Brook St, W1 - 071-408 0881, Fax 071-409 0939
FRENCH
Open Lunch & Dinner Mon-Fri.
The loss of its third Michelin star in 1993 (an event trumpeted in the headlines of every British newspaper) wounded the Roux family's pride more than it deterred their faithful customers. They continue to fill the Mayfair dining room of Le Gavroche (opulent rather than elegant, in our opinion) as if nothing had happened, thus confirming the persistent afterglow of stars declared to be dead. In its glory days, we judged Albert Roux's restaurant to be more than a trifle overrated; conversely (perversely?) we find his punishment unduly harsh and unjustified.
Le Gavroche was the mirror of an age, the symbol of a certain style of restaurant that triumphed in the 1960s and 1970s, epitomised in France by Lasserre. Michel Roux, who has succeeded his father in the kitchens of Le Gavroche, never broke completely with this grandiloquent manner, as illustrated by the perennial papillotes de saumon Claudine, oysters Francine and soufflé suissesse, still fixtures on the menu after umpteen years. Yet Michel Roux also managed quite astutely to catch the 'cuisine bourgeoise' wave at its height, and well he did: in that traditional register, working with superb ingredients, he is undeniably a master. Although he does not attempt to compete

with the culinary innovators and artists of the day, Roux is a first-class professional with a sure sense of timing and a knack for underscoring flavours. His cooking may not bowl us over, but it is beautifully wrought in the classic style. True, one could accuse him of creating confusion when he sets a saddle of rabbit atop herbed risotto and flanks it with superfluous chanterelles, but Roux's talent shines through in his potage parmentier enhanced with truffled tartines, in a delectable pheasant pâté offered with a spiced fig compôte, in a delicate eel mousse, and in his savoury pot-au-feu de canard. Roux's braised lamb cooked to melting tenderness in Madeira and accompanied by spinach studded with plump raisins, is a monument of rich, traditional flavours.

To follow, there are delicious, absolutely classic desserts (wine-poached pears, petit pot an chocolat, tarte Tatin) and petits fours of exceptional quality. The staff are polished without ostentation; the cellar dazzles both by its contents and by the prices it commands (£1,030 for Lafite-Rothschild '61, £69 for the ordinary Pouilly-Fumé from the 'Baron de L'). The atmosphere, we should mention, is not notably jolly. C £55-£60. Set L £36 (inc half bottle of wine), Set D £48.

> *Some establishments change their **closing times** without warning. It is always wise to check in advance.*

 ## The Greenhouse

27a Hays Mews, W1 - 071-499 3331
MODERN BRITISH
Open Lunch Mon-Fri, Sun, Dinner daily.

Gary Rhodes is the chef credited with breathing new life into British cooking and this is the restaurant where he does it. His re-working of British stalwarts such as home-made sausages with onion gravy, braised oxtail and spotted Dick with egg custard, form the hard-core of his menu. These long overlooked dishes are taken back to basics and prepared with the care and sensitivity they deserve. Take faggots, for example, which are painstakingly prepared from pig's offal wrapped in caul and served in a silky-smooth, onion-sweet gravy. On Sundays a traditional British roast lunch is offered, and on Sunday evenings an inexpensive supper menu with dishes such as macaroni cheese with leeks, home-made burgers and shepherd's pie. The restaurant takes its name as a theme and decoration includes an extraordinary topiary sculpture and a collection of stunning food paintings. The location, hidden away in a mews off Grosvenor Square, is surprisingly countrified. C £35. Set Sun L £17.50.

12/20 Langan's Brasserie

Stratton St, W1 - 071-491 8822
MODERN BRITISH

Open Lunch Mon-Fri, Dinner Mon-Sat.

This pioneer of the large brasserie restaurants now so popular in London with its beautifully proportioned rooms hung with an eclectic mixture of pictures, has not changed much since the sad demise of its chef founder Peter Langan. It still buzzes with life, at lunchtime with business men and in the evening with wannabes and stars of stage and screen. The food remains good, sometimes excellent, and specialities such as spinach soufflé with anchovy sauce, liver and bacon and deep-fried skate and chips can't be bettered anywhere. Its reputation as London's most enduringly successful restaurant is intact. And yet, a frisson of excitement has gone. It's the chemistry called Peter Langan. C £25.

 ### Miyama

38 Clarges St, W1 - 071-499 2443
JAPANESE
Open Lunch Mon-Fri, Dinner daily.

It is unusual amongst London's Japanese restaurants to find that the power in the kitchen is also the owner, but Fumio Miyama has established consistently high standards at his Mayfair establishment. It's a pleasing place where a small bar gives way to a deceptively spacious dining room decorated in chic simplicity. The staff, traditionally dressed, glide around offering advice to anyone who wishes to stray from the more familiar dishes. They do an outstanding beef teriyaki and a particularly delicate tempura but it is well worth experimenting with dishes such as horse clam with ginger, and sunomono, in which octopus, mackerel and seaweed are marinated in rice vinegar. Seasonal specialities and sashimi of the day are listed separately. It is also unusual to find a decent wine list in a Japanese restaurant. Warm saké or Kirin beer is one safe option but here they serve a selection of Kentish table wines—all the rage in Japan. C £35. **Set L** £11.50, £18, **Set D** £32, £40.

 ### Mulligans of Mayfair

13-14 Cork St, W1 - 071-409 1370
IRISH
Open Lunch Mon-Fri, Dinner Mon-Sat.
An Irish pub set among the galleries of Cork Street may sound deliciously unlikely, but this place has gained a good West End following. The ground floor is where oysters are washed down with pints of the black stuff in a heartily rowdy atmosphere. In the basement dining room, greater refinement of tone is found, although the food has not sacrificed substantiality of flavour to over-presentation. We wish the waiting staff could find it in themselves to show a little more Irish cheer as they dispense their wares, but there is lots to celebrate on the plate. Good sliced black (or white) pudding is served fried with mustard or calvados sauce (Normandy comes to County Cork via Mayfair!) as a starter, and squid often satisf-

ies. The beef, oyster and Guinness stew will fortify flagging shoppers, as might the boiled ham with a vinegary parsley sauce, while fish may be quite robustly treated, as in a wing of skate with a meat stock sauce, diced vegetables and a heap of champ—mashed potato flecked with green spring onion. Come dessert stage, and the spirit of old Ireland may vanish, leprechaun-like, into the mist to make way for the likes of chocolate truffle and feathered raspberry coulis. Standards have been a little uneven since last year's change of chef, but the place still undoubtedly has individuality and style. Too bad the wine list makes very dull reading. C £28.

 ### Nico at Ninety

Grosvenor House, 90 Park Lane, W1
071-409 1290, Fax 071-355 4877
FRENCH
Open Lunch Mon-Fri, Dinner Mon-Sat.
Whatever became of those bellowing, big-bellied, bad-tempered chefs (known in the trade as 'terrors'), the sort who chucked food critics out of their restaurants for writing reviews they didn't like, and refused to serve diners who preferred their steaks well done? It seems that they are a dying breed. Nico Ladenis carved out quite a reputation for himself at his former restaurants; his outbursts had become the stuff of legend. Did his recent removal to the smart Park Lane district have a calming effect on his colourful nature? One wondered...

Born in Greece, raised in Kenya and now a confirmed Londoner, Nico is the only three-toque chef in the city whose restaurant is family-run. Working with him are his daughter and his half-French half-Romanian wife—the soul of kindness, with a keen wit to boot. The warm wood panelling, flowered fabrics and water-colours on the walls of Nico's spacious, low-ceilinged dining room make an understated setting that may not be memorable, but is perfectly pleasant and comfortable.
Though it seems to us that Nico devotes more time to the dining room than to his stoves, the food prepared by the kitchen staff still bears Nico's inimitable stamp. This is no-frills, classic cuisine that emphasises first-rate ingredients and forthright, focused flavours. Flights of fancy and bold innovations are few: Nico's flawlessly executed menu features robust dishes that keep one's palate fully engaged, whether one chooses the pig's trotters stuffed with morels and sweetbreads; a thick, firm Dover sole in a light, creamy sauce; scallops strewn with sesame seeds in a cèpe sauce; the veal kidney wrapped in filo pastry and accompanied by delicious haricots verts and (less convincingly) by a warm mushroom salad on toast; a plump Bresse pigeon with sweet corn crêpes; or unctuous honey ice cream (though that last was a trifle pale in flavour).
The cheese board is extraordinary, the wines of

excellent lineage and quite pricey: £80 for a Pouilly-Fumé 'Baron de L', £40 for La Rioja's red. It all adds up to a hefty bill. **C** £50. **Set L** £25.

12/20 Oriental

The Dorchester, Park Lane, W1 - 071-629 8888, Fax 071-409 0114
CHINESE
Open Lunch Mon-Fri, Dinner Mon-Sat.

The Oriental arrived with the new-look Dorchester, taking over a banqueting suite next to the famous Terrace. While specialising in Cantonese food, other oriental cuisines and specialities feature periodically. Hence the Oriental provides a showcase for chefs from top hotel restaurants throughout the Orient with regular gastronomic festivals. A simple and elegant décor incorporates authentic silks, fabrics and antiques from the east. The main restaurant on the mezzanine floor stands above three private dining rooms decorated in Chinese, Thai and Indian style. The menu presents Cantonese food at its most impressive relying on rare and expensive ingredients, such as abalone and authentic bird's nest, which are flown in specially from Hong Kong. There are many delights on the menu—dishes that you won't find outside Hong Kong. For example deep-fried eel is served with cinnamon blossom sauce, and pieces of duck are covered in mashed taro and then deep-fried. With the royal cuisine comes the formality of clearly devised courses, lavish presentation and oriental silver

service. The relatively inexpensive set lunch doesn't do the kitchen justice. **C** £35. **Set L** £20, **Set D** £28.

Saga

43 South Molton St, W1
071-408 2236
JAPANESE/SUSHI
Open Lunch & Dinner daily.

Underneath the ground floor sushi bar—one of the largest in London with fourteen stools—the rambling downstairs restaurant seats about 80 in two public areas, and also has private rooms for four or more. In this warm, rustic Japanese décor with brown woodwork, the convoluted vaulting makes a feature of the ceilings. Elegantly dressed, smiling waitresses making every effort to please, offer exceptional service. The manager, French-born, English-educated, M. Leroy, is an enthusiast for Japanese cuisine, able to explain its more abstruse aspects. Menus start with 'Today's special lunch' served with rice, soup, salad and pickles for £6.50; twelve other lunch menus rise to £17 for sushi, with an appetiser, sashimi, a grilled or boiled dish, and soup all included. The 15% service charge is not applied to set lunches. Set dinners run from £35 to £50 or more for a specially chosen meal; in western terms a banquet. The long à la carte offers the expected range of sashimi, sushi, tempura and sukiyaki but look at the interesting 'recommendations' for seasonal, and unusual dishes. Grilled chicken's heart with salt may seem dull until

seasoned with herbed, red pepper, though boiled daisy with sesame sauce is worth trying just once. It was, in truth, one of our few disappointments, amongst many pleasures. Sushi and sashimi are outstanding as is special sunamono—assorted seafoods in mild vinegar. There is a long list of noodle dishes at £5.50 to £9 and notable wappa and other rice dishes at £7.50 to £10. Because of the long opening hours some items are not always available, particularly on Mondays or holidays, but the menus are so wide-ranging that this is unimportant. As well as the usual warm saké there are superior chilled varieties, and several types of shochu, the Japanese spirit, made from buckwheat, barley and sweet potato. In sum this is a very pleasant restaurant, as enjoyable for Japanese-oriented gourmets, as for newcomers to this great cuisine. **C** £44. **Set L** £6.50-£17, **Set D** £35-£50.

Les Saveurs

37a Curzon St, W1
071-491 8919
FRENCH
Open Lunch & Dinner Mon-Fri.

Joël Antunès is the city's up-and-coming young French chef. Trained in the famed Troisgros kitchens in Lyons, he landed up in London after a stint at Bangkok's Oriental. For the moment, Antunès is known only to the 'happy few'. But we lay odds that he may soon give his compatriot, Pierre Koffmann, a run for his money. The premises of the former

Tandoori in Mayfair, purchased by a Japanese group that picked Antunès to run the kitchen, surely lacks the charm and elegance of La Tante Claire. Yet the basement-level dining room is pleasant enough, with its blond panelling, green wallpaper and flower prints; and the many regulars are the knowledgeable sort who can make a restaurant's reputation in record time. A youthful image and solid professionalism are Les Saveurs' twin trademarks. The young French staff obviously adore their work, and it is a positive pleasure to be served by this attentive, discreet, absolutely unaffected crew. The sommelier—he's under 30—feels no need to show off; he speaks with the authority of a true connoisseur, without boring on endlessly as so many wine waiters do. In short, Les Saveurs belongs to the new generation of small, intimate restaurants where fine dining is not a ritual, but sheer enjoyment. In keeping with this outlook, Joel Antunès cooks in a graceful, unstuffy vein.

His cuisine is lovely to behold, yet stops short of excessively 'decorative' effects. His flawless ingredients, precise cooking times and subtly balanced flavours all express the polished proficiency of a disciplined, creative talent. From the salad of warm Dublin Bay prawns set atop exquisite glazed tomatoes to the celeriac rémoulade paired with rich duck foie gras, from the roast turbot and potatoes napped with a sapid

chicken jus to guinea fowl stuffed with black-olive tapenade, from the tiramisù to the roasted pear offered with liquorice ice cream—in a word, from start to finish—the flavours of each dish meld in perfect harmony.

What's more, the bill is far from fearful for food of this high calibre. The worthwhile £29 prix-fixe meal brings three courses plus cheese and dessert. **C** £40. **Set L** £18, **Set D** £29.

10/20 Shogun

Brittania Hotel, Adams Row, Grosvenor Sq, W1 - 071-493 1255
JAPANESE/SUSHI
Open Dinner Tues-Sun 4pm-11pm.

A tunnel leads to the Shogun in the basement of this luxury hotel in Mayfair. The restaurant could be an officers' mess in a medieval Japanese castle—except that the samurai would not have used the comfortable chairs provided. Its appeal is to tourists; most of the Japanese customers sit at the sushi bar. Unlike other Japanese places it is not open for lunch and surprisingly it is owned not by a large corporation, but by Hiromi Mitsuka, one of London's few Japanese lady restaurateurs. She is a charming hostess and although she dresses in elegant western style, not the traditional kimono, she might join you at table for a little vivacious gossip, and playful banter—like a traditional geisha. The Japanese waitresses do wear kimonos to serve graciously, with help from European waiters. Set menus at £30 to £32 offer assorted small hors

d'oeuvres, dobin mushi soup, sashimi, a grill, tempura, a main dish, fruit and green tea. The à la carte menu is not very long, but sashimi and sushi lovers at the bar can choose from the usual appetising refrigerated display. **C** £34.

12/20 Sofra

18 Shepherd St, W1 - 071-493 3320
TURKISH
Open Lunch & Dinner daily.

Healthy eating is owner Huseyin Ozer's buzz word at this acclaimed spot in historic Shepherd Market. Insisting that Turkish food is much more than just kebabs, Ozer, a perfectionist, has devised a menu of the best of Turkish fare and his presence is felt throughout the restaurant, where he meets, greets and solicits comments from guests, proudly handing out business cards on departure. The emphasis is on grilled meat, chicken and fish complemented by fresh vegetables, pulses, olive oil, yoghurt, herbs and spices. Dine inside (ideally near a window) or outdoors at a coveted sidewalk table. Late evening is when the area truly comes alive and the street traffic is an interesting mix. A massive selection of small dishes (meze), ideal for both vegetarians and meat-lovers, comprises the value-for-money 'healthy' lunch—hummus, midye, tava (fried mussels), tabbouleh, kofte and hellim. The à la carte menu is extensive with many notable grills, casseroles and fish options. Turkish wine, whether Karmen (red) or Dorfnal (white) is a perfect foil for the richly flavoured food. Desserts range from apricots stuffed with cream and walnuts to traditional sweet and sticky pastries filled with pistachios. **C £15. Set L £8.45, Set pre- or post-theatre D £9.95.**

Le Soufflé

Inter-Continental Hotel, 1 Hamilton Pl, Hyde Park Corner, W1 - 071-409 3131, Fax 071-409 7460
FRENCH
Open Lunch & Dinner Tues-Sat.

Peter Kromberg, long-standing chef at the Inter-Continental's grand London hotel has had many accolades lavished on his cooking. He is known for his ability to mix different elements and tastes to create excellent dishes, like his immensely popular Lunesdale duck, pan-fried and with crisp potatoes replacing the usual fatty skin. Soufflés, too, which have all but disappeared from 'modern' cooking are given excellent treatment here—both savoury and sweet. However, even the most skilled chefs have their bad days and don't always deliver. On a recent visit Le Choix du Chef (at £43) seemed not to achieve that expected delicate balance needed for a seven-course gourmet meal. After a glass of kir royale came a small helping of excellent fish and crab meat. The tarte de foie gras, truffes et jambon de canard was overwhelmed by the strong ham, and the pastry seemed to have a flat taste. Fortunately the dish was redeemed by the girolles and nut sauce which was just right, being tart and velvety at the same time.

Following a fish course of sea bass and salmon in a vermouth sauce with leeks, a melon sorbet with port gave too strong and too sweet a kick to the taste buds to do what the sorbet in the middle of the meal is supposed to do—refresh and invigorate. We found the main courses, both the pigeon and veal sweetbreads wrapped in filo pastry and the steak, tasty. A small, rather over-done chocolate bread and butter pudding with kumquat sauce was followed by nougat glacé—a frozen dessert of whipped cream and candied fruit. However, at the end of the meal, we did wish there had been more fresh vegetables, or even a salad. Service is extremely good, particularly from the charming and knowledgeable maitre d' who combines just that element of professionalism and friendliness that makes the customer feel at home. A pianist plays at a white piano in the middle of the room. The wine list, almost completely French (there's a small selection of non-French wines) is well chosen and wide-ranging. The décor is hotel dining room style, neither dramatic nor subtle, but designed to make everyone feel comfortable. **C £50. Set L £25.50, Set D £43.**

> *Gault Millau's ratings* are based solely on the restaurant's cuisine. We do not take into account the atmosphere, décor, service and so on; these are commented upon within the review.

NOTTING HILL GATE

12/20 L'Accento Italiano

16 Garway Rd, W2 - 071-243 2201
ITALIAN
Open Lunch & Dinner daily.

This small restaurant, austere in its décor, with a large plate-glass window making up the whole of the front and wooden chairs and tables, is very noisy and produces some very good rustic northern Italian cooking. Meals begin with a basket of excellent fresh bread to be eaten with spicy herb-infused virgin olive oil. Best of the starters are those based on pasta, like tagliatelle verdi with duck ragu. Main dishes are robust also, with osso bucco and bollito misto—the classic boiled meats that come with a delicious parsley sauce—featuring frequently. Fish is well treated as in roast skate which came with brown butter, and roast vegetables are well cooked without being oily. The two-course set lunch is a real bargain. **C £18. Set L & D £10.50.**

L'Altro

210 Kensington Park Rd, W11 - 071-792 1066
ITALIAN
Open Lunch daily, Dinner Mon-Sat.

You walk into L'Altro and feel you are on the fantastic set of an operatic production (apart from the cool jazz playing in the background). Walls are decorated like the outside of a crumbling palazzo and there are some peculiar lights which would look more at home in a Spanish tapas bar. All in all it has a pleasant decadent air, exactly the right kind of ambience for the large plates of fish that arrive after the suitably correct ordering and cooking times. For fish is the name of the game here, though on our last visit there was a dish of baked rack of lamb on offer (at £11 the cheapest entrée dish). Starters might include baby octopus with tomatoes and spices or marinated aubergine with zucchini and peppers with mozzarella, or grilled baby squid with roast peppers. Entrées include mixed grilled fish and shellfish in a delicate basil sauce or whole sea bass baked with radiccio and endives. Desserts are large and very filling and a bit over the top, rather like the whole place. Having said that, the clientele is not the usual hip Notting Hill crowd, but consists of young people clearly there for an occasion and some not so young as well. It's a pleasant mixture. **C** £32. **Set L** £12.50.

12/20 Brasserie du Marché aux Puces

349 Portobello Rd, W10
081-968 5828
INTERNATIONAL
Open Lunch daily, Dinner Mon-Sat. No cards.
At the northerly, less trendy end of Portobello Road, this small corner restaurant is decorated in soft, slightly drab colours enlivened by pictures on the walls and flowers and fruit on a long right-angled bar. Windows on two sides look out onto the street. The adventurous and eclectic cooking produces a short menu which can tempt you with every dish or produce the feeling that there is nothing on it that appeals particularly that day. Dishes like leek and cheese terrine and smoked lamb with celeriac remoulade, as well as borrowings from all over the world to produce a mix of western and Indian tastes such as dhal with courgettes and tomatoes or Indonesian rice to go with well-established kidneys Turbigo, are typical. This very pleasant neighbourhood place, which stays open all day, has a delightful staff. Tables outside in the summer make it a popular resting spot for those weary of the nearby shopping. **C** £20. **Set L** £9.95.

11/20 First Floor

186 Portobello Rd, W11
071-243 0072
MODERN BRITISH
Open Lunch & Dinner daily.
You enter this restaurant located above the Colville pub through an inconspicuous doorway and have to cross a reception area covered in loose pebbles before heading upstairs. The large, circular dining room is a culture clash of baroque and hi-tech, reinvented from the ashes of a trendy drinking club. It's been the breeding ground for some talented young chefs, notably Margot Clayton currently at the French House Dining room. Now, with Michael Knolson at the helm and a new, sharper management, they still dish up fashionable grub such as Thai fish cakes, chargrilled tuna with guacamole, and the ubiquitous sticky toffee pudding, but it's no longer the people's diner that it was. Live jazz on Sunday is a great attraction, and check out the chandelier! **C** £20. **Set D** £27.50

Leith's

92 Kensington Park Rd, W11
071-229 4481
BRITISH
Open Dinner daily.
The summer 1993 refurbishment of Leith's was long overdue. Previously rather grim on the inside with chairs that seemed more suited to an estate agent's office, it is all rather easier on the eye now. Muslin blinds at the windows and plain, stylish mirrors give the restaurant the feel of a pretty, chic, private dining room. Service, led by Nick Tarayan, is as ever perfectly charming and discreet. The wine list, which is his especial preserve, is a document of rare genius, and the readily forthcoming advice for those who wish it is always constructive and helpful. Hors d'œuvres still trundle round on a trolley, and there is fun to be had in mixing and matching yourself a selection. Gull's eggs with spinach are a good bet, but mushrooms à la grecque and marinated collops of monkfish in a vinaigrette are also pleasing. Otherwise, rejoice in the opulent flavours of a salad of pigeon and foie gras with pine nuts and a Cabernet Sauvignon vinegar. Main courses impress for attention to detail,

and for the palpable freshness of produce from the restaurant's own farm. We cannot praise highly enough the rack of lamb with meaty cèpes, bitter turnips and celery, nor the sensitively cooked saddle of venison accompanied by braised celeriac and the robust Scottish haggis, that traditional Scottish dish of sheep's stomach stuffed with chopped lamb's livers and heart, onions and oat meal. Fish, too, is good and may find itself in the company of unlikely but successful vegetable pairings, such as the sautéed brill that comes with fried leeks and mashed cauliflower. Desserts offer a cornucopia of fruit and thrill to the art of combination once again. The hot blackberry soufflé with its sorbet of sloe gin is a winner, as is the autumnally flavoured plum and cinnamon tart with damson ice cream. Even if Notting Hill is somewhat out of your way, Leith's is well worth a detour. **C** £44. **Set D** £25.

12/20 **192**
192 Kensington Park Rd, W11 - 071-229 0482
MODERN BRITISH
Open Lunch & Dinner daily.
This is where London's so-called café society started, and provided the launching pad for numerous 'now' chefs including Alastair Little (of Alastair Little), Rowley Leigh (Kensington Place), Adam Robinson (The Brackenbury), Rosie Gray (River Café) and Sebastian Snow (Snows on the Green) and Maddalean Bonino (Bertorellis). At the end of last year its upstairs bar expanded sideways, losing its

clubby feel (it is now owned by the Groucho Club in Soho) and dual role as a bar/restaurant. The menu, served upstairs and down, is always a good gauge of food fashions. At the moment it's an eclectic mix of rustic cooking, mainly Mediterranean flavours but with a sprinkling of good oriental and Asian spicing. Hence spicy sausages with marinated red onions, goat's cheese and celeriac in choux pastry with a tomato and chive dressing and red mullet with squid, Nero dressing and rouille. Wine merchant John Armit has assembled the wonderful wine list. **C** £20. **Set menu** (weekday) £8.50.

12/20 **Orsino**
119 Portland Rd, W11 - 071-221 3299
ITALIAN
Open Lunch & Dinner daily.
This child of Orso, the Covent Garden media person's restaurant owned by Joe Allen, arrived recently at this cleverly converted pub which sits on the pointed corner of Portland Road. Its triangular shape and windows all round make it feel a bit like being on a ship's deck yet it is remarkably similar in mood to its basement parent. Giant louvered blinds block out the windows and the walls are decorated to give a scrubby effect. This provides a subtle backdrop for the rainbow-coloured wooden chairs. The menu offers an enticing and mixed selection of rustic Italian cooking. Small pizzas with mould-breaking toppings such as goat's cheese, roasted garlic cloves, tomatoes and

herbs, are a highlight of a menu that rarely fails to please. The char-grill is a favoured way of cooking meat and fish, and their inspired assembled salads, with combinations such as warm bitter broccoli, pancetta, new potatoes and balsamic vinegar, are much copied elsewhere. The dessert list is very short but to the point with dishes such as apricot and almond tart with vanilla sauce. An entirely Italian wine list has the good sense to include the Italian equivalent of a pichet. **C** £25.

12/20 **Palio**
175 Westbourne Grove, W11 - 071-221 6624
INTERNATIONAL
Open Lunch & Dinner daily.
A stunning wrought-iron open staircase links the two floors of this restaurant. The menu is a catalogue of all that is fashionable. Hence steamed mussels with greens, lentils and coriander broth; char-grilled squid, two salsas, frites and rocket; and red fruits with mascarpone cream. 'Wozza', as the chef Anthony Worrall Thompson is familiarly called, spearheads the trend here away from formalised menus, with enticing robust soups and salads, things on bread and proper puddings. At lunch the £5 menu is a steal. Noon-till-late opening hours and sensible prices, combined with a lively atmosphere and state-of-the-art music, make it a draw for the young set. There is an intelligent, reasonably priced wine list with fashionable beers. **C** £20. **Set L** £5.

OXFORD STREET

 Masako

6-8 St Christopher's Pl, W1
071-935 1579
JAPANESE/SUSHI
Open Lunch & Dinner Mon-Sat.

London's oldest Japanese restaurant set a pattern for itself, and for its successors. Deep red upholstery, wooden tables, and a few carefully chosen art-works, make for a soberly luxurious ambience. Service is still by Japanese waitresses in traditional kimonos but there are European waiters too; neither show all the elegance and pride in fine service which was such a revelation in the 1960s. The menu is a quite short à la carte divided into sections of appetisers, raw fish, soups, grilled, boiled, fried and special dishes which include sukiyaki and other 'pot dishes'; there is also a long carte of sushi. But many customers, western and Japanese, prefer the simplicity of a set menu. Most dishes are unspecified beyond the traditional succession of raw, boiled, grilled, fried and so on, but the top menus include also kuchigawari and susune zakane both mysteriously translated as 'Food for a change'. On deeper interrogation they turn out to be herring roe and roast duck respectively. Cooking (and preparation of cold food) is always excellent as is the quality of the ingredients. But as in many, but not all Japanese restaurants, the

meal may end with bland tea. Masako is the flagship of the Ninjin group which also include Ginnan (1-2 Roseberry Ct, Roseberry Ave, EC1) the modest Ninjin (244 Great Portland St, W1), also Hiroko and Kashi-Noki housed in the Hilton International Hotels of Kensington and Regent's Park respectively. **C** £37. **Set L** £20, £22, **Set D** £35-£60.

12/20 **Zoe**

12-20 St Christopher's Pl, W1 - 071-224 1122
INTERNATIONAL
Open Lunch daily, Dinner Mon-Sat.

Fashionable once before as Coconut Grove, these premises are now back on the map thanks to celebrity chef Anthony Worrall Thompson's clever menu of 'Town' and 'Country' food. This spurious terminology refers to two long menus providing a clever mix of essentially robustly flavoured, rustic cooking that picks and twists from around the world. Macaroni cheese, presented like a terrine, is served with duck confit, poached ham hock is served with parsley pease pudding and hot potato salad and roast-chilli-rubbed chicken comes with deep-fried okra and garlic potatoes. The ground floor café has its own, marginally more immediate, menu that is full of interesting ideas, and like the restaurant, many dishes may be chosen in small or large sized portions. On sunny days tables are set outside where the sandwich menu—the likes of smoked salmon, ricotta, red onions, fresh capers on

Irish soda bread—is also available. The downstairs restaurant is spacious, comfortable and exceedingly pleasant. The well-chosen, inexpensive wine list offers many wines by the glass. **C** £25.

PICCADILLY

 Café Royal Grill Room

68 Regent St, W1 - 071-439 6320
FRENCH
Open Lunch Mon-Fri, Dinner Mon-Sat.

The most famous clients of the Café Royal Grill Room may have receded into history, but the grandeur of the room has kept the restaurant in the public eye for well over a century. Painted walls and ceiling, sculptured figures and vivid scarlet upholstery make a stunning background for elegant dining. Even the massive, smooth, polished silver serving wagons for the joint of the day look a hundred years old. The only disconcerting hint of austerity is the oddly narrow and at first touch, hard, banquette, but it becomes perfectly comfortable after a few minutes and a glass of house Champagne. It is not known if Oscar Wilde or even the Prince of Wales (later King Edward VII), were serious gastronomes; but they knew what food they wanted and the Grill Room produced it. More recently the kitchen marked time until, in 1992, Herbert Berger arrived as executive chef. More than a year later the fruits of change are beginning to ripen. But soundness in kitchen and dining room takes time to establish, as confirmed by occasional lapses such as the garnish on a superb steak where hair-like pommes paille had somehow become as chewy as leather. Such dishes as tian of lobster with a gâteau of pickled spring vegetables and asparagus coulis show complete mastery of modern 'haute cuisine'; so does the simplicity of escalopes of foie gras with a ragout of celeriac, and truffle sauce. The same regard for the quality of ingredients shows again in the steaks and in an elaborate confection of sweetbreads. Vegetables are treated with due respect, and potato purée is comparable with renowned versions of that seemingly basic dish. The set dinner of three courses and coffee at £32 is excellent value, as is lunch at £22.50. Service is highly skilled with just one modern flaw in evidence: too many waiters asking 'Is everything all right?' The wine list offers great bottles at great prices, but also sound lesser names at reasonable cost. Bourgeois growth clarets are particularly attractive, so it was a surprise to have to ask for a 1983 Bordeaux to be decanted. The Brasserie also offers a short carte and lunch and dinner menus at £14.75. Here too are modern, mostly simple concepts with an occasional flourish. Cooking is generally careful, the flavours interesting and well balanced. A list of 35 wines priced up to £24

is offered, but the whole Grill Room list is available on request. **C** £40. **Set L** from £19.50 (Grill).

🍴 Le Caprice

Arlington House, Arlington St, SW1 - 071-629 2239, Fax 071-439 9040
MODERN BRITISH
Open Lunch & Dinner daily.
Tucked away behind the Ritz, and hidden behind Venetian blinds, very little changes at Le Caprice. Despite some stiff competition—Quaglino's in particular—it remains London's most fashionable restaurant. David Bailey's photographic portfolio, which complements the sharp black, white and chrome interior, ages well, and so does everything about the place. The menu, still bearing the huge influence of former chef Charles Fontaine (now at The Quality Chop House), is a shrewd compilation of tried-and-tested favourites such as steak tartare, eggs benedict and salmon fish cakes with sorrel sauce, plus whatever is state-of-the-art at any given time. It, and every other aspect of this well-run place, is fine-tuned by the omnipresent owners Chris Corbin and Jeremy King. A suitably discerning wine list, like the menu, changes as needs be. Occasionally a place at the bar may be had at short notice, but as a general rule booking is essential several days in advance. **C** £30. **Set menu** £25.

> *Some establishments change their **closing times** without warning. It is always wise to check in advance.*

12/20 Caviar House, La Brasserie

161 Piccadilly, W1 - 071-409 0445, Fax 071-493 1667
RUSSIAN/FRENCH
Open Lunch & Dinner Mon-Sat.
The Caviar House is a relatively new venture, reached through the wood-panelled shop and on the corner of Piccadilly and St James's—which must be one of the best sites in town. The restaurant itself is a light, airy room with a mezzanine as yet little used. The cool, modern décor works surprisingly well given the traditional nature of the place and the food. One disadvantage is the lack of a bar. Comfortable banquette seating around the main wall means that most customers have their backs to Piccadilly and face a wooden boat full of ice, tins of caviar, and bottles of Champagne. A discordant note is the music, which is neither classical nor jazz. The menu consists of various kinds and portions of caviar and fish, and a set menu. The caviar (the five varieties—Sevruga, Oscietre, Royal Black, Beluga, Imperial and then pressed) ranges from 30g of Sevruga at £13.75 to 125g of Imperial at £194, with 50g portions as well. They also serve three different types of Balik salmon and an 'Assiette Royale' of various kinds of fish and shellfish. The £25.50 menu is varied, with seven starters and six main courses. Nothing is particularly adventurous, but all is freshly bought, and well prepared and cooked. From the starters, the Balik salmon—two good thick slices—with

cream and Sevruga caviar, gets you off to a good start. Main courses range from navarin of lamb and salad of Mediterranean prawns served with an interesting chantilly of caviar to a good fillet of brill. Desserts are nicely rich, just what you need if you have kept to caviar and the fish dishes. Coffee and chocolates add £1.75 to your bill. The wine list is short but wide-ranging with the emphasis on France. If you feel particularly extravagant, you can buy any of the products the shop sells on your way out. In any case, the shop is a good lesson in first-rate vodkas, Champagnes not always obtainable in London, and French wines, all reasonably priced. Service is young and good, neither too formal nor too casual. **Set menu £21.50, £25.50.**

11/20 **Criterion Brasserie**
224 Piccadilly, Piccadilly Circus, W1 - 071-925 0909
MEDITERRANEAN
Open Lunch & Dinner daily.
Bob Payton—he of the Chicago Pizza Pie Factory—has joined forces with hotelier Rocco Forte to relaunch Piccadilly's most spectacular dining hall. Its nineteenth century neo-Byzantine architecture is stunning by any standards. Its huge, domed ceiling, inlaid with gold mosaic and semi-precious stones, is divided by a majestic colonnade and supported by marble-clad walls. As befits such a vast space it is put to use from noon til 11.30pm, serving lunch, tea and supper throughout the week, and

brunch and tea on Sunday. The cooking is in the fashionable Mediterranean style, erring towards Italy with lapses into American popular culture. Salmon cake with herb pesto, duck confit wrapped in pastry on rocket salad, and chicken with saffron on a leek and pancetta crostini, rub along with strawberry ice cream sandwich and sticky toffee pudding. Prices are reasonable, brunch more so, but the bargain is the two-course lunch at £10. **C £25. Set L £10.**

 Green's Restaurant and Oyster Bar
36 Duke St, St James's, SW1
071-930 4566, Fax 071-930 1383
BRITISH
Open Lunch daily, Dinner Mon-Sat.
Green's Restaurant and Oyster Bar radiates a comfortable, professional, but at the same time, friendly air. 'Clubby' is the adjective most frequently used to describe the restaurant with its wood-panelled dining room and prints on the walls, but this is not an excluding place. Much of the feeling of welcome is due to the suave and charming owner, Simon Parker Bowles, who is frequently here. And he has trained his staff well. The food is the best of British and the ingredients are chosen with care. After all, what can better oysters in season, smoked salmon, crab, lobster, Dover sole and English lamb when meticulously chosen and simply cooked? Other dishes include shepherd's pie, fish cakes (for which they

have become famous), roast Scotch beef and boiled beef, carrots and dumplings, dishes which have always been championed here. Desserts follow the proverbial British sweet tooth with banana and toffee pie and home-made ice creams. The well-chosen and wide-ranging wine list befits such a restaurant in the heart of club land, owned by a former wine merchant. The restaurant does not appeal to the trendy; this is a traditional place that delivers what it promises: a well-cooked, uncomplicated meal in congenial, old-fashioned surroundings. **C £25. Set Sun L £14.60.**

 Matsuri
15 Bury St, St James's, SW1
071-839 1101
JAPANESE/SUSHI
Open Lunch & Dinner Mon-Sat.
We could suggest that by accident or design this is one of the best sited restaurants in London—adjoining Quaglino's. But there are better reasons for visiting this elegant establishment. The ground floor entrance leads to the cool bar, decorated with colour photographs of the festivals (Matsuri in Japanese) for which the restaurant is named, and a collection of earthenware ninjyo festival mugs. The background of pale wooden panelling is repeated downstairs in contrast to the pale silver-grey walls. The wide staircase is dominated by another piece of festival folk-art, a giant fiery-eyed paper head of a demon.

Teppan-yaki

Some Japanese restaurants offer teppan cooking only. Many more, including some of the best, have a teppan room as one of several options. You sit in a semi-circle at wooden counters fronting the teppan—a giant steep plate on which the main course is cooked. Steaks and prawns or lobster (together or separately) are always offered, and there may be chicken, duck and other seafoods. They are cooked, with vegetables, on the teppan plate using oil and butter, and a wide range of sauces and seasonings.

Some teppan cooks are highly skilled as cooks. Others are showmen who may juggle with the food, and their ultra-sharp knives, during the preparation; a few combine the two. It is all great fun, but there are two features which some people dislike. First you can only sit around the rim of the teppan, which means that you can converse only with those sitting next to you—not ideal if there are more than three in a party. Second is the smell of the cooking, and the cooking medium. However efficient the air extractors, however clean the teppan (both are usually impeccable), the smell of hot oil can be a problem. It may not exist if you take your seat at the teppan early, but when you are finishing the meal, others are being prepared nearby.

Unless otherwise noted, our marks for restaurants which have teppans are for the main room(s) and not for the teppan room.

Coloured fans and bronzes and more photographs are seen downstairs where you choose between the sushi bar seating ten, and the teppan rooms which accommodate 120 around the giant steel plates. You can choose between the teppan set menus or eat à la carte. Main courses include chicken, beef, and duck but the most popular items are seafood (especially lobster) and steaks. These are cooked, with vegetables, on the teppan itself using oil, butter, and much else, including red wine for sauces. Desserts include fried ice cream with a fruit sauce.

But the main attraction is the superb sushi bar. Here you can enjoy both sashimi and sushi at their best, choosing from a wide range of fish and seafood, often including all three cuts of tuna (maguro, chu-toro and o-toro), intensely flavoured sea-urchin roe, grilled eel and extraordinary crisp herring and flyingfish roes. If you like brown crab meat try kanimiso, a soft emulsion blended with tofu, and served in a shiso leaf. This is a paradox of taste, a delicate yet intensely flavoured food for the gods. The sushi bar has another attraction in chef Yamashita whose dazzling skills in preparing the food are matched by his flow of repartee in Japanese and to some extent in English too. Not without cause are sushi chefs compared with English publicans in their rôles of host, entertainer and confidant. C £42.

12/20 Matsuri Teppan Bar
JAPANESE
See text above. **Set L** £9.50-£17, **Set D** £34-£49.50.

The Oak Room
Le Méridien, 21 Piccadilly, W1 - 071-734 8000
FRENCH
Open Lunch Mon-Fri, Dinner Mon-Sat.

The Edwardian dining room of this venerable luxury hotel, transformed by the Meridien chain into one of the smartest in London, is breathtaking to behold—a real jewel. Blond oak panelling, stately mirrors, gilt stucco work and huge chandeliers bathe the Oak Room in a mellow glow, creating an ambience that manages to be both grand and wonderfully relaxing. Surprisingly for a French-owned establishment, the Oak Room's chef, David

Chambers, is English (though he claims some Irish blood as well). True, he is backed up by Michel Lorain, the four-toque chef of La Côte Saint-Jacques in Joigny, who oversees the Oak Room's menu, but it is Chambers and his brigade who actually execute this elegant, intelligent cuisine. The team's technical prowess and opulent artistry are stunning, yet they never get in the way of the food's natural flavours. The marbré of pigeon and foie gras perfumed with anise (a daring but ultimately winning combination); langoustine gazpacho with courgette cream; lightly cooked salmon with magnetout peas in a delicate parsley bouillon; river perch with green lentils; a meltingly tender, robustly seasoned saddle of hare in red wine; succulent duck with coffee-infused chicory; chicken with red cabbage and walnut chutney; and desserts like the lush pear Chiboust or the crisp croustillant of caramelised citrus fruits compose a menu that to our mind represents the best and most abiding sort of cross-Channel alliance: one based on a keen appreciation of fine food! The service, naturally, is of the highest calibre: polished, not ponderous. The cellar is predominantly French, though the rest of the wine-growing world is also well represented. Prices? They are predictably lofty, but tempered by a remarkable fixed-price meal that includes three course, each accompanied by a glass of very good wine. **C** £55-£60. **Set L** £24.50, **Set D** £46.

10/20 Quaglino's

16 Bury St, St James's, SW1
071-930 6767, Fax 071-836 2866
MODERN BRITISH
Open Lunch & Dinner daily.
A shiver of excitement shook London's chic set when, after years of oblivion, Quaglino's re-opened its illustrious doors, sporting brand-new décor and a freshly designed menu. From the first, the 400 covers were besieged with takers—often enough for two seatings at each service. What's more, the frenzy shows no signs of abating. It took two and a half million pounds to turn this basement space into a spectacular brasserie of uncertain style. But stylish it certainly is, with a black-and-white gold staircase straight out of Hollywood which a sparky young crowd love to saunter down, preening and posing for the public. Sir Terence Conran spared no expense to create this most recent jewel in his crown, a restaurant-cum-scene on the order of La Coupole in Paris. Curiously, however, here the ambience is most electric not at night, but at lunchtime.
The young women delegated to welcome patrons obviously have other, more pressing concerns. The waiters, in contrast, are excessively keen: the maître d' exclaimed 'Fantastic' half a dozen times while taking our order. It was not, alas, a word we felt inclined to repeat at the close of a most mundane meal. Although the lavish shellfish bar, set up on a raised platform, is tempting, and the potato cake with finnan haddock decent enough, crab lost amidst a hotchpotch of cucumber and spinach and drowned in soy sauce, stodgy polenta with mushrooms and Gorgonzola, tasteless skate in garlic purée and a merely edible crème brûlée were most disappointing. The vin blanc maison, incidentally, is not one of the glories of French wine-making. These questionable delights incur a bill of £25 per head. **C** £25.

 ## The Ritz Restaurant

The Ritz, Piccadilly, W1
071-493 8181
MODERN BRITISH
Open Lunch & Dinner daily.
Undoubtedly the most beautiful dining room of its kind in London; it emulates the grandeur of Louis XVI with romantic hints of the belle époque in dusky pinks and blues. Elaborate chandeliers drop from a trompe l'œil ceiling, walls are made of marble, a bronze sculpture of Neptune graces one side of the room and gilded decoration abounds. Silver gleams, crystal glistens. Armies of waiters in tail coats glide to and fro; trolleys laden with domes are constantly wheeled between comfortably spaced tables. Vast windows open onto a pretty terrace. So: does the food match the setting? The executive chef, award-winning David Nicholls rises to the challenge for the most part. His cooking carries conviction but

there are inconsistencies that sometimes jar with the demanding prices (some courses are around £30). Whilst he observes the immutable hold of classic French haute-cuisine, he adds a contemporary British flavour, emphasising simplicity and freshness. Thus for starters: native oysters with chilli and shallot vinegars, tortellini of game with pearl onions, bacon and foie gras. Main courses range from cutlets of Southdown lamb with creamed leek, carrot and savoury to roast venison lightly peppered with creamed celeriac and black-currant. We found the flavours well counter-pointed. Puddings are nicely confected, and the cheese board is comprehensive. there is also an imaginative diet menu. The wine list runs to forty pages—the Ritz's famed cellars offer fabulous, and accordingly priced, vintages. That said, our more humble Chateau Garnage '90 did not disappoint. The usually smooth service can be slightly erratic when they are very busy. At weekends there is dinner and dancing, but collar and tie is de rigueur at all times. **C** £45. **Set L** £26, **Set D** £43.50.

 ## The Square
32 King St, St James's, SW1
071-839 8787
MODERN BRITISH
Open Lunch Mon-Fri, Dinner daily.
The décor and food of this stylish restaurant are deceptively simple. Philip Howard does the cooking and he injects humour and intelligence into his menu.

Like his former boss and mentor, Simon Hopkinson at Bibendum, he produces food with concentrated flavours in dishes that manage to be modern and classical all at once. Parfait of chicken livers is served with foie gras, carpaccio or tuna is off-set with a tartare of vegetables and coriander, and roast rabbit comes with warm potato pancake and grain mustard. He gets full marks for presentation, which is artistic without being pretentious. For example, he loves high-rise food—a haystack of tiny spinach leaves are bound with a crab dressing, and roasted sea bass sits on a pile of braised savoy cabbage with mashed potato. Crème brûlée is divided in two with a square sugar crisp perched on top of the cream. The menu changes frequently, shorter and cheaper at lunch, but always exceedingly reasonable considering the high standards. Gold squares and blocks of bright colour are the highlights of a successful minimalist décor by David Collins Associates (who also did The Canteen and La Tante Claire). Interesting wine list. **C** £25.

 ## Suntory
72 St James's St, SW1 - 071-409 0201
JAPANESE
Open Lunch & Dinner Mon-Sat.
It is easy to enthuse about the virtues of a young, innovative chef in his new and fashionable restaurant. It is harder to convey the fullest appreciation of an old-fashioned restaurant which exemplifies restraint

and classical purity. The Suntory is that sort of place. You enter the lounge with its adjoining bar, and relax in comfortable chairs upholstered in Burgundy red looking at a giant calligraphy based on two characters signifying happiness. In the restaurant, tan-coloured furnishings contrast with dark wooden tables and chair frames. The main menu, elegantly printed on embossed silk paper, offers a short à la carte divided into sections Japanese style by cooking method rather than ingredients. Rare 'foreign' intruders are salmon oyako-ae—smoked salmon with salmon roe—and grilled foie gras with teriyaki or vinegar sauce. The quality of ingredients and cooking is all it should be at this level, and presentation is often spectacular, like the special assorted sashimi at £33.60 on an ice mountain in a raised bowl. Oyster and sliced scallop nestle in their shells, and there is a gleaming range of superlative fish—two sorts each of tuna and salmon, sea bass, squid rolled with seaweed and cucumber and salmon roe in its own yellow porcelain bowl. In some ultra-refined dishes, flavours may be over-delicate for western palates. Note komochi-konbu, an appetiser of 'sea-tangle with herring roe', where the sea flavour is secondary to the texture which gives a new meaning to words like 'crisp' and 'crunchy'.
Another room houses a large teppan area where fish and meat are grilled on giant steel plates. Set

menus here are from £49.80 to £64 or you can eat à la carte with main teppan-yaki dishes at £25.80 to £38 with grilled vegetables extra. In the private rooms, exquisite kaiseki banquets cost from £85 per head and are served by kneeling waitresses. As a restaurant owned by a major drinks company they have an extensive and expensive wine list, at the heart of which is a superb range of clarets from Château Beaumont 1988 (£24) and other notable bourgeois growths to classified growths of 1985, 1983, 1982 and 1981. Of the great names only Château Pétrus is omitted. Choice bottles include the 1983 Châteaux Ducru-Beaucaillou, Pichon-Lalande, Lafite, Mouton-Rotschild and Domaine de Chevalier. 'Second wines' of interest include those of Châteaux Palmer, Latour, Margaux and Lafite. **C** £54. **Set menus** £15-£62.50.

10/20 Wiltons

55 Jermyn St, W1 - 071-629 9955
BRITISH
Open Lunch & Dinner Mon-Fri.

For unknown reasons, the favourite restaurant of tycoons, politicians and public figures—mostly men, it should be pointed out. Perhaps the quality of the food and the nature of the service reminds them of the old school days. Orders are taken by elderly men in tail coats and the food is delivered by ladies in black skirts with white pinnies. Celebrated for dishes as antedeluvian as its atmosphere like lobster bisque, omelette Arnold Bennett, sole Walewska and roast grouse, traditional puddings—sherry trifle, apple tart and custard—and savouries like angels on horseback and roes on toast. **C** £45.

PIMLICO

Hunan

51 Pimlico Rd, SW1 - 071-730 5712
CHINESE
Open Lunch Mon-Sat, Dinner daily.

The conservatism of Chinese cookery and cooks is proverbial, so it is only mildly surprising that the menu of London's only Hunan-style restaurant has not changed for thirteen years. Owner Mr Y S Peg, whose 'Cooking Master' was Hunanese, sometimes cooks but is more often in the restaurant. Although many dishes have the same names as Szechuan classics they are more oily here, with the intriguing, faintly bitter undertaste of Hunan pepper. The chef's special Hunan fish soup and lamb in Hunan sauce are typically hot, but it is hot-and-sour prawns that bring floods of tears to the eyes of highly seasoned chilliphiles. Milder appetisers are peppery sesame beef and Hunan-style stuffed mushrooms (English, not Chinese) in a rich, meaty sauce. Glazed toffee lychees make a pleasant change from the usual desserts, and the sweetness cleans the palate. Tea is better than coffee. Service is friendly and helpful in this civilised place which seats fifty amongst masses of potted plants. Musical instruments and Chinese artefacts, plus some decent traditional paintings, decorate cream walls and panels painted in bright yet subtle colours surround the bar. The taste of Hunan is different—and distinctly engaging. **C** £22. **Set D** £20.

12/20 L'Incontro

87 Pimlico Rd, SW1 - 071-730 3663, Fax 071-730 5062
ITALIAN
Open Lunch Mon-Fri, Dinner daily.

Tasteful, elegant and expensive, L'Incontro specialises in Venetian cooking. The owner, Gino Santi, also wrote *La Cucina Veneziana* (Ebury Press, £14.95) which is sold in the restaurant and gives away many of its secrets. Venetian cooking, using a lot of seafood, relies on sage, rosemary and basil. It is worth making sure that you get the daily speciality menu, which is likely to include seasonal risotto and the simpler pasta and fish dishes such as bigola in salsa (short stubby pasta with pounded anchovy), and grilled fresh sardines. A highlight from the à la carte is poached sea bass in balsamic vinegar. You can forget the desserts which are unexceptional. The wine list is mainly Italian. **C** £35. **Set L** £13.50, £16.80.

12/20 Simply Nico

48a Rochester Row, SW1
071-630 8061
FRENCH

Open Lunch Mon-Fri, Dinner Mon-Sat.

The long, narrow room with deep cream walls and rather dull prints has a mirrored dado, a feature common to the décor of all Nico Ladenis' restaurants. But otherwise, this, Nico's own restaurant before he moved to Great Portland Street and then on to 90 Park Lane, seems to lack the sparkle which distinguishes his style. The straightforward menu offers ten choices in each of three courses (or at lunch, two courses only at a reduced price). The only other choice is between chips or pommes purées. Both are good enough to make the choice difficult. We have noticed a certain lack of zing in the execution of simple, but well-conceived, dishes. On a recent visit, fish soup with rouille and croûtons needed more life in the rouille; green peppercorn sauce with roast guinea-fowl was good although it was really a rich cream sauce with green peppercorns. Braised oxtail in wine was excellent, and the vegetable selection was respectable and pleasant despite variable cooking of the cauliflower. Desserts are acceptable, but do not elicit enthusiasm. **Set L** £23, **Set D** £25.

10/20 Tate Gallery Restaurant

Tate Gallery, Millbank, SW1
071-834 6754
BRITISH
Open Lunch Mon-Sat.

Some people go for the mural (Rex Whistler's *The Expedition in Pursuit of Rare Meats*), others for the wine list (laid down over the years and specialising in half bottles and cru classé clarets of good reputation), and some, of course, go for the food. The food at the Tate's basement restaurant is British through and through and has the reputation for sounding a lot more enticing than it really is. Having said that, however, the menu has now been streamlined, shortened and simplified, and is markedly improved. It changes slightly every month but favours red meat and British farmhouse cheeses (to go with those wines). Steak, kidney and mushroom pie, sirloin of beef with Yorkshire pudding and game in season are highlights. The menu and wine list can be ordered in advance, and with notice they will decant wines. **C** £25.

PRIMROSE HILL

11/20 The Big Night Out

148 Regent's Park Rd, NW1
071-586 5768
MODERN BRITISH
Open Lunch Tues-Fri, Sun, Dinner Mon-Sat.

At The Big Night Out in pretty Primrose Hill, you don't get entertainment or cabaret as the name might suggest, but good, solid cooking at reasonable prices. The room that looks out onto Regent's Park Road is white and austere, with dominant pictures on the walls and somewhat uncomfortable chairs. The food, which offers only a small choice is not for vegetarians, concentrating as it does on starters like rillettes of duck and shallots with braised wild mushrooms or lobster ravioli. Main dishes to get excited over include lamb, robust and well cooked with an interesting rosemary-flavoured spinach, and saddle of rabbit which can often be tough and insipid but which turns out here to be strong and succulent. Desserts, like pear soufflé or chocolate cake are good; cheeses are restricted in choice but good of their kind. The wine list is pricey. **C** £20. **Set L** £9.50, £13.50, **Set D** £13, £16.50.

 Odette's

130 Regent's Park Rd, NW1
071-586 5486
MEDITERRANEAN
Open Lunch Sun Fri, Dinner Mon-Sat.

Tucked away in a desirable enclave off Primrose Hill, Odette's is still sufficiently close to town and to Hampstead to draw a media crowd. It's a romantic restaurant—a cosy Langan's—with dim atmospheric lighting and walls tightly packed with old mirrors and pictures. Many prefer the brighter, white-walled, sky-lit room at the rear, and on sunny days the doors are opened onto the attractive shopping street frontage. A succession of talented chefs have passed through Simone Green's well-run restaurant. Lately Paul Holmes has been cutting a dash with an eclectic menu that magpies from around the world. Certain dishes, such as sashimi and tempura are perfect snacking food for the wine bar below, which has its own simplified menu. He is particularly talented with fish which suits his international cooking style well. Hence spicy fish gumbo, hot gravlax with salt cod mash, cucumber, mustard and dill, and scallops with olives and swollen capers served on ribbon pasta. The dessert menu is worth investigating. Espresso chocolate tart, and saffron bread and butter pudding, are fitting ends to a meal here but note, too, the selection of Spanish cheeses served with quince jelly. Bibendum wine merchants, just down the road, supply most of the wines on this intelligently ordered and reasonably priced list. **C £30. Set L £10.**

PUTNEY

12/20 Del Buongustaio
283 Putney Bridge Rd, SW15 - 081-780 9361
ITALIAN
Open Lunch Sun-Fri, Dinner Mon-Sat.
An Italian restaurant in Putney (the second venture of the Italian/Australian owners of Osteria Antica Bologna in Clapham), Del Buongustaio is the kind of place you might expect to find in Italy. It's a jolly, often crowded local restaurant, serving robust food that changes daily. They are fond of casseroling as in the unexpected eel stew, as well as adventurous

combinations such as veal with pungent rocket, often served with filling potato purée or soft polenta. They serve good pastas and vegetarian dishes and fish such as skate or red mullet. Desserts are very good, though very filling. The wine list is, interestingly, Italian/Australian, reflecting the ownership. Australian is not what normally accompanies rustic Italian cooking, but the wines are perfectly complementary. **C £20. Set L £9.50, Set D £19.50.**

RICHMOND

11/20 Ma Goa
244 Upper Richmond Rd, SW15 - 081-780 1767
INDIAN
Open Lunch Tues-Fri, Sun, Dinner Tues-Sun.
The walls of this simple wooden-floored family café are decorated with cartoons and photographs of Goa, and its check tablecloths are covered with cream paper. Helpful, pleasant service is led by the son of the family while his father and 'Ma Goa' herself, cook. He distinguishes between their 'Goan-style' cuisine and 'authentic Goan' which is more spicy and chilli-hot. A short menu is complemented by a blackboard with daily specials. Portions are not too large— but nor are prices—and good quality ingredients are carefully cooked. Fish features strongly, as do fresh vegetables rarely seen outside Indian stores. Rice is good, breads less

so. The short, low-priced, largely Portuguese, wine list includes light red Serradayres, a good match for the food. **C £16.**

SHEPHERD'S BUSH

The Brackenbury
129-131 Brackenbury Rd, W6 - 081-748 0107
MODERN BRITISH
Open Lunch Tues-Fri, Sun, Dinner Mon-Sat.
Hidden away in the residential hinterland between Shepherd's Bush and Hammersmith, some may say that the Brackenbury is not salubrious by any standards. The premises, set back from the road with a small patio, used to be a wine bar, and consist of two split-level rooms divided by a back-facing central stairwell. Décor is functional and pleasant. There are no table cloths or side plates, no fancy cutlery nor designer plates, but the important things like good bread and butter and linen napkins are perfect. At the helm is a young husband-and-wife team, Adam and Kate Robinson, who excel at providing a neighbourhood restaurant with a short, twice-daily menu and a repertoire of dishes that keep prices low. The food is entirely seasonal, making intelligent use of vegetables and relying on the cheaper cuts of meat. Deceptively simple food is packed with flavour and plainly presented. Potato pancake is topped with

RESTAURANTS - SHEPHERD'S BUSH

crème fraîche and salmon caviar; smoked herring and warm potato salad is dressed with good olive oil; and beef stew with carrots and horseradish dumplings leave you in no doubt that the kitchen knows what it's up to. Reasonably priced and carefully chosen wine list. **C £20.**

 Chinon

25 Richmond Way, W14
071-602 5968
FRENCH
Open Lunch Mon-Fri, Dinner Tues-Sat.

When the Triangle wine bar closed, Barbara Deane and her chef/partner Jonathan Hayes moved one door up, and re-invented their restaurant as a bar/café (upstairs) and restaurant (dinner only, downstairs). Hayes is a self-assured and ambitious cook who established a reputation for elaborate re-workings of British classics at the Perfumed Conservatory, the couple's previous restaurant. He's evolved a style that relies on his perfectionism—he likes to do everything himself—and a talent to build up a complex mixture of textures and flavours. His signature dish is caramelised and pan-sealed duck breast, finished in the oven and served with a concentrated jus, a block of swede purée topped with stewed lentils, mashed potato enclosed in Chinese leaves and a filo pastry purse of vegetables. Simpler food is offered in the café and at lunchtime, but flavours are forever concentrated, sometimes overly so, and occasionally he hits the jackpot with peaks of brilliance. It is an

idiosyncratic place that inspires strong reactions—people either love or hate it. The wine list is chosen to suit the quaffing needs of the café as well as the restaurant. **C £30.**

11/20 The Rotisserie
56 Uxbridge Rd, W12 - 081-743 3028
FRENCH
Open Lunch Mon-Fri, Dinner Mon-Sat.

The menu here revolves round the rotisserie which dominates the long narrow room and emits delicious smells. It's located just before the trompe l'œil train at Shepherd's Bush Green and has a low-key frontage that is easy to miss. Inside, it is surprisingly large and simply decorated, run with casual efficiency by a young team. Several imaginative choices for vegetarians, and a small list of fashionably touched appetisers such as gravlax with mustard and dill sauce, and Bayonne ham topped with slices of fresh Parmesan, comprise the short menu. From the rotisserie, Barbary duck, salmon (cooked in a paper bag), chicken and, best of all, rib of beef for two. Accompanied by their excellent chips, this is a decent meal. Well-kept cheeses and a small selection of bistro desserts complete the picture. A modestly priced wine list seems perfectly appropriate. **C £25. Set menu £8.95.**

 Snows on the Green
166 Shepherd's Bush Rd, W1 - 071-603 2142
MODERN BRITISH

Open Lunch Mon-Fri, Dinner Mon-Sat.

Sebastian Snow first made his mark at Launceston Place, and went on to help famous chef Anthony Worrall Thompson establish Bistrot 190 before he opened his own restaurant. He's taken a Provençal theme throughout—the terracotta-blushed walls are hung with blow-ups of sunflowers and lavender is tucked here and there. Tile-topped wooden tables and a matching dresser adorned with bottles of herb-infused olive oil complete the picture. His cooking goes from strength to strength and is a glorious exploration of southern France. Hence rosemary and onion pizza bread with ham, casserole of sausages, beans and duck confit and daube of ox cheeks with red wine, bacon and mash. This is robust cooking that is full of flavour and the menu offers great choice and interest. Desserts are more eclectic—prune and Armagnac galette, caramelised rice pudding and Parmesan cheese with pears. A sensible wine list offers various house wines and plenty under £15. **C £25. Set L £10.50, £12.50.**

*We're always happy to hear about your discoveries and receive your comments on ours. We want to give your letters the attention they deserve, so when you **write to Gault Millau**, please state clearly what you liked or disliked. Be concise but convincing, and take the time to argue your point.*

SOHO

 Alastair Little

49 Frith St, W1 - 071-734 5183
MODERN BRITISH
Open Lunch Mon-Fri, Dinner Mon-Sat.

The Soho that we used to know—sleazy, shabby, exciting—has latterly become a neat and tidy showcase for the world's cuisines. Amidst the Malay, Korean, Hungarian, Italian, Indian, Parisian and British restaurants lined up cheek-by-jowl, this modest establishment attracts no particular attention, with its battered black wooden tables, paper napkins, a ceiling studded with 50 tiny neon tubes, and a few decent pictures and prints on the walls. A nearly illegible menu lists dishes which, on the surface at least, have nothing much to recommend them. But the prices they command (main courses from £16 to £20), though likely to discourage the casual browser, pique the interest of the true connoisseur. Alastair Little's eponymous restaurant is indeed, for those who like this sort of food, the least ordinary eating house in London. Surrounded by establishments that leave no doubt as to their national allegiance, Alastair Little draws inspiration from everywhere, though from nowhere in particular: France, of course, and Italy most of all, with Indian and East Asian touches, hints of Scandinavia (gravlax) and Spain (cheeses). The mix adds up to a Modern British cuisine that is not exactly cosmopolitan, but unfettered and free. Free: there's the word to describe this food, prepared by Alastair Little and a small team led by his enthusiastic sous-chef, Jeremy Lee. It is also generous, wholesome, natural, inventive, adventurous and bizarre. And it is based on ingredients of peerless quality, whether humble (white beans, carrot purée, mussels, salt cod, rabbit) or extravagant (oysters, foie gras, asparagus, morels, game, sea bass, truffles). Little's creations are at once classic and fanciful, even provocative. Consider the splendid Pacific oysters (from Ireland!) presented with incredible herbed meatballs, tender and spicy in the Thai style. Or the carpaccio drizzled with truffled oil and accompanied by grilled artichokes, or potato crêpes with smoked eel and horseradish, or the moreish prune and almond tart. One sees few ruddy-faced trenchermen at Little's tables; instead, the place is filled with elegant or bohemian middle-class types. Likewise, there are no flat-footed, white-aproned waiters but in their place a fleet-footed staff of bright, clever, food-loving young women. The cellar is international (some wines, like the New Zealand Chardonnay and a good Cabernet Sauvignon from Australia, are available by the glass), with more bottles from Burgundy than Bordeaux, as well as interesting selections from Italy, California and Spain, like a wonderful Rioja Ardanza '85. C £35. **Set menu £20.**

 Bahn Thai

21a Frith St, W1 - 071-437 8504
THAI
Open Lunch & Dinner Mon-Sun.

Philip Harris returned from Thailand with a Thai fiancée and opened one of London's first Thai restaurants in Kensington. As its success blossomed he expanded here and created a second, larger Bahn Thai that eventually usurped its parents' popularity. A pioneering menu—complete with hectoring asides—provides an introduction to Thai food, and it is helpful to know that they will obligingly adjust the chilli threshold to suit western palates. The last couple of years has seen the two-storeyed restaurant change and refine its menu to fit in with London's increasingly casual attitude to eating out. The ground floor now concentrates on Thai street food—satay, noodles etc. and upstairs offers a long menu that encompasses the familiar and the esoteric. It is an excellent venue for vegetarians and fish lovers. An intelligently chosen wine list includes many wines under £15. C £25.

Bistrot Bruno

63 Frith St, W1 - 071-734 4545, Fax 071-287 1027
FRENCH
Open Lunch Mon-Fri, Dinner Mon-Sat.

While Bruno Loubet was still the head chef at the celebrated Four Seasons restaurant at the Inn on the

Park, he gave his name and became consultant chef to this modest little bistro that was previously a fish restaurant called L'Hippocampe. For the moment (until his L'Odéon brasserie opens) Bruno is at the helm. His talent is turning ordinary and neglected ingredients into something special. Such things as mackerel, ox cheek, tripe, herrings and scrag end of lamb are elevated to new heights of deliciousness. Slow cooking is a style he particularly enjoys and he is adept, too, at chutneys and pickles which are used as relishes in stuffed pasta and pastry dishes. Loubet also uses ingredients in unexpected ways. Sardine is matched with roast peppers in a tart, and potted oxtail on coleslaw. Co-existing with this imaginative and excellent food are classic French dishes given the Loubet twist. Cold saffron ratatouille is served with a poached egg, roquette and Gorgonzola, and old-fashioned stuffed tomato is served with beans and parsley butter. The eccentric parody of modern bistro design is highly amusing. The wine list is international. C £25.

12/20 Chiang Mai
48 Frith St, W1 - 071-437 7444
THAI
Open Lunch Mon-Sat, Dinner daily.

Vatcharin Bhumichitr, who runs this restaurant, has also written several books on Thai cooking, and here he specialises in food from northern Thailand such as sticky or gelatinous rice which can be combined with red curry beef, coconut fortified sauces, deep-fried yellow egg noodles, curries, peppery sauce. It takes a few moments of acclimatisation to realise that the interior is cleverly designed to resemble an oriental stilt house. The staff wear beautiful clothes made to classic designs from fabrics hand-woven by hill tribes. The menu, intimidatingly long, is thoroughly explained and reveals a predominance of appetisers. It is worth including a Thai salad (hot-and-sour bamboo shoots and prawn are particularly recommended), a soup (traditionally this would be drunk throughout the meal) and something from the vegetarian menu. A sophisticated drinks list includes saké and Thai beer. C £25. **Set menu** £36, £42.

14/20 dell 'Ugo
56 Frith St, W1 - 071-734 8300, Fax 071-734 8784
MEDITERRANEAN
Open Lunch Mon-Fri, Dinner Mon-Sat. Ground floor café: Lunch & Dinner Mon-Sat.

At the height of the recession when Soho's restaurant scene was in the doldrums, along came restaurateur and celebrity chef Anthony Worrall Thompson and set up shop in the unsuccessfully themed Braganza. His menu, interpreted by Mark Emberton, is different on each of the three floors and extols the use of just about every fashionable ingredient and style of cooking going. At its core is an understanding of what the public want, which, currently seems to be inexpensive, tasty, unfussy food served simply and without pretension, and dell 'Ugo also allows for snacking and one-dish meals. The one-pot dishes—simply stewed daubes—matched with a sampling from the outstanding selection of breads, are immensely popular. The other thing that this chef has got right is his pricing. It is possible to spend a packet but much of the menu is priced below most people's expectations. Needless to say, dell 'Ugo buzzes, and despite offering 190 seats, people are turned away every night. The wine list is similarly enlightened. A standard list is augmented by a second list supplied by a different wine merchant each month. C £20.

11/20 L'Epicure
28 Frith St, W1 - 071-437 2829/071-734 2667
FRENCH
Open Lunch Mon-Fri, Dinner Mon-Sat.

The last 'Old Soho' restaurant, opened in 1953, has been doing the same things for so long that it risks becoming fashionable again. The décor is a feast of nostalgia with red banquettes and tub chairs, red velvet curtains and traditional table settings. Service, too, is pleasantly old-fashioned, with long-serving waiters correctly balancing formality and friendliness. Another enduring feature is the flaming torchères around the fascia, the last in London outside club land. They echo the silver lamps in the restaurant on which half the menu is flambéed, the one change being that these lamps are now lined up in the back room and not brought to the table. A score of first courses, main dishes and desserts cooked or finished on them include seafood pancakes, Polish-style sausages with green peppers, entrecôte Diane and crèpes Suzette. They are not the only reminders of the 1950s and earlier. On this menu—although nearly extinct elsewhere—are goujonettes of sole, omelette aux fines herbes and bœuf Stroganoff. However 1994 is not totally ignored. Last year's major success was the fixed-price menu. Furthermore the quality of cooking and ingredients are in tune with today's needs and rather better than one might expect. You may even specify virgin olive oil in the pan instead of butter. Dishes such as Swedish herring with potatoes and aquavit and smoked reindeer are inspirations from Swedish Linnea Tarr who, with her English husband Nigel, has owned and run L'Epicure since 1977. C £26.50. Set L & D £10.90, £14.90.

14 L'Escargot

48 Greek St, W1 - 071-437 6828, Fax 071-437 0790
FRENCH
Open Lunch Mon-Fri (Restaurant), Mon-Sat (Brasserie). Dinner Mon-Sat.
It is too hard to tell yet whether the idea of installing two awarded chefs, David Cavalier and Gary Hollihead, to run this old Trojan was a good idea. The new-look L'Escargot continues its time-honoured tradition of offering a ground floor brasserie (and bar), and a second more expensive and gastronomically ambitious upstairs restaurant. The brasserie menu is French bistro food at its best—dishes such as brandade salad with french beans, trotters with sauce gribiche and bouillabaisse—with a few novelty twists such as fillet of smoked whiting with bubble and squeak. A highlight is a charcuterie trolley. Presentation, however, is more restaurant than bistro. Upstairs, the restaurant menu is a set price for three courses but studded with supplements. Here the style is post-nouvelle-cuisine modernism with elaborate fanciful presentation and over-reduced saucing. By comparison with the brasserie, it seems to steer away from the current trend towards clear, fresh flavours and simplicity. C £30.

12/20 est

54 Frith St, W1 - 071-437 0666
MEDITERRANEAN
Open Lunch Mon-Fri, Dinner Mon-Sat.
It's small but it's smart and much favoured by advertising and media folk, who appreciate its Mediterranean-based, look-we-have-no-choleste rol-or-cellulite, healthy and efficient style of cooking. So there's char-grilled this and polenta with that and asparagus with Parmesan and chicken with artichoke trifolati, stuffed zucchini flowers, spring lamb with mustard pesto, serious salads, proper pasta and optimum olive oil. It's all done with some zing and zap. The menu changes daily. The wine list is short, but perfectly formed, and the place buzzes. Just remember to wear the Armani jeans. C £30.

12/20 French House Dining Room

49 Dean St, W1 - 071-437 2477
BRITISH
Open Lunch & Dinner Mon-Sat.
49 Dean Street is a pub which used to be known as the York Minster but which changed its name to the French House after becoming the favourite hang-out for the Free French during the war. Général de Gaulle ate here during the war and is supposed to have drafted his great speech to the French people in the bar. The downstairs room is a typical Soho pub, but go upstairs and you'll find a small, homely dining room, containing nine tables in all set against a mottled reddish-brown décor and conceding nothing to the latest ideas in interior decoration. The two chefs, Margot Clayton and Fergus Henderson have cooked in a number of stylish, trend-setting restaurants, notably 192 Kensington Park Road, the First Floor and Smith's. Here they produce a confident, simple, mainly British menu which changes daily and which is based on such stalwarts as scallops with rocket and nourishing soups to start with, and substantial main dishes. Good, well selected and cooked game in season, lamb and duck are served with first-rate, no-nonsense vegetables, so partridge is teamed with savoy cabbage and bacon, and braised red cabbage accompanies very tasty grilled lamb. Desserts are good and filling: brown-

bread ice cream is creamy. And in keeping with the old-fashioned feel to the menu, they have maintained Welsh rarebit with Worcestershire sauce. C £20. **Set L & D £22.**

10/20 The Gay Hussar

2 Greek St, W1 - 071-437 0973
EAST EUROPEAN
Open Lunch & Dinner Mon-Sat.
This Hungarian restaurant, now no longer owned by the legendary Victor Sassie, has been a discreet haunt of Labour politicians and lobby correspondents for well over 30 years now. Considering the often delicate nature of the customers' conversations, the Hussar's red velvet upholstered seating, ranged along both sides of the narrow premises, is a little too 'intimate' for either secrecy or comfort. The menu is unchanging and no friend to delicate stomachs. Chilled wild cherry soup, flat omelette of green peppers, fish dumplings in dill sauce and rice, and cold duck with pickled cucumber, is the sort of robust, hearty food to expect. A remarkably good-value set lunch is an excellent introduction, and a relatively calm course can be steered via the likes of chicken and lemon soup, quenelles of carp and sweet cheese dumplings. The off-beat wine list specialises in Tokajio and vintage bottled clarets. C £25. **Set L £15.50.**

Find the address you are looking for, quickly and easily, in the index.

Gopal's of Soho

12 Bateman St, W1 - 071-434 0840
INDIAN
Open Lunch & Dinner Mon-Sun.
As they say, there are lies, damn lies and statistics. But it has to be said that Indian restaurant price differentials are enticing. For only twice the price of a good quality high street Indian, you can eat at what some people call the best Indian restaurant in London. And for this, you enter a whole new realm of experience. Even the starters, so often an empty rite of passage, kick in unexpectedly and deliver surprises. The Mangalore crab (fresh flaked crab cooked with coconut and spices) lived up to its description and transported us to foreign shores. The mashed potato cake patties (reputed to be a recent 'Bombay-side' innovation) brought us reassuringly down to earth—fluffy, crisp and piquant, but above all homely. For the main course, we recommend you avoid the usual middle ground and go for the robustly carnivorous Goanese mutton zacutti or the very unusual fish curry, beautifully textured, rounded and resonant. Both dishes are cooked with coconut and spices. For those who prefer more delicate flavours, the immaculate barbecued chicken Tikka is complemented perfectly by the vegetarian panir Peshawari (cottage cheese cooked with chopped tomatoes, onions and coriander seeds). And if you dare,

treat yourself to a further surprise. The deep ruby smoothness of the Rowan '89 Australian Shiraz pulled all these contrasting flavours and textures together perfectly; at £14.75, a bit more than the average bottle in an Indian restaurant, but well worth it. The wine list has been put together with skill and expertise. After all this, even for a fan, the Indian sweets are a bit of a letdown. Try instead the sorbets which sound interesting if a bit limited in range. Finally, congratulations to chef/owner Gopal (late of Lal Qila and The Red Fort) for having trained his kitchen staff so well that they keep up standards even in his absence. C £18. **Set menus** from £9.75.

12/20 The Lexington

45 Lexington St, W1 - 071-434 3401
MODERN BRITISH
Open Lunch & Dinner Mon-Sat.
Minimalism is the name of the game here. The long, narrow room is lined with dark green leatherette banquettes. It's simple, tasteful and functional. The menu changes daily, is bleak in its descriptions of dishes but appears to follow a formula of a couple of soups, salads and terrines, a pasta dish, and fish, meat and a vegetarian main course. It's modern bistro fare that is a muddle of comfort dishes such as roast lamb sweetbreads with puréed potato and cabbage, and Mediterranean-influenced dishes such as a paysanne salad where everything is finely diced, served with confit of

duck and beetroot and carrot chips, and giant-size gnocchi with a tomato and black olive sauce. The Full Monte gives a taste of all the puddings including pear and apple tatin and crème brûlée. A lively wine list has several wines by the glass. **C** £20. **Set D** £10.

11/20 Manzi's
1 Leicester St, WC2 - 071-734 0224, Fax 071-437 4864
ITALIAN
Open Lunch & Dinner Mon-Sat.
Opened in the late twenties as part of a family-run Italian hotel, Manzi's is an institution amongst literary lunchers and is a sympathetic place for pre- and post-theatre suppers. It's a fish restaurant, proclaiming it with fishy decorations hanging on the walls. Turbot and halibut are specialities, and sole is on offer cooked in more ways than it's possible to imagine. Simple food is the thing to order here, as well as oysters in season, and smoked eel or smoked cod's roe. Steamed or pan-fried fish is exemplary while their battered and deep-fried plaice is outstanding. And they serve the best real English chips in London. Desserts, apart from the flamboyant-looking gâteau, seem an afterthought although their crème caramel is good. The wine list is serviceable. **C** £25.

11/20 Melati
21 Gt Windmill St, W1 - 071-437 2745
MALAYSIAN/INDONESIAN
Open Lunch & Dinner daily.
Note this restaurant's address, for it has no connection with another Melati in nearby Peter Street. This Melati's sister restaurant is **Minang** (see review below). Their à la carte menus have many dishes in common but Melati includes Malaysian and Singaporean dishes as well as Indonesian. Set menus at Melati are less interesting, but one-plate meals such as nasi goreng and mee goreng, and even more the istimewa (special) versions are tasty, varied and substantial, and great value at £4.95 to £6.25. They would put Melati amongst London's best bargain bites. The décor is more basic and the service may be a little less sophisticated than Minang but the cooking is generally reliable. The note on Minang's desserts applies equally here. **C** £23. **Set L & D** £21.25.

11/20 Minang
11 Greek St, W1 - 071-287 1408
INDONESIAN
Open Lunch & Dinner daily.
Floor, ceiling and upholstery in bright, deep ice-blue does not immediately suggest a tropical rain forest, yet it works at this little place, perhaps because the spicing, and chilli-hotness if required, of Sam Alamsjah's cooking makes a touch of coolness desirable, if not essential. There are over 100 dishes on the à la carte menu so it is good news that the set menus include many of the more interesting choices. Actually you can choose your own set menu because when ordering any of the three Riestafels, at £17 to £21.50 per head, you are asked if there are any particular dishes you would like to include or exclude. Many regular favourites are found at their best here—satay of course, as well as pergedel (potato cakes) and murtabak—savoury meat and onion in a crisp pancake parcel. Soup is taken as a separate course or as a side-dish with the main course. There are many recipes for squid (cumi cumi), one of the glories of Indonesian cooking, and tiny fish like miniaturised whitebait are served with crisp peanuts (ikan bilis) or with fried shredded cabbage (sayur kubis). An ideal introduction to this cuisine is the lunchtime mini-Riestafel, £6.50, for soup and eight dishes with rice. Few Asian cuisines offer desserts but Indonesia is the exception. Sam's triple is glorious—three layers in a glass, of pineapple, mango and avocado purées. Tropical fruits are a pleasant alternative. Drink Indonesian beer or red wine which stands up surprisingly well to the spices. **C** £18.50. **Set L** £6.50, **Set D** £12.50.

Ming
35 Greek St, W1 - 071-734 2721
CHINESE
Open Lunch & Dinner Mon-Sat.
Ming is a rather elegant Chinese restaurant north of Chinatown proper, presided over with charm by Christine Yau. It has not followed the fashionable trend of regional authenticity, but tends to a certain imaginative culinary eclecticism within the range of Chinese cooking.

So pick and choose from noodle-based one-dish lunches, Mantou dishes using steamed or grilled bread and Peking dishes, with the odd Cantonese and Szechuan number thrown in for good measure. The cooking has style, wit and imagination. Specialities to look out for are steamed beef with rice flower, ginger duck with pancakes, Ming beef with fresh coriander and onion pancakes, steamed white fish with salted turnip and tree mushroom cake. The clientele are almost as interesting and varied as the wine list which is put together by a food and wine match maestro. C £25. **Set L** from £7.50, **Set D** from £12.

 Red Fort
77 Dean St, W1 - 071-437 2525
INDIAN
Open Lunch & Dinner daily.
   Amin Ali, the owner of this restaurant, received credit for changing the face of Indian food in London. Out went flock wallpaper and meat in a ubiquitous brown sauce and in came a genteel décor and food that wasn't either hot or very hot. Together with relatives and friends from his native Bangladesh he built up a small chain of restaurants with the Red Fort as the jewel in the crown. His pioneering menus have always celebrated refined, Mogul food and honoured its delicate spicing and traditional technique. Cream, butter, yoghurt and baked cheese are frequent ingredients, making this an exceedingly rich and

sumptuous cuisine. Manjit Gill, a celebrity chef and creator of the Bukhara restaurant at the Manrya Sheraton hotel in Delhi, has recently become consultant chef here. His menu is exquisite. Hara kebab is a patty of spinach, bound by gram flour and lentils, stuffed with cottage cheese and raisins, coated with poppy seeds, then pan-grilled with butter. Jumbo prawns are marinated in pomegranate juice and baked with peas, potatoes and tomatoes, and supreme of chicken is flavoured with lemon and stuffed with onion, ginger and mint and pot-roasted with yoghurt. At lunchtime, the buffet menu is terrific value. A startling array of bottles dominate the reception lounge and pin-point the restaurant's other speciality—Indian cocktails. C £30. **Buffet L** £14.95.

11/20 Soho Soho
11-13 Frith St, W1 - 071-494 3491
MEDITERRANEAN
Open Lunch Mon-Fri, Dinner Mon-Sat.
   Most of the more pre-occupying London food fashions of late find emphasis at Soho Soho. Olive oil and balsamic vinegar have their expected outing, and there is much use of pasta, not all of it particulary inspired. High-flavoured items such as offal or tuna seem to work best, often reinforced by a piquant accompaniment such as capers or by vigorous char-grilling. Milder dishes such as a starter of marinated salmon with beetroot suffer from blandness, although we have eaten lamb cutlets and mashed

potato with a rich stock-based sauce that was generous and satisfying. There is a permanent state of pandemonium in the ground-floor café/bar, while the first-floor restaurant—with its gathered curtains and commanding views of Soho doing its thing—offers a more serious menu, but may be as hectic. Good French regional wines will soothe shattered nerves. C £26.

12/20 Sri Siam
14 Old Compton St, W1
071-434 3544
THAI
Open Lunch Mon-Sat, Dinner daily.
   There were those who thought it was bringing coals to Newcastle to open yet another oriental restaurant virtually in Chinatown. However, Sri Siam is a cut above much of its competition and serves reasonably priced, authentic and fresh-tasting Thai food. It's a lively, pleasantly decorated place with helpful young staff, and is a useful any-occasion restaurant. Set meals, which are thoughtfully composed and very generous, are very good value. Choosing from the à la carte provides more interesting and unusual dishes. A Thai version of moules marinières served with Thai herbs, and crab claws stewed in a claypot with herbs and clear vermicelli, are two alternatives to the more popular red, green, yellow and jungle curries that they do so well. A vegetarian menu is also available. C £20. **Set L** from £9, **Set D** from £14.95.

SOUTH BANK

10/20 **RSJ**

13a Coin St, SE1 - 071-928 4554
MODERN BRITISH
Open Lunch Mon-Fri, Dinner Mon-Sat.

An extraordinary wine list that reflects the owner's obsession with Loire wines is a great attraction of RSJ. Many wines are available by the glass and they keep a good stock of half bottles. Matching the keenly priced fine vintages is a reasonably priced menu of anglicised French food. The set lunch is outstanding value, and in all cases the simpler dishes such as duck confit and moules marinières are the wisest choice. The basement brasserie sticks to simpler food—generously made pâtés, and home-made soups—at reasonable prices. Tucked away in the nether regions of the south bank, RSJ is a useful place to know about and popular with folk from the nearby TV stations and magazines offices. C £25. **Set menu** from £13.95.

SOUTH KENSINGTON

 Bibendum

Michelin House, 81 Fulham Rd, SW3 - 071-581 5817, Fax 071-823 7925
MODERN BRITISH
Open Lunch & Dinner daily.

Oh, what a lovely restaurant! Of course, one has first to surmount the indifference of the young 'hostesses' stationed at the first-floor entrance, obviously more concerned with shopping and hairdos than with customers. And one also regrets the absence of a dining-room manager to welcome patrons and offer advice on the menu. Still, it is impossible to resist the sleek, original elegance of this bright and spacious room, done up in blue and white, with a spectacular glass roof, glass panels etched with road maps, white napery, black chairs slipcovered in blue and—the highlight—two stained-glass windows depicting the inimitable Bibendum, and Mich's delightful drawings of vintage cars. The atmosphere seems somehow more suited to lunches than dinner, but the total effect is pure aesthetic pleasure. We bless the day that Sir Terence Conran saved this fine old building, once Michelin's London headquarters, from near-certain destruction.

Always full to the rafters (despite the high-price policy), Bibendum is a must-sample for any visitor to the capital. Not, we hasten to add, that Simon Hopkinson's cooking has us composing rhapsodies. It is honest, unpretentious fare, clever in its way, which has the merit of being deftly executed and forthright in flavour. All these characteristics come together, for instance, in Hopkinson's rich and robust hare soup (very good indeed), his hearty salade de museau, made with the delicate meat from the pig's head, the fresh crab perfumed with coriander and lime juice, the crisply fried salt cod with sauce tartare, the sautéed chicken with chanterelles, and a steak au poivre cooked and seasoned with admirable accuracy. Desserts are excellent, too, notably the poached pears with mascarpone abetted by exquisite little madeleines (for which, we should warn you, the house adds a £2.15 supplement to the £25 prix-fixe menu, hugely popular at lunch).

The wine list entices with top-flight options from all over the globe in a wide range of prices; some are available by the glass. Bibendum wins our praise for serving delicious French baguette and for its attractive ground-floor oyster and shellfish bar, but shame on the slow-coach staff who delivered a bill totalling twice what was actually owed, and then offered only the most perfunctory apology. C £55-£60. **Set L** £25.

12/20 **Bibendum Oyster Bar**

Michelin House, 81 Fulham Rd, SW3 - 071-589 1480, Fax 071-823 7925
MODERN BRITISH
Open Lunch & Dinner daily.

Behind the flower van and the crustacea bar and taking up a fraction of the magnificent Michelin building forecourt, is Bibendum's Oyster Bar. Sadly, it's tiny and though tables do spill into the forecourt, there is always a queue at peak drinking and eating times. A short menu of crustacea, and other fishy delights is augmented by a daily different blackboard list. Langoustine with sauce vierge (tomatoes, garlic and olive oil), crab salad, oysters, plateau de fruits de mer, are served with the same thick and fruity mayonnaise that appears on the restaurant menu. Piedmontaise peppers, Caesar salad and squid with black bean sauce, and always a soup are the sort of dishes you can expect. Excellent Chardonnay house wine, plus small bottles of Champagne are on the appropriate, though pricey, wine list. **C** £25. **Set menu** £20.

 Bistrot 190

190 Queen's Gate, SW7
071-581 5666
MODERN BRITISH
Open Lunch & Dinner daily.
 This address is also the headquarters of the Chefs' Club and one of its leading lights, Roy Ackerman, runs the company that owns this restaurant and Downstairs at One Ninety. Overseeing the kitchens and devising the menus at both places here, and at the company's other restaurants, dell 'Ugo, Zoe and Palio, is Anthony Worrall Thompson. All have similar menus and it was here that the famous chef launched the style. Every fashionable ingredient and style of cooking is reflected here. It mixes and borrows from Italy, France, the Orient and Britain to create a new international cuisine. Spinach matafan (pancake) served with poached eggs, cream and bacon, char-grilled squid with salsa, frites and arugula, and chicory tart tatin with duck livers, are typical examples of his food. Most wines are

offered by the bottle and pichet, and the up-to-the-minute list is augmented by a second list chosen by a different wine merchant every couple of months. The bohemian-style restaurant has a no-bookings policy, but drinks can be taken in the large, next-door bar. **C** £22.

11/20 Bombay Brasserie

Courtfield Close, Courtfield Rd, SW7 - 071-370 4040
INDIAN
Open Lunch & Dinner daily.
 This, the most gracious and beautiful Indian restaurant in London, was converted from a ballroom and themed to convey the opulence of the grand old days of the British Raj. Victorian oil lamps shed a romantic glow over the Indian antiques and artefacts, and the adjoining conservatory is plush with exotic plants. The menu attempts to capture the spirit of Bombay with a list that reflects its cosmopolitan character and so draws on India's varied cuisines. Rich, elegant dishes from the Mogul emperors, wholesome Punjabi fare, fiery spiced fish dishes from Goa, and street snacks from the capital, are all woven into the long menu At lunch, a frequently changing buffet of hot and cold dishes provides an inexpensive way of sampling some of its variety. There is a sophisticated and expensive wine list. **C** £30. **Set L** from £14.95.

10/20 La Brasserie

272 Brompton Rd, SW3
071-581 3089
FRENCH

Open Breakfast, Lunch & Dinner daily.
 La Brasserie was London's first-try approximation of a Parisian café/brasserie. It looks the part, it has a large thirties-style décor with much mirrorwork and a long bar, and a strictly old-fashioned bistro menu. It opens for breakfast and true-to-style provides the day's newspapers which are hung on rods. Throughout the day and until midnight you can simulate your Left Bank experience with rillettes de lapereau, pieds de porc grillés, rump steak grillé and blanquette de veau. This is not a place to take a discerning vegetarian. Daily specials are chalked up on the board. La Brasserie remains popular, specially in the summer when tables are parked outside on the deep pavement, but the quality of its cooking has been usurped by new(er) pretenders on its doorstep. The serviceable wine list has house wine by the half bottle. **C** £20.

12/20 Dan's

119 Sydney St, SW3 - 071-352 2718
FRENCH
Open Lunch Mon-Fri, Dinner Mon-Sat.
 A few paces from bustling King's Road is this relative newcomer to the Chelsea scene. Despite the mildly depressing yellow of the décor, the place has an infectiously animated air. The proprietor, Dan Whitehead, has time to stop and chat, and the small paved area at the back makes for enjoyable outdoor summer dining. We have found the menus

packed with inventiveness, even if the execution has a tendency to occasional clumsiness. Deep-fried king prawns accompanied by a pot of mayonnaise spiked with Pernod invigorate the palate, and that fondness for one strong note of flavour is there again in juniper berries with a baked breast of guinea-fowl, or in the ginger that infused a magret of duck. Desserts may subside into blandness (a pastry base containing nothing but whipped cream and sliced strawberries felt like cholesterol for its own sake), and we have found the coffee disappointing. Wines are overwhelmingly French, limited in choice but well selected. **C** £22. **Set L** £10, £12.50, **Set D** £14, £16.50.

 Downstairs at One Ninety
190 Queen's Gate, SW7
071-581 5666
MODERN BRITISH
Open Lunch & Dinner daily.
Fresh fish dominates the menu at this latest incarnation of a restaurant premises that never seems to make its mark. It's a delightful room, a white-painted, wood-panelled basement with a curtained inner sanctum that is available for private parties. A simulated log fire, walls packed with paintings and several tall green plants give it a bohemian and clubby look. The menu divides into snacking food, appetisers, salads, soups and stews, from the chargrill, pasta and rice, from the pan, fish and chips and then puddings and cheeses. Like the upstairs

bistro, tables are allocated on a first-come-first-served basis. The mood is casual and ways with fish varied, drawing on ideas from the Pacific rim, France and Italy. At the helm is the ubiquitous Anthony Worrall Thompson and the eclectic menu is prepared by Australian Chris Millar. Deep-fried squid is served with chilli mayonnaise, carpacccio of smoked haddock and salmon comes with anchovy ice cream (yes, correct!) and ravioli of lobster is cooked with Chinese greens and a soya dressing. The extensive wine list concentrates on white wine with many under £10. **C** £25. **Set L** £9.95, £12.50.

11/20 **Gilbert's**
2 Exhibition Rd, SW7 - 071-589 8947
MODERN BRITISH
Open Lunch & Dinner Mon-Fri.
Museum visitors in South Kensington often pop into Gilbert's for lunch. It is handy for the tube station and provides an improbably homely atmosphere for such a cosmopolitan area. The interior is a little cramped and bench seating does nothing for bad backs, but the welcome is so warm that much is forgiven. Menus are always short and to-the-point and change frequently, with cooking that has gone for greater simplicity in recent years. Cubes of salmon sautéed with a cream sauce is a gentle lunchtime entrée, while more substantial meats are the main order of the evening. We have found the venison to be not quite adequately tenderised, even in a slow-

cooked, blood-enriched stew, but other French country dishes such as a pork cutlet with an assertive mustard sauce have been more satisfactory. Puddings adopt the English accent once more with liquor-soaked chocolate cake or Derbyshire gooseberry tart flavoured with mint. Coffee is good and strong, and the wine list a rare treat—extraordinarily concise but impeccable in its globetrotting choices. **C** £23. **Set L** £15, **Set D** £20.

12/20 **Grill St Quentin**
2 Yeoman's Row, SW3 - 071-581 8377, Fax 071-584 6064
FRENCH
Open Lunch & Dinner daily.
This is the brasserie version of the Restaurant St Quentin just around the corner on Brompton Road. An enormous basement space offers seats for 140 and takes La Coupole in Paris as its inspiration. It has an immense sense of style and pleasingly simple yet comforting décor. Also, unusual, even in large restaurants, is the generosity of space. Here the tables are large, far enough apart that you aren't forced into eavesdropping. Now part of the Savoy Group, it is run by French staff who operate with a brisk efficiency. Oysters are a speciality—Irish, fines de Claires, Belons and natives—are available in season, and patisserie, cheese and other comestibles are supplied by their food shop (also just around the corner). The main menu is straightforward brasserie food to start, dishes such as smoked herring and potato

salad, goose rillettes and stuffed artichoke, with steak, lamb cutlets, salmon, sea bass and Dover sole from the grill as main dishes. **C** £25. **Set L** £10.50, £13.50.

 ### Hilaire
68 Old Brompton Rd, SW7
071-584 8993
MODERN BRITISH
Open Lunch Mon-Fri, Dinner Mon-Sat.

Much in the way of inventive and satisfying cookery still goes on at Hilaire. Bryan Webb has maintained a stable consistency through difficult economic times, and the aim remains true. It is not, alas, a particularly attractive or comfortable room. A bottle- green glumness is belied by the smart, narrow bow windows that give onto Old Brompton Road. Tables are crammed in, but the crowds do at least enliven the atmosphere and service is extremely proper. Bryan Webb's fondness for Mediterranean ingredients—which, incidentally, predated the current obsession—is such that he can deliver an excellent rendition of Piedmont peppers, grilled to collapse with anchovies and superb olive oil. The neo-Italian tone, however, is solidly buttressed by more familiarly British ways with game, and we especially admire the pungently flavoured roast hare with green lentils on an intensely reduced stock. That more stylistic crossover is taking place than hitherto (but isn't that itself the British mode?) may be seen in a dish of baked turbot with broad beans and strips of salty pancetta. Authenticity is guaranteed in a classic crème brûlée with plenty of vanilla, or in a crèpe filled with sliced apricots and flambéed with brandy. Cheese is always reliable, and coffee vibrantly strong. The added bonus is that a brilliantly imaginative wine list has been put together. It roams the vinous world knowledgeably, and prices are not exorbitant. **C** £35. **Set L** £12.50, **Set D** £25.

 ### Joe's Café
126 Draycott Ave, SW3
071-225 2217
MODERN BRITISH
Open Lunch daily, Dinner Mon-Sat.

Joseph Ettedgui, the rag trade supremo of London, is the Joe in question. And this French-style café is a restaurant conceived as a fashionable pit-stop for those in need of fuelling before or after visiting one of his nearby frock shops. A small frontage, usually with outside tables if the weather can take it, belies its deep snaking interior. Done up like an ocean liner in black, white and chrome, it's the epitome of style and redolent of Le Caprice and L'Express. Lately its food has come onto line, making it a port of call for food lovers as well as clothes-horses. Charles Fontaine, of the excellent Quality Chop House, is now overseeing the kitchen. Gone is the menu of fashionable but soulless food and cynical waiting staff. Now they serve good home-made soups, proper Caesar salad and other stalwarts from the Chop House menu such as salmon fish cake with sorrel sauce, grilled tuna steak with salsa verde and Toulouse sausages, mash and onion gravy. These days it's advisable to book a table. **C** £25.

Lou Pescadou
241 Old Brompton Rd, SW5
071-370 1057
FRENCH
Open Lunch & Dinner daily.

Modelled on a typical Côte d'Azur fish café, Lou Pescadou—which is patois for fisherman—was the brainchild of Pierre Martin, owner of Le Suquet. For some years now it has been owned and run with typical French charm by manager Daniel Chobert and chef Laurent David. Seafood, shellfish in particular, forms the backbone of the menu but other Provençal specialities such as pissaladière and other thin, crisp cheeseless pizzas, are offered too, Bouillabaisse, French oysters, moules, brandade de morue, herring and potato salad, crab-stuffed ravioli, are just some of the snacky dishes on offer. Otherwise, go for the perfectly steamed, grilled and pan-fried Mediterranean fish in season. Thankfully, too, all the trimmings such as bread and butter, and a well chosen wine list, are first-class. One of its great attractions is late opening hours but it is sometimes annoying that they employ a no-bookings system. **C** £30. **Set L** £8.

10/20 Ognisko Polskie
55 Exhibition Rd, SW7 - 071- 589 4635
EAST EUROPEAN

Open Lunch & Dinner daily.

Ognisko Polskie means Polish Hearth Club and it's set in a large terrace opposite Imperial College. The Club offers its members concert rooms, libraries, a bar and even a theatre, but the friendly restaurant is open to the general public, and it's not necessary to speak Polish or to be accompanied by a member to enjoy its marvellously robust, Eastern European food. The quiet, elegant, pale-yellow dining room with its pillars, oil paintings, mirrors and a view onto the gardens is an appropriate venue for a meal with a difference. The menu, printed in Polish and English, changes daily but invariably offers such standards as pierogi malopolskie (cheese dumplings) and sztuka miesa sos chrzanowy, ogorek (boiled beef with horseradish sauce). Such food is not for the faint-hearted, and dessert is likely to be apple or prune-stuffed pancakes. Polish pils lager might be a more sensible alternative to a choice from the wine list, specially if you sample the range of native vodkas flavoured with rowan berry, bison herb and cherries. C £20. **Set L & D** £7.50.

12/20 San Lorenzo

22 Beauchamp Pl, SW3
071-584 1074
ITALIAN
Open Lunch & Dinner Mon-Sat. No cards.

With Princess Diana, Eric Clapton and Mick Jagger all regular patrons (the permanent fixture of marginally discreet paparazzi outside the door in the late evening suggests the celebrity element inside), you can be assured of a good bit of star-gazing most days. The standard Italian fare is less exciting, but traditional pastas and grilled fish do satisfy. At least the helpings are generous and the San Lorenzo pancake, a boozy treat with mascarpone, almond biscuits and pralines, is not to be missed. It is to the credit of the owners, who have now celebrated 30 years in Beauchamp Place, that well-clad ladies-who-lunch and stars who don't mind being ogled continue to flock here. Too distracting, therefore, for a quiet tête-à-tête, but of the two sections—a raised central space surrounded by a more discreet, subtly lit area—choose the latter. C £25.

13/20 San Martino

103 Walton St, SW3 - 071-589 3833
ITALIAN
Open Lunch & Dinner daily.

Walton Street is one of London's little gems, filled with boutiques and smart private terraced houses. Linking Harrod's to Brompton Cross, the trendy shopping intersection with Joseph and The Conran shop at its epicentre, it also houses numerous good restaurants. San Martino has been a resident for more than two decades, and owner Costanzo 'Martino' Martinucci loves to chat with his patrons and grows most of the vegetables and herbs for the restaurant in his own garden in south London. The Tuscan-influenced food is excellent, the menu extensive. Try pasta and fagioli soup with delicate Italian butter beans, served in striking earthenware pots brought back from Brazil by Martino. Pastas are recommended (spaghetti cooked in a paper bag filled with monkfish, scampi, vongole and octopus is a favourite) and the house speciality—whole baby chicken grilled between two bricks—is tender and succulent. Desserts are rich as in crêpes with cream and rhubarb or the traditional tiramisù, the sinful concoction of coffee, chocolate and custard. C £20. **Set L** from £5.50.

12/20 Star of India

INDIAN
154 Old Brompton Rd, SW5
071-373 2901
Open Lunch & Dinner daily.

Despite its many peregrinations since it opened in 1958, The Star of India has always enjoyed a good reputation for its food. Currently its walls and ceiling are decorated with baroque trompe l'œil and outside a huge gold star shines out above the door. The star of The Star is Reza Mohammed, the flamboyantly garrulous owner, who hosts the restaurant. His menu makes for enticing reading and it's advisable to go in a group in order to share several dishes and thus not break the bank. Much is made of vegetables, potatoes in particular, and it is tempting to compose an entirely vegetarian meal. Diced potatoes in a pomegranate dressing, lightly spiced potato croquettes rolled in almonds and fried, and baby aubergines cooked in a mustard seed, tamarind and nut-flavoured gravy. Tandoori dishes are always cooked to order and breads—flavoured nans in particular—are a speciality. A sophisticated drinks list includes various Indian herbal teas. **C** £30.

12/20 Le Suquet
104 Draycott Ave, SW7
071-581 1785
FRENCH
Open Lunch & Dinner daily.

Pierre Martin opened his first London fish restaurant in 1975 when the fishmonger's slab was a thoroughly British affair. He imported French seafood himself and developed a small chain of restaurants now consolidated here. His concept with all of them was to provide a small choice of simply cooked and, where appropriate, lightly sauced and mainly French, seafood. Mussels, scallops and clams are served in many different styles, and the highlight of the menu is the plateau de fruits de mer. A small selection of classic accompaniments, including first-class mayonnaise, decent baguette and a big slab of creamy unsalted butter, is generally just so. The design of Le Suquet, like the others, is very south of France with Provençal print curtains, cane armchairs, tanks of lobsters and bright lighting to show off the colour photos of Cannes harbour. **C** £30.

 Turner's
87-89 Walton St, SW3 - 071-584 6711
FRENCH
Open Lunch Sun-Fri, Dinner daily.

Brian Turner, chairman of the British chapter of the Académie Culinaire and TV chef celebrity, is a high profile chef. He's an omnipresent host, leaving the cooking these days to Peter Brennan, while he works the room and befriends his customers. Classically trained, he worked his way up via the Capital Hotel (where he earned it its awards) and the Greenhouse. His food is restrained, light of touch and elegantly presented in the style that used to be called nouvelle cuisine. He is the first to admit that the trend towards simplicity makes his style of cooking unfashionable, and he has introduced a cheap set lunch with less ambitious creations. The wine list specialises in Chablis and is otherwise traditional and solidly French. It is a charming restaurant, cleverly sectioned off with etched glass partitions and tastefully decorated in blue, cream and gold. **C** £35. **Set L** £9.95, £13.50, **Set D** £23.50, £26.50.

 Walton's
11 Walton St, SW3 - 071-584 0204, Fax 071-581 2848
BRITISH
Open Lunch & Dinner daily.

Waltons continues to hold the prize for the most over-designed restaurant in the capital. So cocooned will you be by layers of fabric that you may well feel you are being tucked up in bed before the evening has begun, and the arrangement of mirrors and curtains is such that—even on a busy night—it can occur to you that there may be nobody else there. Lighting is heavily nocturnal, relieved only by tiny spotlights that pick out the food. This, too, used to suffer from a certain tendency to preciousness. We well remember the broccoli mousse garnished with broccoli sprigs on a broccoli cream sauce dotted with caviar. Things are more recognisably in the English mainstream now, despite the ever-present (and superlative) terrine of foie gras, which perhaps reflects trends elsewhere. We strongly recommend the calf's liver with bacon served with a powerful whole grain mustard sauce that has become something of a stalwart. Salmon fish cakes (that quintessential 1990s restaurant dish) are enriched convincingly with lobster and tarragon, while the beef, served in tender medallions with a well-reduced buttery stock, always delights. Desserts too require more girding of the loins than hitherto. Sticky toffee pudding and solid terrine of white and dark chocolate are the style, and even an iced peach soufflé has impressive density. Coffee remains rather feeble, while the wine list offers an embarrassment of choice but will push up that already stiff bill even higher. **C** £40. **Set L** £14.75 (£16.50 Sun), **Set D** £22 (after 10pm).

> The **C** (A la carte) *restaurant prices given are for a complete three-course meal for one, and service.* **Set L or D or menu** *prices are for a complete fixed-price meal for one, excluding wine (unless otherwise noted).*

STRAND

12/20 The Grill Room

The Savoy, Strand, WC2
071-836 1533, Fax 071-379 5421
BRITISH
Open Lunch Mon-Fri, Dinner Mon-Sat.

A power seating plan of the Savoy Grill's dining room was published a few years ago. The room, particularly at lunchtime, is booked out by the rich and famous, and lesser mortals will have to make their reservations several days in advance. An attraction of the place is the specialities of the day—sausages with mashed potato and fried onions on Monday, steak, kidney and oyster pudding on Tuesday, Lancashire hot-pot on Wednesday, and so on. These English stalwarts aside, the Grill can be relied upon for straightforward grills and roasts, old-fashioned salads (Le Buffet Froid) and classic Escoffier cuisine. Lately there has been a move to include lighter dishes and some enterprising ideas for vegetarians. A fine wine list covers all eventualities. The Grill is run with deferential, efficient service that is quite undiscriminating whoever you are. It's a large comfortable wood-panelled room with chandelier lighting, high-backed sofas and well-upholstered chairs. **C** £40.

 ## The River Restaurant

The Savoy, Strand, WC2
071-836 4343
FRENCH
Open Lunch & Dinner daily.

Tradition is the key word here, and respect for tradition is the primary concern. This is indisputably one of the great dining rooms of London, large, luxurious, comfortable and with window seats that afford fine views through the trees of the Embankment to the river beyond. One of the few restaurants in London where it is possible to dance in the evening to a live band, it is also one of London's busiest. You can rely on chef Anton Edelmann to master with impeccable technique the great classical themes and to use the best ingredients from pheasants and partridges to calf's sweetbreads and kidneys in puff pastry, not to mention the legendary smoked salmon. But he can also personalise these standard dishes with his own discreet touch. The menu offers a choice between tradition and more adventurous ways. Sole rises above banality thanks to a hint of coriander, lobster acquires oriental charm in a spicy sauce and apples give an invigorating accent to calf's liver. If the most impressive wine list confuses, Anton Edelmann has joined forces with sommelier Werner Wissmann to make the choice. The £45 menu comes accom-panied by a glass of wine of their choice to match each course: fillet of John Dory is washed down with Montagny and apple tart with a beautiful Sauternes. As you would expect, service is highly professional here. **C** £40. **Set L** £25.75, **Set D** £31.25, £45.

11/20 Simpson's-in-the-Strand

100 Strand, WC2 - 071-836 9112
BRITISH
Open Lunch & Dinner daily.

Simpson's-in-the-Strand is an institution—the home of traditional British grub dished up in a baronial, gentleman's club-style dining room. The highlight of the menu is the roasts—sirloin of beef, saddle of lamb and Aylesbury duck—which are served from the silver-domed trolleys by long-serving retainers. One of these choices preceded by oysters or the rather wonderful quails' eggs with haddock and cheese sauce, and followed by Welsh rarebit, would make a very fine meal. The daily lunch specials—pork and apple sauce (Monday), boiled silverside with pease pudding, carrot and dumplings (Thursday)—have loyal supporters, and the puddings such as treacle roll, spotted Dick and apple pie are made to closely guarded recipes. **C** £30. **Set L & Pre-theater D** £10.

TOTTENHAM COURT ROAD

10/20 Chez Gérard

8 Charlotte St, W1 - 071-636 4975
FRENCH
Open Lunch Mon-Fri, Dinner daily.

Lately transformed from its agreeably faux-bistro look to a bright, light and post-modernist café, Chez Gérard continues its role as a French grill restaurant.

The speciality is steak frites, chateaubriand for two, which they do beautifully. Prime quality meat is cooked to achieve a crusty surface but leaving the interior meltingly soft. Served with the choice of béarnaise, sauce chateaubriand or sauce verte, it needs no other accompaniment than their crisp pommes frites. A small, fashion-touched selection of appetisers, gravlax tartare and rabbit rillettes, and an excellent cheeseboard are also recommended. There are various set-price meals that are worth checking out. The wine list is appropriately chosen and keenly priced. C £25. Set D & Sat L £15.

 La Gaulette

53 Cleveland St, W1 - 071-580 7608/071-323 4210
MAURITIAN
Open Lunch Mon-Fri, Dinner Mon-Sat.

This is the grown-up parent to Chez Liline in Finsbury Park, Sylvain Ho Wing Cheong's first attempt at bringing Mauritian food to London. Hidden away in a back street in the shadow of the British Telecom tower, it's a pleasant little restaurant dominated by a giant marlin 'sculpture' mounted on the wall. Mauritian cuisine is a glorious melting pot of Indian, Chinese and Creole cooking, all underpinned by French technique, which results in a varied cuisine that can be exotic and spicy and elegant and finely sauced. Ginger, garlic, chilli, curry powder and coriander, together with onions and tomatoes feature frequently, all at once in a ubiquitous Creole sauce. The menu revolves around fish like vacqua, bourgeois, red snapper and parrot fish from Mauritius, and lobster and other shellfish from native shores. Vacqua is cooked with butter and mango, king prawns with chilli, herbs and tomato, and lobster tails are cooked with lemon grass. Tropical fruit makes a fitting finish to the meal. The staff are charming and the experience of a meal here is quite delightful. C £30. Set L £17.95, Set D £22.95.

 Nico Central

35 Gt Portland St, W1 - 071-436 8846, Fax 071-436 0134
FRENCH
Open Lunch & Dinner Mon-Fri.

One expects surprises from master chef Nico Ladenis. In this restaurant, previously his flagship Chez Nico, the usual order of things is reversed and the bargain is dinner when virtually the whole carte becomes a prix-fixe at a remarkable £20 for three courses, service included. Not that it isn't good value for lunch too, for the cooking, although mainly in the 'new Nico' simplified style, is serious and reliable, often showing the flashes of inspiration which has illuminated his work over twenty years in London. Such quality at such prices means that luxurious ingredients rarely appear—only foie gras as a starter which bears a supplement of £6. A welcome innovation is that the menu is entirely in English. Choosing from it is difficult because its originality never goes over the top and every dish reads mouth-wateringly. Starters may include crispy duck with borlotti beans and mustard mayonnaise, mussel minestrone and honey-roast quail with a french bean salad. It was interesting to compare a risotto of cèpes with a similarly named dish at the new flagship, Nico at Ninety. There the classical recipe was not used; the result was different, unusual—and superlative. Here was a classical risotto—and a very good one. Among main dishes cuisine grand-mère is a major influence—but whose grandmother would have cooked lambs' tongues in Madeira sauce with beetroot? Potatoes offer a simple choice of chips or purée while vegetables are a selection, but given that, the four choices make sense and the portions are more than mere tokens. In puddings too some dishes are simple—crème caramel is a reminder of what this masterpiece was before it was spoiled by mass production. Others like chocolate marquise with orange crème anglaise are more elaborate but equally successful. The list of some 40 wines ranges widely with fine bottles from both classic areas and the New World, at ungreedy prices. Macabeo Jaume Serra from Penedes, a full-flavoured dry white at £13.50 is notable, but 1991 La Rosa Bianca (a confusingly named red) is a Tuscan vino da tavola which needs further ageing. Plain walls and a mirrored dado make a suitable background for striking modern pictures. The brightness—some would say harshness—of the lighting is perhaps the one mistake in this pleasant restaurant. Would it be sexist to suggest that this, rather than its site in a business area, accounts for women being greatly outnumbered by men, even at dinner? **C £26.50. Set D £20.**

Pied-à-Terre
34 Charlotte St, W1 - 071-636 1178
FRENCH
Open Lunch Mon-Fri, Dinner Mon-Sat.
Richard Neat, the rising star of Pied-à-Terre, the restaurant he bought after the demise of the ambitious Indian restaurant Jamdani, has spent little time jazzing up the room—merely a lick of paint and some modern art on loan from Richard Hamilton—and he has kept the famously uncomfortable chairs. Neat, who has worked with Joël Robuchon in Paris, with Raymond Blanc at Le Manoir aux Quat' Saisons in Oxfordshire and with Marco Pierre White while he was at Harvey's in Wandsworth, has devoted all his attention to the food. All meals are set price, lunch is the simpler cheaper menu, so it pays to go into training in order to complete the three courses. Neat cooks modern haute cuisine with light sauces, and flavours that bounce off each other. He appears to favour fish and offal and recent impressive dishes have included a tagliatelle of tender langoustine accompanied by a pale green, frothy bouillon made with asparagus, foie gras on a cake of roasted endive surrounded by soft, sweet garlic cloves, and oven-roasted fillet of cod sitting on a mound of mashed potato seasoned with salt cod. Desserts are given the same complex treatment and millefeuille of chocolate and caramelised banana are highly recommended. Service is proper and the wine list tries to be all things to all men with considerable success. **C £36. Set L £19.50, Set D £36.**

12/20 Ragam
57 Cleveland St, W1 - 071-636 9098
INDIAN
Open Lunch & Dinner daily.
To 'know' Indian food without having tasted the southern cooking of Kerala is like 'knowing' European food except for Italian. Keralian cooking is mainly vegetarian, and its dominant flavours include coconut, lemon, mustard seed, pepper, poppy seed and the tangy, citrussy sharpness of tamarind. Order from the pages headed Our Specialities starting with a small bowl of rasam or pepper soup, then choose a dosai—a crisp, rice and lentil flavour pancake, plain or stuffed. Continue with a vadai—spicy lentil cake, or uthappam—'pizza' with lemon or coconut rice. This simple but pleasant café also offers a full list of meat and fish curries but only bigoted carnivores will bother with these. If authentic chilli hotness is a worry take the advice of the helpful waiters and cool the palate with lassi—iced yoghurt drink with mango, peach or pineapple—or the more conventional sweet and salted varieties. **C £12.** Also Sree Krishna, 192 Tooting High St, SW17, 081-672 4250.

11/20 Walsh's
5 Charlotte St, W1 - 071-637 0222
BRITISH
Open Lunch Mon-Fri, Dinner Mon-Sat.
Owned and run by the heirs of the family which started the Wheeler's group of fish restaurants in 1929, Walsh's recalls the original Old Compton Street Wheeler's with a small bar at the front and a warren of small rooms at the back. Coloured and black-and-white sporting prints give a clubby masculine feel to the restaurant. Also reminiscent of the old Wheeler's are fine English native oysters in two sizes, and a menu listing five cooked lobster dishes, three plaice, and nine Dover sole. The quality of both fish and shellfish is superb and the cooking at least reliable in such modern-style dishes as salad St Jacques. Pears in Beaujolais make a subtle dessert. Sole Colbert or lobster Thermidor will please those nostalgic for the 1960s and before. Service up to now may lack the polish which comes with time. The odd carnivore will find two meat dishes offered daily, and yet another pleasure for traditionalists of every age is the revival of the savoury. **C £28.**

TOWER BRIDGE

 Blue Print Café

Design Museum, Shad Thames, Butlers Wharf, SE1 071-378 7031
MODERN BRITISH
Open Lunch daily, Dinner Mon-Sat.

Located on top of the Design Museum and with two terraces that make good use of its stunning river-side views, the Blue Print Café was the now famous restaurateur Sir Terence Conran's first restaurant in Butlers Wharf on the south side of Tower Bridge. It's a sleek, functional, long and narrow restaurant with sliding plate-glass doors that give onto a spacious patio set with tables and shaded by a bright yellow canopy. The kitchen is run by Lucy Crabbe, who 'graduated' from Bibendum, the jewel in Conran's expanding crown. Her menu owes much to her days under Bibendum chef Simon Hopkinson's influence and is an enticing mixture of Mediterranean and British stalwarts. Emphasis is on using good ingredients, simplicity of style and power of flavour. Artichoke heart stuffed with goat's cheese is served as a soufflé and accompanied by two croûtons spread with chunky-cut tapenade; linguine is served in a pool of olive oil leaked from home-made pesto and dusted in freshly grated Parmesan. Patisserie is the kitchen's forte, notably a marvellously gooey, densely flavoured chocol- ate mousse cake and a carefully constructed tower of Charentais melon slices filled with raspberries and sitting in a coulis of red currant. The worldly and keenly priced wine list con- tains several interesting bottles under £12 like Vernuccia di San Gimignano Rocca delle Macie, Oxford Landing Chardonnay and Yalumba Southern Australia. **C** £25.

 Butlers Wharf Chop House

Butlers Wharf Building, 36 Shad Thames, Butlers Wharf, SE1 - 071-403 3403, Fax 071-403 3414
MODERN BRITISH
Open Lunch daily, Dinner Mon-Sat.

Here we have the latest arrival to Sir Terence Conran's collection of restaurants in Butlers Wharf where the menu is a celebration of the best of British cooking. It's an enticing menu that really gets the juices going. Individual steak and kidney pudding is served with its crust oozing with rich, thick gravy; roast pigeon comes with creamy, nutmeggy bread sauce and savoy cabbage; and rare roast beef is accompanied by perfect Yorkshire pudding and horseradish cream. In the kitchen is Rod Eggleston, late of the Blue Print Café and before that a cook at Bibendum, and he is clearly very much at home with his menu. Fish takes centre stage, augmenting the carte with daily blackboard specials, and vegetables are elevated to prime status. Puddings more than pass muster but are not the strength of the kitchen which is too bad because the dessert wine list is outstanding. The décor is Conran's version of a nineties chop house—the precursor of the restaurant proper as exemplified by Charles Fontaine's Quality Chop House—with lots of pale wood, high-backed settles and leather seats. **C** £30. **Set L** £21.50.

12/20 Cantina del Ponte

Butlers Wharf Building, 36 Shad Thames, SE1 - 071-403 5403, Fax 071-403 0267
MEDITERRANEAN
Open Lunch daily, Dinner Mon-Sat.

Part of the complex of Sir Terence Conran's restaurants that goes under the

---

English eating habits

'In England the fork, whether of steel or even of silver, is always held in the left hand and the knife in the right. The fork seizes, the knife cuts, and the pieces may be carried to the mouth with either. The motion is quick and precise. The manoeuvres at an English dinner are founded upon the same principles as Prussian tactics—not a moment is lost.' Faujas de Saint Fond in the early eighteenth century.

---

name of the 'Gastrodome' and with views across the River Thames to Tower Bridge, the large room is dominated by a huge Brueghel-influenced mural, and the simple design is chic meets rustic. A pizza oven sits at one end of the room and a miniature Tower Bridge 'sculpture' at the other. The chairs and tables are plain and beautifully made from wood, and the side lights are suspended on what look like fishing rods. The menu of chef Louis Loizia (who, incidentally, is the only Conran chef not to have worked with Simon Hopkinson at Bibendum), is comparatively short and simple and revolves around pizza and pasta. It does, however, revel in fashionable ingredients and delights in little known terminology. Hence taglioni with crab vellutata, pumpkin and ricotta ravioli served with a slick of melted butter and garnished with balls of carrot, and osso bucco with gremolata, savoy cabbage and polenta. A nice touch is to serve fig biscotti with coffee. The wine list is Italian with several choices under £12; a list of grappas appends the menu. **C** £20.

 ## Le Pont de la Tour

Butlers Wharf Building, 36 Shad Thames, Butlers Wharf, SE1 - 071-403 8403
MODERN BRITISH
Open Lunch & Dinner daily.
The linchpin of Sir Terence Conran's clutch of restaurants down by the river and the arriviste of Butler's Wharf, Le Pont de la Tour is invariably com-

pared to Bibendum, Conran's remarkable restaurant in South Kensington. Like Bibendum, the menu of David Burke (previously Simon Hopkinson's sous chef at that celebrated restaurant) relies on the best and freshest ingredients, simply prepared, and draws its influences from regional France and the Mediterranean, while incorporating the best of British and Irish cooking. London divides between those who think it is as good as Bibendum and those who don't. All agree that it is marginally less expensive. Unlike Bibendum its space—it is enormous—and the separate bar and grill which specialises in shellfish (which can be bought from a shop in the entrance), mean it operates on several levels. Its design is an admirable reflection of Conran's eye for understated style and interest in promoting contemporary art. A huge crustaceous chandelier by Tom Dixon hangs in the bar, and in the restaurant Patrick Caulfield etched the glass screens and hammered the fish-scale leadwork.

The menu changes frequently but the char-grill is a favoured way of cooking meat and fish, and there is a preference for seasonal game and roasts, such as best end of lamb with kidneys, cèpes and potato galette, and côte de bœuf grillée with sauce béarnasie, cooked for two. Other highlights include rare grilled tuna with coriander and chilli, petit salé aux lentilles and sauté of veal sweetbreads with

morels. Best value is pre- and post-theatre menus. The 700-strong wine list with rare vintages is a real speciality. **C** £35. **Set L** £25 (not Sat).

VICTORIA

12/20 La Poule au Pot
231 Ebury St, SW1 - 071-730 7760
FRENCH
Open Lunch & Dinner daily.
In a world of fickle fashions, it is reassuring to find restaurants which have been around for years, which are still serving basically the same food and which are still popular. La Poule au Pot is one such, a French restaurant from whatever decade you discovered it in, decorated in stripped pine, with wooden floors, lacy tablecloths and baskets filled with dried flowers, and for winter warmth, a fireplace. The food, too, owes little to recent fashion, following good, solid, bistro cooking. Escargots in garlic sauce, rocket salad and mushrooms, terrine du chef are followed by mainstays like lapin à la moutarde, guinea fowl, calf's liver and bœuf bourguignon, all well cooked and generously proportioned. To finish, of course, crème brûlée, mousse au chocolat, ice cream and caramel sauce. Their method of serving wine is a novel one. You can order a bottle of a fancy French wine, but their house wine arrives in a huge bottle which is then measured before the bill is

calculated. This restaurant may not be the hottest news in town, but it is solid, fun, good value and extremely French. **C** £22. **Set L** £12.75.

WILLESDEN

 Sabras

263 High Rd, NW10 - 081-459 0340

INDIAN VEGETARIAN
Open Lunch Tues-Fri, Dinner Tues-Sun.

This simple, bright, clean café in an unprepossessing street is owned by the Desai family who cook and serve, with great charm, the finest Indian vegetarian food in London. Some go further in describing it as simply the best Indian food, and the best vegetarian too. Even carnivores who usually find no excitement in vegetarian food may be tempted to convert by the astonishing variety of textures and flavours from Mysore, Surat, Bengal, Gujerat, Bombay, Kerala and other regions. Fresh vegetables are a feature—which is not always the case in oriental vegetarian places. Here they may include such seasonal specialities as karela bitter gourd, dudhi calabash marrow, govar cluster beans and tindora tiny cucumbers. Four sorts of Bombay puri, miniature grain puffs which explode thrillingly in the mouth, include paani puris filled with tamarind water, potatoes and chick peas. The dal tarka served in most Indian restaurants is a tasty thick liquid porridge of lentils with onions and spices. Sabra's even more exciting version explains why Jacob's mess of pottage was so eagerly accepted by Esau in exchange for his birthright. Desserts may include chilled Alphonso mango pulp and home-made pistachio, almond or mango kulfi, Indian ice cream. Many Indian 'pastries' are available, and are often taken away for home consumption by those who find temptation exceeding appetite. To accompany this brilliant cooking there is a choice between properly prepared non-alcoholic drinks such as lassi and a range of Old and New World wines, modest but pleasant bottles at moderate prices. Thalis (set meals on a dish) range from single-plate lunch and early evening meals at £1 to a 'de-luxe thali' of thirteen items for £11. At £2.75 to £3.50 for most dishes, and with only a few items such as south Indian dhosas at £5.95, it is hard to spend as much as £15 per head. At prices which would amply justify an entry in our Bargain Bite classification we must insist on limiting expectations in terms of luxury. But the cooking demands this high rating. **C** £14.

HOTELS

INTRODUCTION

With an official figure from the British Tourist Authority of more than ten million overseas visitors annually plus a further seven million domestic visitors, the demand for quality accommodation in London remains high. The hotel industry has responded with extensive refurbishment programmes and new levels of customer service. The recession taught a few valuable lessons, and the concept of value-for-money, at whatever price level, is now a crucial issue. Not just a bed for the night, many hotel rooms have been turned into individual entertainment centres with satellite TV, VCRs and CD players the norm. And the list of amenities grows—from dressing gowns and designer toiletries to Fax machines and twenty-four-hour butler service. Five-star hotels, also, are racing each other to install fitness facilities, whether it be a couple of stationary bicycles and free weights in a converted room, or a glossy, marble-filled complex, complete with swimming pool, saunas, personal trainers and exclusive lounge areas.

Of course the natural wear and tear of daily passing trade means the life span of any room décor is only a handful of years, but the massive renovation programmes undertaken by a high percentage of London hotels over the last year or so is extremely impressive by any standards. Similarly, hotels have acknowledged the 'personal' factor. Guests want recognition, comfort and security on a hotel visit. While the larger hotels, many of them part of international chains, can offer affiliated services (restaurants and bars, banqueting and conference facilities, business centres and fleets of staff), there is a new breed of hotel in London—the townhouse hotel phenomenon which has seen incredible growth in the last five years. Converted private houses in leafy residential areas, particularly South Kensington, Knightsbridge and Notting Hill, have been joined together, decorated with quality antiques and a very personal, caring service implemented. What they may lack in size (most have fewer than 40 rooms), they make up with charm, style, a very warm welcome and the genuinely personal touch.

LONDON'S PRICES

In the past, London has been castigated for exorbitant hotel room rates and the general cost of living/visiting prices. But now London has stabilised on the world league tables, hovering, according to the British Tourist Authority, around tenth place. It should also be borne in mind that while published rack rates at top hotels remain high, there are many bargains to be had for the intrepid traveller. Check advance purchase packages before departure, investigate corporate rates offered to many businesses, or for the bold, negotiate on the spot. Weekend packages, small group bookings and seasonal savings abound.

CLASSIFICATION & ABBREVIATIONS

We have made classifications purely on the advertised prices of rooms:

Top of the Line: average room rate of £225 or above
Luxury: from £200
First-Class: from £180
Charming Townhouse: from £110
Moderate: from £150
Practical: below £150
Bed & Breakfast: between £60 and £100

However, as we mention, you will find that posted prices vary enormously according to availability, season, day of the week and so on, so it is worth enquiring about any special offers. Our editorial comment will tell you what we think of the hotels, and price does not necessarily mean the best in terms of accommodation, service or ambience. So choose carefully.

CB: continental breakfast
Rms: rooms

EB: full English breakfast
Stes: suites.

RENTING AN APARTMENT

You might also consider the option of renting an apartment, particularly if you are contemplating a longer stay and are quite happy to stock your own fridge and discover your neighbourhood restaurants. Living like a Londoner can be great fun. Renting a house or apartment in London is becoming an increasingly popular option; and greater demand has consequently produced a wider range and choice. The apartments recommended here are only a very few of those available in London. For advice abroad, contact the British Tourist Authority offices. The BTA publishes a booklet listing recommended apartments and apartment services.

When you enquire about an apartment, try to get as much information as you can, as they vary enormously even within the same apartment block. Prices given here, except where indicated otherwise, are for weekly rentals. But there are many options and special breaks, and prices vary according to time of year and availability. Most also offer daily rates, and do not restrict you to a weekly stay. If you stay longer, rates often decrease.

Of the four companies listed here, all of whom deal with large numbers of apartments, we particularly recommend In the English Manner for its delightful townhouses as well as its first-class apartments. They also rent

houses outside London.
Contact:
• *The Apartment Service*, 66 Dalling Rd, W6 0JA - 081-748 4207, Fax 081-748 3972; in USA: *Keith Prowse & Co*, 234 West 44th St, New York, NY 10036 - 212-398 1430, 800-669 8687, Fax 212-302 4251.
• *Barclay International Group*, 150 East 52nd St, New York NY 10022 - 212-832 3777, 800-845 6636, Fax 212-753 1130.
• *In the English Manner*, Lancych, Boncath, Pembrokeshire SA37 0LJ - 0239-77444, Fax 0239-77686; in USA: 515 South Figuera St, Suite 1000, Los Angeles, CA 90071 - 213-629 1811, 800 422 0799, Fax 213-689 8784 and 4092 North Ivy Rd, NE, Atlanta, GA 30342 - 404-231 5837, Fax 404-231 9610.
• *Park Lane Estates*, 48 Curzon St, W1Y 7RE - 071-629 0763, 1-800 284 7385, Fax 071-493 1308.
Recommended apartments:
• *Aston's Budget Studios*, Designer Studios and Designer Suites, 39 Rosary Gdns, South Kensington, SW7 4NQ, 071-370 0737, 1-800-525 2810, Fax 071-835 1419. 60 apts £185-£1,005. Particularly good for budget accommodation, they now also have designer suites in a good Kensington location.
• *Beaufort House*, 45 Beaufort Gdns, Knightsbridge, SW3 1PN, 071-584 2600, Fax 071-584 6532. 22 apts £763-£1,869. In pretty Beaufort Gardens near Harrods, these refurbished, well-decorated and well-equipped suites are in an elegant old building.
• *Central London Apartments*, 48 Bedford Court Mansions, Bedford Ave, Bloomsbury, WC1B 3AA, 071-323 1192, Fax 071-631 3866. 17 apts £275-£1,000. In two buildings, these apartments are well done and within walking distance of the British Museum and Covent Garden.
• *Draycott House*, 10 Draycott Ave, Chelsea, SW3 3AA, 071-584 4659, Fax 071-225 3694. 13 apts £715-£1,800. Located in an old, charming red-brick building, many have their own balconies. Very well decorated in English country style.
• *Durley House*, 115 Sloane St, Chelsea, SW1X 9PJ, 071-235 5537, 1-800 553 6674, Fax 071-259 6977. 11 apts from £190. Fashionable address in Sloane Street, delightful, elegant apartments from the owners of Dorset Square and the Pelham Hotel, thoroughly recommended.
• *Flemings Apartments*, 7 Half Moon St, Mayfair, W1Y 7RA, 071-499 2964, Fax 071-491 8866. 11 apts £1,350-£2,300. Part of Flemings Hotel, they have all the hotel's amenities and a separate entrance. Ideally located in the heart of Mayfair.
• *Fountains*, 1 Lancaster Terrace, Hyde Park, W2 3PF, 071-286 5294, Fax 071-229 3917. 17 apts £1,250-£1,400. These are top-of-the-range apartments, beautifully decorated just north of Hyde Park.
• *Grosvenor House*, Grosvenor House Hotel, Park Lane, W1A 3AA, 071-499 6363, Fax 071-493 3342. 146 apts from £215. Part of the Grosvenor House Hotel, though with its own entrance, the apartments are well decorated and guests can use the hotel's facilities such as the first-rate health club and pool.
• *Hyde Park Residence*, 55 Park Lane, W1Y 3DB, 071-409 9000, Fax

071-493 4041. 120 apts £700-£4,500. Superb accommodation on London's Park Lane, some apartments are on long term lets. The building has all the facilities of a five-star hotel.

• *Lambs*, 21 Egerton Gdns, Knightsbridge, SW3 2DF, 071-589 6297, Fax 071-584 3302. 23 apts £567-£840. Homely rather than elegant apartments in a terraced Victorian house in leafy Egerton Gardens, well located near Knightsbridge.

• *Nell Gwynn Apartments*, Nell Gwynn House, Sloane Ave, SW3 3AX, 071-589 1105, Fax 071-589 9433. 127 apts £240-£700. In an impressive 1930's building, this is a popular location in Chelsea with a health club and garage.

• *One Thirty*, 130 Queensgate, South Kensington, SW7 5LE, 071-581 2322, Fax 071-823 8488. 54 apts £495-£900. Newly re-furbished, in a Victorian building near the museums and Hyde Park, the apartments are well furnished and some have balconies.

• *Orion London Apartment-Hotel*, 7-21 Goswell Rd, EC1, 071-566 8000, Fax 071-566 8130. 129 ensuite studios and apartments from the large French chain near the Barbican centre, but probably aimed more at the business traveller. Designed by a woman, the kitchens have essentials like potato peelers and dishwashers. Rates are £75 per night for a studio sleeping two people, and £105 per night for an apartment sleeping 4.

• *23 Greengarden House*, St Christopher's Pl, W1M 5HD, 071-935 9191, Fax 071-935 8858. 24 apts £770-£,225. In a delightful, secluded place behind Oxford Street, the apartments are quite small, but well decorated and the management is delightfully helpful.

RESERVATION SERVICE

If you arrive without having booked a hotel, the Tourist Information Centres run by the London Tourist Board at Heathrow Airport, Liverpool Street Station, Victoria Station and in Selfridge's department store can book a room for you, though they do not cover every hotel. Otherwise there is a credit card booking hotline run by the LTB open 9am-5pm, 071-824 8844.

TOP OF THE LINE

Average room price £225 upwards.

The Berkeley

Wilton Pl, SW1X 7RL
071-235 6000, Fax 071-235 4330
27 stes £390-£730, 133 rms S £160-£200, D £220-£250 plus VAT. Air cond. Garage. Health club. Restaurants. 24-hr rm service. Ballroom and 4 private rms.

Close to Hyde Park, Belgravia embassy-land and Knightsbridge shopping, the Berkeley is, at 22 years old, the youngest of the Savoy Group's hotels. Discretion is the key here; tucked in a side street off Knightsbridge, it has more of a private home than a modern hotel ambience. Rooms are spacious and service attentive. There are still bells in the rooms to summon valet or maid, but inroads have been made into the twentieth century elsewhere, including very tight security. The Berkeley Restaurant is formal and French, while the lower-ground level Perroquet is more relaxed with an Italian/Mediterranean menu. In true Savoy Group's style, the package is completed with rooftop heated swimming pool and health club (sunbed, sauna, gym, massage and facial treatments), florist, men's and ladies' hairdressers, a private garage and the Minema cinema adjacent which features recent foreign releases and has a separate, smart, two-level café.

Claridge's

Brook St, W1A 2JQ
071-629 8860, Fax 071-499 2210
60 stes £470-£605, 130 rms S £180-£215, D £230-£280 plus VAT. Air cond. Restaurants. 24-hr rm, maid and valet service. Ballroom and 4 function rms.

Fashionable in the most exclusive sense, Claridge's has been patronised by royalty for more than a century. In fact, it feels more like a private club than an hotel, and manager Ron Jones maintains a pleasing mix of tradition and comfort, particularly with the recent upgrading of most rooms (no two are alike). Beside the two restaurants (see Restaurant section), both attracting upscale regulars, serious celebrities and captains of industry, the Causerie, with its good luncheon smörgåsbörd, is popular for pre- and post-theatre dining. Services include hairdressers (both men and women), a travel bureau, theatre desk, florist and membership in the Bath & Racquets Health Club next door for men (gym, steam, squash courts).

The Connaught

Carlos Pl, W1Y 6AL
071-499 7070, Fax 071-495 3262
26 stes £425-£705, 64 rms S £177, D £220-£235 plus VAT. Air cond in most rms. Restaurants. 24-hr rm service. 2 banqueting rms for private luncheon and dinner parties of up to 20.

Built in 1897 and named after Queen Victoria's third son, The Connaught is one of the Savoy Group's hotels that has always set standards for quality British service. The ratio of staff to guests is very high and it shows—quiet exclusive opulence combined with a single objective to be totally British is the style of the Connaught. And total discretion is assumed. There are two restaurants: The Connaught (very formal) and The Grill Room (Georgian-style), both serving a mix of traditional English and French cuisine (see *Restaurant* section). Guests can order excellent room service from the restaurant menus up to 11.30pm, and snacks after that.

The Dorchester

Park Lane, W1A 2HJ
071-629 8888, Fax 071-409 0114
55 stes £330-£1,000, 193 rms S £180-£215, D £215-£240 plus VAT. 30 non-smoking rms. Air cond. Health spa. Restaurants. 24-hr rm service. Ballroom plus 7 banqueting stes.

It is the most spectacular of the great London hotels, but in a discreetly old-fashioned way. The Rolls Royces, Daimlers and stretch Mercedes outside give a hint of the clientele, and celebrities flock here when they want publicity along with tight security and impeccable service and attention. The extensive refurbishment programme has provided the most efficient behind-the-scenes operation—plumbing, heating (and cooling), kitchens and service areas. More to the fore for the visitor, the rooms are now among the best in London. Triple glazed, the large bedrooms have beautiful fabrics and hand-embroidered cushions scattered on the impressive furniture. Bed linen is real linen, and bathrooms are decorated in white Italian marble. Many have separate shower cubicles and twin washbasins. There are call button systems in the rooms for calling valet, maid or waiter room service. And the four roof garden suites, restored to their original patterns, are stunning. The Promenade, just off the lobby, is an elegant meeting space for morning coffee, afternoon tea, cocktails and light snacks. The Oriental Restaurant offers expensive Chinese food in a spectacular décor, and The Grill Room is British. The Terrace is fun for dining with modern French food and dancing to 1940s and 50s bands. The Dorchester Spa offers gym, sauna, steam, massage and beauty treatments and a hairdressers.

Fortyseven Park Street

47 Park St, W1Y 4EB
071-491 7282, Fax 071-491 7281
52 stes £235-£430 plus VAT. CB £12.50, EB £17. Air cond. Business centre. Restaurant. 24-hr rm service. Private dining/meeting rm and lounge area for twenty people.

On a most prestigious Mayfair location, a Relais et Châteaux member and close to the American Embassy and Hyde Park, all suites have dining tables and ensuite kitchens and are ideal for longer stays or for those who need to entertain. Attention to detail in the rooms is noteworthy, with exquisite antiques, interesting fabrics, objets d'art and luxurious bathrooms. Sixty per cent

of the customers are repeat, many of them long-standing Roux brothers fans. The place is run by the celebrated chef, Albert Roux, with his wife, Monique. Their son, Michel, now commands the kitchens at the gourmet restaurant, Le Gavroche. Linked by a corridor, Le Gavroche provides room service meals and private catering. The nearby Grosvenor House health club offers an indoor pool and full spa and fitness facilities.

The Four Seasons Hotel

Hamilton Pl, Park Lane, W1A 1AZ - 071-499 0888, Fax 071-493 6629
26 stes £430-£1,000, 201 rms S £200-£220, D £245 plus VAT. Non-smoking rms on 3 floors. Two rms for disabled. Air cond. Fitness facility. Garage. Restaurants. 24-hr rm service. Ballroom and 4 banqueting stes.

Formerly the Inn on the Park, it was built and is managed by the Canadian-owned Four Seasons Hotels and Resorts, and recently changed its name. The plain façade belies a luxurious interior under the supervision of long-standing manager Ramon Pajares. Views of Hyde Park are soothing. Excellent, large bedrooms are decorated with style with all the expected extras like two telephone lines for the business traveller and comfortable sofas. It has an enviable reputation for professional service and first-rate housekeeping, with baby-listening and baby-sitting services on hand. Of the two restaurants (see *Restaurant*

section for the Four Seasons), Lanes is more relaxed, ideal for late evening, and the fixed-price menus and massive buffet are good. Two bars on the first floor are associated with the restaurants, while the lounge just off the lobby is good for afternoon tea, light meals and drinks. There is a David Morris jewellers.

Inter-Continental Hotel

1 Hamilton Pl, W1V 0QY
071-409 3131, Fax 071-493 3476
42 stes £360-£600, 424 rms S/D £210-£270 plus VAT. CB £11.50, EB £15. Two non-smoking floors. Air cond. Business centre. Fitness facility. Restaurant. 24-hr rm service. Ballroom and 10 function rms.

At the crossroads of Park Lane, Piccadilly and Hyde Park Corner, it is the flagship Inter-Continental property in the UK. Bedrooms are large and comfortable but not ostentatiously decorated. The Coffee House, open throughout the day, has a good view onto the street but is otherwise noteworthy only for its extensive international buffet. The recent refurbishment of the driveway and front entrance, lobby area, ballroom and many function rooms has produced a huge improvement. The business centre is excellent; the fitness facility has a gym and sauna and massages are available.

The Hyatt Carlton Tower

Cadogan Pl, SW1X 9PY
071-235 1234, Fax 071-235 9129
62 stes £350-£2,000, 162 rms £240 plus VAT. 60 non-smoking rms. Air cond. Business centre. Garage. Restaurants. 24-hr rm service. Ballroom and 2 banqueting stes.

The Hyatt Carlton Tower gives 'chain' hotels a good name which translates into individual style, perhaps attributable to the fact that it is located in Belgravia/Knightsbridge, within a stone's throw of the embassy community of Belgravia and the smartest retail area of London. The eighteenth-floor Presidential Suite has wrap-around views, bullet-proof glass, a panic button by the bed and a full-time butler. On the ninth floor you find the Peak health club with state-of-the-art equipment, workout classes and an attractive lounge area for light meals. The Chelsea Room (French) overlooks leafy Cadogan Square, and The Rib Room is one of the best for traditional British beef. Afternoon tea and drinks accompanied by a harpist are fun in the pretty Chinoiserie lounge off the lobby.

The Hyde Park

66 Knightsbridge, SW1Y 7LA - 071-235 2000, Fax 071-235 4552
19 stes £600-£1,500, 167 rms S £195-£275, D £225-£275 plus VAT. CB £11.50, EB £13. 18 non-smoking rms. Air cond. Fitness facility. Restaurant. 24-hr rm service. Ballroom and 23 function rms.

The Hyde Park, with its splendid Edwardian façade, faces Harvey Nichols department store and is very close to Sloane Street and Harrod's. The back and half the bedrooms look out onto Hyde Park itself. A recent restoration includes a major facelift, particularly to the suites, several of which have their own terraces, and the addition of The Restaurant, enfant terrible chef Marco Pierre White's glamorous new lower-ground restaurant (see Restaurant section). Public rooms are gracious with chandeliers, Persian carpets and acres of marble. The afternoon tea is one of London's best, served in the Park Room where the lunch and dinner menu is mainly international, perhaps due to the influence of the general manager, Mr Biscioni.

The Lanesborough

Hyde Park Corner, SW1X 7TA - 071-259 5599, Fax 071-259 5606
46 stes £350-£2,500, 49 rms S £165-£190, D £220-£275 plus VAT. 30 non-smoking rms. Air cond. Restaurant. 24-hr rm and butler service. 4 function rms.

On the site of the former St George's Hospital, the hotel is an imposing new landmark on Hyde Park Corner. Marketed as a country manor house in the heart of central London, it is all large-scale real and reproduction antique furniture, acres of marble and yards of impressive fabric. There can be rather a hushed and reverential atmosphere at times. Rooms are triple glazed and are beautifully furnished. They contain some of the latest equipment, including a Fax machine, all discreetly hidden in the furniture. When guests arrive, they are taken to the room and introduced to a butler who will unpack, pack, run baths, and most importantly, explain the high-tech gadgetry which can be confusing—all in a very traditional British manner. The formal dining room has now been transformed into a banqueting suite. The Conservatory brightens the mood considerably with a rather over-the-top, mock-Oriental theme with massive urns, fountains and trees, particularly quirky for late evening supper dances. The Library buzzes for drinks and light meals, and tea is served in the extremely formal and rather loftily-named Withdrawing Room. Service throughout is faultless if a bit stiff. From personalised stationery and complimentary pressing by a 24-hour butler service on arrival, the package of amenities is commendable. The Royal Suite includes the use of a Bentley and a 24-hour butler.

The Ritz

Piccadilly, W1V 9DG
071-493 8181, Fax 071-493 2687
14 stes £505-£640, 115 rms S £190, D £220-£280 inc VAT. Air cond in stes and executive rms. Restaurant. 24-hr rm service. 3 function rms.

Most people are surprised that the Ritz is no larger than 129 rooms since their international brand name awareness is so strong. Its location, too, at the foot of Bond Street and on the steps of historic

St James's, is ideal. Rooms boast antique furniture, fireplaces, pretty pastels and plush bathrooms. Afternoon tea is a British institution, taken in the stunning setting of the opulent Palm Court. The Louis XIV Restaurant, (generally referred to simply as The Ritz Restaurant), is probably the most beautiful dining room in London, and is classically British in its cooking. There are small shops for jewellery and gifts and guests enjoy fitness membership of the nearby St James's Club.

The Savoy

Strand, WC2R 0EU
071-836 4343, Fax 071-240 6040
48 stes £280-£590, 152 rms S £170, D £195-£260 plus VAT. 50 non-smoking rms. Air cond in most rms. Fitness gallery. Pool. Restaurants. 24-hr rm service. Ballroom and 11 function rms.

The Savoy is best described as an institution and a legend, the feather in the Savoy Group's distinguished cap. Close to both the City and the West End, and within easy walking distance of theatres and Covent Garden, one of its biggest asset is its position facing the Thames and overlooking Embankment Gardens. The bedroom refurbishment scheme is nearly completed, including extravagant bathrooms and art deco décors. The south-facing river-view bedrooms are some of the finest available. Two of the suites were taken by the French Impressionist painter Monet on three separate occasions at three different seasons over

three years. From here he painted the famous bridges series. Since opening in 1889, cuisine has always been emphasised, from, you might say, Escoffier to Edelmann (the current chef). The River Restaurant, overlooking the Thames with dancing in the evening, is formal and old-fashioned. The wood-panelled Grill Room is good for pre-theatre suppers and serious business lunches and offers an extensive wine list. The often-crowded American Bar is good for drinks, while afternoon tea or drinks in the Thames Foyer gives a good chance for people-watching. Upstairs, a Champagne and seafood bar is perched above the entrance drive and ensures a floor-to-ceiling perspective. There is an elegant Fitness Gallery with a swimming pool, massage room, gym and sauna as well as a ladies' and men's hairdresser and beauty treatments. There is also a theatre desk, and the Savoy Theatre is adjacent.

Sheraton Park Tower

101 Knightsbridge, SW1X 7RN - 071-235 8050, Fax 071-235 8231
5 stes £405-£1,200, 280 rms S £205-£270, D £235-£290 plus VAT. CB £9.75, EB £12.75. 4 function rms. 3 non-smoking floors. Air cond. Business centre. Restaurant. 24-hr rm service.

This hotel is in the predictable Sheraton-chain style, but the location is excellent, within ambling distance of the best shops. Efficiency is the key which makes the atmosphere rather functional, but there

are no faults to be found. Beds are large, security is good and housekeeping impeccable. The executive floor service, with butlers, is worth the extra cost. All rooms have wonderful views from the circular tower, though the higher floors are obviously the best. Restaurant 101 is mostly French with some English influence, plus there are two bars and the Rotunda lounge for coffee and tea. Next door the reckless or the seriously rich can play at the independent Park Tower Casino and then take some exercise at the nearby Aquila Health club.

LUXURY

Average room price from £200.

Blakes Hotel

33 Roland Gdns, SW7 3PF
071-370 6701, Fax 071-373 0442
12 stes £475-£575, 40 rms S £125, D £150-£295 inc VAT. 3 non-smoking rms. Air cond in large stes and doubles. Restaurant. 24-hr rm service.

Definitely for travel connoisseurs. Owner Anouska Hempel (aka Lady Weinberg, married to Sir Mark Weinberg, a leading city financier) has created a theatrical setting, befitting her fashion and acting background, in a series of late-Victorian townhouses. The Blakes style is esoteric and highly dramatic with strong themes running through each room's décor, from Biedermeier furniture to black oriental lacquer and a lighter, cosier pineapple motif. There are lots of swagged curtains, trompe l'œil wall treatments and marble in the bathrooms. Room 505 is stunning, with linen, painted floorboards, upholstery, furniture and flowers creating the snowy, all-white canvas. Some might accuse Hempel of over-decoration and fans of minimalism should definitely steer clear. Good in-room amenities, however, include CD and video players. Downstairs, Blakes Restaurant continues Hempel's keen interest in the Orient with Japanese 'Kyoto Country Breakfasts' and an expensive, but beautifully executed, international menu attracting a glamorous clientele.

The Capital

28 Basil St, SW3 1AT
071-589 5171, Fax 071-225 0011
8 stes £270, 40 rms S £157, D £187-£235 plus VAT. CB £9.50, EB £12.50. Air cond. Garage. Restaurant. 24-hr rm service. 2 meeting/private dining rms.

A member of the Relais et Châteaux group, The Capital is just a few steps from Harrod's (delivery of parcels from the store can easily be arranged). They enjoy a high element of returning business travellers; the liveried doorman greets most guests by name. The intimate, pretty, French-inspired restaurant under chef Philip Britten was designed by society stylist Nina Campbell. It offers set-price lunches and a comprehensive wine list supervised by connoisseur and owner David Levin, who also owns L'Hôtel and The Greenhouse Restaurant. His wife, Margaret,

decorated the bedrooms which combine a subtle English country style with Ralph Lauren influences. Guests enjoy fine Egyptian cotton bed-linen, handmade mattresses in the rooms, and lavish marble bathrooms with power showers. Under pinstripe-suited manager Jonathan Orr-Ewing, the service is superbly efficient.

Dukes

St James's Pl, SW1A 1NY
071-491 4840, Fax 071-493 1264
26 stes £330-£605, 38 rms S £185, D £215-£275 inc VAT. CB £8.95, EB £12.50. No air cond, but ceiling fans in all rms. Restaurant. 24-hr rm service. 2 meeting/private dining rms.

Tradition is the key element here in the neighbourhood of St James's, known for its centuries-old shops, tailors and gentlemen's clubs. In a private, very quiet cul-de-sac off St James's Street, this Edwardian building houses an old world, almost clubby and quite masculine hotel. It has a rather formal atmosphere, but excellent service is ensured, particularly from the astute concierge, Thom Broadbent, who has been with the hotel for twenty years. Many rooms have four-poster beds; all are of different shapes and décors with good antiques and marble bathrooms. The Penthouse suite has the bonus of a private roof terrace which can be used for receptions of up to 100 in good weather. There is a lobby sitting room with a fireplace, comfortable sofas and newspapers you can read with your morn-

ing coffee, afternoon tea or drinks. The small cocktail bar, which reputedly makes the best martinis in country, boasts an extensive range of vintage cognacs, while the elegant restaurant focuses on English and French classical food.

Grosvenor House

90 Park Lane, W1A 3AA
071-499 6363, Fax 071-493 3341
72 stes £425-£825, 554 rms S £180, D £195-£425. Some prices inc VAT; more expensive stes inc bfast, rm service dinner, newspapers, minibar, valet service, afternoon tea, express check-in etc, CB £10.25, EB £12.75. Air cond. Garage. Restaurant. 24-hour rm service. 2 ballrooms and 19 function rms.

On the site of the former home of the Duke of Westminster, this is the jewel in Forte Plc's London crown (the group owns eighteen hotels in the capital). Putting it firmly on the hospitality map is the Mayfair address and the enormous ballroom—the Great Room's capacity of 2,000 attracts major balls and art and antiques fairs. Its size makes it slightly impersonal, but bedrooms are large, functional, filled with five-star amenities, and have well-equipped bathrooms. Go to the Crown Club on the fifth floor for executive perks, including a private boardroom. Check in the Restaurant section for the signature dining room, Nico at 90, under Nico Ladenis. Pasta e Fieno is a windowless, serviceable Italian café, while the Pavilion, overlooking Park Lane and Hyde Park, is vast and international, a glitzy version of the obligatory hotel coffee shop. The health club has a pool, gym, sauna and massage.

The Halcyon
81 Holland Park, W11 3RZ
071-727 7288, Fax 071-229 8516
19 stes £275-£550, 24 rms S £165-£185, D £235 inc VAT. CB £9.20, EB £13.80. Air cond. Restaurant. 24-hr rm service. 1 meeting rm.

The celebrity clientele list reads like a Grammy or Oscar awards night—regulars include Tina Turner and Jack Nicholson. It's located away from the centre of town in a classy residential neighbourhood, Holland Park, and is reliably private, discreet and luxuriously appointed. All rooms are furnished with good antiques, some rooms have dramatic designs, and many boast four-poster beds. The Room at The Halcyon, (see *Restaurant* section), features numerous photographs by David Scheiman. The charming walled terrace outside is perfect for intimate al fresco meals in warmer months, while the Vodka bar at the restaurant entrance serves caviar, salmon and lighter meals. On Sunday evening you're entertained by a singer. Guests also have complimentary use of the nearby exclusive Vanderbilt tennis club.

> **Plan to travel?** *Look for* Gault Millau's *other* Best of *guides to Chicago, Florida, France, Germany, Hawaii, Hong Kong, Italy, Los Angeles, New England, New Orleans, New York, Paris, San Francisco, Thailand, Toronto, and Washington, D.C.*

The Halkin
5 Halkin St, SW1X 7DJ
071-333 1000, Fax 071-333 1100
11 stes £325-£425, 30 rms S/D £190-£240 plus VAT. CB £9.50, EB £13.50. Air cond. Restaurant. 24-hr rm service.

One of a kind in London, the stunningly designed hotel is pure Italian, from the minimalist décor to the Giorgio Armani staff uniforms. Chintz has been rejected here in favour of clean, lean lines. Large rooms have bathrooms tucked behind a wall of wood. Rooms boast all the latest techno-gadgetry, from hand-free telephones and remote control lighting to CD players and videos, plus excellent security. The restaurant focuses on modern Italian cuisine and has a handsome adjoining private dining room for parties up to twenty. The bar is adjacent to the lobby.

The Hampshire
31 Leicester Sq, WC2 7LH
071-839 9399, Fax 071-930 8122
5 stes £450-£650, 119 rms S £184, D £220-£281 inc VAT. CB £10.50, EB £13.50. 1 non-smoking floor. Air cond. Business centre. Restaurant. 24-hr rm service. 3 function rms.

For cinema and for theatregoers, or those who thrive on staying in the heart of a city, this is an ideal candidate, for Leicester Square is a non-stop hive of activity with a 24-hour street personality. And the Radisson-Edwardian-owned Hampshire is in the thick of it. Bedrooms are surprisingly pleasant with a rather lavish 'east meets west' décor, although many are too compact. Oscar's Wine Bar is

lively. The Drawing Room is small but good for afternoon tea and provides an invaluable central London meeting place. Suites are spacious, particularly the Penthouse on the seventh floor with its fabulous panoramic views.

The Howard Hotel
Temple Pl, Strand, WC2R 2PR - 071-836 3555, Fax 071-379 4547
28 stes £245-£465, 111 rms S £200, D £226 inc VAT. CB £9.75, EB £13.85. 12 non-smoking rms. Air cond. Restaurant. 24-hr rm service. 5 function rms.

The Howard has one of the lowest profiles of all London's grand hotels, with discretion and privacy the formula for its success among serious captains of industry. Slightly old-fashioned and located on the edge of the City, it is tranquil with sumptuous eighteenth-century decorative touches (friezes, ornate ceilings and marbled pillars). Rooms are equally well done with French marquetry furniture and marble bathrooms. Most have dazzling views of the Thames, and have twin rather than double beds. Le Quai d'Or Restaurant serves classic French haute cuisine and is exceedingly formal. To emphasise the international business appeal, traditional Japanese breakfasts are available at £15.50. The Temple Bar overlooks the pretty, tiered garden area.

The Langham Hilton
1 Regent St, Portland Pl, W1N 3AA - 071-636 1000, Fax 071-323 2340
22 stes £300-£475, 357 rms S £180-£260, D £200-£275

plus VAT. CB £11.50, EB £14.50. Non-smoking floor. 2 rms for disabled. Air cond. Business centre. Fitness facility. Restaurants. 24-hr rm service. Ballroom and 12 function rms.

Originally opened in 1865, the Langham played a key role in London society of the day—Oscar Wilde, Toscanini and Mark Twain were once guests—and now, due in part to its close proximity to the BBC opposite, it continues to draw an intriguing crowd of celebrities. Its reconstruction recently after serving for decades as the headquarters of the BBC is impressive, with marble floors and pillars in public areas, a peach-toned décor and American red oak furniture and fittings in guest rooms. Executive rooms and suites include English breakfast and a complimentary bar. The Memories of the Empire restaurant has an 'east meets west' menu of British classics and international influences, including Californian/Chinese, while Tsar's, decorated in rich royal Russian greens and golds, is a dark and enigmatic bar, serving 107 types of vodka, caviar, seafood and boasting one of the most comprehensive collections of Louis Roederer Champagne in the world. The Chukka bar's polo scenes and equipment are suitably sporty, and it is packed in the early evening and popular for luncheon buffets. The Palm Court is open 24 hours a day for light refreshments, drinks and afternoon tea. Apart from the usual sauna, gym, steam room, solarium, hair

and beauty salon, shop and theatre desk, there is, surprisingly, a small private garden.

London Hilton on Park Lane

22 Park Lane, W1A 2HH
071-493 8000, Fax 071-493 4957
54 stes £300-£1,150, 391 rms S/D £185-£280 plus VAT. CB £12.95, EB £14.95. 4 floors of non-smoking rms. Air cond. Business centre. Restaurants. 24-hr rm service. Ballroom and 12 function rms.

The combination of its Park Lane location and the talented management of Rudi Jagersbacher makes this large hotel work beautifully. Bedrooms, though standardised, are a good size and the de-luxe rooms have pretty light furniture and good fabrics and furnishings. The 28th floor Windows on the World restaurant which serves a reputable buffet lunch and holds amusing dinner dances nightly, has the best view in town—a panorama of Hyde Park, Buckingham Palace and the rooftops of Mayfair and beyond. The famed Hilton efficiency is comforting. Six floors of executive rooms have their own private check-in, a clubby lounge area and business centre. The café/brasserie is functional, St George's bar is only fit for sporting enthusiasts with its six-foot TV screen, but Trader Vic's Polynesian décor and menu is amusing and good value.

Prices for rooms and suites are per room, not per person.

May Fair Inter-Continental

Stratton St, W1A 2AN
071-629 7777, Fax 071-629 1459
51 stes £320-£1,100, 236 rms S £185, D £195-£250 plus VAT. CB £11, EB £13. 1 non-smoking floor. Air cond. Business centre. Health club. Restaurants. 24-hr rm service. 3 function rms plus the May Fair Theatre, for up to 300.

The personality of charming general manager Dagmar Woodward makes this a very personal hotel, full of enthusiastic, professional staff. There are innovative culinary promotions in the restaurants throughout the year, particularly in Le Château, which despite its name, serves a mainly English menu and a good luncheon buffet. It is very clubby and has celebrity pics on the walls. The May Fair Café is a typical all-day hotel restaurant. Bedrooms are comfortable and well equipped if furnished a little predictably by the Inter-Continental chain. Small spa health club boasts a gym, solarium and pool.

Le Méridien

21 Piccadilly, W1V 0BH
071-734 8000, Fax 071-437 3574
50 stes £275-£600, 186 rms S £200, D £215 plus VAT. CB £9.75, EB £12.95. 2 non-smoking floors. Air cond. Business centre. Health club. Pool. Restaurants. 24-hr rm service. 7 function rms.

Le Méridien's Piccadilly Circus location is one of the best addresses in London. Bedrooms benefited from a comprehensive refurbishment programme a couple of years ago and are now awash in pastel pinks and turquoise, good reproduction furniture and chic bathrooms. Delightful afternoon tea in the lounge features a harpist and 40 blends of tea. The formal Oak Room is opulent and grand, with carved wood panelling, a fine French menu and impeccable service. The summery Terrace Garden Restaurant with its glass conservatory ceiling is ideal for grills and light meals and overlooks Piccadilly from the fourth floor. Only the Burlington Bar is a little dark. There is a stunning Champneys health facility with gym, pool, squash court, massage and beauty treatments.

The Milestone

1 Kensington Ct, W8 5DL
071-917 1000, Fax 071-917 1010
36 stes £250-£375, 20 rms S £180, D £210 inc VAT. CB £9.50, EB £13.50. Air cond. Fitness facility. Restaurant. 24-hr rm service.

An attractive Victorian façade decorates this very grand late nineteenth-century former private residence which has excellent views of Kensington Palace just opposite. It is also conveniently close to the Knightsbridge shops. Several of the stunning split-level suites and many of the rooms have king-size four-poster beds. All the rooms are spacious and graciously appointed with beautiful antique furniture. As a listed building, the restoration has been meticulously done according to English Heritage standards, which means original fireplaces, carved wood panelling, high ceilings and large ornate windows. Guests also enjoy very attentive, personal service from the staff. There is 24-hour service both in the Park Lounge and the Stables Bar (originally the carriage house). Cheneston's restaurant serves an international menu with the emphasis on healthy Californian cuisine.

The Regent London

222 Marylebone Rd, NW1 6JQ - 071-631 8000, Fax 071-631 8080
49 stes £280-£800, 260 rms S £160-£180, D £210-£255 plus VAT. CB £10.50, EB £14. Two non-smoking floors. Air cond. Business centre. Fitness facility. Pkg. Restaurant. 24-hr rm service. Ballroom and 9 function rms.

A landmark building (Grade II listed) and former great railway hotel (it is adjacent to Marylebone Station), this grand Victorian Gothic architectural landmark was restored to re-open in 1993. The eight-storey central atrium is its most stunning feature, housing the enormous Winter Garden restaurant/lounge (see *Restaurant* section). Similarly, the rooms, in a beige neutral palette, are among the largest in London and exceptionally well-equipped. The dining room is open throughout the day and is extremely good indeed, a fact not known by a large number of Londoners, let alone visitors. More casual is The Cellars bar with a hot snack menu. The fitness facility has a small pool, sauna, steam room, massage and gym.

Sheraton Belgravia

20 Chesham Pl, SW1X 8HQ
071-235 6040, Fax 071-259 6243
7 stes £300-£415, 82 rms S £175-£245, D £195-£265 plus VAT. Express bfast £6, CB £9.50, EB £11.75. 2 non-smoking floors. Air cond. Business centre. Restaurant. 24-hr rm service. 2 function rms.

Distinctively personal service right from the moment of check-in, seated at an antique leather desk in the lobby with a glass of Champagne, it's hard to imagine the hotel as part of the largest chain in the world. General manager Moyra Beaves is obsessive about detail and runs a tight, professional ship. Bedrooms are smallish but filled with amenities, even if it means the sofa is crammed into a corner. Chesham's Restaurant is a pleasant surprise with a continental cuisine under a French chef who changes the menu daily. A friendly bar is an extension of the lobby with little nooks and crannies for private drinks or afternoon tea.

The Stafford

St James's Pl, SW1A 1NJ
071-493 0111, Fax 071-493 7121
17 stes £290-£430, 57 rms S £184, D £200-£215 inc VAT. CB £8.75, EB £12. 6 non-smoking rms. Air cond in best stes. Restaurant. 24-hr rm service. 4 function rms, including the lower ground wine cellars.

Used as a club for American and Canadian overseas officers in World War II, anecdotes pepper its history. The narrow, dead-end street, discreetly tucked behind St James's, also houses Spencer House, a former home of ancestors of the Princess of Wales. The general ambience is of a refined country house, particularly with the conversion into suites of the original stables of St James's Palace. Rooms are individually furnished, in keeping with the traditional style and fabrics and furnishings are good. An expansive private terrace graces the Terrace Garden suite. The formal restaurant is very pretty, has a reputable wine list and serves a good traditional Sunday lunch from the trolley. Charles has been head barman at the American Bar for 36 years now and has made it into a convenient, convivial luncheon spot or pre-theatre rendezvous point. Crammed with ties, caps and badges, its décor is rather quirky.

FIRST-CLASS

Average room price from £180.

The Athenaeum
116 Piccadilly, W1V 0BJ 071-499 3464, Fax 071-493 1860
16 stes, 107 rms. Price range from £165-£210 plus VAT. Air cond. Valet pkg. Restaurant. 24-hr rm service. 4 conference rms.

At the time of going to press, this prestigious hotel is being totally refurbished following a change of ownership. The goal is a five-star deluxe property. Rooms are being re-constructed to make them larger, furnished in traditional English style (classic rather than chintz) and will have state-of-the-art technology as well as the usual two

telephone lines and VCRs. The pretty lounge which is good for morning coffee or afternoon tea remains but is totally redecorated, the famous bar will continue to stock its 56 different malt whiskys and the restaurant under chef David Marshall will be less formal than before.

Britannia Inter-Continental
Grosvenor Sq, W1A 3AN 071-629 9400, Fax 071-629 7736
14 stes £375-£500, 303 rms S/D £170-£210 plus VAT. CB £8.05, EB £10.75. Air cond. Business centre. Restaurants. 24-hr rm service. 4 function rms.

Popular with local embassies and consulates, the hotel is in the centre of Mayfair facing Grosvenor Square. Superior double rooms are spacious and well-equipped, many with separate stand-up bars, extra seating and massive, luxurious bathrooms. The Adams restaurant serves modern British cuisine, the Best of Both Worlds café has a respectable Anglo-American hot and cold buffet, and the Shogun Japanese restaurant is a good sushi bar. There is also a pub called the Waterloo Dispatch, named after the announcement of victory at Waterloo on the site; the traditional Pine piano bar is for drinks only and there is a cocktail lounge. You can shop in the Georgian shopping arcade at the florist, confectioner and menswear shop.

Prices for rooms and suites are per room, not per person.

Brown's
30-34 Albemarle St, W1A 4SW - 071-493 6020, Fax 071-493 9381
6 stes £245-£400, 114 rms S £165-£175, D £180-£215 plus VAT. CB £11,75, EB £13.75. Non-smoking rms. Air cond. Restaurant. 24-hr rm service. 6 function rms.

There is a quiet revolution going on here since new management took over the day-to-day running of this Forte Plc flagship, and changes look promising. All rooms have been refurbished and many re-configured, eliminating the poky singles and upgrading the bathrooms. And the exceptional Forte housekeeping standards remain. Its two entrances, one in Stratton Street and one in Albemarle Street, provide many anecdotes—allegedly one was for unaccompanied 'ladies' to enter the hotel while regular guests used the other. Brown's Restaurant is formal, serving classical English and French food. But afternoon tea with raisin tea scones in the chintz-filled lounge is a treat not to be missed, nor is the more substantial late afternoon high tea, with grills and fish cakes.

The Churchill Inter-Continental
30 Seymour St, Portman Sq, W1A 4ZX - 071-486 5800, Fax 071-486 1255
37 stes £240-£450, 413 rms S £135-£170, D £145-£185 plus VAT. CB £9.50, EB £12.50. 1 non-smoking floor. Air cond. Business centre. Restaurant. 24-hr rm service. 2 function rms.

A major refurbishment from top-to-toe following the award of the management contract to Inter-Continental means a freshening of everything from carpets and furnishings to the creation of several small meeting rooms in a smart new business centre. Décor in the rooms adopts the British liking of non-matching fabrics and colours, which can be a bit of a jumble in smaller rooms. Clementine's Restaurant (named after Churchill's wife) also received much-needed attention. Now elegantly decorated with warm wood panelling, contemporary British art and nattily striped chairs, the food under chef Idris Caldora is modern Mediterranean. The Club Inter-Continental on the eighth floor has its own check-in, concierge and lounge. The Churchill Bar is a place you can sink into, with deep, club-like leather sofas, myriad Churchill prints and memorabilia and the air of an interesting private study. There is also a spacious lounge next to the lobby for afternoon tea and informal drinks.

The Conrad

Chelsea Harbour, SW10 0XG - 071-823 3000, Fax 071-351 6525
160 stes S £135-£195, D £150-£210 plus VAT. CB £14, EB £16. 1 non-smoking rm floor. Air cond. Fitness facility. Restaurant. 24-hr rm service. 13 function rms.

Applause on three counts—the mesmerising views of Chelsea Harbour with bobbing boats, the fact that all rooms are suites with a separate sitting area, and the influence of a dynamic female general manager, Doreen Boulding. Many people joke

about its inaccessible location, but Marco Pierre White's The Canteen and the Viscount Linley-owned Deals in the same complex have proved extremely successful. Room décor is rather dull, but the Thames is on your doorstep to divert your gaze. The Brasserie and adjacent Drake's Bar come alive on Sundays with excellent jazz buffet brunches (the £28.50 price includes Champagne). Fitness facility includes a gym, pool, steam bath, sauna, massage, and there is a gift shop.

Lowndes Hyatt

Lowndes St, SW1X 9ES
071-823 1234, Fax 071-235 1154
5 stes £275-£400, 73 rms S/D £180 plus VAT. CB £8.25, EB £10.25. 2 non-smoking floors. Air cond. Restaurant. 24-hr rm service. 1 meeting rm.

Very un-Belgravia and definitely un-Hyatt, this intimate, unstuffy, well-run and friendly hotel feels more like a private hotel than part of an international chain. Bedrooms are decorated in attractive blues, greens and pinks and are surprisingly spacious. Brasserie 21—informal with its own bar and a French based, but international menu—has super al fresco tables in summer. If you prefer, you can charge at the restaurants of the neighbouring giant, the Hyatt Carlton Tower. And just next door, the Halkin Arcade is full of shops selling good art, antiques and design.

Prices for rooms and suites are per room, not per person.

The Park Lane Hotel

Piccadilly, W1Y 8EB
071-499 6321, Fax 071-499 1965
46 stes £248.87-£587.50, 274 rms S £152.75-£176.25, D £205.62 inc VAT. CB £9.95, EB £12.95. 1 non-smoking floor. Half the rms air cond. Business centre. Restaurants. 24-hr rm service. Ballroom and 7 function rms.

The Park Lane's extensive refurbishment programme has been working from top to bottom; enquire as to progress at check-in. Rooms are all double glazed and furnished in an appropriately traditional style. All the suites look over the central court or Green Park. At Bracewell's Restaurant, the menu is a mix of French and English, and is formal, pricey and traditional. Its eponymous bar is quite clubby, and the expansive Palm Court Lounge makes a good rendezvous for afternoon tea, light snacks and drinks. The Brasserie on the Park is a modern coffee shop which has occasional worthy food and wine promotions. The men's hair salon is particularly good and the Daniele Ryman shop sells aromatherapy products, including excellent anti-jet lag potions.

The Selfridge

Orchard St, W1H 0JS
071-408 2080, Fax 071-629 8849
2 stes £350, 294 rms S £135-£145, D £150-£295 inc VAT. CB £7.25, EB £10.25. 2 non-smoking floors. Air cond. Business centre. Restaurant. 24-hr rm service. 2 function stes.

Shopaholics will appreciate its proximity to Oxford Street and famous

Selfridge's department store. The approach and driveway are impressive and the busy public rooms are attractive. Bedrooms are adequate and well-equipped, functional rather than luxurious, though housekeeping standards are good. There's a club-like feel to the first floor where you find a chintz-filled central lounge for tea, light meals and drinks and the next-door Fletcher's restaurant (modern English with a French influence). Also here are the Stoves Bar and the Orchard Terrace, an informal brasserie open from breakfast through dinner.

The Westbury
Conduit St, W1A 4UH
071-629 7755, Fax 071-495 1163
19 stes £260-£350, 244 rms S £125-£185, D £145-£185 inc VAT. CB £11.50, EB £11.50. 1 non-smoking floor. Air cond. Free pkg. Restaurants. 24-hr rm service. 4 function rms.

Named after the Long Island Polo Ground in New York and built by a keen polo player (Michael Phipps), the Westbury was opened in 1955. Its enviable location just steps from Bond Street and by the back door of Sotheby's, attracts a well-heeled clientele who love the Mayfair patch. Bedrooms are elegant with dark wood furniture and pretty floral touches, though sizes can vary from box-like to spacious. The Polo Restaurant (also known as the Westbury Grill) serves international fare, the Polo Lounge is open 24 hours for breakfast, lunch, afternoon tea and drinks,

and the Polo Bar serves drinks. Guests can use the nearby Metropolitan Club with its gym, sauna, aerobics classes and pool.

CHARMING TOWNHOUSE

Average room price £110 upwards.

The Basil Street Hotel
Basil St, SW3 1AH
071-581 3311, Fax 071-581 3693
1 ste £238.20, 91 rms S £59-£110.50, D £90.30-£133 inc VAT. CB £5.50, EB £10.60. Restaurant. 24-hr rm service. 3 small meeting rms.

Privately owned, this small central hotel just yards from Harrod's was built in 1910 and although filled with antiques, rich carpets, tapestries and objets d'art, has a very liveable feel. Compared to most Knightsbridge hotels, it exudes an easy, comfortable and charming personality. Each room is a different size, shape, décor and mood, with lots of interesting nooks and crannies. Basil's Wine Bar is charming and apart from the upstairs carvery and salad bar, the women-only Parrot Club is a wonderful retreat for female guests and outsiders and available all day for tea, a glass of Champagne, light meals and snacks.

The Beaufort
33 Beaufort Gdns, SW3 1PP
071-584 5252, Fax 071-589 2834
B&B 7 stes £250, 21 rms S £115, D £130-£225 inc VAT.

Air cond. Modest rm service menu. No restaurant.

Housed in a tree-lined residential square, and ideally situated just 100 yards away from Harrod's and Knightsbridge, this privately owned hotel is unusually decorated with hundreds of original, English, twentieth-century floral water-colours. They set the tone for the individually designed rooms, with their mix of English country house chintz and wood. Prices very generously include breakfast and any drinks from the 24-hour bar, in addition to unlimited food from the modest room service menu like soups, sandwiches and salads, tax, service and membership at the local Nell Gwynn health club.

Cannizaro House
West Side, Wimbledon Common, SW19 4UF
081-879 1464, Fax 081-879 7338
3 stes £225-£320, 42 rms S £105-£125, D £120-£175 inc VAT. CB £6.95, EB £9.75. Year-round weekend tariff £55 per person inc EB (Fri-Sun nights). 5 non-smoking rms. Restaurant. 24-hr rm service. 5 function rms.

Officially in the suburbs, Wimbledon is really a smart, upmarket neighbourhood and a wonderful location for this graceful Georgian mansion on the edge of Wimbledon Common, surrounded by pretty Cannizaro Park. Cannizaro House is close to charming Wimbledon Village with its designer boutiques, trendy restaurants, tea shops and riding stables. Though slightly inaccessible to central London, the place is ideal for a retreat, small conference or pleasant experience of local 'village' life. Bedrooms display a tasteful mix of antique and reproduction furniture, but try to book in the original section of the building where the rooms are larger. The executive rooms boast four-poster beds. Public rooms resemble country house drawing rooms with comfortable couches, fireplaces and huge floral arrangements. The international menu in the restaurant is strong on fish and game, and Sunday lunch followed by a stroll on the common is popular. Summertime evening concerts in the park arranged by the local council are a treat. Inevitably, the hotel is packed during Wimbledon tennis fortnight.

Dorset Square
39/40 Dorset Sq, NW1 6QN
071-723 7874, Fax 071-724 3328
1 ste £165, 36 rms S £90-£100, D £110-£155 inc VAT. CB £7.50, EB £9.50. Air cond in some rms. Restaurant. 24-hr rm service.

A former pair of Regency residences, Dorset Square is intimate and stylish, sister to the Pelham Hotel, evoking the same kind of quiet, country house hotel mood with its pretty drawing rooms with cosy fireplaces. Lots of chintz, swagging, tapestry cushions piled on the beds, good antiques and bountiful floral touches. Private gardens—the original Lord's cricket ground—are accessible to guests, and are particularly pleasant for summertime drinks. There's a small private basement restaurant.

The Draycott
24-26 Cadogan Gdns, SW3 2RP - 071-739 6466, Fax 071-730 0236
25 rms S/D £100-£250 inc VAT. Bkfst £7.95-£10.95. 24-hr rm service. No restaurant.

From the outside, the Draycott looks like a private residence. Inside, it is prettily decorated with antiques and has two delightful public ground-floor rooms, a small library-type room at the front and a large drawing room at the back overlooking gardens which is just right for afternoon tea. Bedrooms vary in size and can be quite small; all are decorated with antiques and paintings and have good bathrooms with Penhaligon toiletries. They do have concierge, Fax and limousine and nanny service available twenty-four hours, though no restaurant. Service can be a little brusque. Guests have free use of the nearby Synergy Centre Health club and the Vanderbilt tennis club.

Durrants
George St, W1H 6BJ
071-935 8131, Fax 071-487 3510
3 stes £185, 93 rms S £60-£80, D £88-£99 inc VAT. CB £5.50, EB £8.25. Restaurant. 24-hr rm service. 3 function rms.

A good and unusual location north of Oxford Street, between Baker Street and Marylebone, and just off Manchester Square where you can browse through the fabulous Wallace Collection, Durrants is a refurbished series of Georgian townhouses giving the overall impression of a clubby, very English welcome. However some rooms are small and a few do not have private bathrooms, so take care when booking. But the staff make up for any shortcomings (it has been family-run for more than 70 years). Durrants Restaurant is informal with a fairly standard international menu selection. The George Bar is popular with residents. Amazingly, their rates have remained the same for three years.

Egerton House
Egerton Terr, SW3 2BX
071-589 2412, Fax 071-584 6540
1 ste £210, 28 rms S £100-£110, D £135-£170 plus VAT. CB £7.50, EB £12.50. Air cond. 24-hr rm service. No restaurant.

A small luxury townhouse true to its description, Egerton House is privately owned by the charming David Naylor Leyland and located in the heart of Knightsbridge. Spread over four floors, its rooms embody the English country house genre, yet it is at the same time unstuffy and intimate. But there is no stinting on luxury, with most rooms overlooking private gardens and all with marble bathrooms. Sensible pricing is its chief allure, particularly noting its proximity to Harrod's, the Beauchamp Place designer shops and the South Kensington museums. An attractive drawing room and study is an ideal venue for afternoon tea or drinks. A dining room downstairs is available for meetings or private dinners up to twenty and is used as a breakfast room.

The Fenja

69 Cadogan Gdns, SW3 2RB
071-589 7333, Fax 071-581
4958
*14 rms £130-£195 inc VAT.
CB £7.25, EB £11.75. 24-hr
snack rm service menu. No
bar or restaurant. 1 small
meeting rm.*

Each room is named after a famous English writer or painter who lived in the area—Rossetti, Belloc, Turner, Jane Austin, Sargent, Augustus John and Whistler. Traditionally furnished with good, bold colours, original pictures, marble busts and a good collection of paintings and prints by eighteenth- and nineteenth-century English artists are scattered throughout the well-sized bedrooms. A nice touch is a drinks tray in each room, equipped with full glass decanters. The Fenja, handily located mid-way between Sloane Square and Knightsbridge, overlooks private Cadogan Gardens which are accessible to guests. It has a very restful, relaxed atmosphere, more like a private house than an hotel, and there is a pretty sitting room. Smoking is not encouraged.

The Franklin

28 Egerton Gdns, SW3 2BD
071-584 5533, Fax 071-584
5449
*4 stes £210, 36 rms S £85-
£135, D £100-£210 plus
VAT. CB £7.50, EB £12.50.
Air cond. 24-hr rm service.
No restaurant.*

In the same private ownership as Egerton House and situated around the corner, the Franklin overlooks a tranquil, leafy garden square. All rooms have tasteful antique furnishings, original oil paintings, traditional fabrics and marble bathrooms, and many boast four-poster beds. The drawing room has a small bar and opens directly onto the garden. Staff are extraordinarily friendly and professional, particularly manager Andrew Phillips who is always on hand to greet guests. The breakfast room is also available as a private function room for up to 20 people.

The Gallery Hotel

8-10 Queensberry Pl, SW7
2EA - 071-915 0000, Fax
071-915 4400
*2 stes £150, 18 rms S/D
£106 inc VAT. CB £7.95, EB
£12. Air cond in public rms
only. Small rm service menu
during day. No restaurant. 1
private meeting/dining rm for
up to 20 people.*

One of London's newest townhouse hotels, the Gallery was originally two Georgian private residences and has been meticulously restored. Close to South Kensington tube station and the museums, its individually designed bedrooms are wonderfully luxurious and many boast private patios. There is a clubby atmosphere in the bar which is ideal for drinks, afternoon tea and light snacks.

The Gore

189 Queen's Gate, SW7 5EX
071-584 6601, Fax 071-589
8127
*6 stes £188-£225, 48 rms S
£98-£109, D £136-£149 inc
VAT. CB £5.75, EB approx
£10. Restaurants. Day-time
rm service. 1 function rm.*

The slightly more sophisticated big sister of Hazlitt's still keeps its bohemian edge with an intelligent, interesting staff, quirky atmospheric décor such as lived-in-look antiques, well-worn Oriental rugs and a fascinating collection of art on the walls, and an air of comfortable decadence. Club rooms have four-poster beds and the room to beg for is the Tudor Room. In a wide avenue of lesser hotels and minor embassies, The Gore stands out on both personality and the quality of its restaurants, Bistrot 190 for breakfast through dinner (7am-10.30am) and the all-fish Downstairs at 190, both orchestrated by Anthony Worrall Thompson, the ubiquitous chef. The Green Room, ideal for drinks or a leisurely break, is a residents' only lounge.

Hazlitt's

6 Frith St, Soho Sq, W1V 5TZ
071-434 1771, Fax 071-439
1524
*1 ste £151, 22 rms S £95, D
£115 plus VAT. CB £5.95.
Day-time rm service menu.
No restaurant.*

Quirky is the best way to describe this bohemian Soho haunt. Once owned by painter-turned-essayist William Hazlitt, born in 1778, all the rooms are named after eighteenth- and early nineteenth-century residents or visitors to the house like Jonathan Swift, Sir Charles Lamb and the Duke of Portland. There are creaky stairs, walls jammed with period pictures, antiques, lots of mahogany, oak and pine, and a general atmosphere of old-fashioned charm and character in this listed building. Rooms vary in size and standards with dark furnishings. Being in the middle of Soho, the clientele is mainly film and music celebrities, but of the low-key sort. Most request specific favourite rooms. They serve an excellent continental breakfast with noteworthy croissants and good coffee. The residents' sitting room is open for light refreshments but there is no liquor license. Nor is there a restaurant, although that would be superfluous; Hazlitt's is located in Soho's premier dining street.

L'Hôtel
28 Basil St, SW3 1AS
071-589 6286, Fax 071-225 0011
1 ste £145, 11 rms S/D £125 inc VAT and CB (in rm or Le Métro). No restaurant.

Just 100 meters from Harrod's in a residential street, rooms may seem small but they are fully-equipped and charmingly decorated in a rural French style. More like an up-market bed and breakfast hotel, it has a welcoming *pension* ambience and the staff treat guests like members of an extended family. The same couple own the more lavish Capital Hotel next door where the bar and restaurant are open to L'Hôtel's guests. Some rooms have coal fire-places. The bustling Le Métro wine bar below carries a full menu from croissants and coffee in the morning to late-evening suppers.

Number Eleven
11 Cadogan Gdns, SW3 2RJ
071-730 3426, Fax 071-730 5217
5 stes £200-£350, 47 rms S £89-£119, D £132-£172 inc service and VAT. CB £8, EB

£10. 24-hr rm service. No restaurant. 2 conference rms.

Number Eleven was one of the first townhouse hotels, and remains quite delightfully old-fashioned. Rooms, which can be small, are being up-graded, as are bathrooms. The Garden Suite has a splendid large drawing room with grand plaster ceiling and many rooms overlook the gardens. The public drawing room is cosy, with a pretty conservatory off the back, and excellent for tea in front of the roaring fire in wintertime. They are affiliated with the health club, Synergy, N°1 Cadogan Gardens which was originally the home of the American Club in the 40s and 50s (see Health & Fitness Clubs section). In keeping with the area, and the *pied-à-terre* feeling, there is a chauffeured Rolls Royce available.

Number Sixteen
16 Sumner Pl, SW7 3EG
071-589 5232, Fax 071-584 8615
36 rms S £55-£95, D £85-£135 inc VAT and CB (served

in the rm). Tea and coffee available all day. No children under 12. No restaurant.

A pristine façade fronts a series of restored early Victorian townhouses in the heart of South Kensington. The ample-sized rooms feature attractive chintz-covered furniture and include many antiques. Small and intimate, it feels like a private home and is used by many guests as a London *pied-à-terre*. The comfortable drawing room has a fireplace, and an incredibly trusting honour system operates in the library bar. A conservatory opens onto the secluded walled garden. Three-quarters of the clientele are regulars with a high level of business people.

The Pelham
15 Cromwell Pl, SW7 2LA
071-589 8288, Fax 071-584 8444
3 stes £225-£260, 34 rms S £115, D £140-£165 inc VAT. CB £8.50, EB £12.50. Air cond. Restaurant. 24-hr rm

Big Ben

Two stories surround the naming of Big Ben, the huge clock and bell in St Stephen's Tower in the Houses of Parliament. During a debate on the naming of this national symbol in the mid-nineteenth century, the large Chief Commissioner of Works, Sir Benjamin Hall was speaking, when an MP piped up 'Why not Big Ben?' The second story is that it was named after a popular Boxer, Benjamin Caunt, the publican of the Coach and Horses in St Martin's Lane who weighed eighteen stone. Knowing the British love of sport, the latter is probably the case.

service. *2 small private meeting rms.*

Opened in 1989, The Pelham is owned by Kit and Tim Kemp who have a keen design eye for the English country house genre. The overall effect is cosy and stylish, from the profusion of flower arrangements (both fresh and creatively dried) and traditional floral prints to fine original antiques and inviting four-poster beds, some with matching teddy bear. Lots of ornaments like clocks, vases, pot pourri and objets d'art are fun, but may make some feel claustrophobic. Bathrooms are attractive and well equipped and concessions to the twentieth century are gently concealed—mini-bars and TVs are hidden under chintz covered tables.

Pembridge Court Hotel
34 Pembridge Gdns, W2 4DX - 071-229 9977, Fax 071-727 4982
B&B 20 rms S £85-£115, D £130-£150 inc VAT. Air cond in some rms. Restaurant. 24-hr rm service for light snacks and drinks.

Privately owned by charming Paul and Merete Capra, who are also restaurateurs (their downstairs restaurant Caps serves mostly Thai food), here is a restored nineteenth-century house facing a quiet, tree-lined garden and located in the Notting Hill area, close to Portobello Road. Bedrooms vary in size, some singles can be small, but the rooms on the top-floor are spacious. Bathrooms have Italian tiles and are well-equipped. Many of the antiques and objets d'art including a large number of fans and the Victoriana in the rooms are from nearby antique shops. The long-standing staff are fiercely loyal, which translates into an excellent, very personal service. Two ginger house cats—called Spencer and Churchill—complete the homely appeal. The décor of Caps restaurant focuses on sporting memorabilia and school caps and is equally informal.

Pippa Pop-ins
430 Fulham Rd, SW6 1DU 071-385 2458, Fax 071-385 5706
Overnight £25 Sun-Thurs, £30 Fri, Sat inc VAT (weekend fee per child of £130); maximum stay 3 nights. 5 large bedrooms accommodate up to 12 children.

Heaven for both parents and children! This bright west London Georgian townhouse specialises in accommodation for children only (aged two to twelve) and presents a loving, fun-filled environment under Montessori-influenced professional supervision. That means toys galore (teddy bears, clowns, games) for both education and play, and when it's fine a large private garden area. Arrival late afternoon, pick-up next day late morning, the package includes home-cooked suppers and breakfasts, magic bubble-baths in the duck and clown bathroom, eight o'clock midnight feasts and bed-time stories. There are night lights and baby alarm intercoms in each room, and security is tight. Open for proper nursery school during the week in term time, the service is also available for hourly baby-sitting (£6), half-days (£22) and full-days (£35).

The Portobello Hotel
22 Stanley Gdns, W11 2NG 071-727 2777, Fax 071-792 9641
B&B 7 stes £170, 18 rms S £70-£85, D £100-£120 inc VAT. 6 rms air cond. Restaurant. Daytime rm service.

Two elegant, six-storey Victorian terraced houses in Kensington were merged to create this eclectic hotel, with many rooms overlooking a delightful private garden. Their smallest rooms are very small (but very inexpensive); other rooms have individual décors, some with delightful floor-to-ceiling windows. Not far from Portobello market, it is also a short, pleasant walk away from Kensington Gardens and Holland Park. Extra touches include goose-down duvets, 24-hour breakfasts and lavish room interiors. Sometimes described as a 'sexy' hotel, it appeals to visiting rock stars and celebrities, and one attic room with sloping ceilings boasts a mirror over the bed. The informal restaurant/bar is open 24 hours. The owners also manage the extremely popular Julie's Restaurant and Wine Bar in nearby Portland Road.

The Sloane Hotel
29 Draycott Pl, SW3 2SH 071-581 5757, Fax 071-584 1348
4 stes £170, 6 rms D £110-£150 plus VAT. CB £6, EB £9.

Air cond. 24-hr rm service. No restaurant.

Tucked away near the King's Road and Sloane Square, The Sloane Hotel is the epitome of intimacy and an absolute gem. The lavish décors are transportable, too—in other words, you can buy most of the antiques from the bedrooms! The owners are inveterate collectors and treat the hotel as if decorating a private residence. The unusual interior design features vintage Vuitton cases, period military uniforms, beautiful carriage clocks, leopard print fabrics, extravagant canopied beds and antique lace. The mix of old and modern is ably executed with well-appointed bathrooms, and all suites are split-level with a separate sitting area. Manager Rebecca Maxwell is a disarming combination of efficiency and charm. From the roof-top reception room and terrace, available for breakfast, light meals, afternoon tea or drinks, guests have mesmerising views of the Chelsea neighbourhood.

Swiss Cottage Hotel
4 Adamson Rd, NW3 3HP
071-722 2281, Fax 071-483 4588
82 rms B&B S £73-£130, D £85-£140 inc VAT. Restaurant. Banqueting/conference rm.

A pretty hotel near Swiss Cottage underground station in terraced houses, rooms are small and well-furnished, and as is the way with small hotels, there are numerous corridors and passages. But there is a delightful and gracious old-fashioned drawing room furnished with antiques and the view over the surrounding residential streets is leafy and restful. A good alternative to central London.

Sydney House Hotel
9-11 Sydney St, SW3 6PU
071-376 7711, Fax 071-376 4233
2 stes £150, 19 rms S/D £90-£130 plus VAT. CB £6.50, EB £9.50, Sydney House bfast £11. Air cond. 24-hr rm service. No restaurant. Small private bfast and meeting rm.

Sydney House Hotel is situated between the King's Road and Fulham Road, in very trendy quarters indeed and close to the Brompton Cross intersection for shopping and restaurants. In a restored parade of mid-nineteenth-century townhouses, it is managed by the affable Swiss owner Jean-Luc Aeby. Each room is individually designed and has unusual details, rich colours and textures, creating a subdued modern mood. Noteworthy are the Chinese Leopard room with Biedermeier furniture, the Royale room with its gilded four-poster bed, the Penthouse with a large terrace, the Paris room with rich reds and toile de Jouy and the more traditional, pretty Wedgwood Blue room. Attentive service adds to the intimate atmosphere.

22 Jermyn Street
22 Jermyn St, SW1Y 6HL
071-734 2353, Fax 071-734 0750
13 stes £205-£240, 5 rms S/D £155 plus VAT. CB £9.50, EB approx £13. 24-hour rm service & take away service from Green's Restaurant & Oyster Bar. No restaurant.

Very much like home as you wish it could be! 22 Jermyn Street is one of London's best private hotel secrets and you could quite easily pass it by in Jermyn Street, for discretion is the key here. No glittering signs, no feathered valets, no shining Rolls Royces will give you any clue as to what is inside. Owner Henry Togna has reshuffled this family property—superbly located near Piccadilly Circus and in historic St James's—into an hotel of charming suites and studios. Here you experience affordable elegance with antique furniture and granite bathrooms, and gracious but friendly service. The desks are the best-equipped in town, with every conceivable staple, paper clip and notepad, as well as Togna's own shopping and restaurant guides, fresh flowers, monogrammed linen and a glass of Champagne on arrival. Even the breakfast tray has a daily weather forecast. Furnishings are comfortable Country Life-meets-sophisticated-central London but not over-chintzed. Everything is possible—from private fittings by nearby tailors to unobtainable theatre tickets. Guests also receive complimentary access to luxurious Champney's health club.

Remember to call ahead to **reserve your room**, and please, if you cannot honour your reservation, be courteous and let the hotel know.

MODERATE

Average room price £150 upwards.

Berners Park Plaza

10 Berners St, W1A 3BE
071-636 1629, Fax 071-580 3972
3 stes £300, 229 rms S £110, D £130-£150 inc VAT. CB £8.75, EB £10.75. 2 non-smoking floors. Restaurant. 24-hr rm service. 5 function rms.

Being half-a-block from Oxford Street and mid-way between Oxford Circus and Tottenham Court Road might suggest a hectic pace, but this hotel is an oasis of calm. Rooms are a jumble of sizes, but pleasantly decorated with a contemporary country house theme, double glazed, and with bathrooms that have both showers and baths. Particularly enjoyable is the Berners Restaurant, a stunning Edwardian dining room with high carved ceilings and an excellent traditional carvery—it was the original ballroom of the nineteenth-century private home of Joshua Berner. A good adjacent cocktail bar offers half-price happy hour drinks from 5pm to 6pm with complimentary canapés.

The Cadogan

75 Sloane St, SW1X 9SG
071-235 7141, Fax 071-245 0994
4 stes £275, 70 rms S £125, D £145-£175. CB £8.50, EB £12.50. 1 non-smoking floor. Restaurant. 24-hr rm service. 2 meeting rms.

Another refurbishment project, this time under the able new general manager Malcolm Broadbent at this useful Sloane Street address, halfway between the Sloane Square and Harvey Nichols/Harrod's triangle. Double-glazed rooms are large and traditionally furnished with sofas, and the bathrooms, with their colourful Portuguese tiles, make a pleasant change from marble. The history of the hotel is riveting, full of anecdotes about former patrons Oscar Wilde and Lily Langtry. The Cadogan Restaurant is very pretty with floral prints and wood trim, and serves modern British food at respectable prices, while the Langtry Drawing Room makes a pleasant afternoon tea break from shopping. Overall there is an intimate atmosphere, like a genteel country house.

The Chelsea Hotel

17-25 Sloane St, SW1X 9NU
071-235 4377, Fax 071-235 3705
7 stes £225-£300, 218 rms S £140-£155, D £155-£175. CB £8.50, EB £10.50. 38 non-smoking rms. Air cond. Restaurant. 24-hr rm service. 2 function rms.

Set amidst the Knightsbridge designer boutiques, the modern Chelsea looks unpretentious but is glossy enough to keep up with the neighbours. Bedrooms are rather small, but a refurbishment package is underway due to new ownership. An attractive central atrium has an impressive stairway up to the mezzanine level where you find a cocktail bar and The First Floor at the Chelsea restaurant. An informal brasserie style rules here at lunch; there's a more formal air at dinner for the Provençal and Italian mixture of cooking. The lobby area proves popular for afternoon tea, breakfast and snack lunches.

The Chesterfield

35 Charles St, W1X 8LX
071-491 2622, Fax 071-491 4793
9 stes £215-£300, 101 rms S £115, D £180 inc VAT. CB £7.95, EB £9.95. 1 non-smoking floor. Air cond in stes. Restaurant. 24-hr rm service. 3 function rms for up to 12 people.

The Mayfair address might lead you into thinking this is a luxury property. True, the public rooms are attractive (a clubby lobby, the refurbished Butler's Restaurant for an international menu and the popular, rather masculine Terrace Bar), but the bedrooms can be disappointing—singles can be small and the décor, to say the least, lacks imagination. Staff can appear offhand, particularly in the Terrace Bar and it's better to opt for room service. Blame it all on a drive for efficiency.

Flemings Mayfair

Half Moon St, W1Y 7RA
071-499 2964, Fax 071-499 1817
6 apt stes £250-£350, 144 rms S £104, D £140-£193 inc VAT. CB £8, EB £10.15. No non-smoking rms. Air cond. Restaurant. 24-hr rm service. 5 meeting rms.

It's a jumble of stairways and nooks and crannies, but a super location in Mayfair and a snip of a price compared to its glossy Park Lane or Piccadilly neighbours. Some rooms can be a bit poky, but apartments offer good value-for-money and have ensuite kitchens and dining areas. The basement level restaurant has an inexpensive buffet lunch daily (£7.50 for a decent three-course meal), plus there's a small bar and comfortable sitting room next to the lobby for afternoon tea and drinks.

The Gloucester

4 Harrington Gdns, SW7 4LH - 071-373 6030, Fax 071-373 0409
13 stes £450-£980, 535 rms S £150-£170, D £165-£185 inc VAT. CB £10.95, EB £12.95. 40 non-smoking rms. Air cond. Business centre. Restaurant. 24-hr rm service. 6 function rms.

When the Rank organisation divested itself of most of its London hotels in 1993, the Singapore-based CDL Co took over this one and embarked on a huge refurbishment programme. There are Reserve Club rooms for executives, with a private lift, check-in and lounge. The regular rooms are good-sized and well-equipped and are being jazzed up a bit in their décor and amenities. The Appleyard restaurant focuses on grills and an international cuisine. There's an all-day Coffee Shop and a spacious Lobby bar for tea, drinks and light snacks. The 24-hour business centre is first-rate.

The Goring

17 Beeston Pl, Grosvenor Gdns, SW1W 0JW - 071-396 9000, Fax 071-834 4393
5 stes £180, 75 rms S £95-£115, D £145-£170 plus VAT. CB £8, EB £11. Some rms air cond. Restaurant. 24-hr rm service. 5 function rms.

Owner George Goring boasts that he has slept in every room and really understands the intricacies of hotel management. Family-run since 1910, it's close to the chaos of Victoria Station and the tourist hordes of Buckingham Palace, and yet tucked away in a quiet side street. Even the façade with its attractive plants and trees, looks inviting. Quality is the buzzword here and old-fashioned service is discreetly undertaken. Some rooms have private balconies overlooking the pretty gardens at the back of hotel. The elegant restaurant combines French and English influences, and there is a bar and 24-hour lounge for drinks, light meals and delightful afternoon tea.

London Marriott

Grosvenor Sq, W1A 4AW 071-493 1232, Fax 071-491 3201
12 stes £220, 223 rms S/D from £160 plus VAT. CB £7.75, EB £10.50. (Executive rms and stes inc bfast). 2 non-smoking floors. Air cond. Business centre. Restaurant. 24-hr rm service. 1 large function rm.

Many rooms overlook impressive Grosvenor Square (although the hotel entrance is in Duke Street) and all are comfortably decorated in quiet pastels. It makes for a pleasant and safe result. Bedrooms are large, with comfortable armchairs and good desks for writing at, though bathrooms can be small. Executive rooms and suites have their own lounge. The Diplomat plays many dining roles, from an informal breakfast and lunch through a comprehensive international dinner menu. The pretty adjacent Regent Lounge and Regent Bar are good for a sumptuous afternoon tea buffet, drinks and light meals.

The Montcalm

Great Cumberland Pl, W1A 2LF - 071-402 4288, Fax 071-724 9180
18 stes (12 duplexes) £230-£320, 98 rms S £150, D £170 plus VAT. CB £9.50, EB £13.50, Japanese bfast £17.50. 5 non-smoking rms. Air cond. Restaurant. 24-hr rm service. 3 function rms.

Named after the eighteenth-century French general, the Marquis de Montcalm, this retreat is just north of frenetic Marble Arch in a private Georgian crescent. Owned by the Japanese Nikko Hotels group, it is meticulously maintained and managed. A substantial refurbishment programme has brought the bedroom décor up to scratch, and the duplex suites are comfortably spacious if a bit tricky with narrow connecting spiral staircases. The light and airy conservatory-style Les Célébrités Restaurant merges French and English cuisine on an extensive menu (and serves Japanese breakfasts to the high proportion of Japanese visitors). The adjacent bar is clubby and cosy with leather chairs, wood panelling, bookcases and a fireplace. Service is pleasant and relaxed, though the first impression of the expansive marble lobby is rather formal. This hotel is certainly a case of reality living up to the promotional material— it really is one of London's best-kept secrets!

Prices for rooms and suites are per room, not per person.

The Mountbatten

Seven Dials, Monmouth St, WC2H 9HD - 071-836 4300, Fax 071-240 3540
B&B 7 stes £393, 120 rms S £153, D £181 inc VAT. 1 non-smoking floor. Air cond in public areas. Restaurant. 24-hr rm service. 3 function rms.

The Earl Mountbatten of Burma provides the theme for this Covent Garden spot owned by Radisson-Edwardian Hotels, and there are mementoes and tributes to India throughout, creating an eclectic mood. Smallish rooms are well-equipped with dark wood furniture and all have marble bathrooms. The country-house style drawing room is good for afternoon tea and informal meetings. The restaurant L'Amiral serves informal French cuisine plus good luncheon specials and there are two bars, the Polo Bar for regular cocktails and Larry's Bar which becomes quite noisy on Fridays with a good disco.

St George's Hotel

Langham Pl, W1N 8QS 071-580 0111, Fax 071-436 7997
3 stes £210, 83 rms S £105-£145, D £125-£175 inc VAT. CB £8.95, EB £10.95. 11 non-smoking rms. Air cond. Restaurant. 24-hr rm service. 5 function rms.

Few London hotels can boast panoramic views of the skyline but the Rooftop Restaurant (15th floor) has a stunning wrap-around vantage point. (It serves rather fussy British food, and offers weekend dining and dancing packages.) Most bedrooms offer the same perspective. The lobby is on the ground floor, and the hotel occupies the ninth to fourteenth floors; external businesses occupy the intervening levels. Its position adjacent to the BBC ensures a regular celebrity clientele while its proximity to Regent and Oxford Streets makes shopping excursions convenient. A much-needed refurbishment project is nearly completed, although room sizes still vary.

St James Court

41 Buckingham Gate, SW1E 6AF - 071-834 6655, Fax 071-630 7587
18 stes £175-£400, 455 rms S/D £130-£165 plus VAT. CB £9.20, EB £13.15, buffet £11.70. 1 non-smoking floor. Half the rms air cond. Business centre. Health club. Restaurants. 24-hr rm service. 3 boardrooms. 4 function rms.

Owned by the well-regarded Taj group of hotels, who also manage the excellent Bombay Brasserie restaurant, the St James Court is well located close to Buckingham Palace. An impressive open-air courtyard connects the hotel bedrooms with an apartment complex of 80 suites which are ideal for longer stays. Good size, well-appointed bedrooms have modern furniture and well-equipped bathrooms. There are three very different restaurants: Auberge de Provence (French with a rustic, atmospheric décor and connected with the legendary Oustau de Baumanière in the south of France), the Inn of Happiness (standard Szechuan Chinese in a plush, high-ceilinged room, popular for Sunday lunch) and the mediocre Café Mediterranée, an all-day brasserie. It shines, however, with frequent Indian food promotions which are well worth making for.

SAS Portman

22 Portman Sq, W1H 9FL 071-486 5844, Fax 071-935 0537
11 stes £200-£700, 261 rms S £110-£150, D £170-£190 plus VAT. CB £7 (in restaurant only), EB £12.50. 4 non-smoking floors. Air cond. Business centre. Restaurant. 24-hr rm service. 9 function rms.

Located opposite the Churchill and close to Marble Arch and Oxford Street shops, the hotel is now owned by the efficient Scandinavian airline, SAS, which has streamlined the whole operation and refurbished most of the hotel. You are assured of good-sized, standard bedrooms and a reasonable package of services and amenities, including an astute security system. The de-luxe double bedrooms have sofa beds, which make this hotel a favourite with families. One novel innovation is the complimentary grab-and-run early morning breakfast of coffee and croissants in the lobby.

Tower Thistle Hotel

St Katharine's Way, E1 9LD 071-481 2575, Fax 071-488 4106
8 stes £275-£295, 800 rms S £115-£145, D £135-£175 inc VAT. CB £7.25, EB £10.25. 5 non-smoking floors. Air cond. Garage. Restaurants. 24-hr rm service.

Part of the expanding Mount Charlotte/Thistle group, it is a massive, modern tower block tucked between Tower Bridge and the colourful St Katharine's

Dock, affording spectacular views from both public and guest rooms. City Club executive rooms (on the seventh and eighth floors) include superior, well-thought out amenities like ironing boards, irons, trouser presses and electronic safes, plus separate check-in. The massive multi-level marble foyer is airily attractive. There are three restaurants: the Princes Room with an international menu, good views and weekend dining and dancing, a traditional carvery and the Which Way West coffee shop/café which transforms itself, curiously, into a nightclub on Thursday to Saturday evenings. The Thames Bar is a bit staid but again, the view is its salvation. The location is handy for both the City and London's number one tourist attraction, the Tower of London.

The Waldorf

Aldwych, WC2B 4DD
071-836 2400, Fax 071-836 7244
30 stes £180-£250, 262 rms S £140, D £160 inc VAT. CB £6.75, EB £12.95. 3 non-smoking floors. Air cond. Restaurant. 24-hr rm service. Ballroom and 8 function rms.

In the heart of theatre land, close to Covent Garden and convenient for the City, the Waldorf's location is excellent. A massive refurbishment has given it a much-needed facelift and both guest and staff reactions have been favourable. A landmark (Grade II listed) building, its rooms echo the Edwardian theme throughout, but it is the public areas which shine, literally, with rich wood panelling and

stained-glass windows. Bedrooms have their own entrance lobby and the new décor, traditionally inspired, reflects the hotel's opulent past, with draped curtains and chandeliers. Bathrooms have period-style washbasins. A traditional British menu and fish specialities appear on the elegant Waldorf Restaurant menu. The informal Aldwych Brasserie is ideal for light meals and pre/post theatre dining. Charming tea dances, known as 'tango teas' take place in the Palm Court Lounge at weekends; otherwise there is regular afternoon tea during the week. Drink either in the oak-panelled Club Bar or the rather ordinary Footlights Bar which tries hard to be a typical English pub.

Whites Hotel

90 Lancaster Gate, W2 3NR
071-262 2711, Fax 071-262 2147
2 stes £300, 54 rms S £135, D £170-£225. Air cond. Non-smoking rms. Restaurant. 24-hr rm service. Pkg. 2 function rms.

This pretty, gracious building, dating from 1866, looks out over the trees of Hyde Park. Behind its imposing façade is a relatively unknown charming hotel which carries on the grand feeling of the outside into the reception area which has a marble fireplace and a panelled writing room. Good sized bedrooms have comfortable chairs, lots of silk furnishings and well-equipped marble bathrooms. The Grill restaurant serves good English and French food, and the bar area is a restful place for a drink.

PRACTICAL

Average room price under £150.

Clifton Ford Hotel

47 Welbeck St, W1M 8DN
071-486 6600, Fax 071-486 7492
5 penthouse stes £175-£400, 196 rms S £130, D £145 plus VAT. CB £10.75, EB £12.95. Air cond. Restaurant. 24-hr rm service. Conference area with 5 syndicate meeting rms.

Just north of Oxford Street, this is part of the small hotel group, Doyle's, which has two hotels in the USA, and is handy for shops and sightseeing. Recent refurbishment means that bedrooms are comfortably kitted out with attractive, although modest, modern décor. The handful of suites, all on the seventh floor with good views, are quite luxurious and highly recommended. Doyle's restaurant (a mainstream mix of English and French food, open daily, breakfast through dinner) is informal and staff are very pleasant. The Howard De Walden Bar is named after the former aristocrat who lived on the premises.

Cumberland Hotel

Marble Arch, W1A 4RF
071-262 1234, Fax 071-724 4621
899 rms S £105, D £120 inc VAT. EB £10. Non-smoking rms on executive floors (2nd and 7th). No air cond. Business centre. Restaurant. 24-hr rm service. Ballroom and 7 function rms.

The Cumberland's lobby can get very busy people with rushing through or milling about, but this is one of the largest hotels in the UK and a good bargain if you don't mind anonymous service. Used by package tour operators, it's popular for its central location (at the west end of Oxford Street just opposite Marble Arch, Speakers Corner and the wonderful expanse of Hyde Park), and the fact that it has the housekeeping stamp of its owners, the hotelier giant Forte. There's a good mix of restaurants: Chinese (Sampans), British (Original Carvery) and an all-day coffee shop, plus two decent bars (Duke's and Austin's). No points for décor, though, in spite of recent upgrades and renovations. Best bet is an executive room with appropriate amenities like trouser presses and hair dryers.

The Forum
97 Cromwell Rd, SW7 4DN
071-370 5757, Fax 071-373 1448
4 stes £170-£250, 906 rms S £105-£125, D £125-£145 inc VAT. CB £7.80, EB £11. 2 non-smoking floors. Air cond. Business centre. Fitness facility. Restaurant. 24-hr rm service. 6 function rms.

Enormous—in fact, the biggest and tallest in the country—it somehow manages to maintain superb efficiency without being too impersonal. Perhaps it's due to its ownership by Inter-Continental Hotels who have their international headquarters in London. Bedrooms may seem functional and modestly equipped but are kept meticulously clean. The very smart Ashburn Restaurant offers an international menu, and the

international Kensington Garden Café is open all day from buffet breakfast to dinner. The Tavern pub offers traditional pub fare and lively Sunday jazz brunches, while Oliver's Lounge next to the lobby does afternoon tea, drinks and snacks. Eleven per cent of the clientele is Japanese, so there is a good range of specialist menus, including an extensive Japanese breakfast.

Novotel London Hammersmith
1 Shortlands, W6 8DR
081-741 1555, Fax 081-741 2120
4 stes £165, 636 rms S £79, D £89 inc VAT. CB £5.75, EB £8.25. 3 non-smoking floors. Air cond. Restaurant. Rm service to midnight. Large exhibition centre, 12 meeting rms.

Owned by the French chain, its West London address may not suit some, but it's accessible to Heathrow, Olympia (the major conference and exhibition site) and is good for conventions and large tour groups. Functional and quiet rooms are comfortable rather than exciting, and the service is very efficient. The Hammersmith neighbourhood is picking up in terms of shopping and restaurants. The large Le Grill restaurant is open all day serving an international menu. The lounge bar also serves snacks.

Royal Court Hotel
Sloane Sq, SW1W 8EG
071-730 9191, Fax 071-824 8381
3 stes £125-£160, 99 rms S £115, D £145 inc VAT. CB £7, EB £9.25. 1 non-smoking

floor. No air cond. Restaurant. 24-hr rm service. 1 meeting rm.

Sloane Square is an impressive address, linking the King's Road (known for trendy, youthful fashion) and Sloane Street (with its designer boutiques). The Royal Court Theatre just opposite shows an interesting mix of contemporary drama. A major re-fit has made the public rooms very attractive, including the Number 12 Restaurant (English and French menu) and the Tavern pub which gets pretty lively in the evenings and at weekends. Bedrooms are enjoying constant upgrades and many have oak furniture and soft colour scemes. Singles, however, remain fairly small. Housekeeping standards are excellent and the staff congenial.

Royal Horseguards Thistle
2 Whitehall Ct, SW1A 2EJ
071-839 3400, Fax 071-925 2263
3 stes £200-£300, 366 rms S £99, D £110, Studio ste £185 inc VAT. Air cond. Non-smoking rms. Restaurant. 24-hr rm service. 12 function rms.

In a grand position just off Whitehall, this hotel comes as a surprise. Originally part of the National Liberal Club, from the outside the building looks like a private club or residence. Walk inside and you're in a large, traditional looking foyer with beautiful ceilings, unlike the usual hotel entrance. Some of the single rooms are small, but the best bedrooms are large and decorated with oak furniture and colourful chintz, very much in the English style; some have a wonderful view of the City. There's a pretty lounge with chandeliers and paintings and rather a masculine, clubby restaurant, Granby's, thoroughly in keeping with the generally ambience of this pleasant hotel.

Royal Lancaster Hotel
Lancaster Terr, W2 2TY
071-262 6737, Fax 071-724 3191
20 stes from £500, 398 rms S/D £125-£153. Air cond. Non-smoking rms. Restaurants. 24-hr rm service. Pkg. Ballroom. 5 meeting rms.

An eighteen-storey modern building overlooking Hyde Park and directly above Lancaster Gate tube station, you enjoy wonderful views over the park from the upper floors, particularly the best rooms on the Reserve Club floors (fifteenth to eighteenth floors) which contain five suites with a drawing room and boardroom. Rooms, which are standard size, are traditionally, though not spectacularly furnished. Downstairs the lounge is a favourite place for tea or a drink; La Rosette Restaurant serves French food and the Brasserie offers a more casual menu of full meals or snacks. Much used by conferences, the hotel has very good technical back-up.

Scandic Crown Victoria
2 Bridge Pl, SW1V 1QA
071-834 8123, Fax 071-828 1099
5 stes £205, 205 rms S £105-£115, D £135-£145 inc VAT. Full buffet bfast £10.50. 5 non-smoking floors. Air cond.

London's statues

London's statues are as singular as the people they depict. Take Sir Joseph Bazalgette (1819-1891) whose statue stands on Victorian Embankment, just near Hungerford Bridge. 'He placed the river in chains' runs the Latin inscription. Sir Joseph was the engineer for the construction of the Victoria Embankment which replaced the old Tudor system of sewerage. By narrowing the Thames, he reclaimed land that was previously marshland and speeded up the flow of the river.

Restaurant. 24-hr rm service. 7 function rms.

Just yards from Victoria Terminal, the address can be both a godsend (you can hoist your own bags from the train) or a nuisance (this chaotically busy neighbourhood sometimes suffers from a down-and-out passing public). Last year's refurbishment gave it a totally modern, new look, including a marble lobby, pretty pastel furnishings and upgraded bathrooms. And if you love Sweden—or Scandinavia in general—its restaurant fare will please. The Gamla Eken, which translates into the name of a Swedish tree, is mainly Scandinavian with an excellent smörgåsbord at lunch; light snacks are also available in the adjacent bar.

The Strand Palace Hotel
Strand, WC2R 0JJ - 071-836 8080, Fax 071-836 2077
784 rms S £89, D £105, Triples (family rms) £120 inc VAT. CB £6.50, EB £8.50. 4 non-smoking floors. No air cond. Restaurants. No rm service. 7 function rms.

Set amidst most of the key West End theatres, this

is an ideal location for enthusiasts. It's a functional operation, run by Forte, and attracts large tour groups. A much-needed major top-to-toe refurbishment of bedrooms has resulted in everything from new beds and furniture to bathrooms and TVs, so standards have greatly improved. There are three restaurants, including Biancone's, an Italian brasserie, the Original Carvery which serves very good traditional British food, and the Café at the Strand, an American-style coffee shop which is open all day; plus two bars which get crowded with a pleasant, buzzing, pre-theatre feel. You can buy typical English country leisure ware at Bolders of the Strand, and there's a jewellers and a Keith Prowse theatre desk.

Topham's Ebury Court Hotel
26 Ebury St, SW1W 0LU
071-730 8147, Fax 071-823 5966
B&B 1 ste, 41 rms S £64 (no bath)-£100, D £89 (no bath)-£150 inc VAT. No non-smoking rms. Air cond. Restaurant.

Limited rm service. 3 small meeting rms.

Being family-run for more than half a century has given Ebury Court a welcoming, friendly ambience, and although its décor and amenities could best be described as old-fashioned, there are moves being made to refurbish and upgrade. Not all rooms have a private bath, but at least they're cosy and comfortable and the price is ludicrously low for its central Pimlico address. Topham's restaurant (mix of English and French) hasn't really found its feet but is fine for breakfasts. The bar is on the lower ground floor. They have many repeat clients who swear by its efficiency and genuine convivial atmosphere.

BED & BREAKFAST

Average room price £60-£100.

Alison House Hotel
182 Ebury St, SW1W 9QD
071-730 9529, Fax 071-730 5494
B&B 11 rms S £28, D £42, Triples £65 (with ensuite bathroom) inc VAT. No restaurant.

Ebury Street, an attractive row of late nineteenth-century terraced houses, is filled with small hotels, some good and some mediocre. This one is consistently commendable, clean and tidy, privately owned and popular with an American clientele, many of them businessmen. All rooms have TVs, hair dryers and basins,

though only one room has ensuite facilities.

Aster House
3 Sumner Pl, SW7 3EE
071-581 5888, Fax 071-584 4925
B&B 12 rms S £52, D £78-£85 plus VAT. No restaurant.

Routinely endorsed by the British Tourist Authority as one of London's best B & Bs, it is family run and professionally efficient with a high record of returning clientele. Set in a pretty residential street in South Kensington, it features lovely bedrooms, many with four-poster beds, all with fridges and TVs. Excellent buffet breakfast.

The Claverley
13 Beaufort Gdns, SW3 1PS
071-589 8541, Fax 071-584 3410
B&B 36 rms (30 with private bathrooms) S £60-£75, D £95-£150 inc VAT. No restaurant.

Pleasant floral décor and good location in a private, quiet cul-de-sac in the heart of Knightsbridge, the Claverley is highly recommended by the British Tourist Authority, and in fact, won their top B & B accolade a few years ago. Good breakfasts and attractive lounge area with complimentary tea, coffee and newspapers.

Elizabeth Hotel
37 Eccleston Sq, SW1V 1PB
071-828 6812, Fax 071-828 6814
B&B 40 rms S £36-£55, D £58-£80, Triples £90, Family rms £75-£80, inc VAT. No restaurant. 1 meeting rm.

The Elizabeth is well located in the heart of Pimlico on an historic

square (the private gardens and tennis court are available to guests) and close to Victoria and Sloane Square. Noteworthy attempts have been made to achieve an authentic mid-nineteenth-century décor with fine prints and portraits. They also have longer-stay self-contained fully-equipped apartments.

Holland Park Hotel
6 Ladbroke Terr, W11 3PG
071-727 5815, Fax 071-727 8166
B&B 23 rms S £37.60-£47, D £47-£63.45, Triple £90 inc VAT. No restaurant.

Charming and intimate, located in a quiet residential area, the building is a curious mix of the old and the new with lots of nooks and crannies, stairways, big windows and a private, very pretty, back garden. The tasteful décor of antiques and Persian rugs is complemented by a thoroughly professional, and congenial staff. Only thirteen rooms have private bath.

Hotel La Place
17 Nottingham Pl, W1M 3FB
071-486 2323, Fax 071-486 4335
B&B 21 rms S £59-£75, D £65-£89, Triples £85-£95 inc VAT. Restaurant.

Close to Marylebone Road and Madame Tussaud's, all rooms have private bathrooms and the standard of décor is excellent following a recent refurbishment and upgrading programme. Good, hearty breakfasts are served in Le Jardin Restaurant (a charcoal barbecue Swiss French cuisine). There is also a useful 24-

hour wine bar and meeting room.

Hotel 167

167 Old Brompton Rd, SW5 0AN - 071-373 0672, Fax 071-373 3360
B&B 19 rms S £54-£65, D £68-£75 inc VAT. No restaurant.

A muted, Scandinavian-influenced décor of soft grey and cream co-ordinating with many good antiques greets the visitor here. The hotel has an excellent location, close to museums like the Victoria & Albert and the Natural History, and to the shops in the Brompton Cross/Fulham Road area. Only double rooms have private baths, although singles are conveniently served with nearby facilities. There is a very gracious and friendly staff.

Manzi's

1-2 Leicester St, WC2H 7BL 071-734 0224, Fax 071-437 4864
B&B 15 rms S £40, D £63 inc VAT. Air cond. Restaurant.

Just off Leicester Square in the heart of Soho, Manzi's is unusual in that its prime purpose is a restaurant, well-regarded for its Italian/seafood menu. Right on the doorstep of many West End theatres and cinemas, its location couldn't be better for the trendy crowd who want alternative accommodation and the bonus of tripping upstairs after a hearty meal. Rooms are fairly basic, but all have ensuite facilities. Check-in is at the reception for the restaurant, so can get busy during meal times. But upstairs, all is calm.

One Cranley Place

One Cranley Pl, SW7 3AB 071-589 7704, Fax 071-225 3931
B&B 9 rms S/D £65-£105 inc VAT. No restaurant.

More like a cosy private home than a small hotel, One Cranley Place is set in a row of Regency houses and boasts a high standard of décor, with antiques and fireplaces in most rooms. Breakfast can be taken in the intimate private lounge/dining room or in bedrooms.

Terstan Hotel

30 Nevern Sq, SW5 9PE 071-244 6466, Fax 071-373 9268
B&B 50 rms S £28-£40, D £48-£52, Triples £60 inc VAT. No restaurant.

Family-owned and situated in a pleasant residential square close to Earl's Court and Olympia exhibition halls, guests enjoy comfortable, simply decorated rooms and only the smallest singles are without private bathrooms. There's a licensed bar and games room.

Windermere Hotel

142 Warwick Way, SW1V 4JE - 071-834 8676, Fax 071-630 8831
B&B 24 rms S £34-£71, D £48-£71, Triples £71 inc VAT. Half-board (3-course dinner) for £8 supplement. Restaurant.

Commended by the English Tourist Board and the British Tourist Authority, and close to the Victoria Terminal, this welcoming and charming hotel enjoys a high level of routine patronage. Light snacks and drinks are available throughout the day in the pleasant lounge and dining

room. Bedrooms are attractive and immaculately kept by housekeeping which is first rate.

AIRPORTS

■ GATWICK

Copthorne London Gatwick

Copthorne, nr Crawley, West Sussex, RH10 3PG - 0342-714971, Fax 0342- 717375
1 ste £190, 225 rms S £98, D £108 inc service and VAT. Air cond. Business facilities. Health club. Restaurants. 24-hr rm service. 11 conference rms. 4 banqueting stes.

This is a slightly different airport hotel, centred around an old sixteenth-century farmhouse and set in 100 acres of gardens and woods in the village of Copthorne, just six minutes from the airport. In keeping with its origins, many bedrooms are in traditional style and log fires and oak beams grace the public rooms. There's a formal restaurant, the informal Garden Room, the Library Bar and the White Swan Pub. For relaxation there's also a croquet lawn and jogging track and nearby golf and horse riding.

Forte Crest Gatwick

North Terminal, Gatwick Airport, West Sussex, RH6 0PH - 0293-567070, Fax 0293-567739
11 stes £120-£160, 457 rms S/D £89 inc service and VAT. Non-smoking rms. Air cond. Business centre. Health club. Pool. Restaurants. 24-hr rm service. 12 meeting rms.

The most notable feature of this large, well-run hotel is the eight-storey high atrium with a cocktail bar and café below. Linked to the airport's North Terminal by a short covered walkway, décor is modern and minimal. Bedrooms are well equipped, though austerely decorated, and the TV system displays flight information as well as viewing. There are several restaurants in this most efficiently run hotel.

Gatwick Hilton International

Gatwick, West Sussex, RH11 0PD - 0293-518080, Fax 0293-28980
Stes £185-£350, 550 rms S £135, D £145-£175 inc VAT. Non-smoking rms. Air cond. Business centre. Health club. Pool. Restaurants. 24-hr rm service. Conference facilities for up to 500.

One of the most impressive of Gatwick's hotels, a pedestrian walkway connects the south terminal with a four-storey central atrium where a life-size replica of Amy Johnson's biplane hangs from the ceiling. Bedrooms are good size and well equipped and the TVs display the latest flight information. There's a health club and pool, two restaurants and two bars, one of which is open 24 hours a day.

Gravetye Manor

Vowels Lane, East Grinstead, West Sussex, RH19 4LJ 0342-810567, Fax 0342-810080
18 rms £85-£140 plus VAT. CB £7. Restaurant.

This is definitely *not* an airport hotel, but arriving or leaving from Gatwick provides the perfect excuse for a de-luxe stay and a delightful dining experience at celebrated Gravetye

Manor. One of the first country house hotels in England, this Elizabethan stone mansion was built in 1598, and still retains its baronial feeling. Public downstairs rooms have magnificent panelled walls and moulded ceilings. The recently refurbished bedrooms are large, comfortable and beautifully furnished with antique furniture and glorious fabrics, while books and magazines are scattered around as if in a private home. The welcome given by Peter Herbert and his staff is proverbial. The gardens also, are renowned— 1000 acres of flower beds and lawns invite guests to stroll outside.

People come from miles around to eat in the restaurant, from a menu that mixes the traditional with the modern. Fish is a favourite here as in a ragout of seafood with Sauternes and grapes, and they smoke their own salmon. Main dishes like roast fillet of Scottish beef and saddle of rabbit or venison show the chef's love of good English ingredients. Set meals run from lunch at £22 to dinner at £26, but the wine list is expensive. If you feel expansive, or want a special treat on arrival or departure, then this is not to be missed.

■ HEATHROW

Edwardian International

140 Bath Rd, Hayes, Middlx, UB3 5AW - 081-759 6311, Fax 081-759 4559
17 stes £450, 443 rms S £153, D £184 inc service and

VAT. Non-smoking rms. Air cond. Business centre. Health club. Pool. Restaurant. 24-hr rm service. 17 conference stes.

Five minutes from the airport, the Edwardian International, part of the small but prestigious Edwardian chain is a comfortable, stylish hotel with a welcoming foyer. Bedrooms are a good size and well decorated, some with four-poster beds, while suites have spa baths and twin washbasins. This is an important residential conference hotel and facilities are excellent for business travellers. There is a pool, gym and health and beauty salon.

Excelsior Hotel

Bath Rd, West Drayton, Middlx, UB7 0DU - 081-759 6611, Fax 081-759 3421
16 stes £295, 826 rms £95 inc VAT and service. Conference facilities up to 800. Non-smoking rms. Air cond. Health club. Pool. Restaurants. 24-hr rm service.

A huge, modern, recently refurbished hotel offering all the comforts of today. Five bedrooms are equipped for wheelchair-bound guests; there is a pool, and the usual health and beauty facilities. Children under fourteen years old can stay free in their parents' room. A grand entrance lobby greets you, and there are extensive conference facilities. Wheeler's of St James's, the fish restaurant chain, runs one of the restaurants and there is a buffet in The Original Carvery.

Heathrow
Hilton

Terminal 4, Hounslow, Middlx, TW5 3AF - 081-759 7755, Fax 081-759 7579
Stes from £195, 400 rms S £135, D from £145 inc VAT. Non-smoking rms. Air cond. Business centre. Health club. Pool Restaurants. 24-hr rm service. 13 meeting rms.

Quite the most spectacular of Heathrow's hotels, all steel and glass and a landmark from the outside, you enter via a huge, high atrium which has a lounge and restaurant beneath it. Bedrooms are well decorated and equipped with all the modern technology international travellers expect. Direct access to terminal 4 is via a covered walkway. Children up to eighteen stay free in parents' room. Adventurously, the latest Zen oriental restaurant has opened here (see *Restaurant* section).

Sheraton
Skyline

Bath Rd, Hayes, Middlx, UB3 5BP - 081-759 2535, Fax 081-759 9150
Stes £300-£450, 352 rms S £140-£150, D £150-£195 inc service and VAT. Non-smoking rms. Air cond. Pool. Restaurant. 24-hr rm service. Conference facilities up to 500.

The Sheraton Skyline is known for the Patio Caribe—a large indoor tropical garden with swimming pool surrounded by palms and with a bar. Just the thing for relaxing in before or after a long flight. Bedrooms are excellently equipped; children up to sixteen years old can stay free in their parents' room, and the banqueting and conference facilities are what you would expect.

REFRESHMENTS
& QUICK BITES

BARGAIN BITES

In the past few years a revolution has occurred among small restaurants and they have come to assume a new importance in our eating-out habits. There are now more good, inexpensive restaurants serving imaginative food than ever before. One trend is for young chefs to take over former pubs, and while keeping pub hours and the bar, using the opportunity to produce first-class cooking. It is a sensible move; the costs of establishing new restaurants, even small ones, are huge. Investing in a better kitchen in a going concern like a pub eliminates much of the expense. And it allows the chef to experiment. One other interesting trend (and where this came from nobody knows) is the transformation of day time 'greasy spoon' type cafés into Thai restaurants in the evening. And in this most welcome of climates, even the humble sandwich has broken free of its cellophane-wrapped straitjacket and emerged—in new chains like Prêt à Manger, Birley's and Café Aroma—as a genuine alternative to a restaurant lunch. The choice is here; everyone should take advantage of it. We have here defined 'bargain' as being possible to eat three courses, without wine or beer, for £15 per person or under, and have indicated the kind of prices you can expect to pay.

■ CAMDEN TOWN

Café Delancey
3 Delancey St, NW1
071-387 1985, Fax 071-383 5314
Open Mon-Sat 8am-midnight, Sun 8am-11pm.

This casual, roomy French brasserie in Camden Town, done out with wooden floors and small tables, is popular with visitors to Camden Lock Market at the weekend and with locals at any time. They follow the brasserie formula successfully: daily specials like baked chicken in a garlic purée crust served with potatoes and a house salad for £8.95, coffee at any time and a relaxed attitude to lingering customers.

Daphne
83 Bayham St, NW1
071-267 7322
Open Mon-Sat noon-3pm, 6pm-midnight.

Daphne is one of the two best choices in an area known for its Greek Cypriot restaurants. While they serve all the favourites from taramasalata to moussaka, they also introduce a more adventurous element with their daily dishes which have a Mediterranean slant, like char-grilled fish or monkfish souvlaki. A pretty décor and a roof garden make this a congenial place where you should reckon on about £14 a head.

*The **prices** in this guide reflect what establishments were charging at the time of going to press.*

L'Ecluse
3 Chalk Farm Rd, NW1
071-267 8116
Open daily noon-10.30pm.

Right opposite the main part of Camden Lock Market, L'Ecluse's French bistro fare consists of tried-and-tested staples like moules marinières, gigot d'agneau and an extensive list of crêpes, both savoury and sweet (the owner comes from Normandy and takes great pride in his cider also). You can spend as little or as much as you like. Noisy, fun and usually crowded.

Nontas
16 Camden High St, NW1
071-387 4579
Open Mon-Sat noon-2.45pm, 6-11.30pm.

The second of Camden Town's good Greek Cypriot restaurants, Nontas has been serving a similar, simply-cooked choice for years to a standard which has remained consistently good. Chicken kebab, for instance, around £5, which can become dry, is moist and redolent of the herbs it was marinated in; moussaka is always freshly made. The relatively recent Ouzerie wine bar next door is a useful place to meet over a bottle of wine (not necessarily Greek Retsina) and snacks.

The Underground Café
214 Camden Town High St, NW1 - 071-482 0010
Open Mon-Sat 6-11pm, Sun 11.30am-4pm (coffee and snacks).

Under the same ownership as the neighbouring Camden Brasserie, this prettily decorated basement has now changed from a predominantly pasta menu to a more general—though still Italian—choice, featuring popular dishes like grilled rabbit with rosemary and white wine served with herb polenta (£8.95) and spicy Italian sausages with braised red cabbage and garlic potato mash (£6.95), and three pasta dishes daily.

■ CHELSEA

Big Easy
332-334 King's Rd, SW3
071-352 4071
Open daily noon-midnight.

One of the new-wave themed restaurants that Londoners have taken to their hearts, the friendly Big Easy is popular with local Chelsea types and parents of small children. Everything from Texas torpedos (deep-fried jalapeños stuffed with cheese) to southern Caesar salad by way of chips 'n' salsa, ribs and steaks and their big selling-point, crabs, which cost between £8 and £9 depending on how big and how the crab is cooked. The menu is littered with notes like: 'How to eat a crab: 1. Put on a bib. 2. Put jewellery in a safe place. 3. Dig in, get messy.' Get the message?

Café de Blank
General Trading Company, 141 Sloane St, SW1
071-259 9331
Open Mon-Sat 9am-9pm.

Part of the Justin de Blank catering empire, this successful café-cum-restaurant is in the basement of the General Trading Company, a shop that has been selling expensive and exclusive household goods to London's fashionable crowd for years. It gets very crowded and the tables are close together, but the customers seem oblivious to their neighbours. The food is an imaginative mix with dishes like smoked salmon, capers, brown bread and salad (£6.20) and bruschetta with spicy avocado salsa (£4.75) making regular appearances. Specials change daily. There is a useful set menu in the evening: two courses for £12.25, three for £14.95 between 6 and 9pm, much used by people going to the local Royal Court theatre.

Chelsea Kitchen
98 King's Rd, SW3 - 071-589 1330
Open Mon-Sat 8am-11.45pm, Sun 9.45am-11.45pm. No cards.

If you were around in the swinging 60s, the chances are that this was your local spot to eat substantially without spending much money. Along with the Stockpot chain (which this is part of), the Chelsea Kitchen still serves good honest fare: stews with potatoes and veg, chicken Madras with rice, and vegetarian dishes, each for less than a fiver. For real traditionalists, puddings come covered in custard. Stripped pine booths, cramped seating and a fun atmosphere have contributed to the long-running popularity of this Chelsea institution.

> Find the address you are looking for, quickly and easily, in the *index*.

■ CHINATOWN

Chueng Cheng Ku
17 Wardour St, W1
071-437 1398
Open Mon-Sat 11am-midnight, Sun 11am-11.30pm.

The dim sum is what attracts customers to this large, old-fashioned Chinese restaurant with a somewhat daunting entrance and décor. Large trolleys trundle around full of steamed dumplings, yam fritters, spare ribs, rice and other delicacies. Staff can be harried so it's best to know what you want. Set meals served all day begin at £9 (minimum two people).

Dragon Inn
12 Gerrard St, W1 - 071-494 0870
Open Mon-Sat noon-11.45pm, Sun 11am-11.45am.

Another dim sum favourite with a wide range, though the one-plate selection of barbecued and roast meats with rice and vegetables is also worth sampling. Service can be good or indifferent, depending on the time of day. Set menus begin at £8.50.

Poons
27 Lisle St, WC2 - 071-437 4549
Open daily noon-11.30pm. No cards.

Now fully licensed, and brighter, the original 'little Poons' from which all the others sprang, is still a tiny nest of rooms serving a huge Cantonese menu. 'Plate dishes' are the most popular—rice or noodles from £3; noodle soups are £2.20 to £2.40. Wind-dried foods (duck, sausage, bacon) brought to this country by Poons, display vivacious strong flavours. Their other introduction, 'original hot pots' also please, especially the challenging stewed bean curd with roasted pork with dried shrimp paste, as powerful a Chinese taste as there is. For many sinophile gastronomes, this café is still the bargain bite of them all.

Tokyo Diner
2 Newport Pl, WC2
071-287 8777
Open daily noon-midnight. No cards.

This former laundrette is now a charming quick eating-house, home from home for many Japanese. You sit on tiny stools at tiny tables in tiny rooms cluttered with Japanese odds and ends and eat donburi—a one-course meal from £3.45 for egg and onion on rice; or a bento box, divided into four compartments, with rice, salad, cooked vegetables and a little raw fish plus a 'main' item such as pork croquette at £6.90 or salmon teriyaki at £11.90. Soups, sushi and ice cream are on offer too.

■ CHISWICK

Bedlington Café
24 Fauconberg Rd, W4
081-994 1965
Open daily 11.30am-2pm, 6-10pm. No cards.

A tiny shrine in the window is the only outward sign that this cramped greasy spoon with its well-loaded fizzy drinks cabinet is anything other than a working man's café.

By night, out come the woks and the lemon grass, and the extended Thai family who run the Bedlington produce inexpensive (main courses are from £3-£5), authentic, everyday Thai food. It's hugely popular, with bookings taken several days in advance, has no drinks license but is strong on atmosphere. The menu is long with few surprises: satay, salads with lashings of chilli and coriander, wafer-thin and well-loaded omelettes and jungle curry with pea aubergine. Good for vegetarians; take your own wine.

Fat Boy's Café
10 Edensor Rd, W4
081-994 8089
Open daily 6.30am-3pm, 6.30pm-midnight.

By day a greasy spoon-type café, by night another successful and popular Thai restaurant serving good, though conventional Thai food—deep-fried starters, curries and many different kinds of noodle dishes. Take your own wine and you'll spend about £12 per person.

■ THE CITY

Birley's
5 Bow Lane, EC4 - 071-248 0358
Open Mon-Fri 8am-3.30pm.

One of the first sandwich bars to offer gourmet sandwiches, Birley's continues to deliver the goods in the City of London, using fresh breads like sultana or honey and excellent fillings. There's also a hot and cold daily special. Mainly catering to City types, they're also useful

on a summer's day for visitors. Branches throughout the City.

Futures!
8 Botolph Alley, EC3
071-623 4529
Open Mon-Fri 7.30am-10am, 11.30am-3pm.

With a name like Futures! we always expect the clients from the predominantly male futures market to be tucking into steak and chips at the very least, and probably wild boar. But no, this is a vegetarian place where muesli and porridge for breakfast and mixed vegetable korma and spinach and mushroom lasagne for lunch are downed by City types with obvious enjoyment. At anything from £1 to £2.90 a dish, they should look happy. In a small alley near St Mary-at-Hill and relatively near the Tower of London, this is a good spot for tourists as well.

Lahore Kebab House
2 Umberston St, E1
071-481 9737
Open daily noon-midnight. No cards.

Not the most salubrious of areas, but venture down to this part of London and you'll find that this basic café prepares some excellent Indian cooking. As the name implies, they specialise in kebabs but are also known for their Punjabi karahi dishes and breads, cooked over flames. Taking your own alcohol, and eating as much as you can, you will probably spend around £9 to £10 if you try very hard.

> *Find the address you are looking for, quickly and easily, in the* ***index***.

Nosherie

12-13 Greville St, EC1
071-242 1591
*Open Mon-Fri 7.45am-4pm.
No cards.*

The dealers in precious stones from nearby Hatton Garden have been using this café for breakfast and lunch for years. But visitors shouldn't be put off. Despite the predominantly local clientele, it's a friendly, welcoming place. Good, filling salt beef sandwiches and smoked salmon-filled bagels are prepared at the front; at the back a small café serves the full menu of gefilte fish, latkes and other Jewish dishes.

■ CLERKEN-WELL

Eagle

159 Farringdon Rd, EC1
071-837 1353
*Open Mon-Fri 11am-11pm.
Lunch & Dinner Mon-Fri. No cards.*

This is what happened when a bright young chef and his restaurant manager bought a pub. Out went the optics, the juke box and the inedible pub grub and in came a bright, open-plan dining-room, a blackboard menu and, behind the bar, a char-grill. The Eagle has spearheaded the new movement to redefine and update the traditional British pub. Open all day, serving coffee and tea as well as fine wine and real ale, it has the air of a bohemian wine bar but is run like a brasserie. David Eyre cooks Italo-Mediterranean, always a hearty soup and usually a stew too, a superior steak sandwich (bife Ana) on home-made ciabatta, and from the grill

merguez sausages, Mediterranean vegetables and chilli-flecked squid. A three-course meal will cost around £12.

The Peasant

240 St John St, EC1 - 071-336 7726
*Open Mon-Fri noon-11pm.
Lunch & Dinner Mon-Fri.*

Not a million miles from the Eagle, in fact just a short walk away, you'll come across The Peasant, another former pub that has become a successful restaurant. The chef is none other than Carla Tomasi who was formerly the chef at Frith's in Soho, a restaurant which despite first-rate food, fell victim to the recession. Italian-based, with dishes like Tuscan bread and bean soup for wintertime blues and sharp, fresh-tasting pastas for summer, the menu is sensibly not divided up into starters and main courses, so you can snack or eat seriously according to your mood and your needs and your pocket. You can eat well for £10 here. The Peasant doesn't hide its origins and the bar is still in place. You can also enjoy a very good selection of draught beers from Adnam's of East Anglia to Theakston's Old Peculiar from Yorkshire. Meals are from £5 to £15, wine is £8 per bottle. All in all, this is a thoroughly welcome new venture.

■ COVENT GARDEN

Ajimura

51 Shelton St, WC2
071-240 0178

*Open Mon-Fri noon-3pm,
Mon-Sat 6-11pm.*

Arguably London's oldest Japanese restaurant, and certainly one of the first to provide a relaxed and informal set-up with an affordable and well-explained menu, Ajimura remains avowedly bohemian with refectory tables, lighting from faded paper lanterns and a rude animal frieze running round the room. Sushi and tempura can be ordered and eaten at the bar, various set meals are built around popular dishes such as sukiyaki, shabu shabu and tempura, there are always dishes of the day and a pre-theatre menu. A nice detail is that you will be offered a selection of saké cups and you choose the one that appeals the most. Set lunch beginning at £7.40 is the best value, dinner prices rise steeply.

Café Casbar

52 Earlham St, WC2
071-379 7768
*Open Mon-Sat 10am-9pm,
Sun noon-6pm. No cards.*

Busy, friendly and always full, Café Casbar is good value with its sandwiches and baguettes, salads and hot daily specials costing around £4. It doubles as a bar in the evenings, so it's a convenient and pleasant meeting place.

Caffé Piazza

17 Russell St, WC2
071-379 7543
Open Mon-Fri 11am-11.45pm, Sun noon-10.30pm.

This newly opened Italian bistro-bar-grill-pizzeria (their own term) is one of the many restaurants bordering Covent Garden

129

Piazza. This means that at least half the customers are tourists, but luckily there are enough regulars to keep standards up. Caffé Piazza is a good place to pop into for lunch or a pre-theatre light meal. Weather permitting, outside tables are best for drinks and people-watching. The two-storey restaurant serves pastas, pizzas and other Italian dishes. Pizzas are from £5.50, starters from £3, main courses cost between £5 and £9. The wine list is fully Italian, and the restaurant also serves Italian beers like Messina, Taurino and Peroni, and fourteen different grappas.

Calabash

The Africa Centre, 38 King St, WC2 - 071-836 1976
Open Mon-Fri 12.30-3pm, Mon-Sat 6-10.30pm.

Calabash is part of the Africa Centre, which includes an art gallery, a craft and book shop, an African bar (with beers and wines from all over the continent) and a disco. Starters you may not be familiar with include aloco, fried plantain served with hot tomato sauce, and vegetarian sambusa which is a pastry stuffed with potatoes, spring onions, carrots and spices. For your main course you can choose between dishes like Nigerian egusi soup cooked in palm oil with melon seeds, fish and African spinach served with yams or rice, or hot chicken stew doro wot from East Africa. Starters are around £2.50 and main courses from £7 to £9.

Cranks

11 The Market, WC2
071-379 6508
Open Mon-Sat 9am-8pm, Sun 10am-7pm. No cards.

Cranks was one of the first vegetarian places in an otherwise carnivore London environment. It flourished and withered and was finally bought-out by the management in 1992. Today it has changed very little, serving solely vegetarian salads (between £2.50 and £4), sandwiches, soups and hot dishes (between £2 and £5) in a stripped wooden décor that takes you right back to the 1960s. Branches throughout London.

India Club

143 Strand, WC2 - 071-836 0650
Open Mon-Sun noon-2.30pm, 6pm-10pm, (Sun to 8pm).

The entrance to this bastion of Indian cooking in London is well hidden and the stairs are narrow, but persevere as the food has kept its authentic character over many years. It's well-known to regulars: at lunchtime it becomes an unofficial canteen for the civil servants and staff from India House and a selection of different nation-alities from the BBC World Service across the road. You can bring your own wine or other alcoholic drinks. The menu is almost equally split between vegetarian and non-vegetarian dishes and special dishes are available on request. The minimum charge is £4 per person which will buy, for example, a vegetable curry and Indian ice cream.

Marché Mövenpick

The Swiss Centre, 10 Wardour St, W1 - 071-734 3130
Open Mon-Sat 8am-midnight, Sun 9am-midnight.

A motorway-style café in a basement might seem rather incongruous for the middle of London—and Leicester Square at that—but any feeling of unease is removed by the sight of the fresh produce that greets you. Much of the food, including steamed mussels, is cooked to order; salads are better than usual; cold meats are imaginative. Though rather confusing (in the way of motorway cafés you're not familiar with), this is a real gem in the Leicester Square area and a good place to meet before the theatre or cinema. You can have coffee and cakes for a couple of pounds, or go for a main dish from £5 to £8.

Neal's Yard Dining Room

1st floor, 14 Neal's Yard, WC2 - 071-379 0298
Open Mon-Sat noon-5pm (Wed to 8pm).

Neal's Yard is the place for wholefood foodies. Apart from the 'World Food Café' as they call themselves, there's Neal's Yard Bakery and Tea Room in the same tiny square. Ingredients and inspiration from all over the world appear on the menu and everything is freshly prepared. Prices vary from soups at £2.50 to hot dishes around £5. Seating overlooks the Yard below.

> *Some establishments change their **closing times** without warning. It is always wise to check in advance.*

Palms Pasta on the Piazza

39 King St, WC2 - 071-240 2939

Open daily noon-midnight.

This good value-for-money restaurant in Covent Garden serves standard food in a fun setting. Best bets are from the grill and include chicken diavola (£6.95) marinated in mustard, white wine, lemon juice and chilli and served with french fries or salad, or fillet of lamb marinated in rosemary oil (both recommended). Pastas are reasonable and tasty and cost from £4.95 for a simple Bolognese to £6.75 for the Orientale blow-out. The young favour the cocktails.

Prêt à Manger

Upper St Martin's Lane, WC2 - 071-377 9595

Open Mon-Thurs, Sun 8am-10pm, Fri, Sat 8am-11pm.

Every time you blink, it seems that another Prêt à Manger springs out of the ground. A phenomenally successful sandwich bar chain, they are aiming for a huge bite of Britain's £1 billion-a-year sandwich business and even making Marks & Spencer (which has ten per cent of this lucrative market) a little nervous. Each Prêt à Manger looks like a stainless-steel high-tech Macdonalds, with counters at the back of their shops from which friendly staff dispense sandwiches, soup, coffee, croissants and any snack they have all day long. They go beyond the usual well-filled sandwich with sushi, sashimi, noodle-based dishes suited to reheating in a microwave oven and American-style baked desserts as well as proper espresso. Very useful if you feel peckish at 8pm on your way somewhere and want a quick, cheap bite, the quality is good and the choice wide. Most people think the two young surveyors who started in a small shop in Putney deserve all their success.

■ EUSTON

Chutney's

124 Drummond St, NW1 071-387 6077

Open Mon-Sat noon-2.45pm, 6-11.15pm, Sun noon-10.30pm.

Chutney's is part of a group with restaurants in Los Angeles and Bombay and this bright, cheerful, very good-value London branch specialises in Indian vegetarian food. With dishes from different parts of the sub-continent, the menu gives a good cross-section. Don't miss the excellent sev poori—fried dough full of potatoes with a little yoghurt and flavoured with different sauces. The set meals beginning at £3.95 are extraordinarily good value.

Diwana Bhel Poori House

121 Drummond St, NW1 071-387 5556

Open daily noon-11.30pm.

The Diwana Bhel Poori has been popular for years with both locals and visitors to this part of London that resembles Little India. A small, basic café with no bookings and a busy atmosphere, a good way to sample the menu is to order a selection of starters like bhel poori, samosa and onion bhajis, leaving out main dishes. The set buffet lunch is £4.95. It's unlicensed, but you can take your own wine and the mango milk shake is delicious.

Great Nepalese

48 Eversholt St, NW1 071-388 6737

Open daily noon-2.45pm, 6-11.45pm.

Just by Euston station, this restaurant is another long-term favourite, and another rather unprepossessing-looking restaurant in this Indian corner of London. Inside, however, it's old-fashioned but relatively smart. Chicken tikka, mutton and curries are moist and well-cooked, masco (deep-fried lentil cakes) and fish masala are worth a visit alone and vegetarians are well looked after. The Nepalese set meal at £9.95 gives a good tour of the country's cuisine. Don't miss the coriander pickle. Service is good.

■ FINCHLEY ROAD

Green Cottage

9 New College Parade, Finchley Rd, NW3 - 071-722 5305/7892

Open daily noon-11.15pm.

This consistently good Cantonese restaurant—handily situated between Swiss Cottage and Finchley Road underground stations—cooks some excellent one-dish meals based on barbecued meats: roasted duck and crispy pork belly, barbecued spare ribs, and a mixture of 'soyed' meats: liver, gizzard, squid and duck wings for the adventurous. Vegetarians are well-catered for: one recommended dish is the 'Buddha's cushion' of stewed black moss with mushrooms and vegetables. Fish feature in dishes like mixed seafood in a potato basket. Set meals vary from £11.50 to £15 per person. Service is brisk, and the décor is not inspiring.

■ FULHAM

Harvey's Café
358 Fulham Rd, SW10
071-352 0625
Open Tues-Sat noon-3pm, Mon-Sat 7.30-11pm. No cards.

Harvey's Café is a room above the Black Bull pub that has been turned into a successful small restaurant, an increasingly popular trend in London these days. Chef/owner Harvey Sambrook prepares a changing menu of Mediterranean-inspired dishes with a Californian slant, making good use of roasted peppers, aubergines and sun-dried tomatoes. The large dining room sports large pictures on the walls, the atmosphere is young and friendly and the service similar. Set lunch served Tuesday to Friday is good value at £5. The pub downstairs has also been taken over by Mr Sambrook and serves light snacks taken from the restaurant menu and a good selection of wines by the glass.

Mamta
692 Fulham Rd, SW6
071-736 5914

Open Wed-Sun 12.30-3.30pm, daily 6-11pm.

One of the few London Indian bhel poori houses to elevate itself above café status, here the décor is elegant and chic and the food prepared with notable attention to detail. Those uninitiated in this style of vegetarian food, made up of several snack dishes, will discover a subtle cuisine of contrasting textures and flavours that is both spicy and delicate. Thali, a complete meal served on a stainless steel tray, is the perfect introduction. Graduate to their dosai, a paper-thin pancake stuffed with potato and onion eaten with a spicy dal sauce and coconut chutney, and sev poori—crisp pastry filled with spiced potatoes, topped with yoghurt, tamarind sauce and sprinkled with fine crisp noodles that look like shredded wheat. Reckon on around £12 for a full meal.

Nosh Brothers Bar and Restaurant
773 Fulham Rd, SW6
071-736 7311
Open Tues-Sat 6-11pm.

Don't be worried by the name, the Nosh Brothers are not a pair of lager louts, but a couple of imaginative young cooks with a good eye for producing a lively and affordable restaurant (around £14 for a good meal). The constantly changing menu features fashionable and well-cooked dishes like pan-fried scallops with coriander and sharp lime pesto, and filling desserts like chocolate rum mousse. There's an intelligent, short

wine list. If you want to talk, try the ground-floor room; if you're a loud group, go down to the basement.

■ GOLDERS GREEN

Laurent
428 Finchley Rd, NW2
071-794 3603
Open Mon-Sat noon-2pm, 6-11pm.

If good Tunisian couscous is what you're after, make your way to this family-run restaurant which uncompromisingly offers nothing but couscous for a main dish (although it does offer a starter of brik à l'œuf—a deep-fried wafer-thin sheet of pastry folded across an egg). The couscous comes with lamb and merguez sausages, with a mixed grill of brochette of lamb, lamb chop and merguez or vegetarian, and ranges in price from around £7 to £10. The cooking is consistently good and the prices reasonable, the décor jolly with gingham check tablecloths and the service friendly.

■ GREAT PORTLAND STREET

Efes Kebab House
80 Gt Titchfield St, W1
071-636 1953
Open Mon-Sat noon-11.30pm.

This family-run kebab house has been serving good, well-priced Turkish food to local office workers since 1974. It squeezes into our bargain bites section by virtue of its good set lunches and dinners at £14 and £15 per person respectively. Most people come for the tender grilled lamb and chicken kebabs preceded by starters like stuffed vine leaves and chicken with walnut sauce. Turkish beer (Efespilsen) is a good accompaniment. Turkish coffee is tongue-tinglingly strong.

■ ISLINGTON

Café Flo

334 Upper St, N1 - 071-226 7916
Open Mon-Fri 9am-11.30pm, Sat 8.30am-11.30pm, Sun 8.30am-11pm.

A remarkably successful chain (like Café Rouge) that produces authentic-looking French bistros at good, cheap bistro prices. The food that is served all day is conventional: baguettes which tend to be stuffed with bland fillings, more successful fish soup, salades tièdes, moules and steak and chips. In the Islington branch the service is good and the atmosphere more relaxed than elsewhere in the chain. We frequently sit there over coffee that has long gone cold, reading a newspaper or watching the world go by. Branches throughout London.

■ KENSINGTON

Café Rouge

2 Lancer Sq, Kensington Church St, W8 - 071-938 4200
Open Mon-Sat 10am-11pm, Sun 10am-10.30pm.

One of the prettiest of the Café Rouge chain with a light, airy interior and views out to a small square,

service is friendly and the brasserie-style food honest and generally well-cooked. Prices for main courses are around £6 to £7. It's frequently full of the young laden down by shopping bags sporting fashionable names sipping coffee and nibbling croissants or taking a long lunch. Branches throughout London.

Sticky Fingers

1a Phillimore Gdns, W8
071-938 5388
Open Mon-Sat noon-11.30pm, Sun noon-11pm.

Bill Wyman left The Rolling Stones and now claims to earn more money from his restaurant. Sticky Fingers is covered with Stones' memorabilia—from old instruments and record covers to Mr Wyman's own photographs of his ex-colleagues. It succeeds because it doesn't try to be anything other than a good hamburger joint for the whole family at reasonable prices (around £5 for large burgers). It is genuinely child-friendly: along with a small portion the staff deliver a colouring book with a 'draw-your-waiter/waitress-competition'. The last time we were there a child broke a glass and the waitress checked first that the little customer was all right before clearing it up. The friendly, young staff work hard and fast.

■ KILBURN

Billboard Café

222 Kilburn High Rd, NW6
071-328 1374
Open Mon-Sat 6.30pm-12.45am, Sat, Sun noon-3pm.

Italy with a touch of California provides the inspiration for the cooking in this surprising café in Kilburn. Bresaola and brushcetta, pastas and grilled meats and well-grilled vegetables with occasional live music are what the predominantly local following go for. American-style Sunday brunch at £6.25 is fun.

■ KNIGHTS-BRIDGE

The Fifth Floor Café

Harvey Nichols, Knightsbridge, SW1 - 071-235 5250
Open Mon-Sat 10am-10.30pm, Sun 11am-4.30pm.

Part of the new look Harvey Nichols, this café on the fifth floor serves a useful purpose for those who cannot get into the restaurant or want a less expensive, quick alternative. It's also a very attractive place, in part of the high-tech food hall. At lunchtime you'll find it full of fashionable ladies with Harvey Nichols shopping bags, tucking into dishes like stuffed squid with lemon dressing (£5.50) or grilled lamb kebabs with aubergine relish. The set daily menu offers three courses for £12.50 and afternoon tea (a particular favourite) is £7.50 for sandwiches, scones with clotted cream and jam, tea or coffee. There's usually a singer between 8 and 10.30pm in the evening and in summer you can sit on the balcony.

> *Find the address you are looking for, quickly and easily, in the **index**.*

Stockpot

6 Basil St, SW1 - 071-589 8627
Open Mon-Sat 8am-11pm, Sun noon-10.30pm. No cards.

One of London's real bargains, the Stockpot chain has been feeding rich and poor for years. We used to eat here as students in our impoverished days and still go there when shopping for clothes rather than books. The wooden floor and stripped pine booths are still the same, as is the menu in general. A starter of melon or avocado salad followed by perhaps a plate of chicken korma with peas, rice *and* chips and finishing off with stewed gooseberries and lashings of custard, plus mineral water will cost around £6. All the Stockpots get very crowded and there is always a queue, but it's well worth the wait. Branches throughout London.

■ LADBROKE GROVE

Canal Brasserie

222 Kensal Rd, W10
081-960 2732
Open Mon-Fri 9am-7pm, evening opening times vary.

Walk in from the bleak surroundings of Kensal Road and you'll be surprised by the startling décor of this old factory on the Grand Union Canal. There's an extraordinary metal sculpture on the wall and a lift with a turret going up and down. Most of the customers at the Canal Brasserie come from the nearby film and recording studios to sample an eclectic modern menu which changes daily and ranges from Thai chicken curry to Italian dishes to couscous. Prices are more restaurant than bargain bite, although you can just get away with our £15 limit. It's a particularly good place in the summer when the atrium gives you a view of the canal. Though lunch is a fixed feast, dinner is moveable, and they often hold special club nights or ethnic food nights, so telephone first to check.

■ MAYFAIR

Joe's Restaurant/Bar

Fenwick of Bond St, 63 New Bond St, W1 - 071-629 9161
Open Mon-Wed, Fri, Sat 9.30am-6pm, Thurs 9.30am-7.30pm.

Fashion designer Joseph Ettedgui has expanded his empire yet again. In-store restaurants have recently become wildly fashionable and Fenwick's has joined the ranks. This, the latest Joe's, opened late 1993 on the second floor and has become the canteen for Vogue staff who work around the corner. On our last visit we spotted the managing editor and designer Katharine Hamnett. And on your way out you can purchase an item from the Joseph boutique. Oh, by the way, the food is fresh, good and moderately priced, with salads (the main things the ultra-thin Vogue staff appear to eat) around £6.

---

*The **prices** in this guide reflect what establishments were charging at the time of going to press.*

■ NOTTING HILL GATE

All Saints

12 All Saints Rd, W11
071-243 2808
Open Tues-Sun 10am-3pm, Mon-Sat 7.30-11.15pm, Sun brunch 10am-3pm.

A crowded, popular hang-out in the heart of Portobello with hefty portions of a wide-ranging menu that goes from roast vegetables with aioli to cod with salsa verde and mustard fruits. Adventurous dishes, costing from £5 for starters and £8 for main dishes, built around what is available and fresh that day make this an exciting small restaurant.

Caps

64 Pembridge Rd, W11
071-229 5177
Open Mon-Sat 6-11.15pm.

An unexpected find this, and part of the delightful Pembridge Court Hotel. Caps, with its unassuming entrance and fun décor, with bare-brick walls and odd artefacts on them offers a menu of good, mixed cooking with more than a nod towards Thailand. Kick off with Thai vegetable spring rolls at £2.95 or Thai steamed salmon mousse at £3.95 (or deep fried brie or mushroom Strognaoff) and progress onto delicious hot Thai noodles, stir-fried with shrimps at £5.95 or just roast duck with black cherry sauce (at £9.45 the most expensive item). Desserts are equally tempting. It's a good local restaurant and somewhere to remember after a hard

Smithfield Market

A horse market, the site of the rowdy Bartholomew Fair (held here from 1123 until 1855), a tournament, jousting and sporting venue, a place of public execution and witch burning, it became a cattle market in 1638. The present buildings date from 1869, some years after Smithfield had become a dead-meat market. Apart from the entertainment value (early morning risers only), this is the place to come for a hearty porter's breakfast at one of the surrounding pubs—bacon, eggs, sausages and tomatoes all washed down with beer.

Saturday's shopping in Portobello Road.

Khan's
13-15 Westbourne Grove, W2 - 071-727 5420
Open daily noon-3pm, 6pm-midnight.
In 1977 when this large attractively-decorated restaurant opened in a former tea-room it was a novelty with its blue walls and colonial atmosphere and good food, a far cry from the standard red-flock places we had grown up with. But although it has now been left behind as Indian restaurants have gone up-market and Indian cooking has improved, it is still a fun place to eat. Purists will look down their noses, but it's worth going for the tandoori dishes. Reckon on around £12 per person.

Standard Indian Restaurant
21-23 Westbourne Grove, W2 - 071-229 0600
Open daily noon-3pm, 6pm-midnight.
Another long-term favourite with Londoners and visitors, this restaurant consistently delivers well-prepared dishes. Surprises are few and far between, as the name implies, but all the dishes are well-cooked; we urge you to try the chana masaladar and chicken tikka masala (a dish you'll find in every Indian restaurant in Britain). The latter is good enough to give you a yardstick for other Indian restaurants' efforts. Set lunch is good value at £7.55.

■ OXFORD STREET

O'Keefe's
19 Dering St, W1 - 071-495 0878
Open Mon-Sat 8am-5pm, Thurs 7.30-10.30pm.
Oh, that there were more such places in London. A cool Mediterranean décor, small tables and friendly staff have transformed what was once just another sandwich bar into a very good café/restaurant. The menu changes daily. On our latest visit, the gumbo soup served with fresh baked bread could have been a meal in itself, but there's a £7.50 minimum at lunch so order carefully. Southern crab cakes with avocado salsa, roasted vegetable salad and vegetarian dishes are typical of the exciting, well-prepared food. Desserts follow the pecan pie/chocolate cake type. Coffee is good.

■ PICCADILLY

Café Sogo
39-45 Haymarket, SW1
071-333 9000
Open daily noon-10pm.
A bargain in the form of a sushi bar in an expensive Japanese department store near Piccadilly Circus is a pleasant surprise. Well-made assorted sushi are £7.80 to £11 at plain wooden tables, or at the bar in this light, airy spot; à la carte is best enjoyed at the bar where you can choose from ingredients in a refrigerated cabinet. Set meals of sushi plus soup are from £8.80 to £13 and are served until 3pm.

Café Torino
189 Piccadilly, W1 - 071-434 1921
Open Mon-Sat 8am-7.30pm, Sun 9.30am-7.30pm.
Café Torino, we always feel, belongs to an endangered species: a self-service café/restaurant in the heart of London which serves honest, unfashionable grub at reasonable prices. It's a gracious if faded place serving cold salads, hot dishes like lasagne, coffee and cakes. You can linger here over a cup of coffee and the staff are pleasant and welcoming—

another plus in an area that is mainly geared to passing trade.

Fountain Restaurant

Fortnum & Mason, 181 Piccadilly, W1 - 071-734 8040
Open Mon-Sat 7.30am-11pm.

It's a mystery that so few people know that this pretty, colonial-style restaurant has such long opening hours. It's a good place for breakfasts which range from a continental breakfast at £4.95 to the filling English variety at £7.95, for snacks and sandwiches throughout the day, afternoon tea, and full lunch and dinner menus. In fact it is a thoroughly useful restaurant with good, though not spectacular cooking operating at nearly full capacity most of the day. The murals on the walls depict Mr Fortnum and Mr Mason on their imaginary travels in the eighteenth century, visiting tea, coffee, cocoa and sugar merchants and growers. The atmosphere is calm and the clientele invariably well-off. If you like the brand of tea you've just drunk, you can, during shop hours, purchase it.

Hard Rock Café

150 Old Park Lane, W1 071-629 0382
Open daily 11.30am-12.30am.

The owner of the Hard Rock Café does his bit for charity: a certain percentage of the profits goes for the homeless and other good causes. The place is packed with rock history: old guitars, photos, posters and record covers are everywhere. Queueing up

for the Hard Rock Café has been a tradition for years for visitors and many people swear it's the best burger place in London at average burger prices.

Pierre Victoire

6 Panton St, W1 - 071-930 6463
Open Mon-Sat noon-4pm, 5.30-11pm.

Pierre Victoire, a bistro which originated in Edinburgh and which now has a branch in Knightsbridge, serves astonishingly cheap, ambitious food. Their £4.90 lunch special includes dishes like millefeuille with mushrooms, jamboyenne de Bayonne and a brandy cream, or avocado with smoked salmon and pork casserole with garlic, small vegetables and fresh mint, followed by desserts or cheese. Coffee is only an extra 50p.

Planet Hollywood

Trocadero, Piccadilly, W1 071-287 1000
Open daily 11.30am-1am.

Planet Hollywood opened with a huge hullaballoo with Hollywood stars Bruce Willis, Sylvester Stallone and Arnold Schwarzenegger. The interior is a Hollywood version of the Hard Rock Café and the burgers are suitable for Rambos and action heroes.

Royal Academy Restaurant

Royal Academy, Burlington House, W1 - 071-439 7438
Open Mon-Sat 10am-5.45pm.

Sweep past the queues for the Royal Academy exhibitions and go down the

stairs to this very popular restaurant. The room is grand with big windows, sculptures and a painted ceiling; the clientele a mixture of tweedy types up from the country and arty types from London. The self-service restaurant does hot dishes from £5 to £6, and a range of imaginative salads based on roast beef, quiche, salmon and more. Eat your first course, then go back for the delicious cakes and desserts—Burlington cake is particularly rewarding.

The Wren at St James's Church

35 Jermyn St, SW1 - 071-437 9419
Open Mon-Sat 8am-7pm, Sun 10am-5pm. No cards.

Located in the beautiful church of St James, the small, bright Wren serves a wholefood vegetarian menu of soups like carrot, cashew nut and apple, jacket potatoes and more substantial dishes. It's a good place to dive into after walking around the Friday and Saturday craft market held in the tiny churchyard on the Piccadilly side. Main dishes are around £4 to £5.

■ PRIMROSE HILL

The Lansdowne

90 Gloucester Ave, NW1 071-483 0409
Open Mon 6-11pm, Tues-Sat 11am-11pm, Sun noon-3pm, 7-11pm. Lunch Tues-Sun, Dinner Mon-Sun. No cards.

The Lansdowne is another of those pubs which have become so well known for their food that they have almost ceased to be pubs as we know them and are now restaurants with a bar attached. There is a daily choice of a soup like roast tomato with pesto, a pasta, a different sandwich or brushchetta and a hot dish like fresh tuna with borlotti beans. The young staff are friendly. It's a good place to stop on any day of the week (except Monday) after strolling along the Regent's Park Canal from Camden Town.

Lemonia
89 Regent's Park Rd, NW1
071-589 7454
Open Sun-Fri noon-3pm, Mon-Sat 6-11.30pm.

Lemonia began in a small restaurant over the road (now renamed Lemonika) then expanded into what was once a pub and is now an elegant, spacious Greek Cypriot restaurant, which is something of an oxymoron. Always popular, its welcoming staff have been known to locals for years, in fact some of them started off down in Camden Town and have, as it were, moved up in the world. Food is tasty, with the meze at £9.25 per person delivering the goods with every dish. Taramasalata is fishy and sharp, halloumi (fried cheese) dry and nicely tart, mixed grill of brochettes of pork, lamb cutlets and meatballs juicy. The wine list is longer than usual and the restaurant continues to have queues at the door.

> *The **prices** in this guide reflect what establishments were charging at the time of going to press.*

■ SHEPHERD'S BUSH

Adam's Café
77 Askew Rd, W12
081-743 0572
Open Mon-Sat 7.30-10.30pm. No cards.

Abdel Boukraa and his English wife Frances serve breakfast-every-which-way during the day, then at dinner time out come the candles and the moody music and their labyrinthine café metamorphoses into a Tunisian restaurant. Recently refurbished and expanded, it now looks more Tunisian than 'caff' and although they keep an impressive list of North African wines, they still operate a bring-your-own-bottle policy. A succession of tasty little appetisers around £2.50 including meatballs, olives with spiced peppers and a bowl of chilli-hot harissa arrive automatically. Couscous, served from a tureen, is the mainstay of a short menu which also offers brik à l'œuf, kebabs, grilled fish and tagine, with sticky pastries to finish. Reckon around £14 per person.

■ SOHO

Andrew Edmunds Wine Bar & Restaurant
46 Lexington St, W1
071-437 5708
Open daily 12.30-3pm, 5.30-11pm.

Although it calls itself a wine bar, Andrew Edmunds is much more of a small French bistro. They do however have a well-chosen wine list with a wide geographical and

price range. Tables close together, a comfortable atmosphere and daily-changing menu of honest food make this a very popular place. You might get venison stew, a range of pastas and good salads with goat's cheese, and deserts like tiramisù. Prices are very reasonable for such good food, and it just squeezes into our bargain bite section—expect to pay around £15 per person.

Café Bohème
13 Old Compton St, W1
071-734 0632
Open Mon-Sat 8am-3am, Sun 10am-11pm.

A hugely popular local hang-out that succeeds well in attracting the young crowds in Soho. It's crowded and friendly and there's often a small jazz group playing in the front bar area. Food is standard brasserie fare of the sandwiches, steak frites variety and prices follow the same pattern—around £6 to £8 for a main dish.

Ed's Easy Diner
12 Moor St, W1 - 071-439 1955
Open Mon-Thurs 11.30am-midnight, Fri, Sat 11.30am-12.30am, Sun 9am-11pm. No cards.

The interior of all the four restaurants is 50s retro with shining steel and suitably unsubtle colours. The juke box is cheap and packed with old rock and roll records for the punters. Hamburgers come big and juicy and around £4 to £5 and are washed down with beer or soft drinks. Branches throughout London.

137

Harry's Bar

19 Kingly St, W1 - 071-434 0309
Open daily noon-3pm, 10pm-6am.

In the days when London shut down at 11pm, Harry's Bar was a godsend. It's still something of a rarity, catering to night owls and early risers with strong stomachs. Food is good and filling with a selection of sandwiches, omelettes and filled jacket potatoes. For £6.95 the Blow Out on the night time menu fills you with typical British breakfast fare; the more delicate might prefer smoked salmon and scrambled eggs.

Jimmy's

23 Frith St, W1 - 071-439 7851
Open Mon-Sat 12.30-3pm, Mon-Wed 5.30-11pm, Thurs-Sat 5.30-11.30pm. No cards.

Jimmy's starts to jump later on when it fills up and gets very loud. It's been here for years, the food is cheap Greek Cypriot standbys like stifado (stew) and all dishes come complete with chips and salad. And it's very cheap, with main dishes around £4 to £6.

Kettners

29 Romilly St, W1 - 071-734 6112
Open daily noon-midnight.

Owned by Peter Boizot who sold the PizzaExpress chain to concentrate on Pizza on the Park, Condotti and Kettners, this old Soho restaurant is something of an oddity: a very reasonably priced hamburger, steak, pizza and salad place in an elegant, old-fashioned setting. The

Champagne bar—on your left as you walk in—is a good meeting place.

Ley-On's

56-58 Wardour St, W1 071-437 6465
Open Mon-Sat noon-11.30pm, Sun 11.30am-10.30pm.

Part of old Soho, just north rather than south of Shaftesbury Avenue, Ley-On's was opened as a Chinese restaurant as long ago as 1926. It's still rather grand if a little faded. The long menu can daunt if you don't know your Chinese food, so we recommend sticking to the dim sum (served from 11.30am to 4.30pm). You can spend as little as £7 or as much as £30 a head, depending on how hungry you are.

Panda Si Chuen

56 Old Compton St, W1 071-437 2069
Open Mon-Sat noon-11.30pm.

A rightly popular Chinese restaurant with a lengthy menu of good Szechuan dishes and set meals from £9.50 to £16.50. Spiced fish, shredded pork with aubergine, herb-marinated beef are all recommended and portions are generous. They serve saké or tea and wine.

Soho Brasserie

23-25 Old Compton St, W1 071-439 9301/3758.
Open Mon-Fri 11am-11pm, Sat noon-midnight, Sun 11am-10pm.

The Soho Brasserie opened before chains like Café Rouge and Café Flo had become popular and was something of a novelty. Now it is one of

many, but still fun. The bar is a good place for a snack, the restaurant behind the long bar serves more substantial meals. Set meals are from £8.95 for two courses.

■ SOUTH KENSINGTON

La Bouchée

56 Old Brompton Rd, SW7 071-589 1929
Open Mon-Fri 9.30am-11pm, Sat, Sun 10am-11pm.

Something of a find in fashionable Old Brompton Road, La Bouchée is a good old-fashioned neighbourhood French restaurant. You can sip a coffee and watch the crowds go by, enjoy bistro-type dishes like goat's cheese salad, snails in garlic butter, or try the good-value set menus. For £4.95 you might get a choice of soupe du jour or poireaux vinaigrettes and saucisses frites. For £6.95 the choice is wider. Food is well-cooked and good value, service is friendly.

Café Lazeez

93-95 Old Brompton Rd, SW7 - 071-581 9993
Open Mon-Sat noon-12.30am, Sun noon-7pm.

Practically next door to Christie's auction rooms, this is, suprisingly, an Indian café/bar downstairs and a restaurant above. The female chef, Sabiha Kasin, cooks 'evolved' dishes, which means that Indian dishes are westernised and made rather more bland. The décor is smart, again unlike an Indian place. For another culture shock, go downstairs for the Indian Welsh rarebit with tomatoes, onions, chillies, black pepper and grated cheese (the latter the only 'Welsh' bit) on toast and grilled at £3.10, or the excellent tandoori cubes of ham, chicken or vegetables marinated in a special 'Lazeez' sauce on lettuce, onions and pepper with rice or rather surprisingly, french fries for £6.10. As their last orders are at 12.30am, they are popular with the late-night crowd.

Daquise

20 Thurloe St, SW7
071-589 6117
Open daily 10am-11.30pm. No cards.

We've been coming to this Polish café/restaurant for years. If you're hungry, then it's a good place for filling Polish food at lunch for around £6. Otherwise, it's best to go for coffee and cakes at any time, particularly if you're footsore after wandering around South Kensington's museums.

■ TOTTENHAM COURT ROAD

Ikkyu

67 Tottenham Court Rd, W1
071-346 6169
Open Mon-Fri 12.30-2.30pm, Mon-Fri, Sun 6-10.30pm.

This busy basement restaurant near Goodge Street underground station is one of the best-value Japanese restaurants in central London. At lunchtime the place becomes hectic with the emphasis on set meals from £6 to £10 of sashimi, sushi, deep-fried dishes and teriyaki. In the evening the pace slows somewhat and the menu widens to include noodle dishes, salads and dishes like fried pork with Japanese leeks.

Mandeer

21 Hanway Pl, W1 - 071-323 0660
Open Mon-Sat noon-3pm, 5.30-10pm.

A cavernous, student-type basement restaurant serving southern Indian and Gujerati food, the Mandeer introduced many an Indian food freak to the continent's vegetarian dishes. 'Mandeer' means temple and there's an air of reverence in this incense-filled place which serves a good value buffet at lunchtime, a wider choice at dinner, fruit juice and organic wine.

Wagamama

4 Streatham St, WC1
071-323 9223
Open Mon-Fri noon-2.30pm, Sat 1-3.30pm, 6-11pm.

From the moment this ramen bar opened, the queues were spilling out onto the street. And it's not difficult to see why. A striking minimalist design, cheerful staff taking orders on computer terminals, a menu based around one-pot dishes or ramen (Chinese-style noodles in broth) combined with char-grilled meat, seafood and vegetables have made this the place to eat. You sit at long wooden tables, turnover is fast and Japanese tea is free. About £9 for a blow-out. Don't miss it.

> *Find the address you are looking for, quickly and easily, in the index.*

■ TRAFALGAR SQUARE

Café in the Crypt

St-Martin-in-the-Fields, Duncannon St, WC2
071-839 4342
Open Mon-Sat 10am-8pm, Sun noon-6pm.

This basement café serves good, basic food to a mixed clientele: tourists from all over the world, priests, business men and not so well-off Londoners. The crypt also has an art gallery, brass rubbing centre, book shop and next door a little chapel for private prayer. Piped classical music softens the stone walls and the food—anything from a sandwich to a large salad, lasagne or chicken with vegetables—is good. The atmosphere is friendly and welcoming which comes partly from the bustle of activity and partly from a more spiritual inspiration: St Martin's was one of the first churches to operate a policy of taking care of London's homeless and somehow the spirit of charity has permeated the place.

Sainsbury Wing Brasserie

National Gallery, Trafalgar Sq, WC2 - 071-389 1769
Open Mon-Sat 10am-5pm, Sun 2-5pm.

Apart from the Tate Gallery, this is (sadly) the only good restaurant in a public museum. It's a restful place with comfortable chairs and tables, friendly staff and a good changing menu which might include char-grilled spicy sausages, pan-fried fillet of salmon with prawn and caper sauce and other modish dishes. Three-course meals range from £9 to £11.25 depending on the main dish. Portions are generous. Or you can just try a baguette filled with hot ham, gruyère and tomato, a side salad for an eminently reasonable £1 or salads ranging in price from £1.80 as a starter to £5.25 as a main course. One great advantage is the wonderful view over Trafalgar Square (the brasserie is on the first floor). If you're in London at Christmas time, you look out at the giant Christmas tree in the Square, lit up with thousands of white lights and often surrounded by carol singers.

■ VICTORIA

Bonjour, Bonsoir
10 Greycoat Pl, SW1
071-222 8866
Open Mon-Sat 8am-5pm. No cards.

In an area of mostly dreary sandwich bars this spacious café with cream walls, black tables and assorted chairs stands out. The French owner seeks to offer 'real food that is fast but not instant'. Not everything is home-cooked and original but much is. Instead of bread with soup there are cheese puffs; pizzas and pies taste, and are, fresh. There is elegant pâtisserie, fine French chocolate, and as an importer of Bizac charcuterie, delicious Loire pâtés in sandwiches to eat here or take away. Continental breakfast—Lavazza coffee, croissant (superb), baguette, butter and jam is probably London's best value at £1.50.

Café Méditerranée
St James Ct, 41 Buckingham Gate, SW1
071-834 6655
Open Mon-Sat 7am-10.30pm, Sun 7.30am-10.30pm.

The rather oddly-decorated and lit Café Méditerranée offers a buffet at lunchtime at £15 per person. It's worth finding out when they have a special festival of foods from different countries. The Taj group, who own the hotel, flies chefs in to create marvellous arrays of different regional foods about four times a year.

■ WATERLOO

Benkei Japanese Eatery
19 Lower Marsh, SE1
071-401 2343
Open Mon-Fri noon-3pm, Mon-Sat 6-10.30pm.

'Eatery' suits this tiny place with seating on bar stools at black counters. West Indian owners with international staff prepare decent sushi, sashimi and tempura; fried, stir-fried and grilled items attest their cheap Japanese authenticity with sugar and MSG galore. Eating à la carte or from a lunch menu costs around £7 per person upwards, excluding service. Tea is free.

The Fire Station
150 Waterloo Rd, SE1
071-401 3267
Open Mon-Sat 11am-3pm, 6.30-11pm.

The Fire Station is just that, a vast, cavernous fire station converted into a vast, cavernous restaurant with an unremittingly high noise level. Located near Waterloo Station and the Young Vic, and just down the road from the famous flower stall run by Buster Edwards—better known as one of the great train robbers—it has been trying to keep its huge numbers of customers happy since it opened in late 1993. There's a strong element of pot luck here; sometimes the food runs out early, at other times there's a good choice. Dishes are inexpensive—around £4 to £6 each, using imaginative materials often discarded in more up-market places for excellent rabbit pâté, skate and lentils, smoked haddock and duck livers. Clientele is mostly young and patient, and many use it as a wine bar rather than a restaurant.

BRITISH FARE

■ COVENT GARDEN

Porters
17 Henrietta St, WC2
071-836 6466
Open Mon-Sat noon-11.30pm, Sun noon-10.30pm.

Popular with both tourists and Londoners, this large, busy restaurant with its mock traditional Victorian interior specialises in pies. Lamb and apricot or Cumberland pie (beef, carrots, onions and tomatoes cooked in ale and herbs topped by potato and cheese), served with vegetables or side salad costs around £7.50. Those with delicate appetites might prefer salmon fish cakes. Puddings are solid and traditional—sticky toffee or steamed syrup sponge are favourites.

■ FINCHLEY

Two Brothers Fish Restaurant

297-303 Regent's Park Rd, N3 - 081-346 0496
Open Tues-Sat noon-2.30pm, 5.30-10.15pm. No cards.

The Manzi brothers, Leon and Tony, whose family started the Manzi's restaurant group, operate this first-rate fish and chip shop where you sit at wooden tables in an attractive blue interior, sampling fresh, crisp fish and excellent chips (and the hollandaise sauce is worth a visit on its own) and bread and butter puddings, all of which will cost around £11 per person.

■ HACKNEY

F Cooke & Sons

41 Kingsland High St, E8
071-254 2878
Open Mon-Wed 10am-7pm, Thurs 10am-8pm, Fri, Sat 10am-10pm. No cards.

Useful if you're visiting the Geffrye Museum nearby, though visitors may find the traditional jellied eels a bit hard to take. Still, at between £2 and £4 a plate you can hardly do better for a bargain bite, and the tiled and mirrored décor takes you back about 100 years.

■ ISLINGTON

Upper Street Fish Shop

324 Upper St, N1 - 071-359 1401

Open Tues-Sat noon-2pm, Mon-Sat 5.30-10pm. No cards.

In the heart of increasingly trendy Islington, this small local is always crowded. The décor is more French bistro than English 'chippie' with wood panelling and mirrors along one wall. Starters include salmon pâté or Pacific oysters, main fish dishes are large and good (costing around £7 to £8 per dish) puddings include bread and butter pudding. You can either bring your own wine (Champagne is traditional) or drink tea.

■ NOTTING HILL GATE

Costas Fish Restaurant

18 Hillgate St, W8 - 071-727 4310
Open Tues-Sat noon-2.30pm, 5.30-10.30pm. No cards.

Excellent fish and chips in a small room which doesn't encourage you to linger. But Costas, which at around £8 for the whole meal is a real bargain, along with its neighbour Costas Grill, has become a Notting Hill institution.

Geales

2 Farmer St, W8 - 071-727 7969
Open Tues-Sat noon-3pm, 6-11pm.

Fresh fish fried in delicate batter served with crisp chips show you what fish and chips should taste like at a price slightly above average (about £9.50 each). Unusually for such a place, they serve good bisque to start though

puddings are designed for large, British appetites. And it's all in a traditional setting: you sit on rustic-style chairs in a pretty restaurant that has been catering to Notting Hill types for fifty years. No booking, but you can sip a glass of wine while waiting.

■ SOHO

Grahame's Seafare

38 Poland St, W1 - 071-437 3788
Open Mon-Sat noon-2.45pm, 5.30-9pm (to 8pm Fri & Sat).

Just near Oxford Street, the dark green banquettes, white linen and pictures on the walls make this an unusual fish and chippery. Even more unusual is the fact that this is a kosher fish and chip restaurant which only just squeezes into our bargain bite section as you will find yourself paying £15 minimum. Starters include smoked salmon and cold bortsch; main course fish is simply and well cooked and the gefilte fish salad substantial and tasty. Motherly waitresses make customers feel at home.

■ ST JOHN'S WOOD

Sea Shell Fish Restaurant and Takeaway

49-51 Lisson Grove, NW1
071-723 8703/071-724 1063
Open Mon-Fri noon-2.15pm, 5.15-10.30pm, Sat noon-10.30pm.

The Sea Shell has been going for years, which is not surprising as it is one of the best-known fish and chip restaurants in London. But there have been complaints in recent years that the restaurant is resting on its laurels. Certainly on our last visit we found both the fish and the chips a bit too greasy. Its premises are smart and spacious and attract a predominantly local London clientele. Prices are quite high (fried plaice on the bone is £8.90 for example).

■ VICTORIA

The Seafresh Fish Restaurant
80-81 Wilton Rd, SW1
071-828 0747
Open Mon-Sat noon-10.45pm.

Fishing nets hang from the ceiling and pictures of boats adorn the walls of this popular and usefully placed (near Victoria station), family-run restaurant, in the same premises since 1965. Except for the scampi, all the fish is fresh. It is skilfully fried—or grilled for £1 extra. If you choose grilled ask for it plain, unless you like it sprinkled with powdered dried herbs. They serve draught beer and some wines. The cost is around £14 per person, but worth it.

CAFES

■ BAYSWATER

Maison Bouquillon
45 Moscow Rd, W2
071-727 0373
Open Mon-Sat 8.30am-9pm, Sun 8.30am-8pm. No cards.

Regulars at this small café will probably throttle us for including their favourite; it's crowded enough already. But it's just far enough away from busy Queensway to escape most of the passing trade and so retains the feeling of a well-loved meeting spot for locals who sit for hours over their newspapers, coffee and pastries.

■ BLOOMS-BURY

Coffee Gallery
23 Museum St, WC1
071-436 0455
Open Mon-Fri 8am-5.30pm, Sat 10am-5.30pm. No cards.

A good place in a street with a large number of ordinary coffee bars with the added attraction of doubling as a small art gallery—the art on the walls changes monthly. Owner Piero Amodio comes from Amalfi so there's a southern Italian influence in the home-made soups, salads and the daily dish (hot in winter, cold in summer). There's a good selection of pastries and desserts and authentic cappuccino. Prices are very reasonable, with sandwiches around £3.50 and main dishes around £3 to £4.

■ COVENT GARDEN

Café Aroma
36a St Martin's Lane, WC2
071-836 5110
Open Mon-Sat 8am-11pm, Sun noon-8pm.

Café Aroma is a rapidly growing chain with new branches opening all the time. All the cafés are fun, with bright colours, good seating and jolly music.

Simple snacks on open shelves include freshly-made sandwiches with fillings like avocado, spinach and red pepper, or lamb tikka. Coffee comes in different roasts and varieties like Café Mexicana—sweet, strong, with a cinnamon stick in the glass and accompanied by an Aztec biscuit. You can either eat in or take away and the price will vary from a couple of pounds to about £5 depending on what you choose. Branches throughout London.

■ HAMPSTEAD

The Coffee Cup
74 Hampstead High St, NW3 - 071-435 7565
Open daily 8am-midnight. No cards.

This small, bow-fronted, old-fashioned and cosy coffee shop in the middle of Hampstead High Street has been attracting local celebrities and visitors for years. The £5.50 breakfast with toast, beans, tomatoes, mushroom, egg and sausage is enough to keep you going all day. A long menu offers sandwiches, grills and hot dishes throughout the day.

Louis Pâtisserie
32 Heath St, NW3 - 071-435 9908
Open daily 9.30am-6pm. No cards.

The same faces have been here for twenty-odd years, and those are just the waitresses! A small, crowded, friendly Hampstead institution serving good coffee and loose-leaf, not tea-bag tea (an increasingly rare occurrence) and a variety of continental pastries which you can also buy from the shop at the front. It gets very busy at peak times but otherwise is a relaxed spot with the atmosphere of a middle-European coffee shop.

KNIGHTS-BRIDGE

Café Minema
43 Knightsbridge, SW1
071-823 1269
Open Mon-Sat 9am-11.15pm, Sun 1pm-9pm.

Sitting in this glass-fronted café is rather like being in a goldfish bowl as the traffic passing by outside in Knightsbridge (or more usually at a halt) has an uninterrupted view. It's a fashionable spot serving Italian-inspired light food such as focaccia sandwiches filled with pastrami and brie for £5, pastas, salads and a hot dish of the day. Espresso comes in glasses. A useful place in an expensive part of London.

Pâtisserie Valerie
215 Old Brompton Rd, SW3
071-823 9971
Open Mon-Fri 7.30am-7.30pm, Sat 9am-7pm. Sun 9am-6.30pm.

This branch of Pâtisserie Valerie which opened sixty-five years after the original in Soho is much smarter than its parent; it caters for the sophisticated of Knightsbridge rather than the raffish of Soho. The menu is more extensive with salads and Italian sandwiches available (around £3.50 each) though most people come for the cakes and coffee.

MARYLE-BONE

Pâtisserie Valerie at Maison Sagne
105 Marylebone High St, W1 - 071-935 6240
Open Mon-Sat 8am-6pm, Sun 9am-6pm. No cards.

Maison Sagne was taken over by Pâtisserie Valerie in 1993 but has changed little. In an interior full of French murals of pastoral scenes, painted mirrors and photos, this is more like a Parisian coffee shop than an English café. But its customers mainly come from the communities that live around here and are more European than English. Good coffee and pastries and a small selection of hot dishes to choose from.

MAYFAIR

Café de Colombia
Museum of Mankind, 6 Burlington Gdns, W1
071-287 8148
Open Mon-Sat 10am-4.30pm, Sun 2.30-5pm (coffee and cakes only). No cards.

Master caterer Justin de Blank does a good job at the Café de Colombia. A small space with a contemporary décor within the Museum of Mankind, the salad-based lunch menu contains choices like home-cured gravlax with dill and mustard sauce and tuna Niçoise salad with lemon, herb and garlic dressing, all around £7. Cakes are good, and pure Colombian coffee first-rate. If you go in the mornings you'll be surrounded by art dealers from Cork Street taking a late breakfast.

NOTTING HILL GATE

Books for Cooks
4 Blenheim Crescent, W11
071-221 1992
Open Mon-Sat 9.30am-6pm. No cards.

A café within a book store? This is a real find. As you walk into the crowded store, the smells of first-rate cooking greet you and lead you through to a tiny room at the back with four or five small tables, surrounded by yet more bookshelves groaning with cooking tomes. Two or three starters and main dishes appear on the menu daily. The last time we went, soup, a light goat's cheese and walnut salad with lambs lettuce and a cappuccino cost around £7 per person. The food is always good and would be praised in any restaurant. The added pleasure of sitting in a tiny room which makes you feel as if you are in a friend's house turns this into a special occasion.

PRIMROSE HILL

Primrose Pâtisserie
136 Regent's Park Rd, NW1
071-722 7848
Open daily 8am-10pm. No cards.

A successful and pleasant café for the actors, writers and other mortals who live in this pretty part of London. Good salads, cakes and croissants at all times of day eaten in the tiny room which seems more like a private home than a café, or outside. A good snack meal will cost round £6.

■ SOHO

Bar Italia

22 Frith St, W1 - 071-437 4520
Open daily 24 hours except 6am-7am. No cards.

A friendly institution which becomes even busier when the cappuccino crowd arrives in the early hours. A large television screen dominates one end; there's an enormous photograph of Rocky Marciano behind the bar, and the regulars talk in Italian. Try to go during a football match when Italy is playing; it's more exciting than the real thing. Bar Italia is a genuine part of old Soho serving no-nonsense café food like pizza and sandwiches to accompany the coffee.

Caffé Nero

43 Frith St, W1 - 071-434 3887
Open Mon-Fri 8am-1am, Sat 9am-1am, Sun 9am-11pm. No cards.

A small Italian coffee bar war broke out when Caffé Nero opened and threatened to take custom away from the long-established Bar Italia opposite. But the two are quite different, with Caffé Nero's ultra-modern interior in marked contrast to the traditional café. Coffee is varied (a particularly tasty one is iced vanilla at £1.50) and there's the usual wide range of Italian pastries.

Maison Bertaux

28 Greek St, W1 - 071-437 6007
Open daily 9am-8pm. No cards.

A tiny café in the middle of Soho where little has changed for decades. In an increasingly fashionable area, they still only serve café-au-lait and pastries. Don't be surprised if occasionally you're swept upstairs at closing time and persuaded to buy a ticket for the small tea room that doubles as a theatre for productions put on by Metin Marlow, who has probably just served you your coffee. Maison Bertaux is a reminder of how Soho used to be.

Pâtisserie Valerie

44 Old Compton St, W1 071-437 3466
Open Mon-Fri 8am-8pm, Sat 8am-7pm, Sun 10am-5.30pm. No cards.

This favourite, busy café has been serving pastries and gâteaux to discerning Soho habitués for decades. This is a place for a continental breakfast, watching the ad men starting their day and the film editors ending theirs.

ICE CREAM

Despite the legendary British sweet tooth, there are very few ice cream parlours in London. You can indulge in a knickerbocker glory in establishments like Fortnum & Mason's Fountain

Restaurant, otherwise make your way to the following.

■ CAMDEN TOWN/ CHALK FARM

Marine Ices

8 Haverstock Hill, NW3 071-485 3132
Open Mon-Sat noon-3pm, 6-10.30pm, Sun noon-7.30pm. No cards.

Marine Ices was popular long before Camden Lock Market drew in the crowds on a weekend. Three generations of the Mansi family have been running the establishment since it opened in 1931 and though there is a restaurant attached, it's the tutti frutti, melon sorbet and huge sundaes that people come for.

■ HAMPSTEAD

Häagen-Dazs

75 Hampstead High St, NW3 - 071-794 0646
Open Mon-Thurs, Sun 10am-11pm, Fri, Sat 10am-11.30pm. No cards.

Häagen-Dazs has won an international reputation and we are prepared to pay higher prices for their ice creams than we are used to. The possibility of combining a large variety of flavours brings out the bizarre in people's tastes. Prices range from £1.20 for a single scoop of frozen yoghurt up to however much you can get into a cone (there is a limit). They do an excellent sundae for £3.25. Also at Häagen-Dazs on the Square, 14 Leicester Sq, WC2, 071-287 9577; Unit 6, The

---

Plan to travel? Look for Gault Millau's other Best of *guides to* Chicago, Florida, France, Germany, Hawaii, Hong Kong, Italy, Los Angeles, New England, New Orleans, New York, Paris, San Francisco, Thailand, Toronto, and Washington, D.C.

Piazza, WC2, 071-240 0236; 138a King's Rd, SW3, 071-823 9326.

PIZZERIAS

■ BLOOMS-BURY

PizzaExpress
30 Coptic St, WC1 - 071-636 3232
Open daily noon-midnight.
Thin crispy dough, thrown in the air like juggling balls by the cooks who work in front of the pizza ovens as you come in, generous fillings like Capricciosa (ham, pepperonata, egg, anchovy, capers, olives, mozzarella, tomato at £5.10) or Veneziana (onions, capers, olives, pine kernels, sultanas, mozzarella, tomato for £3.55 which includes a contribution to the Venice in Peril Fund) and good service make this one of the best of the Pizza-Express chain, and one of the best pizza parlours in town. It was once a dairy and they have kept the delightfully-tiled walls.

■ CAMDEN TOWN

Parkway Pizzeria
64 Parkway, NW1 - 071-485 0678
Open daily noon-midnight.
A popular, local, tiled pizzeria with art deco mirrors and lamps and the usual pizza restaurant marble-topped tables. Pizzas come in a dozen varieties, prices are good and service is brisk. A good bet when visiting Camden Market.

■ CHELSEA

La Delizia
Chelsea Farmers' Market, Sydney St, SW3 - 071-351 6701
Open daily noon-midnight. No cards.
Good Italian pizzas well-priced at around £5 to £6 make La Delizia popular with Chelsea folk and visitors alike, particularly on warm days when you can sit outside in the Chelsea Farmers' Market complex.

■ KNIGHTS-BRIDGE

Pizza on the Park
11 Knightsbridge, SW1 071-235 5550
Open daily 9am-midnight.
Pizza on the Park is a good pizza joint, with a light, stylish interior and excellent pizza ranging from the normal to the adventurous (Prince Carlo with leeks, parmesan, mozzarella, tomato at £5.40) and a Pizza of the month. Many people come for the entertainment, which is first-rate.

California Pizza Company
6 Blandford St, W1 - 071-486 7878
Open Mon-Sat 11.15am-11.15pm.
A suitably 'whacky' West Coast atmosphere in this popular pizza place where peculiar offerings like Passage to India (tandoori chicken, masala sauce, courgette, coriander and cucumber raita for £6.90) are served. Not the place for traditionalists, but fun, young and trendy with a good Californian wine list and in a pretty, light setting.

■ MAYFAIR

Condotti
4 Mill St, W1 - 071-499 1308
Open Mon-Sat 11.30am-midnight.
Prints and paintings on the white walls and excellent pizzas in an attractive restaurant. Good service, along with a wide choice of pizzas as well as different salads, make this a popular spot.

■ NOTTING HILL GATE

Calzone
2a Kensington Park Rd, W11 - 071-243 2003
Open daily 10am-11.30pm.
Good thin-based pizzas and fresh well-seasoned ingredients, including sea food, in a busy restaurant that is smarter than the average pizza joint. Calzone is a good stopover in an interesting area.

■ OXFORD STREET

Chicago Pizza Pie Factory
17 Hanover Sq, W1 071-629 2669
Open Mon-Sat 11.45am-11.30pm, Sun noon-10.30pm.
All the razzamatazz that Chicagoan Bob Payton brings to his London restaurants is here in this roomy basement bar and pizza place, full of memorabilia from Chicago. Londoners were introduced to deep-pan pizzas from Chicago here.

145

They also serve hamburgers and salads and classic cocktails. Child-friendly, it's a good place to come on Sundays to keep the little ones happy.

■ SOUTH BANK

Gourmet Pizza Company

Gabriel's Wharf, SE1
071-928 3188
Open Mon-Sat noon-11pm, Sun noon-10.30pm.

Classic these pizzas ain't, for the Gourmet Pizza Company specialises in pizzas every-which-way but orthodox. They are the only company in the world to have thought up the English breakfast pizza with Cumberland sausage, bacon, tomatoes, mozzarella and mushrooms with baked eggs. And if you think that's not enough you can ask for it served with Black Pudding. Chinese duck pizza? Bresaola pizza? No problem! But really, Mexican lime chicken pizza! If all this strikes you as a bit much, try a more conventional pasta. Otherwise, as they say, Go for it!

PUBS

This well-loved institution has been enjoying a renaissance during the past three years with the liberalising of the licensing laws that allow pubs to stay open during the whole day if they so wish. Particularly in central London, you'll find many of them open from 11am to 11pm Monday to Saturday, though Sunday hours have

remained the same: noon to 3pm and 7 to 10.30pm. As a consequence, many pubs now offer food all day (although this can be a mixed blessing as customers faced with a pub sausage that has taken on the characteristic of shoe leather from sitting under a heater for a few hours have discovered). But generally food has improved, with many pubs offering a wide range of imaginative daily dishes, well-prepared and cooked, and some have even come to rival restaurants in the quality of their cooking. Another change is the widening of brands and types of beer on sale. Although some people may look askance at the availability of such invaders as Fosters, Budweiser, Miller and Lapin Kulta (a strong lager brewed by women in Lapland and inching its way into England), others welcome the chance to sample what the rest of the world drinks. But there is heartening news, too, for those who champion traditional English ales as an increasing number of pubs become independently owned and stock ales that a few years ago were only available locally: Adnams, Benskins, Tetleys, Wadsworths and other varieties from Yorkshire and Suffolk. While pubs must, or course, serve the sophisticated retail customers of the 1990s, these same customers do retain an appreciation for the core values that have been at the heart of the British pub for centuries. The pub is a centre for con-

versation, friendship, tradition and warmth.

■ BELGRAVIA

Antelope

22 Eaton Terr, SW1
071-730 7781
Open Mon-Sat 11.30am-11pm, Sun normal hours. Restaurant Lunch daily.

The upstairs dark-panelled restaurant in this 200 year-old pub is pretty, quiet and relaxing—just the place for a good lunch. The restaurant menu is varied: stuffed trout or beef casserole and home-made puddings, and the wine list includes over 30 decently-priced labels. Downstairs the bar has a good selection of ales and bitters and provides meals and snacks.

Bag 'o' Nails

6 Buckingham Palace Rd, SW1 - 071-834 6946
Open Mon-Sat 11am-11pm, Sun normal hours.

In case you're confused by the name, it comes from the old British habit of anglicising foreign words: Rotten Row is derived from route du roi while Bag 'o' Nails is a distinctly twisted version of bacchanalia. Until 1906, the pub was called the 'Devil & Bag 'o' Nails'. The upstairs Bacchanalia bar serves hot meals which you eat looking onto the back of Buckingham Palace. A good selection of different ales and lagers from around Britain and the Continent is available.

Grenadier

18 Wilton Row, SW1
071-235 3074
Open Mon-Sat noon-3pm, 5-11pm, Sun normal hours.

Restaurant Lunch & Dinner daily.

The Grenadier, charmingly covered with vines and tucked away in a quiet cobbled mews, was the mess for the Duke of Wellington's officers who drank and ate here in the early nineteenth century. Today the pub is a haven of peace and quiet, away from the noise of nearby Hyde Park Corner. Despite the story about the ghost of a Guardsman caught cheating at cards and beaten to death who, it is said, haunts the pub, the Grenadier has a friendly atmosphere. It becomes crowded at lunchtime so arrive early if you plan to eat here.

Star Tavern
6 Belgrave Mews West, SW1
071-235 3019
Open Mon-Thurs, Sat 11.30-3pm, 5-11pm, Fri 11am-11pm, Sun normal hours.

This is an old-fashioned pub in the best sense of the word with real coal fires in winter, upholstered seats, mahogany tables and thankfully, no piped music or slot machines. Food is served at lunchtime and in the evening. In warm weather the outside tables in the cobbled mews, overshadowed by hanging flower baskets, get crowded. The previous landlord, Paddy Kennedy, was a well-known 'character' who had the reputation of not serving you if he didn't like your suit. The present incumbents, who won the *Evening Standard* newspaper's 'Pub of the Year' award in 1992, are welcoming and the pub has become popular with

both locals and visitors. Whether the Great Train Robbery really was planned here in the 1960s remains a matter for discussion.

■ BERMONDSEY

Angel
101 Bermondsey Wall East, SE16 - 071-237 3608
Open Mon-Sat 11am-3pm, 5.30pm-11pm, Sun normal hours. Restaurant Lunch Mon-Fri, Sun, Dinner Mon-Sat.

The Angel, one of the nicest pubs in London, suffers from being in a shabby neighbourhood, but is still worth the trip. The clientele is an interesting mix: in the downstairs bar some people talk about the local soccer team, Millwall, while others are deep in discussion about the latest move by the German Bundesbank. The rest drink their pints on the balcony looking over the river towards the City and Tower Bridge. In the upstairs restaurant a typically British menu offers dishes like Scottish salmon, the Earl of Ronaldshay's sausages and English cheeses.

■ BLOOMSBURY

Lamb
94 Lamb's Conduit St, WC1
071-405 0713
Open Mon-Sat 11am-11.30pm, Sun normal hours.

A friendly local with walls covered with old photographs and prints and the original snob screens—cut-glass panels

above the bar that twisted to protect those who wanted to drink privately from general view. Once providing liquid inspiration for the local writers of Bloomsbury, today the Lamb has a strong local following and an international clientele. You can enjoy games of chess, cribbage and dominoes with your pint and home-cooked bar food. There is a no-smoking room at the back and a few wooden seats outside in the courtyard.

Sun
63 Lamb's Conduit St, WC1
071-405 8278
Open Mon-Sat 11am-11pm, Sun normal hours.

If you're a beer enthusiast, your pilgrimage may well end here for the Sun claims to have the biggest selection of real ales in London. Even the most particular should find something worth drinking among the 60 or so labels in stock. You can also explore the pub's cellars to understand the finer points of beer making and storing. They serve bar snacks at lunch and dinner. But be warned, as the interior is very bare except for the pumps and bottles, this really is a place for the purist.

■ CHARING CROSS

Sherlock Holmes
10 Northumberland St, W1
071-930 2644
Open Mon-Sat 11am-11pm, Sun normal hours. Restaurant Lunch & Dinner daily.

If you want to avoid tourists stay away! Filled with Holmes' memorabilia, this pub is a shrine to all friends of the great detective. Sir Arthur Conan-Doyle popped in now and then in his time and mentioned the pub—then The Northumberland Arms—in The Hound of the Baskervilles. The upstairs restaurant serves a menu with dishes named after different Sherlock Holmes cases (no, there isn't anything with a dog in it!) And his study is re-created on the first floor. Elementary, my dear Watson!

■ CHELSEA

Admiral Codrington
17 Mossop St, SW3
071-589 4603
Open Mon-Sat 11am-11pm, Sun normal hours.

The 'Admiral Cod' as it's locally known is a good place for a pint and a pause while exploring Chelsea. It got its strange name (so we have been reliably informed by a Guards Officer), not because the good admiral won a great naval battle, but because he won a famous victory against the British government over their refusal to pay pensions to sailors and widows of dead sailors. Slightly off the beaten track, this delightful pub also serves good bar food.

Ferret and Firkin in the Balloon up the Creek
115 Lots Rd, SW10
071-352 6645
Open Mon-Sat 11am-11pm, Sun normal hours.

The pub with the longest name in London is quite a walk from King's Road—in fact you have to pass World's End to get there. It

has a wooden floor, skittles to play and pub food at lunchtime. For beer specialists or enthusiasts, all the Firkin pubs are worth a visit as the beer they brew themselves is excellent.

King's Head & Eight Bells
50 Cheyne Walk, SW3
071-352 1820
Open Mon-Sat 11am-11pm, Sun normal hours.

When this 400 year-old pub was in its heyday, eight bells were rung to warn the locals to behave as the monarch sailed past on the river—hence the intriguing name. Today it has a limited view of the Thames but you can just see barges going by across the busy Embankment. A friendly place, you can play traditional games like Shut the Box, Crib or Shoveha' penny, even Monopoly and Scrabble. Apart from the entertainment value, there is a wide selection of beer, wine and malt whisky available as well as food throughout the day. Being a traditional pub, there is a roast on Sunday.

Sporting Page
6 Camera Pl, SW10
071-376 3694
Open Mon-Sat 11am-3pm, 5.30-11pm, Sun normal hours.

This looks more like a restaurant and is, in fact, better for eating than for drinking in. Food varies from sandwiches and French onion soup to steaks and fattening desserts at both lunchtime and in the evening. Its sister pub The Front Page, at 35 Old Church St (071-352 0648), is also good for

meals and is more traditionally decorated with pews, wooden tables and huge old gas lamps lighting the hanging flower baskets outside. They serve lunchtime bar snacks only.

■ THE CITY

Black Friar
174 Queen Victoria St, EC4
071-236 5650
Open Mon-Fri 11.30am-10pm.

The Black Friar is a delightful collection of curiosities. The listed building has an art nouveau interior with bronze reliefs and marble mosaics depicting happy monks at work, and getting happily intoxicated. The side chapel is even more interesting with mosaics and aphorisms on the walls like 'seize the occasion', 'finery is foolery' and 'wisdom is rare'. A note of reality is introduced from the sound of the trains rumbling over Blackfriars Bridge. Bar snacks are available throughout the day.

Ye Olde Mitre
1 Ely Crt, Ely Pl, EC1
071-405 4751
Open Mon-Fri 11am-11pm.

Dark panelling and wooden, rustic tables are typical in this eighteenth-century pub that is justifiably proud of its history. They even have a printed copy of the story of their past history to give to their patrons. Small tables outside between the pub and St Ethelreda's church give extra space for customers enjoying good bar snacks.

■ COVENT GARDEN

Lamb & Flag
33 Rose St, WC2
071-497 9504
*Open Mon-Sat 11am-11pm,
Sun normal hours.*

Famous for its ale, food and bloody history, this busy old pub just off Garrick Street used to be called the 'Bucket of Blood' from the bare-fist boxing once popular on the premises. Now the pleasure is in good beer and food, especially the British cheeses. An open fire, low ceilings and dark panels make the Lamb & Flag one of the most attractive pubs in central London.

Nell of Old Drury
29 Catherine St, WC1
071-836 5328
*Open Mon-Sat noon-11 pm,
Sun normal hours.*

Nell of Old Drury—named after Nell Gwynne, King Charles II's mistress who performed at the nearby Drury Lane Theatre—is a delightful, small, busy pub in the heart of theatreland, with an interior covered with thespian posters. You can order interval drinks from the upstairs Theatre Bar which is a good way to beat the rush at the theatre. Downstairs, bar food like leek and mushroom pie is served all day, and upstairs at lunchtime and during the evening.

The Roundhouse
1 New Row, WC2 - 071-836 9738
*Open Mon-Sat 11am-11pm,
Sun normal hours.*

Real Ale

CAMRA or the Campaign for Real Ale has fought a victorious battle against the big breweries, which at one point wanted to do away with traditional ale and bitter. The reason was simple: you can only store these real British beers for a certain length of time unlike lager (which takes its name from the German word for 'to store'). For those who are interested in the real thing, CAMRA publishes an annual *Good Beer Guide*, the Bible for lovers of real ale. If you are interested in preserving and enjoying the traditional British pub or just want to know where to have a proper pint, contact *CAMRA*, 34 Alma Rd, St Albans, Herts AL1 3BW (0727-867201).

A good place to stop for a refresher while exploring Covent Garden, the Roundhouse is a small pub with a wide selection of real ale and foreign beers. It gets crowded after office hours and patrons often spill outside, weather permitting.

Salisbury
90 St Martin's Lane, WC2
071-836 5863
*Open Mon-Sat 11am-11pm,
Sun normal hours.*

Cut-glass glittering mirrors and brass fittings in a red velvet interior make this one-bar pub near theatreland an attractive pub for the mixture of gay and straight customers.

■ FLEET STREET

Punch Tavern
99 Fleet St, EC4 - 071-353 8338
*Open Mon-Fri 11am-11pm,
Sat noon-3pm, 6-11pm, Sun normal hours.*

The walls are covered with old cartoons from Punch, the satirical and humorous magazine that faded away a few years ago after being a symbol of English humour for a century. The Punch Tavern used to be one of the great journalists' haunts when Fleet Street was at its peak. Today it is an old-world pub with lots of tourists and City suits at lunchtime.

Ye Olde Cheshire Cheese
145 Fleet St, EC4 - 071-353 6170
*Open Mon-Fri 11am-11pm,
Sat noon-3pm, 6-11pm, Sun normal hours. Restaurant Lunch & Dinner daily.*

Rebuilt after the Great Fire in 1666 with high beams and dark panelling, this pub is bustling in spite of losing customers when the Fleet Street newspapers and printing offices moved down to Docklands several years ago. Or, as one of the bar men pointed out, there has been a pub here for 700 years and there will be one here for another 700 years, whatever happens to the rest of the world. Sawdust scattered on the floors in the small rooms, staircases and narrow passages take you back to the days when Dr Samuel Johnson drank here with his literary companions. The restaurant serves traditional British food, and the bar does a good range of snacks daily.

Ye Olde Cock Tavern
22 Fleet St, EC4 - 071-353 8570
Open Mon-Fri 11am-11pm.

A huge, handsome, upmarket pub on four levels, you can escape the noisy main bar, complete with games, in the upstairs cocktail bar. The Carvery Restaurant caters to substantial appetites, less filling bar snacks are available downstairs.

■ HAMMER-SMITH

Blue Anchor
13 Lower Mall, W6
081-748 5774
Open Mon-Sat 11.30am-11pm, Sun normal hours.

This delightful riverside pub which was first licensed under this name in the 1700s is a pleasant place to stop on your way to or from Hammersmith Bridge or the excellent nearby arts complex, the Riverside Studios. On summer evenings the light turns the river view into an Impressionist painting.

Dove
19 Upper Mall, W6
081-748 5405

Open Mon-Sat 11am-11pm, Sun normal hours.

The 300 year-old Dove has contributed more than its fair share to British culture and history. King Charles II is reputed to have drunk here with his mistress Nell Gwynne and the otherwise obscure James Thompson composed 'Rule Britannia' in the bar. The pub is famous for its friendly atmosphere and good bar food that you can enjoy on the terrace overlooking the Thames. Appetites and thirsts—well catered for at the bar—are generally sharpened by the sight of keen oarsmen and oarswomen strenuously rowing their boats past on the river.

Rutland
15 Lower Mall, W6
081-748 5586
Open Mon-Sat 11am-11pm, Sun normal hours.

On a warm summer evening, take your pint, lean against the river wall and reflect on life overlooking the Thames. The more gregarious can chat to the patrons from the next door pub, the Blue Anchor.

■ HAMPSTEAD

Freemasons Arms
32 Downshire Hill, NW3
071-435 4484
Open Mon-Sat 11am-11pm, Sun normal hours.

This large pub with a pretty garden bordering Hampstead Heath serves filling pub food to Hampstead types and visitors. In good weather it's a real pleasure to eat outside. Traditional English Sunday roast beef, a skittle alley and lawn billiards add to the charm.

Holly Bush
22 Holly Mount, NW3
071-435 2892
Open Mon-Fri 11am-3pm, 5.30-11 pm, Sat 11am-4pm, 6-11pm, Sun normal hours.

Just arriving at this picturesque village-style pub is a pleasure. The outside is covered with a vine; inside you'll find Edwardian lamps, old prints and posters and little corners and alcoves with etched glass partitions that ensure privacy. For entertainment, there's usually live music on Wednesdays and Thursdays, and darts and bar games.

Jack Straw's Castle
North End Way, NW3
071-435 8885
Open Mon-Sat 11am-11pm, Sun normal hours. Restaurant Lunch & Dinner daily.

The inn was built as a coaching inn in 1721 and named after the second-in-command of Wat Tyler's 1381 Peasant Revolt against King Richard II. Poor Jack Straw hid in a house on the site, but was caught and executed by the King's men. The inn was later patronised by the Victorian writers Wilkie Collins, W.M. Thackeray and Charles Dickens, but was damaged during World War II and the weatherboarded inn you see today dates only from the 1960s. The upstairs restaurant, advertising itself as perched on 'the roof of London' and high above Hampstead Heath, serves roast pheasant, braised rabbit and game pies—suitable fare for such a history. Downstairs there's a food and cocktail bar and a large garden.

King William IV
77 Hampstead High St, NW3 - 071-435 5747
Open Mon-Sat 11am-11pm, Sun normal hours.

A well-known and long-running gay pub with dark panelling and cottage-style curtains. The predominantly male clientele enjoys hearty snacks and piped music in what is a popular local. There's a beer garden at the back.

Spaniard's Inn
Hampstead Rd, NW3
081-455 3276
Open Mon-Fri 11am-11pm, Sat noon-9.30pm, Sun normal hours.

There's plenty here for history enthusiasts: the pub is named after the Spanish ambassador to the court of James I who lived here, while the infamous highwayman Dick Turpin preyed on his victims from the upstairs windows. Now the upstairs bar is ideal for a meditative drink while downstairs you can enjoy your pint and bar food in antique settles or by an open fire. The pretty garden has an aviary and roses.

■ HOLBORN

Cittie of Yorke
22 High Holborn, WC1
071-242 7670
Open Mon-Fri 11.30am-11pm, Sat 11.30am-3pm.

This huge pub has one of the longest bars in London. Dark, with an extremely high ceiling and small cubicles, it's the place where lawyers and judges gossip about cases over their pub lunches and real ale in comparative privacy. To help the historical atmosphere, the entrance

hall is decorated with medieval-style paintings. The Cittie of Yorke is easy to find—there's a large metal sign and a huge clock outside.

Princess Louise
208 High Holborn, WC1
071-405 8816
Open Mon-Fri 11am-11pm, Sat, Sun normal hours.

The big horse shoe-shaped bar is usually crowded with lovers of real ale as the Princess Louise is well known for its own selection of beers as well as the many different ales from around Britain that it stocks. Fast, friendly staff work between the stone columns and etched mirrors in this old gin palace. In keeping with the latest trend, the pub is also known for its spicy Thai food, served upstairs at lunchtime.

■ HIGHGATE

Flask
77 Highgate West Hill, N6
081-340 7260
Open Mon-Sat 11am-11pm, Sun normal hours.

This old pub with its sash windows and low-beamed bars is charming and full of character. The Flask takes its name from the bottles people used to buy here to fill with water from the Hampstead wells. It has enjoyed its fair share of notoriety—the local hero, Dick Turpin, once hid in the cellars, William Hogarth used to draw here and slightly more recently, Karl Marx, buried in nearby Highgate Cemetery, patronised the place. A large front patio has about

a dozen tables for outside drinking.

■ KENSINGTON

Churchill Arms
119 Kensington Church St, W8 - 071-727 4242
Open Mon-Sat 11am-11pm, Sun normal hours. Restaurant Dinner Mon-Sat.

On one side the wall is covered with pictures of Sir Winston, on the other side with US presidents. A huge collection of jugs and jars hangs from the ceiling and the back of the pub is taken up by a conservatory dining room serving Thai food. This may sound like a hodgepodge, but in fact it's a very successful formula! The Churchill Arms is a popular pub whose regular customers know each other well and it even boasts its own cricket club. The Thai food, only available in the evenings, is authentic; good regional dishes are well-cooked by the resident chefs. At lunchtime the pub also serves traditional British ploughman's food.

■ PIMLICO

Orange Brewery
37 Pimlico Rd, SW1
071-730 5984
Open Mon-Sat 11am-11pm, Sun normal hours.

This elegantly scruffy pub serves its own brewed ales: SW1 for beginners, stronger SW2 for the initiated, Pimlico Porter which is very rich, and a Victoria lager brewed according to old German laws—no chemicals! The Orange Brewery produces 4,320 pints of beer per week, and has a cellar

151

below to mature the product for the right length of time before it's pumped up for the thirsty customers. The curious can book a visit to the cellars. The Pie and Ale Shop next door serves good home-cooked food that is delicious washed down with the Orange Brewery's products. In summer, tables outside facing a little square are very popular.

ROTHER-HITHE

Mayflower
117 Rotherhithe St, SE16
071-237 4088
Open Mon-Sat 11am-11pm, Sun normal hours.

It was from Rotherhithe that the Pilgrim Fathers set sail for America in 1611 and this seventeenth-century inn celebrates them with a model of The Mayflower and other marine memorabilia. To emphasise the ties between the Old and the New World, the Mayflower is the only pub in Britain licensed as a post office and selling both British and American stamps—an interesting fact if not a particularly useful facility. In summer you can brave the windy Thames with a pint on the jetty and in winter stand by an open fire in the beamed bar. Food is good pub fare.

SOHO

Coach & Horses
29 Greek St, W1 - 071-437 5920
Open Mon-Sat 11am-11pm, Sun normal hours.

A good selection of malt whiskys provides an extra reason to visit this famous Soho pub, immortalised by low-life correspondent Jeffrey Barnard in his newspaper columns. The pub has a strong local following of media and creative types.

De Hems
11 Macclesfield St, W1
071-437 2494
Open Mon-Thurs 11am-midnight, Fri, Sat 11am-11pm, Sun normal hours.

Soho has always been the most international of London's 'villages', the place where immigrants from all over the world settled and started to build their lives anew. But this large, spacious Dutch pub seems to be a well-kept secret even among the Sohoites. There's live jazz downstairs and comedy upstairs about once a week.

French House
49 Dean St, W1 - 071-437 2799
Open Mon-Sat noon-11pm, Sun normal hours.

The French House is deeply rooted in history: during World War II Général de Gaulle, leader of the Free French in exile, met his compatriots here. Well-known artists, writers and musicians drank here and the walls are covered with photographs of old and new bohemian regulars. It is like a friendly village pub in the middle of the metropolis. But two more things make the French House unique: it only serves half-pints and customers probably drink more wine than beer. The upstairs dining room has a good reputation (see restaurant section).

SOUTHWARK

Anchor
34 Park St, Bankside, SE1
071-407 1577
Open Mon-Sat 11.30am-11pm, Sun normal hours. Restaurant Lunch & Dinner daily.

In one of London's most historic area—near the sites of the Globe Theatre and the original Clink Prison on Clink Street (hence the good old English expression 'in the clink' meaning in prison)—this wonderfully rambling pub has a restaurant as well as delightful intimate bars like the Financial Times Bar and the Thrale Bar. The Anchor attracts tourists for obvious reasons: the scenic river view from the terrace, good food and the atmospheric, dark-panelled interior. The original pub that stood on this site was destroyed in the Great Fire of London in 1666; it is rumoured that the diarist Samuel Pepys stood here watching the old wooden city burn.

George Inn
77 Borough High St, SE1
071-407 2056
Open Mon-Sat 11am-11pm, Sun normal hours. Restaurant Lunch & Dinner daily.

The surroundings of this beautiful old coaching inn have changed, but the inn itself is still luckily the same. Mentioned first in 1590, the George Inn—one of the last galleried inns in England—was rebuilt after the Great Fire of 1666. Upstairs there is a restaurant; downstairs you can have a meal in the old-fashioned rooms or in the wine bar. Outside tables face the courtyard, where you might catch a play by the local hero, Shakespeare, being performed.

Horniman
Hays Galleria, Battlebridge Lane, SE1 - 071-407 3611
Open daily 10am-11pm.

Hays Galleria is an ambitious riverside development next to London Bridge with shops and boutiques. The spacious, multi-level Horniman—called after Mr Frederick Horniman who made his fortune from importing tea—is decorated with clocks originally made for his office. Clearly a precise man, they show the time around the globe. Good views over H.M.S. Belfast and Tower Bridge and tables outside for picnics make this a useful spot for families with children. There is a carvery and salad bar upstairs.

Market Porter
9 Stoney St, SE1 - 071-407 2495
Open Mon-Fri 7-9am, 11am-11pm, Sat 11am-3pm, 7-11pm, Sun normal hours. Lunch Mon-Fri, Sun, Dinner Mon-Fri.

This remarkable pub, with open fires, wooden furniture and private booths, serves a well-kept selection of real ales—including one brewed on the premises. At lunchtime it gets crowded with both people in suits and local market traders. Like pubs in other markets like Smithfield, the Market Porter is licensed to serve breakfast. Apart from serving an excellent selection of beers from Britain and the continent, this lively

local organises quiz nights and pinball tournaments.

TEA ROOMS

Tea is so quintessentially English it is hard to imagine life in England without the much-loved beverage. But 'I did send for a cup of tea (a China drink)', the diarist Samuel Pepys wrote 300 years ago, 'of which I never had drunk before'. Only 300 years ago! After a lapse, tea, as an occasion in itself, is coming back into fashion. Many London hotels, and other places too, serve an elegant afternoon tea with thin-cut sandwiches, pastries, scones, clotted cream and jam and a choice of Indian or Ceylon teas. While others may include salons de thé, or Italian cafés in a treatise on tea, we have decided (with the notable exception of Emporio

> 'We will, however, forthwith treat on tea, the most popular of our beverages, the one which makes 'the cup that cheers but not inebriates'. The beverage called tea has now become almost a necessary of life.'
> *Mrs Beeton, Book of Household Management, 1861.*

Armani Express) to remain chauvinistic and firmly British. Tea is both a practical treat—if you're going to the theatre, you'll find a substantial tea makes a good

substitute for an often-rushed pre-theatre supper—and a positive pleasure. As soon as you sit down in front of a teapot, life seems to slow down and take on a peaceful feel. Bookings are not normally taken for tea (we have specified where you must book), you just turn up and wait for a table or an armchair. But it's advisable to arrive early as once settled in for a nice cuppa and a chat, the clientele tends to stay put.

■ ALDWYCH

The Waldorf
Aldwych, WC2 - 071-836 2400
Open daily 3.30-6.30pm. Sat, Sun Tea dance 3.30-6.30pm.

The recently refurbished Palm Court provides just the right setting for tea. It comes into its own at the weekend when couples waltz in stately fashion around the floor to the strains of Gregg Davies and the Waldorfians playing a selection from the 1920s and 30s. Tea, which seems pricey at £19.50 per person until you count the entertainment value, includes all the usuals, plus toasted crumpets, presumably because patrons tend to get hungry with all that activity. The Palm Court operates a strict dress code: jackets and ties for the gentlemen, smart dresses for the ladies. And quite right too. Can you imagine dancing around dressed in jeans, while the rest of the non-dancing tea-time regulars look on in horror?

◾ CHELSEA

Oriel

Sloane Sq, SW1
071-730 4275
Open Mon-Sat 8.30am-11pm, Sun 9am-10.30pm.

On the edge of Sloane Square, Oriel is a good place to people-watch while sipping tea and eating old-fashioned toasted tea cakes among other goodies, all for £7.95. The whole place has picked up since the arrival of the new chef David Wilby who has worked with famous chef Anthony Worrall Thompson; the food is good and the waiters are now anxious to please.

◾ CLAPHAM

Tea Time

The Pavement, SW4
071-622 4944
Open Tues-Sun 10am-6pm.

Near Clapham Common, Tea Time is a well-loved local stop. On two storeys, the downstairs room is faintly colonial in atmosphere, highly suitable for a tea shop where they serve generous teas at £3.50 or £6.95.

◾ FINCHLEY

College Farm

The Tea House, 45 Fitzalan Rd, N3 - 081-349 0690
Open Sat, Sun, Bank Hol Mons 2.30-5.30pm.

College Farm, a small farm in the middle of urban north London, is an eccentric place to find a delightful old dairy. Built in 1864, it became a tea house in 1925 and then was restored a few years ago by the energetic Su Russell.

There are blue-and-white Minton tiles on the walls of this octagonal building with windows looking out onto the farm and the fields, solid chairs and tables covered with lace tablecloths, proper tea pots and blue-and-white china and if you take children, a tray of toys for them to play with. Scones are home-made, fresh clotted cream comes with the proper hard crust, and they will refill your teapot as often as you like.

'E.M. Forster never gets any further than warming the teapot. He's a rare fine hand at that. Feel this teapot. Is it not beautifully warm? Yes, but there ain't going to be no tea.'
Katherine Mansfield, Journal, May 1917.

◾ KENSINGTON

Muffin Man

12 Wright's Lane, W8
071-937 6652
Open Mon-Sat 8am-5.45pm.

A small two-storey café which starts serving at 8am when you could, if you felt so inclined, take tea. Set teas range from Devon cream tea at £3.80 to a fuller version at £4.70. It's a useful stop for shoppers in Kensington High Street.

Orangery

Kensington Palace, W8
071-376 0239
Open Apr-Sep: daily 10am-6pm.

A brisk walk through Kensington Gardens or a stroll around Kensington Palace and its remarkable court dress collection should give you an appetite for tea in the Orangery, a severe neo-classical white interior with the odd statue staring at you. It's far enough away from Kensington to feel almost countrified.

◾ KEW

Original Maids of Honour Tearooms

Kew Rd, Kew, Surrey
081-940 2752
Open Mon-9.30am-1pm, Tues-Sat 9.30am-5.30pm.

The Maids of Honour tearooms is just the place to go to after a brisk trot around Kew Gardens. Bow-fronted windows, cottage-style furniture, blue and white china and a startling array of sticky cakes make this restaurant and cake shop one of the longest-running success stories in London. You can consume—or buy—the pastry after which the place is named. Apparently a cook created it especially for King Henry VIII and the recipe, a well-guarded secret, has been passed down through the generations to the Newens family.

◾ KNIGHTS-BRIDGE

Emporio Armani Express

191 Brompton Rd, SW3
071-823 8818
Open Mon-Sat 10am-6pm, Wed to 7pm.

The ultra-chic Emporio Armani Express might seem an odd choice for tea, but sitting staring out over Knightsbridge from a window table, or watching a video of an impossibly thin model on a catwalk and looking into the vast reaches of the shop over a cup of tea and a wider-than-usual tea menu (this is after all, an Italian venture) is great fun. Apart from the usual English fare of cream teas, there are some wonderful chocolate con-coctions, preceded if you so wish by smoked salmon sandwiches.

The Hyde Park
66 Knightsbridge, SW1
071-235 2000
Open daily 4-6pm. Bookings taken.
The Park Room, with its pretty décor, gives a wonderful view over Hyde Park with its sharp greens in summer and golden russets in the autumn. It's such a delightful room it's hardly surprising to dis-cover that this was the place the Queen Mother used to take the young princesses to. The scones are especially good and the teas include Earl Grey, Russian, Pelham Mixture and other mysteries. The price is £11.50.

Richoux
86 Old Brompton Rd, SW3
071-584 8300
Open Mon-Sat 8.30am-9.30pm, Sun 10am-9.30pm.
These three cafés/restaurants are almost over the top in their adherence to tradition. Plump seating, scrolled, patterned wallpaper, mirrors, waitresses in striped dresses and pinafores and

unwelcome muzak are the background against which you can eat and drink any-thing from their full menu all day. But it seems to work; they are always bustling and cheerful. Also at 41a South Audley St, W1, 071-629 5228; 172 Piccadilly, W1, 071-493 2204.

■ MAYFAIR

Brown's Hotel
30-34 Albermarle St, W1
071-493 7020
Open daily 3-6pm.
Tea at Brown's is taken in their dark-panelled sitting rooms, full of comfortable armchairs and sofas and a clientele that ranges from families to single ladies. It has an Agatha Christie air about it and you find your-self looking around at the elderly ladies wondering which might be Miss Marples. It is one of London's old-fashioned treats and one of our top recommendations.

■ PICCADILLY

Fortnum & Mason
St James's Restaurant, 181 Piccadilly, W1 - 071-734 8040
Open Mon-Sat 9.30am-6pm.
The St James's restaurant is one of those places you find almost by accident. Tucked away on the fourth floor, and entered through what looks exactly like an English drawing-room, it's a homely old-fashioned place with homely waitresses and an excellent menu. All the usuals are on the afternoon tea menu at £9.50, but the high tea menu at £11.50 branches out into Windsor toast cov-

ered with potted meat paste, English mustard and grilled mushrooms, and the very traditional Scotch woodcock which is scrambled eggs with an-chovy fillets. Look around you and you find you're sitting amongst the squierarchy of old England tucking in with gusto.

> 'There is nothing yet discovered which is a substitute for the English patient for his cup of tea; he can take it when he can take nothing else; and he often can't take anything else if he has it not.'
> *Florence Nightingale in the Crimea.*

Le Méridien
21 Piccadilly, W1 - 071-734 8000
Open daily 3-6pm.
Afternoon tea is served in the Oak Room Lounge, a light-panelled room decorated with golden trophies and mirrors to the accompaniment of a harp-ist and the gentle buzz of well-filled customers, happ-ily spending £11.50 per person.

The Ritz Palm Court
The Ritz, Piccadilly, W1
071-493 8181
Open daily 3pm and 4.30pm. Booking essential.
Glamorous and glitzy as you'd expect, tea is taken in the gilded Palm Court to the accompaniment of a pianist. It's a far cry from the days when the likes of Douglas Fairbanks, Evelyn Waugh and the unbelieva-

bly wealth Nubar Gulbenkian patronised the place, but is fun and should be on your list of things-to-do-once-in-your-life. Tea is £13.50.

> 'The sooner the tea's out of the way The sooner we can get out the gin, eh?'
> *Henry Reed, 'Two Particular English Vices'.*

■ STRAND

The Savoy
Thames Foyer, Strand, WC2
071-836 4393
Open daily 3.30-5.30pm.

Unashamedly luxurious, you sink into squashy armchairs and listen to a tinkling piano while waiters bring cake plates full of the usual afternoon delights. At £14.85 it's expensive, but they don't ask you to move on.

■ VICTORIA

The Goring
17 Beeston Pl, Grosvenor Gdns, SW1 - 071-396 9000
Open daily 3.30-5pm.

This rarity—a privately-owned hotel now run by the third generation of the Goring family—manages to combine the efficiency of a well-run hotel with the sort of welcome you would expect from an old friend. All this makes afternoon tea in the quiet drawing-room with a splendid ornate mantlepiece and a view over the gardens at the back a special treat. Two fluffy stuffed sheep guard

the open fire and waiters appear unobtrusively, giving a very good impression of being family butlers. All in all, tea at £9.50 per person at the Goring is a pleasure.

■ WIMBLEDON

Cannizaro House
West Side, Wimbledon Common, SW18 - 081-879 1464
Open Mon-Sat 3-5pm, Sun 4-5.30pm. Booking advised.

Built in the early eighteenth century, Cannizaro House was patronised by Victorian figures like Lord Tennyson, Oscar Wilde and Henry James. In winter the full tea is taken in the restaurant (£9.75 per person); in summer you sit under a parasaol on the summer terrace looking out over gardens and parkland with a lighter tea at a lighter price of £4.95.

Forget-Me-Not Tearooms
45 High St, Wimbledon, SW19 - 081-947 3634
Open Tues-Sat 9.30am-5.30pm.

On the edge of Wimbledon Village and near the Common, we recommend the Forget-Me-Not tearooms highly for anyone visiting the area. In winter it's a perfect stop after a visit to Southside House (see Museums: Off the Beaten Track section). Full of personal artefacts and antique china, and with a little light background classical music to aid the digestion, you have a choice of four set teas.

WINE BARS & BARS

It is still true to say that if you're looking for the widest possible selection of wines from all over the world, you're better off in Britain than any other country, and best off in London. For while the French, the Italians, Germans and so on, naturally drink the wines from their own countries, the British, with their miniscule wine industry hampered by government restrictions, taxes and last but not least, the climate, have to venture further afield. Now, good wine bars will have extensive lists covering wines from France and New Zealand, eastern Europe and California, from anywhere, in fact, where interesting tastes are to be found.

Wine bars are attractive places. They have always served good food. Indeed, when they first became popular some twenty years ago, this was one of the factors attracting customers out of the pubs and into the wine bars. They are good places for women to eat together, while women on their own find it just as easy to sit at a bar and order a glass, or eat lunch without attracting the attention they might get in a male-oriented pub. Recently, another type of wine bar has arrived in London—the Spanish tapas bar. Wine bars are often open all day, though they serve full meals only at lunch and dinner time—from around noon to 3pm and from 5.30 to anything up to 11 at night.

With the growth in popularity of wine bars, and the increasing widening of our tastes, not to mention the buying power of the young, other, more eccentric and fun establishments have sprung up. Bars rather than wine bars, they often stay open late and sometimes arrange special evening or Sunday music.

And finally, let us not forget those excellent cocktail bars, still generally found in the grander hotels. Here a cocktail might cost a small fortune, but it gives you the chance to sit in plush surroundings, often entertained by a resident pianist, feeling that the world has not really changed so much.

■ BELGRAVIA

Carriages
43 Buckingham Palace Rd, SW1 - 071-834 0119
Open Mon-Fri 11.30am-11pm.

Located between Buckingham Palace and Victoria Station, Carriages tends to stop people from going where they were originally intending to go. It's an inviting place for a drink: Champagne if you feel rich, otherwise try the cocktails. The pastel-coloured bar with alcoves on the ground floor and Charlie's cellar bar get particularly busy at lunchtime and after office hours. They offer a lunchtime 'menu express' which is a selection of bar food, afternoon teas and pre-theatre suppers.

Ebury Wine Bar
139 Ebury St, SW1 - 071-730 5447

Open Mon-Sat 11.30am-11pm, Sun noon-2.30pm, 7-10.30pm.

One of the first wine bars to open in London and the main bar in the Ebury chain (the others are Carriages, Draycott's in Chelsea and Hoults in Wandsworth), the Ebury Wine Bar has a strong local following. The idea is simple: wine is at it's best when drunk with friends in a jolly, friendly and casual atmosphere. Locals also mutter polite things about the kitchen.

■ CAMDEN TOWN/ CHALK FARM

Cotton's Rhum Shop Bar & Restaurant
55 Chalk Farm Rd, NW1
071-482 1096
Open Mon-Sat 6pm-midnight, Sun noon-11.30pm.

Cotton's stirs up memories of the Caribbean for those lucky enough to have been there. The interior is painted with colours radiating fun and good humour. They serve good cocktails and beers from Americas. Food can be exciting, with dishes like spicy ragga prawns and goat on the menu, but we find the quality fluctuates.

Odette's
130 Regent Park Rd, NW1
071-722 5388
Open Mon-Sat 12.30-2.30pm, 6.30-10.30pm.

One of the very few places to divide their wine list according to the style of the wine which is practical when it comes to finding the right combination of food and wine. Geographically the list covers the

world from California to Lebanon. One of the gems of Primrose Hill, this wine bar is located in the pretty basement of Odette's restaurant where you can enjoy cheaper, still first-rate food than in the restaurant upstairs.

■ CHARING CROSS

Gordon's
47 Villier's St, WC2
071-930 1408
Open Mon-Fri 11am-11pm. No cards.

A dark but cosy cellar with apparently damp walls and an excellent atmosphere, Gordon's has a lived-in look, gathering in a mixed audience of commuters and wine lovers. On summer evenings the crowd spills out into a small garden at the back. The commuters leave early in the evening for trains from nearby Charing Cross or Embankment underground stations, while the rest of the customers tend to linger over the good, basic snacks and wines. The wine list, which is usually chalked on the blackboard, is not the longest in London, but offers a good mix.

■ CHELSEA

Bar Pushkin
84 Sloane Ave, SW3
071-225 0863
Open Mon-Sat 11am-11pm.

A brand new Vodka bar from the same people who brought you Babushka. The style is Imperial Russian with a suitable dose of high drama and lots of vodka. The bar boasts over thirty variations of this 'water of life' in different flavours. The Russian connection continues with bar snacks tailor-made for vodka consumption.

Bill Bentley's

31 Beauchamp Pl, SW3
071-589 5080
Open Mon-Sat 11am-11pm.

The downstairs bar is a small, welcoming room with dark wooden panels and a large selection of wines by the glass. They serve oysters and other delicious titbits for those who want an elegant snack while the upstairs restaurant specialises in fish. The wine list is designed to complement the sea food whether it comes with fins or an unspecified number of claws.

■ THE CITY

Balls Brothers

2-3 Old Change Ct, St Paul's Churchyard, EC4 - 071-248 8697
Open Mon-Fri 11am-9pm.

Balls Brothers have seen the rise, decline and the new rise of wine bars in Britain. When they started some twenty-odd years ago, the customers often ordered the only plonk de plonk they knew. In the yuppie 80s wine bars became one of the symbols of the nouveaux riches and trendy. Today wine bars have settled down as a part of British life and can concentrate on what they are really here for: serving good wines. Balls Brothers ship their own wines and run several wine bars in London. The food is mainly snacks.

Bow Wine Vaults

10 Bow Churchyard, EC4
071-248 1121
Open Mon-Fri 11am-8.30pm.

A real Cockney is, reputedly, born with the sound of Bow church's bells ringing in his or her ears. But there's nothing cockney about the Bow Wine Vaults, situated in Bow Churchyard and with a strong local following. The wine list, with its good selection of bin ends, also attracts customers from all over London. Lunch on smoked salmon or a filling sandwich and travel the world with different wines.

Corney & Barrow Champagne Bar

10 Broadgate Circle, EC2
071-628 1251
Open Mon-Fri 11am-10pm.

As the name says, it's Champagne only in this City bar overlooking Broadgate Circle and next to Liverpool Street station. During the City boom this was the place for young stockbrokers to celebrate their deals with a magnum or two. Despite the relative lack of good deals in the last few years, they still stock a good selection of grandes marques. This is also a good place for a pre-theatre, concert or cinema glass of bubbly before heading for the Barbican Centre.

Leith's at the Institute

Chartered Accountants' Hall, Moorgate Pl, EC2
071-920 8626
Open Mon-Fri noon-2.30pm.

This split-level wine bar-cum-restaurant serves City people in the large base-ment of the Chartered Accountants' Hall. Cooking is of the no-frills school, but the food is delicious and hearty. The chefs also cater well for vegetarians. The bar is on a raised level, allowing the drinkers to observe the eaters at the lower restaurant which has its own, more expensive menu. The wine list is on the expensive side, but offers a neat selection of grapes. As one might expect of the City, and particularly of the rather staid profession of accountancy, men are expected to wear a jacket and tie.

■ COVENT GARDEN

Bar des Amis du Vin

11-14 Hanover Pl (off Long Acre), WC2 - 071-379 3444
Open Mon-Sat 11.30am-11pm, Sun noon-10.30pm.

The serious wine list in this excellent place has wines from around the world, offering tastes from France to California, from Italy to New Zealand. There are three different areas to the Amis du Vin. The bustling downstairs wine bar is famous for its remarkable cheeseboard and reasonably priced wine list, the Café is a traditional brasserie while the Salon offers more intimate meals for dinner 'à deux'.

Le Beaujolais

25 Litchfield St, WC2
071-836 2277
Open Mon-Fri noon-11pm, Sat 5-11pm.

People who want to drink good but inexpensive wines come to this small bar which can squeeze in a maximum of 50 people. Then it's standing room only. The food is described by some as being like a 'French picnic', which is a complimentary remark about the tasty snacks and pies on offer here. Considering this is French, it comes as a surprise to find about 100 ties hanging from the ceiling decorating the otherwise rather sparse interior. But it's full of specialists in the English class system who recognise prominent regiments and public schools among the ties of lesser institutions.

Brixtonian Backayard

4 Neal's Yard, WC2
071-240 2769
Drinks noon-midnight daily, Sat 7pm-midnight, women only. Live music daily 7.30-10.30pm.

Pastel-coloured chairs and breezy staff make the Brixtonian Backayard a jolly place to enjoy rhum (as they spell it). The selection includes something like 200 different brands which are expensive, but they are served in double measures. It is ideal to drop in for one drink on your way to somewhere else. Snacks are available at the bar and there is a small restaurant upstairs if you need something more nourishing.

Christopher's Bar

18 Wellington St, WC2
071-240 4222
Open Mon-Sat 11.30am-11pm.

You'll find this discreet and stylish American bar in the heart of theatreland on the ground floor below

Christopher's restaurant. A large mural depicts long-forgotten celebrities, and behind the bar a television offers the latest from CNN news network. This is the place to sit down with your *International Herald Tribune*. Cocktails are pricey at £5.50, but it helps the bar select its customers. The Champagne cocktails are deceivingly strong. Dress smartly.

Freuds

198 Shaftesbury Ave, WC2
071-240 9933
Open Mon-Sat 11am-11pm, Sun noon-10.30pm. Live jazz on Sunday evenings.

A flight of narrow iron stairs take you down into the basement of Freud's shop, which sells Charles Rennie Mackintosh replica furniture and stylish gifts. The cellar bar is small with barren concrete walls decorated with changing works of art; the seats are not easy chairs and the table tops are made of stone. In spite of this, Freud's is a welcoming place to drop in for a cappuccino or a drink. It get noisier and very crowded in the evening. Snacks are available.

Garrick Wine Bar

10 Garrick St, WC2
071-240 7649
Open Mon-Sat noon-11pm, Sun 12.30-5pm.

This small and friendly bar in the heart of Covent Garden has a tiny ground floor room and a slightly larger cellar. It serves food and is a good place for a glass or a bottle with a friend at whatever time of day.

■ HOLBORN

Bleeding Heart Wine Bar

Bleeding Heart Yard, Greville St, EC2 - 071-242 8238
Open Mon-Fri noon-11pm.

A well hidden, atmospheric wine bar and restaurant at the end of the intriguingly named Bleeding Heart Yard, mentioned in Charles Dickens' *Little Dorrit*, found in a small yard off Greville Street, and definitely worth searching out. You can eat either in the bar or restaurant from a predominantly French menu which changes continuously. Staff are sometimes more fluent in French than English, which is not a negative comment. The wine list covers a good geographical range and is sensibly priced.

■ HOLLAND PARK

Julie's Bar

137 Portland Rd, W11
071-727 7985
Open Mon-Sat 11.30am-midnight, Sun 11.30am-10pm.

Rather expensive wines and generous portions of food are the ingredients in this charming West London bar. If money is no problem, this is a delightful place to relax—it's a cosy bar with stuffed birds in cages and Gothic interiors. On a warm day you can sit outdoors at pavement tables and watch the passers by.

*Some establishments change their **closing times** without warning. It is always wise to check in advance.*

■ ISLINGTON

Almeida

1 Almeida St, N1 - 071-226 0931
Open Mon-Sat 11am-3.30pm, 5-11pm.

Connected to the next door Almeida Theatre, this rather ascetic wine bar comes alive when the theatre audiences stream in. The food is fairly ordinary and the wine list limited, but the place enjoys the patronage of arty Islingtonians and other interesting looking people. The Almeida Theatre is well known as an important venue for strong drama outside the mainstream West End theatre; some of this drama spills over into the wine bar during the intervals and after the shows.

■ KENSINGTON

Church's

20 Kensington Church St, W8 - 071-938 2336
Open Mon-Fri 11am-11pm.

Wine list prices are user-friendly, especially during the happy hours between 5-7.30 pm. For lunch it is worth booking in advance; dinner is served only until 9.30pm. So to enjoy the simple, but well prepared food at Church's, get your times right.

■ KNIGHTS-BRIDGE

Le Métro

The Capital, 28 Basil St, SW3 071-589 6286
Open Mon-Sat 7.30am-11pm.

Around the corner from Harrod's and the Knights-bridge shops, this light-panelled basement bar also serves as the restaurant for L'Hôtel upstairs, and consequently is a useful place for early morning breakfasts. Le Métro shares a kitchen with the Capital hotel and restaurant (also in the same ownership), which explains the high quality of the food. An interesting wine list.

Perroquet Bar

The Berkeley, Wilton Pl, SW1 - 071-235 6000
Open Mon-Sat 11am-11pm.

The Berkeley is a most civilised hotel and this is a most civilised bar with a charming manager. It's small and cosy with the Perroquet restaurant downstairs leading off it. All the usual bar delights are here from Champagne to White Ladys, and Berkeley Champagne cocktails at a not too staggering price (£6.50 to £7.75). Food is good and varied, from soupe du jour to goujonettes de sole frites, and from 7pm until midnight, Tuesday to Saturday, you are serenaded by Leo the pianist.

■ LEICESTER SQUARE

Cork and Bottle

44-46 Cranbourn St, WC2 071-734 7807
Open Mon-Sat 11am-11.30pm, Sun noon-10pm.

One of the pioneering wine bars in London with the accent on Californian and Australian wines, this excellent bar situated almost next to a sex shop stocks in all about 150 different wines from all over the world. The list is always kept up-to-date with special offers. The proprietor's encyclopaedic knowledge and enthusiasm for wine makes the Cork and Bottle one of the most exciting bars in London; and the food is good, too.

■ LONDON BRIDGE

Skinkers

42-46 Tooley St, SE2 071-407 9189
Open Mon-Fri 11.30am-8.30pm.

A Dickensian theme prevails in this atmospheric bar: dark ceilings, black beams, candles and a ghost or two in the vaults. Situated in a converted warehouse underneath railway arches, Skinkers gives a good impression of the past. It feels like a good London drinking spot for mysterious dealings and secret plotting. And to keep your stamina up, they serve a proper lunch with game pies or salmon. The wine list is long and interesting.

■ MARYLE-BONE

The Winter Garden

The Regent London, 222 Marylebone Rd, NW1 071-631 8000
Open Sun-Thurs 9am-1am, Fri, Sat 9am-2am.

This pricey lounge bar with the highest ceiling in London is full, astonishingly, with palms trees. The atrium is about six floors high and has a nicely calming atmosphere. You can eat breakfast here or light snacks, served noon to midnight which include dishes like seared, rare-cooked tuna medallions with a light orange mayonnaise, or roasted chicken breast. Appetisers—served from 5 to 9pm only—vary from oysters and goose liver terrine to prosciutto San Daniele and halibut canapés. This is a relaxing place to meet friends. You can enjoy your drink with unintimidating piano music in the background. But beware, the service can be extremely slow.

MAYFAIR

Dover Street Wine Bar

8-9 Dover St, W1 - 071-629 9813, 071-491 7509
Open Mon-Fri noon-3pm, 5.30pm-3am, Sun 7pm-3am. Cover charge for music £3-£8, entrance free in the early evening. Fri, Sat diners only before 10 pm.

'More than just a restaurant, more than just a wine bar' boasts the slogan, and it is actually quite truthful. The Dover Street Wine Bar offers live music both at lunchtime and in the evening and has even published a CD of its best-loved artists. The menu is varied: from steaks to roasted vegetable salad while the wine list will delight thirsty readers. The young, helpful staff endorse our opinion that the Dover Street Wine Bar is one of the best bars in London. Dress code smart/casual (no jeans or trainers).

Trader Vic's

London Hilton on Park Lane, 22 Park Lane, W1 - 071-493 7586
Open Mon-Sat 5.30pm-1am, Sun 5.30-10.30pm

Decorated as a set for an amateur production of South Pacific, but run professionally. Good value, old-fashioned cocktails with the emphasis on straws, parasols and fruits in big glasses and waitresses in South Sea outfits make Trader Vic's a warm, welcoming and fun bar to visit. Dress code is smart/casual.

NOTTING HILL GATE

Beach Blanket Babylon

45 Ledbury Rd, W11
071-229 2907
Open Mon-Sat 11am-11pm, Sun 11am-10.30pm.

Lavish in a decadent Hollywood style, as strange and charming as the Barcelona cathedral, a post-apocalyptic bar for new bohemians...and the list of varied descriptions goes on and on. BBB used to be a pub, but then Tony Weller and Carmel Azzobardi turned it into the most talked-about bar in 1990's London. Beach Blanket Babylon feels exotic and fun for all ages, a kind of New Age inn. Beer, cocktails, wines and also reasonably priced food make it worth a visit.

Market Bar

240a Portobello Rd, W11
071-229 6472
Open Mon-Sat 11am-11pm, Sun noon-3pm, 7-10.30pm. Live jazz Sunday lunchtime.

Opened by the people who now run Beach Blanket Babylon, this was the first London bar for the new bohemians. Interiors are baroque in their richness, with an extravagant,

slightly decadent feeling. The place buzzes with a mixed crowd from Portobello market and colourful Notting Hill.

Mesón Doña Ana

37 Kensington Park Rd, W11
071-243 0666
Open daily noon-midnight.

One of three wine bars in a small chain, this tapas outpost in Notting Hill Gate is deservedly successful. There's only limited seating at the bar for casual drinking, but the small, typical tapas dishes are so good and relatively cheap that it's worth taking a table, drinking a few glasses of interesting Spanish wine and passing the time of day with friends here. Also Mesón Don Felipe, 53 The Cut, SE1 (071-928 3237); Mesón Don Julián, 125-127 Dawes Rd, SW6 (071-386 5901).

PIMLICO

Chimes of Pimlico

26 Churton St, SW1
071-821 7456
Open daily noon-2.30pm, 6-10.15pm.

In these simply furnished, 'rustic' wine bars, English food, especially pies, are the heart of the menu. In addition, 'from the Garden' they offer salads as well as poultry, beef, ham and fish. Draught cider and perry, 'country wines' and English wines supplement a short, well-chosen, conventional wine list. Also at 91 High St, Wimbledon Village, SW19, 081-946 2471.

■ REGENT STREET

Café Royal
68 Regent St, W1 - 071-437 9090
Open Mon-Sat noon-11pm, Sun noon-6pm.
The central location brings in a mixed clientele, but the prices keep the impoverished away. The bar doubles as a tea room during the afternoon. Beers, wines and spirits are all served, but cocktails are the thing to go for here. Be ready to pay almost £10 for the more refined concoctions. The Café Royal has a real old-fashioned charm from the gilded past (Oscar Wilde and T S Eliot used to meet their friends for a drink here). Either you like it or you don't.

■ SOHO

The Dog House
187 Wardour St, WC2
071-434 2116
Open Mon-Fri 12.30pm-11pm, Sat 6-11pm.
This is a wonderfully trendy watering hole for the young and lively—a cosy cellar bar with small side alcoves with beers and drinks from around the world. The staff can do decent non-alcoholic cocktails or mix classics as required and the bar has a good selection of flavoured vodkas. The Dog House kitchen has received flattering comments, but the place is at it's best as a bar.

Morgan's
4 Ganton St, W1 - 071-734 3830
Open Mon-Fri 11am-10.45pm.
Wooden floors and shades of blue make up the decor in this wine bar just off Carnaby Street. The wine list boasts more than a hundred labels from around the world and in winter you can have mulled wine to keep functional in London's freezing wind. In keeping with the current trend, Morgan's serves Thai food.

Oxygen
18 Irving St, Leicester Sq, WC2 - 071-930 0905

Open daily noon-1am, music 9pm onwards.
This Brazilian oasis in the middle of London operates on three floors. Upstairs there's a Latin restaurant, on the ground floor the bar serves ice-cold cairipinhas and a good selection of imported beers and in the basement you can dance the night away or sit and enjoy live music. The menu includes items such as churrasquinho de carne (barbecued pieces of meat with vegetables char-grilled on a skewer) or mousse de maracuja abacaxi au manga (freshly prepared mousse of passion fruit, pineapple and mango). It's an exotic place.

Shampers
4 Kingly St, W1 - 071-437 1692
Open Mon-Fri 11am-11pm, Sat noon-3pm.
The name suggests bubbly, but actually the wine list covers almost 200 different wines and over twenty Champagnes. This buzzing bar is a branch of the Cork and Bottle and deserves the same compliments. Shampers is nicely hidden in a narrow alley between Regent and Carnaby Street. Reserve a table for meals: a quick bite upstairs or a more leisurely, full agenda downstairs in the basement.

■ STRAND

American Bar
The Savoy, Strand, WC2
071-836 4343
Open Mon-Sat 11am-3pm, 5.30pm-11pm, Sun noon-3pm, 7pm-10.30pm.
This very professional, very traditional and very

Soho Soho!

Some of the first settlers here were French Hugenots, expelled from France in 1685. In a few years, the area was peopled almost exclusively by foreign immigrants who brought their language, customs, food and, latterly, restaurants. A few years ago it had a reputation as one of the sleazier areas of London. Today it's been cleaned up and clubbers and restaurant-goers have replaced street walkers. And where did the curious name come from? It's said to have been the hunting cry of King Charles II as he galloped through Soho Square in pursuit of game some 330 years ago.

expensive piano bar is an absolute must for cocktail aficionados. The latest semi-classic to come from the Savoy's superb bartenders is the Blushing Monarch—a combination of campari, gin, orange curaçao and passion fruit juice. The Champagne cocktails also seem to taste better here than elsewhere, though you pay a price: the cocktails are over £6 each and even beer is priced high above the normal.

We have noted only where establishments do not accept credit cards; otherwise assume that all restaurants, hotels and shops will accept the major credit cards.

■ WATERLOO

Archduke Wine Bar

Concert Hall Approach, SE1
071-928 9370
Open Mon-Fri 11am-11pm, Sat 5.30-11pm.

Just under the railway arches leading in and out of Waterloo station, the Archduke has wooden floors and brick vaults and you can feel the trains passing overhead. But it is handily situated just behind the South Bank Centre and a few hundred steps from the station, and gets busy with both commuters and the theatre and arts crowd. Its food is excellent and well worth making a special visit for. They also have live jazz regularly.

Babushka

173 Blackfriars Rd, SE1
071-928 6179
Open Mon-Sat noon-11pm, Sun noon-6pm.

Babushka means grandmother in Russian, but there's nothing traditional about this newly opened bar—unless your granny has a good head for beer and vodka! During lunchtime and in the evenings, you can listen to music of the jazz variety. Good watering-holes are surprisingly few and far between in the Waterloo area, so Babushka is a welcome addition.

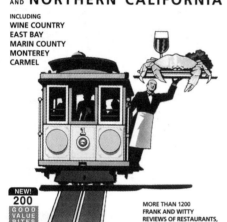

NIGHTLIFE

In the 1970s, the place was known as Swinging London, then life became more serious and for a few years London night life was rather a dull affair with only a few private clubs offering entertainment, dinner and dancing to members. But times changed and the top-notch places like Annabel's and Tramp were soon joined by Stringfellows and others who attracted a more egalitarian crowd.

In the last five years, the London night life scene has exploded with new interests and new ideas, particularly for the young who with a seemingly inexhaustible supply of energy, dance from dusk to dawn, and later, at any number of different venues. Whether it's alternative comedy, disco dancing or jazz you're after, the chances are that you'll be spoilt for choice.

For all the latest information, you should check the listings magazines, the London *Evening Standard* newspaper and the national dailies.

COMEDY & CABARET

The word 'cabaret' has a special meaning to the British, totally different from the continent. Go to a London cabaret and you'll find stand-up comics and musicians rather than topless dancers dressed in jewellery, and jewellery only. There are two major branches of British comedy: the old, and the modern or alternative, although the alternative has become so popular that today it is mainstream. The new alternative comedians started in the 1970s and 1980s as a reaction against old-style humour about women and minorities which they found offensive. They told no jokes about mother-in-laws and racial stereotypes, and they introduced improvised shows, where comedians were asked to act, and react, to the audience's suggestions. Today such shows are immensely popular, though following the jokes can be difficult if you don't know what is currently in the news in Britain. Stand-up comics can still however be rude, sometimes crude and particularly nasty; their humour is definitely not of the old P. G. Wodehouse school of gentle laughter. Audience participation is part of the fun, but if you comment on the artist, be prepared to take a verbal beating. 'Heckling' is totally acceptable, but your comments are supposed to be humorous! Some clubs have 'open microphone' spots, when anybody is allowed to try his or her talent in the very hard business of stand-up comedy.

Taste in humour is a very personal matter, but some of the hottest names on the British comedy circuit currently are Jo Brand, Julian Clary, Kevin Day, Jeremy Hardy, John Hegley, Eddie Izzard, Josie Lawrence, Donna McPhail and Paul Merton. The double act of David Baddiel and Rob Newman play venues usually reserved for the great rock stars only. The comedy circuit changes continually and most of the one-night-per-week-type clubs happen in pubs and small music clubs. The events listed here are correct when going to press and they are also well established.

Canal Café Theatre

The Bridge House, Delamere Terr, W2
071-289 6054
Open Thurs-Sun 10pm. Newsrevue £5.

This delightful building in Little Venice hosts a long running Newsrevue which runs from Thursday to Sunday.

Chuckle Club

Shakespeare's Head, Carnaby St, W1 - 071-476 1672
Open Saturday 8.30pm. Tickets £5.

The Chuckle Club has kept audiences laughing

since 1986 in different venues around London. Shows include both comedians and music.

Comedy Store
Haymarket House, Oxendon St, SW1 - CC Bookings 071-344 4444, Information 0426-914 433
Doors open at 6.30pm, Mon-Sat shows at 8pm, Fri, Sat also at midnight. Tickets £8.

The Comedy Store is the home of new British humour, and the Comedy Store Players are an excellent group of improvisers, some of whom are also regular faces on British television. Their particular skill lies in turning ideas offered by the audience into hilarious, often brilliant pieces of improvised theatre. There is improvised comedy every Wednesday and Sunday, while every Tuesday, Cutting Edge serves up a humorous look at the day's events. Totally up-to-the minute, the show is scripted and planned only hours before going on stage. Every Thursday amateurs have a chance to show their skills with an open microphone. Un-intentional humour is sometimes better than the intended kind. You can dine at the Comedy Store and seats are on a first-come-first-served basis.

Hackney Empire
291 Mare St, E8 - 081-985 2424
Shows and prices vary.

An old theatre saved for the arts instead of being turned into a bingo hall is definitely a rarity. This ravished beauty of a building with its faded gilt ceiling offers a mixture of music, theatre and comedy. It may

be some way from the West End but it is often worth the trip.

Doing the Lambeth Walk

Lambeth Walk was known for its local market and for giving its name to a Cockney dance first made popular in 1937 by one Lupino Lane in the musical *Me and My Girl* at the Victoria Palace.

Jongleurs
The Cornet, 49 Lavender Gdns, SW11
Camden Lock, Dingwalls Bldg, NW1 - 071-924 2766 (bookings for both venues).
Shows Fri 9pm, Sat 7pm, 11pm, Sun 8pm. Tickets £8.

Two clubs both with restaurants and bars. The Camden venue seats 500 people, but still it's essential to book for both places. There is always an interesting and varied collection of performers—from comedians to dancers and mime artists.

Meccano Club
The Market Tavern, 2 Essex Rd, N1 - 081-800 2236
Shows Thurs-Sat at 9pm. Tickets £5.

The basement of this pub provides a venue for many famous names.

Oranje Boom Boom
De Hems, Macclesfield St, W1 - 081-694 1710
Open Wed 8.45pm. Tickets £4.

Different kinds of humour is served weekly upstairs at the Dutch pub, De Hems, in Soho.

Red Rose Cabaret
Red Rose Club, 129 Seven Sisters Rd, N7 - 071-281 3051
Shows Fri and Sat at 9pm, box office opens 8pm. Tickets £6.

An established club offering established names.

DISCOS & CLUBS

'Clubbing' has become such an established pastime that it is possible to go clubbing in London through the whole weekend. Some places serve breakfast and even have early morning dance sessions to keep the customers going. Many of the music venues—like the Marquee, the Borderline and the Jazz Café—also have after-hours club nights.

Some venues run different club nights during the week. Other established clubs have a consistent music policy, but it is still worth checking what is going on. No-body wants to end up in a dinner jacket in a head-bangers' heavy rock ball. On the other hand, it just might be fun...

The club scene is in a constant state of change, and one-nighters come and go before you've got to know their names. Today's trendiest place may well be passé by the time you read this. However, we have listed places which are well es-

167

tablished, some of them clubs that are open every day, some open only once or twice a week. Some of the smaller venues may not accept credit cards, so please check beforehand if in doubt. Many of them have student nights, when entrance fees are reduced to a couple of pounds on production of a valid student card; again check in advance. The only thing for sure is that they are always at the least popular times, beginning or mid week, never weekends. Expect to pay anything from £5 to £12 for a ticket. Many clubs charge less before a certain hour (which could be anything from 10.30pm to 4 am!). But also remember that many of them offer membership and if you're here for any length of time and want to dance every night away at a favourite place, it might be worth joining. In the clubs listed here, drinks prices will start from about £2.50 for a bottle of lager. The general rule is that the later (or nearer to dawn) the time, the more you pay.

Bar Rumba

36 Shaftesbury Ave, W1
071-287 2715
Open Fri-Mon 5.30pm-3.30am. Tickets from £4.

As the name indicates, this is the place for a hot Latin night. They hold special music evenings with house, film soundtracks, jazz and everything to get you moving.

Café de Paris

3 Coventry Rd, W1
071-287 3602
Open Thurs 10pm-4am, Fri, Sat 10.30pm-6am. Entrance £10-£12.

Built in 1908, this Edwardian building, all glitz and plaster work with its distinctive and most un-Edwardian modern lighting rig, echoes to the British and American music put out by the resident DJs to the young.

The Camden Palace

Camden High St, NW1
071-387 0428
Open Tues-Sat 9pm-3.30am, Fri 9pm-6am. Entrance from £4.

This former music hall plays music for different tastes: from indie nights to dance hard-core and sixties' nostalgia events.

Crazy Larry's

533 King's Rd, SW10
071-376 5555
Open Thurs-Sat 10pm-2.30am. Entrance £7.

A large place popular with Chelsea and Fulham locals. The mixed crowd and softer sounds on the dance floor make Larry's more mellow than crazy.

The Dome

178 Junction Rd, NW5
071-281 2195
Open Thurs 9pm-1.30am, Fri and Sat 9pm-2.30am. Entrance £3-£5.

Very popular with students, lovers of indie pop and roots reggae (no ragga), this spacious club with a varied music policy attracts customers from a wide area.

Electric Ballroom

184 Camden High St, NW1
071-485 9006
Open Wed 7.30pm-11.30pm, Thurs-Sat 8pm-2.30am. Tickets about £5.

Music from punk and goth to different styles of dance depending on the

evening. Cheap and cheerful.

Equinox

Leicester Sq, WC2 - 071-437 1446
Open Mon-Thurs 9pm-2.30am, Fri, Sat to 3.30pm. Entrance from £5-£10.

This huge and glitzy main-stream disco used to be called the Empire. Young and fun, it has a student's night on Tuesdays and Wednesdays.

Fridge

Town Hall Parade, Brixton Hill, SW2 - 071-326 5100
Open Tues 10pm-3am, Fri to 5am, Sat to 6am. Entrance from £5.

Continuously one of the hippest clubs in London, the Fridge offers special nights with different themes: Ciao Baby (gay nights) on Tuesdays and Love Muscle on Saturday. The women only Venus Rising evening is a classic on the first Wednesday of every month.

Gardening Club

4 The Piazza, Covent Garden, WC2 - 071-497 3154
Open Mon-Fri 11pm-3.30am, Sat to 6am, Sun to 2.30am. Entrance from £5.

Upstairs it's a cappuccino bar, downstairs it's a collection of small rooms with pumping bass and ever-changing ideas. On Saturday you can usually join the pioneering Club for Life, which might mean music and 'virtual reality trapeze shows'. Another regular event is the Betty Ford Clinic which dries you out with house dancing.

Gossips

69 Dean St, W1 - 071-434 4480

Open Mon-Sat 10pm-3.30am. Entrance from £4.

This friendly and welcoming club is the home for London's longest running one-nighter, 'Gaz's Rockin' Blues'. It's held every Thursday with live bands and a great selection of music from blues to ska. Other special nights have different music policies.

Hippodrome

1 Cranbourn St (corner of Charing Cross Rd), WC2 071-437 4311

Open Mon-Sat 9pm-3.30am. Entrance £4-£10.

The Hippodrome has a magnificent light show and lots of brass in its interior. It is also a meeting place for tourists in London where international audiences spin and bop to the disco music put out by special guest DJs. Prices are cheaper before 10.30pm (£4 Monday to Thursday), but the action only starts to hot up towards midnight. Dress smart/casual (no trainers).

Iceni

11 White Horse St (off Curzon St), W1 - 071-495 5333

Open Wed, Fri, Sat 10.30pm-3am. Entrance £2-£10.

Iceni has three dance floors and serves up a different variety of dance music every night. One of the success stories of 1993, this place will tickle your imagination and inspire your dancing.

Legends

29 Old Burlington St, W1 071-437 9933

Dining & dancing

If you feel like a little light dancing, then the best places to go are London's grand dining rooms, where a small band will provide the music. You have to eat at all these places which are expensive, so the dancing constitutes an added bonus rather than the raison d'être for going.

The best places are *Claridge's* in the main restaurant (Friday and Saturday from 7.30pm to 1am, Brook St, W1, 071-629 8860), *The Dorchester Terrace* (Friday and Saturday 8pm-1am and you can come after the theatre and not for the whole dinner, Park Lane, W1, 071-629 8888), the Palm Court at *The Ritz* (dancing from 10pm to 1am Friday and Saturday, Piccadilly, W1, 071-493 8181), the Rooftop Restaurant at the *St George's* hotel with its fabulous view (Friday and Saturday from 8pm to midnight, Langham Pl, W1N, 071-580 0111), the River Room at *The Savoy* (daily except Sunday from 7.30pm to midnight during the week and later at weekends, Strand, WC2, 071-836 4343), and Windows on the World, another restaurant with great views at the *London Hilton on Park Lane* , (Friday and Saturday, 8.30pm to 2am, 22 Park Lane, W1, 071-493 8000).

Open Fri 10pm-5am, Sat 10.30pm-4.30am. Entrance £5-£15.

The proprietors of Legends have spent a lot of money building the stylish interior. Modern, sleek and glamorous are some of the descriptions used by the punters. Dress code is smart and relaxed, (no trainers or suits).

Limelight

136 Shaftesbury Ave (corner of Charing Cross Rd), WC2 071-434 0572

Open Wed-Sat 10.30pm-3am. Entrance £2-£10.

The Limelight is an extraordinary converted church, where audiences dance to various styles of music. Club nights get both dance floors busy.

Madame Jo Jo's

8-10 Brewer St, W1 071-734 2473

Open Mon-Sat 10pm-3am. Show time 11pm. Entrance £6-£12, table bookings £20 per person.

This civilised, decadent and outrageous transvestite club gathers a very mixed gay and straight audience. Drag acts, cabaret and dancing for the open-minded and fun-loving are on offer. The waitresses in skimpy outfits are of course all male. Don't mind if you feel bemused as well as amused—so does everybody else!

Maximus

14 Leicester Sq, WC1
071-734 4111
Open Mon-Thurs 10.30pm-3am, Fri, Sat 10.30pm-6am. Entrance £6-£10.

Another big place to celebrate in Leicester Square. They do have alcoves for sitting in when the dance floor starts to get too crowded.

Ministry of Sound

103 Gaunt St, SE1 - 071-378 6528
Open Fri midnight to Sat 8am-ish, Sat midnight-Sun 10am. Entrance: £10-£15.

THE club among the clubs for the young and fashionable. This is a huge place with famous DJs and a very trendy clientele. The club's own cinema helps you wind down and chill out after dancing, and they take it very seriously. It's a large New York-style club that believes that dancing is more important than drinking and doesn't serve alcohol. The Ministry is starting its own record label to feed its extremely effective sound system. The club already has its own clothing label.

Le Palais

24 Shepherd's Bush Rd, W6
081-748 2812
Open Thurs 9.30pm-2am, Fri to 3am, Sat 9pm-3am. Entrance £3-£5.

A huge and shiny ballroom with a laser show which glitters against the artificial art deco interior. It hosts glitzy galas and special events now and then, but usually Le Palais functions as a disco. The space-age lights and laser

show attracts up to 2,000 people who like to dress up a little!

Samantha's

3 New Burlington St, W1
071-734 6249
Open Mon-Sat 9pm-3.30am. Entrance £3-£7.

A place for those who like to dress smartly when going out, Samantha's has a selection of bars, split-level dance floor and ornamental pools!

Stringfellows

16 Upper St Martin's Lane, WC2 - 071-240 5534
Open Mon-Thurs 9pm-3am, Fri, Sat 8pm-3am. Non-members allowed in at the discretion of the doormen.

A place where celeb-rities used to come to get photographed by paparazzi. You can still spot familiar faces among the guests, who dine, drink and dance the night away.

Subterania

12 Acklam Rd, Ladbroke Grove, W10 - 081-960 4590
Open Mon-Thurs 8pm-2am, Fri-Sat 10pm-3am. Entrance £6-£8.

Under the motor way flyover in the heart of trendy Notting Hill, this lively club offers live music and dancing. The liberal music policy attracts a very varied audience.

Turnmills

63 Clerkenwell Rd (corner of Turnmill St), EC1 - 071-250 3409
Open Thurs 6.30pm-noon, Fri 7pm-9am, Sat 7pm-3am, then 3.30am to noon on Sun. Entrance £4-£8 (can include dancing lessons).

There's different dancing on offer here: Latin tango, Euro-French rock and jazz

swing. Come early for the lessons and then practice your newly-learned skills later in the evening (or earlier in the morning). They follow a consumer-friendly policy of charging normal pub prices for drinks. Turnmills attracts a very international crowd, and it is rumoured that Parisians travel over (or under) the Channel most weekends for a good evening abroad. 'The Trade' is a mixed gay/straight legend in club land, starting around 3.30am on Sunday and closing about noon!

Wag Club

35 Wardour St, W1
071-437 5534
Open Mon-Thurs 10.30pm-4am, Fri, Sat 10.30pm-6am. Entrance from £5.

Wag used to be notorious for its strict entry policy, but the heady days of the past are long gone and now it caters for different tastes on different nights and gathers a steady crowd of clubbers and onlookers.

GAY BARS & CLUBS

The Angel

65 Graham St, N1
Open Mon-Sat noon-midnight, Sun noon-11.30pm.

A café/bar populated by the local lesbian and gay community.

The Bell

259 Pentonville Rd, N1
071-837 5617
Open Mon 8pm-1am, Tues-Sat 9pm-2am, Sun 5pm-midnight.

A young mixed lesbian and gay audience dance to

the nightly disco in this friendly pub.

First Out Café/Bar
52 St Giles High St, WC2
071-240 8042
Mon-Sat 11am-11pm, Sun 1pm-10.30pm.
Continental style coffee house with a licensed bar downstairs for both gay and lesbian.

Heaven
Under The Arches, Villiers St, WC2 - 071-839 3852
Open Wed-Sun 10.30pm-4am. Entrance £6.
The largest gay club in Britain, with three bars and a massive dance floor with a flashing light show, attracts both gay and straight guests. They have outrageous theme nights.

Kudos
10 Adelaide St, WC2
071-379 4573
Open Mon-Sat noon-11pm, Sun noon-10.30pm.
One sign of the new pink economy boom. Expensive drinks and not so excellent food, but the stylish, modern interior suitable for people-watching makes it worth a visit. Both straight and gay clients.

Wilde's
13 Gerrard St, W1 - 071-494 1060
Open Mon-Sat 7pm-3am.
This is a friendly mixed bar with good music. It also holds meetings and workshops.

Wilde About Oscar
Philbeach Hotel, 30-31 Philbeach Gdns, SW5
071-835 1858
Open Mon-Thurs 7pm-11.30am, Fri-Sat 7pm-midnight.

Maybe the best totally gay restaurant in London with a French-Italian menu. The set dinner menu is £14.50, à la carte is around £17. The downstairs bar is suitable for a quick drink and the Philbeach Hotel is one of the biggest gay hotels in Britain.

MUSIC

Café Royal
The Green Room
68, Regent St, W1 - 071-437 9090
Open Mon-Sat 7pm-11pm. £45 dinner and show, £20 show only.
You can either enjoy a three-course dinner here with coffee and the cabaret for £45, or just come at 8.30pm for the entertainment which starts at 9pm and lasts about an hour and a half, with established names like Bobby Short, Eartha Kitt and Frankie Vaughan.

■ JAZZ

Bass Clef
35 Coronet St, N1 - 071-729 2476
Open Mon-Sat 7.30pm-2am, Sun noon-3pm, 7.30pm-11.30pm. Entrance from £3.
Hidden in the back streets, this small and intimate club offers a fine selection of music from Latin rhythms to jazz and modern beats. They hold club nights for dancing and there is a decent restaurant. All the good comments about the Bass Clef apply to its sister venue, the Tenor Clef next door at 1 Hoxton Sq, 071-729 2476, open daily 7.30pm-midnight.

Dingwalls
Jongleurs, Camden Lock, NW1 - 071-267 1999
Times and prices vary.
The old Dingwalls was an essential club for 70s pub rock and punk. Now the whole of Camden Lock is moving up-market, Dingwalls is situated in a totally new building. The famous name lives on, but the club now shares the premises with the Jongleurs.

Jazz Café
5 Parkway, NW1 - 071-916 6000
Open Mon-Thurs 7pm-midnight, Fri, Sat 7pm-2am. Sat, Sun noon-4pm. Entrance £8-£12.
Their varied music policy covers those things loosely called jazz, but the Jazz Café is not ultra-orthodox about this. At the heart of Camden Town, this stylish club is popular with younger jazz enthusiasts. Tables are strictly for diners, but there is enough room to stand by the bar and enjoy the music. After the live music, the Jazz Café turns into a late night dance club.

Ronnie Scott's
47 Frith St, W1 - 071-439 0747
Open Mon-Sat 8.30pm-3am. Entrance about £12.
This, the most famous of London's jazz clubs is still swinging with big names and you'll have to book or come early if you want to get in. Usually two bands play two sets each during the evening, so you get a lot of jazz. Tables are for diners only, which seems to be the fashion in jazz clubs all over the world. This is a place to listen to the music, so if you want a

conversation, go somewhere else. If you're lucky Ronnie Scott plays his sax; if you're unlucky he tells his jokes. Upstairs at the Tango, DJs play Latin music and exotic grooves. Admission is free for the guests downstairs, otherwise you can buy a ticket for the dance club only. London has gone Latin here for years! The upstairs is open from 11pm to 3am.

Palookaville
13a James St, WC2
071-240 5857
Open Mon-Wed noon-3pm, 5.30pm-1am, Thurs-Sat noon-3pm, 5.30pm-2am.

This little restaurant and wine bar in Covent Garden has small jazz groups, and usually maintains a good balance between the volume of the music and the lively audience. If they're playing your tune, there's a small dance floor to enjoy. Diners around the corner can watch the band on a monitor.

Pizza Express
10 Dean St, W1 - 071-437 9595
Open daily noon-midnight, music from 8.30pm.

Resident all-stars and guest bands entertain regularly in the cellar of this popular Soho restaurant. It's very main stream, more entertaining than adventurous. You have to eat to enjoy the music, but the food is good pizzas.

Pizza On The Park
11 Knightsbridge, SW1
071-235 5550
Open daily 9am-midnight, music from 9pm. Cover charge £15 for music.

This is an elegant pizza restaurant with jazz

standards playing, often world-class.

Prince of Orange
118 Lower Rd, SE16
071-237 2224
Open daily 7.30pm-midnight, Sun 7pm-10.30pm.

This major jazz venue south of the Thames is popular with locals and visitors. At this listener-friendly pub, the jazz is free; you just pay for your drinks.

■ ROCK

Borderline
Orange Yard, off Manette St/Charing Cross Rd, WC2
071-734 2095
Open 8.30pm-11pm, re-opens on special club nights 11.30pm-3am. Entrance from £5.

A small basement club very popular when breaking in new acts. But big bands like REM have played here under a pseudonym. Upstairs at Break for The Border you can dine in a noisy Tex-Mex restaurant, down Tequila Sunrises and listen to the live music.

Brixton Academy
211 Stockwell Rd, SW9
071-326 1022
Times and prices vary.

This large capacity place (4,000) hosts artists who are slightly out of the mainstream, not necessarily alternative but adventurous. The sloping floor gives a good view even from the back. Lots of good rap and reggae.

Dublin Castle
94 Parkway, NW1 - 071-485 1773
Open Mon-Sat 11am-midnight, Sun normal hours. Entrance from £3.

One of the best music pubs in London with a varied booking policy. From jumping blues to rockabilly via reggae and names you thought were long gone. Have a drink at the bar and listen to the music. If you like it, get a ticket and join in at the back to actually see what's going on.

The Falcon
234 Royal College St, NW1
071-485 3834
Open Mon-Thurs 11am-3pm, 5.30pm-11pm, Fri, Sat 11am-11pm, Sun normal pub hours. Entrance from £3.

This very basic 'spit-and-sawdust' pub is a home for new alternative indie bands. It offers the trendiest of gigs in 1994.

Forum
9-17 Highgate Rd, NW5
071-284 2200
Times and prices vary.

The best rock club in London: it's big enough, it books class acts, it's run properly and easy to get to. Its sister venue, The Garage at 20-22 Highbury Corner, N5, 071-607 1818 is smaller and more intimate, open Sun-Wed 8pm-12.30am, Thurs-Sat 8pm-midnight.

Fusilier and Firkin
7 Chalk Farm Rd, NW1
071-485 7858
Open Mon-Thurs 11am-midnight, Fri noon-midnight, Sun noon-3pm, 4pm-10.30pm. Entrance from £3.

A place for a Saturday afternoon dose of rhythm and blues and real ale. In the middle of Camden market, this rowdy, but friendly pub gets easily crowded.

The Grand

Clapham Junction, St John's Hill, SW11 - CC bookings 071-284 2200
Times and prices vary.

A large old theatre converted into the biggest rock venue south of the river in London.

Half Moon Putney

93 Lower Richmond Rd, SW15 - 081-780 9383
Open Mon-Sat 11am-11pm, Sun normal hours. Ticket prices vary.

A long established place for ex-famous musicians to relax and play for pocket money in the large back room. A good blues band really gets the place swinging or wailing or what ever it is they do. Music every evening and also Sunday lunchtime.

Hammersmith Apollo

Queen Caroline St, W6 081-741 4668
Times and prices vary.

This long-running venue used to be the famous Odeon immortalised in the phrase 'No sleep till Hammersmith'—bands used to end their British tours here in Hammersmith and the last gig was often the best, particularly after the hectic life on the road had killed all inhibitions. Legends aside, this old theatre is one of the nicest places to see big names in London.

Marquee

105 Charing Cross Rd, WC2 071-437 6601
Open daily 7pm-11pm, special club nights Fri 7pm-6 am, Sat 7pm-3am. Ticket prices vary.

The legend of the club legends from the 1960s onwards presents mainly heavy rock with goth and indie bands thrown in for good measure. The Beatles are probably the only big British name that has never played the Marquee; during the years superstars are known to return to their roots by playing semi-secret gigs here. A bit of a crumbling place with a glittering history.

Mean Fiddler

24 Harlesden High St, NW10 - 081-961 5490
Times and prices vary.

A bit out from central London but worth a visit, the spacious main club has a balcony giving a good view onto the stage, that is, except when the place gets crowded. It's probably at it's best with big Irish names. But the Mean Fiddler looks surprisingly cosy even when there's only a small audience. The Acoustic Room next door has quieter music. Food is available at the bar and in the Acoustic room.

Roadhouse

Jubilee Hall, 35 The Piazza, Covent Garden, WC2 071-240 6001
Open Mon-Wed 5.30pm-1am, Thurs-Sat 5.30pm-3am, Sun Blues brunch noon-5pm. Entrance £3-£6.

This new venue at the heart of Covent Garden caters for rock fans who are just that bit older. The music is blues-based with some soul and good rocking thrown in for good measure. The décor is American 50s road house, and the food is described as 'global American'. You can dine, have a snack at the bar or just nurse your drink while listening to the music.

Robey

240 Seven Sisters Rd, N4 071-263 4581
Music Mon-Fri 9pm-2am, Sat 9pm-6am (a club night), Sun 5.30pm-10.30pm. Some all-day music marathons. Entrance from £3.

This cavernous, saw dust-floored pub specialises in all-day themes— sometimes it's Irish music from folk to Celtic rap, sometimes psychedelic, sometimes psycho trash. Take your pick. Usually up to eight unknown bands play every night in this spacious North London pub named after the famous music hall artist, Sir George Robey.

Rock Garden

6-7 The Piazza/James St, WC1 - 071-240 3961
Open Mon-Fri 5pm-3am, Sat noon-3am, Sun noon-3pm, 7pm-midnight.

Unknown bands on their way up, or, if you like, at their peak. In the 1970s both The Police and Dire Straits played here. This basement venue where three or four bands play every night, is particularly well located for tourists. Food is available upstairs noon-midnight.

Wembley Arena

Empire Way, Wembley, Middlx - 081-900 1234
Times and prices vary.

The largest indoor place in London always has big names, but the Arena is not the nicest of places to see a concert. Big in size, small in atmosphere.

■ WORLD & ROOTS

Africa Centre
39 King St, WC2 - 071-836 1973
Open Thurs 9pm-2am, Fri 9pm-3am.

During the day the Africa Centre is a place for cultural and political activities, with a craft and book shop and restaurant all packed together. Thursday and Friday nights are for music from all over the huge continent and it becomes a place to dance the night away. The downstairs Calabash is one of the few African restaurants in London open weekdays 12.30pm-2.30pm, 6pm-10.30pm (see *Bargain Bites*, page 120).

Cecil Sharp House
2 Regent's Park Rd, NW1
071-485 2206
House open Mon, Wed, Fri 9.30am-5.30pm, Thurs to 10pm, Sat 7.30pm-11pm. Check times of special concerts. Entrance prices vary.

This is the centre for British folk music and has singers' nights, folk dancing, and a folk music shop. It has lately widened its scope of concerts to roots music from around the world.

Weavers Arms
98 Newington Green, N1
071-354 9501
Open Mon-Sat 11am-11pm, music room 8.30pm-midnight. Sun normal hours.

This large pub serves lovers of American, Irish and British folk and roots music well. There is a large back room for the music; those there just for the beer can stay in the front bar.

PRIVATE CLUBS

Annabel's
44 Berkeley Sq, W1
071-629 2350

Annabel's is one of the most exclusive night-clubs in London. Clientele includes probably more royals around the world than the gossip pages in a tabloid newspaper. Annabel's is a members-only club, the waiting list is extremely long, and there is no temporary membership, so don't even try.

Mosimann's
110 West Halkin St, Belgrave Sq, SW1 - 071-235 9625

See *Restaurant* section, page 25.

Mortons
28 Berkeley Sq, W1
071-499 0363
Open Mon-Fri noon-3am, Sat 6.30-3am.

This exclusive private club, looking out onto Berkeley Square, has, along with Annabel's, one of London's best addresses. You can drink in their excellent bar, and eat in a very pretty first-floor restaurant. Huge mirrors on the walls reflect the dried flower arrangements by the master, Ken Turner; other space is taken up by pictures. The menu follows a satisfying formula with starters like soft shell crab cakes, vegetable terrine or lobster salad. Main courses might include lamb cutlets with red wine and pickled walnuts (highly recommended) or pan-seared salmon. Vegetables are served as a selection in those useful crescent-shaped dishes that have all but disappeared from restaurants and desserts appeal to the sweet-toothed. As one would expect from a club, the wine list appeals. Mainly French, they have a good selection of half bottles. They also offer a vintage selection, the result of a judicious buy of a complete private cellar, with bottles of rare French wines from £200. Service is delightful; if the restaurant manager, John Stephen, is there, get him to advise you on both wine and food. Mortons are offering temporary overseas membership for Gault Millau readers on production of the book for £35 per month. So come out of the cinema or theatre and make your way here for a convivial evening in the restaurant and/or early morning in the bar.

Tokyo Joe's
85 Piccadilly, W1 - 071-409 1832
Open Mon-Sat 8.30pm-3.30am.

This lush private night club requests membership, but you can sort out the details at the door (temporary membership is £5 if you have dinner, £10 just for the disco). The restaurant attracts a clientele used to the little luxuries of life.

Tramp
40 Jermyn St, W1 - 071-734 3174

Membership required and there are many people wanting to join this very exclusive club for the youngish, rich and/or famous. No temporary membership, to join one needs a recommendation from a member.

SHOPS

ANTIQUES

■ ANTIQUE CENTERS

Alfie's
13-25 Church St, NW8
071-723 6066
Open Tues-Sat 10am-6pm.

There is a raffish air to this sprawling maze of almost 200 dealers who occupy a large building, formerly a Victorian department store, at one end of Church Street. An open-air fruit and vegetable market adds to the bustle. Alfie's was established in 1974 and sells everything under the sun from large pieces of furniture to small items of jewellery. There is advertising memorabilia at Liz Farrow's Dodo stand; art deco metalware, Clarice Cliff and Shelley ware at Beth; tins, bakelite products, children's games and commemorative ware at David Huxtable's stand; and Royal Doulton from the turn of the century at The Collector Shop, right next to Alfie's.

Antiquarius
131-141 King's Rd, SW3
071-675 6155
Open Mon-Sat 10am-6pm.

In neat refurbished premises, 120 dealers sell vintage clothing, china, glass, antiquarian books and paintings with a good choice of specialists selling clocks, watches, porcelain, and silver. Among the many stalls, search out the XS Baggage Co which sells antique leather suitcases and bags, and Jasmin Cameron who specialises in eighteenth- and nineteenth-century ink-stands, fountain pens, paint boxes and small silver collectibles. If you're interested in clocks, GS Mathias has fine eighteenth-century longcase clocks among a large assortment of lapdesks and writing boxes.

Bond Street Antiques Centre
124 New Bond St, W1
071-351 5353
Open Mon-Fri 10am-5.45pm.

This small centre with 30 dealers has a good reputation for portrait miniatures, Oriental antiques and silver as well as unusual jewellery at stands like N Bloom and Son, Jacobs, Lack and Archutowski. And for the serious, PMR Antiques specialises in ladies' art deco diamond watches and other jewellery of the period up to 1950.

Chelsea Antique Market
253 King's Rd, SW3
071-352 1424
Open Mon-Sat 10am-6pm.

A scruffy flea-market atmosphere prevails at this rambling, horseshoe-shaped arcade of some twenty dealers where you'll find some fun collectibles. Try Castasides where the stock is all theatre programmes, records of show tunes as well as cinema and theatre posters like the one portraying Elizabeth Taylor and Richard Burton in Private Lives for £30, cheaper than a print and a great talking point. There is an opticals' dealer and Harrington Brothers' books spills over into some half-a-dozen shops.

Gray's Antique Market
58 Davies St, W1 - 071-629 7034
Open Mon-Fri 10am-6pm.

This is an excellent antique market in central London, just by Bond and South Molton Streets and it has some interesting dealers. Britannia has commemorative mugs and plates, especially of royal coronations and anniversaries, while about 95 percent of the top china and pottery wares sold by Solveig and Anita Gray are Oriental ceramics–Chinese, Japanese and Korean–with pieces from 2,000 BC up to eighteenth- and occasional nineteenth-century Imperial ware. They show at some of the top London fairs. The quality is high at this centre, though there's a more informal atmosphere downstairs where you'll find the fascinating Thimble Society of London. Iona Antiques has lovely paintings of animals; right at the entrance is Sean Arnold with a collection of golfing, polo, tennis and other sports memorabilia and vintage luggage, and Paul Lesbirel at Abacus, the very first stall you come to, specialises in a wide range of good, inexpensive silver jewellery.

Gray's Mews
1-7 Davies Mews, W1
071-629 7034
Open Mon-Fri 10am-6pm.

An off-shoot of the main market, the mews has a smart air with a good selection of art deco furniture, scientific instruments, paintings, Oriental china, militaria, fine glassware and jewellery. Guest and Gray have predominantly Oriental ceramics along with a varied and exciting choice of European porcelain, all dated before 1800 such as a Meissen dish from the famous Podewils service, around 1741.

The Mall Antiques Arcade

Camden Passage, N1
071-351 5353
Open Tues-Thurs, Fri 10am-5pm, Wed 7.30am-5pm, Sat 9am-6pm.

Very smart shops offer an exceptional choice of English and continental furniture in the lower level as well as Oriental art, clocks, porcelain, brass, prints and decorative objects. There are 35 dealers on two floors in this London district which is known for its antique shops and arcades. Monika sells period costume jewellery and accessories, Rumours Decorative Arts specialises in Moorcroft pottery, and Mike Weedon has art nouveau and art deco objects. Some dealers keep to their own opening days and hours rather than the Mall's.

■ ANTIQUE MARKETS

Bermondsey Market

Long Lane and Bermondsey St, SE1
Open Fri 5am-2pm.

Sharp-eyed dealers and bleary-eyed tourists rub elbows as they try to spot the bargain of the moment among a large and motley selection of basic stalls long before dawn breaks. The serious buyers, even some high-powered dealers, get there when it opens to look over the silver and paintings. Tourists are more likely to be bewildered at the vast array of second-hand bric-a-brac which includes an eccentric mix from gas masks (who, we wondered would collect these?), old radios, old-fashioned telephones and lots of jewellery, china and glass. Its official name is New Caledonian Market

Camden Passage Market

The Angel, N1
Open Wed 10am-2pm, Sat 10am-5pm.

A pedestrianised path cuts through one of the country's biggest concentration of antiques businesses, about 300 of them in shops, arcades and side streets. Many are open during the week. On market days there is a cheerful ambience, enhanced by little cafés and restaurants. It makes good browsing territory for engravings, prints, jewellery and lots of collectibles. Explore side passages such as Pierrrepoint Row where Drene Brennan has an amazing 2,000 egg cups at her little stall, called the Gazebo, on the top floor. Human nature being what it is, you come away feeling, anything and everything is a potential collectors' item.

Greenwich Market

College Approach, SE10
Open Sat, Sun 9am-6pm.

Tables piled high with a motley collection of second-books, art deco furniture, medals and jewellery. Nearby, the covered crafts market is good for hand-made children's clothes, wooden toys and jewellery. It's more a bric-a-brac than serious market, but no less fun for that, and you can find some bargains.

Portobello Road Market

Portobello Rd, W11
071-371 6960
Open Sat 6am-5pm.

London's best known street market for antiques, bric-a-brac and collectibles gets very crowded on Saturdays as visitors jostle one another to look at the coins, jugs, rugs, ink-stands, silverware and second-hand clothes on display at stalls and in side arcades. Treasures and junk lie side by side. An Information Booth at the junction of Portobello Road and Westbourne Grove gives out a free brochure on the stall holders and galleries, and directs visitors to dealers specialising in the articles they are looking for. It can be a confusing place, changing its personality as you walk along the street. The Notting Hill end has the finer choice of shops and stalls, then there is a fruit and vegetable market, and it all ends with a very scruffy selection of stands selling cheap clothes and bric-a-brac. Note also that there are some 90 antique dealers and art shops open during the week when the market is closed.

■ ART DECO & ART NOUVEAU

Chenil Galleries

181-183 King's Rd, SW3
071-351 5353
Open Mon-Sat 10am-6pm.

Walk into this gallery and you immediately know what it is about—just look up at the stylised painting on the domed ceiling of the hall entranceway. Opened in 1979, it's full of delights for the art deco enthusiast. From a car-shaped tea set, once part of Elton John's collection, to Tiffany signed seals, the choice from the array of dealers is eclectic. Look out for Joana Piotrowski's large display of mirrors, lacquer ware and writing slopes. The neat, brightly-lit shop, called Jazzy Art Deco, specialises in fine furniture from the 1920s to the 1940s such as a classic, semi-circular maple cocktail cabinet.

Editions Graphiques Gallery

3 Clifford St, W1 - 071-734 3944
Open Mon-Fri 10am-6pm, Sat to 2pm.

Three little rooms, jam-packed with sculpture, paintings, lamps, lots of books and ceramics, Erté posters, Lalique vases and collectable artefacts, such as decanters and ice-coolers as well as furniture, make this the best showplace, established in 1966, for the decorative flair of the art nouveau and art deco eras. The seeming jumble of items gives the impression of an eccentric collector's home.

Haslam and Whiteway

105 Kensington Church St, W8 - 071-229 1145
Open Mon-Fri 10am-6pm, Sat to 2pm.

Founded in 1972, this firm has two floors specialising in the arts and crafts period with the furnishings designed by architects of that era that decorated the houses they built. They have glorious items like stained glass by Henry Holliday, a rush-seated bedroom chair by Voysey at £2,250, tiles by William Morris and an umbrella stand decorated with Darwin's monkeys and climbing plants at £3,950 by Mark Marshall. Owner Michael Whiteway has co-written *Nineteenth Century Design.*

John Jesse

160 Kensington Church St, W8 - 071-229 0312
Open Mon-Sat 10am-6pm.

Lalique, Liberty, Tiffany, Daum, Galle—all the famous names are found at this shop specialising in art nouveau and art deco objets d'art, jewellery and all the decorative arts from 1880 to 1950. They have objects like an art nouveau Cartier brooch with a background of diamonds and many small opals, and one by Omar Ramsden with the stunning green stone chrysoprase in the splendid arts and crafts style.

Lewis Kaplan Associates

50 Fulham Rd, SW3
071-589 3108
Open Mon-Sat 10am-6pm.

Art deco is the era this shop deals in, with some magnificent examples of 1930s metal furniture, Daum glass, Puiforcat silver and signed 1940s jewellery by Van Cleef, Cartier and other famous names.

■ AUCTION HOUSES

The quality daily newspapers give details of auctions; otherwise telephone to enquire which particular sales are coming up. Apart from the serious business of buying, previews of sales offer wonderful opportunities to look at antiques before they disappear back into private hands.

Bonhams

Montpelier St, SW7
071-584 9161, Fax 071-589 4072
Open Mon 8.45am-7pm, Tues-Fri 8.45am-6pm, Sun 11am-4pm.
65-69 Lot's Rd, SW10
071-351 7111
Open Mon 8.45am-7pm, Tues-Fri 8.45am-4.30pm, Sun 11am-4pm.

Going under the hammer at this Knightsbridge auctioneers are wide-ranging categories including modern and antique guns, arms, armour and militaria, vintage fountain pens, paintings, water-colours, drawings, prints, furniture, tribal art, clocks and watches, ceramics, books and many other antiquities. The firm reported a record 1993 sales year, helped by pioneering sales such as the art and artefacts of the Near East, mostly Islamic. Rather more informal than the main branch, and less expensive, the Lot's Road galleries hold regular sales of paintings, furniture, prints, silver, jewellery, ceramics and collectibles.

Christie's
8 King St, SW1 - 071-839 9060, Fax 071-839 1611
Open Mon-Fri 9am-4.30pm, Sundays during the sales 2pm-5pm, Tues 9am-8pm.
See *text* below.

Christie's South Kensington
85 Old Brompton Rd, SW7 071-581 7611, Fax 071-321 3321
Open Mon 9am-7pm, Tues-Fri 9am-5pm, Sat 10am-1pm.

A household name associated with the sale of fine paintings, this firm was established in 1766. It quickly became known for its sales of artists' studio works, starting with Gainsborough and continuing with Reynolds, Landseer, Rossetti, Burne-Jones, Leighton, Sargent and others. The smartly refurbished galleries on King Street still have sales of important works of art and Old Master paintings although the range includes anything which collectors covet, whether it be fine wines (for which they have made a name for themselves), vintage cars, English furniture or decorative art objects. Christie's publishes more than 1,200 different catalogues annually from eleven showrooms world-wide. You'll find some of these catalogues for sale in the shop area in the front. The Brompton Road branch in South Ken-sington has a smaller display area but an equally wide range of sale

themes, often connected with seasonal subjects such as Valentine cards. Miniature aircraft, fans, dolls and teddy bears, posters, and everything up to large Oriental carpets are sold.

Phillips
101 New Bond St, W1 071-629 6602, Fax 071-629 8876
Open Mon 9am-7.30pm, Tues-Fri to 5pm, Sun 2-5pm.
10 Salem Rd, W2 - 071-229 9090, Fax 071-792 9201
Open Mon-Fri 8.30am-5pm, Thurs to 7.30pm, Sat 9am-12.30pm, Sun 2pm-5pm.

These busy galleries display for sale arms and armour, musical instruments, Oriental ceramics and books along with the usual collectors' interests such as ceramics, paintings and furniture. The jewellery experts organise some 30 auctions a year world-wide, with London focusing on period and twentieth-century diamond and decorative pieces. By the Bond Street entrance artefacts on display include a cloisonné enamel model of a deer, Qianlong period, and photographs of some rare items sold at its auctions, such as sixteenth-century drawings by Jacopo Ligozzi, sold for a record-breaking £120,300. The firm, which was established in 1796, plans a new shop on the premises to sell catalogues and cards. Usefully, for those with more than just a passing interest in the subject, the Salem Road branch holds talks on Saturday mornings on how to buy and sell at auction.

Sotheby's
34 New Bond St, W1 071-493 8080, Fax 071-409 3100
Open Mon-Fri 9am-5.30pm.

Founded in 1744, these huge galleries extending beyond the small entrance to St George Street and Conduit Street, have a tranquil air. It is a traditional setting for the modern bustle of viewing days and the excitement of the crowds on sales days, when the atmosphere can heighten as lots are sold at the rate of two a minute for thousands of pounds. Like Christie's, Sotheby's offers an excellent advice and valuation service. The busy shop up-front sells its own range of catalogues, and also beautifully illustrated books on art and the decorative arts, including specialist subjects such as *The French Crown Jewels*, *Spencer House* and *Perfume, Cologne and Scent Bottles*.

■ BOOKS & MANU-SCRIPTS

We have included Fax numbers for the antiquarian booksellers as most of them produce catalogues you might want to request.

Bernard Quaritch
5-8 Lower John St, W1 071-734 2983, Fax 071-437 0967
Open Mon-Fri 9.30am-5.30pm.

Dating back to the 1840s, this, the oldest and largest antique book shop in London, can be rather intimidating, catering for serious customers in a very formal atmosphere with each department, from the arts to Islamic culture, run by its own director. Look out for the illustrated medieval manuscripts, called 'leaves' in the trade, usually in a display case by the entrance.

Bertram Rota

9-11 Langley Ct, WC2
071-836 0723, Fax 071-497 9058
Open Mon-Fri 9.30am-5.30pm.

Now run by Anthony Rota, this book shop has a strong literary background. It has the interesting approach of frequently pursuing themes such as collecting the books of both English and American authors that were published by a particular firm. Special short-run editions signed by contemporary authors, like Margaret Atwood, in special papers are an interesting sideline.

Bloomsbury Workshop

12 Galen Pl, off Bury Pl, WC1
071-405 0632
Open Mon-Fri 9am-5.30pm.

Virginia Woolf and her literary and artistic cronies in the Bloomsbury Group— Duncan Grant, Clive Bell, and her sister, Vanessa— are the point of this little corner shop in a newly converted enclave near the British Museum stocking many collector's modern first editions. There are changing exhibitions of work by their off-spring and others connected with the circle.

Henry Sotheran

2-5 Sackville St, W1
071-734 1150, Fax 071-434 2019
Open Mon-Fri 9.30am-6pm, Sat 10am-4pm.

This large wood-panelled shop looks exactly how a fine vintage bookseller's should. It specialises in natural history, with prints and engravings available. The fine books might include a £1,500 bible of 1767 bound in a lavishly tooled design of flowers and thistles, a £500 first edition of Lewis Carroll's *Through the Looking Glass* complete with misprints, or a £500 first trade edition of T E Lawrence's *Pillars of Wisdom*. The shop is strong on travel, exploration and early voyages and look out for the remaindered table by the door which has a good choice. Downstairs is the gallery of The Folio Society which reprints good books with contemporary illustrations and excellent hard-back bindings.

G Heywood Hill

10 Curzon St, W1 - 071-629 0647, Fax 071-408 0286
Open Mon-Fri 9am-5.30pm, Sat to 12.30pm.

Strewn with books and manned by charming staff, this shop is a delight, selling both new and second-hand books and with a specialist children's book section downstairs. The last of the carriage trade booksellers, they also specialise in natural history, illustrated books and volumes on architecture.

Jarndyce Antiquarian Booksellers

46 Great Russell St, WC1
071-631 4220, Fax 071-436 6544
Open Mon-Fri 9.30am-5pm by appointment.

Brian Lake has become the leading specialist in Dickens (including first editions) as well as in eighteenth- and nineteenth-century books, with a strong emphasis on English literature. But his catalogues are full of gems and good ideas, like women's literature, and are amusingly illustrated. Prices, also, are not daunting. The upstairs rooms, which resemble a library more than a book shop look out onto the British Museum.

Maggs Brothers

50 Berkeley Sq, W1
071-493 7160, Fax 071-499 2007
Open Mon-Fri 9.30am-5pm.

The very reassuring atmosphere of a long- established library sets the tone for this grand shop overlooking Berkeley Square where it is advisable to know what you are interested in beforehand. Maggs are one of the oldest and most respected antiquarian book businesses. Early travel books and modern first editions, including foreign language books, are a good theme to explore. This is the place to buy famous autographs—a document signed by Queen Victoria was for sale recently for £350.

Robert Frew

106 Great Russell St, WC1
071-580 2311, Fax 071-631 3253
Open Mon-Fri 10am-6pm, Sat to 2pm, Sun 2pm-6pm.

Prints by Thomas Rowlandson and Arthur Rackham catch the eye in this handsome shop where books on travel and illustrated ones on English literature are stocked.

Sam Fogg

14 Old Bond St, W1
071-495 2333, Fax 071-409 3326
Open Mon-Fri 9.30am-5.30pm.

From the these hushed fourth floor premises, Sam Fogg sells wonderful, luminous medieval and Renaissance illuminated manuscripts from all over the world, with an emphasis on European works and a big collection of Ethiopian origin. Established in 1971, this firm does not sell books, but is the major manuscript dealer in the country, including a wide choice of miniatures, from Armenian to Indonesian to Slavonic.

Simon Finch Rare Books

Clifford Chambers, 10 New Bond St, W1 - 071-499 0474, Fax 071-499 0799
Open Mon-Sat 10am-6pm.

A rarity amid the fashion and jewellery shops of this most prestigious of all London streets, the shop has expanded recently to include a downstairs pre-

mises, in addition to the upstairs room with its sitting-room atmosphere. It specialises in books from the fifteenth to the nineteenth century and prints and artefacts that appeal to passing customers taking time off from buying diamonds and pearls.

Sims Reed

43a Duke St, SW1 - 071-493 5660
Open Mon-Fri 9am-6pm.

The dark wood shelves of this antiquarian book shop display rare, out-of-print and new reference books on fine and applied art from architecture to contemporary design and the shop is probably London's biggest dealer in decorative books with original prints. The telephone calls about first editions attest to the shop's reputation among collections and, in its new corner location, it retains a scholarly atmosphere.

Thomas Heneage Art Books

42 Duke St, SW1 - 071-930 9223, Fax 071 839 9223
Open Mon-Fri 10am-6pm.

Based in royal St. James's, the world's leading supplier of fine art books sells both newly published work, second-hand and collector's items.

Ulysses

40 Museum St, WC1 - Tel and Fax 071-831 1600
Open Mon-Sat 10.30am-6pm, Sun noon-6pm.

There's a comfortable atmosphere and even a wickerwork sofa in the downstairs level of this shop, where neatly-

arranged shelves of collector's items of modern first editions greet the browser. The sister shop across the road stocks vintage travel books.

■ FURNITURE

Bernheimer Fine Arts

32 St George St, W1
071-499 0293
Open Mon-Fri 10am-5.30pm.

European furniture from the seventeenth and eighteenth centuries, Oriental art and porcelain from the second century BC to the eighteenth century are on display in these large premises. Founded in 1985, the firm now also specialises in Old Master paintings with such finds as an oil painting of a Lady Rushout with her daughter by the celebrated eighteenth-century painter Angelica Kaufmann whose works hang in many a stately home.

Pelham Galleries

24-25 Mount St, W1
071-629 0905
Open Mon-Fri 9am-5.30pm.

The emphasis here is on decorative arts and furniture displayed in well laid-out, stylish galleries. Unusual forms of painted and lacquered decoration are well represented, such as a large pair of Imperial Wan-li lacquer wardrobes, around 1600, and a pair of Chinese export lacquer coffers decorated with landscapes, around 1780. Exceptional craftsmanship and interesting historical associations are appealing features of many pieces, like the pair of hand-painted Robert Adams cabinets of 1776 which were thought to have been lost after being removed from a house one hundred years ago. Also on display after three years' restoration work are the wrought-iron railings, 1748, from Chesterfield House in London, demolished in 1937. The parquetry floors based on antique designs in Venetian, Versailles and star patterns are laid out at the Pelham Galleries by the Sinclair Tile flooring company, (071-720 0031, Fax 071-498 3814).

CONTINENTAL & ENGLISH

Anton Chenevière Fine Arts

94 Mount St, W1 - 071-491 1007
Open Mon-Fri 9.30am-6pm.

These impressive showrooms are devoted to ornately designed eighteenth- and nineteenth-century Russian, Austrian, German and Italian furniture along with many objets d'art. Among the display you might find a Russian mosaic malachite tazza of approximately 1820, or an Italian-made rosewood and kingwood Italian-made table, around 1780.

Carlton Hobbs

46a Pimlico Rd, SW1
071-730 3640
Open Mon-Fri 9am-6pm, Sat 10am-5pm.

In the dramatically lit, large showrooms are exceptional choices of eighteenth- and early nineteenth-century English and continental furniture

and works of art such as a pair of gilt and faux bronze French armchairs, 1810, or an Aubusson carpet of 1820.

Jeremy

29 Lowndes St, SW1
071-823 2923
Open Mon-Fri 8.30am-6pm, Sat 9am-5pm.

Brothers Michael and John Hill, are proud to carry on the family tradition of selling high quality English and continental furniture from the eighteenth and early nineteenth centuries from their smart premises in a quiet Knightsbridge street. They have outstanding examples of French, Russian and English decorative art and the Getty Museum in California has bought from them. A very real connection with the past is one of the appeals of old furniture and one piece in particular, a Regency English-made cabinet, 1810, had a hand-written paper in one of the drawers, showing it had once been owned by the Prince Regent's daughter. It read 'Princess Charlotte's own escritoire'.

Jonathan Harris

54 Kensington Church St, W8 - 071-937 3133
Open Mon-Fri 9.30am-6pm.

In these large showrooms are important English, continental and Oriental furniture and works of art, with finds for collectors such as a rare, English shallow mahogany commode with a purple breccia marble top, around 1768, and an ormolu-mounted dressing table, around 1770, which came from the Lords Kinnaird in Perthshire.

Partridge Fine Arts

144-146 New Bond St, W1
071-629 0834
Open Mon-Fri 9am-5.30pm.

This large antiques firm is housed in an impressive building with a grand staircase and marble pillars, built in 1913 as showrooms for Colnaghi, the art dealers. It is the only custom-built gallery of that era still used for the original purpose of showing off masterpieces, now in the form of English and French furniture, silver, paintings of the English and Italian school and hundreds of related artefacts.

G Sarti

55 Jermyn St, W1 - 071-491 0449
Open Mon-Fri 10am-6pm.

Only the sixteenth to the eighteenth centuries are represented in the Italian furniture for which this showy gallery is known. On a recent visit, pride of place was taken by a rare ornately decorated Arte Povera cabinet of 1750 and there was a fine medieval panel depicting two angels crowning the Virgin of Humility, from around 1405-10.

O F Wilson

3-6 Queens Elm Parade, Old Church St, SW3 - 071-352 9554
Open Mon-Fri 9.30am-5.30pm, Sat 10.30am-1pm.

Amid the eighteenth- and early nineteenth-century English and continental furniture are such items as an English-made, cream chinoiserie lacquer box, around 1830, and a decorated sewing box from the same period.

Here you might see a pair of Venetian armchairs from the mid-eighteenth century, Roman gilt wood console tables from around 1750 and Italian statuary marble lions from the nineteenth century. Marble mantelpieces and architectural items are a particular speciality.

EIGHTEENTH- & NINETEENTH- CENTURY ENGLISH FURNITURE

Apter Fredericks
265-267 Fulham Rd, SW3
071-352 1188
Open Mon-Fri 9.30am-5.30pm, Sat by appointment.
The generous windows of Apter Fredericks, a firm which goes back five generations, display some of the fine eighteenth-century English furniture of this leading dealer. Glorious warm mahogany wine cabinets, a George I burr-walnut secretaire tallboy or a gracious George III satinwood chest might stand side by side, or be reflected in a Regency giltwood mirror surrounded by a flamboyant fluted border. Researched with meticulous care, they know the provenance of most of this grand furniture which illustrates the tastes of a past, more gracious age. They have helped form major public collections and furnished the odd royal residence.

H Blairman and Sons
119 Mount St, W1 - 071-493 0444
Open Mon-Fri 9am-6pm.

These are discreet premises for the firm which was founded in 1884, and full of surprises. Customers might come across a 1790 chimney piece by George Brookshaw painted on copper and wood, or an unusual gong designed around 1870 by E W Godwin. Blairmans specialise in eighteenth- and early nineteenth-century English furniture and later English architect-designed furniture and to complement the furniture, you'll find related works in the three showrooms.

Brian Rolleston Antiques
104a Kensington Church St, W8 - 071-229 5892
Open Mon-Fri 10am-1pm, 2.30-5.30pm.
Eighteenth-century English furniture fills the three large showrooms here. On a recent visit, one stunning piece caught our eyes, a William and Mary walnut and oyster veneered laburnum cabinet, profusely inlaid with floral marquetry, with the interior similarly decorated. Also to be coveted was a Regency period rosewood library table with brass inlay and gilded feet at £11,500.

David Pettifer
219 King's Rd, SW3
071-352 3088
Open Mon-Fri 8.30am-6.30pm, Sat to 5pm.
For the last 30 years, David Pettifer has been perfecting his own particular eclectic approach to presenting attractive and unusual items together, with everything from decorative biscuit tins to

Georgian marble busts and recently, a stunning pair of Regency mahogany library English-made armchairs from the 1820s. In keeping with the contemporary need to see objects in context, he holds themed exhibitions. One especially interesting one was *The Library*.

W R Harvey and Co
5 Old Bond St, W1 - 071-499 8385
Open Mon-Sat 10am-5.30pm.
This very traditional firm, established in 1918, holds delightful summer exhibitions under such headings as *The Gentlemens' Library* or *A Cabinet Reshuffle*. Arranged as room settings, they give a very real idea of the life of an eighteenth- or nineteenth-century well-off family. At all times, Harveys displays English furniture, clocks, barometers and works of art from 1690 to the 1830s. Here you will find a Chippendale mahogany bookcase of 1765, or a George III mahogany partners' pedestal desk of 1800.

Hotspur
14 Lowndes St, SW1
071-235 1918
Open Mon-Fri 9am-6pm, Sat to 1pm.
Robin Kern and his brother Brian specialise in museum-quality English furniture in a former delightful townhouse which retains its original character. This is another family business, established in 1924, which currently has three showrooms of mainly eighteenth-century English furniture with many com-

plementary artefacts and objets d'art, from small items like George III silver candlesticks to a beautiful George III mahogany artist's table with a double-rising top of 1755.

John Bly
27 Bury St, SW1 - 071-930 1292
Open Mon-Fri 9.30am-5pm, Sat 10.30am-2pm.

Comfortably laid out with eighteenth-century tables, desks and chairs, this firm was founded in 1888 by the grandfather of the present proprietor, John Bly. He is something of a celebrity among the antique fraternity because of his television appearances on the BBC's excellent *Antiques Road Show* in which viewers send in photographs and brief descriptions of their articles which the experts then identify. Customers may come across John Bly writing his *Daily Telegraph* column at this small, well-stocked shop which has many stylish objets d'art to co-ordinate with the furniture. The firm has its own restoration workshop in Tring, Hertfordshire.

Mallett and Son
141 New Bond St, W1
071-499 7411
See *text* below.

Mallett at Bourdon House
2 Davies St, W1 - 071-629 2444
Open Mon-Fri 9.15am-5.15pm, Sat 11am-4pm.

An institution since 1870, the five floors have been arranged into rooms, with richly-coloured walls to show English furniture,

paintings and decorative objects delightfully laid out as they would be in a fine home. The green dining room, for instance, had a George III pillar table with a set of Sheraton satinwood armchairs, just right for a 1790s dinner party! A recent addition is a room devoted to the later nineteenth and early twentieth centuries which includes interesting examples of Victorian Gothic Revival and the Arts and Crafts movement. Another innovation was to expand the antique glass department with a room in the basement now displaying museum-standard pieces such as air-twist candlesticks from 1745, and Dutch wine glasses, 1790, by David Wolff.

The Christopher Wood Gallery has moved into extensive galleries in Mallett's and holds regular exhibitions of Victorian, Edwardian and pre-Raphaelite paintings as well as eighteenth- and nineteenth-century watercolours and drawings. At Bourdon House, until l953 the townhouse of the second Duke of Westminster, a more eclectic display of paintings, sculpture, objets d'art and garden statuary greets the visitor.

Norman Adams
8-10 Hans Rd, SW3
071-589 5266
Open Mon-Fri 9am-5.30pm.

On the west side of Harrod's, this firm established in 1923, has eighteenth-century English furniture and a wide choice of chandeliers, mirrors and barometers as well as objets d'art from England and

France. A pair of George IV carved rosewood work tables on display had been made by the Banting France Company, the king's cabinet makers, for the great English collector, the first Marquess of Bristol for his stately home at Ickworth in about 1825.

Richard Courtney
112-114 Fulham Rd, SW3
071-370 4020
Open Mon-Fri 9.30am-6pm.

One of the leading dealers in eighteenth-century furniture, important pieces that have passed through their expert hands include a George I veneered walnut bachelor's chest of drawers with the original handles of approximately 1720 and from the same year a wonderful wing chair with walnut legs, still upholstered in its original *gros point* and *petit point* needlework fabric. And a George III commode had splendid marquetry using inlays of harewood, kingwood and rosewood.

Stair & Company
14 Mount St, W1 - 071-499 1784
Open Mon-Fri 9.30am-5.30pm.

In the huge stock of eighteenth-century English furniture and art you might find a rare pair of George III breakfast tables with their tops veneered in rosewood, or a carved George II wood and gilt geso mirror, around 1740. Everything from table candelabra to huge dining room tables gleam importantly in this showroom.

■ ICONS

Maria Andipa Icon Gallery
162 Walton St, SW3
071-589 2371
Open Mon-Sat 11am-6pm.

The golden glow of a medieval altar panel depicting saintly figures with haloes sets the atmosphere of the window display and the exotic interior of this gallery which has become one of Europe's largest collections of fourteenth- to nineteenth-century icons from Russia, Greece, the Balkans, eastern Europe and Ethiopia. Celebrating 25 years of her fascination with these evocative treasures, Maria Andipa was one of the first dealers to open a gallery specialising in Byzantine objects.

■ MAPS & PRINTS

Henry Sotheran
80 Pimlico Rd, SW1
071-730 8756
Open Mon-Fri 10am-6pm, Sat to 4pm.

Sotherans was established in 1815 by Thomas Sotheran whose family firm of booksellers had been founded in York in 1761, still a centre for booksellers today. This branch carries a huge range of topographical and architectural prints by artists such as Piranese, Roberts and Daniells and it positively welcomes browsers.
The print department at 2, 4, 5, Sackville Street, W1, concentrates mainly on original ornithological prints by John Gould although this is principally a book shop.

Japanese Gallery
66D Kensington Church St, W1 - 071-229 2934
Open Mon-Sat 10am-6pm.

Every inch of the walls in this small gallery are covered with colourful wood block prints and Noh masks mainly from the nineteenth century though there are earlier artists too. Birds and flowers jostle with portraits of beautiful women from masters like Utamaro. In the many cases dotted around, Satsuma medicine 'inros', incense burners and tea ceremony pots compete for your attention.

The Map House
54 Beauchamp Pl, SW3
071-589 4325, Fax 071-589 1041
Open Mon-Fri 9.45am-5.45pm, Sat 10.30am-5pm.

Besides antique maps, atlases and globes, the five galleries here offer reference books on the subject of maps and map-making, reproductions and prints and decorative engravings, beautifully presented, most published between 1600 and 1900. Despite its size it has a congenial atmosphere.

The O'Shea Gallery
89 Lower Sloane St, SW1
071-730 0081
Open Mon-Fri 9.30am-6pm, Sat to 1pm.

A must for any map enthusiast—thousands of examples contained in the plan chests are yours for the asking. O'Shea are specialist dealers in fifteenth- to nineteenth-century prints and maps and usefully, the stock can be viewed by county, country or by continent. Prints cover topographical, decorative, natural history, sporting and marine subjects.

The Parker Gallery
28 Pimlico Rd, SW1
071-730 6768
Open Mon-Fri 9.30am-5.30pm, Wed to 8pm, Sat by appointment.

There is always a wide range here of antique prints and engravings with the emphasis on marine, nautical and military sciences, and personalities. They also stock prints on the more light-hearted side of life: games, pastimes and sports.

Jonathan Potter
125 New Bond St, W1
071-491 3520
Open Mon-Fri 10am-6pm.

Ring the bell to gain entry to an upstairs gallery of early maps covering all parts of the known world— a map of the North American Great Lakes with the original Indian names was recently on sale for about £160.

The Schuster Gallery
14 Maddox St, W1 - 071-491 2208
Open Mon-Fri 10am-5.30pm, Sat by appointment.

Illuminated manuscripts and interesting prints of London or botanical subjects greet the customer in this no-nonsense shop where the books are also of the illustrated kind.

---

*The **prices** in this guide reflect what establishments were charging at the time of going to press.*

■ METALWARE

Jack Casimir

23 Pembridge Rd, W11
071-727 8643
Open Mon-Sat 10am-5.30pm.

From fireplaces to candle snuffers, Ray and Michael Casimir carry on a third generation family business in this well-stocked shop, specialising in the sixteenth to nineteenth centuries. The shelves are filled with British and European pewter tankards, copper pots, brass door-knobs and occasional rare items, such as fifteenth-century German braziers in either brass or bronze.

■ ORIENTAL ART

Barry Davies Oriental Art

1 Davies St, W1 - 071-408 0207
Open Mon-Fri 10am-6pm.

Japanese works of art are the speciality of this smart gallery which has some furniture and rare samurai armour. Behind small screens, shelves display fine netsuke, cloisonné, ivory and lacquer ware, such as a three-compartment inro after a print by Utamaro. The firm classifies meticulously the individual artists and schools. In the porcelain range, a Kakiemon blue and white tureen and cover, around 1680, was decorated with mountain landscape. To encourage modern craftsmen in the old traditions, the shop features contemporary lacquer work, especially by Unryuan who has produced a zodiac set of inro and whose work is predicted to rival the old masterpieces.

Eskanazi

10 Clifford St, W1 - 071-493 5464
Open Mon-Fri 10am-6pm.

More like a museum than a shop, this establishment's dramatically lit showcases display Ming porcelain, Tang figures, jade objets d'art and bronze pieces, many with BC dates. Museums and learned institutions refer to Eskanazi's expertise in Chinese antiquities. Its netsuke collection is considered to be the best in Europe, ranging in price from £1,000 to £350,000. One stunning piece of statuary was a gilt bronze figure, half-human, half-monster, cast to hold its carved jade dragon in its head which dated to the second to first century BC.

Michael Goedhuis

30 Eaton Pl, SW1 - 071-245 6359
Open by appointment Mon-Fri.

Amid the Oriental works of art are such fine pieces as a gilt copper rakan, signed Kado, from the eighteenth-century Edo period and a pair of bronze candelabra from the sixteenth-century Ming dynasty. Michael Goedhuis has a wide choice of sculptures, bronzes and ceramics from Japan and China.

Robert Hall

15c Clifford St, W1 - 071-734 4008
Open Mon-Fri 10am-5.30pm.

Established in 1976 and now probably the world's leading dealer in antique Chinese snuff bottles, Robert Hall recently opened this shop to show off his hundreds of pieces, which can be made of glass, agate, jade, enamel or porcelain and range in price from £200 to £400,000. They were originally made for the emperors of the Qing dynasty, becoming extremely popular in the mid-nineteenth century. The equivalent of the European snuff box, the bottle would have a stopper and a little spoon for scooping out the snuff. If you're interested, Robert Hall has written and published books on sale at the shop on this centuries-long habit which has now gone out of fashion.

S Marchant and Son

120 Kensington Church St, W8 - 071-229 5319
Open Mon-Fri 9.30am-5.30pm.

Sidney Marchant founded the firm in 1925 and now son Richard and grandson, Stuart run the business. There are three floors of Chinese pottery and porcelain including a 'blue and white room', jade pieces, works of art and Chinese furniture and Japanese art, porcelain and ivory ware. And what a priceless collection it is. From the 1400s, a fine Chinese early Ming dynasty dish in blue and white porcelain painted with flower-heads and scrolling foliage, and a rare Ming blue and white vase decorated with birds, ducks and flowering branches and trees from the late 1500s. There are annual exhibitions on such themes as the Qing mark and period wares, monochrome and two-coloured and marked imperial pieces.

The Oriental Gallery

4 Davies St, W1 - 071-499 7009
Open Mon-Fri 9.30am-6pm.

In this cosy two-level gallery, the directors Roger Korvens and Gerald Hawthorn are pleased to help collectors and enthusiasts. Their wide-ranging wares include unusual jewellery from China in jade, gold, ivory, coral and turquoise, and furniture such as a sixteenth-century lute table on which the instrument would be played for added resonance. Ming lacquer cabinets, ivory brush pots, porcelain ewers and teapots, cloisonné enamel boxes, bamboo carvings and soapstone figures, all in excellent condition, are also displayed in special exhibitions throughout the year.

Sydney L Moss

51 Brook St, W1 - 071-629 4670
Open Mon-Fri 10am-5.30pm.

At the large, sedate showrooms of this respected dealer are Japanese works of art including paintings, ceramics, jade and netsuke from the eighteenth century, a wide range of Chinese furniture and paintings, snuff bottles, Tang pottery and I-Hsing stoneware. There was a striking pair of bronze seated Buddhist lion-dogs, late Ming, from the sixteenth to seventeenth centuries and a hand-

warmer from the early 1800s for use in the tea ceremony, modelled to look like two puppies.

■ POTTERY & PORCELAIN

Alistair Sampson Antiques

156 Brompton Rd, SW3
071- 589 5272
Open Mon-Fri 9.30am-5.30pm.

English pottery from the seventeenth and eighteenth centuries is the speciality of this shop which has other decorative and interesting items from that period on display, such as English naive painting and brass ware. An eclectic shop, they also have a collection of wonderful English oak furniture from the sixteenth to the eighteenth centuries as well as needlework.

Angela Gräfin von Wallwitz

32 St George St, W1
071-499 6453
Open Mon-Fri 10am-5.30pm.

Continental ceramics are the speciality of this showroom which is in the basement level of Bernheimer Fine Arts. Such items as a Boettger porcelain pagoda, around 1718 and a rare Meissen dish of 1726 are on display along with a selection of other works of art.

Brian Haughton Antiques

3b Burlington Gdns, W1
071-734 5491
Open Mon-Fri 10am-5pm.

A rare collection of Chelsea 'Hans Sloane'

plates with the red anchor mark, 1755-56, take pride of place in this small, smart showroom. One pair was listed as £12,500 and it is believed some of the floral designs were painted from life at the Chelsea Physic Garden, which Sir Hans Sloane presented to the Apothecaries' Company in 1782 and which is now open to the public. A rare pair of St Cloud white figures of seated Chinamen, from around the 1730s, was among the dramatic displays. Mr Haughton is a specialist in first period Chelsea porcelain and first period Meissen.

Constance Stobo

31 Holland St, W8 - 071-937 6282
Open Mon-Fri 11am-5pm, Sat 10am-2pm.

Two Sunderland lustre jugs depicting autumn and winter, an unusual Prattware watch holder and a Staffordshire pottery spaniel jug, one of a pair from around 1850, are found among a large choice of mantel dogs, Staffordshire cow creamers and other pieces of pottery at this corner shop in a quiet enclave near Kensington High Street. Collectors are kept informed about unusual items to add to their shelves, with Sunderland lustre plates of ships and biblical sayings being very popular.

---

*Some establishments change their **closing times** without warning. It is always wise to check in advance.*

Graham and Oxley

101 Kensington Church St, W8 - 071-229 1850
Open Mon-Fri 10am-5.30pm.

Established in 1965, this firm deals in eighteenth- and early nineteenth-century English porcelain from dinner services to important presentation pieces like a Spode *famille rose* dinner service of 1810 priced at £7,800. It is a very popular stop for American buyers and Michael Graham displays at the International Antique Dealers' exhibition in New York. There are also prints and engravings.

Jonathan Horne

66b & 66c Kensington Church St, W8 - 071-221 5658
Open Mon-Fri 9.30am-5.30pm.

From medieval pots to early English pottery up to the arts and crafts era, this firm founded in 1968, has many rarities such as a unique tin-glazed dish decorated with a portrait of Simon Frazer, Lord Lovat, the last person to be beheaded in England. This firm exhibits regularly at the large antique fairs and at Grosvenor House in 1993 displayed a rare and delightful pair of English delftware decorative shoes, 1688, which were probably intended as tokens of affection, and a fine salt-glazed stoneware coffee pot decorated in enamels with scenes of musicians, made in Staffordshire around 1765. The three showrooms display Staffordshire cow creamers, Delft ware and many tin-glazed tiles. Exhibitions about aspects of the collection are held every March.

Klaber and Klaber

2a Bedford Gdns, W8
071-727 4573
Open Mon-Fri 10am-1pm, Sat to 4pm.

This small shop has first class eighteenth-century English porcelain including Bow, Caughley, Lowestoft, Worcester, as well as continental porcelain from Sèvres, Vincennes, Paris and Chantilly. They also stock delightful enamel boxes of the period decorated with the usual messages or souvenir mottoes such as 'A trifle from Worthing'. A few of the shelves have been dubbed the 'bargain basement' and offer slightly imperfect items such as a Delft tile for £20.

■ RUGS & TAPESTRIES

David Black Oriental Carpets

96 Portland Rd, W11
071-727 2566
Open Mon-Fri 10am-6pm, Sat 11am-6pm.

Decorative carpets from Delhi to Donegal are displayed or stand in rolled-up abundance at this cheerful, informal shop. David Black who wrote *Arts and Crafts Carpets*, has actively pursued the idea of specialising in the arts and crafts era. Here you see unusual carpets by Voysey and William Morris among the range, plus ones made in Donegal. There are also vintage carpets from Turkey, India, Persia and some modern carpets, brightly coloured with vegetable dyes, thanks to the Dobag project which the shop is involved in—local craftsmen in Turkey are positively encouraged to use traditional hand-craft methods in making carpets.

C John (Rare Rugs)

70 South Audley St, W1
071-493 5288
Open Mon-Fri 9.30am-5pm.

Established in 1947, this firm excels in its choice of French Aubusson and Savonnerie carpets from the eighteenth and nineteenth centuries. A mid-eighteenth-century French Beauvais tapestry, finely woven in silk and wool, and a mid-Victorian English floral needlework carpet are typical of the finds among the collection which includes hand-made carpets, rugs, textiles and tapestries from Persia, Turkey, India, China, Spain, Italy, France, Portugal, Russia, the Caucuses and England. From his corner premises, proprietor Louis Sassoon gives advice both about carpets and about his collection, which has samples from the sixteenth to the nineteenth centuries.

Keshishian

73 Pimlico Rd, SW1
071-730 8810
Open Mon-Fri 9.30am-6pm.

Eddy and Arto Keshishian track down hand-made, decorative carpets, paying attention to colour balance, the spacing of designs and borders and rarity. They stock carpets from the Far and Near East and from the sixteenth up to the now popular arts and crafts era, with a splendid Donegal carpet from 1900 at £46,000, plus Voysey and Morris carpets. The firm has looms in Turkey which are used to make special carpets for important houses like Spencer House in London.

Linda Wrigglesworth

34 Brook St, W1 - 071-408 0177
Open Mon-Fri 9.30am-5.30pm.

Specialising in Chinese costumes and textiles, the ground-floor suite of this building is arrayed with vibrantly coloured robes from the early nineteenth century like a multi-hued wedding skirt, and decorative panels and fans as well as other accessories, such as hats and footwear worn by attendants to the court. Linda established her business in 1978, intrigued by the symbolism, workmanship and colours of early Chinese costume. She has a special interest in the Qing period, 1644-1911.

Raymond Bernadout

18 Grosvenor St, W1
071-355 4531
Open Mon-Fri 9am-6pm.

The well-established Bernadout family has large showrooms with such finds as a late eighteenth-century French Savonnerie carpet, an early nineteenth-century Persian velvet panel or a late eighteenth-century Uzbekistan velvet Ikat panel, plus important, large and rare carpets from Persia or the Caucuses and other traditional carpet and rug-making countries.

The Textile Gallery

12 Queen St, W1 - 071-499 7979

Mon-Fri 9am-5pm by appointment.

Behind the blue door of this corner Georgian house are comfortable rooms where Michael Frances shows collectors antique textiles from before 1800 as well as carpets, mostly from Persia, India, China and Turkey. Customers can browse through photo albums. The gallery, founded in the late 1960s, has antique embroideries, needlework pieces and wallhangings.

Victor Franses Gallery

57 Jermyn St, SW1 - 071-493 6284
Open Mon-Fri 10am-5pm.

The contrast of nineteenth-century bronze animal sculptures against the rich background of hanging carpets from the Far East give drama to these showy galleries. There was a vivid St George on his charging horse and a bronze stag, 1870, among the display. The carpets come from all over the world, from Russia, Persia, China and Turkestan although the tapestries, including a good selection of small pieces, are mostly European.

---

*We're always happy to hear about your discoveries and receive your comments on ours. We want to give your letters the attention they deserve, so when you **write to Gault Millau**, please state clearly what you liked or disliked. Be concise but convincing, and take the time to argue your point.*

■ SCIENTIFIC INSTRU-MENTS, CLOCKS & WATCHES

Arthur Middleton

12 New Row, WC2
071-836 7042
Open Mon-Fri 10am-6.30pm, Sat 11am-4.30pm by appointment.

A 1733 globe depicts California as an island while others show only blurred edges to the unknown North American coastline. It all depends how far exploration had progressed. Time seems forgotten in this fascinating, old-fashioned shop where antique globes, including beautifully illustrated celestial varieties that depict constellations, are stocked, alongside compasses, telescopes, sextants and other scientific and navigational instruments of the past. Globes range from several hundred pounds for early twentieth-century models to many thousands for the ones made in the 1700s.

Asprey

165-169 New Bond St, W1
071-493 6767
Open Mon-Fri 9am-5.30pm, Sat to 1pm.

Amid its comprehensive antique furniture selection, this famous store has a workshop for clock and watchmakers who undertake the restoration of timepieces and marine chronometers. A plain mahogany two-day, three-tier marine chronometer, made by Parkinson and Frodsham, London, about

1840, costs around £5,500. A silver-cased repeating carriage clock by Jump, with a calendar and phases of the moon, hall-marked 1890, was £65,000.

Garrard
112 Regent St, W1 - 071-734 7020
Open Mon-Fri 9am-5.30pm, Sat 9.30am-1pm.
Longcase and bracket clocks by such master craftsmen of the past as Thomas Tompion, Quare and Vulliamy are sold at this famous shop along with many other Georgian and Victoria makers. There is a wide choice of fine French and English carriage clocks in classic designs as well as French mantel clocks of the eighteenth and nineteenth centuries. Repairs and restoration work are carried out on the premises.

Harriet Wynter
50 Redcliffe Rd, SW10
071-352 6494
By appointment.
Harriet Wynter was one of the first dealers in the specialised world of astrolabes, globes, lodestones, microscopes and telescopes and those wonderful theodolites. She now operates from her house, only seeing serious collectors, and also deals in pictures.

John Carlton-Smith
17 Ryder St, SW1 - 071-930 6622
See *text* below.

Cameron Cuss and Co
17 Ryder St, SW1 - 071-939 1941

Open Mon-Fri 9.30am-5.30pm.
Sharing the same neat premises in the heart of St James's are two experts, with John Carlton-Smith specialising in longcase clocks, especially up to 1830, and carriage clocks up to 1900, as well as vintage barometers. Terence Cameron Cuss, whose business goes back to 1788, concentrates on watches, mostly up to a 1910 dateline, as well as clocks.

Raffety
34 Kensington Church St, W8 - 071-930 1100
Open Mon-Fri 10am-1pm, 2-5pm.
A George III mahogany longcase by Edward Pistor, London, for around £9,000 is the kind of showpiece this shop has by its entrance. Even the doorway has a large clock face over it. The firm deals with English-made clocks, mostly from 1670 to 1860, and also has scientific instruments, barometers and mechanical musical instruments.

Ronald A Lee (Fine Art)
1-9 Bruton Pl, W1 - 071-629 5600
Open Mon-Fri 10am-5pm.
An eighteenth-century longcase clock made by John Shelton in London or an intricately decorated Norwich-made longcase, using the japanning technique, are among the many important timepieces at this informal and friendly dealer, which has no shop front and is located down an off-the-beaten-track, picturesque mews just off Bond Street. Customers

also come looking for good English-made furniture in the large ground level and basement rooms. There are reference books and extensive catalogue information on the shelves by the entrance and it's a good place to begin an obsession.

Trevor Philip & Sons
75a Jermyn St, SW1
071-930 2954
Open Mon-Fri 9am-6pm, Sat 10am-4pm.
Fine old clocks and some unusual objets d'art are displayed in this newly refurbished shop along with scientific instruments, especially navigational ones, which can date back to 1450. Vintage globes are a speciality, particularly from the eighteenth century.

■ SILVER

Asprey
165-69 New Bond St, W1
071-493 6767
Open Mon-Fri 9am-5.30pm, Sat to 1pm.
With a large silver 'factory' on the premises, Asprey's offers its own designs of modern silver ware and exquisite antique silver, especially from the Georgian era. A sugar basket, 1778, with red glass liner, by Burrage Davenport, was £1,250 and a pair of early George III candlesticks £5,500. There are lots of novelties, such as a French-made claret jug in the shape of a duck, 1880, for £4,500, and a Victorian stag's head stirrup cup for £8,500. With its antique glass and furniture and its own work-

shops, Asprey's can comfortably be listed under every shopping category, from leather goods to china.

J H Bourdon-Smith

24 Mason's Yard, SW1
071-839 4714
Open Mon-Fri 9.30am-6pm.

In business for 42 years, John Bourdon-Smith believes antique silver should be bought 'for the love of the article and its useful purpose', and he also thinks it makes a good long-term investment. In a secluded corner of St James's, this family-run shop gleams with coffee pots, platters, tankards, candlesticks, caskets, coasters, tureens, tea sets, salts, snuff boxes, scissors and cutlery, mostly from the Georgian era. Twelve silver dinner plates, made in 1785, engraved with the crest of the Earls of Shrewsbury, cost £9,500.

London Silver Vaults

Chancery House, 53-65 Chancery Lane, WC2
071-242 3844
Open Mon-Fri 9am-5.30pm, Sat to 1pm.

Going through the thick and heavy door, visitors feel they are stepping into a giant underground safe, which turns out to house a series of little rooms where some 30 dealers show fine silver in a no-nonsense fashion. The Vaults have the reputation of offering well-priced Sheffield plate and sterling silver. Look for Vaults 13 and 15 for friendly, expert guidance by E and C T Koopman and Sons, (071-242 8365).

Useful addresses

Antiquarian Booksellers Association, **Suite 2, 26 Charing Cross Rd, WC2H 0DG - 071-379 3041;** *Association of British Picture Restorers*, **Station Ave, Kew, TW9 3QA - 081-948 5644;** *British Antique Dealers' Association*, **20 Rutland Gate, SW7 1BD - 071-589 4128;** *British Antique Furniture Restorers' Association*, **c/o 37 Upper Addison Gdns, W14 8AJ - 071-603 5643;** *Export Licensing Branch*, **Dept of Trade & Industry, Kingsgate House, 66-74 Victoria St, SW1E 6SW - 071-215 8070;** *Furniture History Society*, **c/o Dept of Furniture and Woodwork Design, Victoria & Albert Museum, SW7 2RL - 071-938 8282;** *Historic Houses Association*, **2 Chester St, SW1X 7BB - 071-259 5688;** *International Institute for Conservation*, **6 Buckingham St, WC2N 6BA - 071-839 5975;** *London and Provincial Antique Dealers' Association (LAPADA)*, **535 King's Rd, SW10 0SZ - 071-823 3511;** *National Association of Decorative and Fine Arts Societies (NADFAS)*, **8a Lower Grosvenor Pl, SW1W 0EN - 071-233 5433;** *Provincial Booksellers Fairs Association (PBFA)*, **Old Coach House, Melbourn Rd, Royston, Herts, SG8 7BZ - 0763-248400, Fax 0763-248921;** *Society of London Art Dealers*, **91a Jermyn St, SW1Y 6JB - 071-930 6137;** *Textile Society*, **c/o Victoria & Albert Museum, SW7 2RL - 071-603 5643**

S J Shrubsole

43 Museum St, WC1
071-405 2712
Open Mon-Fri 9am-5.30pm.

An outstanding shop for old Sheffield silver plate, this firm, established in 1918, is popular with connoisseurs. It deals with silver from the late seventeenth to mid-nineteenth century and old Sheffield plate, with items like Georgian tea caddies and a candle holder with a snuffer.

Silver Galleries

111-112 New Bond St, W1
071-493 6180
Open Mon-Fri 9am-5.30pm.

It is a bit intimidating to climb the steps up to the clutch of serious-looking silver dealers but the choice of wares is superb. For that special wedding present, head for A B Bloomstein's large selection of silver and silver plate candelabras, tureens, teapots and platters. Tucked away on the top floor is Brian Beet, open by appointment only (071-437 4975, Fax 071-495 8635) who has silver wine accessories and specialises in silver which is unusual because of its form or its origin. His colonial silver from India, Australia, America and Canada is exceptional and interestingly different from English pieces. His many collectable items include caddie spoons, vinaigrettes and nutmeg graters.

Stanley Leslie

15 Beauchamp Pl, SW3
071-589 2333
Open Mon-Fri 9am-5pm, Sat to 1pm.

Teapots, gravy dishes and tankards by the hundreds hang from a multitude of hooks, giving a silver glow to the shop interior, which has traditional simplicity that long-established silver dealers maintain so beautifully. This is the place to come for a very wide choice of old silver and Sheffield plate.

SILVER & JEWELLERY

Bentley and Co

8 New Bond St, W1
071-629 0651
Open Mon-Sat 10am-5.30pm.

This family-run business, established in 1934, has two floors to show off its antique silverware from the eighteenth century onwards, including complete canteens of English-made cutlery, and a very large choice of English and French period jewellery with a good range of Cartier and Boucheron. A Victorian cultured pearl choker with a detachable brooch was £11,750.

N Bloom and Son

125 New Bond St, W1
071-629 5060
Open Mon-Fri 10am-6pm.

A celebrity expert who has appeared in all the BBC *Antiques Road Shows*, proprietor Ian Harris prides himself on unusual pieces, such as a Victorian gold locket, one side with a Japanese shakudo plaque of a fan-dancing frog, the other showing cranes on a cloisonné plaque, priced at £4,600. The jewellery is mostly from 1860 to 1960, from £200 to £30,000, with some Georgian and Victorian silver. The shop has been welcoming connoisseurs since 1912, when it was founded by Ian Harris's maternal grandfather, Nathan Bloom.

Ermitage

14 Hay Hill, W1 - 071-499 5459
Open Mon-Fri 10.30am-5pm.

Russian works of art, objets de vertu, continental silver and Fabergé pieces are the enticing stock at this little gallery, where historic jewellery can include such finds as a diamond-set brooch, with the initial 'A' and crown, the cypher of the Empress Alexandra Feodorovna, wife of Nicholas 1, which was worn by her lady-in-waiting. In addition, Fabergé's enamel boxes, clocks, frames, Easter eggs and floral pieces were so well documented in sales ledgers in London that their previous ownership enhances their appeal.

Garrard

112 Regent St, W1 - 071-734 7020
Open Mon-Fri 9am-5.30pm, Sat to 1pm.

The antique silver on display at Garrard's often includes pieces made by its founder, George Wickes, who was appointed goldsmith to Frederick, Prince of Wales, in 1735, and by Robert Garrard, who joined the firm in 1792. The tradition continues with modern silver designed and made by its own craftsmen.

Gerald Sattin

14 King St, SW1 - 071-493 6557
Open Mon-Fri 9am-5.30pm, Sat to 1pm.

The sales tickets are a delight to read as Gerald Sattin gives details and interesting facts about his wares, which include English and continental porcelain from the 1720s to about 1860, and glass from the seventeenth and nineteenth centuries along with unusual and collectable silver objects. A very scarce late Victorian sterling silver novelty propelling pencil in the shape of an umbrella came as no surprise, for Mr Sattin is a founder member of the Writing Equipment Society.

Hancocks

1 Burlington Gdns, W1
071-493 8904
Open Mon-Fri 9.30am-5.30pm.

Like many of the specialist silver dealers, this shop, established in 1849, has a wide array of jewellery from the Victorian, Edwardian and art deco eras. The silver ware ranges from £100 to £150,000. An 1873 silver gilt and etched glass claret jug with silver trimming by W G Sissons of Sheffield was £4,250.

Find the address you are looking for, quickly and easily, in the index.

Harvey and Gore

4 Burlington Gdns, W1
071-493 2714
Open Mon-Fri 9.30am-5pm.

A small, bright shop whose stock of silver and old Sheffield plate is the backbone of a firm which was founded in 1723. Among its jewellery display are such choice items as a bracelet from the imperial Russian collection, reported to have been worn by Catherine the Great.

D S Lavender

16b Grafton St, W1
071-629 1782
Open Mon-Fri 9.30am-5.30pm.

Beyond the traditional wood frontage, the walls are bedecked with framed miniatures, a speciality of the firm, established in 1945, which has good antique jewellery and objets d'art such as a Queen Anne snuff box, 1710, and a pair of eighteenth-century lorgnettes. There was a mourning ring for Sir William Pitt, Britain's youngest prime minister, and his sister, Harriet, dated 1806. Some of the miniatures were part of the collection of eighteenth-century royal portraits from the House of Savoy.

Mappin and Webb

170 Regent St, W1 - 071-734 3801
Open Mon-Fri 9am-5.30pm, Sat to 5pm.

The Mappin hallmark was first registered in 1774 and their products are still considered to be the best quality and design of silverware and gifts. Expect to pay £50 for a Mappin plate-embossed biscuit tray. The electro-plated silver plate ware is hand-set using traditional tools. Among the sterling silver gifts are christening mugs for £160, a duck rattle for £130 and picture frames from £65. You'll find antique and second-hand silver here along with beautiful jewellery, clocks, watches, cufflinks, leather gifts, porcelain, including the new Lalique porcelain, and more, all displayed in spacious surroundings. There is a bridal service and at the same address, a firm called Carrington and Co, specialising in regimental silver and sporting trophies. Also at 65 Brompton Rd, SW3, 071-584 9361.

Moira

22 New Bond St, W1
071-629 0160
Open Mon-Fri 9am-5pm, Sat 10am-5pm.

Established in 1985, this showy, sleek shop always has eye-catching, high-quality antique jewellery, with novelty charm bracelets, chunky art deco earrings and signet rings and stylised floral art nouveau pieces. A large diamond ring with the stones set in an unusual twist was £2,490. The well known designers Van Cleef, Arpels, Tiffany and Cartier are well represented along with much stylish 'cocktail jewellery' such as a stunning diamond choker necklace of 1910 by Leonard Matrat.

S J Phillips

139 New Bond St, W1
071-629 6261
Open Mon-Fri 10am-5pm.

Nothing ever seems to change at this fine old shop, founded in 1869, with its wide choice of fine silver on display in traditional glass-fronted tall showcases. Run by the Norton family, it has antique necklaces, brooches, rings and other exquisite pieces. Its wares include a Louis XIV silver gilt dessert service of 36 pieces, from Strasbourg, engraved in 1783 with the arms of Thurn and Taxis, or a set of George III silver salts, 1780, by Robert Hennell in the shape of sea creatures.

Sandra Cronan

18 Burlington Arcade, W1
071-491 4851
Open Mon-Sat 10am-5.30pm.

A polo player herself, Sandra Cronan usually has silver-plated polo trophies and some related artefacts in her tiny arcade shop but her speciality is high-quality antique jewellery. She stages interesting exhibitions such as one on cufflinks through the ages which showed some of the earliest cufflinks made—including a seventeenth century crystal pair belonging to King Charles II.

Tessiers

26 New Bond St, W1
071-629 0458
Open Mon-Fri 10am-5pm.

There are coronets and tiaras in the window of this charming old shop where the silver tankards, tureens and candlesticks are of superb quality. There is a wide-ranging jewellery collection and many objets d'art.

> *Some establishments change their **closing times** without warning. It is always wise to check in advance.*

Wartski

14 Grafton St, W1 - 071-493 1141
Open Mon-Fri 9.30am-5pm, Sat 10am-noon. No cards.

Flower studies, snuff boxes and trinkets including the famous eggs made with wit, charm and humour by the legendary jeweller, Fabergé, make the back of this shop a little retrospective museum of his work. An ancestor of the Wartski family escaped with a dozen of the Imperial Fabergé eggs during the Russian Revolution, so the firm has a historic interest in maintaining its worldwide reputation as keepers of the archives. At the front, amid shelves of antique silver, the work of talented modern craftsmen is displayed, with goldsmith Kevin Coates creating provocative, fantastic necklaces, rings and table sculptures. His opal-faced Ophelia brooch on its own special stand is particularly striking.

TEXTILES & CLOTHING

Gallery of Antique Costumes and Textiles

2 Church St, NW8 - 071-723 9981
Open Mon-Sat 10am-5.30pm.

Their stock is mainly English and French, with some examples of Chinese and Indian textiles. Old fashioned roses are delicately embroidered onto bell-pulls, cushions are covered in a riot of colours and flowers of the fields and hedgerows. Chintzes hang beside antique tassels and swags. The price range is very wide and it's a wonderful place to pick up a shawl or a length of antique material.

Lunn Antiques

21 Cucumber Alley, Thomas Neal's, Shorts Gdns, WC2 071-379 1974
Open Mon-Sat 10.30am-7pm.

Besides the vintage lace and linen, this small shop is decked out with reproduction Victorian night dresses from £24 and children's smocks from £24. Quilts start at £85 and they also stock unusual bed covers and collector's items including beaded dresses from the 1920s.

WALKING STICKS

Michael German

36b Kensington Church St, W8 - 071-937 8566
Open Mon-Fri 10am-5pm, Sat to 3pm.

Hundreds of walking sticks, from 1650 to 1920, mostly with curiously carved handles to appeal to collectors, are on display in these small premises. The average price is between £150 and £200. Collectors are very particular in their tastes; one regular customer collects only dogs' head-handled sticks. A walking stick was once a prestige decorative item shown off at court by royalty, then it became a necessary fashion accessory for gentlemen in the Victorian era. Today it is a collector's item. Michael German also has vintage guns.

AT YOUR SERVICE

CLOTHING REPAIRS

British Invisible Mending Service

32 Thayer St, W1 - 071-487 4292
Open Mon-Fri 8.30am-5.45pm, Sat 10am-1pm.

If you have something special you need mended, this is the place for specialist invisible work that involves taking threads individually from a hem and reweaving them in elsewhere, changing buttonhole sizes and more. Items take about one week.

First Tailored Alterations

85 Lower Sloane St, SW1 071-730 1400
Open Mon-Sat 9am-6pm.

Specialising in leather and suede, this useful place can alter waistbands or reshape suede coats. Items take about one week.

Mr Pany

45 Carnaby St, W1 - 071-437 9107
Open Mon-Fri 11am-9pm, Sat to 6pm.

In central London, Mr Pany offers an express service of same-day repairs for shortening trousers, altering waistbands and shortening dresses. Prices are very reasonable, from £6 to £10.

---

*Some establishments change their **closing times** without warning. It is always wise to check in advance.*

■ DRY CLEANERS

Buckingham Dry-Cleaners
83 Duke St, W1 - 071-499 1253
Open Mon-Fri 8am-6pm, Sat 9.30am-1.30pm.
Particularly noted for cleaning the ball gowns of the smart Mayfair set, they also clean waxed jackets and run a man's shirt service.

De-Luxe Cleaners
30 Brewer St, W1 - 071-437 1187
Open Mon-Fri 8.30am-5.30pm.
De-Luxe are used by local fashion houses, partly because they can clean so fast. They also undertake alterations, repairs and invisible mending.

Jeeves of Belgravia
8-10 Pont St, SW1 - 071-235 1101
Open Mon-Fri 8.30am-5.30pm, Sat to 5pm.
This is the place to take anything precious; they take great care and clean impeccably and wrap your good-as-new garment in tissue paper at the end. They also re-proof raincoats and skiwear, clean and pack wedding dresses, and deal with all household linens including duvets. Free collection/delivery.

Mayfair Laundry
Stirling Rd, W3 - 081-992 3041
Open Mon-Fri 8am-4.30pm.
Established in 1860, they are especially good at starching and finishing stiff collars and dress shirts and

are much used by those who patronise the Jermyn Street gentlemen's shirt makers. Collection/delivery 75p an order.

■ HIRE...

... AN EVENING DRESS

The Merchant of Europe
232 Portobello Rd, W11 071-221 4203
Mon-Sat 11am-6pm.
A really fun place for costume party hire, they specialise in original clothing from the 1920s to the 1970s. So if you want a 1950s look, hire the clothes (around £30) and accessories and get advice from their experts on different periods on hair-styles, make-up and so on.

One Night Stand
44 Pimlico Rd, SW1 071-730 8708
Mon-Fri 9.30am-6pm, Sat 10am-5pm.
For a really special occasion, this shop has cocktail dresses, ball gowns and all the accessories from evening wraps to handbags, everything in fact except shoes. Hire is around £100 and it's best to make an appointment during the busy seasons.

Twentieth Century Frox
614 Fulham Rd, SW6 071-731 3242
Mon-Fri 10am-7pm, Sat 10am-5pm.
Both day wear and evening wear are available from this agency which also sells clothes.

... A FORMAL GENTLEMAN'S OUTFIT

Austin Reed
103-113 Regent St, W1 071-437 2140
Open Mon-Sat 9.30am-6pm.
Formal wear for hire ranges from dinner jackets to morning suits for all special occasions.

Moss Bros
27 King St, WC2 - 071-497 9354
Open Mon-Sat 9.30am-6pm.
The name in formal hire for men (also does ladies dress hire), Moss Bros has been kitting out the elegant for decades. A single-breasted dinner jacket with all the trimmings will cost around £40, double-breasted a few pounds more. Last fitting is half-an-hour before the shop closes and the length of time you can keep the suit is flexible; you can hire on a Thursday for a Saturday occasion.

... A THEATRICAL COSTUME

Angels and Bermans
119 Shaftesbury Ave, WC2 071-836 5678
Open Mon-Fri 9am-5pm.
This famous well-established name has a wonderful stock of period costumes and uniforms as well as animal costumes for hire. Just the thing for a masked ball.

*Some establishments change their **closing times** without warning. It is always wise to check in advance.*

■ HIRED HANDS

Koala Nannies
071-376 7651

Originally started to provide Australian and New Zealand nannies and au pairs, this agency (which at the time of going to press is moving, hence no address) has now expanded and also finds carers, cooks and companions.

Short Cut Services
45 Fernshaw Rd, SW10
071-352 4448

A really useful service that will do everything from getting seats for Wimbledon to organising parties complete with acrobats, conjurors or after-dinner speakers. This company of young fixers enjoys a challenge and have found tight-rope walkers, butlers and helped organise medieval tournaments. They also help with the mundane problems of life like finding a plumber or a locksmith in an emergency.

Universal Aunts
P O Box 304, SW4 0NN
071-738 8937

Established in 1921, Universal Aunts is famous for providing almost everything you need, from daily attendance at an embassy if you're after a visa, to escorting you wherever you want to go. They also act as an employment agency for staff, providing the grand with butlers and the harassed with mother's helps.

Messenger service

If you want something taken door-to-door by car or motor cycle, one of the best is NNG at 071-490 8797 (and they work weekends, too).

■ HOME DELIVERY

Room Service
071-586 5800, Fax 071-586 1222
Delivery times: Lunch Mon-Fri 11am-2.30pm, Dinner daily 5pm-10.30pm.

Customers have a booklet listing a large number of restaurants from the Chicago Pizza Pie Factory to Chutney Mary to Khun Akorn (all in our *Restaurant* section) which offer special take-away meals. You look through the booklet, choose, say, a selection of Lebanese hors d'oeuvres from Al Basha restaurant, phone your order and await your delivery (within the hour unless it is very large). For those with more forethought, you can have a whole Zen restaurant meal for a dinner party.

■ PROPERTY MAIN-TENANCE

N D Management
41 Broxash Rd, SW11
071-738 0151, Mobile 0836-767009

Like all the companies recommended here, the two young directors Nicky Gill and Di Robertson have an efficient and enthusiastic team of helpers. This first-rate company undertakes everything to do with property. They will maintain your apartment or house while you're away, clean, garden, decorate and repair, as well as make travel bookings and theatre reservations. They will even start your Bentley once a week while it is sitting in the garage!

■ SHOE REPAIRS

The Complete Cobbler
28 Tottenham St, W1
071-636 9040
Open Mon-Fri 8am-6.30pm, Sat 9am-1pm.

A family business, George Zorlakkis specialises in trade repairs for big names like Gucci and Charles Jourdan and mends leather handbags and luggage. He can do repairs on the spot and also makes riding boots.

Crispins Cobblers
5 Chiltern St, W1 - 071-935 7984
Open Mon-Fri 8.30am-6pm, Thurs to 7pm, Sat 9.30am-4.30pm.

If you've got a pair of expensive shoes to mend from Churches, Lobbs or Kurt Geiger make your way here. They will re-stitch, replace trims and re-cover scuffed heels on all shoes, not just the best.

BEAUTY

■ BEAUTY SALONS

Body et al
11 Grosvenor Crescent, SW1 - 071-823 1061
Open Mon-Fri 9am-8pm, Sat to 3pm.

Whether it's semi-permanent make-up, shrink-wrap treatment to lose inches in a couple of hours, facial toning for a mini-facelift without surgery, a spa body scrub, collagen replacement to create pouting lips or a firming gel to detoxify the body and combat cellulite, Mavis Parkinson, a health devotee, can offer the latest in techniques at her swish health and beauty clinic. The shrink-wrap sessions cost from £55 for a two-hour treatment.

Delia Collins
19 Beauchamp Pl, SW3
071-584 2423
Open Mon-Fri 9am-6pm, Sat to 1pm.

The white net draping of the large window gives just a discreet glimpse of activity at this long-established beauty salon which deals with customers who appreciate a serious approach to skin care. With more than 40 years' experience, Delia Collins has her lotions and creams made on the premises for facials and massages. Waxing, eyelash tinting, red vein, mole and wart treatments are among the services.

Sher System Studio
30 New Bond St, W1
071-499 4022
Open Mon-Fri 10am-6pm, Sat by appointment.

Helen Sher and her daughter Glenda have developed their own unique beauty treatment, based on an easy warm water therapy: just splash the face regularly in tap water specially treated with Sher crystals. A kit with toner, emollient and other requirements comes in a travel-pack form with light-weight plastic bottles and costs from £130 to £150, which should last about six months. Despite the cost, enthusiastic clients with rejuvenated faces keep rushing back for more. The Shers give lessons in natural looking make-up at £50 a session.

Yves Rocher Beauty Therapy Centre
7 Gees Ct, St Christopher's Pl, W1 - 071-409 2975
Open Mon-Fri 10am-6.30pm, Sat to 6pm.

Managing to combine a cool clinical look with a warm pampered ambience, this reasonably priced beauty centre uses a wide range of powders, creams and oils based on plants, with all treatments perfected at their own laboratories of vegetal biology. A 30-minute facial is around £10.

■ COSMETICS

Cosmetics à La Carte
19b Motcomb St, SW1
071-235 0596
Open Mon-Sat 10am-5.30pm.

Because they have their own factory, Christina Stewart and Lynne Sanders can promise customers that a favourite but discontinued lipstick or foundation can be copied. For their make-up diagnosis and lessons, they use their own brand and Almay hyper-allergenic products. Their other salon is at The Sanctuary in Covent Garden (071-497 0565).

Joan Price's Face Place
33 Cadogan St, SW3
071-589 9062
Open Mon-Fri 10am-6pm, Sat to 5pm.

From model to beauty editor, Joan Price opened the first salon in 1967 to offer make-up sessions as one-to-one lessons rather than just applications of cosmetics. Today a one-hour lesson is £20. The salon stocks some twenty brands in all price ranges. Clients can buy at the salon and as the staff are not on commission, recommendations are genuine. An informal, welcoming approach attracts teenagers and the over-50s. Joan Price did the make-up for Mrs Thatcher's TV appearances. The salon also offers the full range of skin care treatment.

■ HAIR SALONS

Bagley's
58 Upper Montagu St, W1
071-724 8860/723 4576
Open Tues-Thurs 9am-6pm, Fri to 7pm, Sat to 2pm.

A thoroughly friendly salon where owner Gene Bagley listens to what a client asks for and which is recommended to US visitors by regulars from the nearby American embassy. A hair-cut and blow-dry is around £28. They sometimes do the styling for film and TV show casts, with Gene once rising to the challenge of dyeing Sir Laurence Olivier's beard for his role in *King Lear*. Men and children are welcome.

Cadogan Club
18 Lowndes St, W1
071-235 3814
Open Mon-Fri 9am-6pm, Sat to 1pm.

This pleasant Mayfair salon for men and women has always been popular with the fashionable set, with a cut and blow-dry from £40.

John Frieda
75 New Cavendish St, W1
071-636 1401
Open Mon-Sat 9am-5pm.

One of the top names in hairdressing, John Frieda has a third salon in Claridge's Hotel where the colourist is particularly skilful. A cut and blow-dry for ladies is from £29 to £60, for men £24 to £45. Also at 4 Aldford St, W1, 071-491 0840.

Nicky Clarke
130 Mount St, W1 - 071-491 4700
Open Mon-Sat 9am-5pm.

A celebrity in his own right, Nicky Clarke, usually wearing leather trousers and cowboy boots with spurs, cut Fergie's long mane. Other clients include Cindy Crawford, Greta Scacchi, Paloma Picasso and Queen Noor of Jordan. A ladies' cut and

blow-dry for a first time visit is £150, with subsequent visits £95. For men, the first visit is £100, then £70.

Toni and Guy
49 Sloane Sq, SW1 - 071-730 8113
Open Mon-Sat 10am-5.30pm, Thurs to 7.30pm.

This large chain of hairdressing salons prides itself on training its staff at its own large educational centre, not on the client. They have salons around central London, each with a black-and-white facade and a spare-looking interior.

Vidal Sassoon
130 Sloane St, SW1
071-730 7288
Open Mon-Fri 9am-6pm, Thurs to 6.45pm, Sat 8.30am-5.30pm.

The reputation of this internationally known hairdresser is based on the Sassoon philosophy of cutting women's hair to suit the bone structure of the face and achieve a simple 'one-off' feel to the styling. Prices range from £33 to £48 for a cut and finish. Manicures and pedicures are available. Salons throughout London.

Vidal Sassoon Barber Shop
56 Brook St, W1 - 071-493 5428
Open Mon-Fri 9am-6pm, Thurs to 6.45pm, Sat 8.30am-5.30pm.

A salon for men only, the price range for a cut and finish is from £31 to £41.50. Beard trims as well as manicures and hand massages are available.

Worthington's
12 Charlotte Pl, W1
071-631 1370

Open Mon-Fri 9.30am-7.15pm, Sat 10am-5.30pm.

Voted London hairdresser of the year in 1993, Charles Worthington has several salons in central London.

■ SCENTS, SOAPS & TOILETRIES

L'Artisan Parfumeur
17 Cale St, SW3 - 071-352 4196
Open Mon-Fri 10am-1pm, 2pm-6pm, Sat 10am-4pm.

A bespoke perfumeur with a shop in Paris, L'Artisan Parfumeur fits you out with the particular scents that suit you. It's a little boutique of a shop where the art is taken seriously, and you'll be tempted to purchase precious bottles with romantic names like Jardins de Toscane for ladies and L'Eau des Incroyables for gentlemen. And it is no more expensive than a brand name—a 50ml bottle is around £26.50.

The Body Shop
268 Oxford St, W1 - 071-629 9365
Open Mon-Fri 9am-7.30pm, Thurs to 8.30pm, Sat to 7pm.

The founder, Anita Roddick, rediscovered in far-flung countries the natural ingredients used in time-honoured beauty treatments. With its reputation for affordable and environmentally correct products, this nation-wide chain now has a prime position in most High Streets, with 32 London shops full of trendy young women stocking up on jojoba shampoo, passion fruit cleansing gel, honey water toner or dewberry lotion as well as aromatherapy oils, ointments and creams. There are T-shirts about green issues, a wide range of scents, cosmetics and grooming products for men and women. Basket assortments are popular presents. Branches throughout London.

Culpeper
21 Bruton St, W1 - 071-629 4559
Open Mon-Fri 9.30am-6pm, Sat 10am-5pm.

Aromatic food products add extra interest to these herbalist shops which have followed a 'green policy' since the company was founded in 1927. Different curry sachets, jars of ginger and spicy Major Grey's mango chutney tempt the palate. A curry collection in a willow basket is around £17. Nutmeg graters, mulled wine spices, honey and ginger juice cordial are among the foods. As expected, the aromatherapy oils are exceptional, with an attractively boxed starter set for around £17. There are also books, herb-filled pillows, prettily covered hot water bottles, 'make your own' potpourri, scented candles, aroma oil burners and fans. Also at 8 The Market, Covent Garden, WC2, 071-379 6698.

Crabtree & Evelyn
30 James St, WC2 - 071-379 0964
Open Mon-Sat 10am-8pm, Sun 10.30am-5.30pm.

Prettily-packaged hand and body lotions, soaps and bath products are the main attraction of these well-known shops, which also offer jams, preserves, vinegars and teas. Best seller is the Evelyn range, based on a fragrance from the essence of living roses of a variety called Evelyn, which was specially developed for the shops by the rose expert David Austin. Also at 6 Kensington Church St, W8, 071-937 9335; 134 King's Rd, SW3, 071-589 6263; 239 Regent St, W1, 071-409 1603.

Czech & Speake
39c Jermyn St, W1 - 071-439 0216
Open Mon-Fri 9am-6pm, Sat 10am-5pm.

Besides exotic bath oils of frankincense and myrrh, bathroom fittings which make even lavatory roll and brush holders look elegant are the showpieces of these smart little shops. A wall-mounted ivory-coloured porcelain lavatory-brush and holder with a chrome finish costs around £180. Also at 125 Fulham Rd, SW3, 071-225 3667.

J Floris
89 Jermyn St, SW1 - 071-930 2885
Open Mon-Fri 9.30am-5.30pm, Sat 10am-5pm.

Commissions to blend fragrances for the Queen and the Prince of Wales are all in a day's work for the Boddenham family, who have been perfumiers for eight generations and are direct descendants of a Spaniard, Juan Famenias Floris, who first set out his sign here in 1730. Now known for their English flower scents, such as rose, lily of the valley and honeysuckle, the shop sells old-fashioned perfume bottles with silk bulbs and tassels as well as crystal and cut-glass pot-pourri bowls, alabaster soap dishes and tortoiseshell combs.

D R Harris & Co
29 St James's St, SW1
071-930 3915
Open Mon-Fri 8.30am-6pm, Sat 9.30am-5pm.

The original 'Pick-Me-Up' speciality devised by Victorian proprietor, Daniel Rotely Harris, is still sold, from £5.10. No doubt it always did well here in the heart of the gentlemen's clubs. This small shop offers diverse ranges, such as a cucumber and roses cream for facial care, the Arlington line of men's cologne and shaving creams and soaps plus Bewitch silky bath essence. It is a chemist shop where prescriptions can be filled and thus keeps to the original purpose of the shop which was co-founded in 1790 by a surgeon and one of the first pharmaceutical chemists.

Neal's Yard Remedies
2 Neal's Yard, WC2
071-379 7222
Open Mon-Fri 10am-6pm, Wed and Sat to 5.30pm, Sun 11am-4pm.

The striking deep-blue glass bottles, filled with shampoos, bath oils and ready-made lotions, gleam on the shelves in the subdued lighting of this popular shop where the staff are kept busy measuring out herbs, seeds, powders and leaves from giant glass jars for aficionados of natural remedies. To help decide what's good for what, there is a shelf of relevant books to consult. Information about courses and talks about herbalism, essential oils and homeopathy are on display.

Penhaligon's
41 Wellington St, WC2
071-836 2150
Open Mon-Sat 10am-6pm.

These prettily-outfitted shops, whether the Victorian-style interior of the Covent Garden premises or the tiny glass-roofed Mayfair shop, are a pleasant step into a recreated turn-of-the-century past. Fragrances are hand-blended to rediscovered recipes of William Penhaligon, court barber and perfumier extraordinaire in Queen Victoria's reign. The oldest, Hammam, was created in 1872, its exotic name and scent, including jasmine, lavender, rose and sandalwood, inspired by the Turkish baths next to his original shop. Antique perfume bottles and silver table accessories add to Penhaligon's charm. Also at 20a Brook St, W1, 071-493 0002; 16 Burlington Arcade, Piccadilly, W1, 071-629 1416; Royal Exchange, Cornhill, EC2, 071-283 0711.

Les Senteurs
227 Ebury St, SW1 - 071-730 2322
Open Mon-Fri 10am-6pm, Sat to 4pm.

VIP treatment is the norm at this sensually bedecked little shop which doesn't stock the big advertised names in perfumery but 'imports direct from small French and Italian fragrance makers including a sixteenth-century apothecary in a monastery', as Chris Hawksley will explain enthusiastically. His mother, Betty, spends time

fitting a customer to the right scent, which involves trying fragrances, whether flowery or pungent, onto sample cards first. Exclusively made for them is Apogée, an eau de parfum, from £30. There are also lovely room fragrances and bath and beauty solutions.

Trumper's
9 Curzon St, W1 - 071-499 1850
Open Mon-Fri 9am-5.30pm, Sat to 1pm.

The Curzon Street shop opened in 1875 and is lovingly maintained with dark wood panelling and display cases of their fragrances for men, shaving soaps and brushes, reflecting the fact that the founder, George Trumper, ran one of the first exclusive barbershops in London and was court hairdresser. Both shops still provide a barber's service in a soothing and pampered ambience, with face massage and moustache curling on offer. Colognes and after shaves include Wellington, with rosemary and neroli among the ingredients, Astor, with sandalwood and caraway among the base notes, and Wild Fern, which features oak moss and basil. Besides soaps, shampoos, loofahs and sponges, there is a good choice of leather gifts including flasks and cup sets as well as clothes and bathroom brushes. Also at 20 Jermyn St, SW1, 071-734 6553.

---

*Some establishments change their **closing times** without warning. It is always wise to check in advance.*

BOOKS

■ ARTS

Atrium
5 Cork St, W1 - 071-495 0073
Open Mon-Fri 10am-6pm, Sat 11am-4pm.

This welcoming art book shop has a press book of current reviews to browse through on the new publications table. The shelves hold a comprehensive selection of books on photography, architecture, textiles and costume, sculpture, gardens, old masters, stained glass, Islamic and Indian art, Latin American arts, travel, interior design, icons and many other subjects. There are foreign language editions and many exhibition catalogues and the staff take a genuine interest in tracking books down. Events, festivals, readings and other events on the subject of literature and books take place regularly.

BBC Shop
4-5 Langham Pl, W1
071-765 4970
Open Mon-Fri 9am-5.30pm, Sat 9.30am-5.30pm.

An outlet for all the BBC publications, tapes, videos and books, cards and posters, this is smaller than the spacious BBC World Shop but jam-packed with the corporation's products which include coffee table books on some of its series and historical programmes.

BBC World Shop

Bush House, Strand, WC2
071-257 2576
Open Mon-Fri 9.30am-5.30pm, Sat 10am-5pm.

Shows which have been broadcast on the Beeb, as it is sometimes nicknamed, whether radio or TV often produce a publication about the programme, the cast or compilations of favourite scripts. The shop started as an information centre for its millions of listeners world-wide. There are videos, cassettes and CDs about nostalgically remembered shows and current popular programmes, as well as short wave radios.

Cinema Bookshop

13-14 Gt Russell St, WC1
071-637 0206
Open Mon-Sat 10.30am-5.30pm.

The largest book shop on the subject of cinema covering all aspects and catering for everyone from trade to students. They have biographies as well as a good stock of ephemera, posters and photos and carry a good out-of-print section.

Dance Books

4 Cecil Ct, WC2 - 071-836 2314
Open Mon-Sat 11am-7pm.

Founded by a former Ballet Rambert dancer, this shop has books on all types of dance and human movement as well as videos, posters and prints, some of which decorate the walls.

French's Theatre Bookshop

52 Fitzroy St, W1 - 071-387 9373
Open Mon-Fri 9.30am-5.30pm.

This firm, which has published plays since 1830, stocks more than 4,000 play titles in well-assembled order. It has a reference collection of sound effects and dialect recordings to help producers and playwrights. There are also a couple of thousand books on the theatre.

National Portrait Gallery Shop

St Martin's Pl, WC2
071-306 0055
Open Mon-Fri 10am-5pm, Sat to 6pm, Sun noon-6pm.

Attached to the National Portrait Gallery, the shop now also boasts an extensive book shop, which is strong not only on books about art and related subjects, but also on biographies and critical appraisals of the people depicted in the gallery. Books by authors and painters are also included.

Royal Institute of British Architects

66 Portland Pl, W1 - 071-580 5533
Open Mon-Fri 9.30am-5.30pm, Sat 10am-11.30am.

The RIBA, as it is known, has an excellent specialist book shop for anyone interested in architecture and (serious) landscape gardening but in the latter case the books are for professional gardeners rather than the amateur. ('No books about planting potatoes', we were politely informed). They stock foreign publications as well. If you're in the building, an added bonus is the exhibitions the RIBA often puts on.

A Zwemmer

24 Litchfield St, WC2
071-240 4158
Open Mon-Sat 9.30am-6pm.

Two floors are filled with books on artists and every facet of the visual arts with in-depth coverage of medieval, Oriental, twentieth-century art and art history. In the basement, shelves are packed with books on architecture and the decorative arts such as ceramics, fashion, textiles and other crafts. The sister shop in Charing Cross Road stocks books on film, photography and graphic design (80 Charing Cross Rd, WC2, 071-240 1559).

■ COMICS

Forbidden Planet

71 New Oxford St, WC1
071-836 4179
Open Mon-Wed, Sat 10am-6pm, Thurs, Fri to 7pm.

One of London's largest stockists of comics and cartoons. Nobody has counted the selection, but the description is 'two full floors'. Forbidden Planet also sells novels and spin-offs from comics: models, T-shirts and memorabilia.

■ COOKING & FOOD

Books for Cooks

4 Blenheim Crescent, W11
071-221 1992
Open Mon-Sat 9.30am-6pm.

There is a little café at the back of the shop and cooking demonstrations take place upstairs. The shop is notable for its exhaustive selection of food and wine books and is one of the best in the country. From simple cookbooks to exotic cuisine, this shop is a must for anyone interested in food.

Food for Thought, Simon Gough Books

27 Cecil Ct, WC2 - 071-379 1993/8171
Open Mon-Sat 10.30am-8pm.

This fascinating, charming shop specialises in antiquarian, second-hand and modern books on food. If it's *La Cuisinière de la Campagne et de la Ville* by Louis Audot (Paris, 1872), a good first edition of M F K Fisher, Elizabeth David or the latest book of recipes from the latest super-chef you're interested in, this is the place to come to. They will search out specific books for you; they also stock books on herbs, wine, housekeeping and more. Well worth a visit for anyone with the smallest interest in the subject of food.

■ CRIME

Murder One

71-73 Charing Cross Rd, WC2 - 071-734 3483
Open Mon-Wed 10am-7pm, Thurs-Sat to 8pm.

A huge stock of books covers only three topics, but within those includes almost all the books published in Britain. The crime and mystery books section also has many imports from the USA; Heartline covers romantic fiction and New Worlds offers science fiction. They also stock second-hand books.

■ ESOTERICA

Mysteries
New Age Centre

9-11 Monmouth St, WC2
071-240 3688
Open Mon-Sat 10am-6pm.

A zippy purple façade sets the off-beat mood of this psychic and New Age book shop which sells tarot cards, crystal balls, incense, pendulums and other devices for exploring the secrets of the universe.

Skoob Two

17 Sicilian Ave, WC1
071-405 0030
Open Mon-Sat 10.30am-6.30pm.

Part of Skoob, this shop specialises in New Age books, books on the occult and subjects like Greek and Latin, archaeology and ancient religions.

Watkins Books

19 Cecil Ct, WC2 - 071-836 2182
Open Mon-Sat 11am-6pm, Wed 10.30am-6pm.

In this large modern shop you'll find the widest range of books on esoteric themes to do with New Age philosophies: holistic health, eastern religions, and subjects connected with natural health therapies.

■ FEMINIST

Silver Moon
Women's Bookshop

68 Charing Cross Rd, WC2
071-836 7906
Open Mon-Sat 10am-6.30pm, Thurs to 8pm.

All Virago's titles are stocked here, along with books relating to women's issues from women's rights

to giving birth. They hold readings here; consult the listings magazines or telephone for details.

■ FOREIGN LANGUAGES

European Bookshop

4 Regent Pl, W1, and 5 Warwick St, W1 - 071-734 5259
Open Mon-Sat 9.30am-6pm, Thurs to 7.30pm.

These two bookstores specialise, as their name implies, in European books. They concentrate on French, German, Spanish, Italian, Portuguese and Scandinavian books and also in books on English as a foreign language, which today is a huge industry. The Regent Place book shop stocks language books and learning materials; the second book shop is more general.

■ GAY

Gay's the Word

66 Marchmont St, WC1
071-278 7654
Open Mon-Fri 11am-7pm, Sat 10am-6pm, Sun 2-6pm.

A well-stocked shop covering all aspects of life touching on gays, lesbians and sexuality, as well as books on subjects like living with AIDS. Regular author readings are held here. Telephone for details.

*Remember that if you carry a non-British passport, you are entitled to a full refund of the **value-added tax** (VAT). Stores vary in the minimum you must spend in order to claim this. See Basics for details.*

■ GENERAL INTEREST

Compendium
234 Camden High St, NW1
071-485 8944
Open Mon-Sat 10am-6pm, Sun noon-6pm.
A Camden Town institution, catering to the alternative types of NW1, this excellent, out-of-the-mainstream general shop covers subjects from pop music to psychology, semiotics to women's issues. Books on 'Green' topics are particularly well represented here.

Dillons The Bookstore
82 Gower St, WC1 - 071-636 1577
Open Mon-Fri 9am-7pm, Sat to 6pm.
In the heart of literary Bloomsbury, the shop has printed a walking leaflet about some of the authors like Virginia Woolf who lived in the area. This flagship store of a large chain, all very well stocked and organised, is huge and being in the midst of London University has a strong academic section. It is housed in a fantastically decorated Victorian building. Some of the branches specialise: Dillons Arts Bookshop at 8 Long Acre, WC2, (071-836 1359) has a huge range of books on applied and fine art, architecture and related topics and a wide range of specialist magazines and some art posters.

W & G Foyle
113-119 Charing Cross Rd, WC2 - 071-437 5660
Open Mon-Sat 9am-6pm, Thurs to 7pm.
This giant shop is probably London's most famous book seller, an old-fashioned place with countless corridors and shelves, constantly bustling with browsers overwhelmed with choice. It has become a running joke that Foyles definitely has the book you want somewhere but can't necessarily find it. Telephone enquiries are answered by a machine message telling customers that only written enquiries are dealt with.

International newsagents

You can get foreign newspapers at most hotels, in Soho and around the areas visitors throng to, like Knightsbridge. Otherwise try *Gray's Inn News* at 50 Theobald's Rd, WC1 (071-405 5241), *A Moroni & Son* at 68 Old Compton St, W1 (071-437 2847) and *D S Radford* at 61 Fleet St, EC4 (071-583 7166).

Harrod's Book Shop
Harrod's, Knightsbridge, SW1 - 071-730 1234
Open Mon-Sat 9am-6pm, Wed to 7pm.
As is to be expected in a department store of such calibre, Harrod's has a well-stocked book shop, managed by Waterstone's with the same keen enthusiasm which characterises this chain's many branches nation-wide with a strong emphasis on literary book launches and a good selection of finely bound and printed books. The department occupies about an eighth of the second floor with a well-stocked magazine and periodicals area next to it.

Hatchards
187 Piccadilly, W1 - 071-439 9921
Open Mon-Sat 9am-6pm.
Now part of the Dillons book shop chain, Hatchards is still the book shop with cachet, for here top people spend time browsing in the genteel, carpeted rooms. It has all four royal warrants on display (only issued by four members of the royal family) and traditionally sends the royal family a selection of books for their summer holiday reading. There are five floors of books on general subjects with the latest hardbacks by the entrance.

John Sandoe
10 Blacklands Terr, SW3
071-589 9473
Open Mon-Sat 9.30am-5.30pm, Wed to 7.30pm.
Locals speak with real affection about this shop, just off Sloane Square, which is particularly strong on literature and the arts. Lots of paperbacks of fiction, poetry and classics along with the latest hardbacks.

*The **prices** in this guide reflect what establishments were charging at the time of going to press.*

W H Smith & Son

36 Sloane Sq, SW1 - 071-730 0351
Open Mon-Sat 8.45am-6.15pm.

W H Smith & Son is one of the longest established newsagents and booksellers in Britain. They continue to act as good general bookshops, with an emphasis on fiction and travel. Many of their shops concentrate on stationery or computer supplies, but they remain one of the most reliable sources of newspapers and magazines as well as books. Branches throughout London.

Waterstone's

121-125 Charing Cross Rd, WC2 - 071-434 4291
Open Mon-Sat 9.30am-8pm, Sun noon-6pm.

Readings, book launches and signings by authors regularly take place at the lively Waterstone branches which have a name for their literary strength and are a welcome sight in many parts of London. The Kensington High Street branch is spacious. The Charing Cross shop is in a rambling array of rooms and has spread to other premises almost next door. All the branches have an excellent wide selection of books packed on the shelves, displayed invitingly on tables and sometimes stacked on the floor. Also at 193 Kensington High St, W8, 071-937 8432. And branches throughout London.

■ SECOND-HAND

Skoob Books

11a-15 Sicilian Ave, Southampton Row, WC1 071-404 3063
Open Mon-Sat 10.30am-6.30pm.

The largest second-hand book shop in London with around 50,000 titles always in stock, Skoob specialises in second-hand and up-to-date academic books and is the only specialist in scientific and technical books. Apart from that, there's a small antiquarian department and a whole host of other titles. A great shop for browsing in a truly serendipitous manner in slightly shabby surroundings. Ike Ong is the enthusiastic manager who is very approachable if you want advice.

■ SPORTS

Sportspages

Caxton Walk, 94-96 Charing Cross Rd, WC2 - 071-240 9604
Open Mon-Sat 9.30am-7pm.

'The book shop that takes sport seriously' runs the slogan for this specialist shop with a selection of 8,000 titles. Sportspages covers every imaginable sport (excluding chess, board and card games) with books and videos. Titles cover all aspects from training to tactics, from biographies to medical studies.

■ TRAVEL

Daunt Books for Travellers

83 Marylebone High St, W1 071-224 2295
Open Mon-Sat 9am-7.30pm.

This delightful, airy shop on two floors carries a huge and interesting stock of travel books, some 25,000 books in all. Upstairs is the British Isles; ground floor it's Europe; downstairs the rest of the world. They file books how people read them, according to James Daunt, the owner, so together on the Cuban shelves you find the latest book on Caribbean communism and Graham Greene's *Our Man in Havana*. They also have large stockrooms, so if you're after a particular title and can't find it, do ask.

Stanfords

12-14 Long Acre, WC2 071-836 1321
Open Mon, Sat 10am-6pm, Tues-Fri 9am-7pm.

A travel specialist, this shop has a large ground floor devoted to books and guides to everywhere in the world as well as Britain. Downstairs is a well-organised department of maps, including the Ordnance Survey series, for which this shop is justly famous.

The Travel Book Shop

13 Blenheim Crescent, W11 071-229 5260
Open Mon-Sat 10am-6pm.

Shelves jam-packed with travel books to take your

Plan to travel? Look for Gault Millau's other Best of guides to Chicago, Florida, France, Germany, Hawaii, Hong Kong, Italy, Los Angeles, New England, New Orleans, New York, Paris, San Francisco, Thailand, Toronto, and Washington, D.C.

---

mind off the British weather in this full, interesting shop. They stock the usual guides, plus some rare books, kept in locked cabinets and can, for a small fee, try to trace any title. A real enthusiast's shop.

Travellers Book Shop

25 Cecil Ct, WC2 - 071-836 9132
Open Mon-Fri 11am-7pm, Sat to 6.30pm.

In a little street reminiscent of another era, you'll find specialist book stores like this one, stocking Baedekers on the ground floor, those much-loved travel books of the past, and modern guides and second-hand travel books in the basement.

CHILDREN

■ CLOTHING

Anthea Moore Ede

16 Victoria Grove, SW3
071-584 8826
Open Mon-Fri 9am-5pm, Sat 10am-1pm.

If you want that classic look for your child and clothes that look a little like Kate Greenaway's drawings, then this is the shop to come to. It features hand-smocked dresses, white taffeta and velvet party wear, long white night-gowns, tweed coats, romper suits and traditional boy's shirts.

Buckle-My-Shoe

19 St Christopher's Pl, W1
071-935 5589
Open Mon-Fri 10am-6pm, Sat to 7pm.

Nothing but shoes, boots, sandals and fashion trainers rather than the sports variety are sold in this busy shop which caters for children up to ten years old. Moccasins and western boots for the fashion-conscious child with fringing, beading and interlacing come in vivid colours. Even the most particular child should find something here as altogether they stock 85 different styles of shoes, boots and slippers in 300 colourways from both known designers and from their own range.

La Cigogna

6a Sloane St, SW1 - 071-235 3845
Open Mon-Sat 9.30am-6pm, Wed to 7pm.

This is a useful, large, one-stop shop. Besides designer clothes for babies and children, it caters for mothers-to-be and teenagers up to the age of sixteen. They even stock a wide range of hats and shoes.

La Confiture

19 Harrington Rd, SW7
071-581 3432
Open Mon-Sat 10am-6.30pm.

The top range of designer names are on sale here including Babar, Diesel, Gina Dinan, Kenzo, Nik at Pouf, Armore and Edmund along with other exclusive styles from Italy and Spain.

Createx

27 Harrington Rd, SW7
071-589 8306
Open Mon-Sat 9.30am-6pm.

A very well-stocked shop with high fashion French and Italian clothes. Brand names include Catimini,

David Charles, Comme une Image and Petit Bateau.

Joanna's Tent

289 King's Rd, SW3
071-352 1151
Open Mon-Sat 9.45am-6pm.

The children's wear department in the basement is very well-stocked and includes a wide range of accessories.

Oilily

9 Sloane St, SW1 - 071-823 2505
Open Mon-Sat 9.30am-6pm.

Very bright, jolly and original clothing for children in this Oilily store. The Dutch company has caught a mood, and they stock pretty dresses, smocks, casual beach wear and colourful jackets and coats. They also run a range of ladies clothing, in the same style of jolly, casual and colourful.

Patrizia Wigan

19 Walton St, SW3 - 071-823 7080
Open Mon-Fri 10am-6pm, Sat to 5.30pm.

Delightful styles and charming fabrics make the clothes here special. Patrizia Wigan's designer clothes which include casual wear and beautiful dressy garments are known on the international circuit for their very English look. A velvet jacket costs around £55. Also at 72 New King's Rd, SW6, 071-736 3336.

Scott-Adie

53 Godfrey St, SW3
071-352 1718
Open Mon-Fri 10am-5.30pm, Sat to 4pm.

Fiona Hamilton revived a family firm by choosing

this name for her little shop which stocks children's wear made from natural fibres and with a classical theme. There is a wide range of tartans and Liberty prints. Popular lines are reversible clothing and Bumble Bee hats and gloves. The shop does a 'bunny basket', custom-filled to deliver to hospitals to welcome new babies.

Trotters

34 King's Rd, SW3 - 071-259 9620
Open Mon-Sat 9am-6pm, Wed to 6.30pm.

A lively place where children up to the age of eight come to have their hair cut while gazing at goldfish swimming in tanks. With a juice bar, this makes an excellent one-stop shopping place for toys, videos, shoes, books and games. Also at 127 Kensington High St, W8, 071-937 9373.

Young England

47 Elizabeth St, SW1
071-259 9003
Open Mon-Fri 10am-5.30pm, Sat to 1pm.

Hand-smocked dresses, tailored coats, formal dresses, swim-wear, night-dresses and dressing gowns, all with a traditional appeal, are sold in this well-stocked shop, catering for children up to the age of eight. Natural materials are used, such as taffeta, wool and cotton. Everything is well-made with generous hems, linings on wool products, net petticoats with party dresses and matching accessories. A red tartan dress at £147 had its own head-band, pony-tail scrunch, little purse and detachable collar. Wool

coat-dresses and sailor-look garments are popular.

If you need help

The following agencies are invaluable for getting baby sitters, au pairs or nannies. *Koala Nannies*, **071-376 7651**, and *Universal Aunts*, **071-738 8937**.

■ FURNITURE

Dragons

23 Walton St, SW3 - 071-589 3795
Open Mon-Fri 9.30am-5.30pm, Sat 10am-5pm.

A white four-poster bed has pride of place in the back of this long shop which has miniature armchairs, tables, desks and hand-painted furniture by three artists, including one who specialises in Beatrix Potter animals. Other furniture has stencilling, hand-painted floral designs, sponging, gilding, lacquering and a wide range of decorative techniques for pretty children's rooms. The shop stocks everything from rag dolls to enamel bread bins which make colourful and unusual containers for toys.

The Nursery Window

83 Walton St, SW3 - 071-581 3358
Open Mon-Fri 10am-5.30pm, Sat to 4.30pm.

Fabrics and wallpaper for children's rooms are in

abundance at this shop which also stocks a wide choice of changing mats and bags, cot quilts, hooded towels, pram quilts, weekend bags, play mats, lampshades, bibs, blankets and everything else to make a baby's room cosy.

■ TOYS, GAMES & BOOKS

Absolute Balls

61 Broadwick St, W1
071-437 0985
Open Mon-Sat 10am-6pm.

Learn to juggle or ride a unicycle at this brightly-lit shop where owner Colin Milton is happy to demonstrate his unusual wares. There are juggling beanbags at £3.50 each and gift sets of three balls for £12.50. Colin Milton says some of his customers are stressed executives who want to take up a hobby to help them unwind, but professional and amateur performers also use the shop, which is supplied by products made in its own factory. There are also spinning plates, boomerangs and special clothing.

Benjamin Pollock's Toy Shop

44 The Market, Covent Garden, WC2 - 071-379 7866
Open Mon-Sat 10.30am-6pm.

Model theatres and intricate cardboard cut-outs of old-fashioned theatres with all the accoutrements are the delightful wares at this shop, which also has puppets, traditional toys, rag dolls and teddy bears.

Children's Book Centre

237 Kensington High St, W1
071-937 7497
Open Mon-Sat 9.30am-6.30pm, Tues to 6pm, Thurs to 7pm.

A bright well-organised shop with books arranged by age and by subject, it is usually full of kids, sometimes sprawled on the floor, perusing a book or watching the latest video on a TV set. They stock a wide choice of fiction and educational books for young children, toys, cuddly bears and cassettes. The staff are knowledgeable and understanding.

The Disney Store

140-141 Regent St, W1
071-287 6558
Open Mon-Sat 9.30am-7pm.

Mickey Mouse is represented on T-shirts, mugs and other products but so are all the other Walt Disney characters from Pinnochio to Snow White. Adults and kids are sometimes inspired to sing along with the characters on the multi-screen video. There are two floors, with the lower level full of stuffed toys and its own travel centre which arranges trips to the various Disneylands.

The Doll's House

29 The Market, Covent Garden, WC2 - 071-379 7243
Open Mon-Sat 10am-7pm.

Attractive dolls' houses and everything to furnish them with are the speciality of this shop which caters for collectors as well as children. Some, like the

half-timbered, thatched house are fabulous. Handcrafted furniture and little household accessories, even pot plants and bowls of fruit are in abundance in charmingly vaulted premises on the lower ground floor. Kits are available at around £115.

Early Learning Centre

36 King's Rd, SW3 - 071-581 5764
Open Mon-Sat 9am-6pm, Wed to 7pm.

Always very busy, this welcoming shop geared to children, not adults, has a wide selection of games, books, puzzles and other cheerful products to encourage children to play and learn. There is a special area where kids are usually putting giant building blocks up or having a go at some new game. Also at 225 Kensington High St, W8, 071-937 0419.

Frog Hollow

15 Victoria Grove, W8
071-581 5493
Open Mon-Sat 9am-5.30pm Sun 11am-5.30pm.

Frogs are well-represented in this shop which is known mainly for its exceptional range of toys, books, tapes and everything to amuse children.

Hamleys

200 Regent St, W1 - 071-734 3161
Open Mon-Sat 10am-6pm, Thurs to 8pm.

A very large department store which has nothing but toys and items for children has made this address famous. It is always thronging with children

looking at toys from the cheap and cheerful items to top-of the range. Adults are just as likely as children to find entertaining toys.

Just Games

71 Brewer St, W1 - 071-734 6124
Open Mon-Sat 10am-6pm.

From the obscure to the obvious, the trivial to the important games like chess and Mah Jong, this shop stocks everything that a board game enthusiast could want, including books on the subject.

The Kite Store

69 Neal St, WC2 - 071-836 1666, 071-836 2510
Open Mon-Fri 10am-6pm, Sat 10.30am-5.30pm.

The cheerful window display of brightly coloured kites says it all: this shop has do-it-yourself kits and high-powered designer kites in every shape imaginable.

London Kite and Juggling Company

10a Foubert's Pl, W1
071-437 4552
Open Mon-Sat 10am-7pm.

There are almost 30 different types of juggling balls, lots of kites and roller blades here. Proprietor Stephen Alway says the most unusual product he sells are fireballs.

Puffin Book Shop

10 The Market, Covent Garden, WC2 - 071-379 6465
Open Mon-Sat 10am-8pm.

At the time of going to press, the book shop was moving into this address adjacent to the Penguin Bookshop. They stock all the excellent Puffin books as well as good children's books from other publishers. As they are connected to the Penguin Bookshop, they are hoping that reluctant teenagers who usually rebel at the idea of a 'children's book shop' will also be persuaded to browse among their titles.

■ WHERE TO ENTERTAIN CHILDREN

The Little Angel Marionette Theatre

14 Dagmar Passage, Cross St, N1 - 071-226 1787

The Ugly Duckling, *Sleeping Beauty*, Christmas opera and more, all done with marionettes have been delighting children for years at this tucked away theatre in Islington.

Unicorn Theatre for Children

6/7 Gt Newport St, WC2
071-836 3334

Year-round professional entertainments for children from old favourites like Pinnochio to commissioned new works.

Polka Theatre for Children

240 The Broadway, Wimbledon, SW19
081-543 4888

Well worth making the journey out to Wimbledon for a performance at the delightful Polka Theatre for Children which has a very wide variety of shows for all ages.

DEPARTMENT STORES

Some department stores are a definite 'must' to visit and this compilation features the ones British people visit and Londoners themselves put on top of their lists of places to shop.

Fenwick

63 New Bond St, W1
071-629 9161, Fax 071-409 1890
Open Mon-Sat 9.30am-6pm, Thurs to 7.30pm.

From inexpensive to designer label, the women's clothes and accessories attract a wide range of customers looking for the right hand bag or outfit without prices getting out of hand. It stocks top and middle-range designer names like Georges Rech, Jasper Conran and Jean Muir, Nicole Farhi, Paul Costelloe and Mondi and has always been known for its lingerie. It has a limited menswear department and two restaurants, including the new Joe's. Founded in 1891 in its present corner location, here is a pleasant, comfortable place to shop in, never as hectic as the nearby Oxford Street scrum.

Fortnum & Mason

181 Piccadilly, W1 - 071-734 8040, Fax 071-437 3278
Open Mon-Sat 9.30am-6pm.

Fortnum & Mason stays in an agreeable time warp with its glittering chandeliers, opulent packaging and the world-famous array of luxury food and wine. And though prices have changed from

early eighteenth-century days when a baronet in Berkeley Square paid a mere £5 for six dozen bottles of the finest claret, this very traditional department store is a monument to the elegance of a past age—the assistants in the food hall wear tail coats. The exterior is famous for its clock—the figures of Mr Fortnum and Mr Mason greet each other as the hour is struck. The original duo founded this remarkable store in 1707 to cater for the aristocracy of St James's. Mr Fortnum was a footman in the Royal Household who knew the exact grocery requirements of the royal family, and Mr Mason supplied the delivery wagons. There is life beyond the food hall; upstairs there are departments for clothes for both adults and children and a restaurant.

Harrod's

Knightsbridge, SW1
071-730 1234, Fax 071-581 0470
Open Mon-Sat 9am-6pm, Wed to 7pm.

Harrod's is so vast (it occupies a 4.5 acre block) and so famous that it has become a tourist attraction in its own right. And well it should be, with its magnificent exterior and equally impressive departments inside which include, on the ground floor alone, the new Egyptian Hall for gifts, a glittering perfume hall and the renowned food hall— well known for its Edwardian picture-tiles and daily changing sculpture of fish. Harrod's began as a small Victorian grocery store, but from its early beginnings was always in the forefront of fashion. It was the first London shop to install an escalator—because the manager hated lifts. This 1898 novelty proved such an excitement for the first clients that an attendant had to be stationed at the top to give out brandy or sal-volatile as appropriate to the gentlemen and ladies overcome by the experience. Today the list of its departments and services goes on and on, and includes a bank, theatre and safe-deposit boxes, justifying its claim to sell anything and everything. The January sale which usually begins around the 5th of the month brings the whole of Knightsbridge to a halt.

Harvey Nichols
109-125 Knightsbridge, SW1 - 071-235 5000, Fax 071-235 8560
Open Mon-Fri 10am-7pm, Wed to 8pm, Sat to 6pm.

Of the two department stores in Knightsbridge (the other one is Harrod's), Harvey Nichols has the kudos for being the top showplace for fashion designers, stocking most of the big national and international names. Prices match, though they do stock their own brand names and some designers who produce excellent, less expensive ranges. It is all very well laid out, and easy to shop in. Lately it has changed ownership and the new regime has challenged Harrod's in another way, by opening a high-tech, exciting food hall with restaurant, café and bar.

Liberty
210-220 Regent St, W1
071-734 1234, Fax 071-734 8323
Open Mon-Sat 9.30am-6pm, Wed 10am-6pm, Thurs 9.30am-7.30pm.

Founded in 1875 at the height of the arts and crafts movement which aimed at making objects both beautiful and useful, Libertys with its mock Tudor half-timbered façade on one side and carved stone façade onto Regent's Street, is a picturesque sight. Inside, it rambles through various floors and departments. From the Oriental department and gifts in the basement to the galleried display of Persian rugs on the top floor, a bazaar-like ambience prevails which makes it unique in London. Liberty's fabrics are famous the world over, with the peacock feather scarf one of its oldest and most distinctive designs. Accessories in that famous print material, their own design jewellery range called Amuelti, antique jewellery, Italian leatherware and furnishing fabrics are also things to seek out.

Marks & Spencer
458 Oxford St, W1 - 071-935 7954, 071 486 5379
Open Mon-Sat 9am-7pm. No cards.

Marks and Sparks, M and S, call it what you will, Marks and Spencer has become the very backbone of the nation's shopping. While it is best known as the place to buy top quality, reasonably priced knitwear and underwear, M and S sells everything from shoes to hats, toiletries to plants, and still does

not take credit cards. The showplace for all its latest products is the Marble Arch branch, so called because it is near that landmark. Here, the company tries out designs it has especially commissioned, often from young designers just out of art school, so you will find clothes here that are often sharper and with a younger slant than at any of the 300 other shops around the country. The company recently went into food retailing which has proved an enormous success. Using specific chefs to develop new ideas, M and S is now acknowledged as one of the major forces in the food business. And it all started as a penny market stall in 1884. Branches throughout London.

Peter Jones
Sloane Sq, SW1 - 071-730 3434, Fax 071-730 9645
Open Mon-Sat 9am-5.30pm, Wed to 7pm.

Chelsea's only department store holds the wedding lists for the well-born, well-heeled and well-connected town-and-country set, an ideal place for distinctive fabrics, linens, china, glass, antiques and fashionable gifts as well as clothes and accessories. A bonus here is that both its coffee shop and licensed restaurant have views over London's roof tops.

Selfridge's
400 Oxford St, W1 - 071-629 1234, Fax 071-495 8321
Open Mon-Sat 9.30am-7pm, Thurs to 8pm.

It is unfair to describe Selfridge's as the 'poor man's Harrod's' because the huge store stocks designer names and expensive goods among its vast range of products. But the phrase sums up the feeling that Londoners do look upon this store with the loyalty they would show to a local shop. Selfridge's, easily the biggest store on Oxford Street, retains its reputation for convenience and breadth of choice for central London shopping. Everyone heads there automatically to compare full ranges of products, from cat flaps to camcorders to cashmere coats to cut crystal. There is even a service arcade in the basement for key-cutting, shoe repairs and dry-cleaning. There are several eating places, including self-service and waitress service restaurants, cafés, an ice cream parlour and a couple of bars. The food hall is very well stocked.

Sogo

Piccadilly Circus, SW1
071-333 9000
Open Mon-Sat 10am-8pm.

The biggest department store in Japan chose a very central London location for its premises, which features some very British fashion names, such as Dunhill, Aquascutum, Burberrys, DAKS, Jasper Conran and Paul Smith. International names are well represented with Karl Lagerfeld, Etienne Aigner and Hanae Mori. Stocking china, crystal, leather accessories, make-up, modern and antique jewellery and Japanese-made giftware in the Fuji boutique, and boasting a travel agency, this compact two-floor department store

is understandably popular with Japanese visitors, who also appreciate the adjoining Sogo café which has even has 'sushi for children' on the menu.

FASHION FOR HIM & HER

There was a time when there was a clear distinction between men's shops and those catering for women only. But in the last few years, this distinction has blurred. Many designers (and shops) now cater for both sexes, and many women, particularly, now wear men's clothes, claiming that jeans, for example, are better cut for men than for women. So we have divided this section into three parts: Clothing For Him and Her, Menswear and Womenswear. And our Young Chic & Street fashion section includes both unisex and those shops that cater for one or the other. If you're confused, think of the designers!

Agnès B.

Floral St, WC2 - 071-379 1992
Open Mon-Sat 10.30am-6.30pm, Thurs 10am-7pm.

The casual, chic French clothes of Agnès B. (now a grandmother) with 'Agnès B.' T-shirts are at the top of this converted warehouse which overlooks the rooftops of Covent Garden. A young family can get it together here, with the bébé range, including tot's berets at £15. Smart women's day wear and suits along with frothy tops

for the evening are on the second floor. Menswear takes over the ground and basement. Also at 111 Fulham Rd, SW3, 071-225 3477.

Alfred Dunhill

30 Duke St, SW1 - 071-499 9566
Open Mon-Fri 9.30am-6pm, Sat 10am-6pm.

The curved counters of gleaming wood were designed to give the impression of going aboard ship in a more stylish era, and the clothes at this department store have that edge of looking traditional in a stylish way. Double-breasted blazers, linen trousers, cotton shirts as well as leather accessories, watches, fragrances, umbrellas, fountain pens and all manner of small artefacts complete the Dunhill look, which adheres to the philosophy 'it must be the best'. There is an extensive ladieswear department also. Dunhill's started as a tobacconist shop for which it is still famous. In a specially set aside area you find a walk-in humidor and an amazing choice of cigars, tobaccos, lighters and other accessories.

Austin Reed

103-113 Regent St, W1
071-734 6789
Open Mon-Sat 9.30am-6pm, Thurs to 7pm.

The studied conservative look is this department store's hallmark, with five floors devoted to putting that look together, especially with Austin Reed's own label. It is known for its reasonable price range. The Options shop has separates, suits and accessories for women.

Browns
23-27 South Molton St, W1
071-491 7833
*Open Mon-Sat 10am-6pm,
Wed to 7pm.*
This stalwart among the favourite places to find top designers looks like a house which has broken through the neighbouring walls and become a series of cosy rooms. Moschino, Max Mara, Donna Karan and Sonia Rykiel are among the many lines. The menswear department is at one end with equally top names on offer like Dolce and Gabbana and Byblos on two floors.

Comme des Garçons
59 Brook St, W1 - 071-493 1258
*Open Mon-Sat 10am-6pm,
Thurs to 7pm.*
A minimalist interior contains a rack of quirky, ultra-fashionable men's clothes from Rei Kawakubo, usually in black. There are women's clothes, often in filmy fabrics, including evening skirts and see-through blouses. Downstairs you'll find more conservative, but still stylish and stylised jackets and trousers.

Designer Sale Studio
241 King's Rd, SW3
071-351 4171
*Open Mon-Fri 10am-7pm,
Sat to 6pm, Sun noon-6pm.*
An all-year-round sales shop stocking Italian designer clothes for men and women, this two-level corner shop, in business since 1988, has such bargains as a Krizia silk and wool ladies' suit for £375, instead of £900, and a

Bagutta men's suit for £295 instead of £710.

Emporio Armani
191 Brompton Rd, SW3
071-823 8818
*Open Mon-Sat 10am-6pm,
Wed to 7pm.*
Providing a relaxed large store environment which young men and women prefer for shopping, this designer shows his more affordable lines of tailored and casual clothes in those famous neutral colours here. The smartly-dressed sales assistants wear the clothes with just the right air of nonchalance. Also at 57-59 Long Acre, WC2, 071-917 6882.

Esprit
6 Sloane St, SW1 - 071-245 9139
Open Mon-Sat 10am-6.30pm, Wed to 7pm.
Their own brand of stylish casual wear for women (menswear is found in the two other shops) is mostly made in Germany with jeans and a wide range of sweaters, shirts, trousers, skirts usually in neutral colours and complementary gloves, hats, scarves and belts. Look out for the American-made 'Esprit collection' line featuring natural wool from West Virginia sheep and knitted by a local women's co-operative group. Also at 165-167 Kensington High St, W8, 071-376 0012; 82 King's Rd, SW3, 071-589 7211.

The General Leather Company
56 Chiltern St, W1 - 071-935 1041
*Open Mon-Fri 10am-6pm,
Sat to 5pm.*

A good place for finding that perfect leather jacket as they design as well as manufacture collections of leather, suede and sheepskin garments. Popular with people who prefer made-to-measure clothes, which are often a must where leather and suede are concerned, they will also alter old models and do repairs.

Jaeger
200 Regent St, W1
071-734 8211
*Open Mon-Sat 9.30am-6pm,
Thurs to 7pm.*
Among the top names for that completely put-together look combining elegance with well-cut simplicity for men and women, this large, airy shop has a large choice of suits and separates with well-bred style.

Jones
13 Floral St, WC2 - 071-240 8312
Open Mon-Sat 10am-6.30pm, Sun 12.30pm-5.30pm.
Strange contraptions and overhead lighting from operating theatre lamps enhance the off-beat atmosphere of this large shop which has English street fashion clothes under £500 and an extremely wide range of international high fashion. Two Belgians—Dries Van Hoten and Dirk Bikkenberg—are popular and Jean Paul Gaultier, Miyake, Fujiwara and many avant-garde designers are also represented. There is a women's shop next door, where the highly original designs of another Belgian, Ann Demeulemeester, hit the right eclectic note.

211

Chunky, high-soled leather boots sell like hot cakes in both shops.

Joseph

77 Fulham Rd, SW3
071-823 9500
Open Mon-Sat 10am-6.30pm, Wed to 7pm, Sun noon-5pm.

One of the first designers to provide a large all-in-one shop with clothes for men and women, it remains popular with young customers looking out for the whole Joseph range and a select few other designers plus arty gift items. There is subdued lighting on the ground floor. The menswear occupies the basement floor and stocks designers like Dolce and Gabbana, Kenzo and Dries van Noten.

Katherine Hamnett

20 Sloane St, SW1 - 071-823 1002
Open Mon-Fri 10am-6.30pm, Wed to 7pm, Sat to 6pm.

In this dramatically decorated shop, one of Britain's top designers shows her idiosyncratic, Italian-made clothes for men and women. For the latter, go for beaded 'hot pants' at £175, a black velvet suit with wide lapels at £775, a sequinned waistcoat at £290 or simple jeans for £70.

Kilgour, French and Stanbury

8 Savile Row, W1 - 071-734 6905
Open Mon-Fri 9am-5pm.

This is one of the few tailors in Savile Row that makes suits for ladies although it is best known as a gentleman's tailor (see *Menswear/Tailors* section). The Queen orders her riding wear from equestrian tailor Bernard Wetherill who shares the premises.

Nicole Farhi

27 Hampstead High St, NW3 - 071-435 0866
Open Mon-Sat 10am-6pm, Sun noon-6pm.

Constantly in the pages of fashion magazines, Nicole Farhi produces a well-cut stunning effect in shades of pale grey and brown. For women, a classic coat is £400, a cream rib cardigan £140, a knitted waistcoat £100. The Hampstead shop is the only one that stocks her men's range (equally as sophisticated and elegant), but the large stores like Harrod's, Harvey Nichols and Selfridge's carry both the men's and women's styles. Branches throughout London.

Paul Smith

40-44 Floral St, WC2
071-379 7133
Open Mon-Fri 10.30am-6.30pm, Thurs to 7pm, Sat 10am-6.30pm.

The pizzazz of Paul Smith's designs make him popular with celebrities. The sprawling network of little rooms in this shop makes cosy browsing for floral ties, distinctively patterned shirts, zany waistcoats alongside antique sunglasses and pens. The suits on the ground floor feature unusual touches such as a cuff that is cut to veer out; downstairs the suits are more conservative. There has been a Paul Smith for boys from five to fifteen for a couple of years. In keeping with the prevailing trend, he has launched a women's range of suits and separates at a new shop at number 40.

Racing Green

193-197 Regent St, W1
071-437 4300
Open Mon-Fri 10am-7pm, Sat to 6.30pm.

Chunky knits, storm jackets, Oxford-style or brushed check shirts, sweatshirts, T-shirts and own label jeans at this large new shop attract men and women who like comfortable casual clothes in strong colours. The 'twill traveller' shirts at £32 come in deep, unusual shades such as lavender, pale peach, dark coral, pumpkin and pewter. Women like the rib leggings and separates. such as a pleated skirt, £40, and V-neck tunic top, £42. Children's wear is for seven to twelve year olds. There are accessories such as desert boots, lambswool gloves and scarves, belts and socks. Mail-order catalogue available.

Romeo Gigli

62 South Molton St, W1
071-495 6730
Open Mon-Sat 10am-6pm, Thurs to 7pm.

The myriad of zany, multi-coloured lamp-shades suspended from the ceiling set the off-beat style of this new boutique, which the designer has created himself to show off clothes with flair. Menswear is lined along one side, ladies the other. A separate shop, Gigli, with even sparkier clothes for younger tastes, is down the road.

The Scotch House

2 Brompton Rd, SW1
071-581 2151
*Open Mon-Fri 9.30am-6pm,
Tues 10am-6pm, Wed
9.30am-7pm, Sat 9am-6pm.*

Unrivalled for the quantity of its quality wool and cashmere clothes, The Scotch House has 300 tartans, a reference book, a wide range of kilts, including ankle-length ones for the evening, and an excellent children's department. Those society weddings where the pageboys look like miniature Highlanders have relied on this shop for years. Kilts are beautifully finished with leather-bound edges, and there are lots of sweaters to match from all the top brand names plus lamb's wool throws and scarves. The Brompton Road branch is the largest. Also at 84 & 191 Regent St, W1, 071-734 0203.

Simpson's

203 Piccadilly, W1 - 071-734 2002
Open Mon-Sat 9am-6pm, Thurs to 7pm.

A sushi bar at lunchtime is one of the attractions of this most English of department stores. It started as a three-week Japanese products promotion four years ago and attracted so many new customers, Japanese, European and British that they have kept it. Simpson's has a large number of departments selling international designer clothes for men and women as well as its famous range of men's clothes under the DAKS label. Overcoats, raincoats, tweed jackets and high quality suits with all the appropriate accessories are on sale.

Vivenne Westwood

44 Conduit St, W1 - 071-439 1109
Open Mon-Sat 10.30am-6pm, Thurs to 7pm.

Undisputedly the most influential British designer with great 'street cred', Vivienne Westwood has her main collection for men and women on sale at the Conduit Street shop, where velvet, lacy and image-imprinted bustiers, fake fur-trimmed jackets and extremely high-soled shoes take pride of place. The Davies Street one is set aside for evening wear and made-to measure. It has a dramatic lower level where the floor and changing room curtains display a photographic pattern of long wavy pre-Raphaelite tresses. Her original shop in King's Road keeps to her classics and styles which appeal to the younger fashion set. Also at 6 Davies St, W1, 071-629 3757; 430 King's Rd, SW1, 071-352 6551.

■ OUTERWEAR

Aquascutum

100 Regent St, W1 - 071-734 6090
Open Mon-Sat 9.30am-6pm, Thurs to 7pm.

That distinctive khaki pattern with a touch of red makes this firm's rainwear the drawing card but the pattern appears in other garments too, and there is a wide variety of classic British-made clothing for men and women. The showerproof coat first started selling in 1851, the year of the Victorian Great Exhibition, held to show off good British inventions. Some things have not changed.

Burberrys

18-22 Haymarket, W1
071-930 3343
Open Mon-Fri 9.30am-6pm, Thurs to 7pm, Sat 9am-6pm.

The famous black-and-gold Burberry check appears as a lining on solid trench coats, which have earned a world-wide reputation for being quintessential rainwear. It was created by Thomas Burberry in the 1870s, and fast gained the reputation of being untearable, rainproof, virtually crease-proof yet cool and comfortable. Meryl Streep wore one in *Kramer versus Kramer*, Michael Douglas in *Wall Street* and Warren Beatty in *Dick Tracy*. A wool-lined trench coat is £615, unlined is £450. Besides pure-cotton waterproofs, this department store has other lines of clothing plus sweaters, shawls, umbrellas and luggage. It is an excellent one-stop shopping expedition for that all-round English look. Also at 165 Regent St, W1, 071-734 4060.

R M Williams

179-181 Regent St, W1
071-434 0061
Open Mon-Sat 9.30am-6.30pm.

The classic Akruba bushwhacker hats that Prince Charles wears during his Australian visits are one of the best-selling items here, along with Australian-made moleskin trousers, oilskin jackets and hand-crafted boots. The racks are full of cotton, denim or linen shirts and jeans, trousers and shorts for men and women, with a line of sturdy skirts for ladies, too. Established some 60 years ago, this Aussie firm pays attention to detail, with only the best quality buttons, zips and rivets. The over-all great outdoors look is devastatingly romantic à la Indiana Jones. Also at 15 Kensington Church St, W8, 071-937 4333.

■ SHOES

You will find more designs for feet in *Menwear, Women's Wear* and the *Young Chic & Street Fashions* sections.

The Natural Shoe Store

21 Neal St, WC2 - 071-836 5254
Open Mon-Tues 10am-6pm, Wed-Fri to 7pm, Sat to 6.30pm, Sun noon-5.30pm.
The Natural Shoe Store has the clear aim of selling sensible footwear that doesn't look like an orthopaedic nightmare. You'll find good walking shoes and well-fitting office shoes which don't rub and punish the foot at this useful address. Also at 325 King's Rd, SW3, 071-351 3721.

■ YOUNG CHIC & STREET FASHIONS

Ally Capellino

95 Wardour St, W1
071-494 0768
Open Mon-Fri 11am-6pm, Sat 10.30am-6pm.
Non-faddy, softly-shaped separates mainly for women as well as dresses

and coats, all in a youthful mood, are the staple of this five-year old Soho shop, whose 'hearts of oak' range aims to produce up-to-date styles at affordable prices. The jewellery has a heart motif, too. For an idea of prices: a vinyl peasouper coat was £149.

Amazon

7a Kensington Church St, W8 - 071-376 0630
Open Mon-Fri 10am-6pm, Thurs to 7pm, Sat 9.30am-6pm.
Amazon started as one small shop and has proceeded to take over its neighbours, now stretching over five premises in fashionable Kensington Church Street at 1, 3, 7a, 7b, 19 to 22. It buys up seconds and discontinued lines from a wide variety of sources and sells them astonishingly cheaply. The stock changes rapidly, so if you see something you like, buy it; it may be gone the next day.

American Classics

398, 400 & 404 King's Rd, SW10 - 071-352 2853
Open Mon-Sat 10am-6.30pm.
Two of these shops sell new clothing and the third concentrates in second-hand, or vintage clothing. The selection includes lumberjack shirts, highway patrol leather jackets and jeans. Also American Classics Junior, 615 Fulham Rd, SW6, 071-610 1113.

American Retro

35 Old Compton St, W1
071-287 1092
Open Mon-Sat 10.15am-7pm.
Highly Stylish American clothes and accessories in

the styles of the past and coming decades. Leather jackets, lingerie, underwear, shoulder bags, sun-glasses, cigarette lighters and also post cards and books. Also at 14 Pembridge Rd, W11, 071-243 2393

Daniel James

70 Kensington High St, W8
071-937 4207
Open Mon-Sat 10am-7pm.
One's idea of T-shirt or sweatshirt is turned upside down in a Daniel James shop. Maybe you can call these clothes high style T-shirts in the widest possible sense: they are full of rich patterns, finely crafted details, applications and features borrowed from history or religious iconography. These clothes go well with more expensive designer creations. Real gems and affordable with prices from £30 to £70. Branches throughout London.

The Duffer of St George

27 D'Arblay St, W1
071-439 0996
Open Mon-Sat 10.30am-6.30pm.
Duffer's own label produces anything from knitwear to leather jackets and denim outfits. This is one of the best shops for casual menswear. T-shirts with 'Disco sucks' printing don't come much more sarcastic than here. Definitely clothing for clubbers. The Covent Garden branch has a selection of suits. The name, if you're interested, refers to a character in a classic children's book about school life. Also at 29

Short's Gdns, WC2, 071-379 4660.

Flip
125 Long Acre, WC2
071-836 4688
Open Mon-Sat 10am-7pm, Thurs to 8pm, Sun noon-6pm.

Two floors of second-hand American clothing and 'ready-loved' Levi's. You can find silly frilly shirts and suede jackets with cowboy fittings, semi-slick evening-wear and heavy grunge shirts. More fun than haute couture.

Gigli
38-39 South Molton St, W1
071-493 1230 ext 263
Open Mon-Sat 10.30am-6.30pm, Thurs 10am-7pm.

Fun waistcoats in zany colours and bright designs for young people hang on racks suspended from the ceiling by nautical ropes, fitting in with the modern approach to shopping when even the background is a designer product.

Hyper-Hyper
26-40 Kensington High St, W8 - 071-938 4343
Open Mon-Sat 10am-6pm, Wed to 7pm.

Young British designers are being promoted everywhere these days, but this market-style complex was one of the first forums for up-and-coming uninhibited work. Design students from overseas know this is the place to head for to see some 70 young designers' clothes.

John Richmond
62 Neal St, WC2 - 071-379 6020
Open Mon-Sat 10am-7pm.

Street chic

The incredibly popular *Camden Lock* (**Camden Town, NW1**) is at its busiest on Saturday and Sunday afternoons, but many of the shops in the surrounding area and the indoor market stay open all week. Particularly good for young street fashions, many shops specialise in chunky shoes while others offer everything from the 1960s hippies look to contemporary leather ware. Velvet hats, flowery shirts, silk waistcoats, some clearly from manufacturers, others hand-made, make this a mecca for the young.

Stylish jackets, suits, dresses and shirts for the young-at-heart. The richness of baroque is combined with the 90s look in some of the most extravagant and timeless clothes in this Covent Garden shop. John Richmond jackets have the rare advantage of looking both trendy and almost classic.

Kensington Market
49-53 Kensington High St, W8
Open Mon-Sat 10am-6pm.

Everything in street fashion and life-style for the converted: second-hand jeans, army surplus, new designers, clothes from Asia, jewellery, music, a hair dresser, café, tattoo parlour and even a tarot and palm reader. Floor after floor offers stalls with different items. If you don't find what you are looking for here, then maybe you don't know really known what you are looking for.

Michiko Koshino
70 Neal St, WC2 - 071-497 0165
Open Mon-Sat 11am-7pm.

Japanese Michiko Koshino has adopted Britain as her second home and the Brits have returned the compliment by loving her designs. This very ascetic shop shows Michiko's formal (if you can use that word here) clothing and leisure wear. She favours strong contrasts in her shapes and colours.

Miss Selfridge
40 Duke St, W1 - 071-629 1234
Open Mon-Sat 9.30am-6pm, Thurs to 8pm.

A good place for young fashionable clothes at reasonable prices. All the latest fashions come here and they also have make-up and accessories.

Pam Hogg
5 Newburgh St, W1
071-287 2185
Open Mon-Sat 10am-6pm.

Blonde, Scottish designer Pam Hogg is often photographed for magazine spreads wearing her own blatantly body-conscious clothes, a favourite with clubbers. PVC trousers, slashed, skin-tight body suits, wet mesh-look tops, sequinned bustiers and all sorts of studded, see-through or neon-coloured latex garments are sold in this little shop. One dress, daringly slashed throughout its skimpy material was £195. 'Not for shrinking violets' reported one fashion magazine.

Red or Dead Clothing

Thomas Neal's, Earlham St, WC2 - 071-240 5576
Open Mon-Fri 10.30am-7.30pm, Sat 10am-7pm, Sun noon-6pm.

A wide selection here of essential Red or Dead fashion for party people and for those who like sensible Doc Marten clothes. From leather jackets to belts, from waistcoats to trousers and T-shirts with style.

SHOES

Red or Dead Shoes

33 Neal St, WC2 - 071-379 7571
Open Mon-Fri 10.30am-7.30pm, Sat 10am-7pm, Sun noon-6pm.

Red or Dead make shoes which are a far cry from slim and elegant Italian classics. These shoes bring back memories of the extremes of the 1970s platform days and some are clearly inspired by Frankenstein's monster and then turned into footwear. More fun than most shoe shops! Branches throughout London.

Shellys

14-18 Neal St, WC2
071-250 3726
Open Mon-Sat 9.30am-6.30pm, Thurs to 7.30pm.

With chunky leather shoes and boots in vogue among the young street-smart fashion set, always bustling Shellys branches have sprung up to offer Doc Martens and Lumberjacks galore along with other must-have lines, sometimes in outrageous colours, for men and women. They are comfortable shoes so sometimes a tourist mother, buying presents for her sons and daughters, has been seen buying a pair for herself. Also at 266-270 Regent St, W1, 071-287 0939; and 159 Oxford St, W1, 071-437 5842.

FLOWERS & PLANTS

Cameron Shaw

279 New King's Rd, SW6
071-371 8175
Open Mon-Fri 9am-6pm, Sat 10am-5pm.

Dried flower sculptures are created with wit and humour by the sister-and-brother team of Kerry and Russell Longmuir. The final effect might be a moss-covered bicycle or the corner of a wheat field (from about £80). They also supply top furnishing stores.

Edward Goodyear

45 Brook St, W1 - 071-629 1508
Open Mon-Fri 8.30am-5.30pm.

Part of Claridge's hotel but with its own façade, this long-established florist has been arranging country flowers for high society since 1880—including the head-dresses and bouquets for the present

Princess of Wales's bridesmaids.

Fast Flowers

339 Fulham Rd, SW1
071-352 8618
Open Mon-Sat 10am-6pm.

Dainty dried 'rose trees' (costing from £28) in the window of this turquoise-fronted shop catch the eye. Inside, flowers and pretty jugs from £15 look picturesque against the red-tiled floor.

Felton and Sons

220 Brompton Rd, SW3
071-589 4433
Open Mon-Fri 8.30am-5.30pm, Sat to noon.

From its large corner shop in the heart of fashionable Kensington, Felton's—lit by a chandelier—offers a good service to a regular clientele who appreciate their traditional arrangements.

The Flowersmith

34 Shelton St, WC2
071-240 6688
Open Mon-Sat 10am-6pm.

Bouquets of exotic and esoteric country flowers 'guaranteed to gain attention' for £20, a striking posy arrangement for £15 and woodland 'configurations' of amaryllis against a moss, bark and twigs background in a glass tank at £28 are just some of their imaginative ideas. Unusual vases and baskets and a bonsai clinic are also popular.

Kenneth Turner

21 South Audley St, W1
071-355 3880
Open Mon-Sat 9am-5.30pm.

Quite simply, the best designer of dried flower arrangements in Britain, possibly in the world. Kenneth Turner creates the most fabulous decorations for private homes, weddings, clubs and hotels and flies around the world for clients. In the shop you can be inspired by, and buy, wonderful small trees with elaborate decorations, moss-covered baskets and scented candles. A real cornucopia!

Moyses Stevens
157-158 Sloane St, SW1
071-259 9303
Open Mon-Fri 8.30am-5.30pm, Sat to 4.30pm.
A wheelbarrow full of roses, with neatly arranged masses of seasonal flowers amid garden ornaments, greet the customer at this top florist with imaginative designs.

Pulbrook & Gould
127 Sloane St, SW1
071-730 0030
Open Mon-Fri 9am-5.30pm, Sat 10am-2pm.
A large, glamorous showplace, established some 30 years ago by Susan Pulbrook and Rosamund Gould, the eponymous shop became known for its innovative, natural approach to flower-arranging, and for its use of masses of white flowers. Apart from flowers, they sell quality gardening accessories like special aprons (around £17) and gardener's skirts in dark green cotton with useful deep pockets (£19). The latest venture is the Lady Pulbrook Flower School which passes on its techniques in one-day sessions. They cost £145 and include flowers and lunch.

■ FLOWER MARKET

Columbia Road Market
Columbia Rd, E2
Open Sun 8am-12.30pm
Try and visit this delight market on a Sunday morning, even if you don't want to buy flowers. If you do, you can get some real bargains here (and some bad buys, remember this is a typical street market). The shops in this picturesque Victorian street cater to the gardening fan and are full of delightful ceramics, urns, garden furniture, vases and accessories. A number of good small cafés add to the atmosphere.

■ GARDENING

Avant Garden
77 Lebury Rd, W11
071-229 4408
Open Mon-Fri 10am-6pm, Sat to 4pm.
Clifton Nurseries in Little Venice, one of the best known garden centres and design businesses in London was started by Joan Clifton who has now opened this odd, delightful shop in trendy Ledbury Road. Not just the expected wrought-iron chairs and tables are on display. You'll also find original candelabra, amphorae and pot stands, as well as gardening tools like her 'Monet' watering cans, buckets and jugs (from £28 to £50). An inspiration to the aspiring indoor and outdoor gardener.

FOOD

■ EVERYTHING YOU NEED

Anyone even moderately interested in food should visit the food halls of the big department stores. Recently the 'Big Three'—Harrod's, Fortnum & Mason and Selfridge's—have been joined by a glittering new food hall in Harvey Nichols. We have also included here several smaller shops that nonetheless cover the whole spectrum of gastronomic endeavours.

Fortnum & Mason
188 Piccadilly, W1 - 071-734 8040
Open Mon-Sat 9.30am-6pm.
Fortnum & Mason, established in 1707, is definitely one of the 'must see' sights for food lovers. The food hall is very grand and very traditional. Most of the myriad goods on display here are own label. Everything is so attractively displayed it is easy to lose track of time among the jams, jellies, condiments and sauces. Then, of course, there are wines, fresh fruits and vegetables and an excellent selection of cigars. Around 200 cheeses are on offer at any one time, as well as sausages, smoked fish, pâtés, hams, fresh pasta, traditional English pies, and freshly ground coffee. For sweet lovers there are mouth-watering pastries and chocolates. Fortnum & Mason are justly famous for their food hampers as well.

Markets

The concept of the street market is alive and well in London, and there are several that are worth a visit both for local colour and for the variety of goods for sale. The best in central London is Soho's *Berwick Street Market* (Mon-Sat 9am-5pm), known for fruits and vegetables and other assorted produce. For an idea of what an old-fashioned country market was like, *Kingston Market*, Kingston-upon-Thames (Sat 9am-5pm), held in the old village square, is worth a visit. Meats and vegetables as well as ethnic foods are on offer at *Shepherd's Bush Market*, Shepherd's Bush (Mon-Sat 9am-5pm) and *North End Road Market* in Fulham (Mon-Sat 9am-5pm). *Brixton Market* (Mon-Sat 9am-5pm) has a staggering array of Afro-Caribbean produce, a wide selection of meats and excellent fish from around the world. *Portobello Road Market*, a mecca for antique lovers, sells food as well as very good fish. Try *Spitalfields Market* in Spitalfields, EC1, for organically grown vegetables (Sundays only).

Harrod's
Knightsbridge, SW1
071-730 1234
Open Mon, Tues, Sat 10am-6pm, Wed-Fri to 7pm.

Harrod's is one of London's greatest tourist meccas, particularly just before Christmas when the famous white lights are on outside and the crowds thicken to a real throng. Harrod's has a reputation as a supreme retailer of quality, and the food halls are justly famous. You'll find everything here, from the most traditional British fayre to continental and eastern delicacies. If you feel the need for American-style fudge brownies or Pop Tarts, you'll find these here, too, in the supermarket section. For the indulgent, their ready-made hors d'oeuvres are a treat.

And remember, if by some strange chance you don't see what you want, just ask; there is nothing that Harrod's can't get.

Harvey Nichols
109-125 Knightsbridge, SW1
071-235 5000
Open Mon-Fri 10am-7pm, Wed to 8pm, Sat to 6pm.

Until recently, Harvey Nichols, (or Harvey Nicks, as it's band of fashion-conscious aficionados call it) was a fashion shoppers-only establishment, with a good brasserie attached. Since then, the fifth floor has been totally given over to food, so those as dedicated to the most up-to-date Donna Karan as to the most up-to-the-minute designer pasta can shop till they drop under one roof.

The feeling is decidedly hi-tech—stainless steel and polished wood being the order of the day. Delicacies include fruit and vegetables, magnificent cheeses, an excellent assortment of continental meats, and a large selection of gourmet tins and bottles from around the world. There is also a first-rate wine shop, coffee shop, and restaurant.

Partridges of Sloane Street
Sloane St, SW1 - 071-730 0651
Open daily 8.30am-10pm.

Just off Sloane Square, Partridge's, established in 1972, is just as posh as its surroundings. It is not a large shop, but everything is here: exotic fruits and vegetables, wine, freshly baked breads, ground-to-order coffees, and an assortment of ready-made dishes each day such as ratatouille, whole poached cold salmon, several types of quiche, and salmon coulibiac. Also a good selection of cold meats and salamis, caviar, biscuits, and wine. They roast their own chickens daily; this is a good place to buy an impromptu meal.

Le Pont de la Tour
36 Shad Thames, SE1
071-403 4030
Open Mon-Fri 8.30am-10pm, Sat, Sun to 6pm.

Le Pont de La Tour is part of Sir Terence Conran's Thameside 'Gastrodome', 'a collection of food-related activities which appeal to those who are particularly interested in the variety and quality of food and drink.' Incorporated into this grand scheme are a spice and oil shop (a wide array of spices, all ground on the premises, is on display, and a selection of olive oils are open for tasting), a food store offering fresh fruit and vegetables, breads baked at the gastrodome by Neville Wilkins, products from France, Italy, Spain and Britain, and a smoked fish and crustacean shop (choose from smoked trout, smoked salmon, haddock, mackerel, kippers, mussels, clams, and oysters, to name a few). There's a wine shop as well.

The Real Food Store
14 Clifton Rd, Little Venice, W9 - 071-266 1162
Open Mon-Fri 8.30am-7.45pm, Sat to 6pm.
Manager Kevin Gould describes The Real Food Store as 'a healthy grocers'. It's an apt description, for the shop is a cross between a health food and a gourmet food shop, combining the best of both worlds. Amongst the vitamins, smoked tofu and organically grown vegetables, you'll find carefully chosen products from 50 to 60 countries around the world. Lavender honey from Provence, organically grown almonds from Spain, Iranian dried apricots, olives flown in weekly from Provence with a selection available for tasting, Neal's Yard cheeses, olive oils and the shop's own label products like pesto sauces and mincemeat. You won't find anything with refined sugar, artificial colours or flavours, MSG, or E-numbers—which makes

Gould difficult for his suppliers, but they are beginning to catch on. Opening soon is a demonstration kitchen where Britain's best cooks can show their stuff.

Selfridge's
400 Oxford St, W1 - 071-629 1234
Open Mon-Sat 9.30am-7pm, Wed to 8pm.
Unlike the quintessentially English Harrod's and Fortnum & Mason, Selfridge's approach is pancultural. Here you get a taste of food from around the world. There are good ranges of British meats, cheeses, biscuits, mustards and condiments, but perhaps more prominent are the international foods. A huge Lebanese counter sells sweets made with almonds, pistachios, pastry and honey, as well as kibbeh, tabbouleh, and labna; an Indian counter offers a number of curries to take out. Fans of Chinese, Mexican, Italian, Kosher and French food won't be disappointed either. There are usually small titbits on offer to taste before buying.

■ BAKERIES & PATIS-SERIES

Bagatelle
44 Harrington Rd, SW7
071-581 1551
Open Mon-Sat 8am-8pm, Sun to 6pm.
The owners have succeeded in their aim of creating a little piece of Paris in London. Bagatelle is a traditional French pâtisserie and traiteur, pro-

ducing about 50 types of pastries, breads like baguettes, old-fashioned white, walnut, and raisin (all made with French flour), and caters for small and large parties. There are hams, terrines, pâtés and quiches, and mouth-watering ready-made dishes to take away, including their speciality: ballotine of guinea fowl with foie gras mousse.

Cannelle
166 Fulham Rd, SW10
071-370 5573
Open Mon-Fri 8am-8pm, Sat 8.15am-7pm, Sun 9am-7pm.
The minimalist interior of this fashionable pâtisserie is in stark contrast to the lush goodies on offer. Delicious colourful cakes and pastries, croissants, pains au chocolat and rich hand-made chocolates vie for attention with a selection of terrines and salads. A good place to sit and enjoy a pot of tea or a coffee and sample the tempting delicacies. Also at 26 North Audley St, W1, 071-409 0500; 221 Kensington High St, W8, 071-938 1547.

Carmelli Bakeries
128 Golders Green Rd, NW11 - 081-455 3063
Open Mon-Thurs 7am-midnight, Fri 7am-1pm, Sat 6.30pm-Sun midnight.
Carmelli supplies the local community and the whole of the north London Jewish community with breads like cholla, bulka, plain and onion bagels and an assortment of cakes including Madeira and honey. The shop is always packed with people buying huge amounts of bread and cakes which are baked

practically around the clock. They also produce bagels with lox and cream cheese and egg and onion to take out.

Clarke's
122 Kensington Church St, W8 - 071-229 2190
Open Mon-Fri 8am-8pm, Sat 9am-4pm.

Proprietor Sally Clarke, a transplanted Californian, opened the shop as an offshoot of Clarke's, her next-door restaurant. Clarke's breads (delicious creations like Parmesan bread, apricot bread, rye bread with poppy seeds, black olive bread, and walnut bread) first gained the adulation of Londoners in the restaurant; here, you can buy them along with the assortment of English cheeses from Neal's Yard, home-made ginger nut and gingerbread man cookies, rhododendron honey, Whittards teas and Monmouth's coffees—which you can savour in the shop.

Jane Asher's Party Cakes
24 Cale St, SW3 - 071-584 6177
Open Mon-Sat 9.30am-5.30pm.

This shop, run by actress Jane Asher, supplies customers with wonderful whimsical cakes. In addition to the 500 designs on offer, you can design your own cake—as many people do—and the shop will make it up for you to your specifications: from Mickey Mouse to a cake in the shape of a bottle of Château Margaux! The small, delightful tea room

serves croissants, coffee, tea, and light lunches.

Justin de Blank Hygienic Bakery
46 Walton St, SW3 - 071-589 4734
Open Mon-Fri 7.30am-6pm, Sat to 1pm.

The smell of freshly baked bread overwhelms you; the bread is baked downstairs and the odours waft out into the street. The company uses brick ovens which have been in use for over 125 years to bake their wholemeal loaves, cottage loaves, olive bread, cheese and onion bread and brioches. They also make sweets, quiches, and pasta and hot dishes to take out for lunch.

Neal's Yard Bakery
6 Neal's Yard, WC2
071-836 5199
Open Mon-Fri 10am-5.30pm, Sat 10am-5pm.

This little bakery in the heart of Neal's Yard turns out artisan-style breads. Each day they produce large and small whole-wheat loaves, three-seed loaves, and sunflower seed, cheese and herb, olive and garlic, fruit and malt, and sourdough loaves.

Pâtisserie Valerie
44 Old Compton St, W1
071-437 3466
Open Mon-Fri 8am-8pm, Sat to 7pm, Sun 10am-6pm.

A favourite haunt of bohemian art students, tourists and Londoners, Valerie's is packed at any time of the day. Valerie's draws the crowds with its array of French-style pâtisserie in simple surroundings. The gâteaux are

a treat to the eye, and the profiteroles to die for. Also at 215 Old Brompton Rd, SW3, 071-823 9971.

■ CHEESE

Cheeses
13 Fortis Green Rd, N10
081-444 9141
Open Mon-Sat 9.30am-5.30pm, Sun noon-3pm.

You could easily miss this tiny shop in Muswell Hill but seek it out for the vast amount of cheeses in stock (between 110-160 at any given time). They specialise in farm-made cheeses, where the milk is produced and the cheeses made in the same place. Cheeses made from cow's, ewe's, and goat's milk come from all over the world, though Britain and France are most strongly represented.

International Cheese Centre
21 Goodge St, WC2
071-631 4191
Open Mon-Fri 8.30am-6.30pm, Thurs to 7.30pm, Sat 10.30am-6.30pm.

With anything from 350-400 cheeses from ten countries available at any given time, the International Cheese Centre offers an impressive range. English cheeses, mostly farmhouse cheeses, are best represented, with France not far behind. A good proportion are made with unpasteurised milk, and—helpful for strict vegetarians—the list shows which cheeses are made using vegetarian rennet. Also a good selection of biscuits, jams, sauces, and mustards made by small suppliers. Also at Liverpool

St Station, EC2, 071-628 2343.

Jeroboam's

24 Bute St, SW7 - 071-225 2232
Open Mon-Fri 9am-6pm, Sat to 2pm.

This well-loved cheese shop has a loyal following. The focus is primarily French, though there are cheeses (about 130 varieties) from Britain and Ireland, Italy, Spain and even one from Croatia! Also in stock is a selection of French wines, pasta, breads from Sally Clarke and a huge round French country loaf flown over weekly. They make gift boxes and baskets to order. Also at 51 Elizabeth St, SW1, 071-823 5623.

Neal's Yard Dairy

17 Shorts Gdns, WC2
071-379 7646
Open Mon-Fri 9.30am-6pm, Sat to 5.30pm.

It is probably true to say that Randolph Hodgson has single-handedly saved true British and Irish cheeses from virtual extinction. The shop opened in 1979 with Hodgson and his wife Jane Scotter making and selling their own cheese. Now the business has expanded to include farm-produced cheeses from throughout Britain and Ireland. Every cheese in this shop has been handmade by a real person using real milk from real animals, and properly 'brought up' on the premises, turned by hand, and aged to perfection before being offered for sale. Hodgson wants people to know that 'cheeses are living things', and to keep what he calls the 'human

factor' he puts the maker's names on the cheese he or she produces. The vast majority are made from unpasteurised cow's, sheep's and goat's milk. There is also yoghurt, fromage frais and cream, and breads from Sally Clarke.

Paxton & Whitfield

93 Jermyn St, SW1 - 071-930 0259
Open Mon-Fri 9am-5pm, Sat to 4pm.

This delightful, busy shop tucked away in picturesque Jermyn Street has been in business since 1797, and is a must for cheese lovers. Service is friendly, so if you want to taste any of the 250 well looked-after cheeses on offer, just ask. A good selection of hams, meats and pies, as well as coffee, tea, chutneys and pickles is on offer and they offer an excellent mail order service.

■ CHOCOLATE & CONFEC- TIONERY

Charbonnel et Walker

One The Royal Arcade, 28 Old Bond St, W1 - 071-491 0939
Open Mon-Fri 9am-5.30pm, Thurs to 6pm, Sat to 4.30pm.

Who says the British can't make chocolate? These famous chocolates are hand-crafted in Tunbridge Wells, Kent—although there was a French factor when the company was founded in 1875. They are very English in style, with names like English violet and English rose. The

shop, tucked into the Royal Arcade, is well worth a visit.

Rococo

321 King's Rd, SW3
071-352 5857
Open daily 10am-6.30pm.

If you have a genuine passion for real chocolate, visit this shop, set up in 1983 by Chantal Coady, who, while working part-time at Harrod's to finance her art degree, worked at Harrod's chocolate counter. She became hooked and after a great deal of research, opened up shop, wrote the authoritative and up-to-date book *Chocolate: Food of the Gods*, available at the shop, and has become probably the country's foremost expert on chocolate. Here you will find bars of 'cru' chocolate—each type coming from specific beans from specific plantations. The top chocolate, Grand Cru Manjari Pure Criollo 64 percent, made from the rarest cocoa from the Caribbean, has a fruity flavour and a velvety, quick-to-melt feeling in the mouth. An experience not to be missed. There are also hand-made English truffles which even at £20 per lb sell out every day. The shop has an innate sense of fun: some of the gourmet chocolate is wrapped in painted silver to resemble brightly coloured fishes, and there are numerous scary looking chocolate dinosaurs on display.

We have noted only where establishments do not accept credit cards; otherwise assume that all restaurants, hotels and shops will accept the major credit cards.

■ COFFEE & TEA

Algerian Coffee Stores
52 Old Compton St, W1
071-437 2480
Open Mon-Sat 9am-7pm.

Passing through Soho, you'll be aware of this shop from the delicious aroma of freshly ground coffee. This is a real find for coffee and tea addicts, with a large array of exotic coffees and teas from around the world, and they are particularly strong on fruit-flavoured and herbal teas. They also sell Arabic spices, chocolate-covered coffee beans and chocolate-covered figs. A range of cafetières, espresso makers and high-tech Alessi kettles are on display in the front window.

Angelucci Coffee & Tea Merchants
23b Frith St, W1 - 071-437 5889
Open Mon-Sat 9am-5pm, Thurs to 1pm.

This tiny corner shop, still run by the Angelucci family, has stood in the same place for its entire 60-year history. Very little, it appears, has changed in that time, and the shop has a wonderful, old-fashioned atmosphere. Choose from 34 coffees from around the world—Puerto Rico, Angola, Kenya and Haiti, to name a few—or make up your own blend. You can buy as little as a quarter pound.

---

*Find the address you are looking for, quickly and easily, in the **index**.*

Drury Tea and Coffee Co
3 New Row, WC2 - 071-836 1960
Open Mon-Fri 8.30am-6pm, Sat 11am-5pm.

This well-known company has been in London for over 50 years. The shop is bright, friendly and traditional. Teas are from Sri Lanka, India, China, Formosa, and Africa, and there are flavoured teas as well. Try China Rose Tippy Golden Darjeeling, or one of Drury's traditional blends, like English Breakfast. You can buy infusers, teapots and accessories here. Also at 37 Drury Lane, WC2, 071-836 1960; 1-3 Mepham St, SE1, 071-836 2607.

H R Higgins
79 Duke St, W1 - 071-491 8819
Open Mon-Wed 8.45am-5.30pm, Thurs, Fri to 6pm, Sat 10am-5pm.

The company was founded in 1942 by Mr H R Higgins, who wanted to become *the* coffee man in London. It is still in family hands, presided over by Mr Higgins' semi-retired daughter. The coffees come from Colombia, India, Sumatra, Costa Rica, Mexico, Tanzania, Jamaica, Guatemala, Ethiopa, Brazil, and Java. The company now sells tea as well as coffee, and gift packs of both coffee and tea. The people at Higgins are helpful, and in a small tea room downstairs you can sit and enjoy a good cuppa.

Monmouth Coffee Company
27 Monmouth St, WC2
071-836 5272

Open Mon-Sat 9am-6.30pm, Sun 11am-5pm.

Probably the best place to buy coffee in London. In addition to being retailers, the Monmouth Coffee Company imports their own Arabica beans from Colombia, Kenya, Nicaragua, Costa Rica and Papua New Guinea and roasts them on the premises six days a week. They stock 21 types of coffee at all times, each available in medium and dark roasts or a combination. You can sit and sample the varieties at the back of the shop. You can even buy green (unroasted) coffee beans and roast them yourself (instructions provided).

The Tea House
15 Neal St, WC2 - 071-240 7539
Open Mon-Sat 10am-7pm, Sun noon-6pm.

In keeping with this particular patch of Neal Street, The Tea House has a distinctly Oriental air, and if loose tea in a myriad flavours is your bag, stop in. The Tea House stocks teas from China, India, Japan, Sri Lanka, Taiwan, Kenya, Russia, Turkey and South Africa, and has a huge assortment of fruit, flower, and flavoured teas like quince, mango, caramel, or coconut. Upstairs, a good assortment of unusual teapots, including one in the shape of a brontosaurus, greets you.

Twinings
216 Strand, WC2 - 071-353 3511
Open Mon-Fri 9.30am-4.30pm.

Tea lovers shouldn't miss this wonderful, rather eccentric shop. Not only can you find a wide selection of all Twinings' varieties as well as tea towels, tea pots and infusers, there's also a little museum at the back which traces the family firm's long history (it was founded in 1706), of which the company is justly proud.

Whittard of Chelsea Ltd

73 Northcote Rd, SW11
071-924 1888
Open Mon-Sat 8.30am-5.30pm.

Whittards was established in Chelsea in the 1860s. The main branch is now in Clapham's Northcote Road, but the other shops maintain a traditional ambience. Coffee and tea are pretty much on an equal par here, and all their speciality teas and Arabica coffees are imported specially for them. Darjeeling First Flush, a true tea-lover's brew is available here (at £22 per lb at time of writing) and there are fruit teas and commercial blends as well. A range of wacky teapots rounds out the goods on offer. Branches throughout London.

■ FISH, MEAT & GAME

Allen & Co

117 Mount St, W1 - 071-499 5831
Open Mon-Fri 3am-4pm, Sat 5am-1pm.

Established in Mayfair for over two hundred years, and here for one hundred and ten years, this is one of the best butchers in town. The shop is traditional, the meat is first-class. It comes as no surprise to learn that Allen's supplies some of the best kitchens in London, from the nearby Connaught to Le Méridien. But they are equally good with the general public, and will produce any kind of cut needed. Long may they remain on a prime site in the middle of Mayfair, providing the kind of service any community would love.

Bute Street Boucherie

19 Bute St, SW7 - 071-581 0210
Open Mon-Fri 7am-6pm, Sat to 5pm.

A top-class butcher who caters for the choosy tastes of the large local French community with Scotch beef, Dutch veal, English lamb, game, and free-range poultry. French cuts of meat are always possible and they stock a selection of French tinned goods like cassoulet.

Boucherie Lamartine

229 Ebury St, SW1 - 071-730 3037
Open Mon-Fri 7am-7pm, Sat to 2.30pm.

With its baskets of fresh vegetables, herbs and wild mushrooms, this shop has everything to please the eye and the palate. Quintessentially French, it is part of the Albert Roux empire. Cheeses come in twice a week from Paris, as does the bread, though it is actually baked here; even the vegetables, which are always of the finest quality the season has to offer, are flown in from Paris. At the butcher's counter you can buy prepared and tied meats to order, and genuine boudin blanc and boudin noir sausages. Try any of the seasonally-inspired, prepared dishes to take away, like daube of beef and hare cooked in red wine. Pâtisserie is courtesy of Albert Roux. Here is the next best thing to shopping in Paris.

The Caviar House

161 Piccadilly, W1 - 071-409 0445
Open Mon-Sat 9am-10pm.

Though the Danish-owned Caviar House has been operating internationally since 1950, this is a relative newcomer to Piccadilly. The purpose of the shop, which incorporates a brasserie as well, is to show that caviar is not just a luxury product for the rich. On offer is Iranian Sevruga, Oscietre, Beluga, Imperial, Royal Black, and Classic Grey caviars, as well as caviar pressé which has a distinctive taste and texture. Knowledgeable staff answer any questions you might have about caviar, and a full range of complementary goods—wine, vodka, chocolates—is on offer.

Curnick

170 Fulham Rd, SW10
071-370 1191
Open Mon-Sat 8am-5.30pm.

The meat on display here—crown roast of lamb, larded pheasants, oxtail—is top quality and expertly butchered. The beef is of particular interest as it comes from free-range cattle on Curnick's own farm in Colgate, near Horsham, Sussex. This very obliging butcher will prepare any cut of meat you like.

A Dove & Son
71 Northcote Rd, SW11
071-223 5191
Open Mon, Wed 8am-1pm, Tues, Thurs-Sat 8am-5.30pm.
The shop was opened in 1889—and has the document on the wall to prove it. Now third generation, this family butcher offers excellent quality meats, mostly free-range. The lamb comes from Sussex, the beef from Aberdeen, and in season, a wide array of game is available. Home-cooked hams and a good range of cheeses from France and England, all from small suppliers who don't supply supermarkets, add to the attraction.

The Highgate Butchers
76 Highgate High St, N6
081-340 9817

Open Mon-Sat 8am-5.30pm.
Highgate residents are lucky in their top-notch local butcher. This is a small shop, tucked into a row of small shops in Highgate village's picturesque High Street. The meat is all very good quality, and Adrian the butcher can handle special requests for customers, such as crown roast of lamb, boned saddle of lamb and Dutch veal. A long list of speciality sausages is on offer, including the traditional English favourites of Cumberland, alongside the more adventurous lamb and mint, beef and Guiness and (ahem) Jurassic Pork, to name a few—all freshly made on the premises.

Jarvis & Sons
56 Coombe Rd, Kingston-upon-Thames, Surrey
081-546 0989
Open Tues-Thurs 8.30am-5pm, Fri 8am-5pm, Sat to 4pm.

Sausages

An interesting development over the past few years has been the rebirth of interest in the great British 'banger', or sausage. A mere five years ago, most British sausages were indistinguishable from a piece of bread, but all that has changed due to public demand for a return of the brawny, meaty, real thing, and the dedication of numerous butchers. Today, good butchers make their own sausages, which are once again a source of pride and enjoyment. For the best in London try the following: *Simply Sausages*, Hart's Corner, Farringdon St, EC4, (071-329 3227); *Biggles*, 66 Marylebone Lane, W1, (071-224 5937); *O'Hagan's Sausage Shop*, 192 Trafalgar Rd, SE10, (081-858 2833); and finally *Jefferies*, Coombe Rd, Kingston-upon-Thames, (081-547 3588) for best-ever venison sausages.

Easily one of the best fishmongers in the London area, everything here is flappingly fresh, and the staff are very knowledgeable. It is one of the few places where you can get first-rate sushi and sashimi cuts, so Japanese Londoners travel miles to buy here. For the more traditional British taste, there are usually jellied eels on offer. In the autumn, this is the place for game—wild duck, pheasant, quail, grouse, venison and hare.

Lidgate's of Holland Park
110 Holland Park Ave, W11
071-727 8243
Open Mon-Fri 7.30am-6pm, Sat to 5pm.
Lidgate's, established in 1850, is, quite simply, one of the best butchers/charcutiers in the country, and possibly the best in London. The panelled walls, piled high with goodies, are festooned with myriad awards that Lidgate's has earned throughout its 144-year history. All the beef, lamb, pork, chicken and eggs are free range, and proprietor David Lidgate keeps in touch with the farmers who rear the animals that end up at Lidgate's. In addition to the usual cuts of meat comes a touch of the exotic—marinated wild boar cutlets (in season) with sesame, ginger, and olive oil, spatchcocked poussin with paprika and pepper, marinated rump, and a number of beautifully turned noisettes of lamb. Not to be missed are Lidgates famous pies—lamb and leek, steak and kidney, cottage, game, and

coq au vin pie, all freshly prepared daily. They have a good selection of English and French cheeses.

Wholefood Butchers

31 Paddington St, W1
071-486 1390
Open Mon-Thurs 8am-6pm, Fri to 6.30pm, Sat to 1pm.

All the meat sold here is organically produced, which means that it comes from animals that have been allowed to grow, feed, and develop naturally without artificial growth stimulants or hormones; the ground on which they graze must also adhere to strict requirements. The meat is all of the best quality, and in season there is game as well as duck, goose, and turkey eggs.

■ GOURMET SPECIAL-ITIES

I Camisa & Son

61 Old Compton St, W1
071-437 7610
Open Mon-Sat 8.30am-6pm.

It is difficult to see how I Camisa crams so many Italian specialities into such a small area. Inside the shop you could be in Italy, and many of the customers are as fluent in Italian as the owners. Both fresh (different varieties made daily) and dried pasta, and an excellent array of salamis are specialities along with a good range of Italian olive oils, and a small, carefully chosen wine selection. The shop is very busy so you might have to queue, giving a good opportunity to sniff and browse.

Carluccio's

30 Neal St, WC2 - 071-240 1487
Open Mon-Thurs 11am-7pm, Fri 10am-7pm, Sat 10am-6pm.

Owners Antonio and Priscilla Carluccio have done much to elevate Italian cuisine to cult status in the UK in recent years. In their Italian shop you can find the new gastronomic treats they search out on their annual 'hunting trips' to Italy. Delicacies might include fresh cuttlefish pasta, white Alba truffles in brine, and marinated aubergines. Olive oils from all over Italy, a wide selection of Italian cheeses and salamis, cooked pasta dishes and antipasti are available. The lazy cook can choose from set-price, ready-prepared, four-course meals which they can deliver. Antonio Carluccio is a mushroom fiend so if you are in London in September, you'll find a wonderful assortment of hand-picked fungi, gathered from secret sources around the suburban London area, and truffles flown over fresh from Italy.

Finn's

4 Elystan St, SW3 - 071-225 0733
Open Mon-Fri 8am-5pm, Sat 8am-2pm.

A small friendly shop where you are assured of a warm welcome, and top-quality food. A favourite with their loyal customers is honey and mustard sausages. Finn's specialises in food you can take home to eat—always two or three soups, prepared meat, vegetables, and fish dishes. In addition there is a range of jams (made in Yorkshire),

flavoured olive oils and vinegars, chutneys and flavoured mustards made on the premises. They even make their own muesli. If it's a party you have in mind, Finn's can organise that too.

R Garcia & Sons

248-256 Portobello Rd, W11 - 071-221 6119
Open Mon-Sat 9am-6pm, Thurs to 1pm.

Notting Hill's large Spanish community flock to this family-run shop which has been in Portobello Road, and in the same family, since its opening. Manager Rafael Garcia is happy to assist with any questions customers have. This mini supermarket stocks all things Spanish—excellent quality canned fish products, paella rice, Spanish biscuits and turron (a Spanish confectionery), plus a wide selection of Spanish and Italian olive oils, cheeses, proper chorizo and eighteen different kinds of olives!

Lina Stores

18 Brewer St, W1 - 071-437 6482
Open Mon-Sat 6am-5.45pm.

A neighbourhood Italian delicatessen with a warm atmosphere, the shop is full of the scents of fresh basil, sage, parsley and tarragon. They stock De Cecco dried pasta, fresh pasta, home-made ravioli, Italian cheeses and meats, and sacks of various rices for risotto and semolina for polenta. You can have fresh coffee ground to order. Ask to sample the numerous antipasti on display with fresh ciabatta bread.

Mauro's Pasta

229 Muswell Hill Broadway,
N10 - 081-883 2848
*Open Tues-Sat 11am-8pm,
Thurs to 6pm, Sun to 4pm.*

The front window of Mauro's is bright from Mauro's multicoloured fresh pasta—green, yellow, based company recently opened in the Thomas Neal shopping complex. They stock a good range of gourmet goods, including Mauro's pasta sauces, cheeses from France, Italy, Spain and Britain (you can taste before you buy), red, black and white, made with spinach, saffron, beetroot, squid's ink and egg, in various shapes, lengths, and sizes. Mauro also makes dried pasta in unusual flavours, like wild mushroom, carrot, anchovy, and bitter chocolate. To complement them are ten to fifteen different home-made sauces available daily, and home-made antipasti.

Mortimer & Bennett

Unit 14, Thomas Neal's Complex, WC2 - 071-240 6277
Open Mon-Sat 10.30am-7pm.

The Covent Garden branch of the west London-

Ethnic foods

Part of the fun of food shopping in London is discovering the enormous diversity of ethnic foods on offer. If you like *Chinese food*, China-town, just off Leicester Square should not be missed. Here, Loon Moon (071-734 9940) and Loon Fung (071-437 1922) supermarkets, both in Gerrard Street, are worth an extended perusal. If you're into *Thai food*, the best place to go is Talad Thai (081-789 8084). Bayswater's Peking Supermarket (071-243 3006) stocks *Chinese, Vietnamese, Malaysian*, and *Philippine foods*. Brixton is the place for *Caribbean food*, and numerous small shops with a staggering array are found near Brixton station. Try Muji with shops at 38 Shelton St and 26 Great Marlborough St for all things *Japanese*.

---

smoked salmon, pâtés, fresh pasta and agnolotti, coffee, tea, and olive oil. The staff are friendly and eager to help, so don't hesitate to ask questions. Also at 33 Turnham Green Terr, W4, 081-995 4145.

Randall & Aubin

16 Brewer St, W1 - 071-437 3507
Open Mon-Fri 8am-6.30pm, Sat to 6pm.

This shop transports you straight to Provence. Staffed with friendly, knowledgeable people, it is stocked with wonderful produce—cheeses, game, meats, sausages, picture-perfect breads (including sourdough and proper French baguettes), olive oils, vinegars and dressings galore, all beautifully displayed and kept. Their clientele is used to being pampered and aren't disappointed. The pâtés are beautifully turned out—try goose rillettes and duck confit. They make sandwiches to take out.

The Rosslyn Delicatessen

56 Rosslyn Hill, NW3
071-794 9210
Open Sun, Mon 9am-6pm, Tues-Sat 9am-7pm.

Near the High Street, the Rosslyn Delicatessen draws Hampstead's discerning palates. Service is friendly and knowledgeable, and you can taste any of the 100 to 120 cheeses in stock before buying. A small pâtisserie at the back offers an assortment of sweets, continental hams and sausages, a good selection of French, wholemeal and ciabatta breads, jars and bottles of mustards, oils, vinegars, coffee and tea. The lazy gourmet can enjoy several cooked dishes on offer daily, such as chicken roulade and beef Wellington. Christmas hampers are a speciality.

Tom's

226 Westbourne Grove, W11 - 071-221 8818
Open Mon-Sat 8am-8pm, Sun 10am-2pm.

'Tom', who is Tom Conran, son of restaurateur Sir Terence Conran and nephew by marriage of Antonio Carluccio, shows that good taste runs in the family. This busy little aqua-and-blue west London market packs a lot into a small space. The influence is largely Italian, with a selection of single estate Italian olive oils, but France is not left out with a French cheese selection that includes Reblochon and Epoisses. There is a selection of ready-prepared dishes to take out (lemon and parsley gnocchi, char-grilled vegetables with Herbes de Provence and olive oil), and arguably the best gourmet sandwiches in town made with ciabatta.

Le Traiteur Français
142 Notting Hill Gate, W11
071-229 7185
Open Mon-Sat 9am-7pm.

Such places are found everywhere in Paris, but too seldom in London. This is a proper traiteur—they do outside catering—and one of the best places for French regional delicacies like choucroute and large, plump andouillette sausages. A wide assortment of breads includes traditional baguette, breads made with olives, onions, sun-dried tomato, and walnuts, as well as pain rustique. The breads are made in London, by a French baker, using French flour, traditional French techniques, in a French oven—even using French water! Butter croissants and brioche (not, I am assured, made with part-butter and part-margarine) are good. French cheeses are flown over twice a week.

Villandry
89 Marylebone High St, W1
071-487 3816
Open Mon-Fri 9.30am-7pm, Sat to 5pm.

This rustic-looking shop is packed with delicacies

from Britain, the Continent and the US. Try cheeses from Neal's Yard and the famous Philippe Olivier in Boulogne, cakes and bread from Tuscany and Paris or dried beans from Dean & DeLuca. Or chocolates from Valrhona and chillies from Mexico. Wines come exclusively from Paris's Le Grand Filles et Fils who specialise in the smaller producers. Villandry also has a restaurant that is open for lunch during the week.

■ HEALTH FOODS

Neal's Yard Wholefoods Ltd
21-23 Shorts Gdns, WC2
071-379 8553
Open Mon-Wed 9am-7pm, Thurs to 7.30pm, Fri to 7pm, Sat to 7.30pm, Sun 10am-5.30pm.

Holidaying health food (or 'whole food' as it's called in Britain) freaks should go to this spacious, friendly shop, as it has just about everything healthy under one roof. You'll find all sorts of untreated dried fruits and nuts, herbal teas, bags of spices from around the world (very good value), and organic rice, as well as vegeburgers, tofu and vegetarian pies and doorstop loaves of wholemeal bread.

Wholefood
4 Paddington St, W1
071-935 3924
Open Mon 8.45am-6pm, Tues-Fri to 6.30pm, Sat to 1pm.

Part of the same company as Wholefood Butchers, Wholefood echoes the belief in pro-

ducts without artificial colourings, flavours, or chemical additives. Seasonal organically grown vegetables are available, as well as breads, preserves, honeys, free-range eggs, fruit juices, pasta, cheeses and yoghurt and a selection of organic wine. They also stock a good range of books and health care products.

Wild Oats
210 Westbourne Grove, W11 - 071-229 1063
Open Mon-Fri 9am-7pm, Tues 10am-7pm, Sat to 6pm, Sun 10am-4pm.

Wild Oats is a three-storey emporium selling everything for the whole food enthusiast including more than twenty types of bread and twenty two breakfast cereals. They have organic baby food and products for people with food allergies. Recent excitement took over when they found a delicious new wholemeal pasta called Vita-Spelt Angel Hair pasta. Staff, led by the owners Stephen and Jan Mosbacher, are expert and enthusiastic.

■ WINES & SPIRITS

It may seem strange, but London—and all of England, in fact—is an excellent place to shop for wine. Because England has no long tradition of wine production, there is, instead, a long tradition of importing wine. A visit to any of the main wine shop chains (liquor stores are known here as 'off-licences') will reveal an excellent selection of wines from around the world—from California, New Zealand, and South Africa as well as those from France and Italy. The best wine shop chains are Oddbins and Nicolas (look in the telephone directory for your local branch), but for the avid wine fan, the following independent shops are recommended.

Berry Bros & Rudd
3 St James's St, SW1
071-396 9600
Open Mon-Fri 9am-5pm, Sat to 1pm.

Few wine merchants in London have such an 'olde worlde', Dickensian feel as this excellent shop. And that's because Berry Bros & Rudd has stood in this spot since the mid-eighteenth century, and very little in the shop has changed—apart from the wines. In addition to traditional red Bordeaux and Vintage Port, on which Berry Bros is very strong, there is a good selection of wines from California, Australia, and New Zealand. They stock an array of single malt Scotch whiskies, and a fairly large selection of half bottles, too.

Corney & Barrow
194 Kensington Park Rd, W11 - 071-221 5122
Open Mon-Sat 10.30am-8pm.

With its main office in the ultra-conservative City, London's financial district, and a shop in the eternally arty Portobello area, Corney & Barrow attracts wine lovers from a large spectrum with a wide range of top quality wine. For the pin-striped City gent all the Bordeaux first growths and top-name Burgundies (particularly

Leflaive and Matrot), while for the bohemian crowd there is a well-chosen list of house wines and wines from the New World. Corney & Barrow tends to instil loyalty—it's a wine shop with many fans, largely due to friendly, knowledgeable service.

La Vigneronne
105 Old Brompton Rd, SW7
071-589 6113
Open Mon-Fri 10am-9pm, Sat to 7pm.

Master of Wine Liz Berry, the 'vigneronne' herself, is the genius behind this well-stocked little shop. Liz makes frequent travels to the Continent, particularly France, and knows all of the producers' wines—and most of the producers themselves—on a first-name basis. This being the only La Vigneronne, Liz is not confined by size, so if there's something good, but not much of it, she can stock it until it runs out. For this reason, the shop is well worth a visit, as there are wines here that you won't find elsewhere. Speciality areas are Alsace (Marc Kreydenweiss), and the Languedoc-Rousillon region in southern France, about which Liz has written a book.

Wine Cellars
153-155 Wandsworth High St, SW18 - 081-871 3979
Open Mon-Fri 11.30am-8.30pm, Sat 10am-8.30pm.

Canadian David Gleave, a Master of Wine, in charge of the wine buying at Wine Cellars, has a passion for all things Italian, so there is a heavy bias toward Italian wines. But even if not an ardent Italian fan, you'll

find much to please as Australia, New Zealand, France, California and Germany are well represented. And for the foodie, there is a small but well chosen selection of Italian olive oils, like Villa di Vetrice and Tenuta di Capezzana, maize flour for polenta, pasta flour, chestnut flour, and chickpea flour. David Gleave cannot help throwing a few recipes into the wine list, so the shop is worth going to for all sorts of reasons.

GIFTS

Up-market gifts are available at many of the shops listed under sections such as china, leather, jewellery and department stores but this list features some small or specialist shops. In keeping with the times, museums shops have greatly improved beyond the well-stocked postcard counter and we have noted our favourites here. However most museum shops are first-rate so if you have a specialist interest, check in the museum section for more.

Annabel Jones
52 Beauchamp Pl, SW3
071-589 3215
Open Mon-Fri 10am-5.30pm, Sat 10.30am-4pm.

The ground floor has delightful jewellery (look for the star and flower ranges) while the lower level has clever, covetable giftware, which includes glass globes, in blue, green and yellow, used as match strikers. Among the silverware are heart-shaped clocks, dice-shaped paperweight clocks, egg-timers, cigar tubes, miniature gardener's trugs to be used as salt cellars, watering cans, champagne coolers, novelty pepper mills and many other objects, including picture frames, pens and enamel cufflinks.

Asprey
165-169 New Bond St, W1
071-493 6767
Open Mon-Fri 9am-5.30pm, Sat to 1pm.
'It can be done' is the motto of the resident artists so expect to see an extravagant showpiece on display by the entrance, just past the doorman, something like a rock crystal barrel supported by silver gilt rearing horses set with precious stones and priced at £457,500. From the filigreed white wrought-iron trim and arches around the outside to the fifth floor, this is the ultimate gift shop with both tradition and a sense of frivolity. Look for the multi-coloured ostrich wallets, purses and handbags in hot pink, green purple and yellow, jewellery and more.

Barclay & Bodie
7-9 Blenheim Terr, NW8
071-372 5705
Open Mon-Sat 9.30am-5.30pm.
A wonderful source of ideas for gifts, and some delightful boxes to put them into in this elegant St John's Wood shop. Practical as well as pretty, their French Provençal oven-to-tableware consists of hand-painted dishes which come from the oven or microwave and then fit into

woven baskets. They stock all sorts of goods like bags, pewter boxes, initialed ladies handkerchiefs and something we could not resist—miniature tea pots in the shape of garlic heads, cabbages and cauliflower. Just the thing for a collector.

Best of British
27 Short's Gdns, WC2
071-379 4097
Open Mon-Sat 10.30am-7pm.
British-made products which are different and cover a wide price range (anything from 50p up), is the idea behind this shop. There are Nottingham lace runners at £8.25, jewellery made from dyed heather stems, fun, goose-shaped cloth bags at £30 plus hand-blown glass kaleidoscopes, needle-work kits, sweaters, carved house plaques and pretty dishes. Two floors make for rewarding browsing.

Blewcoat School
The National Trust, 23 Caxton St, W1 - 071-222 2877
Open Mon-Fri 10am-5.30pm, Thurs to 7pm.
Inside this early 1800s building, an historic attraction in its own right, are products designed and produced for the National Trust, the body which maintains stately homes, country houses and much of the English countryside. The building was once a school for poor children: look for the little figure of a boy and girl on the back outside wall. The fabric designs of the aprons, tea towels, tea cosies and the printed designs of diaries and paper products are

based on authentic patterns from its properties like palatial Ickworth, in Suffolk, or are specially commissioned like the calico one for Styal, a restored Victorian cotton factory outside Manchester, which makes the cloth itself.

British Museum
Great Russell St, WC1
071-636 1555
There is a book shop, children's shop and a gift shop which sells very good reproductions of hundreds of items from the museum's collection, from Roman earrings to an Egyptian cat.

Cartoon Gallery
44 Museum St, WC1
071-242 5335
Open Mon-Fri 11am-5.30pm, Sat to 4pm.
Humour is a particular national characteristic that frequently doesn't export well, but you'll find the reasonably priced original cartoons irresistible if you have an insight into British humour. Started by Mel Calman, they have a permanent selection as well as changing exhibitions, T-shirts and postcards.

Contemporary Applied Arts
43 Earlham St, WC2
071-836 6993
Open Mon-Sat 10am-6pm, Thurs to 7pm.
A cool, spacious art gallery which gives its artefacts plenty of room. There are fun multi-coloured clocks which resemble collage sculptures showing planes and sputniks and other machines flying around a clock face. Beautifully

For the left-handed

This is a wonderful and eccentric idea and a delight to visit. Their best selling range is scissors, but they also sell items such as a left-handed sickle. Oh yes, and their catalogue opens back to front, that is from the back, or rather the wrong way to a right-handed person... if you see what we mean! *Anything Left-Handed*, 57 Brewer St, W1, 071-437 3910, open Mon-Fri 9.30am-5pm, Sat to 2pm.

crafted and designed vases, pitchers and bowls are on display in the lower floor along with ceramics, jewellery, textiles, glassware, metal, wood work and more.

Crazy Pig Designs
38 Short's Gdns, WC2
071-240 4305
Open Mon-Sat 10.30am-5.30pm.
A Santa Fe ambience is what this shop uses to show off the strange, chunky silver jewellery that craftsmen make on the premises. A skull motif runs through many designs; other oddities include pendants at £117, made from 2,000 year-old prehistoric fossilised mammoth or walrus tusk. Semi-precious stones, garnets, amethysts and haematite's feature in some work. Customers' own designs can be made up.

The Egyptian House
77 Wigmore St, W1
071-935 9839
Open Mon-Sat 9.30am-6.30pm, Thurs to 7.30pm.
From the hieroglyphs on the ornately decorated façade to the turquoise highlights of many of the hand-crafted figures, this colourful shop is a showplace for products from Egypt, including hand-knotted silk carpets for £1,000. Among the crafts represented are ceramics, weaving, embroidery, brass hammering and wood-inlay techniques. Fun products include colour-your-own papyrus kits and little Egyptian cat statues for £8.

Equinox
78 Neal St, WC2 - 071-497 1001
Open Mon-Sat 9am-7pm, Sun 10am-6pm.
This astrology shop has the sun, moon and stars as well as star signs imprinted on teapots, mugs, glassware, aprons, keys rings, T-shirts, candle-holders, candles, paper party napkins, cards and a wide selection of gift ware. There are lots of posters of the sky at night and an extensive range of astrology books here. A bright, modern shop, it can prepare astrological charts while you wait.

Eximious
10 West Halkin St, SW1
071-235 7828
Open Mon-Fri 9.30am-5.30pm, Sat 10am-4pm.
This beautiful shop looking like an elegant private drawing room contains a first-class collection of gifts and accessories for your home. By appointment to The Prince of Wales they sell a wide collection from lacquered wooden planters to architectural bookends. They can monogram items for you, and will also produce personalised enamel boxes with your house, favourite horse, cat or just a message. Their mail order catalogue is a delight to browse through.

Gallery Shop
Crafts Council, 44a Pentonville Rd, N1 - 071-278 7700
Open Tues-Sat 11am-6pm, Sun 2-6pm.
Well away from the centre, this shop has a constantly changing range of contemporary crafts created by artists who make sculptures, design scarves, carve wood and produce ceramics, pottery and glass. The hand-made jewellery is wonderful but it is possible to buy hand-made automata too. It is part of the National Centre for the Crafts and also houses an information centre, exhibitions space and café.

Graham & Green
7 Elgin Crescent, W11
071-727 4594
Open Mon-Fri 10am-6pm, Sat 9.30am-6pm.
Eye-catching windows in the middle of the Portobello district attract passers-by into this shop which is crammed full of original items. Watch for items like a cast-metal fast car at £40, planters and candle-sticks.

Halcyon Days

14 Brook St, W1 - 071-629 8811
Open Mon-Fri 9.15am-5.30pm, Sat 9.30am-5.30pm.

Charming enamel boxes are decorated with themes like Victorian flowers from the Victoria and Albert Museum archives or specific designs made for anniversaries or celebrations. Some have messages like 'Thank you'; others display sporting pursuits. A recent Christmas box, (£65), showed a village church and old-fashioned carol singers. The enamel is put on copper in Bilston, Shropshire and each box has a certificate of authenticity. Antique enamel boxes and other wares such as pot-pourri baskets, mirrors, spill vases and photo frames fill the shelves and cabinets.

Janet Fitch

25 Old Compton St, W1
071-287 3789
Open Mon-Sat 11am-7pm, Sun 1pm-6pm.

A showcase for British craftsmen, making charming, fun jewellery. A pair of unusually wrought heart earrings by Julie Cook are £26. Janet Fitch has compiled a book called *The Art and Craft of Jewellery* and the products display some of the techniques described using glass, ceramics, leather, acrylics, semi-precious stones, beads and wooden pendants. There are velvet hats, collage wall-hangings, ties, scarves and cards. A third shop has opened in Covent Garden's Thomas Neal's Yard complex. Also at 2 Percy St, W1, 071-580 8710.

London Transport Museum

The Piazza, WC2 - 071-379 6344
Open daily 10am-6pm.

The London Underground map is the most popular selling item, but the reproductions of the best transport posters of previous decades make charming souvenirs; the originals were works of art commissioned regularly to promote the destinations along the route.

Monograms & More

Whiteleys, 151 Queensway, W2 - 071-792 3394
Open Mon-Sat 10am-8pm, Sun noon-6pm.

Thanks to its computerised embroidery service, this shop promises to put initials, names or messages on customers' own items while they shop. It stocks its own cheerful array of bags, caps, towels, T-shirts, sweatshirts, robes and pet accessories to which it can add embroidery. It costs £5 for up to seven letters, one inch high. Lots of shops in the Whiteleys complex help you pass the time while they complete the embroidery.

Museum Store

37 The Market, The Piazza, Covent Garden, WC2
071-240 5760
Open Mon-Sat 10.30am-6.30pm, Sun 11am-5pm.

Museums from all over the world have some of their products on sale at this first floor shop making its collection of gifts very eclectic; they even have reproductions of Vatican Library illuminated manuscripts. Also at 50

Beauchamp Pl, SW3, 071-581 9255; 4a-5a Perrins Ct, NW3, 071-581 9255.

National Portrait Gallery Shop

St Martin's Pl, WC2
071-306 0055
Open Mon-Fri 10am-5pm, Sat to 6pm, Sun noon-6pm.

A wonderful array of postcards with the faces of the famous and historic people featured in the gallery make this shop a must, along with such giftware as Henry VIII paperweights, bookmarks depicting his wives and finely published art calendars and address books.

Naturally British

13 New Row, WC2
071-240 0551
Open Mon-Sat 11am-7pm, Sun noon-5pm.

Hand-made products from crafts people all over Britain are packed into the two floors of this busy shop. Even the gangway rope on the staircase can be made to order. Hand-painted fire screen figures, brightly coloured wooden flower boxes and key cupboards, Victorian-style night-gowns, Welsh tapestries and love spoons and personalised pub signs are among the shop's wide range.

Neal Street East

5 Neal St, WC2 - 071-240 0135
Open Mon-Sat 10am-7pm, Sun noon-6pm.

More like a bazaar than a shop with everything from the Orient, from cards and notebooks to kimonos, folk craft, brightly coloured bed coverings, cloth bags, scarves, I Ching books and sculptures of Buddha.

Nina Campbell

9 Walton St, SW3 - 071-225 1011

Open Mon-Fri 9.30am-5.30pm, Sat 10am-4pm.

A delightful shop well worth a visit for its mixture of goods, many of which you'll be tempted to buy for your own home as well as for gifts. Go particularly for objects covered in her heart and sprig motif, which include both china and soft goods like small and large boxes. You can also get small tables here and brass table lamps complete with her special shades.

Ogetti

135 Fulham Rd, SW3 071-581 8088

Open Mon-Sat 9.30am-6pm.

High-tech or unusually crafted items are on display in the minimalist atmosphere. Expect the unexpected: a domino set with Picasso decorations, a letter opener inlaid with pear, cherry, apple and other fruit woods, swizzle stick spoons and beautiful multi-coloured glass tumblers.

Past Times

164 Brompton Rd, SW1 071-581 7616

Open Mon-Sat 9.30am-5.30pm.

The interesting theme behind this shop's products is that all eras of history are represented whether it is a medieval manuscript jigsaw puzzle or a compact disc of Gregorian chants. A heraldic woollen sweater is £50. Laid out in chronological order, the varied

giftware includes tapestry kits, jewellery, card games, calendars, satchels, candles and cards.

Royal Academy of Arts

Burlington House, Piccadilly, W1 - 071-223 0091

Open Mon-Sat 9am-6pm.

You'll find good gifts here, most of them unique to the Royal Academy. They commission work in connection with their exhibitions and also have a very good range of designs made by the Royal Academicians. Their ceramic plates and bowls are excellent.

The Spotted Duck Mk II

117-119 Fulham Rd, SW3 071-589 0369

Open Mon-Sat 10.30am-5.30pm.

Jam-packed with those special little buys that some gift shops have a knack of finding, this store's shelves are overflowing with miniature cars, unusually-patterned boxer shorts, stuffed toys, fragrant candles, pretty bottles, picture frames, massage balls, magnifying glasses and all sorts of knickknacks. The original shop is in Salisbury, which may explain the unusual name.

Tate Gallery Shop

Millbank, SW1 - 071-887 8000

Open Mon-Sat 10am-5.50pm, Sun 2-5.50pm.

The most popular selling item is its visual pun 'Tate by Tube' poster, showing a tube of paint spelling out the name of this art gallery and promoting travelling by London underground to

get there. From a 5p bookmark to a framed print around £200, this spacious shop has wonderful art publications and fun art T-shirts.

These Foolish Things

Whiteley's, 151 Queensway, W2 - 071-792 1121

Open Mon-Sat 10am-8pm.

Alice in Wonderland tea cosies, stained-glass hanging window decorations, small flowery boxes, pewter frames, scented candles, painted cat doorstops, Woods of Windsor scents, fine art address books—the list of knickknacks is inspiring.

Tiffany & Co

25 Old Bond St, W1 071-409 2790

Open Mon-Sat 10am-5.30pm.

They have a wonderful stock of jewellery in their three-storey shop, and on two floors a select choice of leather and silver gifts, scarves, picture frames, clocks as well as handsome silver cutlery, china and crystal. You can find gifts in all price ranges from a matching sterling silver T-clip retracting pencil at £45 to the fabulous and fabulously priced.

Victoria & Albert Museum Shop

Cromwell Rd, SW7 071-938 8500, Mail order 071-938 8623

Open daily 10am-5.50pm (Mon noon-5.50pm).

With its spacious room—it is in the woodwork gallery—and its large changing stock, this is a good gift-hunting place especially for exclusive items made to coincide with exhibitions, like that on Pugin, as well as its limited edition products matching new galleries, such as the recently opened glass gallery. There are excellent books on decorative arts and even a little Crafts Council shop with a wide range of crafts including hand-made jewellery.

HOME

The Conran Shop

Michelin House, 81 Fulham Rd, SW3 - 071-589 7401
Open Mon-Sat 9.30am-6pm, Tues 10am-6pm, Sun noon-5pm.

Some consider this the most exciting shop in London, both for its wide range of specially commissioned merchandise and for its location. You'll find it inside the fantastic art nouveau building that was once the headquarters of the Michelin tyre company. It's impossible to miss, with its motoring motifs and stained-glass windows. As the shop's buyers travel extensively there are antiques and curious artefacts from all over the world, like a 150-year old ceremonial elephant from Rajistan for £12,500. As the shop works with contemporary designers and manufacturers, much of the furniture collection is exclusive to them. They also stock more than 200 fabric designs, exclusive bed-linen and garden furniture.

The Dining Room Shop

62-64 White Hart Lane, Barnes, SW13 - 081-878 1020
Open Mon-Fri 10am-5.30pm, Sat 10.15am-5.30pm.

Just the shop to come to for a wonderful selection of antique tables, chairs, glass, china, table linen, very pretty lace and cutlery. In fact everything you need for the most elegant of dining rooms.

The General Trading Company

144 Sloane St, SW1
071-730 0411
Open Mon-Sat 9am-5.30pm, Wed to 7pm.

A place where you can find every kind of pretty household object from a candle-stick to a library pole holder with antiqued-hide covering, this is an institution among the local fashionable 'Sloane Ranger' set and still the top place for a traditional wedding list for young brides. All the departments—antiques, upholstery and furniture, Oriental, garden, stationery, kitchen, linen, cutlery, china, glass—cater for shoppers with an appreciation of good design. The shop holds all four Royal Warrants (a Royal Warrant is granted by the Queen, the Queen Mother, the Duke of Edinburgh or the Prince of Wales), and is only one of eleven other companies in the country to share this honour.

Habitat

196 Tottenham Ct Rd, W1
071-631 3880
Open Mon-Sat 9.30am-6pm, Thurs to 7.30pm.

Still a good all-round place for well-designed, patterned chairs, tables, chairs and sofas, along with dinner services, throw rugs, blinds, bed linen, lamps and cutlery.

Heal's

196 Tottenham Ct Rd, W1
071-636 1666
Open Mon-Wed 10am-6pm, Thurs to 8pm, Fri to 6.30pm, Sat 9am-6pm.

With three floors of stylish, modern furniture and a wide range of imaginative and exciting decorating accessories, Heal's seems out on a limb on this busy through street dominated by computer and high-tech shops, but it is a must for visitors who appreciate good craftsmanship. The company began as bedmakers and its hand-made beds are still famous and sought after. Its reputation for being a fore-runner in the arts and crafts movement in the 1920s is maintained today: Heal's is a good place for one-offs, exclusive designs and new ideas.

India Jane

140 Sloane St, SW1
071-730 1070
Open Mon-Sat 10am-6pm, Wed to 7pm.

Everything here (with the very odd exception) is imported from India, hence its name. It's a colourful, good collection of both

---

Remember that if you carry a non-British passport, you are entitled to a full refund of the **value-added tax** *(VAT). Stores vary in the minimum you must spend in order to claim this. See* Basics *for details.*

And also...

One of those shops where you walk in and say 'Why hasn't anyone done this before?' V V Rouleaux aka Annabel Lewis has searched through the shops of Paris and New York to come up with the greatest selection of *ribbons*, *trimmings* and *braids* you're ever likely to see. It's a veritable treasure-house for designers, milliners, stylists and ordinary members of the public after delightful specialist ribbons. V V Rouleaux, 201 New King's Rd, SW6, 071-371 5929 and 23 King's Rd, SW3, 071-370 4413, (Mon-Sat 10am-6pm).

If you thought *stencilling* was hard, then just make your way to *The Stencil Store* at 91 Lower Sloane St, SW1, 071-730 0728 (Mon-Sat 9.30am-5.30pm) and you'll be inspired to put paint to stencil and convert your room into an architectural haven, or an English garden. Chests of drawers can be transformed overnight. Here they sell stencil designs, paints and sticks, books, sponging kits and special paint effects. If you're still not sure, they run a morning course outside London at *Chorley Wood*, telephone 0923-285577 for details.

furniture and small objects, linens and rugs, planters and china.

Jerry's Home Store
163-167 Fulham Rd, SW3
071-225 2246
Open Mon-Fri 10am-6pm, Sat 9.30am-6pm.

The look of stylish comfortable American homes appealed to Jeremy Sacher so much that he decided to introduce the look to London in this airy store where popcorn makers, cookie jars, brightly coloured cups and plates make a cheerful display. The large room downstairs has a New England feel, from the expansive sofas, gleaming wooden tables, lamps and accessories.

Much of the merchandise is made in America.

Laura Ashley
256 Regent St, W1 - 071-437 9760
Open 9.30am-6pm, Thurs to 7pm.

The company prides itself on holding on to their customers from childhood to grand-motherhood, designing patterns which mix and match with each other in the distinctive Laura Ashley style (although this is no longer confined to the original country flowers look). A new design team was brought in recently to celebrate the company's fortieth anniversary and has helped revamp the look further.

Muji
26 Gt Marlborough St, W1
071-494 1197
Open Mon-Sat 10am-6.30pm, Thurs, Fri to 7pm.

Where to list this fascinating store was a problem, as it stocks all manner of Japanese-style things, from futons to minimal-designed Japanese clothing, from shrimp rice crackers to wonderful household goods and stationery. Also at 38 Shelton St, WC1, 071-379 1331.

Nice Irma's
46 Goodge St, W1 - 071-580 6921
Open Mon-Fri 10am-6pm, Thurs to 7pm, Sat to 5pm.

A wonderfully cheerful shop on two levels with well-priced objects and furnishings for the home such as hand-spun wool rugs from India, from £13 to £70, brightly coloured quilts from £27 to £50, decorative ceramics, unusual candle-holders and candelabra, even prettily patterned dressing gowns for under £35. Lots of knickknacks, many from the Far East join the jewellery, glassware and stylish paper flowers.

Les Olivades
7 Walton St, SW1 - 071-409 2938
Open Mon-Fri 9.30am-5.30pm, Sat 10am-5pm.

A shop that gives you an instant feeling of summer, Les Olivades is all about Provence, with fabrics for curtains (which they can have made up) or table cloths, painted furniture, clothes, fabric shoes and all manner of pretty dried flowers, bags and accessories.

Purves & Purves

83 Tottenham Ct Rd, W1
071-580 8223
*Open Mon-Sat 9am-6pm,
Thurs to 7.30pm.*

A delightful general shop which sells contemporary furniture and furnishings run by a husband-and-wife team who enjoy their buying trips—and it shows in the collection of merchandise. Particularly eye-catching are some of their definitely different lamps, such as green resin tree lamp made in France for £85.

■ CHINA & GLASS

Bridgewater

739 Fulham Rd, SW6
071-371 9033
Mon-Fri 10am-5.30pm, Sat to 5pm.

Spongeware is an old technique of decorating pottery which Emma Bridgewater has revived for her own charmingly-shaped and designed English china. Everything from delightful small mugs for small children to large pasta and salad dishes in a variety of colours. You can have pieces personalised with a name or commission pieces. She also sells through other small and large shops, like Harvey Nichols, which often carry two or three designs exclusive to them. Twice a year, in January and the summer, they have good sales of seconds.

Chinacraft

71 Regent St, W1 - 071-734 4915
*Open Mon-Sat 9am-6pm,
Thurs to 7.30pm.*

Chinacraft makes a full range of dinner service and crystal ware which is stocked in other large London shops. For novelty and souvenir items which range from life-sized china dogs to the Lilliput Lane range of houses, try their main shop. Branches throughout London.

Contemporary Ceramics

7 Marshall St, W1 - 071- 437 7605
Open Mon-Sat 10am-5.30pm, Thurs to 7pm.

Since 1960, the members of the Craft Potters Association have had a large, bright gallery in which to sell their distinctive highly original pieces, from everyday domestic ware to collectable statuary, pots and vases and some jewellery. There are changing exhibitions and a large stock of books and magazines on ceramics, plus some potters' tools. The floral bowls and mugs at £13 by Clive Davies, a tall bird jug at £49 by Molly Curley, and odd, primitive conversation pieces by Peter Clough were eye-catching, but the whole wide-ranging display makes excellent browsing,

The Glasshouse

21 St Alban's Pl, N1
071-359 8162
Open Mon-Sat 10am-6pm.

The Glasshouse used to be in Covent Garden, but the four designers—Annette Meech, David Taylor, Fleur Tookey and Chris Williams have now moved to Islington where they continue to produce delightful original glass, selling only their own work.

The range goes from repeated designs like their glass shells at around £5 and napkin rings at £6,50 to the most splendid one-off pieces for hundreds of pounds. At the gallery and shop you can actually see them blowing which adds to the experience. They also undertake restoration work.

Lawleys

154 Regent St, W1 - 071-734 2621
Open Mon-Sat 9.30am-6pm.

At ground level, this appears an average-sized shop with china, jewellery and novelties like the Swarovski glass animals, but go up the curving staircase, for here the premises stretch on and on displaying all the leading china manufacturers and a cutlery corner.

Reject China Shop

134 Regent St, W1 - 071-434 2502
*Open Mon-Sat, 9am-6pm,
Thurs to 8pm.*

When this shop began some 35 years ago, a lot of 'seconds' were being released by the china manufacturers, so the Beauchamp Place shop was started as a centre for bargain hunters. Today, although the company retains the name, their shops stock mostly high quality china, though still retaining a seconds area, clearly distinguished both by labels and a more cluttered display. There are lots of amusing items, too, like teapots on legs. Also at 34 Beauchamp Pl, SW3, 071-581 0733.

The Tea House

15 Neal St, WC2 - 071-240 7539
Open Mon-Sat 10am-7pm, Sun noon-6pm.

Astonishingly shaped teapots on the upper level attract visitors as much as the wide variety of tea on the ground floor. Sherlock Holmes looking for a clue, a couple dancing, a snowman, a cottage—any subject can inspire a teapot maker. Brightly coloured plain-shaped teapots make an appearance as do fortune-telling teacups and books.

Thomas Goode

19 South Audley St, W1 071-499 2823
Open Mon-Sat 9.30am-5.30pm.

Not only does the outside look like a grand townhouse with marble columns and two blue and white urns in the niches, it feels wonderfully traditional inside as well, reflecting its status as an institution for gentrified shopping since 1845. There is a flamboyance along with tradition and unexpected nooks to explore through the various rooms, like tables decked out with a wide array of coloured glassware and the antique knickknacks corner where old mother-of-pearl handles are now attached to make-up brushes. This is an exclusive shop; even the hard-back catalogue which is more like a coffee table book, costs £25.

Villeroy & Boch

203 Regent St, W1 - 071-434 0240/1239
Open Mon-Sat 10am-6pm.

Rich colours used within distinctive designs have been the trademark of this firm's tableware since its 1748 formation. The company, which gives out reliable information as to how long it will continue with a particular range (useful if you're purchasing a whole dinner set), also stocks delightful items like their Paloma Picasso range. Downstairs there are rejects, with up to 30 percent off some bargain items.

Waterford Wedgwood

158 Regent St, W1 - 071-734 7262
Open Mon-Sat 9am-6pm, Thurs to 7pm.

Stretching an impressive length while remaining on one level, the shop's name says it all and stocks all the ranges produced by these two famous manufacturers. At Christmas, it decorates its trees with its beautiful cups and saucers. You can get inspiration from their tables laid out for different occasions, including a whole dinner party.

Wilson and Gill

137 Regent St, W1 - 071-734 3076
Open Mon-Sat 9.30am-6pm, Thurs to 7pm.

Art on your everyday table was the intention of the original Philipp Rosenthal in 1900, an ideal still pursued by the firm which submits designs to a jury of independent judges before making delightful pieces with amazing motifs like The Voyage of Marco Polo or Medusa, plus limited editions. The name Rosenthal is writ large outside this shop which bears its original name of Wilson and Gill, a famous jewellers which became the first shop allowed to have a Rosenthal outlet.

■ FABRICS, FURNISHINGS & INTERIOR DESIGN

THE ENGLISH STYLE

Before World War II, Paris and New York were the most important centres for interior decoration. But for the last few years, it has been London that people flock to for inspiration. In 1972 Mrs Munro (see below) helped organise an exhibition in Paris called *Le Style Anglais*, which consolidated the English approach to interior design. Unlike much European design which is often very formal, it is based both on practical consideration (that is comfort and ease is taken into consideration) and on the eternally beautiful English style as epitomised by the chintzes and antiques found in English country houses. From being an exclusive look, it can now be seen everywhere, a move helped by the early popularity of Laura Ashley. But English design is not just chintz and grand country houses. We have included shops that follow a totally different style also. Many of the shops we recommend here undertake commissions and offer an interior decorating service; others may just sell wallpapers and fabrics.

Barclay & Bodie
7-9 Blenheim Terr, NW8
071-372 5705
Open Mon-Sat 9.30am-5.30pm.

You could be in somebody's drawing room in this excellent shop, apart from the odd shower curtain decorated with Greek and Roman statues in view. They stock a certain amount of Victorian antiques here, but this is mainly a shop for well-designed accessories for the home, from a Parisian navy gingham cotton frame for pictures to candle sconces, padded hangers and rugs.

Cath Kidston
8 Clarendon Cross, W11
071-221 4000
Open Mon-Fri 10.30am-5.30pm, Sat 11am-4pm.

As an interior decorator Cath achieves an unfussy, bright look, based on her own taste for unusual fabrics and wallpaper designs and a love for 1950s' simplicity. She recently opened this shop in a villagey corner of posh Holland Park, where renovated tables, chairs and dressers of her favourite era are sold along with the interesting fabrics and artefacts she discovers on her visits to antique and bric-à-brac markets. Expect to find mirrors, ironing boards, duvet covers, children's furniture and more in this fun shop.

Colefax & Fowler
39 Brook St, W1 - 071-493 2231
Open Mon-Fri 9.30am-1pm, 2pm-5.30pm.

When the firm started in the 1930s, John Fowler took the romantic spirit of late eighteenth-century decoration as his inspiration. Now the famous Colefax and Fowler firm is located in a Georgian house in Mayfair which has survived modernisation and which shows off the great swags of fabrics and floral wallpapers and antique furniture to perfection. The firm is famous for creating that certain English style so characteristic of the large English country houses of the well-to-do.

David Hicks
Albany, Piccadilly, W1
071-437 2499
By appointment only.

Overseas visitors who are planning to live in London can no longer head for the David Hicks shop to browse for ideas, for this internationally acclaimed interior designer now only runs a decorating service, transforming houses into comfortable, elegant residences.

Designers Guild
267 and 277 King's Rd, SW3
071-351 5775
Open Mon-Fri 9.30am-5.30pm, Wed, Sat 10am-5.30pm.

Every decorative device combined with stunning, often dramatic wallpapers and curtain materials make this an inspiring showroom to visit. N°277 King's Road offers the exclusive Designers Guild range of fabrics and wallpapers, while the sister shop stocks cushions and ceramics as well. They offer a complete designer service.

Global Village
247/249 Fulham Rd, SW3
071-376 5363
Open Mon-Sat 9am-6pm.

Encouraging trade between the West and third-world countries, Global Village has a large collection of accessories for the home with exotic origins. You'll find gold-sunburst wall hangings, rattan furniture, birdcages, linen cushions and beaten silver photograph frames here in a delightful mix.

Jane Churchill
135 Sloane St, SW1
071-730 6379
Open Mon-Sat 9.30am-5.30pm, Tues 10am-5.30pm, Wed 9.30am-7pm.

Wallpapers and fabrics, many based on old designs which are re-coloured, create a co-ordinated range complete with pleated lampshades, towels, bed linen and many accessories to match.

Joanna Wood
48a Pimlico Rd, SW1
071-730 5064
Open Mon-Fri 10am-6pm, Sat to 4pm.

A very English look is apparent in the prettily finished objects—hat boxes, stationery and desk accessories, lamp-shades, miniature china boxes, table mats and coasters, freeze-dried rose heads with pungent aromas, plant pots, visitors' books and cushion covers. The furniture and fabrics are equally distinctive in this shop which offers an interior decorating service.

Mary Fox Linton
239 Fulham Rd, SW3
071-622 0920
Open Mon-Fri 9am-5.30pm.

Her own designs are translated into fabrics, wallpapers and carpets to achieve that completely together English look for a house.

Mrs Monro Ltd

16 Motcomb St, SW1
071-235 0326
Open Mon-Fri 9.30am-5.30pm, Fri to 5pm.

Started in 1927 by Geraldine Monro, the company is now run by her daughter, Jean Monro, whose particular love is eighteenth-century taste. Her most famous work was the decorating and furnishing of N°1 Royal Crescent, Bath (see *Bath*). But mostly Jean Monro and director John Lusk work privately, creating delightful designs all over the world based on the English country house look with antique furniture, china, furniture and period chintzes. Although primarily an interior design firm, they also have some beautiful chintzes on show, the designs for which they have researched and discovered in old books and old houses. They then have them made up either for private clients, or for their showroom.

Osborne & Little

304-308 King's Rd, SW3
071-352 1456
Open Mon-Fri 9.30am-5.30pm, Wed and Sat 10am-5.30pm.

A strongly traditional range of floral and striped wallpapers, mostly designed in England, make this a first stop for Londoners planning to re-decorate their homes along classic lines using good quality materials.

Sanderson

112-120 Brompton Rd, SW3
071-584 3344
Open Mon-Sat 10am-6pm.

Recently opened at this location, the Sanderson name is famous for a particular 'quality' look in their fabrics and wall-papers. On two floors, they also stock rugs, accessories and furniture.

The Shaker Shop

25 Harcourt St, W1
071-724 7622
Open Mon-Sat 10am-6pm.

Admiration of the totally simple and practical style of the furniture of the Shakers in America—a religious group who broke away from the Quakers in the late 1700s—led Liz Shirley and Tim Lamb to open their first shop selling chairs, tables and other products made at the Shaker Workshops in Massachusetts. The unusual and definitely non-English sight of chairs hung on the wall first brought curious customers into the shop. So many were impressed by the pure lines and craftsmanship of the trestle and candle tables, the wall cupboards and even the peg rails that there is now a second shop where they also sell fabrics. Also at 322 King's Rd, SW3, 071-352 3918.

Simon Horn Furniture

117/121 Wandsworth Bridge Rd, SW6 - 071-731 1279
Open Mon-Sat 9.30am-5.30pm.

The French bateau boat is not a design particularly well known over here, but it will be if Simon Horn has anything to do with it. He designs these delightful wooden beds which are hand-built in materials like solid cherrywood. If you have a children's room where you want something special, try his child's *bateau lit* that serves as cot, child's bed and then sofa (in that order) at £980.

Timney Fowler

388 King's Rd, SW3
071-352 2263
Open Mon-Fri 9.30am-6pm, Sat 10am-6.30pm.

First of all this textile husband-and-wife designer team brought strong black-and-white graphics and designs to the London scene. Now colour is used for the fabrics, cushions, wraps, scarves and boxes in equally dramatic images, influenced by medieval stained glass, rococo panache, or even the crown jewels. Devotees of their signature range of Roman emperors' head and mythological scenes will find these are still available. Quirky sidelines are popular such as the venture with Linda McCartney to produce scarves displaying images from Linda's photography.

Viaduct

1-10 Summers St, EC1
071-278 8456
Open Mon-Fri 9.30am-6pm, Sat 10.30am-2pm.

James Mair, a former architect, stocks 'cutting-edge' furniture in his showroom on the ground floor of an old print warehouse in Clerkenwell. In the huge well-lit space he sells Martin Ryan's Romany chair with splayed steel legs and birch laminate seat, £125, Philippe Starck's door handles at £13 a pair and lights and other accessories by top

European and English designers.

KITCHEN-WARE

David Mellor
4 Sloane Sq, SW1 - 071-730 4259
Open Mon-Sat 9.30am-5.30pm.
Devoted to the well-appointed kitchen, the ground floor stocks glassware from Poland, Finland, Spain as well as English Dartington. Downstairs are clay cooking pots, bright blue earthenware, corkscrews, aluminium moulds and other items to make your cooking life easy and enjoyable. The shop also has bottles of special olive oils and jars of sauces, aromatic olives, olive pesto and sun-dried tomatoes.

Divertimenti
44-45 Wigmore St, W1
071-935 0689
Open Mon-Fri 9.30am-6pm, Sat 10am-6pm.
Full of people looking for the perfect gadget, the best pot to cook in, pretty ochre-toned earthenware, the right coffee-pot, small items like white net coverings for keeping food, this is an atmospheric shop with browsers roaming the two floors of pots, plates, cookery books and culinary miscellania. Also at 139-141 Fulham Rd, SW3, 071-581 8065.

Elizabeth David Cook Shop
3 North Row, The Market, WC2 - 071-836 9167
Open Mon-Fri 10.30am-8pm, Sat, Sun 11am-5pm.

Le Creuset pots and pans in yellow, orange, blue and dark green are displayed in abundance on the small ground floor. There are more up the wooden stairs where all the kitchen gadgets, coffee makers, jelly moulds, icing equipment and kitchen necessities are kept along with a small selection of cookbooks, some by the influential cook herself.

Richard Dare
93 Regents Park Rd, NW1
071-722 9428
Open Mon-Fri 9.30am-6pm, Sat 10am-5pm.
This kitchenware shop may seem small but it carries a very good professional range of kitchenware, suspended from the ceiling, piled high on shelves and stacked on the floor. Good earthenware pottery alongside asparagus steamers and fish kettles and a delightful ambience in this residential neighbourhood.

LIGHTING

Aktiva Systems Ltd
8 Berkley Rd, NW1
071-722 9439
By appointment.
Aktiva is part of the very successful, small design company John Herbert Designs (at the same address) and Aktiva is their furniture and lighting design arm. Spare and architectural, the elegant lighting appeals to private clients as well as architects and designers. Their speciality is low voltage spotlight and decorative wall lights.

Artemide
17 Neal St, WC2 - 071-240 2346/2552
Open Mon-Fri 10am-6pm, Sat 10.30am-5pm.
Home and office lighting and furniture for lovers of Italian style. Minimalist, strict and simple features, elegant and considered details make for expensive lighting.

Besselink & Jones
99 Walton St, SW3 - 071-584 0343
Open Mon-Fri 10am-5.40pm, Sat to 4pm.
The clutter of lamps in the window indicates how jam-packed the shop is with antique lamps, handmade lampshades and many new lamps, designed in traditional style. The sign says 'wonderful lamps'. The firm operates at Harvey Nichols although the vintage lamps are mostly at this shop.

Christopher Wray's Lighting
600 King's Rd, SW6
071-736 8434
Open Mon-Sat 9.30am-6pm.
Christopher Wray stocks an amazing collection of one-offs and a lot of Tiffany-style lamps. Prices vary, depending on whether the item is reproduction or not.

London Lighting Company
135 Fulham Rd, SW3
071-589 3612
Open Mon-Sat 9.30am-6pm.
Forty manufacturers from all over Europe are represented in this huge gallery devoted to lamps and lights in the contemporary tradition. One of their suppliers has the rights to the Bauhaus

designs and makes lamps based on the original styles. There is also a wide choice of overhead lights to illuminate paintings.

■ LINEN

Descamps
197 Sloane St, SW1
071-235 6957
Open Mon-Sat 9.30am-6.30pm, Wed to 7pm.

Classic pyjamas but with some fun designs also, this bright shop has a large selection of French ranges of sheets, table linen, quilt covers and an upstairs room for nursery accoutrements.

Frette
98 New Bond St, W1
071-629 5517
Open Mon-Sat 10am-6pm.

It is almost intimidating to find so many shelves of neatly wrapped-up towels in a long gallery of a room and in so many colours. There are bathrobes made in the same thick towelling by the factory in Italy. They also stock sheets, pillowcases and bedspreads and everything can be matched.

The Irish Linen Company
35 Burlington Arcade, W1
071-493 8949
Open Mon-Fri 9.15am-5.45pm, Sat 9.30am-4.30pm.

A wonder in white is how this little corner shop looks with all its stock draped around. The linen comes only from Ireland and there are even tea cosies in the fabric at around £20.

The Monogrammed Linen Shop
168 Walton St, SW1
071-589 4033
Open Mon-Fri 10am-6pm, Sat to 5pm.

A white-fronted shop which has lots to choose from, including practical picnic rugs with a waterproof underside in a selection of bright colours and various sizes. It takes only a few days to have products monogrammed.

The White House
51-52 New Bond St, W1
071-629 3521
Open Mon-Fri 9am-5.30pm, Sat to 1pm.

The best known of London's linen shops is expensive, but the stock really is beautiful and includes the kind of items you buy once in a lifetime. A delicate pink cotton voile sheet set, which includes an embroidered top sheet, plain bottom and two pillow cases, costs around £2,000, while a silk-satin night-gown and jacket cost over £1,000. They sell towels with daintily scalloped edges, dressing gowns, exquisitely made lingerie and many matching accessories, a range of table cloths and hand-embroidered dining room linen. The shop will undertake commissions to custom-make one-off designs of all the above. More like a traditional department store, there is a children's designer clothes section with hand-smocked dresses for four to five year olds around £350 as well as clothes on

the conservative, even staid, side for men and women.

■ SILVER

Kings of Sheffield
319 Regent St, W1 - 071-637 9888
Open Mon-Fri 10am-6pm, Sat to 5.30pm.

These shops sell well-priced silver-plated canteens of tableware, made in their factory in the cutlery-making centre of Sheffield. A three-piece carving set costs £93; in stainless steel, the price is £48, while at the top of the sterling silver selection, the price is £260. The firm provides cutlery cases and tables. Branches throughout London.

IMAGE & SOUND

■ MUSIC

INSTRUMENTS

Blanks
273 Kilburn High Rd, NW6
071-624 7777
Open Mon-Sat 10am-5.30pm.

A large department store of musical ideas from guitars and sheet music to brass and traditional Irish folk instruments.

Foote's
10 Golden Sq, W1 - 071-734 1822 for percussion, 071-437 1811 for orchestral instruments
Open Mon-Fri 9am-6pm, Sat to 5pm.

Anything from educational percussion to orchestral

*The **prices** in this guide reflect what establishments were charging at the time of going to press.*

brass, strings and accessories. Chas E Foote's short-term hire is very practical for those impractical musicians who leave their Stradivarius on a train on the day of a Royal gala performance. Good rental service for schools and parents who want their child to learn on a good instrument.

London Rock Shop
26 Chalk Farm Rd, NW1
071- 267 5381
Open Mon-Sat 10am-6pm.

Three floors with amps, guitars and keyboards for rock musicians of all ages and styles. Anything from a busker's amplification to hi-tech sampling stations can be found here.

Rose Morris
11 Denmark St, WC2
071-836 0991 for equipment, 071-836 4766 for printed music
Open Mon-Fri 10am-6.30pm, Thurs to 7pm, Sat to 6pm.

Six floors of instruments, amplification, soft ware, tutorial videos and accessories. The basement is full of electric guitars, the ground floor has a selection of printed music, the first floor is packed with professional keyboards, the second with digital pianos, acoustic guitars are stored on the third floor and recording equipment on the fourth.

SPECIALISTS

Accordions of London
365a Kilburn High Rd (corner of Loveridge Rd), NW6 - 071-624 9001

Open Mon-Sat 10.30am-6pm, Sun 12.30-4pm.

A specialist shop with a range from beginners' instruments to concert accordions and related instruments and a repair, estimate and spare parts service. The shop even has accordions made specially for them in Italy, one of the very few countries where they are still manufactured.

All Flutes Plus
5 Dorset St (off Baker St), W1
071-935 3339
Open Mon-Fri 10am-6pm, Sat 10am-4.30pm.

The name gives it all away: sales, repairs and rentals of quality flutes with an odd recorder and saxophone thrown in. New and second-hand instruments and accessories.

Andy's
27 Denmark St, WC2
071-916 5080
Open Mon-Fri 10am-8pm, Sat 12.30pm-6.30pm.

Andy's is one of those shops where they really love what they are doing. And that is vintage guitars (but they are also good at selling them!). The ground floor is dedicated to electric instruments, guitars and basses of all shapes and ages, the first floor to beautiful acoustic instruments. Prices are sensible and service is expert. This is a serious shop; Bob Dylan has been spotted browsing through the vintage selection. The shop's repair service is used by super professionals like Brian May of Queen. The workshop also makes guitars and has a 'finder service' for those who want a particular instrument. To give a chance to

acoustic players, Andy has opened a music café in an old forge near the shop. Andy's Forge is at 22 Denmark Pl, WC2 (next to Tottenham Ct Rd station), 071-916 5080. Check the varying opening times.

J & A Beare
7 Broadwick St, W1
071-437 1449
Open Mon-Fri 9am-12.15pm, 1.30pm-5pm.

These violins are almost for virtuosi for Beare's quietly elegant shop is not for the time-wasters. J & A Beare has a long tradition as violin makers, repairers and retailers. It is best to book an appointment if you want to see their antique instruments. Here quality goes before quantity.

Bill Levington
144 Shaftesbury Ave, WC2
071-240 0584
Open Mon-Sat 9.15am-5.30pm.

Bill Levington specialises in brass and woodwind instruments, so the shop has anything from trumpets to sousaphones. Other things to blow or to breath through are bagpipes, recorders and top grade flutes. Get your brass band equipped here!

T W Howarth
31-35 Chiltern St, W1
071-935 2407
Open Mon-Fri 10am-5pm, Sat to 3pm.

London's premier woodwind shop gets larger every time you pass them. Now they occupy three shops; N°31 has oboes and bassoons, N°33 saxophones and N°35 clarinets. T W Howarth is a full service shop for the woodwind players and their instruments.

Macari's
92-94 Charing Cross Rd, WC2 - 071-836 2856
Open Mon-Sat 10.30am-5.30pm.
An excellent shop for guitars, amplifiers and accessories, they have a good selection of vintage guitars from a 1930s lap steel to twelve-string Stratocasters and more conventional instruments.

Professional Percussion
205 Kentish Town Rd, NW5
072-485 0822
Open Mon-Sat 10am-6pm.
A large selection of drum sets and ethnic percussion instruments from different corners of the world and a repair and hire service.

Ray Man
29 Monmouth St, WC2
071-240 1776
Open Mon-Sat 10am-6pm.
The tiny, crammed shop on Neal Street seemed full even without customers and the new premises just around the corner will probably soon be as packed as the previous address. Ray Man specialises in Eastern and African instruments from gongs and flutes to the most complicated stringed things you've ever seen. And most of them are playable as well as beautiful.

Spanish Guitar Centre
36 Cranbourne St, WC2
071-240 0754
Open Tues-Sat 10.30am-6pm.
A selection of acoustic guitars from £60 beginners

Denmark Street

You can see couples walking down Denmark Street: she is bored while his eyes are gleaming. Not every woman loves shopping, especially if it is window shopping for guitars and other instruments. For Denmark Street is *an oasis for every budding musician.* It's full of music shops offering everything that can be banged, plucked, hit, rattled, programmed, blown or used otherwise to make any kind of noise. The dozen or so shops serve customers from young beginners to seasoned professionals. The price range is very wide and you can find anything from a child's practise drum kit to a complicated sampling station.

models to £7,000 virtuoso instruments. More than just a shop, you can learn to play by having lessons at the centre.

Synthesiser Service Centre
6 Erskine Rd, NW3 - 071-586 0357
Open Mon-Fri 9.30am-5.30pm.
Not a shop but a place to get your keyboards and amplifiers repaired. The centre is used by some famous people and service is efficient and friendly. Expect to wait about two weeks to get your machinery back from their workshop.

RECORDS

CLASSIC & EASY LISTENING

The Coliseum Shop
31 St Martin's Lane, WC2
071-240 0270
Open Mon-Sat 10am-7.30pm.

Next to the English National Opera, the Coliseum shop is dedicated to opera from its beginnings to today. They also sell a wide selection of opera videos.

Covent Garden Records
84 Charing Cross Rd, WC2
071-379 7635
Open Mon-Fri 10.30am-7.30pm, Sat 10am-7pm.
An excellent selection of classic and contemporary music on CD.

Dean Street Records
58 Dean St, W1 - 071-734 8777
Open Mon-Sat 10am-6.30pm.
West End original cast recordings, hits and misses from Broadway, nostalgia and music from films are stocked in a record shop to get sentimental over.

*The **prices** in this guide reflect what establishments were charging at the time of going to press.*

Dress Circle
57-59 Monmouth St, WC2
071-240 2227
Open Mon-Sat 10am-7pm.
Recordings and videos of musicals, soundtracks, celebrity nostalgia and memorabilia. For those who love musical entertainment.

The Royal Opera House Shop
James St, WC2 - 071-240 1200
Open Mon-Sat 10am-7.30pm.
Everything from CD's to libretti, from books to First Night perfume and Royal Opera silks and videos.

GENERAL

HMV
150 Oxford St, W1 - 071-631 3423
Open Mon-Sat 9am-7 pm, Thurs to 8pm.
HMV's megastore is a bit difficult to find your way around. The ground floor covers the mainstream in pop, rock, reggae and soul. No big surprises here, but things get better a floor down. Jazz, folk and world music from all over the globe are well represented with Indian music from films, country from America, Latin pop songs and Ethiopian jazz. The classic section is also excellent.

Tower Records
1 Piccadilly Circus, W1
071-439 2500
Open Mon-Sat 9am-midnight, Sun 11am-10pm.
If you have a severe need to buy a CD of, say, Fauré's *Requiem* or Miles Davis's *Sketches of Spain* late at night, then go to Tower Records, the

second megastore in the area. The ground floor has a vast selection of pop and rock and imports. The first floor has a huge collection of classical and contemporary music, jazz, country and world music. Their useful free monthly magazine called *Top* tells you about new releases and forthcoming concerts.

Vinyl Solution
231 Portobello Rd, W11
071-229 8010
Open Mon-Sat 11.30am-6.30pm.
A mini-megastore on two floors. Dance music from swing-beats to rare grooves is situated in what they coyly call the "bassment". Upstairs it's indie, trash, noise and hardcore. Vinyl Solution has everything from collectable reggae to classic soul and 60s psychedelia, and a good second-hand department.

Virgin Megastore
14-30 Oxford St, W1
071-631 1234
Open Mon-Sat 9.30am-8pm, Thurs 10am-8pm, Sunday noon-7pm.
The original megastore still has a wide selection of music from every area. But Virgin also sells videos, T-shirts, books, magazines, notes, cartoons, games and concert and aeroplane tickets. It is purely a matter of taste which of the megastores you prefer, but Virgin is the best organised of the three with good listening facilities.

*Find the address you are looking for, quickly and easily, in the **index**.*

SPECIALISTS

Beanos
27 Surrey St, Croydon, Surrey, CRO 1RR - 081-680 1202
Open Mon-Fri 10am-6 pm, Sat 9am-6pm.
This is the largest second-hand record store in Britain and is reasonably priced for normal records and hugely expensive for collectors' items.

Black Market
25 D'Arblay St, W1
071-437 0478
Open Mon-Sat 10am-7pm.
Noisy and buzzing with house, hip hop and rap, Black Market also sells merchandise like baseball caps.

Cheapo Cheapo Records
53 Rupert St, W1 - 071-437 8272
Open daily noon-10pm.
A huge selection of music from folk to psychedelia, from classical to children's songs.

Daddy Kool Music
9 Berwick St, W1 - 071-437 3535
Open Mon-Fri 10.30am-6.30pm, Sat to 7pm.
Reggae, ska and generally Jamaican music from the last few decades is stocked at the intriguingly named Daddy Kool which also sells second-hand records and rarities.

The Folk Music Shop
Cecil Sharpe House, 2 Regent's Park Rd, NW1
071-485 2206
Open Mon-Fri 9am-5pm, Sat 10am-6pm.
Cecil Sharpe collected a huge amount of British folk music on the nineteenth

century and had this home of British folk named after him. It stocks folk music from both home and abroad.

Mole Jazz

291 Pentonville Rd, N1
071-278 8623
Open Mon-Sat 10am-6pm, Fri to 8pm.

Just across the street from King's Cross Station, this shop is always packed with enthusiasts. Records, cassettes, books and posters are well organised and you can listen to the music before buying. They also have a special collector's section with rarities.

Ray's Jazz

180 Shaftesbury Ave, WC2
071-240 3969
Open Mon-Sat 10am-6.30pm.

Small, but packed with wonderful recordings from Dixieland to avant-garde and with good listening facilities. The friendly staff know their stuff and are honest in their comments. They have a good selection of second-hand albums. There is a silent auction for rare records: they are put on display and customers put in their bids within a given time.

Rock On

3 Kentish Town Rd, NW1
071-485 6469
Open daily 10.30am-6pm.

For the collectors of rockabilly, 60s soul and all records interesting. Records are usually second-hand and the staff knows their prices.

Rough Trade

16 Neal's Yard, WC2
071-240 0105
Open Mon-Sat 10am-6.30pm.

This indie specialist stocks all the unknown independent record companies you can imagine (and some more, too) from around the world, and a good selection on fanzines. Also at 130 Talbot Rd, W11, 071-229 8541.

Sounds of China

6 Gerrard St, W1 - 071-734 1970
Open daily noon-8pm. No credit cards.

The shop, which stocks both classical and popular Chinese music, also sells books and magazines.

Stern's African Record Centre

116 Whitfield St, W1
071-388 2756
Open Mon-Sat 10.30am-6.30pm.

Good selection of African, Caribbean and Latin music at reasonable prices and an information point for world music concerts in London.

SHEET MUSIC

Boosey & Hawkes

295 Regent St, W1 - 071-580 2060
Open Mon-Fri 9am-6pm, Sat 10am-4pm.

This shop which includes publisher Peters Edition's special department, celebrates printed music by covering everything from educational music to classical, opera, jazz and pop.

Foyle's

119 Charing Cross Rd, WC1
071-437 5660
Open 9am-6pm Mon-Sat, Thurs till 7pm.

One floor of this massive book shop is dedicated to sheet music and music books.

Music Sales

8-9 Frith St, W1 - 071-434 0066
Open Mon-Fri 9.30am-5.30pm.

The showroom gives a good idea of the variety in the Music Sales catalogue as it covers music from Hummel and Handel to solo tuba, fretwork fireworks of the Spanish guitar and disco rhythms of Abba.

Schott

48 Great Marlborough St, W1 - 071-287 2854, 071-439 8282
Open Mon-Fri 9am-5.30pm.

All classical printed music from early times to contemporary, and miniature scores for orchestras or solo pieces for recorder, educational music and books.

■ PHOTO-GRAPHY

Fox Talbot

154 Tottenham Ct Rd, W1
071-387 7001
Open Mon-Sat 9am-5.30pm.

Specialising in second-hand cameras, Fox Talbot stock names like Leica, Canon, Minolta and Nikon but they can get any make of camera. They have a limited range of large format film. The Strand shop is strictly for professionals. Also at 443 Strand, WC2, 071-379 6522.

Jessop Photo Centre
67 New Oxford St, WC1
071-240 6077
*Open Mon-Sat 9am-6pm,
Thurs to 7pm.*

There are so many camera shops in London that it can become most confusing. But Jessops is one of the best for amateur equipment and their staff are friendly and helpful. They carry a large stock of everything the amateur might need.

Keith Johnson & Pelling
93 Drummond St, NW1
071-380 1144
Open Mon-Fri 9am-5.30pm.

This is the biggest photographic company in Europe, a real professional's place with a superb range of equipment including Hasselblads and film. They also have a comprehensive hire section. Book well in advance, as serious equipment is sometimes difficult to come by. There is also a first-class repair service.

Silverprint
12b Valentine Pl, SE1
071-620 0844, Fax 071-620 0129
Open Mon-Fri 9.30am-5.30pm.

The place to come to for special papers imported from India and Japan (among other places) that you will not get elsewhere. No cameras on sale here; they are in the business of supplying processing, developing and printing materials and very special chemicals. So expert and specialised are they that they have been known to export an order to Malaysia—of paper from Japan! They have a first-rate catalogue and mail-order service.

JEWELLERY

■ CONTEMPORARY DESIGNERS

André Bogaert
5 South Molton St, W1
071-493 4869
Open Mon-Fri 10am-5.45pm, Sat 10.30am-5.30pm.

Modern, spare designs are to be found here from silver key rings to fabulous rings in eighteen-carat gold, set with diamonds (at £18,000). He also designs pieces using vermeil—laying eighteen-carat gold over silver.

Electrum Gallery
21 South Molton St, W1
071-629 6325
Open Mon-Fri 10am-6pm, Sat to 1pm.

Barbara Vartlidge's small but comprehensive showcase for contemporary jewellery by more than 90 artists from all over the world usually has exhibitions along a theme or promotes a new artist. Vicki Ambery-Smith, for instance, produces architecturally-inspired jewellery, such as Shakespeare's Globe. Wendy Ramshaw, who creates distinctive ring sets, recently received an OBE honour for her contributions to art.

The Great Frog
51 Carnaby St, W1 - 071-734 1900
Open Mon-Sat 10.30am-6.30pm.

Silver and semi-precious stones predominate in the designs of Carol and Pat Reilly, who have been selling off-beat jewellery for twenty years. The shop has photographs of wild pop groups, wearing such accessories as a wild-faced belt buckle or an articulated ring, looking like miniature armour. There is also a cowboy theme and lots of rings with a skull motif. Popular selling items include leather and feather earrings or pendants.

Lesley Craze Gallery
34 Clerkenwell Gdn, EC1
071-608 0393
Open Tues-Fri 10.30am-5.30pm, Sat to 5pm.

A showcase for some of the best contemporary designers, this now has two gallery spaces. One has work by contemporary designers permanently on display; the other has exhibitions. Recent exciting exhibitions have been 'Today's Jewels—Paper to Platinum' and one on Wendy Ramshaw. Lesley Craze is keen to promote commissions for her stable of jewellers, and some exhibitions have included drawings and information on techniques which all adds to the interest.

Merola
178 Walton St, SW3
071-589 0365
Open Mon-Sat 10am-6pm.

Imaginative designs by Maria Merola include novelties such as cherub earrings at £65 and there is always a wide range of decorative crosses. This jewel of a shop glitters with vintage costume pieces particularly by the designer Miriam Haskell.

Theo Fennell

177 Fulham Rd, SW3
071-352 7313
Open Mon-Fri 10am-7pm, Sat to 5.30pm.

As a silversmith, Theo Fennell has transformed London icons into souvenir miniatures, such as a traditional phone booth and post box. As a jeweller, he designs strikingly original pieces with personal statements. Recently he set a blue sapphire into an acorn-shaped brooch for an aristocrat who wanted to auction it for a charity that carried that symbol. His smart corner shop is a favourite of the town-and-country set for his wide range of traditional jewellery as well as novelty items.

■ COSTUME JEWELLERY

Butler & Wilson

20 South Molton St, W1
071-409 2955
Open Mon-Sat 10am-6pm, Thurs to 7pm.

Magazine fashion editors regularly turn to the big, bold necklaces and bracelets found here, most recently the chunky jet look, which explains why top models and celebrities pop in. Owners Nicky Butler and Simon Wilson were originally antique jewellers and still display some old and art nouveau pieces, especially at the Fulham Road branch. They also stock accessories like T-shirts and sunglasses and gifts like diamanté picture frames. Also at 189 Fulham Rd, SW3, 071-352 3045.

Ciro

9 New Bond St, W1
071-491 7219
Open Mon-Fri 9.15am-5.30pm, Sat 10am-5pm.

Tiaras at £500 appeal to brides who are looking for a glittering well-made headpiece in a shop known for its wide choice of jewellery of cirolite stone, a quality faux diamond. The shop, which has been in Bond Street since 1917, has built its reputation on its original speciality of fine imitation and cultured pearls. Also at 61a Brompton Rd, SW3, 071-489 5884.

Cobra & Bellamy

149 Sloane St, SW1
071-730 2823
Open Mon-Sat 10.30am-6pm.

Tania Hunter and Veronica Manussis set their own distinctive designs, most recently in fabulous amber, at their little black-and-white boutique. Look out for silver pieces and objets d'art.

Fior

31 New Bond St, W1
071-493 0101
Open Mon-Sat 9.30am-6pm.

The most amazing array of bejewelled evening bags, either gold or silver-plated, are eye-catching specialities here. They come in scrunchy as well as square, round, oval and novelty shapes—including a tortoise or a hare—ranging from £100 to £600. Other unusual buys are Salvador Dali-style watches with melted down faces, sold as wristwatches or pendants, and starting at £79. Discreetly displayed inside the shop is a royal warrant 'By appointment to HRH the Prince of the Netherlands'. Also at 27 Brompton Rd, W1, 071-589 0053.

Kenneth Jay Lane

66 South Molton St, W1
071-499 1364
Open Mon-Sat 9.30am-5.30pm, Thurs to 6.30pm.

A stylish but classic look is the aim of designer Ken Lane, who says that 'glamour is all year round'. His showy creations are made to be cherished and collected, lasting far beyond a fashion season. There are good reproduction ranges in the style of Bulgari, Cartier, Boucheron and Van Cleef. Strings of pearls are from £48 and a twist of several strands of pearls off-set with blue and green stones is £120. Also at 30 Burlington Arcade, W1, 071-499 1364, and 58 Beauchamp Pl, SW3, 071-584 5299.

Kiki McDonough

77 Walton St, SW3 - 071-581 1777
Open Mon-Sat 10am-6pm.

A favourite with the smart set, Kiki McDonough designs and produces delightful jewellery, drawing on inspirations from all ages and from all parts of the world. Using precious metals and stones, a gold, pearl and diamond choker at £5,200 or an eighteen carat gold, diamond and sapphire eternity ring at £1,900 both have a timeless quality. She produces a catalogue or you can go along to the pretty showroom and shop in Walton Street for a leisurely look.

Van Peterson

117 Walton St, SW3
071-589 2155
Open Mon-Sat 10am-6pm, Wed to 7pm.

Van Peterson is run by a husband-and-wife team who design charming, up-to-date fashionable pieces, particularly heart-shaped items. The shop also has an adjoining premises which sells antique jewellery items such as jet chokers from the 1930s and vintage Rolex and Cartier watches.

■ FINE JEWELLERY

Adler

13 New Bond St, W1
071-409 2237
Open Mon-Fri 9.30am-5.30pm, Sat 10am-3pm.

Now Vienna-based, the third generation of the Adler family keeps the opulent influence of the Ottoman civilisation in their striking pieces influenced by the designs of their grandfather, Jacques Adler, who had a workshop in Constantinople in 1910. Look for the Seraglio multiple ring with several gold hoops linked by a bar and studded with diamonds set off by round sapphires, rubies and emeralds. In-house designer Dominique Bott will undertake new commissions or re-design old jewellery.

Asprey

165-169 New Bond St, W1
071-493 6767
Open Mon-Fri 9am-5.30pm, Sat to 1pm.

Aspreys is an institution, full of beautiful things, including their own designed pieces. This is also a place to come for antique jewell-ery and they have a good art deco selection too.

Boodle & Dunthorne

128-130 Regent St, W1
071-437 5050
Open Mon-Sat 9.30am-6pm.

Tiny but flawless diamonds are set in the Excelsius range at the shop, usually just called Boodles, which makes a diamond cluster ring more affordable, from £755. Almost 200 years old, this family business started in Liverpool, opening a branch in London six years ago and most recently in Regent Street. Rebecca Hawkins, chief designer, is still Liverpool-based. The company sponsors the work of young designers and crafts people. Interesting pieces to commission are hand-painted enamel brooches or necklaces, featuring customers' homes or other favourite subjects. Also at 58a Brompton Rd, SW3, 071-584 6363.

Boucheron

180 New Bond St, W1
071-493 0983
Open Mon-Fri 10am-6pm, Sat 10.30am-4pm.

Famous for its perfume in the diamond ring-sha-ped bottle, this family business was founded in Paris in 1858. It has designers both here and in France, creating its signature look of combining gold and rock crystal to make stunning necklaces, from £8,500, highlighted by the different colours of the semi-precious stones used like blue lapis lazuli or pink tourmalines. The austerely elegant wood-panelled shop seems designed for serious shoppers.

Cartier

175 New Bond St, W1
071-493 6962
Open Mon-Fri 10am-6pm, Sat to 5pm.

Synonymous with classic French design since it opened in 1909, the London branch sells its own brand fragrance from £28 and watches from £600, with its most popular item being the classic three-coloured gold triple ring at £600. Gift items include a monogrammed inkwell at £240. It has a showcase of vintage Cartier pieces on sale and sometimes advertises Cartier's search for objets, jewels and watches made before 1970.

Collingwood

171 New Bond St, W1
071-734 2656
Open Mon-Fri 10am-5.30pm, Sat to 5pm.

Collingwood, in existence for two hundred years and holding Royal Warrants, stocks watches and jewellery and will also undertake commissions.

David Morris

25 Conduit St, W1 - 071-499 2200
Open Mon-Fri 10am-6pm, Sat to 5pm.

This small shop carries a range of David Morris's distinctive designs that make him one of Europe's foremost jewellers, and some of the new 'boutique range' of signature pieces. He will undertake commissions and is especially popular for jewellery set with pink and yellow diamonds.

Find the address you are looking for, quickly and easily, in the index.

247

Garrard

112 Regent St, W1 - 071-734 7020
Open Mon-Fri 9am-5.30pm, Sat 9.30am-1pm.

The Queen entrusts Garrard to spring-clean the crown jewels in the Tower of London annually so it is not surprising to learn that they have played a part in the making of some of them, like Queen Victoria's little crown which she wears in all her later portraits. The firm set the famous Cullinan diamond in the Imperial State crown which the Queen wears at the State Opening of Parliament every November. As a gift emporium, the shop's range includes leather goods and china, including little Hebrend dishes at £11, all packed in Garrard packaging which displays all four Royal Warrants.

Heller Pearls

26 Conduit St, W1 - 071-629 1805
Open Mon-Fri 9.30am-5.30pm.

Beautiful strings of lapis lazuli, turquoise, jade and other semi-precious stones adorn the window along with the cultured pearls which were once Naomi Heller's trademark. She now considers coral jewellery her speciality. You can design your own with guidance from Mrs Heller.

Ilias Lalaounis

174 New Bond St, W1
071-491 0719/0673
Open Mon-Fri 10am-6pm, Sat to 5pm.

At their Athens workshops, the four daughters of the family are the sixth generation carrying on the tradition of producing high quality, opulent-looking gold jewellery, inspired by Greek tradition and Byzantine influences.

Paul Longmire

12 Bury St, SW1 - 071-839 5398
Open Mon-Fri 9am-5pm.

Traditional or modern, antique or custom-made cufflinks to express a client's personality or his coat of arms—all are found in the world's largest collection at this shop, which has its own heraldic reference library. Paul Longmire and his son, Rupert, a designer, welcome a challenge, even portraying a client's children, pet or car in enamel, using colour photographs for reference. There is an ever-changing display of Longmire's own colourful enamelled, patterned cufflinks from £280. They also make enamel brooches, pendants, bracelets, earrings and blazer buttons.

Philip Antrobus

11 New Bond St, W1
071-493 4557
Open Mon-Sat 10am-5pm.

This venerable firm founded in 1815 made the engagement ring given to the Queen by HRH Prince Philip. It now carries a good range of antique and Victorian pieces and also modern jewellery. They are known for their workshop which makes up specially commissioned pieces.

Richard Ogden

28 Burlington Arcade, W1
071-493 9136/7
Open Mon-Fri 9.15am-5.30pm, Sat to 5pm.

With one of the largest and most beautiful collection of rings in the country, proprietor Richard Ogden finds that engagement and wedding rings are popular sellers. His fine antique and traditional jewellery ranges from £50 to £15,000.

Tiffany & Co

25 Old Bond St, W1
071-409 2790
Open Mon-Sat 10am-5.30pm.

The décor is not opulent considering the international fame of this jewellery shop, which shows off its designer rings, brooches and necklaces from the likes of Paloma Picasso and Elsa Peretti on the ground floor. This includes its Tiffany signature collection.

The Watch Gallery

100 Jermyn St, SW1
071-930 9488
Open Mon-Fri 10.30am-6.30pm, Sat to 6pm.

A Champagne bar for customers to 'take their time' while considering a purchase, a catalogue which wins design awards and is a collector's item in its own right, and many limited edition pieces are all part of this shop's individual approach to selling watches since the firm was founded in 1984. Breitling watches are the most popular, with fun watches from £25. Branches throughout London.

Watches of Switzerland

5, 14, 15 New Bond St, W1
071-493 2716
Open Mon-Sat 9am-5.30pm.

There are many branches of this company, selling a wide range of watches, but in this corner of New Bond Street are a trio of their specialist showrooms. N°5 is the Rolex centre, N°14 is for Chopard and N°15 is the Patek Phillipe specialist where the Ivor Spencer School for Butlers even sends its trainees for tuition about the care of the expensive watches their employers might own. Branches throughout London.

Crafts flair

Just over the river and a little along from the South Bank Centre you'll find a collection of young crafts people in Gabriel's Wharf. It's an excellent hunting ground for first-class jewellers, woodworkers and clothes designers and there are good small cafés where you can sit beside the river looking out onto the scene. *Gabriel's Wharf*, **56 Upper Ground, Waterloo, SE1, 071-620 0544, open Tues-Sun 11am-6pm.**

LEATHER & LUGGAGE

Asprey
165-169 New Bond St, W1
071-493 6767
Open Mon-Fri 9am-5.30pm, Sat 9am-1pm.

Still a family business, Asprey's dates back to the 1780s when an ancestor of Huguenot descent worked as a silk printer and craftsman of fitted dressing cases. His son, Charles, went on to make more portable cases in leather and moved in 1848 to the present premises where luggage is still hand-stitched and gold-tooled. A black hide flight bag is £280.

Barrow & Hepburn
25 Bury St, St James's, SW1
071-925 2578
Open Mon-Fri 9am-5pm.

Until recently an exclusive business making fine leather goods for gentlemen, the Royal Maundy purses and Ministerial despatch boxes, this company founded in 1780, has just opened its first retail shop. They stock a delightful and impressive range of leather goods, including luggage and those wonderful Gladstone bags, brief cases and small hand-crafted leather items like stud boxes.

The Coach Store
8 Sloane St, SW1 - 071-235 1507
Open Mon-Sat 9.30am-6pm.

The American company Coach, which has been making very high-quality, durable, classic handbags and small leather goods since 1941 stocks all its ranges in the relatively new Sloane Street shop. These handsome, classic designs, hand-crafted in the best leather might be on the expensive side—from £75 to £390—but the bags last for ever, and as with all the very best leather, improve with age and handling.

Gucci
27 Old Bond St, W1
071-629 2716
Open Mon-Fri 9.30am-6pm, Sat to 5.30pm.

This famous designer name has gone discreet, fed up with all the copies made of his chunky linked double G. Now the initial range is an overall delicate pattern in leather, with handbags from £180 up.

The silk flowered scarves are pretty enough to frame, which is how the Gucci offices around the world decorate their walls. Also at 17 Sloane St, SW1, 071-235 6707.

Hermès
155 New Bond St, W1
071-499 8856
Open Mon-Sat 9am-6pm.

From leather gloves, belts, bags to brief cases, Hermès is the automatic choice for shopping for customers fond both of the familiar fat 'H' logo and the distinctive scarves. Often sporting a horsy motif, one shows Buckingham Palace and the Queen on horseback along with 'Paris' under its trademark. Clothes for men and women are also available at this brightly-lit, corner shop, where even the Calèche perfume has a horse and carriage on its label. Also at 176 Sloane St, SW1, 071-823 1014.

Loewe
130 New Bond St, W1
071-493 3914
Open Mon-Sat 9.30am-6pm.

From suede suits to leather-and-suede luggage, the elegant products from

249

Hermanos Loewe include hand-bags, purses and brief-cases, embellished with a logo that is one of the most prestigious among leather ware shops.

Louis Vuitton
149 New Bond St, W1
071-409 0155
Open Mon-Sat, 9.30am-6pm.
Of course, there are plain, beautifully designed leather bags but everyone seems to want that famous LV splashed everywhere, no doubt because the name is synonymous with glamorous travel. Each shop has those fabulous solid trunks, reminiscent of sea-going voyages. Also at 198 Sloane St, SW1, 071-235 3356; 7 Royal Exchange, Cornhill, EC3, 071-283 9913.

Mulberry
11-12 Gees Ct, St Christopher's Pl, W1 - 071-493 2546
Open Mon-Sat 10am-6pm, Thurs to 7pm.
For that perfect English country look, this large shop in a trendy, tucked away alleyway of boutiques is the place to find everything—from satchels to chic little handbags, from bags to belts, from manicure sets to key rings. Their clothes are very appealing, and they introduce new designs each season, including waxed raincoats. Also at 185 Brompton Rd, SW1, 071-225 0313.

Pickett Fine Leather
41 Burlington Arcade, W1
071-493 8939
Open Mon-Fri 9am-6pm, Sat to 5.30pm.
One person makes a crowd in this cupboard of

a shop, but what a marvellous cupboard, packed with hundreds of wallets, handbags and briefcases in all colours.

Revelation
170 Piccadilly, W1 - 071-493 4138
Open Mon-Sat 9.30am-6pm.
The shop is on two levels and has divided its displays. On ground level there is a very wide range of small leather items such as wallets and purses, while downstairs there is a grand selection of suitcases and briefcases.

MENSWEAR

■ ACCESSORIES

HATS

Bates
21a Jermyn St, SW1
071-734 2722
Open Mon-Fri 9am-5.30pm, Sat 1pm-4pm.
One of those endearing places that seem to have been here forever and adds to the charm of a street known for established family businesses, Bates the Hatter, which is what the staff say when answering the telephone, designs its own traditional tweed flat cap, which sells from £35. This apart, there is an overwhelming choice.

Herbert Johnson
30 New Bond St, W1
071-408 1174
Open Mon-Fri 10am-6pm, Sat 10am-5pm.
Jack Nicholson's hat in *Batman*, Indiana Jones's hat in *Raiders of the Lost Ark*,

Rex Harrison's hats in *My Fair Lady* and Peter Sellars' 'lucky' hat as *Inspector Clouseau* are among the cinematic headgear made by this traditional hatters which has catered to high society and the military since 1899. This family business has an in-house design team for such interesting projects as well as for your ordinary trilby. Alongside 100 styles of hats always on display are accessories like fancy waistcoats, scarves and silk dressing gowns.

James Lock & Co
6 St James's St, SW1
071-930 5849
Open Mon-Fri 9am-5.30pm, Sat 9.30am-12.30pm.
A legendary hat-maker established in 1676 to kit out the nearby court of St James, this shop became famous for the 'coke' or as it is better known, the 'bowler' made for William Coke in 1850. It was transported to America to become the 'Derby'. Hats have made a come-back and this is the place to come to find anything from a cap for country pursuits to a straw boater for watching cricket.

SHIRTS & TIES

Harvie & Hudson
77 & 97 Jermyn St, SW1
071-930 3554
Open Mon-Sat 9am-5pm.
Rolls of striped, checked or plain blue, navy or pink poplin cotton line the back of N°97, ready for measurement here to be made up at the workshop at N°77. Keeping to a very traditional look, the shop's own designers decide

which subtle colour changes should take place to keep up with the seasons. The material is woven in Scotland, along with a range of ties to complement the colour exactly. Regular customers tend to buy several shirts and ties in the colourways, knowing their wardrobes will always be co-ordinated.

Hilditch & Key

37 Jermyn St, SW1 - 071-734 4707
Open Mon-Fri 9.30am-6pm, Sat to 5.30pm.

In business since 1899, the ready-to-wear range is excellently made, with the cutting done by hand using two-fold cotton poplin in a wide range of stripes and solid colours. Well-known for a distinctively shaped collar, the shirts have fine single-needle stitching, extra length to the body and real mother-of-pearl buttons. The hand-made-to-order shirts are cut and made at N°73. This shop also sells hand-slipped ties and fine quality pyjamas and dressing gowns. Also at 73 Jermyn St, SW1, 071-930 5336.

Thomas Pink

35 Dover St, W1 - 071-493 6775
Open Mon-Fri 9.30am-6pm, Sat to 5pm.

Quality, a conservative look with a certain cachet and reasonable prices make this shop a must for young men. There are two outlets in the City of London but the Dover Street and Jermyn Street shops are the most central. Their best-selling, pure cotton poplin shirts are around £40. Little silk knot cufflinks which punctuate the cuffs with delightful twists of colour are £5. Boxer shorts are £12. Also at 85 Jermyn St, SW1, 071-930 6364. Branches throughout London.

Turnbull & Asser

71-72 Jermyn St, SW1
071-930 0502
Open Mon-Fri 9am-6pm, Sat to 5pm.

Quite why flamboyant stripes and conservatism go hand in hand is a mystery but this shirt maker is acknowledged as the top place for custom-made shirts which achieve that combination to perfection. The minimum order is six shirts, which will last for years, especially if they are sent back for regular repairs, which can include replacing the collar in a contrasting stripe or plain colour. There is a large ready-to-wear selection. The firm makes shirts for the Prince of Wales.

SHOES

Church's

58-59 Burlington Arcade, W1 - 071-493 8307
Open Mon-Sat 9.30am-6pm.

Sensible penny loafers for £120, a pair of Oxford brogues for £170, this shop is one of the branches of a famous Northampton-based manufacturer. Well-made, they tend to last for ever, particularly if well repaired and looked after. But after all, they are of a timeless English classic style, so you may well find yourself handing them down to your son. Branches throughout London.

Deliss

41 Beauchamp Pl, SW1
071-584 3321
Open Mon-Fri 9.30am-5.50pm, Sat noon-4pm.

This working cobbler's shop makes shoes for both men and women, using some exotic materials along with ordinary leather, such as elephant and crocodile. Men's shoes start from £449.

Edward Green

51 Burlington Arcade, W1
071-499 6377
Open Mon-Sat 9am-5.30pm.

There is a showcase of smart shoe models for men who can then be fitted to have shoes made-to-measure from £350. The company also does its own range of wallets and bags. Men's shoes made by this discerning firm, whose motto is 'English master shoemakers to the few', have that classic look in which the arcade shops and those on nearby Jermyn Street pride themselves.

Fratelli Rossetti

196 Sloane St, SW1
071-259 6397
Open Mon-Fri 9.30am-6pm, Sat 10am-5.30pm.

Fratelli Rossetti produce the kind of brogues that originated in Britain but were refined abroad. Wonderfully detailed, punched and decorated in first-rate Italian leather, these elegant shoes look good with both formal and more casual wear.

---

*The **prices** in this guide reflect what establishments were charging at the time of going to press.*

J. Lobb
9 St James's St, SW1
071-930 3664
*Open Mon-Fri 9am-5.40pm,
Sat to 4.30pm.*

The pungent and evocative smell of leather greets the customer to this venerable cobbler's shop, which looks as it does when it was founded in 1850 by John Lobb who wanted to be the 'best bootmaker'. Made-to-measure shoes for both men and women cost from £1,500, with a time-consuming process to get the measurements right. There are 3,000 wooden lasts in storage. Designs are classical only. The holder of three Royal Warrants, Lobbs made boots for the Duke of Wellington. They also do ready-to-wear shoes.

Kurt Geiger
70 Jermyn St, SW1 - 071-839 5133
Open Mon-Sat 9.30am-5.30pm.

A men's shoe shop with many continental designers such as Ferragamo, Bruno Magli, Stemar as well as English makes.

New & Lingwood
53 Jermyn St, SW1 - 071-493 9621
*Open Mon-Fri 9am-5.30pm,
Sat 10am-5pm.*

Known as an excellent shirtmaker, this shop has wonderfully woody brown shades in its classic men's shoes as well as velvet slippers with hand-embroidered monograms and motifs. There are many other accessories to complete a gentleman's wardrobe. Old Etonians shop here, having been introduced to the firm's branch near the famous school as boys.

Salvatore Ferragamo
New Bond St, W1 - 071-629 5007
Open Mon-Fri 9.30am-5.30pm, Sat 9.30am-5pm.

Very elegant well-made Italian shoes for men (and for women) in this Bond Street shop attract both City types and visitors.

R E Tricker
67 Jermyn St, SW1 - 071-930 6395
Open Mon -Fri 9.30am-5.30pm, Sat to 5pm.

All-leather shoes for men are made in Northampton, the historic centre of the English footwear industry, for this old-fashioned shop which offers a made-to-measure service. Besides classic brogues and tasselled penny loafers, velvet monogrammed slippers are popular. The walls are lined with wooden lockers, adding to the olde-worlde charm.

WAISTCOATS

Georgina von Etzdof
149 Sloane St, SW1
071-823 5638
Open Mon-Sat 9.30am-6pm, Wed to 7pm.

While you're buying a scarf for a female, take time to look at the individually designed silk waistcoats (£185) and ties (£42.50). Fun, smart and eye-catching.

Tom Gilbey
Waistcoat Gallery
2 New Burlington Pl, W1
071-734 4877
Open Mon-Sat 9.30am-6pm.

These works of art go well beyond the flamboyance of any mass-produced waistcoats with Tom Gilbey producing some which could be described as art collages due to the decorations sewn on fine rich materials.

WOOLLENS

Berk
46 Burlington Arcade, W1
071-493 0028
Open Mon-Sat 9am-5.30pm.

This small shop in Burlington Arcade which is a mecca for wool fans stocks cashmere in its own label and in the Ballantyine range.

N Peal
192 Piccadilly, W1 - 071-437 0106
Open Mon-Fri 10am-6.30pm, Sat 10am-6pm.

N Peal has a wonderful range of cashmere and other wool sweaters and cardigans for men. Subtle colours and good designs make this well-established firm one of the first stops for woollens. They are expensive, but they last and are classic in design. Branches throughout London.

Westaway
& Westaway
65 Great Russell St, WC1
071-405 4479
Open Mon-Sat 9am-5.30pm.

A wonderful shop for both sexes, they sell particularly good cardigans and V-neck sweaters for men at extremely reasonable prices. Also a good place for scarves.

*Some establishments change their **closing times** without warning. It is always wise to check in advance.*

■ GENERAL

Blazer

117b Long Acre, WC2
071-379 0456
Open Mon-Sat 9.30am-6.30pm, Thurs to 7.30pm.

A pleasantly co- or- dinated look to the suits, shirts and ties, with smart suits ranging between £225 and £350, shirts around £35 and equally reasonably priced accessories in this busy shop. The casual clothes in Long Acre N°36 lean towards the American pre- ppy look. Always popular are the soft, wide-cut Dehavilland shirts. Also at 36 Long Acre, WC2, 071- 379 6258; 90 New Bond St, W1, 071-409 2841.

Christopher New

56 Neal St, WC2 - 071-379 1024
Open Mon-Fri 10.30am-7pm, Sat to 6.30pm.

This menswear shop has distinctive clothes, mostly by Christopher New, who is known for his richly patterned shirts and knitwear, made in Britain. One shirt with a crayon motif was £75, a tiger- patterned, printed cord shirt was £65 and hand-knit sweaters are around £175. The emphasis is on in- formality and fun with accessories such as striped socks and bold ties by En- glish Eccentrics.

Hackett

20 Piccadilly, W1 - 071-734 0868
Open Mon-Sat 9.30am-6pm.

For a while the descrip- tion 'young fogey' was bandied about to describe that pleasant, conservative look reminiscent of prev-

ious decades. This firm started to make its own gar- ments in 1984, copying the vintage clothing the founders came across in market stalls, like perfect 1930s Lobb shoes for £2. The firm now sells brushed cotton shirts, tweed sports jackets, hand-knit sweaters, plus-fours and all manner of clothes for events like polo and race meetings. The Piccadilly shop shares premises with J C Cording, supplies of Barbour, the best of the waxed weather- proof coat manufacturers whose whole range of waterproofed products is here. Branches throughout London.

Kent & Curwen

29 St James's St, SW1
071-409 1955
Open Mon-Fri 9.30am-6pm, Sat to 5pm.

A jolly, jaunty air pre- vails, thanks to the brightly striped blazers and caps, usually worn at sporting events like the Henley Regatta. Many of these are official colours to be worn strictly by the members of a particular club, regiment or school, but there are ad- aptations of the striped look. The jackets are some- times bought by visitors from overseas for weddings and occasions where an English atmosphere is needed. Chunky cricket sweaters with their bold stripe trims are popular, and women buy them too.

Moss Bros

27 King St, WC2 - 071-497 9354
Open Mon-Fri 9am-5.30pm, Thurs to 7pm, Sat to 6pm.

Moses Moses started selling second-hand suits in

1860; his sons, under a new company name, Moss Bros, found themselves lending a formal suit to an unsuccessful stock-broker just once too often so they started charging him for the loans in 1897. Thus, suit hire was born. Still outfit- ting formal occasions, in- cluding a 'cocktail collection' of hire clothes for ladies, the Covent Gar- den shop has dark panelled walls stretching back to rooms which include a traditional barber shop. Among the many racks of men's clothes are the newly introduced Hugo Boss range, Pierre Cardin and Chester Barrie suits and cashmere coats. Also at 88 Regent St, W1, 071- 494 0666.

Sam Fisher

76 Neal St, WC2 - 071-836 2576, Fax 071-408 1458
Open Mon-Sat 10.30am-7pm.

Lots of British-made sweaters as well as shirts, jackets and shoes are at the Covent Garden branch. The two in the arcade are stacked with cashmere, wool and cotton knits mostly for men, who can also choose from silk accessories including waistcoats, ties and socks. Also at 22-23 and 32-33 Burlington Arcade, W1, 071-493 4180/6221.

Xerxes

1 St Christopher's Pl, W1
071-224 2640
Open Mon-Sat 10.30am-8pm.

Coming across little boutiques in tucked-away places adds to the fun of discovery when shopping, with this place a good find as it specialises in two designers, Alfredo from Italy and Thome Schulz from Germany. The suits and brightly patterned ties have a continental flair.

■ LARGE SIZES

High & Mighty
83 Knightsbridge, SW1
071-589 7454
Open Mon-Fri 9am-6pm, Thurs to 7pm, Sat to 5.30pm.

The ready-to-wear suits and garments here are made for men who are very tall, six foot three inches and more. Also short men who are very wide are catered for, with chest sizes from 40 to 60 inches. Also at 145-147 Edgware Rd, W2, 071-723 8754.

■ TAILORS

Blades of Savile Row
8 Burlington Gdns, W1
071-734 8911
Open Mon-Sat 9.30am-5.30pm.

A lovely shop furnished in country-house style, this smart tailors offers a wide selection of ready-to-wear suits from £400, made with computer technology. There are hand-finished suits from £540 and hand-painted ties. Pin-stripe, grey and Prince of Wales check remain firm favourites with customers who may find this shop less formidable than some of the more austere tailoring establishments in Savile Row itself.

Anderson & Shepppard
30 Savile Row, W1 - 071-734 1420
Open Mon-Fri 8.30am-5pm.

People speak with awe about this establishment, considered to be the tops in the tailoring network. The company's policy is never to advertise and its reputation for perfectly cut and crafted suits makes it popular with American visitors. If you're recommended by someone, they will try to match the cutter your friend has, to achieve a similar look or feel. Prince Charles's double-breasted suits are made here.

Dege Savile Row
10 Savile Row, W1 - 071-287 2941
Open Mon-Fri 9am-5pm.

The Duke of Westminster, who regularly heads the list as the richest man in Britain, buys his suits here. The company name is well-known but the shop houses several tailors and is celebrated for its equestrian and military background.

Henry Poole
15 Savile Row, W1 - 071-734 5985
Open Mon-Fri 9am-5pm.

In typically discreet Savile Row style, this firm has been going since 1806 and has occupied the present building since 1887. It received its first Royal warrant from Queen Victoria for making under-stated and elegant suits.

Gieves & Hawkes
1 Savile Row, W1 - 071-434 2001
Open Mon-Sat 9am-6pm.

Admiral Nelson and the Duke of Wellington shopped here over a century ago. The firm sells mostly ready-to-wear suits, using the latest computer technology to get the sizing right. A large shop with a genteel ambience, it is well-stocked with scarves, belts, shirts and accessories.

Hogg Sons & J B Johnstone
19 Clifford St, W1 - 071-734 5915
Open Mon-Fri 8.30am-5pm.

Two tailoring establishments share these traditional-looking premises. The work room is on the ground floor where customers can catch a glimpse of the meticulous attention to detail. The front shop stocks some ready-to-wear clothes, including women's jackets. Sara Haydon is the only women proprietor in Savile Row.

H Huntsman and Sons
11 Savile Row, W1 - 071-734 7441
Open Mon-Fri 9am-1pm, 2pm-5.30pm.

One of the venerable names of Savile Row, this firm has been well-respected for its top quality menswear since the 1920s when it started making suits. It has a distinctive range of well-fitted jackets and blazers. A two-piece suit costs from £700. Like many other Savile Row tailors, the shop sends staff twice a year to the USA to fit customers.

Kilgour, French & Stanbury
8 Savile Row, W1 - 071-734 6905
Open Mon-Fri 9am-5pm.

This famous old firm gives the reassuring feeling that comes from tradition and quality. Its tailors take pride in making a suit from beginning to end, not using piecemeal methods. Suits are all hand-made, using traditional skills, and cost from about £1,500. The firm also makes ladies' suits. There are some 5,000 material patterns to choose from. It shares the premises with another famous tailor, the equestrian specialist Bernard Wetherill, which is why a saddle prop is on hand to get measurements absolutely right. This is sent to Buckingham Palace when the Queen orders new riding wear.

SPORTING GOODS

■ CLOTHING & EQUIPMENT (GENERAL)

Lillywhites
Piccadilly Circus, SW1
071-930 3181
Open Mon-Fri 9.30am-7pm, Sat to 6pm.

This five-floor department store with a famous address has the widest all-round choice of sportswear and equipment for any sport. There are departments devoted to baseball, hockey, squash, golf, tennis, badminton, darts, football, everything from archery to Wimbledon products. Customers might get confused finding their way around this bewildering abundance in a rambling series of rooms and departments, but don't worry, the staff are particularly knowledgeable here.

YHA Adventure Shop
14 Southampton St, WC2
071-836 8541
Open Mon-Wed 10am-6pm, Thurs, Fri to 7pm, Sat 9am-6.30pm.

A truly enormous choice of parkas, knapsacks, sleeping bags and every piece of equipment for camping and mountain climbing is stocked in the enormous Covent Garden branch. Even in winter when the ski equipment takes up space, there is a geodesic dome tent set up and the staff talk customers through the intricacies of its maintenance. A lightweight nylon, hexagon-shaped tent for a family is around £135. The Arctic explorer Sir Ranulph Fiennes and mountaineer Chris Bonnington use YHA cooking and camping equipment on their adventures. Once part of the Youth Hostel Association, the company is now privately owned but there is a membership department (071-836 1036) at the shop for people who wish to join and want to make bookings at a hostel. Also at 174 Kensington High St, W8, 071-938 2948.

■ FISHING

Farlow's
5 Pall Mall, SW1 - 071-839 2423
Open Mon-Fri 9am-6pm, Sat to 4pm.

This corner shop in the Royal Arcade could be a one-stop shopping place: it stocks the best cane trout rods and carbon-fibre salmon rods and a full range of tackle for every type of fishing. Farlow's stocks its outdoor clothes range in a separate shop.

House of Hardy
61 Pall Mall, SW1 - 071-830 5515
Open Mon-Fri 9am-6pm, Sat to 4pm.

A distinguished name in angling circles and a rival to Farlow's, Hardy's stocks all the best-quality fishing requisites in a neatly arranged modern shop: cane rods, special salmon flies, its own brand of safety vest, Barbour garments, unusual carved walking sticks, videos on fishing, hand warmers and sporting prints. It now has a computerised service for booking services such as salmon fishing on the Tweed.

■ HUNTING & SHOOTING

Boss & Co
13 Dover St, W1 - 071-493 0711
Open Mon-Fri 9.30am-5pm.

The present owner Tim Robertson is the great-grandson of the founder. The firm still hand-makes 'Best Guns Only' to the original designs. There is nothing smart about the Dickensian-looking shop but this is the specialist maker of Boss single trigger guns including the famous Boss Over and Under in 210, 28, 20 and 12 gauge. It has recently resumed making side-by-side Express Double rifles. All firearms are made to order, taking from eighteen months to three-and-a-half years.

Holland & Holland

33 Bruton St, W1 - 071-499 4411
Open Mon-Fri 9am-5.30pm.

Suppliers of rifles to the Duke of Edinburgh and founded in 1835, this shop has a handsome reception area where small cannons, framed bullet arrangements and old engravings and newspaper articles are on show. It goes a great length to the back rooms where the firearms are displayed. The shop sells antique and second-hand rifles and guns as well as imported makes. It has an extensive range of seriously sensible country clothes and accessories.

James Purdey & Sons

57 South Audley St, W1
071-499 1801
Open Mon-Fri 9am-5pm.

The top people's gunsmith, this Mayfair shop sells its own famous brand name in premises which retain an established-for-decades feel. Old royal warrants remain painted on the window frontage obscuring the view inside except for the mounted stags' heads. The guns and rifles, all handmade, are works of art and are collector's items. They are displayed and sold in the corner shop which has an adjoining more modern shop on Mount Street for accessories and a top quality range of outdoor clothing and footwear from woollen shawls for ladies to tweed hats.

William Evans

67a St James's St, SW1
071-493 0415

Open Mon-Fri 9.30am-5.30pm.

Smart apparel for the country, including leather-lined wellington boots and Barbour waxed coats are for sale along with cartridge belts and bags and framed shooting caricatures. An order for a gun, which can cost £52,000, takes about two years to complete. Besides new Sidelock and Boxlock game guns and rifles, there is a wide range of second-hand guns, both their own brand and well-known makes.

■ RIDING

Gidden's

15d Clifford St, W1
071-494 2388
Open Mon 9.30am-6pm, Tues-Fri 9am-6pm, Sat 10am-3pm.

A traditional saddle maker, the firm makes its own attaché cases and passport holders among the wide range of leather goods in stock. They recently opened their pattern books from the turn of the century to put the distinctive, old-style saddle drawings on to silk scarves, which look charming and sell at £113.

Swaine Adeney

185 Piccadilly, W1 - 071-734 4277
Open Mon-Sat 9.30am-6pm, Thurs to 7pm.

A hunting scarlet jacket catches the eye and sets the horsy note among the products and clothes available in this general store with shooting equipment, saddles, riding boots, tweed shooting jackets, suede waistcoats and finely-made umbrellas. A

red cavalry twill frock jacket in 100 percent wool is £325 and a black cavalry twill riding skirt is £90. The shop has changed its image somewhat by featuring a wider range of classically designed clothes for men and women. An equestrian print blouse in 100 per cent silk is £185.

■ SAILING

Captain O M Watts

45 Albermarle St, W1
071-493 4633
Open Mon-Fri 9am-6pm, Sat to 5pm.

Walk into this specialist, serious sailing suppliers and you can almost smell the ozone and hear the sea. They stock everything for sailors from small items to clothing and charts. The knowledgeable staff offers expert advice when needed.

■ SKIING & MOUNTAIN-EERING

Alpine Sports

215 Kensington High St, W8
071-938 1911
Open Mon-Fri 10am-7pm, Thurs to 8pm, Sat 9am-6pm, Sun 11am-5pm.

Brightly-coloured ski clothes are up front, a Nervica concession with more glamorous colours of one-piece ski suits, around £279 to £330, is at the back, and on the lower ground floor are ski equipment or camping supplies, depending on the season. There is a walk-in tunnel of a rock surface for customers to try out the climbing boots and lots of ski boots. Custom boot fitting is a fine art, costing £10 an hour.

Ellis Brigham Mountain Shop
30-32 Southampton St, WC2
071-240 9577
Open Mon-Fri 10am-7pm, Sat 9.30am-6pm, Sun 11am-5.30pm.
Even the door handle is ski-shaped at this specialist shop which sells snowboards along with the Raichle and Salomon ski boots. The shop also has a good choice of back-up products for winter and summer sports.

Snow & Rock
188 Kensington High St, W8
071-937 0872
Open Mon-Fri 10am-7pm, Sat 9am-6pm, Sun 11am-5pm.
The name says it succinctly since this large shop has skiwear and trekking gear in a good range of styles at reasonable prices. It has a climbing wall to try out the boots on, and in summer a very good choice of tents and camping equipment. The range of essentials is wide, from silk weight underwear at £30 to hand-and-finger exercise gadgets and a boot lab.

STATIONERY & PENS

Interlude
17 Cucumber Alley, Thomas Neal's, 31 Earlham St, WC2
071-379 3139
Open Mon-Fri 10.30am-6.30pm, Sat to 6pm.
This little shop and its friendly, interested staff offering the Yard-o-Lead propelling pencil, the Mont

Blanc celebrated Meristerstuck pen and fine stationery are a surefire attraction for tourists to Covent Garden's newest shopping enclave.

The Italian Paper Shop
11 Brompton Arcade, SW1
071-589 1668
Open Mon-Sat 10am-5.30pm, Wed to 7pm.
Lots of marbled books and note-pads alongside pretty boxes are shown in stylish disarray in the window of this trendy arcade shop, a magnet for stationery lovers in an area more famous for its fashion shopping. The marbled products are in the peacock design produced by Il Papiro of Florence. Gift wrap paper and stationery in the traditional Florentine border pattern is also sold.

Justfax
78 Long Acre, WC2
071-240 0317
Open Mon-Fri 9.30-6pm, Sat 10am-6pm.
All the big names in loose-leaf diary organisers have their products neatly arranged on racks and shelves in this small corner Covent Garden shop which also sells pens and pencils by well-known names. Its sister shops have a wider range of pens. Also at 43 Broadwick St, W1, 071-734 5034; 1 Berkeley Sq, W1, 071-491 7176.

Letts of London
3 Shepherd St, W1 - 071-499 2620
Open Mon-Fri 9.30am-5.30pm.
The traditional leatherbound desk and pocket diaries sold here have a dis-

tinctive lineage since the original concept of diary was hit upon by the firm's founder, Thomas Letts, a stationer who combined a calendar with a journal in 1812. By 1838 he was producing 28 varieties. Although the shop sells address books and fine stationery, diaries are a seasonal business so it shares premises with Mayfair Trunks, which sells top quality leather briefcases, document and attaché cases. The shop will also make repairs to briefcases.

Paperchase
30-34 Haymarket, SW1
071-925 2647
Open Mon-Sun 10am-7pm.
The original Georgian bay window front, the Victorian high desk in the corner and a resident ghost are features from the past at the Haymarket shop. Stretching into a back room and a larger brightly-lit annexe, the shop displays cards, postcards, calendars, boxes, pot pourri and general stationery products. Branches throughout London.

Papyrus
48 Fulham Rd, SW3
071-584 8022
Open Mon-Sat 9.30am-6pm.
Branching out from Bath, this shop has two sides to its services. In true cottage-industry style, a team of craftsmen do their own design, book-binding and marbling to produce photo albums and all manner of desk accessories. It is also a design and print business of letterheads, invitations and stationery.

Penfriend

Bush House, Strand, WC2
071-836 9809
Open Mon-Fri 9.30am-5.30pm.

Almost a little museum of the craft of writing utensils and curios like Georgian skirt-lifters, lorgnettes and early pencil sharpeners, the shop has a genial proprietor, Peter Woolf, who beams when visitors come to browse in the shop located in an off-beat arcade that includes the BBC Word Service Shop. He sells fully-restored vintage pens such as Mentmore, Conway Stewart, Onoto and Swan, which he often supplies for films, TV series and photo shoots. There is also a huge range of modern pens and their workshop will repair pens. Also at 34 Burlington Arcade, W1, 071-499 6337.

Scribbler

39 Neal St, WC2 - 071-240 6221
Open Mon-Fri 10.30am-6.30pm, Sat 10am-6.30pm, Sun 12.30pm-5.30pm.

For a wide choice of greetings cards, brightly coloured stationery and related products, even T-shirts, this popular corner shop has a pleasantly fun range. Also at 173 Kensington High St, W8, 071-938 1861.

Smythson

44 New Bond St, W1
071-629 8558
Open Mon-Fri 9.15am-5.30pm, Sat 10am-1.30pm.

As stationers to the Queen, this is really a small department store of quality paper products and leather goods sold by polite, knowledgeable young men. There is hand-bordered, water-marked stationery at almost £15 for 25 sheets plus matching envelopes and hand-blocked wrapping paper with a fleur-de-lys pattern at about £5 for two sheets. Among the quality pens for sale are novelties such as quills and glass dip pens. There are American edition diaries from £10.50. The most unusual item is a deluxe leather picnic case for two, with china plates and cups at £950.

Walton Street Stationery Company

97 Walton St, SW3 - 071-589 0777
Open Mon-Fri 10am-6pm, Sat to 5pm.

Aficionados of lush writing paper enthuse about this tiny shop which stocks Crane's 100 percent cotton paper in many colours and takes orders for engraving and printing.

TOBACCONISTS

Astley's

109 Jermyn St, SW1
071-930 1687
Open Mon-Sat 10am-6pm.

The octagonal-shaped entrance is designed to have as much display space as possible to show off the hundreds of pipes, some intricately carved, some antique. It sells its own brand of pipe tobacco along with accessories such as tobacco pouches and humidors.

Benson & Hedges

13 Old Bond St, W1
071-493 1825
Open Mon-Fri 9.30am-5pm.

The cool, clean-cut, efficient look of the shop belies its historical tradition of selling tobacco products, pipes and cigarettes since 1870. There is a range of small leather gifts.

Davidoff

35 St James's St, SW1
071-930 3079
Open Mon-Sat 9.30am-6pm.

A showy, spacious store with the best selection of Havana cigars in their own walk-in humidor. This famous shop also sells cognac, lighters and top quality smoking accessories.

Desmond Sauter

106 Mount St, W1 - 071-499 4866
Open Mon-Sat 9am-6pm.

Antique smoking memorabilia is one of the attractions in this old square-shaped shop with a glass walk-in humidor taking pride of place among the wooden fixtures. They sell exclusive smoking products in hall-marked silver, boxes and decorative pipes.

Inderwicks

45 Carnaby St, W1 - 071-734 6574
Open Mon-Sat 9am-6pm.

Incongruous among the fashion shops, this long-established little shop has an amazing array of pipes for sale, with subtle differences such as stem length and size taken into account by serious smokers, who can order a pipe made-to-measure.

James J Fox & Robert Lewis

19 St James's St, SW1
071-493 9009

*Open Mon-Fri 9am-5.30pm,
Sat to 4.30pm.*

The sign says James J Fox but this little shop is home to two well-known cigar merchants. It is devoted to high quality cigars from all over the world made with traditional care and attention to detail. James Fox also runs the tobacco department at Harrod's.

Shervingtons
337-338 High Holborn, WC1 - 071-405 2929
Open Mon-Fri 8.30am-6pm.

Established in 1864, this shop is set in a half-timbered building which dates to 1545, so there is a special atmosphere to enjoy while perusing the full range of pipes, tobaccos and smoking products.

G Smith and Sons
74 Charing Cross Rd, WC2
071-836 7422
*Open Mon-Fri 8.30am-6pm,
Sat 9am-5.45pm.*

A specialist in hand-blended snuff, which is available in some 50 aromatic varieties, this small shop stocks its own brand of tobacco as well as antique snuffboxes and little spoons for taking snuff.

WOMEN'S WEAR

■ ACCES-SORIES

HATS

David Shilling
5 Homer St, W1 - 071-262 2363

Open Mon-Fri 10am-6pm by appointment.

Booking is essential at this internationally famous salon. Although he designs clothes and home furnishings as well, David Shilling's name has become synonymous with hats and with reviving an interest in dramatic styles. His haute couture creations always appear in the newspapers after the Ascot Races, with the name of the wearer often tacked on as an afterthought!

The Hat Shop
58 Neal St, WC2 - 071-836 6718
*Open Mon-Fri 10am-6pm,
Sat 10.30am-6pm.*

As befits Covent Garden, this shop's windows are full of the latest headgear to catch the eye of fashion-conscious young women. Inside you find traditional hats along with men's bowlers, trilbies and top hats. The shop will also spruce up a hat to fit in with the new season's fads.

Herbert Johnson
30 New Bond St, W1
071-408 1174
*Open Mon-Fri 10am-6pm,
Sat to 5pm.*

Founded in 1899, this family business has a millinery department for women and an in-house design team. Dozens of styles of hats are on display.

Lock & Co
6 St James's St, SW1
071-930 5849
*Open Mon-Fri 9am-5.30pm,
Sat 9.30am-12.30pm.*

This quaint shop sees more women entering its hallowed portals since it opened a millinery depart-

ment recently with pretty hats for occasions like Ascot but also traditional straw hats for garden parties in the summer. Hats are from £60 to £280. With four milliners, two on the premises, there is plenty of advice, all given with quiet friendliness.

Stephen Jones
29 Heddon St, W1 - 071-734 9666
Open Mon-Fri 9.30am-5.30pm by appointment.

In the calm, beige-carpeted basement premises of this gently-spoken designer, there are dozens of sample hats on mannequin heads, from flirty, feathery shapes to the wide-brimmed look. Stock hats are from £50 to £150, and custom-made from £110 to £400. The latter may involve two or three fittings as well as discussions about materials and colours.

SCARVES

Georgina von Etzdof
149 Sloane St, SW1
071-823 5638
*Open Mon-Sat 9.30am-6pm,
Wed to 7pm.*

A wonderful shop for that one-off scarf that can give your wardrobe an unexpected lift. Georgina von Etzdof designs her own fabrics and patterns in an exotic fashion and produces two collections a year. Try the shot pleated chiffon scarf at £248 for a really special accessory, or a more modest silk and linen scarf. Chiffon, chiffon satin and more in a whole host of glorious colours.

SHOES

Bertie
36 South Molton St, W1
071-493 5083
*Open Mon-Sat 10am-7pm,
Thurs to 8pm.*

Chunky-chic is the way young women's fashion shoes seem to be. This little shop and its branches caters for the demand with a wide choice of comfortable shoes mostly in varying shades of brown or black. Branches throughout London.

Church's
58-59 Burlington Arcade, W1 - 071-493 8307
Open Mon-Sat 9.30am-6pm.

This shop, which sells its shoes through big department stores as well, originally comes from Northampton, home of shoe makers. Its women's shoes look like clones of men's styles, sensible and comfortable with old-fashioned chic. Not all the shops feature women's footwear. Branches throughout London.

Deliss
41 Beauchamp Pl, SW1
071-584 3321
Open Mon-Fri 9.30am-5.50pm, Sat noon-4pm.

In the village atmosphere of this richly endowed shopping street, it seems right to find a working cobbler's shop with customers being measured for hand-made shoes in full view of the window frontage. Lizard, crocodile, elephant and ostrich skin are among the shoe and boot coverings available. Other hand-made products include matching bags and belts. Ladies shoes start from £355.

Emma Hope
33 Amwell St, EC1 - 071-833 2367
Open Mon-Sat 10am-6pm.

Emma Hope produces two kinds of shoes: classical, but extremely classy styles for daytime, very wearable, very distinctive in the best fashion, and a delightful collection of wedding shoes, which can also double as special occasion shoes. They come in both leather and materials like satin, often with delightful bows and decorations. Again, although extremely pretty, these are not frivolous shoes but have a timeless classicism to them. On one hand you are transported back to the eighteenth century and on the other, you look extremely elegant.

Fratelli Rossetti
196 Sloane St, SW1
071-259 6397
Open Mon-Fri 9.30am-6pm, Sat 10am-5.30pm.

Stylish Italian shoes from a Milanese family who still own the business. Their shoes are classic and fashionable at the same time, made on proper lasts in traditional manner and beautifully detailed.

Gina Shoes
42 Sloane St, SW1 - 071-235 1440
Open Mon-Sat 10am-6pm.

Gina shoes have been around for years now, but this is their first retail venture under their own name. They hope to get into Europe from here, and from the looks of the customers and the shoes, should have no trouble. An English, in fact London-based firm, their shoes which start at £100 are fun and stylish. They have a particularly good and very popular line in high-heeled party shoes.

Hobbs
Unit 17, The Piazza, Covent Garden, WC2 - 071-836 9168
Open Mon-Sat 10.30am-6.30pm, Thurs to 7.30pm.

Well known for the classy yet fashionable designs that appeal to all ages, Hobbs shoes are comfortable and they keep within a reasonable price range. Some styles keep going; some new ones are introduced seasonally. Most of their shops also carry a good range of their clothes, and they are particularly strong on suits and sweaters. Branches throughout London.

Johnny Moke
396 King's Rd, SW1
071-351 2232
Open Mon-Sat 10.30am-6.30pm.

For the past ten years, this designer's shop has perched in a bend of the road which overlooks the busy, tail-end stretch of the King's Road. A witty use of straps and buckles make his ladies' shoes stylish and individual and a favourite with fashion-spread editors as well as an international clientele. Shoes can be hand-made in about four weeks, at about £170, with the customer choosing material and fabrics.

Manolo Blahnik
49-51 Old Church St, SW3
071-352 3863
Open Mon-Fri 10am-6pm, Sat 10.30am-5.30pm.

Sexy, flamboyant, original, comfortable, clever, irresistible are the adjectives used by this designer's customers about his Italian-made shoes, appealing to those looking for glamour on their feet. Only women's shoes are made, usually in small batches of fifteen. They are on display in this spartan little shop in a charmingly quiet corner of Chelsea.

Pied à Terre
19 South Molton St, W1
071-493 3637
Open Mon-Sat 10am-6.30pm, Thurs 10.30am-7.30pm.

First introduced in the 1970s, this firm has several branches selling Italian-made shoes mostly for women, although there is a selection for men at some branches. The designs are made in small production runs and the in-house designers react quickly to changing fashion trends. The price range is from £60 to £110. Some of the shops sport a 'Pied à Terre Rouge' sign, which indicates they carry a small range of hand-made shoes for women in the £110 to £160 price range. Branches throughout London.

Robert Clergerie
67 Wigmore St, W1
071-935 3601
Open Mon-Sat 10am-6pm, Thurs to 7pm.

Chunky hand-bags in navy, dark green or black sport the signature logo of this Paris-based designer, whose handsome, French-made, hand-stitched shoes for women are on display in this small shop, which also has a small range of classic designs for men.

The unfussy look is apparent even in dressy shoes, like the ladies' scarlet satin shoes, fastened with a strap and a single delicate button, at £189.

Salvatore Ferragamo
New Bond St, W1 - 071-629 5007
Open Mon-Fri 9.30am-5.30pm, Sat to 5pm.

The elegant Italian-made shoes attract customers to this glamorous, brightly-lit shop, where they stay on to browse and buy belts and bags. This is another firm which keeps expanding its accessories range. They now sell dramatic scarves and a growing line of smart women's clothes specially designed for them. A pair of calf and lizard trimmed shoes cost £165.

Small & Tall Shoe Shop
71 York St, W1 - 071-723 5321
Open Mon-Sat 10am-5pm, Thurs to 7pm.

As the name suggests, this shop caters for those people who find such difficulty with sizes. They stock shoes for small English sizes of thirteen to two-and-a-half, (American one to four-and-a-half and European 31 to 34) and large English sizes eight-and-a-half to eleven (American ten-and-a-half to thirteen, and 42 to 46 European). Their shoes are stylish, fashionable, and foreign made (the British who will not acknowledge that people are not all built the same). They also specialise in wedding and party shoes for all sizes in pretty styles at not outrageous sizes. A thoroughly useful find!

Stéphane Kélian
49a Sloane St, SW1
071-235 9098
Open Mon-Sat 10am-6pm, Wed to 7pm.

This designer, who is also extremely successful in Paris, is known for seamless, hand-woven shoes, some of which are on sale for £235 a pair. Besides his own label of French-made shoes for women and men, his workshops make shoes for such designers as Claude Montana, Kenzo, Issey Miyake and Jean Paul Gaultier. Also at 11 Grosvenor St, W1, 071-355 3201.

■ AFFORDABLE CHIC

Hobbs
47 South Molton St, W1
071-629 0750
Open Mon-Sat 10am-6pm, Thurs 10.30am-7.30pm.

The fashionably chunky shoes are excellent and the complementary clothes from cashmere blend coats at £300 to flower-print tea dresses at £139, are popular with career women. Branches throughout London.

Jane & Dada
20 St Christopher's Pl, W1
071-486 0977
Open Mon-Sat 9am-6pm, Thurs to 8pm.

Occupying two premises, this shop has women's wear at reasonable prices, reflecting the latest styles in lots of choices, whether it be outerwear including coats and jackets or informal clothes with shirts from £35 to £85, and trousers £50 to £90. This is a good place to head for when browsing for a wide selection in a cosy ambience rather than a department store environment. Also at 59 Hampstead High St, NW3, 071-431 0708.

Karen Millen
46 South Molton St, W1
071-495 5297
Open Mon-Sat 10am-6.30pm, Thurs to 8pm.
Once one of the designers at Pied à Terre, Karen Millen has a good line of understated separates in neutral colours for office wear, with jackets around £115 and skirts from £60. Branches throughout London.

Monsoon
264 Oxford St, W1 - 071-499 2578
Open Mon-Sat 9.30am-6.30pm, Thurs to 8pm.
Going from strength to strength, this firm keeps opening larger shops offering consistently lovely silks from Thailand, knitwear from Hong Kong and other printed clothes made in the Far East. They have also made a name for themselves with well-cut linen suits and waistcoats. Branches throughout London.

Old England
18 Beauchamp Pl, SW3
071-584 1100
Open Mon-Sat 10.15am-6pm.
Cashmere and silk combination knitwear, especially the skirt and long tunic top, is popular with customers. Prices are from £125. There is a wide selection of fine shawls, throws and scarves as well as pure cotton men's and women's shirts. Run by Jean Kitson, this shop would suit visitors

who like personal attention in a small place rather than browsing in a department store.

Phase Eight
97 Lower Sloane St, SW1
071-823 4094
Open Mon-Sat 9.30am-6pm, Thurs to 7pm.
A well-coordinated shop which stocks pretty clothes for casual/smart occasions. Their own in-house design team produces most of their stock, though they also have names like French Connection. It's a good place to come to for a dress for a summery occasion or a slightly more tailored suit. Branches throughout London.

Pied à Terre
9 South Molton St, W1
071-629 0513
Open 10am-6.30pm, Thurs to 7.30pm.
The shop name means shoes first of all to customers but there are several shops, like one of the South Molton branches, which have 'Basics for Women' clothes to complement the shoes. The garments are designed in-house using fabrics from all over the world in the colours of the season, with separates and dresses between £40 and £70. Other Pied à Terre shops stock shoes only. Branches throughout London.

Susan Woolf
9-13 Brompton Rd, SW3
071-584 7047
Open Mon, Tues 10am-6.30pm, Wed to 8pm, Thurs, Fri to 7pm, Sat 9.30am-6.30pm.
This is an excellent shop to find casual/smart thoroughly co-ordinated

outfits in materials like silk, wool and linen. Their range is well designed in a mix-and-match effort. With two collections a year, they manage to keep up with the latest colours and fashion details while still producing clothes that do not date. Their Brompton Road shop, with its unexpected fireplace in the back, is delightful to wander around. Branches throughout London.

Whistles
12 St Christopher's Pl, W1
071-487 4484
Open Mon-Sat 10am-6pm, Thurs 10am-7pm.
With some 50 new lines a season the shop philosophy is to spot up-and-coming designers, especially from France, so that the clothes from suits to evening wear always have a varied appeal. Branches throughout London.

■ DESIGNERS

All the top continental and Japanese names are to be found in London with their distinctive, stylish clothes. But we have included here some of the interesting British designers who have made a name for themselves on the international circuit. Like designers world-wide, many of them have started immensely successful ready-to-wear outlets with less expensive clothes that are individual and notable. We have also included here shops which have a range of designer wear. Happy hunting!

Amanda Wakeley

80 Fulham Rd, SW10
071-584 4009
*Open Mon-Sat 10am-6pm,
Wed to 7.30pm.*

This young, very successful British designer recently opened her first shop for her own label of ready-to-wear clothes for women. She continues her made-to-order business, by appointment only, at the same premises. Understated, elegant and fluid, the dresses, suits, knitwear and separates make a striking impact, matched up with shoes and accessories. Look for wide, see-through evening trousers, skirts cut on the bias and long, sleeveless waistcoats. Trousers are from £350, jackets from £470, an evening dress from £500 and scarves are £80.

Betty Jackson

311 Brompton Rd, SW3
071-589 7884
Open Mon-Sat 10am-6pm.

Betty Jackson designs smart clothes for women of all ages and has won many awards for her popular separates, dresses and other garments. Her versatility led her to produce Betty Jackson designs as Vogue and Butterick patterns for dressmakers. Opened in 1991, the shop sells everything from leather coats to evening wear—a floral silk top was £398.

Brown's Own Label

50 South Molton St, W1
071-491 7833
Open Mon-Sat 10.30am-6.30pm.

To promote young British designers and to show off the more affordable ranges of Brown's in-house

team this shop opened recently across the way from the main Brown's which caters for both men and women. Trouser suits are around £320. Changing exhibitions focus on different British artists such as silk scarves by textile designer Neil Bottle, or twisted jewellery by Slim Barratt.

Bruce Oldfield

27 Beauchamp Pl, SW3
071-584 1363
*Open Mon-Fri 10am-6pm,
Sat 11am-5.30pm.*

Only custom-made clothes are on offer, with customers choosing from a rack of model dresses and then being fitted. The cost is approximately £3,000 but it is good value, Bruce Oldfield explains, pointing out that the same price would buy only an off-the-peg dress from a top international designer. There is a friendly atmosphere and no appointment is necessary.

Caroline Charles

56-57 Beauchamp Pl, SW3
071-589 5850
Open Mon-Sat 10am-5.30pm, Wed to 6.30pm.

A country house, complete with fire blazing in the hearth in winter, houses this designer's knitwear, suits and evening dresses, which can best be described as 'occasion clothes'. The mother of the bride will head here as will Ascot-goers and Glyndebourne Opera devotees. There are also stylish casual clothes.

The Changing Room

10a Gees Ct, St Christopher's Pl, W1
071-408 1596

Open Mon-Sat 10.30am-6.30pm, Thurs to 7.30pm.

A butcher's block and a large wooden-framed mirror provide a simple background in this small shop which has a dozen or so designers including Plantation, Lesley George, Betty Jackson, No Name Studio and Tehen.

Junior Gaultier

18 Foubert Pl, W1 - 071-287 3761
Open Mon-Sat 10am-6pm, Thurs to 7pm.

We make no apology for including Jean Paul Gaultier here, as he has made London his home. A French-made Victorian fountain in the middle of the shop creates a picturesque background to the 'diffusion' range of Jean Paul Gaultier, with his own label jeans, waistcoats, shirts, leather bags, sunglasses and his first perfume for women in the distinctive Madonna-shaped bottle. Despite the raunchy packaging it is a pretty floral scent with orchid, iris vanilla and amber in the ingredients. The mainstream Gaultier collection is at Draycott Avenue. Also at Galerie Gaultier, 171-175 Draycott Ave, SW3, 071-584 4648.

Kanga

8 Beauchamp Pl, SW3
071-581 1185
Open Mon-Sat 10am-6.30pm.

Georgette dresses with flirty shapes in sharp pinks, blues, yellows and other vibrant colours intertwined in intricate patterns were designed by Lady Tryon, nicknamed Kanga and an old friend of the Prince of Wales, to create a dressy

Good as new

Of the resale clothes stores in London, the best and oldest is *Pandora Dress Agency*, at 16 Cheval Pl, SW7, 071-589 5289, where the wealthy bring their once (or maybe twice) worn dresses and stock up on a new lot.

outfit which wouldn't crush when packed. Made in Hong Kong, they used to be one size but now come in small, medium, large and extra-large, ranging from £300.

Lucienne Phillips
89 Knightsbridge, SW1
071-235 2134
Open Mon-Sat 9.30am-6pm.

The indomitable Lucienne holds friendly court in her busy shop, where her policy for the past twenty years has been to stock clever, up-and-coming British designers along with established names. Jean Muir's designs first appeared at Harrod's when Lucienne was a buyer there and are, of course, now sold at this shop along with Arabella Pollen, Jean and Martin Pallant, Penny Green and other top names. Celebrities shop here, and Lucienne takes pride in a clippings book which shows Elizabeth Taylor, for instance, at an awards ceremony wearing a jacket bought at her shop. This is

a comfortable place to look at a wide array of designer fashions.

Margaret Howell
24 Brook St, W1 - 071-495 4888
Open Mon-Sat 10am-6pm.

Known for her understated, comfortable, fluid skirts, jackets, shirts and separates for men and women, Margaret Howell shows off a collection in the neutral tones of taupe, beige, ivory, grey, with an occasional hint of pale pink. Mixing and matching her designs guarantees a totally co-ordinated, very modern/traditional English look. Also at 29 Beauchamp Pl, SW3, 071-584 2462.

Paddy Campbell
8 Gees Ct, St Christopher's Pl, W1 - 071-493 5646
Open Mon-Fri 10am-6pm, Thurs to 7pm, Sat 10.30am-6pm.

This designer's attention to detail, such as distinctive buttons on her simply cut suits, make her clothes look special. From hats to evening wear, the look is spot-on for her many regular customers who like an under-stated look.

Roland Klein
7-9 Tryon St, SW3 - 071-823 9179
Open Mon-Fri 9am-5.30pm, Fri to 5pm.

One-off designs in this delightful shop which you find through a tiny gate into a courtyard. They have a limited range of suits (which you can buy as jacket and skirt separately), dresses for summer occasions and smarter cocktail wear. Although they do not undertake com-

missions, they can make up any style you see in your own size if it is not in stock.

Ronit Zilkha
34 Brook St, W1 - 071-499 3707
Open Mon-Sat 9.30am-6.30pm.

From tailored suits with snazzy details to fluid evening wear, this triangular-shaped corner shop has eye-catching clothes. Typical of her style is a body-skimming viscose tunic with draped front and wide-legged trousers, around £500, looking both formal and relaxed. Also at 187 Brompton Rd, SW3, 071-823 8415.

Space NK
41 Earlham St, WC2
071-379 7030
Open Mon-Sat 10am-5.30pm, Thurs 10.30am-7pm, Sun noon-5pm.

The empty expanses of this unusual shop caused comment when it opened, but the distinctive carrier bag with the shop's logo is now one of the familiar sights in Covent Garden. There is a careful selection of unusual clothes for women by designers such as Liza Bruce, Abe Hamilton and Oguri. Shoes by Espace and belts and bags have been chosen to be eye-catching. Particularly popular are the smart accessories and hand-crafted jewellery. There are soaps, candles, stationery and a cosmetics counter of SheUemura products as well as an aromatic oils counter of Espa products. Men's fashions are to be introduced. Herbal teas and healthy snacks are available at the snack counter.

Wardrobe

3 Grosvenor St, W1
071-935 4086
*Open Mon-Sat 10am-6pm,
Thurs to 7pm.*

Since 1973, Susie Faux has been a godsend to busy, successful women who come to her shop for overall advice on a complete look from hosiery to make-up. The clothes are mainly from Italian, French and German designers, including Erreuno, Mani, Strenesse and Antonio Fusco. The all-important, well-cut jacket, perhaps by Jil Sanders, is often a focal point in choosing garments for the new season. The sales staff really do advise, and records are kept for regular customers so any new purchases will keep the co-ordinated look—the latter also helps husbands and boyfriends buy the right gift. Also at 17 Chiltern St, W1, 071-935 4086.

■ EVENING & SPECIAL OCCASION

Anouska Hempel

2 Pond Pl, SW3 - 071-589 4191
Open Mon-Fri 10am-6pm.

Models of very special dresses in fabulous materials and rich colours glow against the black, dramatic décor of the showroom of Anouska Hempel. An Australian, she also owns Blakes Hotel, beloved by the international media crowd. The tailoring is superbly done, with velvet evening tops from £1,500 which have such precisely beaded edging that the stitches are in-

visible. These are special occasion clothes for women with great flair.

Bellville Sassoon

18 Culford Gdns, SW3
071-581 3500
Open Mon-Fri 9.30am-5.30pm.

This large, stark, L-shaped showroom is brightly-lit and with a stylised décor which has, most notably, an unusual ceiling design of curled-back furls looking like a cloud opening up. Along the walls are the racks of stunning evening gowns, in red or black and other solid colours, with cocktail dresses and special occasion clothes all designed and made in Britain, with David Sassoon still the top designer.

Droopy & Browns

99 St Martin's Lane, WC2
071-379 4514
Open Mon-Wed 10.30am-6.30pm, Thurs to 7.30pm, Fri to 7pm, Sat 9.30am-5.30pm.

Founded in York in 1972 by the designer Angela Holmes, this company is strong on wedding dresses (best to make an appointment for these), evening wear and smart day suits and dresses, with all the fabrics coloured, dyed and woven to Angela's own specifications to complement her designs. The London shop's dress racks are always brimming with stunning, romantic clothes and matching hats. It is an informal, fun place to browse. A wool crepe suit with a mid-calf length skirt costs around £450, a high-waisted dress with well-fitted bodice and swirling bias-cut skirt £295 and there are blouses and skirts for £110 each.

Monsoon Twilight

67 South Molton St, W1
071-499 3987
*Open Mon-Sat 10am-6pm,
Thurs to 7pm.*

A newly developed range of velvet and silk clothes for the evening are the speciality of this off-shoot from the original boutiques and there is another branch in Covent Garden Market. A little lace evening dress is around £70.

Tatters

74 Fulham Rd, SW3
071-584 1532
*Open Mon-Fri 10am-6pm,
Sat to 5pm.*

From funky thirteen year-old girls to 70 year-old matrons, this shop is the place to go for evening wear for frothy little dresses, important-looking ball gowns, lovely tops and lots of velvet and satin garments to wear in the evening.

Zandra Rhodes

85-87 Richford St, W6
081-749 3216
Mon-Fri 9.30am-5.30pm, by appointment.

Printed velvets are among the new ranges designed by this flamboyant personality, whose colours and patterns have always added extra zing to her very showy clothes of chiffon and organza. Samples are on display, with a dress starting from £750. After fitting, it will take about 6 to 8 weeks for an order to be completed.

---

*Some establishments change their **closing times** without warning. It is always wise to check in advance.*

■ LARGE SIZES

Long Tall Sally

21 Chiltern St, W1 - 071-487 3370
Open Mon-Fri 9.30am-5.30pm, Thurs 10am-7pm, Sat 9.30am-4pm.

One of fourteen outlets nation-wide, this shop commissions manufacturers, who supply the High Street fashion stores, to re-proportion the current styles to fit women from five foot nine up. From teenagers to any age the range of clothes includes leggings and jeans among the casual wear as well as business suits and special occasion dresses.

1647 Ltd

69 Gloucester Ave, NW1 071-483 0733
Open Mon-Sat 10am-6pm.

A thoroughly useful shop started by comedienne Dawn French and ex-architect Helen Teague to produce both casual and party clothes for the larger lady. The name refers to their terms of reference— from the conventional 16 to size 47. They produce four ranges a year in different types of fabrics like jersey, linen and silk and prices are very reasonable, from £35 to £125. Styles are deliberately loose rather than fitted and they name their sizes small, medium and large rather than by the usual manufacturers' sizing. All the clothes are designed and made in their own workshops. They have a large mail-order business and the shop stocks extra colours and designs.

■ LINGERIE

Bradleys

85 Knightsbridge, SW1 071-235 2902
Open Mon-Fri 9.30am-6pm, Wed to 7pm, Sat 10am-6pm.

Flamboyant lingerie and sexy underwear along with cotton night-gowns and sensible pyjamas and slippers are included in the wide selection in this large shop which has top designers from all over the world, including Christian Dior, Nina Ricci, Ambade and the Cotton Club. From teenagers to grand-mothers, this shop can out-fit them all.

Courtenay House

22 Brook St, W1 - 071-629 0542
Open Mon-Sat 10am-6pm, Thurs to 7pm.

Behind the maroon façade is a handsome room with a sofa adding a personal touch. Ivory, white and cream colours dominate the beautifully-made night-gowns and elegant pyjamas with matching robes which hang on the rack. Satin, lace and silk underwear also comes in dainty, shimmering under-stated colours.

Fogal

51 Brompton Rd, W1 071-225 0472
Open Mon-Sat 9.30am-6pm, Wed to 7pm.

Luxury hosiery is the only product of this shop which has pantyhose in the window sometimes bearing the price tag of £165. Inside, prices start from £6.50. It is the quality of the fibres used and the hand-finishing which make some

of the products so pricey. One pair had 1000 crystals sewn up the side. Also at 36 Bond St, W1, 071-493 0900; and 25 Burlington Arcade, W1, 071-493 8130.

Janet Reger

2 Beauchamp Pl, SW3 071-584 9360
Open Mon-Sat 10am-6pm.

Designer Janet Reger was responsible for putting glamour back into underwear and lingerie. In this elegant white-walled shop, skimpy knickers hang importantly and incongruously, each pair on its own hanger. Again pale colours dominate the night-gowns and robes.

Rigby & Peller

2 Hans Rd, SW3 - 071-589 9293
Open Mon-Fri 9am-6pm, Wed to 7pm, Sat 9.30am-6pm.

As corset-maker to the Queen, this firm offers a discreet made-to-measure service for underwear, despite the rather bright colours of some of the ranges on the racks by the entrance and in its large windows. Bathing suits, one and two-piece, in a very wide choice and in all sizes, are on display at the back.

■ MATERNITY

Maman Deux

79 Walton St, SW3 - 071-589 8414
Open Mon-Sat 9.30am-6pm.

An odd little shop which sells unusual gifts such as little pillows with slogans like 'never complain, never explain', it has clothes for pregnant women who don't want to look dull. The stock includes jeans, smart suits, dresses and bathing suits.

■ PETITE SIZES

Celia Loe
68 South Molton St, W1
071-409 1627
Open Mon-Sat 10am-6pm.
With twelve shops in Singapore, where she has her clothes made, Celia Loe designs for petite women, five foot four inches and under. These are dressy clothes, some in ultra-bright colours, which look particularly striking in the suits.

■ WOOLLENS

Berk
46 Burlington Arcade, W1
071-493 0028
Open Mon-Sat 9am-5.30pm.
A small shop stocked with neatly folded piles of cashmere sweaters, Berk has its own label and also stocks the extensive Ballantyne range, all in appealing colours. Also at 61 Brompton Rd, SW3, 071-589 8000.

Edina Ronay
141 King's Rd, SW3
071-352 1085
Open Mon-Fri 10am-6pm, Wed to 7pm.
Elegant hand-knit garments which fit beautifully have established this designer, but there are also tailored separates in the best fabrics—linens, silks and wools. Among the raffish boutiques of this long road, this corner boutique is a high-quality discovery.

Geo Trowark
10a St Christopher's Pl, W1
071-487 4556
Open Mon-Sat 10am-6pm, Thurs to 7pm.
Not wool products but languidly lovely sweaters, hand-knitted in indigo dye cotton and chenille, and scarves at £26 are popular items among the Artwork lines. A smart herringbone tweed-effect jacket is £235. This tiny shop's products are so popular a larger branch opened recently in Covent Garden. Also at Unit 13, Thomas Neal's, Earlham St, WC2, 071-240 5940.

Joseph Tricot
28 Brook St, W1 - 071-629 6077
Open 9.30am-6pm, Thurs 10am-7pm.
The speciality of this Joseph outlet is knitwear for women, with glamorous, long-line silhouettes. A pure new wool sweater in shades of grey-black costs from £145. Fun fabrics appear, such as cotton lengths finely woven into a multi-coloured tapestry-effect against a red background for £240. In the back room, there are some Joseph clothes on sale, such as men's suits and silk parkas.

Marion Foale
13-14 Hinde St, W1
071-486 0239
Open Mon-Fri 10am-6pm, Sat to 5pm.
The solid colours and the tasteful appeal of these high quality, hand-knits in silk, cotton and wool yarns for women are a pleasure to wear. The shop is run with sedate flair.

Moussie
109 Walton St, SW3
071-581 8674
Open Mon-Sat 10am-6pm.
Designer Moussie Sayers has a flair for cheerful designs for her sweaters which start in price from £130. Her shop has other women's clothes too.

Patricia Roberts
60 Kinnerton St, SW1
071-235 4742
Open Mon-Sat 10am-6pm.
In this quietly located corner shop, with one room lined with shelves of yarns, Patricia Roberts has her range of sumptuously textured sweaters, with angora jackets, or angora highlights within a cable pattern background. In business for 25 years, this designer likes to add a witty theme to casual styles, including perhaps a jockey and related horsy motifs. She also stocks a wide variety of handsome, classical styles, with sweaters starting from about £280.

N Peal
192 Piccadilly, W1 - 071-437 0106
Open Mon-Fri 10am-6.30pm, Sat to 6pm.
This roomy branch in Piccadilly stocks a wide selection of famous cashmere goods from N Peal, the company that was one of the first to redesign the ordinary cardigan or twinset and turn it into a high fashion item. On the corner of Burlington Arcade and Piccadilly you find the original small store, displaying elegant cashmere separates in tranquil, fashionable colours with coral one of the prettiest shades. For a choice of traditional

London's markets

There are plenty of *open-air craft markets* in London—try the stalls in the middle of *Covent Garden* for interesting hand-made items by young designers, the daily market at the church of *St Martin-in-the-Fields* and on Fridays and Saturdays the collection of stalls at *St James's Church*, Piccadilly.

cashmere sweaters in a variety of colours try N°37 which also stocks scarves, stoles, and sweaters for men. Branches throughout London.

Pringle of Scotland
93 New Bond St, W1
071-705 4600
Open Mon-Sat 9.30am-6pm, Thurs to 7.30pm.
The entire knitwear collection of this famous firm is on display in this new airy shop, including dresses, skirts, jackets as well as pastel-coloured cashmere dressing gowns and lots of sweaters. Cashmere/silk dresses are alluring, with thigh-high slits in the skirts. To complement the look,

Celtic symbols appear in the range of jewellery, which is made in precious metals, including eighteen-carat gold, enamel and gemstones.

Shirin Cashmere
11 Beauchamp Pl, SW3
071-581 1936
Open Mon-Sat 10am-6pm, Wed to 7pm.
Founded in 1982, this family business designs and makes in its own factory, glamorous but wearable dresses, coats, jackets, separates and legwear, all in cashmere, or in silk knitwear. Each season brings its own new clever motif in the patterns of some garments, like im-

ages of belts and sunglasses. A gun-metal, fluid, calf-length cashmere dress was £425. The styles are timeless. Upstairs there is a useful cashmere clinic which will wash and re-dress any cashmere garments to make them look like new.

Westaway & Westaway
65 Great Russell St, WC1
071-405 4479
Open Mon-Sat 9am-5.30pm.
There is something reassuring about shops like this one, where shelves are lined with sweaters and the tables are laden with tartan scarves which match the sensible skirts hanging on the rack. A wonderful place for traditional woollens at reasonable prices and particularly favoured by young Italians. A sister shop, called Westaway's Real Shetland Shop, down the street at N°92, specialises in the distinctively patterned sweaters hand-made by crofters in the Fair Isles of Scotland.

ARTS

& LEISURE

ART GALLERIES

■ CONTEM-PORARY

GEOGRAPHY

The Bond Street Area has long been acknowledged as the heart of the established art scene, but in recent years it is less of an indicator of a gallery's status. Two alternative groups of galleries are now well established to the west and to the east of central London, showing slightly more 'advanced' art, the real avant-garde being shown in quite isolated galleries in the heart of the East End.

While most galleries do not close for the month of August, it is advisable to check on all opening times before making a visit if it is out of the way as some galleries are only open when an exhibition is on show.

Anderson O'Day Gallery

255 Portobello Rd, W11
071-221 7592
Open Mon-Wed by appointment, Thurs-Sat noon-5.30pm.

A pioneer of this now established gallery area, Prue O'Day presents new art with a fresh and energetic view, fitting with the bustling activity outside in the street. Always thought-provoking but never aiming to shock, she shows the work of young British artists to watch for in years to come: Jeffrey Denis, Simon Gallery, Maria Chevska.

Annely Juda Fine Art

23 Dering St, W1 - 071-499 3100
Open Mon-Fri 10am-6pm, Sat 10am-1pm.

Founded in 1960 by Annely Juda and jointly run since 1967 with her son David, this gallery is known world-wide for its exhibitions of Constructivism, Dada, Russian Avant-Garden, Bauhaus and de Stijl. Since moving into the present space, it has been revitalised and some of the best international contemporary artists like Ackling, Fulton, Nash, Caro and Christo now join the classics of Kandinsky, Mondrian, Rodchenko, Schwitters and Chillida.

Anthony d'Offay Gallery

9, 21 & 23 Dering St, W1
071-499 4100
Open Mon-Fri 10am-5pm, Sat 10am-1pm.

Anthony d'Offay started his gallery in the tiniest of spaces, developing spectacularly into one of the most important international venues when, in 1980, a Joseph Beuys installation opened the first of several museum-like galleries. A real galaxy of celebrated artists, including Andre, Gilbert & George, de Kooning, Morley, Richter, Turrell, Warhol and Long, demonstrate the breadth of d'Offay's interests. The catalogues should not be missed on any account.

Benjamin Rhodes Gallery

4 New Burlington Pl, W1
071-434 1768
Open Mon-Fri 10am-6pm, Sat 10.30am-1.30pm.

This is an understated gallery with a very English feel about it. Committed to searching out new art but definitely within a traditional arena, Benjamin Rhodes is not attracted to conceptual art forms, preferring the quiet confidence of Eileen Cooper or wild exuberance of Zadok Ben-David.

Bernard Jacobson Gallery

14a Clifford St, W1
071-495 8575
Open Mon-Fri 10am-6pm, Sat 11am-5pm.

The sign above the door says 'Modern English Masters' and this is no false declaration. The results of Bernard Jacobson's 25 years of dealing in this area are on the walls, from Bomberg, Abrahams and Weight to the new additions of Glynn William's and Maggi Hambling. Comprehensive gallery publications sometimes include conversations with the artists and provide a personal insight into the work.

Curwen Gallery

4 Windmill St, W1 - 071-636 1459
Open Mon-Fri 10am-5.30pm, Sat 10.30am-1pm.

Set up to act as a showcase for the prints made at the Curwen Studio, the gallery now promotes artists working in all media. British masters such as Ben Nicholson, William Scott and Henry Moore are still dealt with but the overall emphasis in the monthly exhibitions is the introduction of new work, including Paul Neagu and Martin

McGinn. This said, the company is still actively involved in the publishing of limited edition prints, resulting in an annual 'Salon des Graphiques'.

England & Co
14 Needham Rd, W11
071-221 0417
Open Tues-Sat 11am-6pm.

Australian Jane England specialises in retrospective exhibitions of overlooked British artists of the 1940s, 50s and 60s. Ralph Rumney, William Green, Paule Vézelay are among those rediscovered thanks to her efforts. As well as producing these scholarly reassessments she organises annual thematic shows which often use all the small space and more, so it's worth checking if additional gallery space is being used.

Flowers East
199-205 Richmond Rd, E8
081-985 3333
Open Tues-Sun 10am-6pm.

This is the flagship gallery of several run by Angela Flowers and her son, Matthew. Making a brave move to the East End, into what is now a complex of spaces, has enabled the showing of large-scale sculpture and painting, plus the initiation of a separate graphics/print department. The enormous warehouse space means there is always plenty of work on show, from such varied artists as Patrick Hughes, Peter Howson, Nicola Hicks and Kevin Sinott. Angela Flowers Gallery is also at 5 Silver Pl, near Lexington St, W1, 071-287 8328.

Francis Graham-Dixon Gallery
17-18 Great Sutton St, EC1
071-250 1962
Open Mon-Sat 11am-6pm.

This area was once tipped as one where galleries would re-locate but the hoped-for boom evaporated. This one remained, consolidated and continues to delight. Francis Graham-Dixon runs an annual programme of young and established British, European and American artists, all beautifully hung in a space which seems all the more cool and airy in contrast to the narrow streets of this former jewellery quarter.

Gimpel Fils
30 Davies St, W1 - 071-493 2488
Open Mon-Fri 9.30am-5.30pm, Sat 10am-1pm.

The Gimpel family have built on their long association with established artists but are not trapped by their 50 year's history. In fact they are one of the few galleries to take on 'difficult' new art in the West End. Terry Atkinson and Andrea Fisher are two of the many young artists being given a chance alongside established artists like Niki de Saint Phalle.

Hamiltons
13 Carlos Pl, W1 - 071-499 9493
Open Mon-Fri 10am-6pm, Sat 11am-7pm.

A treasure trove of a photographic gallery. On entering, the line of framed work stretching the length of the gallery is a daunting sight. However for the persevering photo fan there are some real classics here, including Richard Avedon, David Bailey, Helmut Newton and Anselm Adams. Exhibitions of new work from contemporaries such as Linda McCartney, Irving Penn and Herb Ritts are mounted with panache.

Jill George Gallery
38 Lexington St, W1
071-439 7343
Open Mon-Fri 10am-6pm, Sat 11am-4pm.

A lively gallery hinting at its one-time genesis as a graphics and print gallery. Limited edition and monoprints are usually on show downstairs, paintings upstairs. Jill George has a policy of showing younger artists and believes in working with architects and interior designers often on commissions.

JPL Fine Arts
26 Davies St, W1 - 071-493 2630
Open Mon-Fri 10am-5.30pm. And by appointment.

A haven of France in the centre of London, lovingly stocked with Impressionist and Post-Impressionist paintings, pastels and watercolours. Christian Neffe presents mostly domestic-scale works from Monet, Sisley, Signac, Vuillard, Dufy, Marquet and many more in an intimate atmosphere devoid of pretentiousness but reverentially hushed.

Karsten Schubert
41-42 Foley St, W1 - 071-631 0031
Open Tues-Fri 10am-6pm, Sat 11am-3pm.

The main strength of German dealer Karsten Schubert is in the choice of new sculpture. Work by

Rachel Whiteread (who was the Tate Gallery Turner Prize winner in 1993), Alison Wilding, Michael Landy, Anya Gallaccio and Thomas Locher are among those who might stimulate a reaction of pleasure or anger, according to taste. It's interesting to see the gallery has broadened its base to include establishment artists Bridget Riley and Ed Ruscha.

Lisson Gallery

67 Lisson St, NW1 - 071-724 2739
Open Mon-Fri 10am-6pm, Sat 10am-5pm.
Geographically isolated but right at the centre of the art world, if not making most of the running in its promotion of artists in Britain and abroad. Nicholas Logsdail has been based in the Bell Street area for 30 years but it is in this present purpose-built gallery that museum-like shows from artists such as Dan Graham, Anish Kapoor, Tony Cragg and Juan Munoz have made the gallery's reputation unassailable. The architect Tony Fretton designed both the gallery and its addition and the dextrous use of space makes a visit worthwhile. As an example of architecture designed for art it is an unusual, if not unique, opportunity in London.

Marlborough Fine Art

6 Albermarle St, W1
071-629 5161
Open Mon-Fri 10am-5.30pm, Sat 10am-12.30pm.
This is one of the most important galleries for twentieth-century works.

Behind the scenes the estates of Francis Bacon, Barbara Hepworth, Kurt Schwitters and Graham Sutherland are dealt with, while in the gallery careful exhibitions of paintings and sculpture from gallery artists such as R B Kitaj, Paul Rego, Steven Campbell and Frank Auerbach are usually presented as one-person shows. The gallery also has a department of contemporary graphics.

Paton Gallery

London Fields, 282 Richmond Rd, E8 - 081-986 3409
Open Tues-Sat 11am-6pm, Sun noon-6pm.
One of the few platforms for emerging talent from the post-graduate art schools in London. Graham Paton moved to this gallery complex from Covent Garden but continued his interest in new painting with new vigour. Both abstract and figurative work from the crème-de-la-crème of the Royal College of Art, Royal Academy, Slade and Chelsea Schools of Art are not only shown but successfully sold to major collections world wide.

The Photographer's Gallery

5 & 8 Great Newport St, WC2 - 071-831 1772
Open Tues-Sat 11am-7pm.
This was the first independent gallery in Britain devoted to photography and has, since its foundation in 1971 by Sue Davies OBE, maintained its reputation as the venue for contemporary photographic work. It has al-

ways shown innovative work alongside classic images, playing a major role in establishing key names; Irving Penn, Andre Kertesz and Lartigue were all first shown here. The present director aims to make it both accessible and welcoming to a broad cross section of the public. Housed in two buildings, it holds 24 exhibitions a year in several gallery spaces, the largest of which, the Brandt Room, is in N°8 Newport Street, along with the excellent book shop. The print sales room and library are in N°5 over another extensive showing area.

Raab Boukamel Gallery

9 Cork St, W1 - 071-734 6444
Open Mon-Fri 10am-6pm, Sat 10am-4pm.
The fact that this was originally a German gallery is reflected in the work it shows: Hödicke, Fetting and other major contemporary painters who Ingrid Raab has introduced to London from Raab Berlin. With a recent new partnership, new directions are possible; the established department of photographic art has a distinct American feel with works by Sherman, Serrano, Lagerfeld and Skogland.

Rebecca Hossack Gallery

35 Windmill St, W1
071-409 3599
Open Mon-Sat 10am-6pm.
This gallery has two areas of specialisation, showing a selection of contemporary British art and

art of a non-European tradition. Several shows each year feature work by Australian Aboriginal artists and contemporary African artists. The gallery has a sculpture garden in the West End connected to its second gallery in Piccadilly.

Redfern Gallery

20 Cork St, W1 - 071-734 0578
Open Mon-Fri 10am-5.30pm, Sat 10am-5pm.

From its beginning in 1936, Redfern's gave one-man exhibitions to young painters, printmakers and sculptors, and the inclusion of young artists in mixed shows and as published print editions has never changed. Famous for its stock of works by well-known artists, ranging from paintings by Gauguin, van Gogh, Matisse and Monet to Hockney, Bacon and Tapies it is perhaps a touch complacent for new, modern works, but for artists established in the 1950s and 60s, it remains true to the tradition of Proctor, Tindle and Neiland.

Special Photographers Company

21 Kensington Park Rd, W11
071-221 3489
Open Mon-Fri 10am-6pm, Sat 11am-5pm.

This is a fine art photography gallery and agency which introduces unknown and internationally recognised photographers, such as Herman Leonard, Edward Sheriff Curtis, Joyce Tennison, Holly Warburton and Laura Wilson, in both group and one-person

---

---

shows. There is always plenty to see on the two floors of this small gallery and it is all very well presented. The annual 'music' theme exhibitions are popular events and have featured photographs of Bob Marley, Jimi Hendrix and the Rolling Stones.

Victoria Miro Gallery

21 Cork St, W1 - 071-734 5082
Open Mon-Fri 10.30am-5.30pm, Sat 11am-1pm.

Victoria Miro picks her artists with care and presents precise exhibitions in her equally careful precise space, re-designed by Claudio Silberstrin in 1990. The mood of the gallery suits works by Alan Charlton, Ian Hamilton Finlay and Richard Tuttle, although some may find the austerity a little severe.

Waddington Galleries

5a, 11, 12, & 34 Cork St, W1
071-437 8611
Open Mon-Fri 10am-5.30pm, Sat 10am-1pm.

Cork Street is truly Leslie Waddington's territory, with a series of separate galleries, plus a graphics department, all within a few yards of each other. Works by Picasso, Dubuffet, de Kooning, Matisse, Picabia and Gris are in stock, and one-person exhibitions take place in the corner gallery. The younger artists dealt with include Mimmo Paladino, Barry Flanagan and Michael Craig-Martin.

Zwemmer Fine Photographs

1st floor, 28 Denmark St, WC2 - 071-379 6250
Open Tues-Sat 11am-7pm.

Francis Hodgson, the Manager, combines an extensive knowledge of photography with an enthusiastic confidence gained over years of working in the field, to create exhibitions which are skilfully selected and displayed. The gallery is not limited to any type of photography or any period, but reflects his 'minor leanings to East European and Russian photography'. Browsers are welcome, which is to be expected from a member of the Zwemmer group, who specialise in the publishing and retailing of books on the arts. The book shops are a short walk away, in Charing Cross Road, and, like the gallery, are a joy to anyone looking for a place which cares about art as much as they do.

■ EIGHTEENTH- NINETEENTH- TWENTIETH- CENTURY ART

Agnew's
43 Old Bond St, W1
071-629 6167
Open Mon-Fri 9.30am-6.30pm.

Established in 1867 and situated in a sumptuous 1870's building, this family firm is the thoroughbred of painting and print dealers. Behind a modest exterior lies a luscious array of paintings from the English eighteenth and nineteenth centuries, prints from artists of the French tradition—Vuillard, Redon, Bonnard, Picasso, Lautrec, alongside, interestingly, sculpture from British contemporary artists including Dame Elisabeth Frink.

Arthur Ackermann & Peter Johnson
27 Lowndes St, SW1
071-235 6464
Open Mon-Fri 10am-5pm, Sat 10am-noon by appointment.

A good mixture of sporting, equestrian and landscape scenes in the best English tradition. Oils, drawings and water-colours from the eighteenth

and nineteenth centuries, including Henry Bright of the Norwich School, are now the mainstay of the stock but Ackermann and Johnson also show two contemporary painters: Ken Howard and Douglas Anderson.

Chris Beetles
8 & 10 Ryder St, St James, SW1 - 071-839 7551
Open Mon-Sat 10am-5.30pm.

Chris Beetles deals mainly in Victorian and contemporary water-colours and illustrations. The great variety of the stock means there is always a wide range of work on view from the likes of Arthur Rackham, Albert Goodwin and Helen Allingham. Each Christmas since 1990 he has issued a catalogue describing his voluminous stock, featuring more than 100 artists from 1780 to the present day.

Christopher Wood Gallery
141 New Bond St, W1
071-499 7411
Open Mon-Fri 9am-5.30pm, Sat 11am-4pm.

Christopher Wood is one of the foremost specialists in fine Victorian, Edwardian and Pre-Raphaelite pictures and works of art. Established in Belgravia in 1979, it joined the Mallett Group in 1988 and is situated on the second and third floors of the Mallett Building, through which it is reached. It shows nineteenth- and twentieth-century English and European paintings, as well as sculpture, ceramics,

nineteenth-century gothic furniture and works of art. One gallery is devoted to eighteenth- and nineteenth-century water-colours and drawings.

The Fine Art Society
148 New Bond St, W1
071-629 5116
Open Mon-Fri 9.30am-5.30pm. Telephone for Sat opening times.

The Fine Art Society is one of the most distinguished in London. Founded in 1876, it quickly established a rapport with such nineteenth-century luminaries as Ruskin, Whistler and Millais. This is still the area it excels in, and in more recent years it has pioneered the revival of interest in late nineteenth- and early twentieth-century British painting, most particularly the (original) Glasgow boys—Guthrie, Lavery, Melville and Crawhall—and the founder members of the New English Art Club.

Frost & Reed
16 Old Bond St, W1
071-629 2457
Open Mon-Fri 9am-5.30pm.

Although Frost & Reed can trace its history back through 186 years of fine art dealing, don't get the idea that this is a dusty archive. A recent buy-out by Tony Neville and two co-directors has re-invigorated the gallery, with six shows a year of really good eighteenth-, nineteenth- and twentieth-century sporting pictures, including Stubbs and Munnings, as well as important Impressionist and Post-Impressionist water-colours and drawings. As if this wasn't enough, the gallery also has a policy of showing living artists in the downstairs area.

The Lefevre Gallery

30 Bruton St, W1 - 071-493 2107
Open Mon-Fri 10am-5pm.

The choicest examples of French Impressionist paintings are shown in this long-established family business. Once in a while they also feature work outside that tradition, but only of twentieth-century greats like Picasso or Georgia O'Keefe. The selection of catalogues, spanning many past years, is impressive in displaying the works that have gone through the gallery, although whether the oyster-pink interior is well suited to either Redon or Renoir is debatable.

The Maas Gallery

15a Clifford St, W1 - 071-734 2302
Open Mon-Fri 10am-5.30pm.

On entering the gallery it feels as if you are in someone's sitting room— the fire will be lit on cold days and the scale of the rooms is domestic. The Maas Gallery specialises in Victorian and Pre-Raphaelite drawings, paintings and water-colours, and here you will see the works of Burne-Jones and Alma-Tadema among others of that period in a correct setting. Five exhibitions of British contemporary art are held each year in addition to the stock work on show.

Mathof Gallery

24 Motcomb St, SW1
071-235 0010
Open Mon-Fri 9.30am-5.30pm, Sat by appointment.

Brian MacDermot founded the Mathof Gallery in 1975, when *The World of Islam Festival* was about to be held in London. He concentrates on the paintings of Arabia and the Orientalist movement (not to be confused with oriental art), many depicting the customs of the Arab peoples. These works, although created by Europeans, can claim a place in the history of the Arab nations. Aside from this they are stunning, especially as presented here, in beautiful hand-carved frames covered in gold leaf.

Paul Mason Gallery

149 Sloane St, SW1 - 071-730 3683/7359
Open Mon-Fri 9am-6pm, Sat 9am-2pm.

For over 25 years, Paul Mason has been a specialist dealer in eighteenth- and nineteenth-century marine and sporting pictures and prints. The gallery has an extensive collection of oil, water-colour and gouache ship portrait pictures by the better-known Port artists, plus many equestrian portraits, mostly from 1780-1890.

Peter Nahum

5 Ryder St, St James's, SW1
071-930 6059
Open Mon-Fri 10am-5.30pm.

Peter Nahum left Sotheby's in 1984 to open his gallery in St James's specialising in paintings, drawings and sculpture of the highest quality from the nineteenth and twentieth centuries. Since that time he has handled the majority of important Victorian painting coming onto the

market, including works by Burne-Jones, Millais, Tissot, Denis, Alma-Tadema and Watts. As he is a television personality, academic, lecturer and author in addition to being an advisor to many official departments of art, one can only envy the energy and enthusiasm for his chosen subject which results in the stock of sublime works.

Pyms Gallery

13 Motcomb St, SW1
071-235 3050
Open Mon-Fri 10am-6pm, Sat by appointment.

There is a very wide range of work on display here, with an interesting emphasis on the Irish eighteenth, nineteenth, and twentieth centuries, including work by Lavery and Orpen. French Naturalism as represented by the Barbizon School along with some British late nineteenth and early twentieth century—from Sickert to Nicholson— makes for a real mix of European flavours.

Richard Green

4 & 33 New Bond St, W1
39 & 44 Dover St, W1
071-493 3939
Open Mon-Fri 10am-6pm, Sat 10am-2.30pm.

Each of these four departments has a particular specialism—British, sporting and marine paintings; Victorian and European paintings; and fine Old Master paintings—and each is worth visiting. With a collection which includes works by Pieter Brueghal, Canaletto, James Seymour, Barend Cornelis Koekkoek, Alfred Sisley, Boudin and Sir Alfred Munnings, it is one of the most comprehensive to be seen outside a museum.

Richard Philp

59 Ledbury Rd, W11
071-727 7915
*Open Mon-Sat 10am-6pm
(but check Sat opening times
before visiting).*

On two floors of an elegant building just off Portobello Road, the equally elegant Richard Philp has a stock which spans a millennium. Roman and Greek sculpture occupy the same space as Old Master drawings alongside early Elizabethan or Jacobean portraits. However this is no casual selection. Perhaps one has to know the man to get to the heart of the obsession, and he has a reputation for awkwardness which may dismay the timid, but you can feel the genuine delight in works of art here.

Spink & Son

5-7 King St, SW1 - 071-930 7888
Open Mon-Fri 9am-5.30pm.

Rather like the British Empire, Spinks feels as if it has known better days of glory. The kernel of an illustrious past is ever present, but the current reality seems that it is still living in the past. Not surprising when one considers Spink's was established in 1666 and grew to be one of the largest and most all-encompassing antiques establishments in England. Each room is relatively small and contains a selection of artefacts, mostly particularly Indian, southeast Asian and Islamic art. The Fine Art section usually researches and displays nineteenth- and twentieth-century art, but it is difficult

to feel inspired by the exhibitions, although occasionally exceptional works are displayed.

Thomas Gibson Fine Art

44 Old Bond St, W1
071-499 8572
Open Mon-Fri 10am-5pm.

A delightful interior, very stylishly decorated for English tastes—all minty and mossy greens—and, moreover, classic works well shown both upstairs and in the small basement. It is refreshing to see works as disparate as those by Craigie Aitchieson and Giacometti on show at the same time.

OLD MASTER SPECIALISTS

P & D Colnaghi & Co

14 Old Bond St, W1
071-491 7408
Open Mon-Sat 9.30am-6pm.

A reverential hush pervades the interior, hinting at the impeccable provenance of Colnaghi's. The company goes all the way back to 1760, and whilst concentrating on Italian and French schools up to the early 1800s, also has carefully selected Old Master paintings on view, including English paintings. The plush surroundings complement the works, which are allowed ample viewing space—as befits the quality of paintings destined for major collections in the world.

Harari & Johns

12 Duke St, St James, SW1
071-839 7671
Open Mon-Fri 9am-5.30pm.

Philip Harari and Derek Johns met whilst working at Sotheby's and formed their own business in 1981. As specialists in Old Masters they have achieved international acclaim for discovering lost masterpieces and showing in their gallery rare works never previously exhibited. In addition, three annual shows present displays of European painting and sculpture.

John Mitchell & Son

160 New Bond St, W1
071-493 7567
Open Mon-Fri 9.30am-5.30pm, Sat by appointment.

This independent family firm was established in 1930 and the current owner, Peter Mitchell—a well-known specialist dealer in flower paintings—is assisted by his son James. They offer a small, rigorously selected stock of paintings, water-colours and drawings from the seventeenth to nineteenth century. The mention of the great Lyonnais flower painter, Antoine Berjon, is liable to unleash lengthy eulogies. Visitors will find a relaxed and helpful reception here.

Johnny Van Haeften

13 Duke St, St James's, SW1
071-930 3062
Open Mon-Fri 10am-6pm.

Here, on green baize-lined walls, are real gems of seventeenth-century Dutch and Flemish Old Masters. Johnny Van Haeften has extended family in Holland, but is not Dutch; however it is hard to imagine anyone more in tune with Dutch painting. These are works to be enjoyed and marvelled over in a small gallery before they are whisked off to some lucky museum.

Lane Fine Art
123 New Bond St, W1
071-499 5020
Open Mon-Fri 10am-6pm.

This is one of many galleries in the Bond Street area that were built specially to exhibit paintings, and it shows. Top-lit, the red-and-green interior displays to their best advantage the examples of British painting from the sixteenth to early nineteenth century which is the gallery's specialism, most particularly early English portraits and marine and sporting pictures from masters such as John Knox and George Stubbs.

Leger
13 Old Bond St, W1
071-629 3538
Open Mon-Fri 9am-5.30pm.

Based in this entire building since the 1930s, Leger has made quality an underlying aim and here the quality of each work, whatever its price, is assured. The best of British oils and water-colour paintings from 1720 to 1850 can and should be seen here in this very accessible atmosphere— Gainsborough, Turner, Girton, Adam, Payne—alongside lesser-known but equally respected artists.

Raphael Valls
11 Duke St, St James's, SW1
071-930 1144
Open Mon-Fri 9.30am-5.30pm.

In a bustling, rather faded, atmosphere are paintings, drawings and water-colours (mostly)

from the Dutch and Flemish tradition. European Old Maters such as Ruisdael, Arellano and Van Goyen are being dealt with, and not behind the scenes, but relax and browse through the hub-bub, it's well worth it.

Simon Dickinson
58 Jermyn St, SW1 - 071-493 0340
Open Mon-Fri 9.30am-5.30pm. An appointment is not always necessary, but advisable.

Whilst it is possible, and indeed encouraged, by Simon Dickinson for the casual visitor to see the selection of Old Master and British paintings on show, the strength of this organisation is in finding important pictures from private collections.

Whitfield Fine Art
180 New Bond St, W1
071-495 6488
By appointment.

Clovis Whitfield is one of the most important, and charismatic, dealers in Old Master Italian paintings from the sixteenth to late eighteenth century. He recently won a prize for identifying a work by Lanfranco and his quiet confidence is apparent in the feel of this tasteful space. Drawings are also shown, along with Florentine and Venetian frames which are of the same period.

Wildenstein & Co
147 New Bond St, W1
071-629 0602
Open Mon-Fri 10am-5.30pm.

A venerable institution which deals in Impressionist and Old Master

paintings. Shimmering silver-grey crushed velvet walls and period furniture set the scene for the occasional Van Gogh or Leonardo da Vinci sketch. Handy for the auction rooms and perfect for those dreaming of owning a masterpiece.

HOBBIES & SPORTS

■ ART COURSES

London's local authorities run large numbers of courses. If you're here for some time, get *Floodlight* from any book store. This is a useful booklet published annually and listing every possible course with full details from butterfly-spotting to macramé. For private courses, try Sotheby's and Christie's. They both run a variety of courses, some lasting a year and leading to an academic qualification, others lasting anything from a day to a month and aimed at the person with a general interest in the subject.

Christie's Education
63 Old Brompton Rd, SW7
071-581 3933, Fax 071-589 0383

Evening courses cover fine and decorative arts and music and wine courses (see below).

Sotheby's Educational Studies
30 Oxford St, W1 - 071-323 5775, Fax 071-580 8160

Sotheby's run a specialised month-long

course each summer as well as evening study courses, day and weekend courses throughout the year in fine arts, ceramics, furniture and wine (see below).

■ ART SUPPLIES

Brodie & Middleton
68 Drury Lane, WC2 - 071 836-3280/9, Fax 071-497 8425
Open Mon-Fri 8.30am-5pm.
A major shop for stage design and theatrical make-up since 1840 in the heart of London's theatre world, Brodie and Middleton sell everything for thespians from stage dyes and blood capsules to special brushes and paints for theatre sets.

L Cornelissen & Son
105 Gt Russell St, WC1 071-636 1045, Fax 071-636 3655
Open Mon-Fri 9.30am-5.30pm, Sat 9.30am-5pm.
We love the old-fashioned chests of drawers and displays in this 'Artists' Colourmen' specialists, established in 1855. You'll find unusual items here like lapis lazuli paints as well as an extensive range of the best brushes, painting knives, glues and pastels, gilding materials and papers.

Falkiner Fine Papers
76 Southampton Row, WC1 071-831 1151, Fax 071-430 1248
Open Mon-Sat 9.30am-6pm. Closed Fri 1-2pm.
Falkiner stock a wide range of good and rare international hand-made papers for water-colours, drawings and printmaking

such as kozo (oriental mulberry paper), vellum, parchment and beautiful hand-marbled papers in both large and small quantities.

Green & Stone
259 King's Rd, SW3 071-352 0837, Fax 071-351 1098
Open Mon-Fri 9.30am-5.30pm, Sat 9.30am-6pm.
Near the Chelsea College of Art, Green and Stone sell almost everything for the artist. But this is the place to go if you want gilding materials such as real or fake gold, glazes for special effects and varnishes that will give a surface an aged or cracked look for an instant antique.

T N Lawrence & Son
117-119 Clerkenwell Rd, EC1 - 071-242 3534, Fax 071-430 2234
Open Mon-Fri 9am-5pm, Sat 10am-4pm.
Founded in 1859 in Bleeding Heart Yard, this shop has moved and expanded. Apart from being the only place for wood engraving materials, they also specialise in tools for all kinds of engraving, 'Golden' acrylics from the USA, materials for etching and ranges of paints and paper for book binders. In fact if it's paper you're after, Lawrence is world-famous for their wide range of rare supplies.

Rowney
12 Percy St, W1 - 071-636 8241
Open Mon-Fri 9am-5.30pm, Sat 10am-5pm.
Established in 1789 as a perfumery selling paints and pigments for cosmetics, Rowney's is now the

largest UK manufacturer of artists' paints. As you can imagine, their shop contains the widest possible range of paints.

Tiranti
27 Warren St, W1 - Tel and Fax: 071-636 8565
Open Mon-Fri 9am-5.30pm, Sat 9.30am-1pm.
Tiranti's has been supplying materials for sculptors for over 100 years. But added to the mallets and chisels for stone sculpting and clays for modelling in the past, they now also supply dental plaster (apparently good for modelling), silicon rubber resins and more for the contemporary artists.

Winsor & Newton
51 & 52 Rathbone Pl, W1 071-636 4321
Open Mon-Fri 9am-5.30pm, Sat 9.30am-1pm.
In business for 150 years, they produce a very wide range of paper and paints and are particularly useful in supplying oil paints in small sizes, which are normally only available in large quantities.

■ BICYCLING

Bicycling in London, as in any city, can be hazardous and should be undertaken with care. All the following shops carry a wide range of accessories including protective helmets which you should wear. Deposits on hiring vary, but reckon on anything from £40 to £50 for a week's deposit.

> *Find the address you are looking for, quickly and easily, in the **index**.*

On Your Bike

52-54 Tooley St, SE1
071-357 6958
Open Mon-Fri 9am-6pm, Sat 9.30am-5.30pm.
Major stockists of mountain bikes, touring and racing bikes, they hire by the day, week, month or longer. Daily rates begin at £8, and they have a special weekend rate.

Portobello Cycles

609 Goldborne Rd, W10
081-960 0444
Open Mon-Wed, Fri, Sat 10am-5pm.
A general bicycle shop which hires by the week only.

Yellow Jersey Cycles

44 Chalk Farm Rd, NW1
071-485 8090
Open Mon-Sat 9am-6pm, Sun 11-5pm.
Open seven days a week, this friendly shop specialises in mountain bikes and hybrids (town-type mountain bikes). Weekly hire starts at £45.

■ BRASS RUBBING

This peculiarly English hobby has many devotees. You'll find a lot of them carefully rubbing the impressions of knights and ladies, dogs and coats-of-arms at the two main brass rubbing centres.

London Brass Rubbing Centre

St Martin-in-the-Fields Church, Trafalgar Sq, WC2
071-437 6023
Open Mon-Sat 10am-6pm, Sun noon-6pm.

Westminster Abbey Brass Rubbing Centre

North Cloister, Westminster Abbey, SW1 - 071-222 4589
Open Mon-Sat 9am-5.30pm.

■ COOKING

Le Cordon Bleu

114 Marylebone Lane, W1
071- 935 7621
Attracting both professionals and amateurs, Le Cordon Bleu offers a wide range of courses in the culinary arts from specialised short courses, demonstrations and daytime courses in classic cuisine, guest chef lecturers and tastings to advanced pâtisserie training. Unashamedly French, it issues certificates and diplomas on the professional courses, and has an arrangement with the Paris Cordon Bleu school whereby students can transfer between the two. Facilities are excellent since it was taken over by Andre Cointreau and the school offers restaurant-like conditions for the aspiring chef.

Leith's School of Food & Wine

21 St Alban's Grove, W8
071-229 0177
If you want to learn about restaurant management, wine or how to plan a sophisticated dinner party menu in one easy Saturday morning lesson, this is the place to come. But Leith's is also one of the most important schools for people who want to go into catering as a career, from cooking in a restaurant, to cooking for

directors. Courses run for different lengths of time and many lead to professional qualifications recognised the world over for their high standards.

■ DANCE

Dance Works

16 Balderton St, W1
071-629 6183, Fax 071-499 9087
Open Mon-Fri 8am-10pm, Sat, Sun 10am-6pm.
Dance Works offers over 100 classes to choose from, including Russian classical ballet, contemporary, salsa and tap, all taken by experts. They also teach martial arts, have various fitness studios and a rehearsal space used by TV, film and video companies.

Pineapple Covent Garden

7 Langley St, WC2 - 071-836 4004, Fax 071-836 0806
Open Mon-Fri 9.30am-8.30pm, Sat 9.30am-6.30pm, Sun 10.30am-3.30pm.
Seven studios offer 180 classes a week in every kind of dance from contemporary to jazz. They also have a hydra gym.

■ GARDENING

The English Gardening School

66 Royal Hospital Rd, SW3
071-352 4347, Fax 071-376 3936
Established in 1983, the school which is for both professionals and amateurs, offers various options from one-day workshops on general subjects such as the English cottage garden tradition, roses and plant groupings

to one-year courses in subjects like Garden Design and Botanical Illustration which lead to a professional qualification.

The Royal Horticultural Society

80 Vincent Sq, SW1
071-834 4333

The RHS as it's popularly known, runs the famous Chelsea Flower Show. But they also have monthly flower shows in their splendid halls in Vincent Square. Like a mini-Chelsea but entirely indoors, each show concentrates on a theme or species from dahlias and rhododendrons to their Great Autumn Show. Telephone for details, and also for details of admission to their comprehensive library.

■ GOLF

Richmond Park

Roehampton Gate, Richmond Park, SW15 - 081-876 3205

Two beautiful eighteen-hole golf courses to play on for only £9 a day Monday to Friday, or £12.50 Saturday or Sunday. They hire out golf clubs but you must have your own golf shoes. Playing times are governed by the Park opening times and can be eccentric (no playing during deer culls for instance), so get all the details on the telephone first.

■ HEALTH & FITNESS CLUBS

There are a number of good health and fitness clubs in London. Although the most economical way to enjoy them is to take out a year's membership, many of them have shorter memberships of one month, one week or just one day. In addition, many offer special days which include use of the facilities and special offers on beauty treatments. All clubs try to be flexible so it's worth talking to the membership secretary to see what you can arrange. Most also offer beauty treatments and it is not necessary to take out membership for those.

Champneys The London Club

Le Méridien, 21 Piccadilly, W1 - 071-437 8114, Fax 071-494 0876
Open Mon-Fri 7am-11pm, Sat, Sun 8am-9pm.

A swimming pool, fully equipped gym, cardiovascular room, dance studio and squash courts are some of the many facilities this luxurious club offers. They have an overseas membership of one, three or six months, priced from £250 to £1,050 and a special day for £95 which gives you the use of facilities, lunch and one treatment. Annual membership is from £840 to £1,440 plus a joining fee.

Crystal Palace National Sports Centre

Norwood, SE19 - 081-778 0131
Open Mon-Fri 8am-10pm, Sat 8am-8pm, Sun 8am-6pm.

This huge and impressive complex is the premier sports centre in Britain. While it holds leading competitions on both the international and national circuit (frequently televised), it is also open to the public. Facilities are superb and include an Olympic-size pool, a diving pool, football pitches as well as six floodlit all-weather courts and ten squash courts.

The Dorchester Spa

The Dorchester, Park Lane, W1 - 071-495 7335, Fax 071-495 7351
Open daily 7am-9.30pm.

The place to come to for pampering, the Spa offers everything from eyelash tinting to assorted body wraps, massage, waxing and any treatment you can think of. There is also a fully-equipped gym and work-out studio, solarium and whirlpool bath. Rates are very reasonable: £30 a day to £1,050 for a year and no joining fee. Hotel guests have free use of the club.

The Gym at the Sanctuary

11 Floral St, WC2 - 071-240 0695
Open Mon-Fri 7.30am-9pm (Wed to 10pm), Sat, Sun 10am-5pm.

A useful, inexpensive place in the middle of Covent Garden for women only. Housed in an old banana warehouse, it's one of our favourite locations for swimming, sunbeds and aromatherapy. Membership is only £99 per year and the daily rate is £10; classes are around £2 per hour. There's also a category which may be useful even if it's hardly flattering called Over Forty Fatty which costs £300 for six weeks. If you book treatments, you do not need to take out the day membership and you can use all the facilities.

The Harbour Club
Watermeadow Lane, SW6
071-371 7700, Fax 071-371 7770
Open daily 6.30am-11.30pm.

This spectacular £7 million development which opened in 1993 is impressive. Spread over four levels, it never feels crowded. There's a 25-metre ozone pool, crèche, ten indoor and four outdoor tennis courts plus the unique feature of the Real Tennis court (originally the game of royalty). Membership is high, from £1,995 plus joining fee. They have off-peak membership, but no temporary memberships.

Holmes Place Health Club
188a Fulham Rd, SW10
071-352 9452, Fax 071-376 3517
Open Mon-Fri 7am-11pm, Sat, Sun 9am-9pm.

This is the place for celebrity-spotting but those famous faces (and bodies) look quite different when working out on the state-of-the-art machines or trying to keep up with the aerobics, dance, step classes and yoga. Yearly membership is £650 plus joining fee; monthly membership is from £195 (off-peak) to £280.

Jubilee Hall
20 The Piazza, WC2
071-379 0008
Open Mon-Fri 6.30am-10pm, Sat, Sun 10am-5pm.

In Covent Garden's former Flower Market, this popular club offers

membership and is open to non-members. Huge number of classes include contemporary jazz, cardio plus and something called fat attack workout which is surprisingly popular. The gym is large and light and they also have martial arts classes and a treatment centre. Prices are very reasonable: classes are only £4 each for non-members while membership ranging from £45 to £500 makes this one of the best deals in London.

Jubilee Sports Centre
Cairo St, W10 - 081-960 9629, Fax 081-960 9661
Mon-Fri 7am-10pm, Sat, Sun 8am-8pm.

A 30-metre pool, sports hall, squash courts, sunbeds and multi-gym are just a few of the facilities at this excellent centre. Although you have to take out membership, a yearly one is only £27.50. Membership here gives you membership at the Porchester Centre (see below).

The Hogarth Health Club
1a Airedale Ave, W4
081-995 4600, Fax 081-742 1494
Open Mon-Fri 6.30am-11pm, Sat 9am-9pm, Sun 10am-9pm.

See *text* below.

Lambton Place Health Club
Lambton Pl, Westbourne Grove, W11 - 071-229 950, Fax 081-742 1494
Open Mon-Fri 7am-11pm, Sat, Sun 9am-9pm.

See *text* below.

Mecklenburgh Health Club
Mecklenburgh Pl, WC1
071-813 0555
Open Mon-Fri 7am-10pm, Sat, Sun 9am-9pm.

Excellent facilities at all these health clubs which also offer good-value days. Lambton Place's 'Top to Toe' includes use of the gym, swimming pool, steam room and spa and 10% off the normal tariff prices for beauty treatments and hairdressing—all for £20 for the whole day. Lambton Place also has a sports injury clinic for the serious. The subterranean Mecklenburgh Health club has a restaurant overlooking the pool and a huge gym with the kinds of machines that are used in American Olympic training centres. Annual membership rates vary from £685 to £1,125.

London Central YMCA
112 Great Russell St, WC1
071-637 8131, Fax 071-436 1278
Open Mon-Fri 7am-10.30pm, Sat, Sun 10am-9pm.

Accessible to the general public, they offer a swimming pool, fitness classes, weight training, badminton, basketball and gymnastics. You can join as a member or just turn up and take temporary membership for the day. Rates are very good: the weekly membership is only £32.50; yearly memberships are equally attractive.

*The **prices** in this guide reflect what establishments were charging at the time of going to press.*

Marshall Street Leisure Centre

14-16 Marshall St, W1
071-287 1022, Fax 071-798 2006
Open Mon-Fri 7.15am-9pm (Mon to 7pm), Sat 8am-8pm.

Excellent facilities at very good rates: for instance swimming for a member is £1.70, for a non-member £2.20, and aerobics classes are £3.35 for members, £4.10 for non-members. Sandwiched between Oxford Street and Regent Street, they offer swimming lessons, life-saving courses, special gym facilities, saunas, steam rooms and sunbeds.

N°1 Synergy

1 Cadogan Gdns, SW3
071-730 0720, Fax 071-730 5217
Open Mon-Fri 8am-9pm, Sat 8am-6pm.

Housed in what was the home of the American Ladies Club in the 1940s and '50s, Synergy offers all the usual facilities as well as acupuncture, Shiatsu, reflexology and more. Guests at Number Eleven Cadogan Gardens (see *Hotel* section) can use the club for free; outside members can join on a monthly basis for as little as £58, or try a health and beauty day for £65.

■ HOT AIR BALLOONING

Balloon Safaris

27 Rosefield Rd, Staines, Middlx, TW18 - 0784-451007, Fax 0784-440200

For a truly different view of England, try going up in the skies in a hot-air balloon for £99 per person. The company flies from dif-ferent venues in the south-east and the balloons can take up to sixteen people, and yes, you do have a pilot on board. A voucher would make a truly unusual gift!

■ ICE SKATING

Broadgate Ice Rink

35/36 Broadgate Circle, EC2
071-588 6565
Open end Nov-end Mar: Mon noon-3pm, Tues-Fri noon-3pm, 4-7.30pm, Sat, Sun 11am-1pm, 2-4pm, 5-7pm.

London's only open-air ice rink and consequently operating only in winter-time, it's a pretty place in the middle of the impress-ive new Broadgate development in the City. You can hire skates, buy equipment and book skating lessons.

Queen's Ice Skating Club

17 Queensway, W2
071-229 0172

At the time of going to press, this famous rink was being re-furbished so tele-phone for details.

■ RIDING

Riding in Hyde Park is one of London's singular pleasures. Book in advance at any of the following stables for every day ex-cept Mondays. Prices are around £25 per hour and they can lend you hats if necessary.

If you want to go further afield, Richmond Park is delightful.

Bathurst Riding Stables

63 Bathurst Mews, W2
071-723 2813

Ross Nye

8 Bathurst Mews, W2
071-262 3791

Roehampton Gate Stables

Priory Lane, SW15 - 081-876 7089

■ NEEDLE-WORK

COURSES

The Embroiderers' Guild

Apt 41, Hampton Ct Palace, East Molesey, Surrey, KT8 9AU - 081-943 1229, Fax 081-977 9882

Exhibitions, classes, a library, shop and study schemes are all run by this crafts-based organisation. They have 11,000 members in the UK and overseas who receive a Newsletter giving news of the Guild's activities.

Royal School of Needlework

Apt 12a, Hampton Ct Palace, East Molesey, Surrey, KT8 9AU - 081-943 1432, Fax 081-943 4910

The School was founded in 1872 by a daughter of Queen Victoria and friends, with the purpose of showing the beauty of hand-crafted needlework and of finding suitable employment for ladies of gentle birth in straitened circumstances. Today the School designs and makes banners for the military, un-dertakes all kinds of commissions, does smocking, and stretches customers' own work—everything in fact to do with the gentle art of needlework. They also hold open days, exhibitions, classes and private lessons throughout the year.

SUPPLIERS

Ehrman
14-16 Lancer Sq, Kensington Church St, W8 - 071-937 8123
Open Mon-Sat 9.30am-6pm, Thurs 9.30am-8pm.
A treasure trove for needlework enthusiasts, Ehrmans stocks Kaffee Fassett, Annabel Nellist, Candace Bahouth and other designers. You can see everything made up before you buy the kit or appropriate materials (though sadly one's own efforts never quite look as good). They also sell loose canvases, tapestry wools and stationery.

Liberty
210-220 Regent St, W1
071-734 1234
Open Mon-Sat 9.30am-6pm, Thurs 9.30am-8pm.
This department store has an excellent needlework department staffed by people who are themselves experts.

Tapisserie
54 Walton St, SW3 - 071-581 2715
Open Mon-Fri 10am-5pm, Sat 10am-4pm.
If you're after one-off traditional English and Continental designs, make your way to this small but well-stocked shop. Antique themes are designed by their own team and you

can get a picture of your own adapted to a canvas. All their canvases come with wools.

■ SHOOTING

Holland & Holland
Ducks Hill Rd, Northwood, Middlx, HA6 2SS - 0923-825 349, Fax 0923-836 266
The famous gunmakers Holland and Holland have a shooting school 50 minutes by underground from central London where for about £75, two people can clay-pigeon shoot for an hour.

■ SWIMMING

For outdoor swimming

Try *Highgate* (men) and *Kenwood* (women), both off Millfield Lane, N6 (081-340 4044) or *Hampstead* (mixed bathing) at the Hampstead Ponds, off East Heath Rd, NW3 (071-435 2366).

Apart from pools attached to health clubs (see above), there are a number of good central London pools. Local authorities all have swimming pools and have lists available at local libraries. Otherwise for indoor swimming try:

Chelsea Sports Centre
Chelsea Manor St, SW3
071-352 6985

Porchester Centre
Queensway, W2 - 071-792 2919

Crystal Palace National Sports Centre
Norwood, SE19 - 081-778 0131

■ TENNIS & SQUASH

Squash is very difficult to play on a casual basis in London. You have either to be a member of a club, or book a local authority court. **The Jubilee Sports Centre, Porchester Centre** and **Crystal Palace Centre** are good bets to try. The **Squash Rackets Association**, The Salons, Warple Way, W3 (081-746 1616) can supply lists of clubs.
The top tennis tournament is, of course, the All England Lawn Tennis Championships at Wimbledon first held in 1877. (*All England Lawn Tennis* and *Croquet Club*, Church Rd, Wimbledon SW19, 081-946 2244). It's difficult to get tickets for this world event, but if you want to pay a premium, ticket agencies can often supply tickets—look in the classified section of major national newspapers. The enthusiastic can try queuing for return tickets after lunch on the day; it's fun, cheap and you often get to see a good four hours or so of tennis. An equally enjoyable event (though less prestigious), played on grass courts in a club small enough to see the players properly, is the Stella Artois tournament at *Queen's Club* (the run-up to

Wimbledon). For information on tennis and on where to play in London, contact the **Lawn Tennis Association** or the **Lawn Tennis Federation**, both at Queen's Club, Barons Court, W14, 071-385 4233/2366.

There are not many indoor tennis courts in London, but two clubs can provide play on a casual basis if their courts are not full. Both offer various kinds of yearly membership: individual, corporate and family.

The Carlton Tennis Club

Alfred Rd, Westbourne Green, W2 - 071-286 1985, Fax 071-289 2028
Open daily 7am-11pm.

Three indoor courts with well-laid Escotennis carpet surfaces and good lighting. Coaching is £16 per hour; if they just hit the ball back at you it's £10 per hour. Their current fitness studio is being upgraded at the time of going to press; hopefully they will have a swimming pool as well as extra steam rooms in 1994. Non-members pay £20 per person Guest Fee and an hourly court fee varying between £12 and £20. Yearly membership starts at £650, plus joining fee.

The Vanderbilt Racquet Club

31 Sterne St, W12 - 081-743 9816/9822, Fax 081-740 0440
Open daily 7am-11pm.

This club offers eight indoor tennis courts and one show court with good spectator facilities, stretch and fitness classes, a beautician, bar and restaurant and special treatment centre for sports injuries and general conditions such as stress, spinal pain and migraine. Yearly membership begins at £795 plus joining fee. Temporary membership for overseas residents is £130 per calendar month.

■ WATER SPORTS

Within London, water sports centres are concentrated in Docklands. Getting out on one of the old docks is an exhilerating experience, though the whole great Docklands development has been moving at a snail's pace for several years. Hours vary according to the time of year and amount of daylight.

Docklands Water Sports Club

King George V Dock, Gate 14, Woolwich Manor Way, E16 - 071-511 7000, Fax 071-511 9000
Open Summer: daily except Wed; Winter: Thurs-Sun.

This is the club to go to for wet-biking and jet-skiing. You can either bring your own craft or hire from the centre.

Docklands Sailing and Watersports Centre

Westferry Rd, Millwall Docks, E14 QS - 071-537 2626
Open Summer: daily; Winter: times vary.

A day membership means you can windsurf, sail, canoe and go dragon-boating—where you sit in a canoe with 22 people accompanied by a dragon and a gong. All very Hong Kong, they will tell you.

Royal Docks Waterski Club

Gate 16, King George V Dock, Woolwich Manor Way, E16 - 071-511 2000
Open Summer: daily during hours of daylight; Winter: Wed 11am-4pm, Sat, Sun 10am-4pm.

This specialist water-skiing club teaches everyone from beginners up to competition standard skiers. The rate of £15 (£52 for four lessons) covers tuition and all equipment if necessary (including wet suits) for fifteen minutes.

■ WINE COURSES

Christie's Education

63 Old Brompton Rd, SW7 071-581 3933, Fax 071-589 0383

Christie's auction some of the world's greatest wine. They also run two wine courses, an introductory evening course on five consecutive Tuesday evenings, and a special master class course which takes a closer look at classic wines and vintages.

Sotheby's Educational Studies

30 Oxford St, W1R 1RE 071-323 5775, Fax 071-580 8160

Both varietal and regional courses on offer here throughout the year, covering tastings of Cabernet Sauvignon and Merlot, New World wines and more.

Wine Wise

107 Culford Rd, N1
071-254 9734

Wine expert and author Michael Schuster holds tastings (some with food) with wines ranging from the everyday drinking wines to the world's great vintages. The beginner's course takes six evenings and covers wines from all over the world as well as related subjects like the right kind of glasses to use, decanting etc.

HOUSES TO VISIT

Londoners are particularly proud of their famous residents; walk around any area and you'll see blue plaques galore on the outside of different houses telling you who lived there and when. Even more enjoyable, given our intense curiosity about how other people live, is seeing private homes. Happily London has more than its fair share, from the Queen's official residence to Dr Johnson's small house in the City.

Buckingham Palace

SW1 - 071-930 5526
State rooms open Aug & Sep: 9.30am-5.30pm. Changing of the Queen's Guard May-Aug: 11.30am; Aug & Sep: alternate days but subject to change without notice.

Buckingham Palace opened to the general public for the first time in August 1993 to help fund the restoration of parts of Windsor Castle after a hugely damaging fire.

Imposing? Yes. Comfortable, beautiful, homely?

Who lived where

Walking around London's streets you'll notice blue plaques on the sides of houses telling you which famous personage lived there and when. You'll be surprised—an Indian poet in the Vale of Health on Hampstead Heath, Mozart in Ebury Street, Handel in Brook Street. There are some surprising finds as well as some obscure ones. To qualify a candidate must have been dead for at least twenty years and born more than one hundred years ago and to have made some positive and important contribution to human welfare or happiness.

No. But what everyone agreed on was the quality of the art, much of which was purchased by the (thankfully) spendthrift George IV. It's a huge place, functioning as both office and home and used for ceremonial state occasions like banquets for visiting heads of state.

What the visitor sees are the Throne Room, Picture Gallery, Drawing Rooms, Grand Staircase and other impressive State rooms. The general opinion is that this is a place for the art lover, rather than royal watchers, though you do see the door through which the Royal family makes a sudden and dramatic entrance before formal dinners, and pass through the Music Room where Princess Diana used to tap dance in happier days. And the souvenirs you can purchase on your way out make it all worthwhile, even if they are on the pricey side (cufflinks for £40, Palace desk blotters for £25).

Thomas Carlyle's House

24 Cheyne Row, SW3
071-352 7087
Open Apr-end Oct: Wed-Sun 11am-5pm. National Trust.

'A most massive, roomy, sufficient old house... Rent £35'. So wrote Thomas Carlyle in 1834 of his new lodging in fashionable Chelsea. Left as he and his wife Jane had it, it's a modest house where he wrote some of his greatest books like *The French Revolution* and *Frederick the Great*. Personal touches—his hat hanging by the garden door, a screen his wife decorated—bring this little house to life.

Charles Dickens House Museum

48 Doughty St, WC1
071-405 2127
Open Mon-Sat 10am-5pm.

Many of the rooms are laid out exactly as they were when Dickens sat at his desk and wrote *Oliver Twist* and *Nicholas Nickelby*, and finished *Pickwick Papers*. The only one of Dickens's London homes to survive (he lived here from 1837 to 1839), it was bought by the Dickens Fellowship in the 1920s and has enough mementoes to satisfy the most enthusiastic fan: first editions, portraits, his terrible colour schemes and carpet, his desk and chair and personal items such as marked-up prompt copies for his lucrative readings.

Fenton House

20 Hampstead Grove, NW3
071-435 3471
Open Mar: Sat, Sun 2-6pm; Apr-Oct: Mon-Wed 11am-5pm, Sat, Sun public hols 11am-6pm. National Trust.

This pretty, gracious William and Mary house built in 1693 is full of early keyboard instruments (which are kept in full working order and used for concerts held in the house), fine eighteenth-century furniture and a magnificent collection of porcelain. The formal garden is a delight on a sunny day and as the house is surrounded by other old Hampstead mansions, the sense of the past is palpable.

Freud Museum

20 Maresfield Gdns, NW3
071-435 2002
Open Wed-Sun noon-5pm.

In 1938 Sigmund Freud (1856-1939), the founder of psychoanalysis, escaped war-time Vienna and arrived in leafy Hampstead. Until his death here a year later, he worked surrounded by his possessions in what was a replica of his Vienna consulting rooms. His collection of antiquities, his working library and papers and the famous desk and couch are all on display. On his death in

1939 his daughter Anna kept the house as it was; it was opened as a museum in 1986.

Ham House

Ham St, Richmond - 081-940 1950
Open Mar 30-end Oct: Mon-Wed, Sat 1-5pm, Sun 11.30-5.30pm; Nov-wkend before Christmas: Sat, Sun 1-4pm. National Trust.

Standing by the River Thames, Ham House was built in 1610 but came into its own with the redoubtable Countess of Dysart (c1626-98) and her second husband, the Duke of Lauderdale. In an age which valued comfort and elegance, the Duchess spared no expense. The house passed to the Duchess's son by her first marriage, a man as miserly as his mother was prodigal, and declined. But as a result the house remained in its original form and now appears locked in the past. The grand rooms contain wonderful furniture and fabrics while the kitchens are full of roasting spits, scrubbed wooden tables and even a seventeenth-century mouse trap.

Iveagh Bequest

Kenwood House, Hampstead Lane, NW3
081-348 1286
Open daily: Apr-Sep 10am-6pm; Oct 1- Mar 31: 10am-4pm. Admission free.

A magnificent mansion remodelled by Robert Adam in 1764, this neo-classical house set high on Hampstead Heath in landscaped gardens was rescued by Edward Cecil Guinness, 1st Earl of Iveagh, in 1925 and given to London. The library is

the architectural highlight, but the real glory of the house is its collection of treasures: paintings many national galleries covet and the very finest English eighteenth-century furniture. It's beloved by locals—children and dogs play in the grounds, families picnic beside the lake. Now administered by English Heritage, it holds a series of highly popular open-air summertime concerts by the lake. (Look in national newspapers for details).

John Keats House

Keats Grove, NW3 - 071-435 2062
Open Apr-Oct: Mon-Sat 10am-1pm, 2-6pm, Sun 2-5pm; Nov-Mar: Mon-Fri 1-5pm, Sat 10am-1pm, 2-5pm, Sun 2-5pm. Admission free.

The Romantic poet John Keats (1795-1821) lived from 1818 to 1820 in this small Regency house in a Hampstead side street and penned *Ode to a Nightingale* in the garden. A love letter to his fiancée, Fanny Brawne, who lived next door (he died in Rome of consumption before the marriage could take place), her engagement ring and many other small mementoes as well as books and letters fill this pretty, rather sad house.

Sir John Soane's Museum

13 Lincoln's Inn Fields, WC2
071-430 0175
Open Tues-Sat 10am-5pm.

The son of a brick-layer, John Soane (1753-1837) rose to become one of Britain's leading architects. He designed the Bank of England, Dulwich Picture Gallery and more, and as an art patron accumulated and commissioned a wide variety of works. The astonishing result is an eclectic collection remaining much as he left it, and both the house and the collection are full of surprises. The already crowded walls of the picture gallery unfold to reveal yet more paintings (such as William Hogarth's *Rake's Progress* series which cost £570 in 1802); the Monk's Parlour is full of grotesque Gothic casts; a vast sarcophagus stands in the crypt. Seek out the design for his wife's tombstone: it inspired Britain's old-style red telephone boxes.

John Wesley's House and Chapel
49 City Rd, EC1 - 071-253 2262
Open Mon-Sat 10am-4pm, Sun noon-2pm.

John Wesley, the founder of the Methodist church, laid the chapel's foundation stone in 1777 and lived in the house next door in the last years of his life. Five storeys high but only two rooms deep, it's rightly plain with bare wooden floors and little furniture. The chapel where Baroness Thatcher was married is also austere, with columns made from ships' masts.

Dr Johnson's House
17 Gough Sq, EC4 - 071-353 3745
Open May-Sep: Mon-Sat 11am-5.30pm; Oct-Apr: 11am-5pm.

Dive into Hind Court off Fleet Street and then into Gough Square for a glimpse of eighteenth-century life. Dr Samuel Johnson (1709-84) lived

here from 1749 to 1759, compiling his great dictionary in the attic, surrounded by six assistants and scribes who stood at high desks, industriously scratching away with their quill pens. But go for the atmosphere and the sense of peace in this hectic part of the City of London. As the day comes to an end, it's easy to imagine the good Doctor putting down his pen, snuffing out his candle, and walking out for ale and good company at the nearby taverns.

Leighton House
12 Holland Park Rd, W14
071-602 3316
Open Mon-Sat 11am-5.30pm. Admission free.

The flamboyant, purpose-built studio and house of Pre-Raphaelite painter Lord Leighton is a rare sight in fashionable Kensington. Built at the height of the Victorian Aesthetic movement for the wildly fashionable portrait painter, the high point is the Arab Hall added in 1879 to accommodate the Islamic tiles he acquired on his travels and Walter Crane's gilt mosaic frieze. Paintings by Leighton and his contemporaries hang in the richly decorated rooms.

Linley Sambourne House
18 Stafford Terr, W8
071-937 0663
Open Mar-Oct: Wed 10am-4pm, Sun 2-5pm.

Built in the 1870s, N°18 was the home from 1874 to 1910 of Linley Sambourne, book illustrator and political cartoonist for the satirical magazine

Punch. As you enter the cluttered, olive-green hall with its small fireplace, dinner gong and heavy curtains to keep dangerous draughts at bay and wander through the rooms, the years slip away. The house is a perfect, almost totally intact example of a late Victorian, early Edwardian home.

Spencer House
27 St James's Pl, SW1
071-499 8620
Open Feb-July, Sep-Dec: Sun guided tours only 10.30am-4.30pm.

Spencer House was built in the mid-eighteenth century for John, first Earl of Spencer in fashionable St James's, conveniently close to the monarch at St James's Palace. The former London home of the present Princess of Wales's family, it has been sumptuously and correctly restored by Lord Rothschild who currently leases the houses and is one of the very few examples surviving of an eighteenth-century townhouse. The Spencer family was noted for its art collection and legendary and lavish entertaining, and for a few thousand pounds, you too can hire the house and dine in the gilded surroundings.

Southside House
Wimbledon Common, SW19 - 081-946 7643
Open Oct-May 31: Tues, Thurs, Sat, Bank hols. Guided tours only every hour 2-5pm.

This is a house where the phrase 'entering a time warp' has real meaning. Lived in continuously by the same family since it was built in 1687, this small red-brick mansion which has been left mercifully un-restored, is full of odd fam-ily treasures—the pearls worn by Marie Antoinette at her execution and the cuff links given by King Edward VII to Axel Munthe, the doctor who became famous for his work with the poor in southern Italy and who wrote the best-seller *The Story of San Michele* in the 1920s. To the surprise of the fashionable world Axel Munthe wooed and married the society beauty Hilda Pennington whose family owned the house... but that's another story. Visit this atmospheric house, so full of ghosts. Each time you enter a room you feel that the occupants of the past have just closed the far door quietly behind them, leaving you to enjoy their house for a few minutes before they return.

MUSEUMS

London has some of the best museums in the world, both large and small, so we have divided this section into major museums and those we think you should see for their specialist inter-est or idiosyncratic nature. We have noted where ad-mission is free; otherwise there is an admission charge. If you are in London over a public holi-day, please check opening times.

Barbican Gallery
Barbican Centre, Silk St, EC2
071-638 4141
Open Mon-Sat 9am-11pm, Sun, public hols noon-11pm.

The art gallery which holds some first-rate ex-hibitions is housed on the fifth floor of this piece of 1960s city planning. The residential, commercial and arts complex was built on a site destroyed during World War II and opened to the public in the 1980s. To many people it's a nightmare to navigate, but persist as it contains two theatres, a concert hall, cinemas, library and a con-servatory on the roof. It's always a lively place to visit, and the exhibitions are of major importance.

Bethnal Green Museum of Childhood
Cambridge Heath Rd, E2
081-980 2415
Open Mon-Thurs, Sat 10am-5.50pm, Sun 2.30-5.30pm. Admission free.

This delightful treasure house in the East End of London is housed in one of the temporary train-shed buildings that were put up for the original Victoria and Albert Museum (which it is still part of) in South Kensington. Re-erected piece-by-piece in 1872, the cast-iron building now con-tains the nation's toy box. Walk inside and you're magically transported back in time through your own childhood to the seventeenth century. What delights and reassures is the fact that children's pleasures have changed so little. Dolls' houses from three centuries still attract crowds of small children pointing out miniature pia-nos, plates and furniture; others clamour to put money into the machine that makes the model

trains go round their eter-nal circle. It's a wonderful mix of toys and games, dolls and magic lantern shows, model railways and board games from all over Europe. They hold special children's workshops every Saturday at 11am and 2pm.

British Museum
Great Russell St, WC1
071-636 1555
Open Mon-Sat 10am-5pm, Sun 2.30-6pm. Admission free. (Special evening open-ing: 1st Tues of the month 6-9pm, Feb-Dec, admission £5).

The British Museum, one of the world's greatest museums, was started by the physician Sir Hans Slo-ane (1660-1753) who sug-gested in his will that the government buy his private collection. This they did and in 1753 passed the British Museum Act for London's (and the world's) first public museum. Benefactors gave generous-ly and the collect-ion rapidly outgrew the origi-nal location in Montagu House, Bloomsbury. George II bequeathed the Royal Library of 10,500 volumes (1757), Sir William Hamilton gave his antique vase collection (1772), the famous Greek Marbles from the Parthenon and Erech-theum from Greece were bought from Lord Elgin in 1816 and George III donated his library of 120,800 books in 1823. The present neo-classical building (1823-38) designed by Robert Smirke now houses some four mill-ion objects, divided bet-ween different depart-ments (Greek and Roman,

Egyptian, Ethnography, Prehistory and Roman Britain, Oriental, Coins and Medals, Medieval and Later Antiquities, Prints and Drawings, Western Asiatic and Japanese Antiquities). There are so many treasures—Egyptian mummies, the Portland Vase, the glorious Lindisfarne gospels, the Sutton Hoo ship burial, the magnificent Chinese art—it is impossible to see them all in one visit. The best way to explore the museum is to pick up a map in the front hall and choose one or two particular topics or galleries to wander around. And then come back for your favourites.

Courtauld Institute Galleries

Somerset House, Strand, WC2 - 071-872 0220
Open Mon-Sat 10am-6pm, Sun 2-6pm.

Housed in grandiose Somerset House (1776-86), the Courtauld Institute Galleries contain one of the best collections of Impressionist and Post-Impressionist paintings outside France. But apart from such masterpieces as Manet's *Bar at the Folies-Bergeres* and Van Gogh's *Self-Portrait*—part of the original gift of textile magnate, Samuel Courtauld (1865-1947)—you can feast your eyes on paintings by Rubens, Tiepolo and Van Dyck as well as British paintings, Roger Fry's pictures, art works by the early twentieth-century London Bloomsbury Group and the Omega Workshops, drawings and more. It's an important collection

housed in impressive surroundings and there's a good book shop attached. The Witt Library, open to art historians and dealers by private application, contains the most complete catalogue of Western paintings in the world.

Hayward Gallery

South Bank Centre, SE1
071-928 3144
Open Tues-Wed 10am-8pm, Thurs-Mon 10am-6pm.

One of London's main venues for major exhibitions, its stark concrete exterior and interior cause some people to shudder. But the exhibitions are of such a high standard that purists should overcome their horror and venture inside.

Imperial War Museum

Lambeth Rd, SE1 - 071-416 5000
Open daily 10am-6pm.

Perhaps it is appropriate that the Imperial War Museum, dedicated to the paraphernalia and story of twentieth-century war, should be housed in the former Bethlehem Hospital for the Insane ('Bedlam') built in 1811. The museum with its huge guns outside and the machinery of war inside is impressive. So, too, is the story of the social effects of war: the deprivation, food rationing, air raid precautions and censorship. Extracts from wartime films, radio programmes and literature, paintings and photographs are on display as are strange artefacts like Montgomery's caravan office and the German straw overboots for protec-

tion against Russia's cold. The museum is kept up-to-date: the most recent exhibits relate to the Gulf War of 1991.

Institute of Contemporary Arts

The Mall, SW1 - 071-930 3647
Open daily noon-11pm.

Established in 1947 by art critics Herbert Read and Roland Penrose to help British artists in the way American artists were by the Museum of Modern Art in New York, the Institute holds a lively and continual series of exhibitions, films, theatre and talks. It moved into Carlton House Terrace in 1968.

Madame Tussaud's Waxworks and The Planetarium

Marylebone Rd, NW1
071-935 6861
Open Sep-Jun: Mon-Fri 10am-5.30pm, Sat, Sun 9.30am-5.30pm; Jul-Aug: daily 9am-5.30pm.

One of London's greatest tourist attractions which you should try to avoid at peak times like school holidays, Madame Tussaud's began as a museum in 1835 when the redoubtable lady stopped touring England with her waxworks—originally death masks of many of the best-known victims of the French Revolution—and made a permanent exhibition. The scope is endless and international: from King Henry VIII to Nelson Mandela and is continually being added to. In the 'Garden Party' section you mingle with life-like models of celebrities; Man's gruesome side is displayed with a grim catalogue of torture and punishment in the ever-popular 'Chamber of Horrors'; a stylised London taxi cab takes you through London's history in 'The Spirit of London'.

The London Planetarium next door has a cinema showing the mysteries of the planets and the solar system and a separate Space Trail exhibition. Compared to similar exhibitions in France or the USA, it is limited, but nonetheless worth seeing.

Museum of Garden History

Lambeth Palace Rd, SE1
071-2661 1891
Open 1st Sun in Mar-2nd Sun in Dec: Mon-Fri 11am-3pm, Sun 10.30am-5pm.

This was started as a labour of love by Rosemary Nicholson in what was the shut and decaying church of St Mary-at-Lambeth, beside the Archbishop of Canterbury's London home, Lambeth Palace. With the help of dedicated gardeners, who included Lady Salisbury of Hatfield House and the Queen Mother, the church opened as a museum in 1979, dedicated to the history of gardening in Britain. It's officially the Tradescant Trust, called after the Tradescants, father and son, who were gardeners to seventeenth-century monarchs, and dedicated plant hunters in Russia, Europe and particularly the Americas. They were also the Salisbury family's gardeners. The museum has good changing exhibitions, and the churchyard, which has a knot garden planted with seventeenth-century plants, is a delightful place to sit in on a summer afternoon. The Tradescants are buried in the churchyard, alongside Captain Bligh of *Bounty* fame.

Museum of London

150 London Wall, EC2
071-600 3699
Open Tues-Sat 10am-5.50pm, public hol Mon, Sun noon-5.50pm.

Arranged chronologically, the museum tells the story of London in an intriguing way with each section providing a vivid idea of what living in London was like throughout the ages. You pass through a Roman kitchen, see the Cheapside Hoard of jewellery cascading down a chimney just as it was found, walk past eighteenth-century prisons, grocers' shops, through elegant Regency London to the city of the Suffragettes, the Blitz and the Swinging Sixties. One of the high points is the cinematic experience of watching the Great Fire of London: Samuel Pepys' contemporary account is read with suitable solemnity while the model of London appears to burn and crash to the ground in front of your eyes. The museum offers a delightful visual experience, holds frequent exhibitions and in the cinema shows a changing programme of classic British movies from the days when Britain had a movie industry.

Museum of Mankind

6 Burlington Gdns, W1
071-437 2224
Open Mon-Sat 10am-5pm, Sun 2.30-6pm. Admission free.

In the somewhat unexpected surroundings of the back of elegant and aristocratic Burlington House, you'll find the British Museum's Ethnographic Department. It's a small but interesting collection where Eskimo snow spectacles are displayed alongside human head mascots from the Amazon and West African jewellery. Changing exhibitions on the second floor are particularly effective in dis-

---

Friends of...

If you're in London for any length of time, consider becoming a Friend of one of your favourite museums. Although the main purpose of these organisations is to raise much-needed funds, becoming a Friend is rather like joining a club. You pay a yearly membership and receive news about the museum, free admission to exhibitions as well as the possibility of enjoying specially arranged holidays. Many of them also organise evening viewings which are only open to Friends. The Friends of the Royal Academy can take guests to private views for free, and use the special club Room which is one of the best in London.

playing objects against the settings they come from.

Museum of the Moving Image
South Bank, SE1 - 071-401 2636
Open daily 10am-6pm.

A fascinating journey through the history of moving pictures from the earliest flickering experiments with zeotropes and magic lanterns to holograms and beyond. Exhibits come in all sorts of guises; the section on Charlie Chaplin (born in nearby Kennington) is illustrated with clips from his films and artefacts from his life like his indispensable cane. Actors dressed in appropriate costumes invite you into a cinema to watch a silent movie, aboard a 1919 Lenin Agitprop train for an excellent piece of early Russian propaganda, or to try for a part in an early Hollywood film. The amazing technology allows the artistic to draw their own cartoons and the ambitious to watch themselves reading the news.

National Army Museum
Royal Hospital Rd, SW3
071-730 0717
Open daily 10am-5.30pm. Admission free.

The museum records five centuries of the British Army from 1485 to the present day with weapons, paintings, tableaux, dioramas and film clips. Students of military history should write to the Director for a reader's ticket to the comprehensive, rare collection of manuscripts, books, maps, drawings and more.

National Gallery
Trafalgar Sq, WC2 - 071-839 3526
Open Mon-Sat 10am-6pm, Sun 2-6pm. Admission free.

The National Gallery came into being in 1824, many years after other national galleries in Europe had opened, when King George IV persuaded a philistine government to buy 38 major paintings, including works by Raphael and Rembrandt. Today this large and comprehensive collection, housed in the neo-classical William Wilkins building of the 1830s and in the new, controversial Sainsbury Wing (the original design for which caused Prince Charles to enter the architectural arena when he declared it a 'monstrous carbuncle') provides a first-class panorama of European painting from Giotto to the French Impressionists. Modern and British paintings are housed in the Tate Gallery. The masterpieces here are well known: the Leonard da Vinci cartoon, Velazquez's *Rokeby Venus*, *The Baptism of Christ* by Pierro dell Francesca, Van Eyck's *Arnolfini Marriage* and *The Haywain* by John Constable. Divided into sections covering Early Renaissance (1260-1510) in the new Sainsbury Wing, High Renaissance (1520-1600), English, French and German Painting (1800-1900) and more, the galleries are compact and easy to wander through.

National Portrait Gallery
2 St Martin's Pl, WC2
071-306 0055

Open Mon-Fri 10am-6pm, Sat 10am-6pm, Sun 2-6pm. Admission free.

If you want to know what a favourite, famous or infamous British writer, King, Queen, Prince or Princess, poet, artist or villain looked like, go to the National Portrait Gallery which shows British history through its people. Covering five centuries of portraiture, the earliest portraits include a Hans Holbein cartoon of King Henry VIII, while the latest, new galleries include photographs, sculptures and pictures of contemporary figures. The latter is a difficult section; who will be considered important enough to be preserved in years to come? As the collection concentrates on the sitter rather than the artist, it is a complete mixture: works by some of the world's greatest artists hang alongside some fairly mediocre efforts. The collection, arranged chronologically, gives an insight into different age's ideals of beauty: sloping shoulders and long noses in the eighteenth century, gamin waif-like looks in the 1990s.

Natural History Museum
Cromwell Rd, SW7
071-938 9123
Open Mon-Sat 10am-5.50pm, Sun 11am-5.50pm. Admission charge but free Mon-Fri 4.30-5.50pm, Sat, Sun, public hols 5-6pm.

More than 65 million species make up one of the world's largest collections of animals, plants, fossils and minerals which was founded originally on the private collection of the celebrated physician Sir

Hans Sloane whose collection also helped found the main British Museum. Traditional displays alongside interactive techniques prompt questions about ecology and evolution, the origin of the species and how human beings have developed. It has some spectacular new exhibits including the popular permanent Dinosaur Exhibition and one on insects (Creepy-Crawlies), both of which display life-like models. The building is worth a visit in itself: a huge cathedral-like space designed by Alfred Waterhouse using revolutionary Victorian building techniques and covered outside with a stone zoo of animals and plants.

The museum incorporates the former Geological Museum which tells the story of the Earth. The Earth Galleries explore our planet and its natural resources; the gemstone collection draws students of gemology from all over the world who come to see the unique fibrolite, the orange sapphire, tourmalines and other priceless gems. After wandering through the extraordinary mixture of fossils, minerals, a re-enactment of an earthquake, a chunk of the Moon and more, you emerge bewildered and astounded by the complexity of the planet.

Queen's Gallery

Buckingham Palace Rd, SW1
071-799 2331
Open Tues-Sat 10am-5pm, Sun 2-5pm.

A small gallery and surprisingly little visited, the quality of the exhibits is a revelation. But why should

this be a surprise? The Queen's collection of paintings and furniture is one of the finest and most valuable in the world. (Sir Anthony Blunt, for 30 years her art adviser until exposed as the 'third man' and a Soviet spy in 1979 and stripped of his knighthood, was a noted world expert.) The selection is comprehensive; particularly rich in old masters like Michelangelo, Raphael and Leonardo, displays will often also include drawings by Hogarth, Stanley Spencer and Topolski among others. The well-stocked shop sells all kinds of high-quality royal 'souvenirs'.

Royal Academy of Arts

Burlington House, Piccadilly, W1 - 071-439 7438
Open daily 10am-6pm.

A splendid institution housed in the equally splendid Burlington House, Piccadilly, the Royal Academy of Arts was founded in 1768 by Sir Joshua Reynolds with King George III as patron. Although most widely known for its Annual Summer Exhibition (held for over 200 years), the Royal Academy has some of the best exhibitions in London such as recent surveys of American Art and Italian Art, drawings from the Getty collection and shows of major individual artists. The light, airy Sackler Galleries, designed by English modern architect, Norman Foster, house visiting exhibitions. Each elected Academician (a roster of names which includes every major British artist in-

cluding contemporaries Alan Jones, David Hockney and Elisabeth Frink and architects Richard Rogers and Norman Foster) has to give a piece of work before receiving a Diploma signed by the Sovereign. Along with bequests, gifts and purchases, this makes for an impressive collection of British Art over the past 217 years. Some is on show, some can be seen by appointment, much is on loan to other institutions and exhibitions.

Royal Air Force Museum

Grahame Park Way, NW9
081-205 2266
Open daily 10am-6pm.

A must for anyone interested in the history of aviation and the story of the Royal Air Force with aircraft displayed in a vast hall. The museum has three separate sections: the RAF Museum, the Battle of Britain Museum and the Bomber Command Museum. There are also effective exhibits of room settings, air raid shelters and command posts which convey a very real atmosphere.

Science Museum

Exhibition Rd, SW7
071-938 8000
Open Mon-Sat 10am-6pm, Sun 11am-6pm. Admission charge but free Mon-Fri 4.30-5.50pm, Sat, Sun, public hols 5-6pm.

The Science Museum will thrill even the most unscientific-minded. Leaving aside the new Space Exploration Galleries and Launch Pad, (a first-class hands-on exhibition for children), the museum with its five floors of exhibits brings such varied subjects as medical history, the art of navigation, the weather, computers and transport to life. Exhibits range from a magnificent collection of scientific instruments and apparatus originally belonging to King George III in the eighteenth century, Puffing Billy, the earliest surviving locomotive (1813), to Apollo 10. How scientific discoveries and progress have transformed our lives plays an equally important part, and there are enough interactive displays to satisfy the most avid seeker after scientific discovery, from age three upwards.

Tate Gallery
Millbank, SW1 - 071-887 8000
Open Mon-Sat 10am-5.50pm, Sun 2-5.50pm. Admission free but charge made for major exhibitions.

The Tate Gallery, which has space to show only a small part of its vast holdings, contains two major national collections: British art from the sixteenth century to 1900 and international modern art from the Impressionists to today. The gallery is always sparking off one major row after another as the great British public fulminates against wasting public money on collections of bricks or toys. Whatever your predilections, it's a lively, always interesting collection which is in the process of being re-hung (another source of controversy). Built through the generosity of sugar millionaire Sir Henry Tate, who also gave his own collection, the latest major addition is Sir James Stirling's Clore Gall-

---

Keeping out of step

If you're crossing Albert Bridge in Chelsea, look for the sign that demands that troops break step while marching over it. The vibrations, it was felt, might cause it to collapse.

---

ery which houses the extensive collection of JMW Turner's works.

Victoria & Albert Museum
Cromwell Rd, SW7
071-938 8500
Open 10am-5.50pm (Mon noon-5.50pm). Donation suggested.

The V and A as it is popularly known, is officially the National Museum of Art and Design and the largest decorative arts museum in the world, covering a mind-boggling seven miles of galleries. Opened in 1857 with the accent on design and craft in commerce, it was the brain-child of Prince Albert and civil servant Sir Henry Cole (who, incidentally, sent the first Christmas card in 1843). The massive, comprehensive museum is arranged in a unique way. It is divided into galleries devoted to art and design to express the style of an age (such as Europe from 1600 to 1800), and into study collections which concentrate on materials and techniques. The Dress collection, the Historic Musical Instruments Collection, the Indian Gallery (which contains the greatest collection of Indian Art outside India, a legacy of the British Empire), the

Chinese Gallery, the new Japanese Toshiba Gallery and the fabulously valuable Jewellery Gallery all merit visits. Unless you have a specific purpose in mind, the best way to enjoy the museum is just to wander through it at random. That way you discover unexpected sections, like the vast metalwork department, full of snuff-boxes, arms and armour, watches, clocks, locks and salt cellars, or the extraordinary Cast Courts which turn out to be two galleries containing Victorian plaster casts of Europe's great sculptures and masonry originally made as teaching aids. As so much of Europe's art is eroding with pollution, this was not such a crazy idea after all.

Wallace Collection
Hertford House, Manchester Sq, W1 - 071-935 0687
Open Mon-Sat 10am-5pm, Sun 2-5pm. Admission free.

One of the greatest private collections of European art in the world, the Wallace Collection includes among its many treasures a display of eighteenth-century French paintings that rivals the Louvre's. Four generations of the Hertford family acquired wisely—the collection includes superb eighteenth-century English portraits, Sèvres porcelain and armour. The family enjoyed sometimes scandalous relations with the English and French Royal families, and the third Marquess appears as the dissolute Lord Stayne in Thackeray's *Vanity Fair*. The house is magnificent; they certainly had a good setting to enjoy themselves in.

Whitechapel Art Gallery
80 Whitechapel High St, E1
071-377 0107
Open Tues-Sun 11am-5pm (Wed to 8pm). Entrance free except for one show a year, usually a major retrospective in the summer.

Since the 1960s, this has been the mecca of innovative art under a series of high profile directors. Catherine Lampert's current exhibition programme has taken on a more lyrical mood, reflecting her interest in British painters like Lucien Freud. Two elegant main galleries, the upper one totally top-lit, are used for one-person contemporary shows and retrospectives.

■ OFF THE BEATEN TRACK

Bank of England Museum
Bank of England, Bartholomew Lane, EC3 - 071-601 5545
Open Mon-Fri 10am-5pm, also Easter-end Sep: Sun 11am-4pm.

'The Old Lady of Threadneedle Street' (as the bank was named by the playwright and politician

Sheridan) was set up in 1694 to raise money for foreign wars, came under government control in 1766 and was nationalised in 1946. The museum tells the story of the 'banker's bank' (and a surprisingly exciting one it is), and the story of the development of the financial system with displays from glittering gold bars to dealing desks.

HMS Belfast
Morgan's Lane, Tooley St, SE1 - 071-407 6434
Open mid-Mar-Oct 31: 10am-5.30pm; Nov 1-mid Mar: 10am-4pm.

The cruiser *HMS Belfast*, the Royal Navy's last big-gun ship, became a floating museum in 1971. During World War II, this floating city with 800 men on board had the unenviable task of guarding Russian convoys and in 1943 helped sink the greatest single danger to the Russian lifeline, the German battle cruiser *Scharnhorst*. Part of the ship has been left as it was; the rest relates to the history of the Royal Navy. In these days of nuclear weapons the whole ship has a curiously old-fashioned feel; was war really like this?

Clockmakers' Company Collection
Guildhall Library, Aldermanbury, EC2 - 071-606 3030
Open Mon-Fri 9.30am-4.30pm. Admission free.

It's a good thing to try to go to the museum in the morning when this large collection (some 600 watches and 30 clocks dating from the sixteenth to the nineteenth centuries) chimes, bongs and tinkles

the hours. But at any time, the collection holds surprises. The oldest surviving clocks date from the 1300s; by 1675 English watches using hair-springs could run to within an accurate two minutes a day; in 1752 the world's first watch to compensate against the effects of heat and cold was made; by 1785 there were self-winding watches. You come away wondering where our need for accurate timing will lead.

Crafts Council Gallery
44a Pentonville Rd, N1
071-278 7700
Open Tues-Sat 11am-6pm, Sun 2-6pm. Admission free.

The national centre for crafts shows work by Britain's foremost craftspeople. Britain has always had a reputation for producing first-rate craft items, and this gallery endorses that view. There's always something new and interesting to see in frequently changing exhibitions of silver, jewellery, woodcarvings, pottery and more. The shop is an excellent source of good, one-off items and presents you won't find elsewhere. Otherwise you can find out which designer attracts you and commission work from them.

Cutty Sark
King William Walk, SE10
081-853 3589
Open Apr-Sep: Mon-Sat 10am-6pm, Sun noon-6pm.

This absurdly small vessel now permanently marooned in Greenwich, was built at Dumbarton, Scotland in 1869 as one of the fast clippers used to race across the Atlantic and Pacific Oceans in the nineteenth century carrying first tea, then wool. In 1871 she won the annual China to London clipper race taking a mere 107 days. The brave clipper's last sea voyage was in 1938; she became a museum in 1957. On board you see the complex rigging and masts characteristic of the great days of sail; below deck the cramped quarters of the seamen are full of prints, instruments, odd personal artefacts and the Long John Silver Collection of wooden figureheads.

Design Museum

Butlers Wharf, Shad Thames, SE1 - 071-407 6261
Open daily 10.30am-5.30pm.

Inevitably full of trendy, well-dressed people, this brain-child of Sir Terence Conran is solely devoted to the design of mass-produced everyday objects from chairs to cars, lemon squeezers to radios. International design is displayed in temporary exhibitions with different themes and there's an exciting interactive section where you can research details on the history and design of every object you can think of. You want to know about chairs? Legs of chairs? History? Famous designers? Just follow the instructions on the screen. The Blueprint Cafe (see *Restaurant* section) is an excellent watering-hole; otherwise try a cappuccino in the cafe museum and observe the other visitors.

Walks around London

There are a lot of excellent companies taking you on walks through every part of London concentrating on the fascinating and frequently disreputable side of London's history. Many of them also have historic pub walks, which is an excellent way to meet people. You can get information on the following by telephoning direct or from *London Tourist Board* **offices.** *Citisights of London* **(071-955 4791),** *Historical Tours* **(081-668 4019, Fax 081-668 4019) and** *Original London Walks* **(071-624 3978) are all highly recommended.**

Dulwich Picture Gallery

College Rd, SE21 - 081-693 5254
Open Tues-Fri 10am-1pm, 2-5pm; Sat 11am-5pm, Sun 2-5pm.

England's oldest public art gallery was designed by the imaginative Sir John Soane (see the John Soane Museum) and opened in 1814. His use of skylights which gave the rooms natural light made it the model for most subsequent art galleries. The twelve galleries and mausoleum contain a splendid collection of Old Master paintings belonging to Dulwich College.

Fan Museum

12 Crooms Hill, Greenwich, SE10 - 081-858 7879/ 081-305 1441
Open Tues-Sat 11am-4.30pm, Sun noon-4.30pm.

Fans may seem at first an unlikely subject for a museum, but this one is full of surprises. The museum shows fans in themed exhibitions like those decorated with children or flowers; there is a perman-

ent display on the history and materials used in fan making, and a craft workshop which holds fan-making classes and undertakes conservation and restoration.

Fawcett Library

London Guildhall University, Old Castle St, E1 - 071-320 1189
Open term time: Mon 11am-8.30pm, Wed-Fri 10am-5pm. Holidays: Mon, Wed-Fri 10am-5pm.

Britain's main reference collection on women is the direct descendant of the London Society for Women's Suffrage, founded in 1867. It holds over 50,000 books, pamphlets and leaflets, periodicals, boxes of papers on relevant organisations, newspaper cuttings and photographs, autographed letters and posters. The library is part of the university, but non-members can use it on a daily basis. Dedicated feminists as well as those with a general interest in the women's movement will find it invaluable.

Florence Nightingale Museum

St Thomas's Hospital, Lambeth Palace Rd, SE1 - 071-620 0374
Open Tues-Sun 10am-4pm.

Florence Nightingale, born into a well-to-do Victorian family, became a nurse (*not* a profession for a lady) and was sent to the Crimean War. Her reorganisation of Scutari Hospital and fame as 'the lady with the lamp' (she sat at the deathbeds of 2,000 men, believing no-one should die alone) turned out to be only a small part of her achievements. On her return home she became a tireless campaigner for hospital reform and set the standards of nursing care and training we know today. The museum tells the story of this formidable lady's remarkable life with room sets, pictures, and personal memorabilia.

Geffrye Museum

Kingsland Rd, E2 - 071-739 9893
Open Tues-Sat 10am-5pm, Sun, Mon, public hols 2-5pm.

This delightful museum is housed in a charming collection of alms-houses which were built for the poor in 1715. In the centre of the former furniture-making area in the East End, it became a museum in 1911. The interior is arranged as a series of room settings taking you through the story of English furnishings and decorative tastes, from a 1600 panelled Elizabethan room through the elegance of the Georgians to the 1950s. Outside there's a walled herb garden to wander around. It is a charming

place and especially good to visit around Christmastime when there is always a special display.

Guards Museum

Wellington Barracks, Birdcage Walk, SW1 - 071-930 4466/3271
Open Sat-Thurs 10am-4pm.

If you're a military enthusiast, this is a must, full of tableaux, weapons, uniforms, models and dioramas to illustrate the battles that the five famous Guards regiments have taken part in.

Horniman Museum

100 London Rd, Forest Hill, SE23 - 081-699 2339
Open Mon-Sat 10.30am-5.30pm, Sun 2-5.30pm.

The tea merchant, Frederick Horniman, clearly a man with a tremendous curiosity about his fellow human beings, had this art nouveau museum built in 1901 to house all the odd objects he had collected on his travels—everything from Navajo paintings to objects you'd be hard put to to name if there wasn't a handy description nearby. Most famous is the collection of 6,000 musical instruments from all over the world. Displayed in the music room, you can hear, through headphones, hundreds of different instruments.

London Dungeon

Tooley St, SE1 - 071-403 0606
Open Apr-Sep: 10am-6.30pm; Oct-Mar: 10am-5.30pm.

The sort of ghoulish place children love and parents shudder at, full of the more bloodthirsty parts

of British history and naturally accompanied by shrieks and groans. Even the entrance is fun: you enter a dark and different world, lit by candles. Their most popular exhibit? The Jack the Ripper Experience, they cheerfully tell you.

London Transport Museum

The Piazza, Covent Garden, WC2 - 071-379 6344
Open daily 10am-6pm.

Don't pass this one by thinking it's just full of old vehicles. It's a lively place, with lots of hands-on exhibits for children, and yes, lots of old but interesting vehicles from the original horse-bus of 1829 to trams and tube trains. The art collection is interesting too: London Transport has always commissioned first-rate artists for their posters, including Graham Sutherland and Paul Nash.

Lord's Cricket Ground Gestetner Tours & Museum

St John's Wood, NW8
071-289 1611, Tours: 071-266 382

A visit to the Cricket Museum will not give you an insight into the game visitors find so distressingly obscure, but it will provide you with a bit of amusement (if such a thing can be allowed with such a revered institution). It was not, it turns out, such a gentleman's game: the first rules state the width of the bat as early cads were making bats wider than the wicket behind them. There are paintings and objects, a talking head of W G Grace and eccentric objects like the stuffed sparrow killed by a cricket ball in play. And you do see the famous, and it has to be said, very beautiful rooms and grounds. The opening times are about as confusing as the game: the museum is shut during the 'closed season'—that is when there are no matches, though the tours operate then (at noon and 2pm). No tours however at major matches or preparation time... You must telephone ahead for details and booking.

National Sound Archive
29 Exhibition Rd, SW7
071-589 6603
Open Mon-Fri 9am-5pm, Thurs 9am-9pm. Admission free.

Most Londoners will look baffled if you ask them about the National Sound Archive. But it's one of those well-kept secrets that the few people who have discovered it rave about. And not surprisingly. A branch of the British Library, it contains 900,000 discs, some from the start of recording in the 1880s. If you want to hear an 1880's recording of Queen Victoria, Tennyson reading one of his own poems, wildlife sounds, international ethnic music or even the complete repertoires of our two main theatre companies, this is the place to come to. You can arrange to hear recordings, but you must go through the library procedure which includes research and booking. For the enthusiast, it's an extraordinary collection of ghostly voices from the past.

Drinking fountains

In 1859 the Metropolitan Free Drinking Fountain Association was established to supply drinking water to combat the dreadful water shortages, cholera and intemperance rife in London's poorer areas. By 1886 they had established 594 though few remain today.

The Old Operating Theatre, Museum & Herb Garret
9a St Thomas' St, SE1
071-955 4791
Open Jan 6-Dec 14: Tues-Sat 10am-4pm.

The oldest surviving operating theatre in the country was built in 1822 from part of the herb garret. With its banked seats for students to watch as surgeons performed their grisly tasks before the days of anaesthetics and antiseptic surgery it is just like a theatre. The herb garret, used by the Apothecary of nearby St Thomas's, has objects like instruments for the ancient art of cupping and trepanning. With such reminders of the crude medicine of the past, you emerge doubly grateful for being born in the twentieth century. They hold lectures at 2.30pm on the first Sunday of every month on the history of Old St Thomas's Hospital and Guy's and the history of health care.

Percival David Foundation of Chinese Art
53 Gordon Sq, WC1
071-387 3909
Open Mon-Fri 10.30am-5pm. Admission free.

If you're at all interested in Chinese porcelain, you must see this important and relatively unknown collection of beautiful Chinese ceramics made between the tenth and eighteenth centuries. Percival David (1892-1964) was a Governor of the School of Oriental and African Studies and gave his collection to London University. It is an exquisite collection; many of the pieces were once owned by Chinese emperors.

Royal College of Music Museum of Instruments
Prince Consort Rd, SW7
071-589 3643
Open Wed in term time: 2-4.30pm.

Housed in the prestigious Royal College of Music which has had as pupils Benjamin Britten, Ralph Vaughan Williams and other leading British musicians, this valuable collection of around 500 instruments must be on your list if you have an interest in music and the means of making it.

Royal Mews
Buckingham Palace Rd, SW1
071-799 2331
Open Wed noon-4pm, plus other days during summer.

Subject to closure at short notice.

This collection of royal vehicles is housed in the old stables and coach houses of the Palace which were built by John Nash in 1825. Of major interest is the 1761 gold state coach of George III weighing a massive four tons and pulled at walking pace by eight horses. But don't miss the glass coach used for royal weddings or the splendid royal cars. The harnesses are among the finest in the world, and some of the magnificent heavy horses are stabled here.

Saatchi Gallery

98a Boundary Rd, NW8
071-624 8299
Open Fri-Sun noon-6pm. Fri free entry; Sat, Sun charge.

This spectacular space, converted by architect Max Gordon from an old paint factory for Charles Saatchi in 1985, is one of the few venues for viewing large-scale contemporary work in its correct setting. The Saatchi Collection of International Contemporary Art is displayed in changing exhibitions, with young British artists being featured in the future, along with guest exhibitions. The Richard Wilson piece *20:50* on permanent display is stunning and should not be missed.

Shakespeare's Globe Museum

1 Bear Gdns, SE1 - 071-928 6342
Open Mon-Sat 10am-5pm, Sun 2-5.30pm.

After setbacks galore, the project to rebuild Shakespeare's Globe Theatre on the old Bankside site seems to be going ahead steadily. In the meantime, Shakespeare lovers should visit this small museum in a warehouse on the site of a seventeenth-century bear-baiting pit. The museum tells the story both of the Elizabethan theatre and of disreputable Southwark where the theatres were built, away from the Puritanical City fathers who forbade such pleasures. It's well worth telephoning to find out about their lunchtime events: poetry, jazz and performances of Elizabethan music.

Tea & Coffee Museum

The Clove Bldg, Maguire St, Butlers Wharf, SE1
071-378 0222
Open Nov 1-Mar 31: 10am-5.30pm; Apr-Oct: 10am-6pm.

This museum, devoted to the history of the much-loved beverages, tea and coffee, is housed down by the warehouses where cargoes were brought ashore. It's the brain-child of Edward Bramah, former tea merchant and taster, whose huge and comprehensive collection of teapots, coffee pots and general tea and coffee making machinery forms the main bulk of the museum. If you go, you're likely to meet Mr Bramah. He's a mine of information, so get him to take you around his favourite exhibits if you can. And do have a cup of tea or coffee in the café—the taste (particularly of the tea) will remind you of the past glories of the drink before the almost universal use of the dreaded tea-bag.

Theatre Museum

Russell St, WC2 - 071-836 7891
Open Tues-Sun 11am-7pm.

Despite the fascinating collection of theatrical memorabilia—from death masks, to playbills, costumes to make-up boxes—this is a surprisingly static museum. Nonetheless, if you love the theatre it's worth a visit.

Tower Bridge Museum

SE1 - 071-403 3761
Open Apr 1-Oct 31: daily 10am-6.30pm; Nov 1-Mar 31: 10am-5.15pm.

Tower Bridge (1886-94) was one of London's wonders with its ability to open 135 feet high for ships to steam through. The museum has been rebuilt and now has all sorts of animatronic characters and special effects which create the past. It's also a good place to go for the spectacular views and, cleverly, there are pictures of the same views through the ages, showing how much London has changed. The Bridge is not just for show; it is still raised an average of ten times a week to allow tall ships to pass.

Wimbledon Lawn Tennis Museum

Church Rd, Wimbledon, SW19 - 081-946 6131
Open Tues-Sat 10.30am-5pm, Sun 2-5pm.

Lawn tennis grew out of Real Tennis in the 1870s; in 1875 one croquet lawn at the All England Croquet Club was transformed into a tennis court and the new game became all the rage. The museum is both great fun (lots of good exhibits often displayed in appropriate room settings) and informative. Did you know that Bunny Austin was the first man to wear shorts on the Centre Court (1933), that each racket uses 33 feet of animal gut and that 33,000 bath buns and eighteen tons of strawberries are consumed every Wimbledon fortnight?

PARKS & GARDENS

Battersea Park

Albert Bridge Rd, SW11
071-871 7530
Open daily dawn-dusk.

London's second large park to be created not for royalty, but for Londoners (the first being Victoria Park in the East End) was opened on marshy fields beside the river by Queen Victoria in 1853. Its delightful ornamental lake, Old English Garden and carriage drives made it an instant success with the Victorians, who used it almost exclusively for the great new craze of bicycling which was forbidden in royal Hyde Park. In 1985 the Peace Pagoda, one of more than 70 built around the world, was opened. Today the park contains a botanical garden, deer park, the Festival Pleasure Gardens (part of the 1951 Festival of Britain), tennis courts, boating lake and a children's zoo with monkeys, snakes, deer, otters and a reptile house.

At Easter there is a special Easter Day parade.

Chelsea Physic Garden

Swan Walk, SW3 - 071-352 5646
Open Apr-Oct: Wed, Sun 2-5pm.

Tucked away in a peaceful corner of Chelsea, this delightful garden was founded by the Worshipful Society of Apothecaries in 1673 to grow plants for medical study, following Pisa (1543) and Oxford (1621). Internationally important, the garden conducted a two-way traffic: plants were sent from all over the known world to be cultivated and studied here, while the first cotton seeds were packed up and sent from Chelsea down the Thames and on to the new colony of Georgia. Today it is a small, pretty four-acre garden of herbs, flowers, trees, and medicinal plants grown in a newly-established area. Pharmaceutical companies around the world are once again researching the uses of natural drugs from plants grown in Chelsea—the garden has come full circle, it seems. It's a wonderful place for a summer afternoon. To the sound of birdsong and the distant hum of traffic on the Chelsea Embankment, you can stroll around the ancient trees, historical walks and the first rock garden in this country, installed in 1772.

Chiswick House

Burlington Lane, W4
081-994 3299
Open Apr 1-Oct: daily 10am-1pm, 2-6pm, Nov-Mar: daily 10am-1pm, 2-4pm.

Though called Chiswick House, it is really the gardens that people come to see. The house, modelled on a Palladian villa, was never intended to be lived in, but was built in 1725-1729 by the third Earl of Burlington, specifically to show off his works of art and as a place to entertain his friends. The gardens, full of delightful eighteenth-century temples and grottoes, were the first to move away from the formal Dutch style of gardens so popular up to then and epitomised by those at Hampton Court Palace. Only one or two of the little buildings remain, but the garden makes a delightful informal park and people come from miles around to see the camellias housed in the early nineteenth-century conservatory.

Crystal Palace Park

Sydenham, SE19 - 081-778 7148
Open daily dawn-dusk.

This park where Joseph Paxton's great glass house was re-erected after the Great Exhibition in 1851, was formally opened in 1854 by Queen Victoria and became one of the showplaces of Victorian London. Fires in the vulnerable glass 'Crystal Palace' however took their toll and the park's importance and attraction gradually declined. The last and most disastrous fire was in 1936 when the flames were visible from Brighton, 60 miles away. Today it is best known for the Victorian prehistoric stone monsters; there's also a boating lake, a children's zoo and the

Crystal Palace National Sports Centre.

Green Park

SW1 - 071-930 1793
Open daily 5am-dusk.

Full of daffodils in springtime, this small 53-acre park was once part of Henry VIII's hunting ground. Charles II made it into a royal park, and being a monarch who liked his pleasures built a snowhouse in the middle of it to keep his wines cool in summertime (you can still see the mound). During the eighteenth century it was a known haunt for duelling, highwaymen, ballooning and for grand fireworks displays which reached their height in 1748 at the celebration of the end of the War of the Austrian Succession. Today it's a good place to hire a deck chair on a summer afternoon, or just to stroll around, away from Piccadilly's hustle and bustle.

Greenwich Park

SE10 - 081-853 2608
Open daily 6am-dusk.

Greenwich enjoyed its best days under the Tudors. Henry VIII was born here and retained a particular fondness for the park where he hunted deer and jousted. The park was first enclosed in 1433, but what we see today was created later by Louis XIV's gardener, Le Nôtre, who designed the gardens at Versailles and was invited by Charles II to do a similar job for him. The park is magnificent, rising from river level gently to the Queen's House and up to the top of the hill and the Royal Observatory. It's worth the climb to the top, though the wonderful symmetry of the original design is marred today by towering Canary Wharf.

Hampstead Heath

NW3 - 081-348 9945
Open daily 24 hours.

Some 790 acres of rolling hills, meadows, woods, ponds and lakes, this is one of London's wonders, an area of open spaces and great vistas which through legislation will be kept in perpetuity for the people's enjoyment. Lying between the hilltop villages of Hampstead and Highgate, it's a collection of properties added to the Heath over the years. Parliament Hill became part of the Heath in 1889, Golders Hill Park in 1898 and Kenwood in the 1920s. Further small areas were added subsequently (such as the delightful, secret Hill Garden signposted off the road beyond Jack Straw's Castle) and today it constitutes a 'green lung' for Londoners. At weekends it's full of people flying kites, jogging, having picnics and exercising their dogs. On the three main holiday weekends of Easter, May and late summer there's a popular funfair at South End Green.

Highgate Cemetery

Swain's Lane, N6 - 081-340 1834
Eastern Cemetery open Apr-Oct: daily 10am-5pm, Nov-Mar: daily 10am-4pm. Western Cemetery Apr-Oct: guided tours only Mon-Fri noon, 2pm, 4pm, Sat, Sun 11am-4pm; Nov-Mar: Mon-Fri noon, 2pm, 3pm, Sat, Sun 11am-3pm.

The most fascinating of all London's Victorian cemeteries, Highgate opened its western part in 1839. A perfect example of exotic High Victorian taste with an Egyptian Avenue, a street of family vaults and the Circle of Lebanon, famous names which lie peacefully here include Tom Sayers (last of the bare-fisted fighters), scientist Michael Faraday, the poetess Christina Rossetti and writer Mary Ann Evans (George Eliot). Many have elaborate tombstone, with dogs, angels and other figures watching beside them. Rescued by the Friends of Highgate Cemetery, it is being sensitively restored and remains one of London's great nature reserves. In the newer Eastern Cemetery, the most famous tomb is (still) that of Karl Marx.

Holland Park

Abbotsbury Rd, W14
071-602 9487
Open Apr-late Oct: 7.30am-10pm (but can vary); late Oct-Mar: 7.30am-4.30pm.

A relatively late addition to London's parks, this small, intimate place full of wooded areas, rhododendrons and azaleas as well as the odd peacock the visitor comes across unexpectedly, was made into a public park in 1950. It stands in the former grounds of Holland House, a splendid mansion bombed during the war. Holland House, now a student hostel, forms the backdrop for the annual outdoor Holland Park Theatre which performs mainly opera (for details call the

Central Library, 071-937 2542 x 2295). The former Garden Ballroom is now The Belvedere Restaurant (see *Restaurant* section).

Hyde Park
W2 - 071-262 5484
Open daily 5am-midnight.

This huge 619-acre park, made up of Hyde Park and Kensington Gardens, has been a royal park since 1536 when King Henry VIII seized the lands of Westminster Abbey at the Dissolution of the Monasteries. The monk's loss is our gain; it was turned from a hunting and hawking park for the indefatigable Henry VIII into a public park by Charles I. Protector Cromwell sold it off; Charles II took it back again and created the road which became the place for polite society to see and be seen. When William and Mary came to live in Kensington Palace they had 300 lamps hung from the trees along the *route du roi* (or Rotten Row as it became anglicised as). However even this eminently sensible precaution did nothing to deter the gangs of notorious highwaymen who, along with the duellists, continued to haunt the park. The Serpentine was created by damming the Westbourne river in the 1730 and during the 1814 celebrations for the defeat of Napoleon the complete Battle of Trafalgar was re-enacted on the lake. The park continues to be a place for entertainment today: both Mick Jagger and Luciano Pavarotti have each held a concert here and Speaker's Corner (by Marble Arch) continues to provide a platform for anyone with a cause and a loud voice.

Regent's Park
NW1 - 071-486 7905
Open daily 5am-dusk.

Another acquisition of Henry VIII, it became part of the town plans of the Prince Regent who commissioned John Nash in the early nineteenth century to design an extremely grand 'garden city' for his aristocratic friends within the park. Fifty-six villas in a variety of classical styles were planned though only eight were finally built. It's a beautiful and gracious park with Nash's terraces around the edge and Queen Mary's Rose Garden in the centre. In the summer, the Open Air Theatre puts on a season of plays while the boating lake is famous for its wide variety of water birds. The future of London Zoo, which has been in Regent's Park since 1830, is in doubt, as it is considered too small for the animals which roar, glide, slide and trot inside it. If you're here on Easter Monday, the annual parade of horses and carriages around the Outer Circle is worth seeing and brings back the slow pace of a past age.

Richmond Park
Kingston Vale, SW15
081-332 2225
Open daily 7.30am-dusk.

King Charles I first enclosed this huge park of 2,470 acres in 1637 with an eight-mile wall to form a hunting park. Today herds of deer still wander through these relatively wild areas of woods and bracken-covered heath. Big enough to absorb five cricket pitches, two golf courses and twenty-four football grounds without the public being aware of them, the park has two eighteenth-century lakes, beloved by anglers, and the Isabella Plantation, full of rhododendrons.

Royal Botanical Gardens
Kew, Richmond, Surrey
081-940 1171
Gardens open daylight hours. Telephone first for seasonal house and museum opening hours.

First planted in 1759 by George III's mother, this 288-acre garden is the most complete public garden in the world. Sir Joseph Banks (1743-1820) who went round the world with Captain Cook established the garden as an international plant centre, sending gardeners and plant-hunters off to every known continent to collect specimens for the magnificent collection. The gardens contain glorious Victorian heated palm houses (wonderful to dash into on a cold winter's day), trees, flowers, formal and informal gardens as well as royal buildings like tiny Kew Palace, the Orangery and much more.

*We're always happy to hear about your discoveries and receive your comments on ours. We want to give your letters the attention they deserve, so when you **write to Gault Millau**, please state clearly what you liked or disliked. Be concise but convincing, and take the time to argue your point.*

THEATRE & MUSIC

No city in the world has a richer or more varied theatrical life than London. Always the capital of English-speaking theatre as well as a melting-pot of international talents, in the last couple of decades Andrew Lloyd Webber and a small group of British directors and designers have made London a serious competitor with New York for the musical crown as well. Only in opera and dance is London outshone by a few other centres of excellence boasting of stronger traditions and deeper purses.

The 'West End' is London's equivalent of Broadway—a relatively small area bounded by Shaftesbury Avenue and the Strand which for 300 years or so has been the heart of theatreland. Most theatres in this area were built between 80 and 110 years ago. Beautiful gilded interiors, a sense of history, and occasional discomfort can help or hinder your enjoyment, so choose carefully. London has too many theatres producing too many different plays to mention more than a few, and to give some guide lines as to what to expect. But if you are uncertain as to what to see, the Friday *London Evening Standard* and the weekend quality national newspapers publish helpful summaries of all the main plays and performances.

■ MUSIC

CLASSICAL

London offers daily more than a dozen chances to listen to classical or contemporary music with artists varying from international stars to ambitious students. The following list is only a selection of some of the venues. Many places have music either at lunchtime or in the evenings. Check the details from a newspaper or call the venue in advance.

Barbican
Barbican Centre, Silk St, EC2 Information 071-638 4141, CC bookings 071-638 8891

Anything from full-scale symphonies in the main concert hall to performances of chamber and folk music in the various foyers.

South Bank Centre
South Bank, SE1 - 071-928 8800

Three halls with music from pop to Prokofiev. The Royal Festival Hall is the biggest venue with good acoustics for symphonies or great choral works. The Queen Elizabeth Hall is smaller, suitable for chamber music and visiting opera productions. The Purcell Room seats under 400 people and is used for recitals, readings and debut concerts by new artists. Book shops, bars, cafes, exhibitions and foyer concerts make the South

Bank Centre a pleasant place for a concert-goer.

British Music Information Centre (BMIC)
10 Stratford Pl, W1 - 071-499 8567

The BMIC which promotes contemporary British music and has a music library, also hosts small concerts and recitals.

Royal Albert Hall
Kensington Gore, SW7 071-589 8212

A beautiful round building with everything from Eric Clapton to the best symphony concerts. It's probably best known in Britain at least, as the home of the annual BBC Promenade concerts ('the Proms'). Tickets for the Proms can be bought on the day of performance, but long queues build up early, so take a cushion or camping stool with you. The 'Promenaders' then sit in the middle of the hall or high up in the balconies. It's the thing almost every English person will have done once.

Royal College of Music
Prince Consort Rd, SW7 071-589 3643

The place for students' showcase concerts.

St John's Smith Square
Smith Sq, SW1 - 071-222 1061

Chamber and symphony orchestras play in this con-

*Some establishments change their **closing times** without warning. It is always wise to check in advance.*

verted church. Concerts are frequently recorded by the BBC and the atmosphere is very special.

St Martin-in-the Fields

Trafalgar Sq, WC2 - 071-930 1862

St Martin's is world-famous for its concerts which range from lunchtime recitals to Mozart by candle light in the evening. On the east side of Trafalgar Square, the church is one of London's landmarks.

Wigmore Hall

36 Wigmore St, W1
071-935 2141

The recently-refurbished Wigmore Hall is an intimate and pleasant place for small-scale concerts. Good acoustics and a friendly atmosphere have made it probably the most loved of London's classical venues. There is music every night.

IN CHURCHES

The following churches have concerts regularly at lunch time or in the evenings.

Holy Trinity

Sloane Sq, SW1 - 071-730 7270

St Anne and St Agnes

Gresham St, EC2 - 071-373 5566

St James Piccadilly

Piccadilly, W1 - 071-437 5053

St Mary-le-Bow

Cheapside, EC2 - 071-248 5139

St Pancras Parish Church

Euston Rd, NW1 - 071-387 8250

OPERA & DANCE

Three of London's largest theatres are devoted to opera and dance. Two are the homes of major resident companies, the third of visiting ones. In addition there are a couple of venues largely devoted to modern dance, and experimental small-scale touring opera companies visit sporadically.

Royal Opera House

Bow St, WC2 - 071-240 1066

'Covent Garden', as the Royal Opera House is invariably called, is London's premier home of opera and ballet. Designed by E M Barry in 1858, this opulent theatre boasts a magnificently-chandeliered Crush bar itself the size of a small theatre. In repertory, style and philosophy Covent Garden is on the international circuit of grand opera attracting the leading artists of the world. Under its musical director, Sir Georg Solti, the or-

Buying tickets

The most convenient way is by phone direct to the theatre box office; only rarely is a booking charge made and tickets can be paid for by credit card or reserved up to 30 minutes before curtain-up. Most theatres are centrally located so you can often stop by in person to buy your tickets and check seat locations. For sell-out musicals try reputable theatre ticket agencies who make a booking charge (enquire the percentage). The cheapest way to buy tickets for many shows is at the *Leicester Square* half price ticket booth. Theatres with a surplus of unsold tickets deliver them for sale at half price plus a 50p charge. Tickets go on sale for the day of performance only at 2.30pm for evenings and noon for matinees (limit two per person). You have no choice of seats (you get the best available), but for the cost of a half hour in the queue this is a great way of economising on the cost. As seats for the English National Opera, The National and the RSC are often included the choice is wide. As in every capital in the world it is not a good idea to buy tickets through sellers on the street. You pay exorbitant prices often for bad seats. If you want to see a 'hot ticket' show before you set out, go through your travel agent or telephone the theatre direct.

chestra is marvellous, especially when he is conducting. Although its dependence on peripatetic international stars means there is no very identifiable house style, at their best, productions are as great as any in the world. Despite 2,096 seats, productions sell out and the best seats are expensive at over £100. However, there are 65 rear amphitheatre tickets (one per person) available on the day of performance from l0am—queuing from 8am should ensure a ticket for most productions—and up to 58 standing places are available on the day 90 minutes before curtain-up. Covent Garden is also the London home of the Royal Ballet, Britain's premier dance company.

Coliseum

St Martin's Lane, WC2
071-836 3161

London's largest theatre, with 2,356 seats, has been home to the English National Opera (ENO) since 1968. Built in 1904 by prolific theatre architect, Frank Matcham, the Coliseum was originally a variety theatre, then home to lavish spectaculars and briefly a down-at-heel cinema before its rebirth as an opera house. ENO's present singular character stems from its origins as a touring company with the mission to bring opera to new audiences in the provinces. To do this it needed a permanent company, mostly British—soloists as well as chorus—and it chose to sing everything in English for greater accessibility. Today it has turned these

traditions to good effect: its soloists are drawn from a small but increasingly excellent pool of largely British talent. Because they work closely together more of an ensemble feel has developed, and with it a more committed acting style than is normal in opera.

Sadlers Wells

Roseberry Ave, EC1
071-278 8916

Devoted to music and dance this rather stark, 1,500-seat 1930s theatre has a broad and exciting repertoire featuring visits from major touring companies in opera (Glyndebourne), light opera (D'Oyly Carte), dance (London Contemporary Dance Theatre) and the more experimental (Black Light Theatre Company of Prague). Slightly off the main tourist track, it is always worth checking what is playing here. The two principal small, experimental venues for dance are The Place, 17 Dukes Rd, WC1 (071-387 0031) and The Cockpit, Gateforth St, NW8 (071-402 5081). Both offer enthusiasm, youth, talent and the feeling of participation in and exploration of the new.

■ THEATRE

FRINGE THEATRE

The West End theatre is fed by the creative ferment of the fringe, London's equivalent of New York's 'Off Broadway'. It ranges from the well-established—indeed subsidised—theatre to small rooms in pubs.

Almeida

Almeida St, N1 - 071-359 4404

Since the artistic direction was taken over by actors Iain McDiarmid and Jonathan Kent, this tiny 1837 building has become acknowledged as the most exciting theatre outside the West End. It stages a mixture of premieres (by authors as notable as Harold Pinter) and the classics, adorned by stars who give their services for the Actors Equity minimum wage and directed by the two principals and celebrated guests. With a capacity of only 300 in an arena layout, intimacy as well as excitement is guaranteed. Located in Islington (near the Camden Passage Antique market) the theatre is an easy ten-minute walk from the Angel underground station.

Hampstead

Swiss Cottage Centre, Ave Rd, NW3 - 071-722 9301

Housed in a shed-like building, the Hampstead Theatre in its 25 years of existence has sent many successes to the West End. Most productions are of new plays so prediction of what you might see is impossible, but this is the sort of venue always worth giving the benefit of the doubt. With permanent tiered seating this is an unusually comfortable way of visiting the Fringe. The theatre is adjacent to Swiss Cottage underground station.

King's
Head Islington

115 Upper St, N1 - 071-226 1916

This is deservedly the most famous of all London's pub theatres. It puts on a broad repertoire of new plays in a cramped room where you can eat beforehand (honest, good-value-for-money, ordinary food). The atmosphere is special and on the right night can offer great excitement. It is located in Upper Street 100 yards before Almeida Street.

Theatre Royal, Stratford East

George Raffles Sq, E15
081-534 0310

A tiny Victorian theatre located deep in the East End of London but conveniently close to Stratford tube station and subsidised mostly by local government, this theatre caters primarily for the local community but has a long history of developing popular works which transfer to the West End from its days as the Theatre Workshop under Joan Littlewood in the 1960s through to the present. Often the work will be of only parochial interest, but look out for their enjoyable and traditional Christmas pantomimes (a strange mixture of fairy tales, comedy and modern bawdy that is uniquely English).

MUSICALS

On any given night in the West End more people are watching musicals than all the other forms of theatre put together. The names of many of the between fifteen and twenty or more shows will be familiar since the musical is international. Many of the current crop of musicals have come from Andrew Lloyd Webber and have been occupying the same theatres for years. But there are good reasons for seeing such familiar works in London—this is where many originated and the eagle eye of the original director ensures standards are maintained, competition to take over leading roles is intense, and many of the theatres they occupy are among the West End's most beautiful.

Drury Lane Theatre Royal

Catherine St, WC2 - 071-494 5060

This is one of the most magnificent of London theatres and the oldest site in continuous use (since 1663). It deserves its royal title—Nell Gwynne delighted King Charles II and both King George I and George III survived assassination attempts here. On a more artistic plane, David Garrick played in the eighteenth century as did the mighty Edmund Kean in the nineteenth. The pre-

---

Backstage tours

One of the best ways of discovering more about the theatre is to go on a backstage tour. The three mentioned here also take you beyond the stage, into the auditorium and the changing rooms and give you a good potted history of the place. There's nothing more exciting—and daunting—than standing on the stage staring out into the footlights and beyond. The experience should sort out the serious from the dilettante aspiring thespians. *Drury Lane Theatre Royal*, **Catherine St, WC2 - 071-494 5060;** *National Theatre*, **South Bank, SE1 - 071-633 0800;** *Royal Shakespeare Company*, **Barbican Centre, Silk St, EC1 - 071-628 3351.**

---

sent vast edifice (it seats 2,237), with its classical exterior, cupola-topped entrance and twin staircases leading to the Grand Salon Bar, was designed by Benjamin Wyatt in 1812. Since 1989 director Nicholas Hytner's acclaimed production of *Miss Saigon* has filled every seat.

Her Majesty's

Haymarket, SW1 - 071-494 5400

Phantom of the Opera is one of Andrew Lloyd Webber's most popular shows and opened eight years ago at this attractive 1896 theatre, which changes its gender to Her or His Majesty's according to who is on the British throne at the time.

London Palladium

Argyll St, W1 - 071-494 5000

Another huge theatre (capacity 2,298), the Palladium was for many years the home of variety shows and 'to play the Palladium' was the ambition of every singer and comedian on both sides of the Atlantic. For the past few years these lavish acts have been replaced by musicals.

New London

167 Drury Lane, WC2
071-405 0072, CC bookings
071-404 4079

Designed in 1973 by theatre designer Sean Kenny, the New London has been home to *Cats* since Trevor Nunn's first production opened here in 1981. Be warned 'latecomers are not admitted while the auditorium is in motion'!

Palace

Cambridge Circus, W1
071-434 0909

Owned by Andrew Lloyd Webber, this magnificent former opera house, dating from 1891, is one of the few West End theatres not hosting one of his works. Beautifully refurbished inside and out, it became home to director Trevor Nunn's production of *Les Misérables* in 1984.

SUBSIDISED THEATRE

One of the reasons London retains its pre-eminence with English-speaking theatre is because of state subsidy. The subsidised theatres not only offer some of the best productions of a range of plays from the classic to the contemporary, they are also a training ground for Britian's best actors, directors and designers, as well as transferring productions to the commercial West End. The two main companies are the Royal National Theatre and the Royal Shakespeare Company, both of whom occupy permanent purpose-built London homes.

National Theatre

South Bank, SE1 - 071-928 2252

Opened in 1976, Sir Denys Lasdun's Royal National Theatre is a modernist concrete and glass building beside the Thames. It offers three contrasting theatre spaces and includes areas to relax with a drink and a snack, admire the sunset over the river, or enjoy a free informal concert or exhibition. It teems with life before or after the show and is always a pleasure to visit. For the last five years the artistic director has been Richard Eyre who has taken the company to new heights following in the footsteps of Lord Olivier and Sir Peter Hall. He pursues a deliberately eclectic policy using directors from other companies around the country and top British stage and screen actors in conjunction with a dedicated ensemble permanently attached to the company. This marriage of the established with the new offers constant surprises and revelations and is reflected also in the breadth of works presented—native and foreign, originals and translations. The three auditoria offer distinct theatrical experiences. The largest, the Olivier, seats 1,100 in an amphitheatre facing a large, open stage equipped with magical mechanical devices for spectacles in large-scale works. The most conventional is the proscenium-arched Lyttleton which seats 900. The experimental Cottesloe seats up to 400, has flexible seating and offers everything from theatre-in-the-round to more conventional layouts. Despite the greater comfort and luxury of the two larger theatres, the Cottesloe can often be the most thrilling of the three because it offers wonderful intimacy with the actors. Many of the National's finest productions sell out completely. But don't despair—a limited number of seats for each production are sold on the day of performance at 9.30am. Queue from 8.30am or before to be sure of a chance of a seat.

Barbican

Barbican Centre, Silk St, EC2
071-638 8891

As its name suggests, one of the main purposes of the Royal Shakespeare Company is to produce the works of the Bard, but it also embraces new plays and classics from the entire world repertoire. Originally based in Stratford, Shakespeare's birthplace, where it was founded over 100 years ago, the company now divides itself between its three theatres there and its two in the Barbican in London. The company is more of a repertory one than the National in that one team of actors plays first the

Stratford theatres and six months later comes to London. The Artistic Director, Adrian Noble, has almost as wide a range of directors as the National, and productions are exciting and innovative. The building itself is something of an architectural folly: it opened in 1982 but dates in conception from a futuristic vision of the 1960s. Inside the building it's easy to get lost—get there early. But the two auditoria are magnificent. The main theatre is almost spherical giving even those in the remotest seats—the 'gods'—a good view of the large stage. The Pit is also impressive: it is small with a capacity of only 180-240, with the action three-quarters in the round so the audience feels a real involvement.

The Royal Court

Sloane Sq, SW1 - 071-730 1745

The third most important subsidised theatre is the tiny 395-seat Royal Court in Chelsea's Sloane Square (next to the tube station of that name). Built in 1888, it has always been an important venue for new writers. Once it was George Bernard Shaw, Sir Arthur Pinero and Granville Barker, then in the 1950s John Osborne and the revival of realistic English drama, and in 1994 it has a new, exciting, young Artistic Director, Stephen Daldry. The minute studio Theatre Upstairs (capacity 60-80) is an important venue for radical new writing.

WEST END THEATRES

Plays—with the notable exception of *The Mousetrap* at St Martin's Theatre—do not have long runs, but a few pointers as to what to look for can be given. Since retiring from a long and distinguished reign over first the RSC then the National, Sir Peter Hall is now an independent producer of plays and opera. His preference is generally for classic works produced with clarity and style and with distinguished casts. Contemporary English farce is something of an acquired taste but its best exponent is the Theatre of Comedy under the direction of Ray Cooney. If you enjoy double entendres and simple fun, these productions are fast and professional and very popular with their fans.

Theatre Royal

Haymarket, SW1 - 071-930 8800

Second only to the Drury Lane Theatre Royal for a sense of history, the Haymarket was originally built in 1720 and rebuilt in 1821 by John Nash. A beautiful theatre is not in itself a reason to choose a production, but it is a wonderful bonus and the Theatre Royal's track record in choosing productions is good.

OUT

OF LONDON

INTRODUCTION

The fortunate visitor to London has more than the delights of the capital to explore. With Bath a mere 90 minutes away by train, Brighton, Oxford and Cambridge about an hour and even York only two hours away, it is worth taking a day trip into this green and pleasant countryside. But once there, you may well find so much to see that you decide to stay longer. So here we make some suggestions: where to stay, what to do, what to see and of course, where to eat.

BATH

On the practical side: we have indicated hotel prices, and where breakfast is included. You will find, however, that there are so many special weekend/weekday/Champagne breaks, and that prices vary so much according to the season and to availability, that the prices printed here are more an indication of what you might expect to pay.

Bath, a mere hour and fifteen minutes by train or under two hours by car, has been welcoming tourists for nearly 2000 years and is a 'must' for any trip out of London. According to legend, Bath's famous hot spring was discovered by Prince Bladud, son of King Lear, expelled by his people after contracting leprosy. He became a swineherd and each day took his pigs into the forest, foraging for acorns. To his horror, he discovered that the pigs, too, were contaminated with a skin complaint. He roamed further and further into the forest until one day he saw the pigs miraculously cured after rolling in a muddy pool. He immediately plunged in himself to find that the miracle waters had worked for him, too. Such is the legend.

What we know for certain is that the Romans discovered the hot spring and built a whole complex of baths around it, plus a temple to the goddess Minerva. The city became known as Aquae Sulis, and saw its first tourist influx—Romans from all over Britain. By AD 410, Rome was under siege and the Romans abandoned their most northerly province. The baths fell into disuse and the Roman buildings were plundered for their valuable Bath stone until the Middle Ages, when Bath once more became a thriving city with the hot spring and one medieval bath in use. In 1702, Queen Anne, advised by her doctors to take the waters at Bath as a cure for gout, set a new trend and yet another influx of tourists set Bath on a course of expansion.

Three men were largely responsible for the city we see today: Ralph Allen, a stone quarry owner, and the architects John Wood the Elder and John Wood the Younger. Together they set about building the most splendid new Georgian city, with terraces and crescents and circles of houses, all in mellow, golden Bath stone. Throughout the eighteenth century, the whole of the fashionable world came to Bath to take the waters and enjoy the balls and assemblies presided over by 'Beau' Nash, Master of Ceremonies—Dr Johnson, Richard Sheridan, Jane Austen and Lord Nelson, to name but a few. But in the early nineteenth century, the young and fashionable followed the Prince Regent to the newly discovered seaside resort of Brighton for their summers, and Bath was left to the staid and the elderly.

In 1879, when digging out new sewers, the borough engineer discovered the remains of the **Roman Baths**. Extensive excavations were made and once more, tourists flocked to Bath. As recently as 1980, the Temple area was excavated and a new museum opened in 1983.

The twentieth-century tourist sees a city on two levels: below ground, a network of Roman baths and temple, and above ground, the most glorious Georgian city, built, like Rome itself, upon seven hills. The delights of this city do not end with its architecture however; there is a **Museum of Costume**, the headquarters of the **Royal Photographic Society**, the preserved Georgian house at **N°1 Royal Crescent**, art galleries, an **American Museum**, shops, restaurants and hotels to suit every budget. A day trip will give the visitor a tantalising glimpse of a fascinating city and the desire to return, but to get a full appreciation of Bath, it really is worth spending several days here.

The Roman Baths (0225-461111) are open November to end of February Monday to Saturday 9am-5pm, and 10am-5pm on Sunday. Summer opening times are 9am-6pm daily.

N°1 Royal Crescent (0225-428126) is open March-November Tuesday to Sunday 10.30am-5pm, and from November 1 to December 11 Tuesday to Sunday 10.30am-5pm.

Further information from the Tourist Information Centre, The Colonnades, Bath St (0225-462831).

Gault Millau's ratings are based solely on the restaurant's cuisine. We do not take into account the atmosphere, décor, service and so on; these are commented upon within the review.

■ RESTAURANTS & HOTELS

11/20 **Alfresco Restaurant**
Bath Spa Hotel, Sydney Rd, Bath, BA2 6JF
0225-444424, Fax 0225-444006
INTERNATIONAL
Open Lunch Mon-Sat.

Lunch or an informal dinner may be taken in the Alfresco. Here the cooking is eclectic, with influences from the Far East, Mediterranean and old England and can range from a starter with a glass of wine to a full three-course meal. Starters average around £5, and main courses £8 to £12. **C £20.**

Bath Spa Hotel
(See restaurant above)
6 stes from £219, 94 rms £125-£195 inc VAT. Health spa. Pool. Tennis. Restaurants. 24-hr rm service.

Set in seven acres of beautiful grounds, this splendid Georgian house is a mere ten minutes' walk from the centre of Bath. Public rooms are airy and spacious with wonderful displays of fresh flowers. Bedrooms are individually decorated with every luxury the guest could want, including sumptuous mahogany and marble bathrooms with Penhaligon's toiletries. Residence of the hotel confers automatic membership of the well-equipped health and leisure spa with its swimming pool and jacuzzi. Restaurants: *Alfresco Restaurant*, above, and *Vellore Restaurant*, below.

14 **Clos du Roy**
1 Seven Dials, Saw Close, Bath - 0225-444450
FRENCH
Open Lunch daily & Dinner Tues-Sat. Pre-theatre menu from 6pm and after show.

No stranger to Bath, the talented Philippe Roy has staged a comeback from the village of Box to a stunning new site in the Seven Dials Centre, next to the Theatre Royal. The theme of the restaurant is musical with a white grand piano as a central feature and with the dining room opening out onto a balcony. The cooking is what one would expect from such a fine chef, with some excellent value set-price menus. The two-course lunch at £8.95 might include a timbale of smoked chicken with walnut oil dressing and a poached fillet of salmon with dill on a bed of green lentils. Game (in season) features prominently on the good-value dinner menus with, for example, a poached fillet of venison garnished with pomme purée and a pomegranate sauce. The accompaniments are simple and superb: exquisite fresh breads and rolls and wonderful unsalted French butter. Wines are predominantly French with reasonably priced house selections at £8.95. C £20. Set L £8.95, Set D £22.

Dower House Restaurant

Royal Crescent Hotel, 16 Royal Crescent, Bath - 0225-319090, Fax 0225-339401
FRENCH
Open Lunch & Dinner daily.

A leisurely stroll through the delightful gardens of this superb listed building brings you to the Dower House Restaurant. The décor is a muted apricot and the restaurant has a serene feel to it with formal but unobtrusive service. The cuisine is very much in the modern idiom and the presentation a feast for the eye as much as for the palate, a notable example being medallions of venison with a compote of apple, shallots, chestnuts and orange. Fish, too, is presented with great care: scallops on a ginger jus and monkfish with red wine fish sauce. Desserts are not neglected either with a dream of a chocolate tart and orange sauce. The comprehensive wine list offers an unusually large selection of half-bottles. C £25. Set L £14.50-£18.50, Set D £28.

Fountain House

9/11 Fountain Buildings, Landsdown Rd, Bath, BA1 5DV - 0225-338622, Fax 0225-445855
B&B 14 stes £120-£250 inc VAT.

Situated in one of Bath's beautiful Georgian terraces, this all-suite hotel is particularly suitable for families. Guests have all the facilities of an hotel: continental breakfast, maid service and so on, but with the advantage of extra space and privacy. The suites consist of one, two and three bedrooms plus sitting room and fully equipped kitchen and one or two bathrooms.

11/20 Garlands Restaurant

7 Edgar Buildings, George St, Bath - 0225-442283
MODERN BRITISH
Open Lunch Tues-Sun, Dinner daily.

Owners Tom and Jo Bridgeman run this delightful little restaurant in the centre of Bath. The cooking is sound and reflects modern trends, with starters such as filo pastry pouches filled with mixed cheeses and garnished with sun-dried tomatoes and olives. Main courses show original touches, such as succulent medallions of pork coated in pesto and bread crumbs and finished with lemon and sage, and followed by refreshing chilled lemon tart, served with lashings of clotted cream. They have recently opened a café for lighter, cheaper meals. C £20. Set menus £16.95-£19.50.

New Moon

 Seven Dials, Saw Close, Bath - 0225-444407
FRENCH
Open daily 9am-11pm.

Being both restaurant and brasserie, this is a welcome new addition to a city already well served with restaurants. In the morning, fresh croissants and pain au chocolat are served, while at lunchtime the brasserie menu comes into action. The bias is definitely French, with Toulouse sausages in shallot cream sauce highly recommended. In the evenings a more formal à la carte menu is presented with perhaps warm chicken mousse with onion confit, green peppercorn sauce and crispy bacon, followed by steamed fillet of salmon garnished with a dry vermouth, tomato concassée and dill cream sauce, and ending with excellent home-made ice creams or sorbet. Light lunch is around £7. C £16. Set L £7, Set D £14.50, £17.50.

Olive Tree Restaurant

Queensbury Hotel, Russel St, Bath - 0225-447928, Fax 0225-446065
INTERNATIONAL
Open Lunch Tues-Sat, Dinner Mon-Sat.

Although part of an hotel, the Olive Tree has a loyal, local, non-resident clientele, being both informal and moderately priced, with a set three-course menu of £17 served from Monday to Friday. A strong Mediterranean influence pervades the cooking, for instance a first course of a crostini of Mediterranean vegetables with pinenuts and Parmesan, followed by a fine osso bucco braised in wine with tomatoes and garlic. Desserts owe more to the native English tradition and include a mouth-watering rum and orange bread and butter pudding. **C** £20. **Set D** £17.

 ## Priory Hotel Restaurant

Weston Rd, Bath, BA1 2XT - 0225-331922, Fax 0225-448276
INTERNATIONAL
Open Lunch & Dinner daily.
The Priory Hotel has an excellent long-serving chef in Michael Collom who retains the same dishes and the same loyal local following. His kitchen serves several dining rooms with sound, skilled cooking: rack of lamb with garlic and rosemary, scallops in pastry with tomato sauce, and filling desserts like hot apple pie with Calvados sauce and a good selection of British and continental cheeses. The wine list is expensive. Service in this old-fashioned, comfortable dining room and hotel is impeccable. **C** £30. **Set L** £20.50, **Set D** £29.50-£32.

Priory Hotel

(See restaurant above)
B&B 21 rms £85-£195, DB&B £195-£225 inc service and VAT. Restaurant. Pool.
Unusually for Bath, the architecture of the priory is gothic rather than Georgian. Situated a little way from the centre, but in a peaceful residential area right by Bath's golf course, it has all the ambience of a country house hotel but with the amenities of the city. Fresh flowers abound, and books and magazines are scattered around. Bedrooms, some with a separate area, are furnished with antiques and equipped with all the amenities you expect from such a fine hotel.

Queensbury Hotel

Russel St, Bath, BA1 2QF - 0225-447928, Fax 0225-446065
B&B 22 rooms £89-£149 inc service and VAT. Restaurant.
This delightful townhouse hotel is located in a quiet street, close to Bath's architectural gems of the Circus and the Royal Crescent. Bedrooms are very well equipped, with nice extras like books and magazines. Housekeeping is of an ex-

tremely high standard and there is a lovely courtyard garden to relax in on summer evenings. Restaurant: see *Olive Tree Restaurant*, above.

Royal Crescent Hotel

16 Royal Crescent, Bath, BA1 2LS - 0225-319090, Fax 0225-339401
13 stes £265-£360, 31 rms £98-£195 inc VAT. Exercise pool. Restaurant. 24-hr rm service.
Not only is this hotel located in the centre of Bath's most famous crescent, it also affords wonderful views across the city to the countryside beyond. It boasts four-poster beds, antique furnishings and an eye-catching sixteenth-century tapestry from Brussels. The hotel offers every comfort, including twenty-four hour room service and plunge pool and is set in a delightful garden with a croquet lawn. Restaurant: see *Dower House Restaurant*, above.

12/20 Vellore Restaurant

INTERNATIONAL
Bath Spa Hotel, Sydney Rd, Bath - 0225-444424, Fax 0225-444006
Open Lunch Sun, Dinner daily.
What was once the ballroom of a stunning Georgian house is now the restaurant at the heart of this grand hotel. Chef Jonathan Fraser uses first-class local ingredients for a simple but robust cuisine, presenting a subtle blend of natural flavours. From the set price menu, we chose hot crispy duck leg with sugar-glazed plums and an olive salad, followed by a simply cooked but delicious escalope of calf's liver with red currants and ginger and an exemplary rich chocolate Belgium torte. Coffee is good with wonderful petits-fours and service was attentive. The comprehensive wine list includes many bottles from the New World. **C** £35. **Set D** £34.

COLERNE

 ## Lucknam Park Restaurant

Lucknam Park Hotel, Colerne, Wiltshire, SN14 8AZ - 0225-742777, Fax 0225-743536
MODERN BRITISH
Open Lunch & Dinner daily.
Everything about this opulent country house hotel radiates elegance, from the 200 handsome acres outside to the im-

peccably furnished bedrooms inside. The dining room is every bit as elegant as one would expect of a 1720 Palladian mansion and is presided over by head chef Michael Womersley whose credentials are impressive. He has worked with Raymond Blanc at the Manoir aux Quat' Saisons and Michel Guérard in France. He has since developed a modern British style of cooking, with classic dishes being given a light and imaginative touch. A first course might be a gâteau of foie gras, truffle chicken and pistachio, served with brioche toast, followed by roast breast of pheasant filled with a spiced mince of its meat on a port wine sauce. The wine list is presented by vintage, so a knowledge of good years is helpful. The cheeseboard offers an excellent selection of English farmhouse cheeses. **C** £25. **Set L** £19.50, £22.

Lucknam Park Hotel

(See restaurant above)
B&B 11 stes £275-£380, 31 rms £100-£275 inc VAT. Health spa. Pool. Tennis. Restaurant.
Lucknam Park is the result of great expense and care; reputedly more than £4 million went into its refurbishment which transformed a run-down country house into a heavenly hotel, located on the edge of the Cotswolds and six miles northeast of Bath. Even in an area well served with grand country house hotels, Lucknam Park stands out, set as it is in 200 acres of parkland. From the moment you roll down the avenue of ghostly beech trees and glimpse the wisteria-clad frontage, you know you are in safe hands. Inside, the grand dimensions of the rooms, the subtly varied furnishings and the acres of marble speak of calm, old-fashioned luxury. The leisure spa is very well equipped with facilities like a gym, whirlpool bath, sauna and beauty salon. And there is a good old-fashioned snooker room.

HINTON CHARTERHOUSE

 Homewood Park Restaurant

Hinton Charterhouse, nr Bath, BA3 6BB
0225-723731, Fax 0225-723820
FRENCH

Open Lunch & Dinner daily.
If you can't stay at this elegant, peaceful country house hotel set in well-groomed grounds five miles south of Bath, try to visit for a meal. You'll be warmly welcomed, installed in a comfortable dining room and served commendable food. Lunch is a pleasant, fairly simple affair, offering a set three-course meal that might include a warm salad of pink roasted quails and pan-fried foie gras, followed by a roulade of lemon sole and lobster with a lobster sauce, and ending with a mouth-watering hot apple and cherry strudel with local clotted cream. The dinner menu is longer and more elaborate, but both meals rely heavily on the restaurant's excellent fish. Sea bass is served with a sauté of fennel and oyster mushrooms, for instance. Game, too, is strongly represented: a light feuilletté of puff pastry is filled with a ragout of pheasant breast, flambéed with whisky and with a medley of wild mushrooms; a saddle of venison comes marinated in red wine with rosemary and juniper. Desserts are strong on chocolate with such delights as a chocolate mousse layered between chocolate meringue discs with strawberry fritters. Good sorbets, an extensive, attractive cheeseboard, including a number of west country varieties, and excellent coffee with home-made petits-fours, make for an elegant finish. The wine list is long and interesting and includes a number of Australian and Californian wines as well as a strong French selection. **C** £25. **Set L** £18.50, **Set D** £29.50.

Homewood Park Hotel

(See restaurant above)
B&B 15 rms £90-£125 inc service and VAT. Tennis. Restaurant.
Only six miles south of Bath, Homewood Park is an ideal place to stay if you're looking for tranquillity and some good food. Built mainly in the eighteenth and nineteenth centuries and set in ten acres of gardens and woods, Homewood's young and enthusiastic owners offer a charming welcome. All fifteen rooms are luxuriously appointed and the elegant lounge, complete with log fire, provides just the right atmosphere of a private country house, particularly on the croquet lawn.

■ LIGHT MEALS

Canary Café

Queen St, Bath - 0225-424846
Open daily 9am-8pm (Jan to 5.30pm).
Located in a charming side street in the centre of Bath, this is an ideal stop for morning coffee, a light lunch, afternoon tea or early supper. Indeed, the Canary is noted for its coffees and teas of over forty different varieties. One luncheon speciality worth trying is 'Somerset Rabbit'—a version of Welsh rarebit made with red wine and local Cheddar cheese. Of note, too, is the wholesome steak-and-kidney pudding, served in winter. At teatime there is a wonderful selection of home-made cakes. Main courses are around £5.

Pump Room Restaurant

Pump Rooms, Bath - 0225-444477
Open daily 9am-4.30pm.
Situated above the Roman Baths, this elegant room serves morning coffee with 'Bath' buns, plus excellent light lunches and teas. The spaghetti carbonara, while not perhaps totally authentic, is nonetheless good; salads are light and refreshing and there's always a home-made soup of the day. Service is young and friendly, if a bit slow, but as meals are often accompanied by the first-class Pump Room Trio or the resident pianist, this is not too much of a penalty. Main courses are around £6 to £7.

Woods

9-13 Alfred St, Bath - 0225-314812
Open Mon-Fri 11am-11pm, Sat noon-11pm, Sun noon-2.30pm, 6.30-10.30pm.
This little brasserie/restaurant has long been a favourite amongst Bath's residents, not least for the daily £5 lunchtime specials. The smoked chicken, avocado and toasted almond with basalmic vinaigrette and garlic bread is popular along with terrine of wild boar, duck, port and juniper served with toast and home-made chutney. The restaurant is more formal and serves a three-course lunch for £9.50: perhaps home-made leek and potato soup, followed by loin of pork, pan-fried with garlic and anchovy butter, and a raspberry bakewell tart on a fresh fruit coulis for dessert. **Set D** £9.95-£17.50.

■ PUBS

Bath has so many good restaurants and brasseries, that pubs tend to be worth visiting more for soaking up the friendly local atmosphere than for food. Two such are the **Old Green Tree**, 12 Green St and **The Star**, The Paragon, near Guinea Lane.

BRIGHTON

In the 1750s the unusual and healthy effects of sea bathing brought Brighton to the attention of the fashionable, and this small south coast fishing village became the place to see and be seen. Early visitors included Dr Samuel Johnson and Mrs Thrale, followed some years later by George, Prince of Wales whose highly scandalous goings-on set the seal of success on the little seaside resort. In 1785 he secretly married Mrs Fitzherbert, a young Catholic widow, and turned his 'superior farmhouse' by the sea into the wildly extravagant **Royal Pavilion**. Its fantastic onion domes outside and ornate decorations within, mixing Indian, Chinese and even gothic with wild abandon, made it one of the wonders of the age. The Prince Regent filled his extravaganza full of fabulous furniture—gilded wood cabinets, a couch shaped like an Egyptian river boat with crocodile feet, mirrors, and everywhere delightful details like flying dragons, painted serpents and the like that scroll their way up the walls and over the ceilings.

But Brighton also offers the visitor reminders of a more modest past. To the west of the Royal Pavilion lies the area known as 'The Lanes'—narrow, twisting alleyways that once housed seventeenth-century fishermen's cottages and now house antique shops. The *Palace Pier* takes you forward to the great days of the cross-Channel steamers to Dieppe. Today it gives visitors a good idea of traditional English seaside life.

Only a one-and-a-half to two-hour car drive, or a one-hour train journey from London, Brighton is a delightful town, a mixture of elegant Regency architecture (look out for *Lewes Crescent* and *Sussex Square* in Brighton and *Brunswick Square* and *Adelaide Crescent* in Hove), and cheerful vulgarity. In May the town stages the *Brighton Arts Festival*, now one of the largest in England; throughout the year the *Theatre Royal* stages productions from London, and the *Gardner Centre* at the University of Sussex is known for music and drama. The **Museum** and **Art Gallery** contains some remarkable art nouveau and art deco furniture and decorative art, while **Brighton Sea Life Centre** provides a view of British marine life from shrimps to stingrays and sharks as you walk through Europe's largest underwater tunnel.

The Royal Pavilion in the centre of Brighton (0273-603005) is open October to May daily 10am to 5pm, and June to September daily 10am to 6pm.
Brighton Museum and Art Gallery, adjacent to the Pavilion in Church Street (0273-603005) are open from Monday to Saturday (except for Wednesday) from 10am to 5.30pm, and Sunday 2 to 5.30pm.
The Brighton Sea Life Centre, Marine Parade (0273-604234) is open daily from 10am to 6pm and later in summer.
*For further information contact the **Tourist Information Centre** at the Town Hall, Church Rd, Hove (0273-778087) and at Marlborough House, 54 Old Steine (0273-323755).*

■ RESTAURANTS & HOTELS

12/20 Bottoms Restaurant
Topps Hotel, 17 Regency Sq, Brighton
0273-729334, Fax 0273-203679
BRITISH/FRENCH

Open Mon, Tues, Thurs-Sat Dinner.
The basement of this small hotel is just big enough to take residents and a few others who come to sample simple, but well-cooked British food with a French accent. Favourite dishes include little queen scallops grilled in garlic and butter, potato pancakes with smoked salmon, crisp duck, venison in red currant sauce and fresh, delightfully done vegetables. The menu is a set-price one for two courses, and puddings, of the home-made ice cream and bread and butter pudding variety, are extra. The wine list is reasonable. **C £20. Set D £18.95.**

10/20 Browns
3-4 Duke St, Brighton - 0273-323501
INTERNATIONAL
Open daily 11am-11.30pm.
Part of the Browns chain, with outlets in Oxford and Cambridge, this is a jolly brasserie just on the edge of the Lanes which successfully manages to be all things to all men. Food varies from pizza, salads and hot sandwiches to steaks and fish and daily blackboard specials. The house wines are good value. It's a fun place for a family and has a children's menu and mother's room. **C £18.**

Dove Hotel
18 Regency Sq, Brighton, BN1 2FG - 0273 779222/3
B&B 8 rms £35-£65 inc service and VAT.
Next door to Topps Hotel and restaurant, this small family-run place is very welcoming and friendly with its simple décor and reasonable-sized bedrooms. You have to arrange for a light evening meal in advance; breakfast is served either in your room or in the basement restaurant.

Grand Hotel
King's Rd, Brighton, BN1 2FW - 0273-321188, Fax 0273-202694
B&B 8 stes £460-£1020, 200 rms £125-£225 inc VAT. Health spa. Pool. Restaurant. 24-hr rm service.
The Grand is Brighton's best known hotel, right on the sea front, and with, appropriately, a grand, luxurious feel with its marble floors and columns, plaster ceilings and a central staircase to make an entrance down. Victorian–style furnishings in the public rooms and

chintzy bedrooms, some with sea views, add to the feeling of solid comfort. They have rooms especially for female executives, facilities for the disabled, a fully equipped health spa, the Midnight Blues night club and the King's restaurant. Even if you're not staying here, try to take tea in the pretty conservatory, overlooking the sea.

12/20 Langan's Bistro
1 Paston Pl, Brighton - 0273-606933
INTERNATIONAL
Open Lunch Tues-Fri, Sun, Dinner Tues-Sat.
Another of the late, lamented, Peter Langan's restaurants, this smaller version of Langan's Brasserie in London near the marina serves some exotic, if expensive food, using fashionable ingredients like ravioli with wild mushrooms, monk-fish, Dover sole with tapenade, calf's liver, lamb and guinea fowl. Fun and rewarding. **C** £20. **Set L** £14.50.

Old Ship Hotel
King's Rd, Brighton, BN1 1NR - 0273-329001, Fax 0273-820718
B&B 152 rms from £49 per person inc VAT. 24-hour room service.
One of the oldest sea front hotels, it has a considerable history attached, dating back to the fifteenth century. In the eighteenth century when it became fashionable, Paganini played in the ballroom. The large wood-panelled lobby has antiques, most of the bedrooms have modern bathrooms. Children up to twelve stay and eat free when sharing their parents' room.

Topps Hotel
17 Regency Sq, Brighton, BN1 2FG - 0273-729334, Fax 0273-203679
B&B 14 rms £45-£99 inc service and VAT. Restaurant.
Paul and Pauline Collins run this delightful small hotel in a pretty Regency square in the middle of Brighton. There is one main public room, full of books, and fourteen delightfully furnished bedrooms varying in size, with sofas and fresh flowers; two have a four-poster and balcony. Bathrooms are also better than average for a small family-run hotel, with good toiletries and dressing gowns provided. The atmosphere is friendly and service is atten-

tive. Restaurant: see *Bottoms Restaurant* above.

CAMBRIDGE

Cambridge is known, by visitors particularly, for its great and ancient university. The city itself lies on the edge of England's strange fenlands, 'a low dirty unpleasant place' as the seventeenth-century diarist John Evelyn unflatteringly described it. But disregard this description; Evelyn went to Oxford and even 300 years ago the rivalry between these two great seats of learning was acute.

A mere hour's train ride away from London, or a one-and-a-half to two-hour car journey, Cambridge is worth staying in and spending a day or two wandering around. The *Tourist Information Centre* organises excellent walking tours of the city; otherwise you can take a bright green bicycle free from a bike park and see the city from the student's viewpoint. If you don't have time to see everything, you should make for the colleges of St John's, Trinity, Clare, King's, Queens', Corpus Christi, Peterhouse and Jesus. Cambridge is compact, a delightful place at any time of year, from spring when the crocuses and daffodils blaze with colour along the Backs, on a lazy summer's day when you can punt down the river, and even in winter when the easterly wind whips around the buildings and sends you scurrying for cover. Most colleges allow you to wander at will, but try to avoid mid-April to June during examination time as many colleges are closed to the public.

Scholars arrived in Cambridge in 1209 but the first college, Peterhouse, was only founded in 1281, followed by Clare in 1326, Pembroke in 1347,

Gonville in 1348, Trinity Hall in 1350, and Corpus Christi in 1352. In the next two hundred years, ten more colleges followed, including the well-known King's (1441) and Trinity (1546). Women were finally allowed a college for themselves in 1873 with Girton. Currently the university consists of 31 colleges; the latest, Robinson College, was founded in 1977.

From the *River Cam*, the view of the colleges is one of the most inspiring and beautiful sights in Britain. A walk along the 'Backs', as this section of the river is known, shows the red medieval brickwork of *Queens' College*, the elegant façade of *Clare College*, the soaring spires and great windows of *King's College* chapel (well-known for its Christmas carol concert, broadcast throughout the world), and the bridge of *St John's*. But Cambridge is not just about beautiful buildings. This is the city where Isaac Newton worked on the Laws of Motion, where Rutherford split the atom in the Cavendish Laboratories and Watson and Crick discovered the secrets of DNA. Today Cambridge is known as one of the centres of the high-tech industry..

For a short walk, start at **Magdalen College**, founded in 1542, and boasting the outstanding *Pepys library*. Cross Magdalen Bridge and walk south down Bridge Street and you come to the delightful round *Church of the Holy Sepulchre*. Opposite you enter **St John's College** (1511) through a gateway bearing the arms of the founder, Lady Margaret Beaufort, mother of Henry VII. The dining hall's original hammer-beam roof dates from the sixteenth century; the chapel is only nineteenth century but it's worth trying to get to evensong here—the singing from the choristers is as good as the equally sublime singing at King's. Next door is **Trinity College** (founded by Henry VIII in 1546), the largest and one of the most beautiful colleges, with 700 students and a master appointed by the Crown. Its *Great Court* surrounds a magnificent octagonal fountain fed by pipes originally installed by the monks. Trinity also boasts one of the most famous *libraries* in England, built by Sir Christopher Wren between 1676 and 1685 and containing a statue of one of the more notorious Trinity students—Lord Byron. Trinity has had its fair share of famous and infamous students, including Isaac Newton, Pandit Nehru, Kim Philby, Guy Burgess and Anthony Blunt (the Fourth Man), as well as members of the royal family like Prince Charles.

Gonville and Caius (pronounced Keys) comes next, founded by Edmund Gonville in 1348 and re-founded and enlarged by Dr Caius in 1557. It is known for the three gates that symbolise the three stages in a student's life: the *Gate of Humility*, the *Gate of Virtue* and the third, the *Gate of Honour* which leads you into *Senate House Passage*. South of here stands charming and gracious **Clare College**, first founded in 1326 then much altered twenty years later by Lady Elizabeth of Clare, a granddaughter of Edward I. It's worth wandering past the gardens and over *Clare Bridge*, the oldest in Cambridge, dating from 1640.

Then you come to the great glory of Cambridge—**King's College**—founded by Henry VI in 1441 and connected with Eton College. The centrepiece of Henry VI's grand architectural design is the *chapel* which took some 70 years to complete and which over-awes the visitor with its delicate stone fan-vaulted roof, the early sixteenth-century wooden organ screen and organ case, *The Adoration of the Magi* by Rubens, and the rich stained-glass windows. The chapel is both magnificent and important; its late Perpendicular style makes the transition from the last great era of medieval church building to the more secular age of the Renaissance.

Every college tells you something about the past—an endless and fascinating journey. **Corpus Christi**, founded in 1352 by two town guilds was the result of the ordinary townspeople's desire for what had been an aristocratic education, and gives an impression of what a medieval college looked like. **Queens' College**, founded three times, twice by the wives of English kings (and therefore called Queens', not Queen's), is a delightful red-brick building. At the back, you find the famous wooden *Mathematical Bridge*, built in 1749 and so called because its structure is held together without benefit of nails. **Peterhouse**, found down Trumpington Street, is the oldest college. **Jesus College** (1496) was built on the sight of an old nunnery; some of the buildings are incorporated into the college.

Venture further afield if you can: to classical **Downing**, to **Emmanuel** where John Harvard was a student, and to **Sidney Sussex**, the college of Protector Oliver Cromwell who in 1649 had King Charles I beheaded. The portrait of Cromwell in the *dining hall* is covered over when the Royal Toast is drunk, his head (only) is buried in the *chapel*. The gardens are some of the best in Cambridge.

But Cambridge holds other delights, too. The **Botanic Garden** offers 40 acres of wonderful, exotic, and ordinary, plants. The **Fitzwilliam Museum** has extensive Egyptian, Greek and Roman collections and a huge collection of English pottery and porcelain as well as paintings and illuminated manuscripts. The **Scott Polar Research Institute** shows mementoes of Captain Scott's journey to the South Pole. **Kettle's Yard Art Gallery** holds exhibitions of contemporary paintings. From the university church of **Great St Mary's** you get panoramic views of the city; in **Little St Mary's** you can see the memorial to Godfrey Washington which bears stars and stripes—believed to be the origin of the United States' flag. If you're in Cambridge during July, the *Cambridge Festival* features music, theatre and exhibitions. And finally there's a fun outdoor market on *Market Hill* from Monday to Saturday. As we mentioned at the beginning, Cambridge merits more than a day's visit.

*Fitzwilliam Museum, Trumpington St (0223-332900) is open Tuesday to Saturday 10am to 5pm, and Sunday 2.15-5pm. Further information from **Cambridge Tourist Information Centre**, Wheeler St (0223-322640).*

■ RESTAURANTS & HOTELS

10/20 Browns
23 Trumpington St, Cambridge - 0223-461655
INTERNATIONAL
Open Lunch & Dinner daily.

Set in an old hospital building of Addenbrookes opposite the Fitzwilliam Museum, this cheerful, useful all-day bistro which is part of the Browns chain serves everything from hot sandwiches to burgers, daily fish specials to chocolate puddings. Child-friendly with a special children's menu, and with prices not designed to break the bank, this is an informal place, much patronised by students. **C £15.**

Garden House Hotel
Granta Pl, Mill Lane, Cambridge, CB2 1RT
0223-63421, Fax 0223-316605
4 stes £295, 114 rms £86-£168 inc VAT. Restaurant. 24-hr rm service.

This modern hotel, ideally placed on the banks of the river Cam, has a bar and lounge looking out onto the pretty view. It has impressive, if slightly impersonal modern public rooms and well-appointed, standardised bedrooms, some with a river view. Children under sixteen years old, sharing their parents' room, stay free. Service is friendly. There is one formal restaurant, Le Jardin and the Riverside Lounge which is ideal for snacks. One of Cambridge's delights is to take tea on the lawns here.

 Midsummer House

Midsummer Common, Cambridge - 0223-69299

INTERNATIONAL

Open Lunch Sun-Fri, Dinner Tues-Sat.

In a city surprisingly bereft of gastronomic treats, Midsummer House stands out. It is in the most splendid position: set between the Common and the river, with a garden and first-floor balcony looking straight out onto the water and a conservatory where most of the action takes place. (But it's difficult to find; get directions when you book.) Quite a formal restaurant, prettily decorated and full of flowers, they prefer smart dressers. The cooking, from the Bavarian chef/owner Hans Schweitzer, can be on the complicated side—in the modern idiom but classically based. The menu is priced from two courses up to six, so you can eat delicately or treat yourself. Depending on the time of year, starters might include cream of asparagus soup with asparagus spears and the intriguing tea-smoked seafood brochette—salmon, prawns and monkfish delicately flavoured and moist on a bed of avocado and papaya salad. Main dishes reflect the classical base with some innovations—chicken armoricaine with lobster and shrimp sauce or aiguillette of beef with roasted garlic potatoes. Desserts include light soufflés of fruit (passion fruit and lime are favourites). The wine list is quite extensive, French based and with welcome half bottles. C £25. Set L £13.95-£40, Set D £24-£40.

12/20 Twenty Two

22 Chesterton Rd, Cambridge - 0223-351880

INTERNATIONAL

Open Dinner Tues-Sat.

This pleasant terraced-house restaurant run by two lecturers at the local catering college continues to please with its set menu that uses ingredients like wild mushrooms, pigeon, lamb and duck. Very good desserts include English flavours like rhubarb. A good wine list includes descriptions that are designed to illumin-

ate not confuse and prices begin around £8. **Set D** £19.50-£23.

University Arms Hotel

Regent St, Cambridge, CB2 1AD - 0223-351241, Fax 0223-315256

B&B 115 rms £60-£150 inc service and VAT. Restaurant.

A large Edwardian building on the edge of the city centre, the hotel overlooks famous Parker's Piece with its cricket pitch. The décor is formal and standardised but comfortable. It boasts an oak-panelled restaurant and several bars (Fenners Bar has over 100 whiskies to choose from).

SIX MILE BOTTOM

Swynford Paddocks Hotel

Six Mile Bottom, Newmarket, CB8 0UE 063-870 234, Fax 063-870 283

B&B 15 rms £70-£128 inc VAT. DB&B £50-£150. Tennis. Restaurant.

Once the home of Colonel Leigh and his wife Augusta, half sister to Lord Byron, the 'mad, bad and dangerous to know' poet was a frequent visitor here. (The hotel provides a detailed account of the scandalous relationship). Now it is a gracious, white mansion set in pretty countryside and next door to a stud (Newmarket is at the heart of the flat-racing country), a few miles from Cambridge. Surrounded by gardens, complete with croquet lawn, the interior is delightful. The reception area is galleried; other public rooms are comfortably and stylishly furnished. Bedrooms, individually decorated, have lovely views and some have four-poster beds. The dining room serves rather formal food from fresh, local ingredients.

∎ PUBS

Fort St George, Midsummer Common, stands just beside the river and shares the same view as Midsummer House and serves good lunchtime snacks. There's a rewarding walk along the towpath to the pub from Magdalene Street Bridge. In a side street near Parker's Piece, **The Free Press**, 7 Prospect Row, serves good, cheap food in its small, crowded bars.

HAMPTON COURT

Like all the great palaces of the past, **Hampton Court Palace** sits gracefully on the banks of a river. For the Thames acted as a highway, bringing goods for the greater comfort of the nobles, as well as the characters of history: ambassadors, guests, mistresses and spies. King Henry VIII, an avaricious man, watched while Cardinal Wolsey spent some fifteen years building this splendid place. Then he claimed it as a 'gift' from his despondent servant and proceeded to add to it, installing a tennis court (today the oldest surviving 'real' or 'royal' tennis court in the world and still used) and several wings. Subsequent monarchs also enjoyed this splendid red-brick building and filled it full of magnificent art, furnishings and tapestries. It is an extraordinary statement of royal wealth, magnificence and pomp.

In March 1986 a fire destroyed the *King's Apartments*, one of Sir Christopher Wren's masterpieces added between 1689 and 1694 for the reigning monarchs William and Mary. Fires have always been a danger in royal and noble residences, but this one was extensive and particularly alarmed the heritage industry, charged with looking after so many historic buildings. But the technical expertise and the high degree of historical authenticity brought to the restoration over a six-year period means that what we see today is a genuine re-creation of the old apartments.

As work began, exciting discoveries were made. Graffiti drawn by Wren's artisans was found behind the panelling, and between the floors, sackfulls of seashells which had provided sound and heat insulation centuries ago, came to light. Ironically, another disaster proved advantageous. The great storms of autumn 1987 uprooted six ancient, protected oak trees in Kent and they provided the timber for the new roof trusses. The great blue-and-gold vaulted ceiling of the *Chapel Royal* is a masterpiece; the *Haunted Gallery*, where the headless ghost of Catherine Howard, Henry VIII's queen, is reputed to have run screaming after her execution, appears undisturbed. After the six-year, £13 million restoration, the King's apartments are revealed in all their glory—much as they looked on their completion at the end of the seventeenth century.

With the opening of the apartments have come other innovations for the public now visiting the Palace. Guides and odd characters dressed in period costume show you around the palace, answer questions and, perhaps picking at the fruit and sweetmeats piled high on the dressed tables, give you a sense of the opulent past. You walk through several centuries of architectural and artistic highlights, past Brussels tapestries, and masterpieces by Caravaggio, Brueghel, Sir Peter Lely and Mantegna. The imposing *Great Hall* with its hammer-beam roof has been painstakingly restored, and once again the kitchens are warm with fires and full of pots and pans.

The exterior is no less magnificent and the gardens are replanted at each successive season, making them some of the finest public gardens in the country. Also to see are the *Maze*—albeit now looking rather small—the *Privy Gardens*, the *Great Fountain* and the *Great Vine*, planted in 1769.

You can get there easily by car (about fifteen miles southwest of London), by rail from Waterloo station (two trains an hour taking 31 minutes) or by Green Line Coach from Victoria, taking about an hour (telephone 081-668 7261 for details).

Hampton Court Palace is open from mid-March to mid-October Monday 10.15am to 6pm and Tuesday to Sunday 9.30am to 6pm, and mid-October to mid-March on Monday from 10.15am to 4.30pm, and Tuesday to Sunday 9.30am to 4.30pm. Last admission is 45 minutes before closing time. For enquiries telephone 081-781 9500.

■ RESTAURANT

   Le Petit Max

97a The High St, Vicarage Rd, Hampton Wick - 081-977 0236
FRENCH
Open Lunch Sun, Dinner daily. No cards.

By day a café called Bonzo's under a railway bridge in Kingston, in the evening a brilliant small restaurant led by the entrepreneurial Marc and Max Renzland and chef Matthew Jones who has worked at Gidleigh Park in Devon and Bibendum. The place is cramped, the décor uninspiring, but the food is a revelation. The menu changes according to what they buy, but ranges from foie gras or crevettes to cassoulet, rack of lamb or sweetbreads with rocket. Desserts are very good. There is no wine list, but you can get wine from the shop next door. The menu is a set-price one, but there are tempting supplements so you will probably find yourself paying more. It's well worth the trip, but telephone first as they do sometimes close at the beginning of the month. **Set D £16.95.**

OXFORD

Oxford is a rewarding city to get to know, with more obvious life and verve than its rival Cambridge. The city is known for Oxford sausages, Frank Cooper's Oxford Marmalade (no longer made here), Oxford University Press, the covered market, which nobody should miss, and lately for the fictional but oh-so-believable Inspector Morse. And like every city with a long history, Oxford has its fair share of odd facts and stories of the 'Did you know?' variety. Did you know, for instance, that three crones sitting at Carfax gave Shakespeare the inspiration for the three witches in Macbeth? Or that Lawrence of Arabia canoed along the underground city stream firing a pistol up St Aldate's grating? One odd thing is not fiction, however. Did you know that Christ Church time is five minutes later than Greenwich Meantime? If not, you soon will as Great Tom, the six-ton bell in Tom Tower, rings 101 times (one for each founder member of the college) at 9.05pm every night.

Most visitors, however, come to see the University. Spring and autumn are the best seasons to visit when the streets are (slightly) less full and the colleges are open to visitors. Examination time—May and June—are the worst as many colleges are closed. The *Oxford Information Centre* organises walking tours of the colleges and the city conducted by Blue Badge Guides which last two hours. You can rent a bicycle by the day, week or term from *Dentons* (0865-53859) or from *Pennyfarthing* (0865-249368). Or you can wander at will through the halls, quads and gardens of the medieval and later buildings. For Oxford's beauty is not so immediate as that of Cambridge; you have to seek it out down small passages, through gateways into College quads (at Cambridge they're called 'courts') and along alleyways.

Now with 35 colleges, the University began with a group of English students expelled from Paris in 1167. But it was not until 1249 that the first college, University College, was founded, to be followed by Merton in 1264 and Balliol around 1266.

Start at the centre of the old city, *Carfax*, meaning the crossing of the four ways. South along St Aldate's you come to **Christ Church** (known familiarly as 'the House') the grandest college and the home of Alice in Wonderland; Lewis Carroll—a mathematics don here—wrote it for Alice Liddell, the dean's daughter. By a quirk of history, its college chapel became the smallest cathedral in England. The *hall* of the college is the largest in Oxford, with a richly carved hammer-beam roof and splendid portraits of former students and dons hanging on the walls. Along Blue Boar Street, you come to **Corpus Christi College**, founded in 1517 and the first college at which Greek was taught. Again the *hall* is worth seeing, as is the *library*, one of the most picturesque in Oxford. Nearby **Merton College** possesses some of the oldest buildings in Oxford. Its *gateway tower* was built in 1418, the *chapel* was built in the last decade of the thirteenth century while the *library* is one of the oldest medieval libraries in England (1371–78), and was the first to store books upright in shelves instead of lying them flat in presses.

Along the High Street (east of Carfax) you come across the university church of **St Mary's**. It's well worth climbing up the spire high above the rooftops. From here you look over the mellow buildings and understand the inspiration of the nineteenth-century poet Matthew Arnold who described Oxford as 'That sweet city with her dreaming spires'.

Behind the church you come to a cluster of fascinating buildings like **Brasenose College** (so called after its brazen or brass door knocker) with its handsome *gateway tower* and modern buildings by architects Powell and Moya who built many new additions to both Oxford and Cambridge colleges. Here also, you come across **All Souls College**, founded in 1438 by King Henry VI and dedicated to the souls of all those who fell in the Hundred Years War against the French. It has a warden and fellows but no undergraduates; the fellows are among the most distinguished in British intellectual life.

The **Sheldonian Theatre** was the first work of Sir Christopher Wren. Built in 1663–1669, this impressive semi-circular and rectangular building is used for degree-giving ceremonies. It is also frequently used for concerts; go if you can for the acoustics and the sense of the past. Impossible to miss is the splendid **Radcliffe Camera**, built to house Dr Radcliffe's science library, and now part of the world famous **Bodleian Library**. One of the six copyright libraries in Britain, the Bodleian, which receives a copy of every single book published in the United Kingdom, was named after Sir Thomas Bodley, diplomat and fellow of Merton, who gave 2,000 books for the new 1602 library.

Like Cambridge, Oxford is a city where you wander at will, either discovering new sights or if you are a frequent visitor, rediscovering your favourites. Try to see **New College** in New College Lane, founded in 1379, with a particularly fine *chapel* adorned with Epstein's statue of Lazarus, and gardens bounded by the old city wall. **Magdalen College** (1458) is worth seeking out for its famous fifteenth-century *Bell Tower*, *lawns*, *river walk* and *deer park*, as well as its three *quads*; **Worcester College** (1713) for its delightful *gardens* and half-secret lake.

And if colleges *pall*, Oxford has other attractions. The **Botanical Garden** in the High Street—the oldest in Britain—was founded as a 'Physic Garden' in 1621. The **Ashmolean Museum** in Beaumont Street, founded by Elias Ashmole in 1683 contains the university's art and archaeological collections, and oddities like twelve cartloads of the 'Cabinet of curiosities' of the Tradescants, father and son, great gardeners and collectors. The **Pitt Rivers Museum** is one of the world's great anthropological collections in an extraordinary Victorian setting. The internationally known **Museum of Modern Art** shows paintings, sculpture, photography, design, advertising, architecture, performance, folk art and crafts. It also has a good book shop. *Music at Oxford* presents various concerts and music festivals throughout the year. *Blackwell's* book shop in Broad Street is a large and comprehensive book shop, a delight to browse through. And *The Oxford Story* gives you the chance to take a ride through scenes from the University's past.

But if, after looking around Oxford, you're in danger of being too impressed, just recall the song in *Wind in the Willows* by Kenneth Grahame: 'The clever men at Oxford
Know all that there is to be knowed.
But they none of them know one half as much
As intelligent Mr Toad.'

The Ashmolean Museum, Beaumont Street (0865-278000) is open Saturday 10am to 4pm and Sunday from 2 to 4pm. Music at Oxford can be contacted on 0865-864466.

The Oxford Story at 6 Broad Street (0865-790055) is open daily April to October from 9.30am to 5pm (last admission), July and August from 9am to 6.30pm (last admission) and from November to March from 10am to 4pm (last admission). Further information from the Oxford Information Centre, St Aldate's (0865-726871).

■ RESTAURANTS & HOTELS

11/20 Al-Shami
25 Walton Crescent, Oxford - 0865-310066
LEBANESE

Open Lunch & Dinner daily.

Still good value, this Lebanese restaurant, located between Somerville and Worcester Colleges, continues to serve decent food in its crowded dining room. Main dishes are preceded by a huge plate of crudités and olives. Hot and cold hors d'oeuvres continue to please: humus, fatayer (spinach patties) and spicy sausages. Most main dishes are chargrilled; desserts like filling paklava finish the meal. Iryan yoghurt is traditional; the wine list is short but good with an excellent Château Musar from Lebanon. **C** £18.

13/20 Bath Place Restaurant
4-5 Bath Pl, Holywell St, Oxford, OX1 3SU
0865-791812, Fax 0865-791834
FRENCH
Open Lunch Wed-Sun, Dinner Tues-Sat.

Down a tiny cobbled alleyway, this collection of seventeenth-century cottages, ultimately owned, as is most of Oxford, by one of the colleges, has been transformed into a family-run hotel/restaurant. The dining room has a formal atmosphere and the food is serious while the pretty presentation reminded us of the days of nouvelle cuisine. Fish is treated well, as in scallops and langoustine tails for a starter and paupiette of turbot and salmon mousse. More hearty ingredients such as rabbit also make an appearance, accompanied by savoy cabbage and spices; spring lamb is suitably pink; desserts are delicious and grand—like a splendid millefeuille of bitter chocolate and raspberries. The wine list runs to some very good bottles, some as half bottles. **C** £25. **Set Sun L** £19.50.

Bath Place
(See restaurant above)
B&B 2 stes £115-£125, 8 rms £70-£100 inc VAT. Restaurant.

Just the place for a romantic weekend, this small, atmospheric hotel is right in the centre of Oxford, but remains quiet as it is situated in its own small alleyway just off Holywell Street. It is more a restaurant with rooms than an hotel, but bedrooms have a pretty décor and are equipped with colour TV and mini-bar. Breakfast is served either in your room or in the dining room.

DB&B: Dinner, Bed & Breakfast.

10/20 Browns
5-11 Woodstock Rd, Oxford - 0865-511995
INTERNATIONAL
Open Lunch & Dinner daily.

The Browns here is housed in a less impressive location than the Cambridge Browns but the general ambience, jolly service and honest-to-goodness food is the same. Prices are very reasonable: around £6 for a good hamburger and the same for spaghetti and this is the sort of place where you can linger over coffee. **C** £15.

12/20 Cherwell Boathouse
Bardwell Rd, Oxford - 0865-52746
BRITISH
Open Lunch Wed-Sun, Dinner Tues-Sat.

On the river Cherwell, the best way to arrive is by punt, although more cautious and sensible souls will drive here. It's a delightful setting, particularly in summer when the light plays on the river and its banks and you sit in the converted boathouse looking over the scene. Menus change weekly and are restricted to three items per course. Starters and main dishes always have a vegetarian alternative. Starters might include leek and potato soup or a pasta, main dishes are strong on fish like red snapper, sea bream or shellfish as well as good hearty dishes like hare in a pepper sauce. Desserts revert to the traditional English mode and become puddings: rhubarb and ginger fool or home-made ice cream. There are good British cheeses. The wine list interests with its good mixture of the serious and the relatively light, and is strong on French wines. All in all, the Cherwell Boathouse is well worth a detour—by punt or by car. **Set L & D** £16.

Cotswold House
363 Banbury Rd, Oxford, OX2 7PL - 0865-310558
B&B 7 rms £48 inc VAT.

At this friendly no-smoking B&B in north Oxford, about two miles from the city centre, you get a warm welcome from owners Jim and Anne O'Kane. All the rooms, which are nicely though not spectacularly furnished, have a colour TV, fridge and a hair drier. Traditional English breakfast pleases and although they have no restaurant, there are enough pubs and restaurants nearby. A short bus ride from a stop almost outside the front door takes you into the centre.

15 North Parade
15 North Parade, Oxford - 0865-513773
FRENCH
Open Lunch daily, Dinner Mon-Sat.

In a narrow street just to the north of the city centre, this pretty neighbourhood restaurant is as popular as ever. As with all good neighbourhood places, the constant presence of the charming owner Georgina Wood is a strong factor. So is the cooking from new chef Colin Gilbert who spent a stint in the south of France and who has brought some of those sunny flavours to north Oxford. Good bread and olives alert you to the possibilities and you are not disappointed. Menus change weekly and might include roast fillet of salmon with fresh tomato, basil and olive oil sauce, baked goat's cheese with provençal vegetables or seafood soup. Meat appears with pigeon, duckling or lamb cutlets with tapenade and fish again in darne of salmon with seafood sauce. Cooking is light of touch, and pretty to look at. Vegetables are excellent. Crème brulée is both light and satisfying and the short but international wine list gives a good choice. **C** £23. **Set L** £11.75, £13.75, **Set Sun L** £12.95, **Set D** £19.50.

Old Parsonage Hotel
1 Banbury Rd, Oxford, OX2 6NN - 0865-310210, Fax 0865-311262
B&B 4 stes £190, 26 rms £97.50-£125 inc VAT.

Privately owned, this creeper-clad stone house was built in 1660 and was reopened as an hotel after extensive renovation in 1991. In the interim, among other things, it served as Oscar Wilde's base. It is beautifully done with individually furnished bedrooms, complete with every comfort including two showers in the well decorated marble bathrooms, pretty fabrics and furnishings, a garden and roof garden. There are nice personal touches around the hotel, good flowers and exemplary service. There is no restaurant, but the Parsonage Bar serves some excellent food: salmon fish cakes with mayonnaise, calf's liver, steak. There's a good wine list and commendable wines by the glass. Otherwise you can trot across the road for a good snack or meal at Brown's, in the same ownership.

Randolph Hotel

Beaumont St, Oxford, OX1 2LN - 0865-247481, Fax 0865-791678
4 stes £150-£250, 105 rms £110-£140 inc service and VAT. Restaurant.

The Randoph has a splendid neo-Gothic façade and is one of Oxford's more recent landmarks (it was built in 1864). For long the place where parents came to stay while visiting their student offspring, it is comfortable in a grand hotel manner with an oak-panelled foyer and sweeping staircase. Public rooms are elegant and bedrooms vary in size from small to extensive. The Spires Restaurant serves traditional food and a wine bar nestles in the vaults which are open Monday to Saturday 11am to 11pm. It is also a good place for high tea—all very traditional.

12/20 Restaurant Elizabeth

82 St Aldate's, Oxford - 0865-242230
FRENCH
Open Lunch & Dinner Tues-Sun.

Still a bastion of classic French cuisine, with the emphasis on traditional dishes which it does very well indeed. Set in small rooms in a charming fifteenth-century house with windows looking out onto Christ Church, dishes like pâté de foie de volaille, rack of lamb, the old favourite duck à l'orange and the fabled crème brulée continue to please a clientele which has also changed little. The wine list is legendary with old bottles and new discoveries, particularly in the Rioja section (the chef and proprietor are both Spanish). C £25. Set L £15.

11/20 Whites

16 Turl St, Oxford - 0865-793396
FRENCH
Open Lunch daily, Dinner Mon-Sat.

Restaurant and wine merchant, you walk past the bar and down into the restaurant to find dark wooden chairs and tables and Dali prints on the walls. The menus vary in price according to the number of dishes, and in the well thought-out menus from £21 upwards, according to the glass of wine you select for each course. Food is traditional and good. You might choose from crab or onion soup, chicken liver pâté or scallops in puff pastry to start, veal with oyster mushrooms, fish with pasta or grilled lamb. The wine list changes regularly and comes up to expectations. C £25. Set L & D £11.50, £13.95, £21-£26.95.

GREAT MILTON

 ## Le Manoir aux Quat'Saisons

Great Milton, nr Oxford, OX44 7PD - 0844-278881, Fax 0844-278847
FRENCH
Open Lunch & Dinner daily.

What is Raymond Blanc's secret? Disciplined creativity, cooking times accurate to a second, matchless—mostly local—ingredients are part of it. But Blanc's true genius lies in his rare sense of harmony, evident in the way he marries flavours in a dish, and the dishes on the menu. Then there is his approach to people and the beauty and comfort of his old manor set in ravishing, verdant grounds.

Arriving at Le Manoir is magical. The mellow stone of the fifteenth-century houses, the manicured gardens, tennis courts, pool and kitchen garden are pure enchantment. Visitors are charmingly welcomed, and whisked off to delectably decorated guest rooms, some of which can be improbably frilly.

A brisk tour of the grounds, and then the feast begins. The courteous manager Alain Désenclos offers an aperitif, then Raymond Blanc appears at the same time as the amuse-gueules, a sumptuous foretaste of what is to come. We sampled a little dish composed of lobster and—yes—swedes, and a langoustine bisque with the lingering finish of a fine wine. Blanc helps the diners select their meal, either the £59.50 sampling menu of four courses plus dessert, or seasonal specialities, or such Manoir classics as bouillabaisse en gelée, truffled squab stuffed with boudin blanc, quail fillets with bacon-flecked potatoes in a wild mushroom essence, l'assiette de caramel au café...

By the time you read these lines, Raymond Blanc's prolific imagination will doubtless have added new creations to the menu he invents and executes with his gifted English sous-chef, Clive Fretwell. We can only hope that your meal will be as superb as the one we had in the Manoir's beamed, cream-coloured dining room, with its still lifes and French scenes by an American disciple of Matisse. Our meal began with a scallop tartare of glistening freshness seasoned with a limpid vegetable jus, truffle and Japanese shiso leaves; a terrine of lime-marinated red mullet bound by a smooth salt-cod brandade and surrounded by glossy green seaweed, further enhanced by a sauce of oysters and sour cream (a stunning composition of colours and tastes) and a plum ravioli filled with spinach, Parmesan, meat juices and white truffles, a mite massive, but joyously Italian in spirit. A mix of truffles, onions and lightly smoked bacon swaddled in a golden crust—a real explosion of flavours—gives the lie to those who hold that modern chefs lack the technique of their elders. Delightfully simple and utterly satisfying was the so-called 'civet' of shellfish embellished with a little caviar, seaweed and tart cucumber. A tender roast woodcock benefited from an Hermitage sauce bringing out the bird's deep, latent flavours. Concluding the meal were rare Welsh cheeses and gorgeous, delicately crafted deserts: a thin slice of crystallised pineapple offered with sorbet and molten caramel and a parfait presented in a cup so thin and finely worked than one can scarcely believe it is made of chocolate. C £65. Set L £29.50-£59.50, Set D £59.50.

Le Manoir aux Quat'Saisons

(See restaurant above)
3 stes £325-£375, 16 rms £165-£275 inc service and VAT. Outdoor pool. Tennis. Restaurant.

What can one say about this glorious and now famous manor house, standing by the church in Great Milton and just seven miles from Oxford? The restaurant is sublime (see review), one of the best in the country while the hotel is a delight. Surrounded by parkland and gardens, with its own vegetable and herb gardens, it's a warm Cotswold stone manor house. The downstairs rooms are full of comfortable squashy sofas and chairs, beautiful flowers and antique furniture. Warming fires glow in the grates in winter. Bedrooms are individually decorated with lovely fabrics and furnishings, although some guests find

the total effect a little overpowering. Some bedrooms are in the converted stable block and most of them have a private terrace overlooking the grounds. Even the dovecote is a suite. Bathrooms are equally elegantly done; service is suitably attentive. It is expensive, but it is worth it. If you are completely bowled over by the cooking, you can learn some of the secrets (the talent comes from inside you) at Le Petit Blanc Ecole de Cuisine. The cooking school operates several five-day courses, from October to Easter, ranging from £875 per person to £1,025 per person.

■ PUBS

Oxford has its fair share of pubs. Try the **Eagle and Child**, 49 St Giles, known locally as the Bird and Baby. J R Tolkein used to drink here, as did C S Lewis; the firelit parlours are very welcoming. In the ancient **Turf Tavern**, Bath Place, tall customers bang their heads on the picturesque beams. **The Bear**, Alfred St, behind Christ Church, dates from 1242 and has a collection of 3,000 ties from schools, colleges, clubs and regiments.

STRATFORD-UPON-AVON

Had it not been for an accident of birth on 23 April, 1564, Stratford would have remained a sleepy market town. As it is, *William Shakespeare* was born there on that date and as early as the eighteenth century tourists began to flock to the town. Remarkably, despite a huge Shakespeare industry, Stratford is still a delightful market town with the pretty River Avon running peacefully through it and a wealth of fine Tudor timber-framed and Georgian houses. As to the life of Shakespeare, we know very little, only that he was born in a house in Henley Street, known as the Birthplace, the eldest son of John Shakespeare and Mary Arden, and that shortly afterwards he was baptised in Holy Trinity Church. We suppose that he probably attended the Grammar School in Stratford (still standing), but have no firm documentary evidence. At the age of eighteen he started courting, and subsequently married, Anne Hathaway, some eight years his senior. They had three children: Susannah and the twins Judith and Hamnet. He then disappears from the records for some time but was obviously making a name for himself, for he subsequently appears as actor-manager of the Globe Theatre in London, with his plays being performed before the Court of Elizabeth I. By 1597, he had made enough money to purchase New Place, the largest house in Stratford and was able to retire here in 1610. On April 23, 1616 (his 52nd birthday), he died and was buried in Holy Trinity Church. Such are the scant details of Shakespeare's life.

Far more rewarding for the modern visitor are the large number of buildings associated with him that are still standing and are open to the public. First on the list must be **Holy Trinity Church**, worth seeing not only for the Shakespeare tombs and Memorial but also for the beauty of its architecture and tranquil setting beside the river. The **Birthplace** and **Anne Hathaway's Cottage** are obvious places of pilgrimage, but less well known (and therefore less crowded in high season), is **Mary Arden's House** in the village of Wilmcote, just outside Stratford. The Ardens were substantial yeoman farmers, as will be seen from the size of the house. The farm buildings contain displays of rural life from Shakespeare's day onwards and they hold frequent falconry displays. Like all the Shakespeare properties, the guides within the house are knowledgeable and entertaining; here at Mary Arden's House they give wonderful descriptions of life in Elizabethan England. Other properties open to view include **Harvard House**, home of Katherine Rogers, mother of John Harvard, **New Place** and **Hall's Croft**, home of Shakespeare's daughter Susannah, and of course the **Royal Shakespeare Theatre**, home to the Royal Shakespeare Company.

Shakespeare's Birthplace is open from March to October, Monday to Saturday 9am to 5.30pm, and from 10am to 5.30pm on Sunday. Winter hours are from 9.30am to 4pm Monday to Saturday, and 10.30am to 4pm on Sunday.

*Mary Arden's House is open from March to October, Monday to Saturday 9.30am to 5pm, and 10am to 4pm on Sunday. Winter hours are Monday to Saturday 10am to 4pm, and 1.30 to 4pm on Sunday. Further information from **Stratford Tourist Information Centre**, Bridgefoot (0789-293127).*

■ RESTAURANTS & HOTELS

Alveston Manor

Clopton Bridge, Stratford-upon-Avon, CV37 7HP - 0789-204581, Fax 0789-414095
3 stes £165, 105 rms £80-£110 inc VAT. Restaurant.

This big, reliable hotel is easy to find but is also next to a busy road junction, which is not the most tranquil of settings. Inside however, a suprisingly cosy atmosphere prevails, with small oak-panelled rooms, creaking stairs and deep carpets. Bedrooms are comfortable and well-appointed.

Dukes Hotel

Payton St, Stratford-upon-Avon, CV37 6UA
0789-269300, Fax 0789-414700
B&B 2 stes £100, 22 rms £45-£85 inc VAT. Restaurant.

Dating from 1820, this centrally located hotel was originally two Georgian townhouses. The hotel is furnished with antiques and bedrooms are well-equipped, all with private facilities like satellite TV.

Falcon Hotel

Chapel St, Stratford-upon-Avon, CV37 6HA
0789-205777, Fax 0789-414260
B&B 1 ste £99, 73 rms £70-£94 inc VAT.
Restaurant.

The main part of this hotel dates from the sixteenth century, but it has a modern extension at the rear and a charming walled garden. Bedrooms and bathrooms are well-appointed and the one suite has a four-poster bed. The hotel is situated in the heart of Stratford, within walking distance of the Royal Shakespeare theatre and major tourist attractions.

Shakespeare Hotel

Chapel St, Stratford-upon-Avon, CV37 6ER
0789-294771, Fax 0789-415411
B&B 5 stes £120-£150, 63 rms £85-£125 inc VAT. Restaurant.

A lovely creaky old building, dating back to 1637, but with all modern comforts. Period furnishings and open fires give a warm atmosphere to the public rooms. Bedrooms are named after characters from Shakespeare's plays and include four-poster rooms and suites.

10/20 Sir Toby's

8 Church St, Stratford-upon-Avon - 0789-268822
FRENCH
Open Dinner Wed-Sat.

This is a cheerful bistro in a town sadly lacking in good restaurants. Diners include many theatregoers, hence the early opening times of 5.30pm to 9.30pm. They feature dishes like home-made fish ravioli with prawn sauce for starters, chicken with olives, rosemary and thyme with a wild mushroom sauce as a main dish, and traditional bread and butter pudding. Good, reasonably priced house wines. C £15.

Stratford House

18 Sheep St, Stratford-upon-Avon, CV37 6EF
0789-268288, Fax 0789-295580
B&B 11 rms £78-£82 inc VAT. Restaurant.

A delightful little hotel, centrally located, yet on one of the quieter streets in Stratford. The building is Georgian and has a peaceful walled garden at the rear. Log fires welcome you in winter and there is a restaurant and bar in the conservatory.

Bedrooms are nicely furnished and have floral prints.

ALCESTER

12/20 Billesley Manor Restaurant

Billesley Manor Hotel, Alcester, Warwickshire, B49 6NF - 0789-400888, Fax 0789-764145
MODERN BRITISH
Open Lunch & Dinner daily.

Just three miles from Stratford, the oak-panelled dining room of Billesley Manor makes a pleasant venue for a formal lunch or dinner. Fresh, locally bought ingredients are well-presented and feature flavoursome combinations in the modern idiom such as lamb with basil and turnip purée and breast of chicken stuffed with mango. Vegetables are abundant; the hot chocolate soufflée and crème brulée to finish with are impeccable. The very good wine list sticks mainly to French bottles. C £ 34. Set L £17, Set D £26.

Billesley Manor Hotel

(See restaurant above)
2 stes £180-£205, 39 rms £99-£135, inc VAT (and EB Fri, Sat, Sun). Pool. Tennis. Restaurant.

Billesley Manor is a sixteenth-century manor house, set in eleven acres of gardens and now a fine hotel just three miles from Stratford. It is believed that Shakespeare may have written *As You Like It* here. Wood panelling covers the walls of the public rooms and bedrooms vary from well laid-out modern rooms to period rooms furnished with four-poster beds. Service is of a high standard with staff both helpful and efficient.

ALDERMINSTER

12/20 Bell Bistro

Alderminster, Warwickshire - 0789-450414
INTERNATIONAL
Open daily noon-2pm, 7-9.30pm.

Just outside Stratford, this old coaching inn calls itself a pub/bistro and that's just what it is. The emphasis is on the food and it is of a standard way above usual pub fare. The kitchen is presided over by Vanessa Brewer and a team of young helpers and all the food is freshly prepared and home-made. During the week a good-value two course lunch for £5.95 might consist of faggots in a rich gravy with new potatoes, followed by divine chocolate bread pudding. In addition a lengthy list of interesting dishes on the blackboard includes dishes such as crispy-topped lamb in cider; a whole blackboard is devoted to fish dishes. In summer the set lunch is replaced by an excellent cold buffet with good salads and rare roast beef. On Sundays there is always a roast and it's usually packed, so it's well worth booking. Main dishes are between £6 and £8.

Ettington Park Hotel

Alderminster, Stratford-upon-Avon, CV37 8BS - 0789-450123, Fax 0789-450472
B&B 5 stes £180, 48 rms £145, DB&B £190. Helipad. Pool. Tennis. Restaurant.

This remarkable neo-gothic pile has recently been refurbished and now has a wonderful Victorian conservatory and an elegant, spacious drawing room. Bedrooms are individually furnished with superb views across the gardens and surrounding countryside; bathrooms are full of toiletries. The fourteenth-century chapel is now in use as a small conference room. They have a sauna and solarium as well as fishing, riding and clay pigeon shooting for the more energetic.

■ PUB

Slug and Lettuce

38 Guild St, Stratford-upon-Avon - 0789-299700
Open Summer: daily 11am-11pm, Winter: daily 11am-3.30pm, 5.30-11pm.

Pine tables and chairs and flagstone floors with rugs give a nice 'farmhouse kitchen' feel to this popular pub. In summer there is a pretty terrace where meals or drinks can be taken. An extensive range of bar food includes home-made soups, black pudding with tomato, bacon and cheese, or chicken breast baked with avocado and bacon. Desserts are very good indeed.

Plan to travel? Look for Gault Millau's other Best of *guides* to Chicago, Florida, France, Germany, Hawaii, Hong Kong, Italy, Los Angeles, New England, New Orleans, New York, Paris, San Francisco, Thailand, Toronto, and Washington, D.C.

WINDSOR

Windsor Castle, where the kings and queens of England have lived for 900 years, dominates the small town and the surrounding countryside. First a wooden fortress built by William the Conqueror in 1066, a day's march or twenty miles from his other castle, the Tower of London, the present collection of buildings is a mixture of architectural styles. Three sections—Upper, Middle and Lower Wards—give dramatic views over the river and countryside. Entering the castle through *Henry VIII's Gateway* into the *Lower Ward* takes you into the *Horseshoe Cloisters*. To your right stand the little houses of the *Military Knights of Windsor*, an order founded by King Edward III as the 'Poor Knights of Windsor'. One of the glories of the castle is *St George's Chapel*, begun in 1478 and reminiscent of King's College Chapel in Cambridge, but full of tombs (ten monarchs are buried here) and monuments of royalty.

But what most visitors come to see are the *State Apartments*, the formal rooms used by the reigning monarch for ceremonial, State and official occasions. Open to the public when the Royal family is not in residence, they vary from Charles II's small rooms to the *Garter Throne* room and the extravagant *Waterloo Chamber*, built to celebrate the famous victory over the French in 1815. Some of the impressive art collection is on display on the walls, the furniture throughout is very grand. Before going into the State Apartments you come to what is many people's favourite: *Queen Mary's Dolls' House*, created by the architect Sir Edwin Lutyens for the young Queen Mary and given by the nation to her in 1923. It is a wonderful world in miniature, with every single detail thought out from tiny cabin trunks to the plumbing.

Walk over the river bridge at the bottom of the town and you enter **Eton**, a delightful small town best known for *Eton College*, founded by Henry IV in 1440. Built of mellow red brick, it exudes exclusivity and expense. It is after all, one of Britain's leading public (private) schools with more than its fair share of distinguished old boys.

Windsor is about 27 miles west of London, a short car journey. Trains from Waterloo Station run regularly and take about 45 minutes (071-928 5100). Green Line Coaches (081-668 7261) run from Victoria Station, taking approximately 45 minutes.

Windsor Castle is open daily throughout the year (except when the Royal family is in residence), 10am to 5pm from April to October and to 4pm November to March. Last admission is one hour before closing. Telephone 0753-831118 to check.

■ RESTAURANTS & HOTELS

BRAY-ON-THAMES

Waterside Inn
Ferry Rd, Bray-on-Thames, nr Windsor - 0628-20691, Fax 0628-784710
FRENCH
Open Lunch Wed-Sun, Dinner Tues-Sun.

The Waterside has held its position as one of the top restaurants in Britain for many years. It is not difficult to see why: the tranquil riverside setting could hardly be bettered, its proximity to London guarantees its clientele and the name Michel Roux ensures that standards of cuisine and service rarely slip. This is truly dining on the grand scale, starting with drinks on the delightful riverside terrace before stepping inside to start with a delicious amuse-bouche. Cooking is firmly rooted in the classical French tradition but in line with modern tastes, with lighter sauces and increased use of olive oils and

basil. It would be hard to beat the lobster and crab ravioli served with a crustacean oil flavoured with basil. During the week a three-course Menu Gastronomique is served at lunchtime for £28 with wines available by the glass (not included in the price), so it is possible to enjoy all that the Waterside has to offer at an affordable sum. For those who decide to go the whole hog, there is the five-course Menu Exceptional at £58 per person (minimum two people). Dishes are taken from the main à la carte menu and represent some of the finest creations of the Waterside. A perfect starter of grilled scallops served on a confit of tomato and shallot might be followed by a fillet of red mullet served on a bed of diced squid and red pepper with a red wine sauce. The palate is then refreshed by a pink champagne sorbet before succulent rosettes of loin of lamb, pan-fried and garnished with baby onions, girolles and spinach served with a piquant juniper sauce. The choice then lies between perfectly ripened French cheeses from Philippe Olivier or the most wonderful and old-fashioned sounding, but fresh-tasting, crêpe soufflé Grand Marnier, served with segments of oranges, the whole ending with coffee and petits-fours. And of course, anything that involves the art of the patissier is brilliant. The wine list is long and comprehensive, French, and expensive. If you feel like staying, there are six smart bedrooms, some with views of the river and an electric launch is available for hire. **C** £45. **Set L** £28, **Set D** £58 (five courses).

SHINFIELD

Shinfield is a mere half hour from London's Heathrow Airport, an hour from the city itself, and twenty miles west of Windsor and well worth the trip.

L'Ortolan
The Old Vicarage, Church Lane, Shinfield, nr Reading - 0734-883783, Fax 0734-885391
FRENCH
Open Lunch Tues-Sun, Dinner Tues-Sat.

With the exception of an outstanding salt-cod tartlet (served as an amuse-gueule) and an extremely delicate dish consisting of an enormous oyster (difficult to cut in its shell, even harder to swallow at one gulp) in caviar jelly on a bed of spinach and salmon, chef John Burton-Race's other offerings lacked the personality that their descriptions and ravishing presentations had led us to expect: slices of brawn with carrots, leek and duck rillettes in a lentil and cress vinaigrette; a hefty ravioli filled with potato purée in an ethereal herbal sauce with wild mushrooms and asparagus; nice, firm turbot with chanterelles, truffles and green vegetables in a creamy leek-butter sauce; dainty desserts flavoured with dark and white chocolate, coffee and caramel, escorted by ice creams, all artistically arranged to resemble a painting by Mondrian. Every single dish roused the appetite, each one married all manner of delicate and clever ingredients; yet the end products were consistently too sedate.

Perhaps we ought to have looked to the more rustic options—all, incidentally, French-inspired, doubtless the legacy of Burton-Race's stint with Raymond Blanc twelve years ago—like the boudin au cidre or lotte in a tangy mustard sauce, lusty pheasant with sauerkraut, the dark chocolate soufflé or pineapple swirled with mandarine sabayon.

Yet as a worthy successor to the irascible Nico Ladenis who preceded him here, Burton-Race is an imaginative chef with personality to spare. He is poised for a brilliant future, if one is to believe the man's self-promotion, an odd mix of ambition and detachment, firm faith in French cuisine and the belief that British chefs are now among its top practitioners (all his sous-chefs and assistants are English). We salute Burton-Race's bold inclusion of native wines in his wide-ranging cellar which contains mainly Burgundian wines. The English Old Buxter with its admirable balance of acidity and fruit is worth many a Muscadet, and the peach-scented dessert wine bears comparison to a good Loupiac. C £40. Set L & D £21.50-£52.

WATER OAKLEY

Oakley Court Hotel

Windsor Rd, Water Oakley, nr Windsor, SL4 5UR - 0628-74141, Fax 0628-37011

11 stes from £245, 81 rms from £125 inc VAT. 9-hole golf. Restaurant.

Just three miles west of Windsor, Oakley Court is a grand Victorian manor house built in the then prevalent and extraordinary gothic style, on the banks of the river Thames and surrounded by 35 acres of gardens. If it looks familiar, think back to the Dracula films; they were filmed here, using only candles to light the entire place. Log fires, traditional furnishings, a wood-panelled library and well appointed bedrooms, some with four poster beds, make for great comfort. It is believed that Général de Gaulle stayed here; it was, apparently, the headquarters in England for the French resistance. It's a good place to relax on the nine-hole pitch-and-putt golf course or the croquet lawn; they also have coarse fishing and punting on the river and can arrange golf, tennis and more in the vicinity. It has one grand restaurant—The Oakleaf—presided over by Murdo MacSween who serves grand food with an oriental spicing. There is a table d'hôte lunch at £18.75 per person, and dinner at £29 per person. The wine list is comprehensive.

YORK

Y ork is one of Britain's best preserved medieval cities and only two hours from London by train. It is probably true to say that to get an idea of what the City of London once looked like you should visit York.

Founded by the Romans in AD 71 as a fortress to quell the rebellious northerners, York was first known as 'Eboracum'. With the departure of the Romans successive invasions followed, but of these early settlers, it was the Vikings who left the greatest mark on the city, not least by the fact that the gates are still called bars and the streets are called gates. (Logical once you know that the Danish word for street is gaten). The Norman conquerors found a thriving little city which they promptly sacked (those rebellious northerners again), but they did build the magnificent city walls which we still walk on today. In the Middle Ages York became the most important city in the north as its massive Minster church—the largest north of the Alps—testifies. By the eighteenth century, York was also the most fashionable, and the 'Beau Monde' came from far and wide for the balls and assemblies and to occupy the graceful Georgian houses built to accomodate them. By great good fortune, the Victorian Industrial Revolution largely passed York by, and instead the city became a refuge for the mill owners of the neighbouring towns. Thanks to this happy accident of history, the modern visitor can feel that, in York, he steps back in time.

The best way to start a visit to this intriguing city is to walk around the *walls* which enclose the 263 acres of medieval York. From here you gaze down upon the web of narrow streets with names steeped in history: *Spurriergate* named after the spur makers, the *Shambles* from 'fleshammels' (once a row of butchers' shops), and the curiously named *Whip-Ma-Whop-Ma Gate*, derived from a whipping post where criminals were thrashed. Dominating the skyline is the great **York Minster** which took over two hundred years to build. It has some of the finest medieval stained glass in Britain and is a 'must' for any visit to York. One of the most exciting recent developments in York was the excavation of the *Viking settlement* in Coppergate and the opening of the **Yorvik Centre**. The visitor boards a 'time car' and is whisked back through history to a reconstruction of the Viking community of over 1,000 years ago. Everyday sights, sounds and even smells are re-created and the time-traveller gets a very real feel for life in a Viking town.

The car passes through the actual excavation site and finally the visitor walks through an exhibition of everyday items from the 'dig': woollen socks, shoes and, rather surprisingly, hornless Viking helmets.

No visit to York is complete without seeing the **Castle Museum**. Partly housed in the old prison, the visitor sees the highwayman Dick Turpin's cell (the residents of York are particularly proud of this famous resident), and walks through reconstructed *Victorian streets* containing, among other shops, a butcher, a baker and a candlestick maker. It is essentially a museum of everyday life and some of the twentieth-century exhibits—vacuum cleaners, television sets and so on from the recent past—will bring a pang of nostalgia.

Medieval buildings such as the *Merchant Adventurer's Hall*, scores of churches, narrow streets, the **National Railway Museum**, the eighteenth-century **Fairfax House**, the city walls and gates, the Minster, the Yorvik Centre and excellent shops. Truly, York has something for everyone.

Yorvik Centre is open April to October daily from 9am to 7pm, and from November to March daily from 9am to 5.30pm.
The Castle Museum *is open April to October Monday to Saturday from 9.30am to 5.30pm and Sunday from 10am to 5.30pm, and November to March daily 9.30am to 4pm.*
Further information from **York Tourist Office***, De Grey Room, Exhibition Sq (0904-621756).*

■ RESTAURANTS & HOTELS

12/20 Ivy Restaurant
Grange Hotel, Clifton, York, YO3 6AA
0904-644744, Fax 0904-612453
MODERN BRITISH
Open Lunch & Dinner daily.
The new chef at this excellent restaurant, much loved by the locals, produces some interesting fixed-price menus based on

fresh local ingredients. Three courses each with a choice of seven dishes for £19 make this good value for money. A very commendable starter of braised local rabbit with small vegetables and fresh rosemary might be followed by a supreme of Gressingham duck with glazed apples and crispy leeks. Their desserts are famed in York and are definitely for the sweet-toothed: chocolate and rum torte, dark-and-white chocolate parfait with red currants and their oven-baked peaches with a nut caramel sauce. The wine list is sensible and sensibly priced. The brasserie in the former cellars serves more informal meals. Open from 10am for breakfast, it usefully also serves after-theatre suppers. **Set L** £12.50, **Set D** £19.

Grange Hotel

(See restaurant above)
1 ste £165, 29 rms £85-£140 inc VAT. Restaurant.
Located just outside the city walls, this welcoming hotel has been converted from an elegant Regency townhouse. The drawing room has an open fire and fresh flowers, while the downstairs morning room always has a good selection of newspapers and magazines. An old house means bedrooms vary in size but are prettily furnished with antiques and decorated in the English country house style. Service, led by the charming manager, is young, friendly and efficient.

Judges Lodging Hotel

9 Lendal, York, YO1 2AQ - 0904-638733, Fax 0904-679947
B&B 13 rms £85-£150 inc VAT. Restaurant.
The Judges Lodging used to be the official residence of the Assize court judges and dates back to 1710. Now it is a comfortable, small hotel in the heart of York. Bedrooms, some with four-posters, are well equipped and there is a cosy lounge area. In addition to a more formal restaurant, light lunches are served in the Judges Bar, housed in the original wine cellars.

12/20 Melton's

7 Scarcroft Rd, York - 0904-634341
INTERNATIONAL
Open Lunch Tues-Sat, Dinner Mon-Sat.
Good value, simple décor and sound, often adventurous cooking are the order

of the day here. Delicious grilled vegetables with celery and capers in olive oil might be followed by a dish like fillet of brill with lobster sauce, then white chocolate parfait. Seafood is often included. The cheeseboard has a fine selection of English and Irish cheeses and the short wine list gives good value. C £20. **Set L & D** £10-£18.

12/20 Middlethorpe Hall Restaurant

Middlethorpe Hall, Bishopsthorpe Rd, York, YO2 1QB - 0904-641241, Fax 0904-620176
MODERN BRITISH
Open Lunch & Dinner daily.
Located just outside York, this William and Mary house, converted to an hotel, has an elegant, panelled dining room. There are fixed-price menus for both lunch and dinner and the cooking of Kevin Francksen shows a good classical training. From the dinner menu, light smoked salmon parcels with lime dressing, followed by a breast of pheasant with a compote of garlic and shallots, and finally an iced raspberry parfait with plum compote was first-rate. Service is formal and the wine, though expensive, is of good quality. C £30. **Set L** £14.90, £16.90, **Set D** £29.95.

Middlethorpe Hall

(See restaurant above)
7 stes £165-£189, 23 rms £83-£164 inc service and VAT. Restaurant.
Middlethorpe Hall overlooks the racecourse. The entrance hall often has a log fire blazing and the public rooms feature some fine antique furniture. Bedrooms are individually decorated with Edwardian–style bathrooms and every luxury expected of a country house hotel is available. Service is of a high standard and very friendly.

12/20 19 Grape Lane

19 Grape Lane, York - 0904-636366
MODERN BRITISH
Open Lunch & Dinner Tues-Sat.
In the heart of medieval York, it is delightful to find a restaurant serving English food, albeit very much in the modern idiom. Ingredients are good and fresh and the cooking generally well executed. Light lunches are offered, perhaps a smoked

duck salad with raspberry vinaigrette, and a fixed-price dinner menu. This might start with a robust terrine and be followed by one of the excellent fish selections, a North Sea medley for instance. Desserts fittingly owe more to the old English tradition with sensational Yorkshire treacle tart on offer. An interesting wine list, with French and New World selections and with house wines from Georges Dubœuf. **C** £10. **Set D** £18.95.

■ LIGHT MEALS & PUBS

Bettys
6-8 St Helen's Sq, York - 0904-659142
Open daily 9am-9pm. Pianist 6-9pm.

Bettys is an institution in York but it is somewhat ironic that this quintessentially English tea room should have been founded by Frederick Belmont, a young Swiss confectioner in the 1920s. The result is the best of both worlds—Swiss confectionery and cakes combined with English tradition. The tea rooms are vast and still preserve the feel of the twenties. Also a good venue for a light lunch or an early supper, one of the most notable dishes is Yorkshire rarebit, made with Theakstons' Ale and served with ham. Other rarebits are equally tasty and served with Bettys' notable home-made chutney. Swiss specialities are not forgotten and the spring onion and mushroom rösti is well worth sampling. Main dishes average from £5 to £7.

The Black Swan
Peaseholme Green, York - 0904-625236
Open Mon-Sat 11am-11pm, Sun noon-3pm, 7-10.30pm.

Everyone's idea of a pub, the Black Swan is timber-framed and dates back to the fifteenth century. Bar food (not served Sunday or Monday evenings) includes giant Yorkshire puddings with a variety of fillings, steak and onion pie, salads etc. Yorkshire puddings start at £1.95.

The Old Starres
Stonegate, York - 0904-623063
Open Mon-Sat 11am-11pm, Sun 11am-3pm, 7-10.30pm.

In Stonegate, close to the Minster, this pub makes a welcoming haven after a morning's sightseeing. Walls have been stripped to reveal their original panelling. Bar food (not served weekend evenings) includes sandwiches and hearty pies like steak and kidney, and a good vegetable pie. Main dishes are around £3 to £4.

335

TASTES

THE WORLD DINING & TRAVEL CONNECTION

Want to keep current on the best bistros in Paris? Discover that little hideaway in Singapore? Or stay away from that dreadful and dreadfully expensive restaurant in New York? André Gayot's Tastes newsletter gives you bimonthly news on the best and worst in restaurants, hotels, nightlife and shopping around the world.

☐ **YES**, please enter/renew my subscription to TASTES newsletter for 6 bimonthly issues at the rate of $40 per year. (Outside U.S. and Canada, $50.)

Name_____

Address_____

City_____State _____

Zip_____Country _____

Phone   (   )   --

☐ Enclosed is my check or money order made out to Gault Millau, Inc.

☐ $_____

☐ Charge to: __ AMEX __ MASTERCARD __ VISA   Exp. _____

☐

Card# _____ Signature _____

310 /94

FOR FASTER SERVICE CALL 1 (800) LE BEST 1

BASICS

ARRIVING IN LONDON

Getting into London from any of the three major airports is relatively easy. From *Heathrow* (fifteen miles from London) the **Piccadilly line** underground takes you into central London in about 45 minutes and departs every five minutes (tickets cost £3). But note that there are only escalators to get you down to the trains and very few stations in central London have lifts. If you want to stay above ground, **Airbus A1** takes about one hour to get to Victoria or **A2** takes the same time to get to Russell Square. They leave approximately every twenty minutes, stop at various places en route and cost £5 single, £8 open return. Signs at the airport indicate the route and the stops. A taxi will cost around £35. Beware mini cabs or private drivers touting for custom in the airport; they can be expensive, so you should only take a licensed black cab.

From *Gatwick* (29 miles), a fast and frequent train service takes 30 minutes into Victoria Station (£8.60 single, £16.90 return). **Flightline buses 777** depart at 5.20am, 6.50am, 7.50am then on the hour every hour to 10pm, seven days a week. They take anything from 90 minutes to two hours depending on the time of day and cost £7.50 single, £11 return. A taxi will cost at least £45 and take from an hour and a half to two hours.

From *Stansted* (37 miles) the **Stansted Express** train from Bishop's Stortford station departs every 30 minutes and takes 45 minutes to arrive at Liverpool Street Station (£7.50 single, £14.40 return). **National Express** or **Cambridge Coach Services** depart every hour, taking around 90 minutes to arrive at Victoria Coach station and depending on the day of travel will cost either £6.75 or £8 single. A taxi will cost between £35 and £40 and take about the same time.

GENERAL ENQUIRIES

Heathrow
081-759 4321

Gatwick
0293-535353

London City Airport
071-474 5555

Stansted
0279-680500

GETTING AROUND

■ PUBLIC TRANSPORT SYSTEM

London's public transport system is one of the biggest, oldest and most complex in Europe, so expect overcrowding at peak times—between 8am and 9.30am and 4.30pm to 6.30pm.

It is also expensive compared to other cities. The most economical tickets are *Travelcards*—daily, weekly or monthly passes giving you unlimited travel on all forms of transport in set zones. Make sure you get the right ticket for the right zone as there are six which stretch from city centre into outer suburbia. Most major sights are contained within zones one and two. You can buy these tickets at train or underground stations and at newsagents showing a special 'Red Pass' agent sign. Weekly and monthly passes require a passport-sized photograph. One-day Travelcards (no photo needed) cannot be used before 9.30am Monday to Friday. For zones 1 and 2 a day card costs £2.70, a weekly one £13 and a monthly card £50. Visitors coming from abroad can buy a *Visitor's Travelcard* which includes transport between Heathrow and London, virtually unlimited use on British Rail trains, the underground and buses as well as discount vouchers for some tourist attractions. You can only buy this abroad at British Rail International offices and it varies according to the exchange rate. Remember that there is a complete ban on smoking on London Transport. Apart from the fact that you can be fined up to £1,000 for the offence, you will find yourself confronted by irate passengers if you try.

■ BUSES

The most pleasant way for a visitor to travel around London is by bus, though it can be very time-consuming. Bus stops are of two kinds: compulsory stops shown by London Transport signs with a white background, and request stops shown by signs with a red background. For the latter you have to hold out your hand to indicate to the driver to stop.

Many of the newer buses are one-man operated and you pay your fare to the driver as you get on. Do not try to pay with large notes—you risk the wrath of the queue. Night Buses exist on several popular routes from 11pm to 6am. The routes are prefixed with the letter 'N'. Travelcards do not operate on night buses.

If you want to take a bus to almost *anywhere outside central London*, from Aberdeen to Athens, you'll probably go from the main coach station on Buckingham Palace Road (about five minutes walk from Victoria railway station). There are two main companies for national travel: **Green Line**, 081-668 7271, and **National Express Rapide**, 071-730 0202.

CARS

Driving in London can be a nightmare if you don't know your way around. And there is the added hazard of possible clamping for illegal parking or for over-running your time on a meter. But if you do plan to go outside London into the countryside, hiring a car is a good idea, particularly from an airport. Here we give the main numbers for car-hire firms. Look in the telephone directory for local branches.

Avis	**Budget**
081-848 8765	0800-181181
Eurodollar	**Europcar**
0895-233300	071-387 2276
Hertz	**Smiths Self Drive**
081-678 1799	0709-853566
Thrifty	**Woods**
0494-442110	0737-240291

TAXIS

There are taxi ranks at railway stations and other convenient locations. You can hail a cab on the street whenever you see the yellow 'Taxi' or 'For Hire' sign lit up. Usually you give a tip of between ten and fifteen per cent of the cost of the journey. You can call a taxi on **Radio Taxicars** (071-272 0272), **Computer Cabs** (071-286 0286), **Ladycabs** (women-only

drivers, 071-254 3501) and **My Fare Lady** (women-only drivers, 081-458 9200).

TRAINS

To get to outer London and beyond, British Rail runs trains every day except *Christmas Day* and *Boxing Day* (December 25 and 26).

Charing Cross Station
Strand, WC2 - 071-928 5100
Connections for south London and the southeast of England.

Docklands Light Railway (DLR)
Connects Docklands with the City, Stratford and Greenwich. Trains run from Monday to Friday from 5.30am to 9.30pm, about every eight minutes.

Euston Station
Euston Rd, NW1 - 071-387 7070
Connections for northwest London and northwest England, the Midlands, North Wales, Scotland, and Ireland via Holyhead.

King's Cross Station
Euston Rd, NW1 - 071-278 2477
Connections for northeast London, the east and northeast of England, and the east coast of Scotland.

Liverpool Street Station
Bishopsgate, EC2 - 071-928 5100
Connections for east and northeast London, Essex and east Anglia.

Paddington Station
Praed St, W2 - 071-262 6767
Connections for west London, Oxford, Bristol, Plymouth, the west of England, South Wales, Ireland via Fishguard.

Thameslink Service
Connects Luton Airport with south London, Gatwick Airport and Brighton via West Hampstead and Blackfriars.

> *Remember that if you carry a non-British passport, you are entitled to a full refund of the **value-added tax** (VAT). Stores vary in the minimum you must spend in order to claim this. See Basics for details.*

Victoria Station
Buckingham Palace Rd, SW1 - 071-928 5100
Connections for south London, Gatwick airport, southwest England and the Channel ports for the Continent.

Waterloo Station
Waterloo Rd, SE1 - 071-928 5100
Connections for south London and the south of England.

■ UNDERGROUND

Known as the 'tube', the London underground has eleven lines and 273 stations and is the oldest in the world, having opened on January 10, 1863. Tube trains run every day except Christmas Day from around 5.30am to just after midnight, but this is not always the case on lines running to outlying stations.

You can get tickets either from a ticket office or from an automatic machine which will indicate whether it will give change or not. Select the ticket type you need, then your destination and the cost of the fare is automatically displayed. Remember to keep your ticket as you will need it at the end of the journey. Penalties for fraud are severe—from £200 for travelling without a ticket.

■ LONDON TRANSPORT

Docklands Travel Hotline
071-918 4000
24-hours.

London Travelcheck
071-222 1200
24-hours.
Frequently updated travel news.

London Buses
071-222 5600

London Underground
071-222 5600

Lost Property
200 Baker St, NW1 - 071-486 2496
Open Mon-Fri 9.30am and 2pm.
Recorded message. Individual enquiries handled by letter or personal visit between.

Travel Information
071-222 1234
24-hours.

TOURS

■ BY BUS

A good way to see London is from the top of a double-decker open-topped bus. The **Original London Sightseeing Tour** (071-828 7395) runs from four central London departure points close to underground stations: Baker Street, Marble Arch, Haymarket and Victoria Station. They last an hour and a half and have a choice of eight language commentaries and an English-speaking guide. You can buy tickets on the bus, from any London Transport station or London Tourist Board Information centre and at most central London hotels.

A foreign view

'That which makes the dwelling in this City very diverting is the facility of going out into the Fields, as to Knightsbridge, where is an excellent Spring Garden, to Marylebone, where is a very good Bowling-Green, Islington is famous for cakes, as Stepney is for bunns.'
From the diary of the *French traveller*, **Sorbière, 1698.**

The **Big Bus Company** (081-944 7810) offers much the same service, an hour-and-a-half tour in an open-top bus, departing from Marble Arch, Piccadilly (The Ritz hotel), Victoria (Royal Westminster Hotel) and Victoria Coach Station. Prices range from £9 for adults for a two-hour tour to £17.50 for a half-day and anything between £44 and £54 for a full day depending on the company and whether lunch and entrance fees are included.

Other companies offering bus tours lasting from two hours to a full day include:

London Pride, 0708-631122; **Frames Rickards,** 071-837 3111; **Harrod's,** 071-581 3603.

■ BY CHAUFFEURED LIMOUSINE

Avis (Luxury Cars)
071-917 6703

Camelot Chauffeur Drive
071-235 0234

Europcar Interent
071-834 6701

Kensington & Chelsea Cars
071-603 6660

■ BY PRIVATE CAR & DRIVER-GUIDE

Take-a-Guide Ltd
43 Finstock Rd, W10 - 081-960 0459, Fax 081-964 0990
One of the oldest and best driver-guide company.

Good Company
48 Prince of Wales Rd, NW5 - 071-267 5340, Fax 071-284 0765
Or try this smaller company.

■ BY RIVER & CANAL

Travelling through London by river is a wonderful experience as you see the riverside buildings from a different angle and travel effortlessly.

Trips go from Westminster Pier and Charing Cross Pier regularly, winter and summer. They take twenty minutes to the Tower of London and 50 minutes to Greenwich. You can just go to the piers and take the next boat; they depart every 30 to 45 minutes, depending on the time of year and cost around £3 single to the Tower of London, £4 return, and £4.40 single to Greenwich, £5.40 return. For more information call **Catamaran Cruisers,** 071-987 1185 or **Westminster**

Passenger Service Association, 071-930 4097.

Bateaux London/ Catamaran Cruisers
Charing Cross Pier, Victoria Embankment, WC2 - 071-839 3572, Fax 071-839 1034
A luxury restaurant cruiser which has good food and a wonderful panoramic view of the riverbanks. Three cruises per day include lunch (£28), tea (£20) and dinner (£46), all accompanied by live music. Board at Temple Pier on Victoria Embankment.

Canal Trips

The *Regent's Park Canal* is worth seeing. Narrow boat cruises on Jason's Trip start opposite 60 Blomfield Rd, Little Venice, W9, daily at 10.30am, 12.30pm and 2.30pm, plus 4.30pm at weekends, 071-286 3428. From *Camden Town*, try the Jenny Wren which you board at Camden Lock.
For *a different dining experience,* the same company runs My Fair Lady. You get a good lunch or dinner and initial talk from Paddy Walker who owns the company, and a trip past the London Zoo to Little Venice and back—an excellent few hours entertainment. *My Fair Lady,* 250 Camden High St, NW1, 071-485 4433 or 071-485 6210. The costs vary from £4 for the canal journey between Little Venice and the Zoo (in either direction) to £16.95 for the Jenny Wren lunch cruise and £26.95 for the dinner cruise.

■ GUIDE BOOKING AGENCIES

Guild of Guide Lecturers
The Guild House, 52d Borough High St, SE1 071-403 1115, Fax 071-378 1705

Tour Guides Ltd
2 Bridge St, SW1 - 071-839 2498, Fax 081-839 5314

AT YOUR SERVICE

■ TOURIST INFORMATION

British Travel Centre
12 Regent St, Piccadilly Circus, SW1
Open Mon-Fri 9am-6.30pm, Sat, Sun 10am-4pm (May-Sep Sat 9am-5pm).

Heathrow Terminals 1, 2, 3
Underground Station Concourse, Heathrow Airport, Middlesex
Open daily 8.30-6pm.

Liverpool Street Underground Station
London, EC2
Open Mon 8.15am-7pm, Tues-Sat 8.15am-6pm, Sun 8.30am-4.45pm.

Selfridge's
Basement Services Arcade, Oxford St, W1

Victoria Station Forecourt
Victoria Station, SW1
Open during store hours.

■ USEFUL ADDRESSES

RELIGIOUS SERVICES

BAPTIST

London Baptist Association
1 Merchant St, E3 - 081-980 6818

BUDDHIST

The Buddhist Society
58 Eccleston Sq, SW1 - 071-834 5858

EVANGELICAL

Whitefield House
86 Kennington Park Rd, SE11 - 071-582 0228

JEWISH

Liberal Jewish Synagogue
28 St John's Wood Rd, NW8 - 071-286 5181

United Synagogue (Orthodox)
Woburn House, Tavistock Sq, WC1
071-387 4300

MOSLEM

Islamic Cultural Centre
146 Park Rd, NW8 - 071-774 3363

PROTESTANT

Church of England
St Paul's Cathedral, EC4 - 071-248 2705

QUAKERS

Religious Society of Friends
173-177 Euston Rd, NW1 - 071-387 3601

ROMAN CATHOLIC

Westminster Cathedral
Victoria St, SW1 - 071-834 7452

■ EMBASSIES

Australian High Commission
Australia House, Strand, WC2 - 071-379 4334

Canadian High Commission
Macdonald House, 1 Grosvenor Sq, W1
071-629 9492

French Consulate General
21/23 Cromwell Rd, SW7 - 071-581 5292

New Zealand High Commission
New Zealand House, 80 Haymarket, SW1
071-930 8422

United States Embassy
24 Grosvenor Sq, W1 - 071-499 9000

The **prices** in this guide reflect what establishments were charging at the time of going to press.

■ PHONE DIRECTORY

Police, Fire and Ambulance Services
999 or 112

Doctorcall
081-900 1000

Medcall
0459-131313
24-hours.
Doctor service.

Emergency Dental Care
071-837 3646
24-hours.

Eastman Dental School
256 Gray's Inn Rd, WC1 - 071-837 3646
Private and National Health Service care.

Samaritans
071-734 2800
24-hours.
Helpline for all emotional problems. Local telephone directory will list your nearest branch.

LATE-OPENING CHEMISTS

Bliss Chemist
5 Marble Arch, W1 - 071-723 6116
Open daily 9am-midnight.

Boots the Chemist
Piccadilly Circus, W1 - 071-734 6126
Open Mon-Fri 8.30am-8pm, Sat 9am-8pm, Sun noon-6pm.

■ BUREAUX DE CHANGE

Almost every bank in central London operates a bureau de change, and there are numerous private enterprises which change money also.

Exchange rates vary quite widely, even between branches of the same bank. Otherwise try any of the three central exchanges listed here.

American Express
6 Haymarket, SW1 - 071-930 4411

Chequepoint
13-15 Davies St, W1 - 071-409 1122

Exchange International
Victoria Station, SW1 - 071-630 1107

Thomas Cook
45 Berkeley St, W1 - 071-408 4179

■ TAX-FREE SHOPPING

Value added tax (VAT) of 17.5% is charged on almost all goods in Britain except, most notably, on books, food and all children's clothes, and is almost always included in the advertised price.

Non-European Community visitors to Britain staying for less than three months can claim back VAT.

Take your passport with you when shopping. You must fill in a form in the store when you buy the goods and then give a copy to Customs when you leave the country. You may also have to show the goods to Customs, so make sure they are accessible. The tax refund will either be returned by cheque or attributed to your credit card—although in that case you may pay a service charge. Most stores have a minimum purchase threshold, often £50 or £75. If your goods are shipped directly home from the shop, VAT should be deducted before you pay.

GOINGS-ON

There is so much going on in London it is difficult to decide what to see, but here we give a brief month by month summary.

English national holidays are January 1, Good Friday, Easter Monday, the first and last Mondays in May, last Monday in August, December 25, 26. When December 25, 26 fall on a weekend, extra holidays are given on the preceding Friday or following Monday/Tuesday. If New Year's Day falls on a weekend, the first Monday in January is usually a Public Holiday.

For further details of any of these events, you can contact the London Tourist Board at 071-730 3488.

■ JANUARY

London
International Boat Show
Earl's Ct, SW5 - 071-385 1200

World of Drawings
and Watercolours
The Park Lane Hotel, Piccadilly, W1
071-499 6321
One of the biggest and most prestigious international art fairs.

Art Show
Business Design Centre, Upper St, Islington, N1 - 071-359 3535
The annual exhibition of work by living artists from around the world produces some wonderful surprises. Prices range from £50 to £20,000.

■ FEBRUARY

Chinese New Year
Celebrations throughout Chinatown.

■ MARCH

Chelsea Antiques Fair
Chelsea Town Hall, SW3 - 071-352 1856
A popular antiques event stretching over ten days and held twice a year (September).

International
Spring Gardening Fair
Olympia, W14 - 071-603 3344
Organised by the Royal Horticultural Society and often overlapping into April.

■ APRIL

London
Original Print Fair
Royal Academy of Arts, Piccadilly, W1
071-439 7438
The longest-running event of its kind in the world, attracting print dealers from around the world.

■ MAY

British Antique Dealers'
Association Fair
Duke of York's Headquarters, King's Rd, SW1
One of the two official antique dealers' organisations, the BADA show is a popular, excellent antiques fair with an international clientele.

Royal Windsor Horse Show
Home Park, Windsor - 0753-860633

Chelsea Flower Show
Royal Hospital, Chelsea, SW3 - 071-828 1744
Probably the most famous flower show in the world and one of the most difficult to get tickets to. Contact the Royal Horticultural Society for details (071-834 4333).

■ JUNE

Beating Retreat by the Massed
Bands of the Household Division
Horse Guards Parade, SW1 - 071-414 2357

Trooping the Colour
Horse Guards Parade, SW1 - 071-414 2357
Celebration of the Queen's official birthday on June 11.

International Ceramics
Fair and Seminar
The Park Lane Hotel, Piccadilly, W1
071-499 6321
The fair of ceramics—the most commonly collected of all antiques—combines the best dealers and an interesting lecture programme.

Stella Artois Championship
Queen's Club, W14 - 071-225 3733
The 'run-up' to Wimbledon—small and delightful.

Royal Academy
Summer Exhibition
Royal Academy of Arts, Piccadilly, W1
071-439 7438

One of the largest public art exhibitions in the world and the event that, in the days when such things mattered, announced the beginning of the London social season.

Olympia Fine Art & Antiques Fair
Olympia, W14 - 071-603 3344

Grosvenor House Art and Antiques Fair
Grosvenor House, W1 - 071-499 6363

The most prestigious antiques and fine art fair in the world, with top dealers mainly from Europe and the United States. Not to be missed if you are even a little interested in the subject.

Royal Ascot Race Meeting
Ascot, Berks - 0344-22211

One of the best flat race meetings in Britain.

Wimbledon Lawn Tennis Championships
All England Lawn Tennis Club, SW19
081-946 2244

■ JULY

BBC Henry Wood Promenade Concerts
Royal Albert Hall, SW7 - 071-589 8912

Stretching into September with daily concerts which cover almost the whole spectrum of the music world.

Royal Tournament
Earl's Ct, SW5 - 071-385 1200

When the army shows off in a wonderful display of might and skill, orchestrated so well it puts many operatic directors to shame.

■ AUGUST

West London Antiques Fair
Kensington Town Hall, W8 - 071-937 5464

■ SEPTEMBER

Chelsea Antiques Fair
Chelsea Old Town Hall, SW3 - 071-352 1856

A popular antiques event stretching over ten days and held twice a year (March).

■ OCTOBER

Horse of the Year Show
Wembley Arena, Wembley - 081-900 1234

Show-jumping from the world's top competitors.

Park Lane Antiques Fair
The Park Lane Hotel, Piccadilly - 071-499 6321

■ NOVEMBER

RAC London to Brighton Veteran Car Run
Hyde Park, London to Brighton

When the 'old crocks' gather to drive in stately manner to Brighton.

Lord Mayor's Show
The new Lord Mayor parades through the streets of the City of London. It always takes place on the second Sunday in November, and there are fireworks along the river at the end of the day.

Remembrance Sunday Ceremony
Cenotaph, Whitehall, W1

International Art and Antiques Fair
Harrod's, Knightsbridge, SW1 - 071-730 1234

World Travel Market
Earl's Ct, SW5 - 071-385 1200

One of the biggest travel trade shows in the world.

■ DECEMBER

Olympia International Show Jumping Championships
Olympia, W14 - 071-373 8141

MENU SAVVY

A guide to international food terms.

CHINESE

Boa bun: dim sum item; small, steamed buns, white in colour, stuffed with a variety of minced fillings (often chicken, shrimp, pork or lotus beans)

Bird's-nest soup: soup that has been thickened and flavoured with the gelatinous product derived from soaking and cooking the nests of cliff-dwelling birds

Bok choy: Chinese white cabbage

Dim sum: figuratively 'heart's delight'; a traditional meal featuring a variety of small dumplings, buns, rolls, balls, pastries and finger food, served with tea in the late morning or afternoon

Egg roll: crêpelike wrapper stuffed with pork, cabbage or other vegetables, rolled up, and deep-fried or steamed

Fried rice: cooked, dried rice quickly fried in a wok with hot oil, various meats or vegetables and often an egg

Hoisin: a sweet, rich, dark brown sauce made from fermented soy beans; used as a base for other sauces

Lychee: small, round, fleshy fruit; used fresh, canned, preserved and dried

Mu shu: a delicate dish of stir-fried shredded pork and eggs rolled up in thin pancakes

Oyster sauce: a thick, dark sauce of oysters, soy and brine

Peking duck: an elaborate dish featuring duck that has been specially prepared, coated with honey and cooked until the skin is crisp and golden; served in pieces with thin pancakes or steamed buns, and hoisin

Pot sticker: dim sum item; dumpling stuffed with meat, seafood or vegetables, fried and then steamed

Shark's fin soup: soup thickened and flavoured with the cartilage of shark's fins, which provides a protein-rich gelatin

Shu mai: dim sum item; delicate dumpling usually filled with minced pork and vegetables

Spring roll: a lighter version of the egg roll, with fillings such as shrimp or black mushrooms

Szechuan: cuisine in the style of the Szechuan province; often using the peppercorn-like black Chinese pepper to make hot, spicy dishes

Thousand-year-old-eggs: chicken, duck or goose eggs preserved for 100 days in ashes, lime and salt (also 100-year-old-eggs)

Wonton: paper-thin, glutinous dough wrapper; also refers to the dumpling made with this wrapper, stuffed with minced meat, seafood or vegetables

Wonton soup: a clear broth in which wontons are cooked and served

FRENCH

Agneau: lamb

Aïoli: garlicky mayonnaise

Américaine or armoricaine: sauce of white wine, Cognac, tomatoes and butter

Andouille: smoked tripe sausage, usually served cold

Anglaise (à l'): boiled meats or vegetables

Ballottine: boned, stuffed and rolled poultry

Bâtarde: sauce of white roux

Béarnaise: sauce made of shallots, tarragon, vinegar and egg yolks, thickened with butter

Béchamel: sauce made of flour, butter and milk

Beurre blanc: sauce of wine and vinegar boiled down with minced shallots, then thickened with butter

Beurre noisette: lightly browned butter

Bière: beer

Bigarade: bitter orange used in sauces and marmalade

Bisque (crayfish, lobster, etc.): rich, velvety soup, usually made with crustaceans, flavoured with white wine and Cognac

Blinis: small, thick crêpes made with eggs, milk and yeast

Bœuf: beef

Bœuf bourguignon: beef ragoût with red wine, onions and lardons

Bombe glacée: moulded ice cream dessert

Bordelaise: fairly thin brown sauce of shallots, red wine and tarragon

Boudin noir: blood sausage

Bouillabaisse: various fish including scorpionfish cooked in a soup of olive oil, tomatoes, garlic and saffron

Bourride: sort of bouillabaisse usually made with large white fish, thickened with aïoli; served over slices of bread

Brie: cow's milk cheese with a soft, creamy inside and a thick crust, made in the shape of a disk and sliced like a pie

Brioche: a soft loaf or roll, often sweetened and used for pastries

Brochette: on a skewer

Canapé: small piece of bread topped with savoury food

Canard: duck

Carbonnade: pieces of lean beef, first sautéed then stewed with onions and beer

Carré d'agneau: rack of lamb

Cèpes: prized wild mushroom, same family as the Italian porcini

Chanterelles: prized wild mushroom, trumpet-shaped

Charcutière: sauce of onions, white wine, beef stock and gherkins

Charlotte: dessert of flavoured creams and/or fruit moulded in a cylindrical dish lined with ladyfingers (if served cold) or strips of buttered bread (if served hot)

Chasseur: brown sauce made with shallots, white wine and mushrooms

Chèvre (fromage de): goat (cheese)

Choucroute: sauerkraut; often served with sausages, smoked bacon, pork loin and potatoes

Citron: lemon

Chou-fleur: cauliflower

Clafoutis: a dessert of fruit (usually cherries) baked in an eggy batter

Confit: pork, goose, duck, turkey or other meat cooked and sealed in its own fat

Coquilles St-Jacques: sea scallops

Côte d'agneau: lamb chops

Coulis: thick sauce or purée, often of vegetables or fruits

Court-bouillon: stock in which fish, meat and poultry are cooked

Crème chantilly: sweetened whipped cream

Crêpe Suzette: crêpe stuffed with sweetened butter mixture, Grand Marnier, tangerine juice and peel

Croque-monsieur: grilled ham and cheese sandwich

Croûte (en): in pastry crust

Crudités: raw vegetables

Daube: beef braised in red wine

Écrevisses: crayfish

Entrecôte: 'between the ribs'; steak cut from between the ribs

Épinards: spinach

Escalope: slice of meat or fish, flattened slightly and sautéed

Escargots (à la bourguignonne): snails (with herbed garlic butter)

Financière: Madeira sauce enhanced with truffle juice

Florentine: with spinach

Foie gras: liver of a specially fattened goose of duck

Fondue: a bubbling pot of liquid into which which pieces of food are dipped—most commonly cheese and bread; can also be chocolate and fruits or various savoury sauces and cubes of beef. Also, vegetables cooked at length in butter and thus reduced to pulp

Forestière: garnish of sautéed mushrooms and lardons

Frangipane: almond pastry cream

Galantine: boned poultry or meat, stuffed and pressed into a symmetrical form, cooked in broth and coated with aspic

Galettes and crêpes (Brittany): galettes are made of buckwheat flour and are usually savoury. Crêpes are made of wheat flour

Gâteau: cake

Gelée (en): in aspic; gelatin usually flavoured with meat, poultry or fish stock

Génoise: sponge cake

Granité: lightly sweetened fruit ice

Gratin dauphinois: sliced potatoes baked in milk, sometimes with cream and/or grated Gruyère

Grenouille: frog (frogs' legs: cuisses de grenouilles)

Hollandaise: egg-based sauce thickened with butter and flavoured with lemon

Jambon: ham

Julienne: vegetable soup made from a clear consommé, or any shredded food

Lait: milk

Langouste: rock or spiny lobster

Langoustine: saltwater crayfish

Lapin: rabbit

Lièvre: hare

Limon: lime (also, **citron vert**)

Lotte: monkfish or anglerfish; sometimes called "poor man's lobster"

Madrilène (à la): garnished with raw, peeled tomatoes

Magret (Maigret): breast of fattened duck, cooked with the skin on; usually grilled

Médaillon: food, usually meat, fish or foie gras, cut into small, round 'medallions'

Moules marinière: mussels cooked in the shell with white wine, shallots and parsley

Nantua: sauce of crayfish, white wine, butter and cream with a touch of tomato

Noisettes: hazelnuts; also, small, round pieces of meat (especially lamb or veal)

Nougat: sweet made with roasted almonds, egg whites, honey and sugar

Œufs: eggs

Pain: bread

Parfait: sweet or savoury mousse; also a layered ice cream dessert

Parisienne: garnish of fried potato balls

Paupiettes: thin slices of meat stuffed with forcemeat and shaped into rolls

Pissaladière: tart with onions, black olives and anchovy fillets

Poires: pears

Pommes: apples
Pommes de terre: potatoes
Poulet: chicken
Provençale (à la): with garlic or tomato and garlic
Quiche: tart of eggs, cream and various fillings (such as ham, spinach or bacon)
Ratatouille: stew of aubergines, tomatoes, bell peppers, courgettes, onion and garlic, all sautéed in oil
Rémoulade: mayonnaise with capers, onions, parsley, gherkins and herbs
Rissoles: type of small pie filled with forcemeat
Rouille: sort of mayonnaise with pepper, garlic bread soaked in bouillon, olive oil and possibly saffron
Sabayon: fluffy, whipped egg yolks, sweetened and flavoured with wine of liqueur; served warm
Saint-Pierre: John Dory; a white-fleshed fish
Salade niçoise: salad of tomatoes, hard-boiled egg, anchovy filets, tuna, sweet peppers, celery and olives (also can include green beans, potatoes, basil, onions and/or broad beans)
Sole meunière: sole dipped in flour and sautéed in butter with parsley and lemon
Soissons: garnished with haricot beans
Sorbet: sherbet
Spätzle: round noodles, often made from eggs
Steak au poivre: pepper steak; steak covered in crushed peppercorns, browned in a frying pan, flambéed with Cognac; also sauce deglazed with cream
Tapenade: a paste of olives, capers and anchovies, crushed in a mortar with lemon juice and pepper
Tartare: cold sauce for meat or fish: mayonnaise with hard-boiled egg yolks, onions and chopped olives
Tarte: tart, round cake of flan; can be sweet or savoury
Tarte Tatin: upside-down apple tart invented by the Tatin sisters
Tortue: turtle; also, a sauce made with various herbs, tomato, Madeira
Tournedos Rossini: beef sautéed in butter, served with pan juices, foie gras
Truffe: truffle; highly esteemed subterranean fungus, esp. from Périgord
Vacherin: ice cream served in a meringue shell; also, creamy, pungent cheese from Switzerland or eastern France
Viande: meat

INDIAN

Aloo: potatoes
Aloo papri chat: crisp poori stuffed with chick peas and potatoes and served with a sour sauce with spicy yoghurt

Bhaji: deep-fried snacks of vegetables in a spicy batter, usually onions and potatoes, served with spicy flavoured chutney
Bharta: a dish cooked and puréed
Bhatura: round, lightly leavened and deep-fried bread
Bhel poori: crisp poori piled with puffed rice, potatoes, onions, sev (vermicelli) and with fresh coriander, usually served with tamarind sauce and chutneys
Biryana: Moghul dish of seafood, meat or chicken marinated in lemon juice, yoghurt, onions, garlic and ginger and stewed with saffron rice
Chapati: unleavened, thin, round bread made from wholemeal flour and in central India often used instead of rice
Dal: lentils
Garam masala: best known of the ground, aromatic Indian spice mixtures, containing no turmeric
Ghee: clarified butter, regarded in India as the purest food because it comes from the sacred cow, giving a rich, buttery taste
Gosht: lamb
Kachori: pastry stuffed with spiced mung beans, served with tamarind chutney
Kofta: balls or dumplings of ground or mashed meat or vegetables, grilled or fried and often stuffed with spices or diced nuts
Korma: powder or aromatic spice, with white pepper instead of chilli powder and used in mild curries cooked with yoghurt
Kulfi: milk ice cream flavoured with mango, pistachios or almonds
Masala dosai: ground rice or semolina and lentil pancake filled with potatoes and onion and served with spicy coconut chutney
Mughlai: method of cooking using cream, yoghurt, almonds and pistachios
Murgh: chicken
Naan: soft-textured bread made from white flour leavened with natural yeast and baked by moistening one side and attaching it to the inside of a tandoor oven. May have poppy or sesame seeds or onion added
Paper dosai: very thin pancakes with potato and onion, served with coconut chutney
Parathas: crisp, layered, buttery breads served plain or stuffed
Poori: whole-wheat bread, like a chapati, fried, usually in ghee, and puffed into a ball. Served with vegetarian foods, particularly dal (lentil), potato and bean dishes. Cooked pooris can be stuffed with hot curried fillings as a quick snack
Poppadum: flat, dried wafers of lentil, rice or potato flour, deep-fried and served as a snack. Can be highly spiced
Potato poori: crisp poori piled with potatoes and onions, sweet and sour sauce, yoghurt and sev (vermicelli)

Pilau: rice stir-fried in ghee then cooked in stock and served with fish, vegetables or meat

Raita: yoghurt dish

Samosas: crisp, deep-fried triangular pastry stuffed with spiced vegetables like onions and served with chutney or yoghurt

Sev poori: crisp poori piled with potato and onions and sweet and sour sauce and with sev (vermicelli)

Tamarind: a tree producing flat, bean-like pods which have become essential in Indian cooking. Often made into a chutney as a dip for deep-fried snacks

Tandoor: barrel-shaped mud or clay oven used for roasting meats and baking bread (moistened and placed against the sides of the oven)

Tandoori: fish or meat marinated in spices and yoghurt and cooked in a tandoor, usually dyed a characteristic bright orange

Thali: complete meal on a tray with each curry, relish and dessert in separate bowls or katori, plus bread or rice

Tikka: minced or diced

Vindaloo: very hot dish seasoned with ground roasted spices and chillies with vinegar and/or tamarind. A speciality of central and western coastal India with a strong flavour

ITALIAN

Acciughe: anchovies

Aceto: vinegar

Aglio: garlic

Agnello: lamb

Agnolotti: crescent-shaped, meat-filled pasta

Agrodolce: sweet-and-sour

Amaretti: crunchy almond macaroons

Anatra: duck

Anguilia: eel

Aragosta: spiny lobster

Arrosto: roasted meat

Baccalà: dried salt cod

Bagna cauda: hot, savoury dipping sauce for raw vegetables

Birra: beer

Biscotti: cookies

Bistecca (alla fiorentina): charcoal-grilled T-bone steak (seasoned with pepper and olive oil)

Bolognese: pasta sauce with tomatoes and meat

Bresaola: air-dried spiced beef; usually thinly sliced, served with olive oil and lemon juice

Bruschetta: toasted garlic bread topped with tomatoes

Bucatini: hollow spaghetti

Calamari (calamaretti): (baby) squid

Calzone: stuffed pizza turn-over

Cannellini: white beans

Cappelletti: meat- or cheese-stuffed pasta ('little hats')

Carbonara: pasta sauce with ham, eggs, cream and grated cheese

Carciofi (alla giudia): flattened and deep-fried baby artichokes

Carpaccio: paper thin, raw beef (or other meats)

Cassata: ice cream bombe

Cavolfiore: cauliflower

Ceci: chick peas

Cipolla: onion

Conchiglie: shell-shaped pasta

Coniglio: rabbit

Coppa: cured pork fillet encased in sausage skin

Costata: rib steak

Costoletta (alla milanese): (breaded) veal chop

Cozze: mussels

Crespelle: crêpes

Crostata: tart

Fagioli: beans

Fagiolini: string beans

Farfalle: bow-tie pasta

Fegato: liver

Fegato alla veneziana: calf's liver sautéed with onions

Fichi: figs

Finocchio: fennel

Focaccia: crusty flat bread

Formaggio: cheese

Frittata: Italian omelette

Fritto misto: mixed fry of meats or fish

Frutti di mare: seafood (esp. shellfish)

Funghi (trifolati): mushrooms sautéed with garlic and parsley

Fusilli: spiral-shaped pasta

Gamberi: shrimp

Gamberoni: prawns

Gelato: ice cream

Gnocchi: dumplings made of cheese (di ricotta), potatoes (di patate), cheese and spinach (verdi) or semolina (alla romana)

Grana: hard grating cheese

Granita: sweetened, flavoured grated ice

Griglia: grilled

Insalata: salad

Involtini: stuffed meat or fish rolls

Lenticchie: lentils

Maccheroni: macaroni pasta

Manzo: beef

Mela: apple

Melanzana: aubergine

Minestra: soup; pasta course

Minestrone: vegetable soup

Mortadella: large, mild Bolognese pork sausage

Mozzarella di bufala: fresh cheese made from water-buffalo milk

Noce: walnut

Orecchiette: ear-shaped pasta

Osso buco: braised veal shanks

Ostriche: oysters
Pane: bread
Panettone: brioche-like sweet bread
Panna: heavy cream
Pancetta: Italian bacon
Pappardelle: wide, flat pasta noodles
Pasta asciutta: pasta served plain or with sauce
Pasticceria: pastry; pastry shop
Pasticcio: pie or mould of pasta, sauce and meat of fish
Patate: potatoes
Pecorino: hard sheep's-milk cheese
Penne: hollow, ribbed pasta
Peperoncini: tiny, hot peppers
Peperoni: green, red of yellow sweet peppers
Pesca: peach
Pesce: fish
Pesce spada: swordfish
Pesto: cold pasta sauce of crushed basil, garlic, pine nuts, Parmesan cheese and olive oil
Piccata: thinly-sliced meat with a lemon of Marsala sauce
Pignoli: pine nuts
Polenta: cornmeal porridge
Pollo: chicken
Polipo: octopus
Pomodoro: tomato
Porcini: prized wild mushrooms, known also as the boletus
Prosciutto: air-dried ham
Ragù: meat sauce
Ricotta: fresh sheep's-milk cheese
Rigatoni: large, hollow ribbed pasta
Riso: rice
Risotto: braised rice with various savoury items
Rucola: arugula
Salsa (verde): sauce of parsley, capers, anchovies and lemon juice or vinegar
Salsicce: fresh sausage
Saltimbocca: veal scallop with prosciutto and sage
Sarde: sardines
Semifreddo: frozen dessert, usually ice cream with or without cake
Sgombro: mackerel
Sogliola: sole
Spiedino: brochette; grilled on a skewer
Spumone: light, foamy ice cream
Tartufi: truffles
Tiramisù: creamy dessert of rum-spiked cake and triple-crème cheese
Tonno: tuna
Torta: cake
Tortelli: pasta dumplings stuffed with greens and ricotta
Tortellini: ring-shaped dumplings stuffed with meat or cheese and served in broth or in a cream sauce

Trennette: thin noodles served with potatoes and pesto sauce
Trota: trout
Uovo (sodo): egg (hard-boiled)
Uva: grapes
Uva passa: raisins
Verdura: greens, vegetables
Vitello (Tonnato): veal in a tuna and anchovy sauce
Vongole: clams
Zabaglione: warm whipped egg yolks flavoured with Marsala
Zafferano: saffron
Zucchero: sugar
Zucchine: courgettes
Zuppa: soup
Zuppa inglese: cake steeped in a rum-flavoured custard sauce

NEAR EAST

Borek: feta cheese fritter served as an appetiser, sealed with beaten egg and deep-fried
Borscht: thick Eastern European soup of beets and boiled beef, often garnished with a dollop of sour cream
Cacik: yoghurt salad with chopped cucumber and garlic
Falafel: crushed chick peas made into patties and deep fried, served with sesame sauce
Hummus: cooked chick peas crushed with sesame oil, lemon juice and garlic
Imam bayildi: Turkish speciality of cold cooked aubergines with olive oil and lemon juice which can be stuffed with onion, tomatoes, peppers, parsley and garlic
Kebab: small pieces of marinated meat grilled or roasted, originating in Turkey
Kibbeh nayeh: crushed wheat and raw ground lamb eaten with raw onion and mint in olive oil
Kofte: meatballs of lamb with mint
Moutabal: roast aubergines with sesame oil, lemon juice and garlic
Tabbouleh: salad of crushed wheat, parsley, tomatoes and onions with olive oil and lemon juice

JAPANESE

Amaebi: sweet shrimp
Anago: sea eel
Awabi: abalone
Azuki: dried bean; azuki flour is often used for confections
Ebi: shrimp
Enoki (Enokitake): delicate mushrooms with long stems and small caps
Hamachi: yellowtail
Hibachi: small, open charcoal grill

Hirame: flounder
Ikura: salmon roe
Kaiseki: multi-course menu of luxury dishes reflecting the seasons with the use of seasonal foods and artistic dinnerware and presentation
Kani: crab
Kappa: cucumber
Kobe beef: cattle raised in exclusive conditions (frequent massages and a diet featuring large quantities of beer), which results in an extraordinary tender, very expensive beef product
Konbu: dried kelp; used in soup stock, for sushi and as a condiment
Maguro: tuna
Maki: rolled
Mako: shark
Mirugai: giant clam
Miso: soup; soybean paste from which a savoury broth is made, usually served with cubes of tofu or strips of seaweed
Ono: wahoo fish; a relative of mackerel often compared in taste to albacore
Ramen: Chinese soup noodles
Saba: mackerel
Sake: salmon
Saké: traditional rice wine served hot or cold
Sashimi: thinly sliced raw fish, ususally served with soy sauce and wasabi
Shabu shabu: similar to sukiyaki; beef and vegetables cooked tableside in a broth
Shiitake: prized cultivated mushroom, dark brown with a large cap
Shoya: soy sauce
Soba: buckwheat noodles
Sukiyaki: braised beef and vegetable dish with broth added after cooking
Sushi: rounds of vinegared rice wrapped in dried seaweed with a center of raw fish or vegetables, served with wasabi and soy
Tai: snapper
Tako: octopus
Tamago: egg
Tamari: dark sauce similar in composition and taste to soy; often used for dipping
Tempura: deep-fried, batter-dipped fish and vegetables
Teriyaki: a marinade of soy and sweet sake, used on meat, fish and poultry
Tofu: bean curd, processed into a liquid and then molded into large cubes
Toro: fatty belly cut of tuna
Udon: wheat noodles
Unagi: freshwater eel

Uni: sea-urchin roe
Wasabi: a hot, spicy condiment made from the roots of Janapese horseradish, chartreuse in colour
Yakitori: a dish of pieces of chicken and vegetables, marinated in a spicy sauce, skewered and grilled

THAI

Kaeng (or **Gaeng**): large and diverse category of dishes: loosely translates as 'curry'
Kaeng massanan: a variety of coconut-milk curry
Kaeng phed: a red, coconut-cream curry
Keang som: a hot-sour curry
Kapi: fermented shrimp paste; vital ingredient in nam phrik, or dishes flavoured with hot chilli sauce
Kai (or **Gal**): chicken
Khai: egg
Khoa: rice
Khoa phad: fried rice
Khoa suai: white rice
King: ginger
Kung: prawns
Lab (or **Larb**): dish of minced meat with chillies and lime juice
Mu: pork
Nam: sauce
Nam pla: fish sauce
Nam phrik: a hot chilli sauce
Nuea: beef
Ped: duck
Phad: fried
Phad king: fried with ginger
Phad phed: fried hot and spicy
Phad Thai: pan-fried rice noodles with chicken, shrimp, eggs, peanuts and bean sprouts
Phrik: chilli pepper
Pla: fish
Si racha (or **Sri racha**): spicy chilli condiment
Tom: boiled; often refers to soups
Tom kha kai: chicken coconut-cream soup flavoured with lemongrass and chillies
Tom yam kung: hot-sour shrimp soup flavoured with lemongrass, lime and chillies
Yam: flavoured primarily with lime juice and chillies, resulting in a hot-sour taste; usually 'salads' but can also be noodle dishes or soup
Yam pla: raw fish spiked with lime juice, chilli, lemongrass, mint and fish sauce

T

U